PROTECTION OFFICER TRAINING MANUAL

PROTECTION OFFICER TRAINING MANUAL

Seventh Edition

International Foundation for Protection Officers
P.O. Box 771329, Naples, FL 34107

An imprint of Elsevier Science
Amsterdam   Boston   Heidelberg   London   New York   Oxford
Paris   San Diego   San Francisco   Singapore   Sydney   Tokyo

Butterworth-Heinemann is an imprint of Elsevier Science.

∞   Recognizing the importance of preserving what has been written, Elsevier Science prints its books on acid-free paper whenever possible.

Library of Congress Cataloging-in-Publication Data

Protection officer training manual/International Foundation for Protection Officers. – 7th ed.
   p. cm.
   Includes bibliographical references and index.
   ISBN 0-7506-7456-3 (alk. paper)
1. Police, Private—Training of—United States—Handbooks, manuals, etc. 2. Private security services—United States—Handbooks, manuals, etc. I. International Foundation for Protection Officers.

HV8291.U6P76 2003
363.28'9—dc21

2003050337

British Library Cataloguing-in-Publication Data
A catalogue record for this book is available from the British Library.

The publisher offers special discounts on bulk orders of this book.
For information, please contact:

Manager of Special Sales
Elsevier Science
200 Wheeler Road
Burlington, MA 01803
Tel: 781-313-4700
Fax: 781-313-4882

For information on all Butterworth-Heinemann publications available, contact our World Wide Web home page at: http://www.bh.com.

10 9 8 7 6 5 4 3 2 1

Printed in the United States of America

DEDICATION

"To the men and women who hold the front lines of the fight for our safety and security, those that have fallen and those still with us."

CONTENTS

CONTRIBUTORS

Ronald R. Minion, CPP, CPO
Founding Director, International Foundation for Protection Officers. Mr. Minion is a former member of the Royal Canadian Mounted Police and Founder of one of Canada's largest Security Service Companies. He is a graduate of Mount Royal College and Columbia Pacific University and is a longtime member of the American Society for Industrial Security (ASIS). He is a past ASIS Chapter Chairman and Regional Vice President and was named International Regional Vice President of the Year. He was the recipient of the ASIS President's Certificate of Merit and was the first examined Certified Protection Professional (CPP) in Canada. Ron is best known for his continuing efforts to develop professional growth opportunities for Private and Public Security Personnel.

Sandi J. Davies
Executive Director, International Foundation for Protection Officers. Ms. Davies began her career in contract security in 1980, with a primary focus on personnel administration. She became deeply involved in training, and was instrumental in developing Security Officer training programs for a major national guard company. Her interest in security training grew, and in 1988 she joined the newly founded IFPO as an administrative assistant. In 1991 she was named executive director of the IFPO and has been a driving force in Foundation program development and administration. Sandi is a longtime member of the American Society for Industrial Security (ASIS), having served in various executive positions at the chapter level.

Rich Abrams, CPO, CPOI
George A. Barnett, CPO
Colin Best, CPO
Patrick C. Bishop, CPP
Dr. Norman R. Bottom, CPP, CPO, CST
R. Lorne Brennan, CPO
John Christman, CPP
Tom M. Conley, MA, CPP, CFE, CPO
David J. DeLong, CPP
Francis J. Elliot, CPP
Martin A. Fawcett, CPO
Richard P. Fiems, MA, CPO, CSS, CPOI
Michael A. Hannigan, CPO
Christopher A. Hertig, CPP, CPOI
Arthur A. Holm, CPO

Glen Kitteringham, MSc., CPP, CPOI, CSS, CPO
Thomas E. Koll, CPP
Michael Krikorian, CPP
Johnny May, CPP, CPO
Cole Morris, CPP, CFE, CPO
Denis A. O'Sullivan, CPP, CPO
Philip P. Purpura, CPP
David L. Ray, LL.B
John Ryan, CPO
Jill Segraves, CPO
Cecelia Sharp
Michael Stroberger, CPO, CSS, CPOI, CLSD, CPP
Charles T. Thibodeau, M.Ed., CPP, CSS
Christopher L. Vail
Jeff B. Wilt, CPP, CPO

INTRODUCTION

Introduction
Code of Ethics
Chapter Summary Review

Introduction

By Ronald R. Minion, CPP, CPO
Sandi J. Davies

PURPOSE

The purpose of this manual is to provide a current, useful, consolidated *Security Officer Training Manual* that provides "need-to-know" information for protection officers throughout the security industry. This manual serves as the course text for the Certified Protection Officer (CPO) program. Many security professionals also find the contents of this manual helpful in their day-to-day security management responsibilities.

GENERAL INFORMATION

The first edition of the *Protection Officer Training Manual* (POTM) originated with the birth of the International Foundation for Protection Officers (IFPO) in 1988. Twelve dedicated security professionals from the United States and Canada had a vision: to create an organization that would provide meaningful career opportunities for line security officers throughout North America.

To succeed, the newly formed board of directors of the IFPO realized that a certification program was needed, along with a professional training manual. Hence, POTM, first edition, was created to serve as the course text for the Certified Protection Officer (CPO) program. The IFPO, the CPO program, and POTM all proved to be vital components in the realization of the aims and objectives of the foundation.

Today, the IFPO is the recognized catalyst in the development of professionalism throughout the private security industry. Thousands of security officers, who have earned the CPO accreditation, have gained knowledge and professional career enhancement. And, they have unselfishly provided encouragement and information to their colleagues and employers. Hence, a new dimension of opportunities has spread through the security industry.

The first edition was simple, short, and limited in scope, but included enough information to help the security officer better understand his/her roles, duties, and responsibilities. However, since that simple beginning, each subsequent edition has brought new and enlightening information to the security professional. POTM is now considered the leading training manual for line security officers.

Feedback has been the most significant factor, which has led to a standard of excellence for this new manual. We have received countless letters of appreciation for the depth and quality of the sixth edition, but these same enthusiasts have been liberal with their recommendations for changes and improvements, and we have listened. Ongoing dialogue with security managers, supervisors, consultants, educators, and, of course, protection officers has enabled us to develop and maintain a training manual that will serve future learning.

The seventh edition has 12 units and 43 chapters. The contributors to the seventh edition are among the best writers, academics, and practitioners in the security community. This talented group of professionals has generously provided readers of this superior manual with unique opportunities to acquire current asset protection and life safety information. These writers are simply outstanding individuals who deserve recognition and appreciation for their service to the security community.

The International Foundation for Protection Officers is supported by a team of security professionals throughout North America who, year after year, work diligently on behalf of the foundation and what it stands for. Because of these men and women, who are committed to excellence and remain steadfast in their obligation to high standards of service, the IFPO continues to be successful. You all deserve our thanks.

EXPANDED PROTECTION ROLES

In the past decade, a new kind of private justice has emerged to facilitate private/public corporate protection. For a number of reasons, not the least of which is a burdensome public justice system and declining police availability to protect business and industry, management has undertaken to develop and maintain a "self-protection" posture.

Corporations that once required limited security measures have now placed personnel and asset protection as organization priorities to sustain a safe and productive work environment.

An integral part of this overall protection process is the professional security manager and supervisor, complemented with a security staff capable of attending to ongoing protection needs. While public law enforcement and private protection roles have many similarities, asset protection is becoming a paramount concern for every public organization.

Who will assume the responsibility for protecting private and government organizations? We suggest that a new, effective, enlightened protection officer is essential to assist management with the responsibilities of personnel, asset, and information security. Public law enforcement organizations lack the human and financial resources required to enhance organizational safety and security.

Police organizations will continue to maintain a reactive posture, while protection groups must undertake to develop even more effective integrated security systems. There must be better communication and role appreciation developed among public police and private security organizations. This is a different task that requires a creative approach initiated by security and police administrators.

There should be cooperation, resulting from mutual understanding and a "joint venture" approach to crime prevention. When we consider that there are more than two—and soon to be three—private security employees to every one public law enforcement officer, there must be cost-effective benefits available to governments and free enterprise that recognize the important role of private security in our modern society.

MANUAL FORMAT

The contents of this manual are sometimes quite basic. However, every security supervisor and manager should fully understand all of the information contained herein so as to provide better leadership and interpretation of officer responsibilities.

This edition is divided into 12 units. The material contained in each unit is arranged so as to provide the reader with a smooth flow of related security information. The final part of the manual is a Miscellaneous section that contains a variety of material that is either too short to constitute a complete chapter or not relevant to any other part of the manual.

At the conclusion of each chapter there are 10 questions of the fill-in-the-word, multiple-choice, and true/false variety. Before the reader proceeds to the next chapter, it is vitally important to be able to answer each question correctly.

CERTIFIED PROTECTION OFFICER (CPO) PROGRAM

The *Protection Officer Training Manual* is the course text for the Certified Protection Officer (CPO) program.

The CPO designation is a professional accreditation that can be earned by completing a self-pacing course based on this manual.

Briefly, a candidate must complete the following stages of progression to earn the CPO designation.

- Submit application for enrollment
- Successfully complete a midterm examination
- Successfully complete a supervised final examination (A proctor may be located within the candidate's organization or community.)

(Both examinations are based on the contents of this manual.)

CERTIFIED PROTECTION OFFICER (CPO) FINAL CHALLENGE PROGRAM

The CPO Final Challenge concept reduces the time of study required in that the midterm examination process has been eliminated. The only requirement in this program is to write the CPO final examination. A suitable proctor must be identified to supervise this portion of the program.

The CPO program is an internationally recognized certification for protection officers.

Contact the International Foundation for Protection Officers (IFPO) for more information regarding the Certified Protection Officer and/or other programs.

CONCLUSION

The term *protection officer* frequently appears in this manual. What is a protection officer? A protection officer is the individual whom this manual is intended to serve, including the following:

- A non-police person employed in private or public security.
- An individual committed to fulfilling a functional role in the modern security community.
- An individual who provides security from a fixed location or in the capacity of a patrol officer.

Indeed, the manual is a useful tool for security supervisors and managers, but the primary beneficiary is the protection officer.

The editors of the **Protection Officer Training Manual** *are honored to work with so many outstanding security professionals since the planning of the first edition . These talented and dedicated security professionals have worked tirelessly in supporting, promoting and contributing to the International Foundation for Protection Officers and all of its worthwhile programs. "We could not have done it without you!"*

Protection Officer Code of Ethics

The Protection Officer Shall

I	*Respond to employer's professional needs*
II	*Exhibit exemplary conduct*
III	*Protect confidential information*
IV	*Maintain a safe & secure workplace*
V	*Dress to create professionalism*
VI	*Enforce all lawful rules & regulations*
VII	*Encourage liaison with public officers*
VIII	*Develop good rapport within the profession*
IX	*Strive to attain professional competence*
X	*Encourage high standards of officer ethics*

PROTECTION OFFICER CODE OF ETHICS

Today business and the public expect a great deal from the uniformed security officer. In the past there has been far too little attention paid to the ethical aspects of the profession. There have to be solid guidelines that each officer knows and understands. More importantly, it is essential that each manager and supervisor performs his or her duties in a manner that will reflect honesty, integrity, and professionalism.

Every training program should address the need for professional conduct on and off duty. Line officers must exhibit a willingness to gain professional competency and adhere to a strict code of ethics that must include the following:

Loyalty

To the employer, the client, and the public. The officer must have a complete and thorough understanding of all of the regulations and procedures that are necessary to protect people and assets on or in relation to the facility assigned to protect.

Exemplary Conduct

The officer is under constant scrutiny by everyone in work and public places. Hence, it is essential that he/she exhibit exemplary conduct at all times. Maturity and professionalism are the key words to guide all officers.

Confidentiality

Each officer is charged with the responsibility of working in the interests of his/her employer. Providing protection means that the officer will encounter confidential information that must be carefully guarded and never compromised.

Safety and Security

The foremost responsibility of all officers is to ensure that the facility that must be protected is safe and secure for all persons with lawful access. The officer must fully understand all necessary procedures to eliminate or control security and safety risks.

Deportment

Each officer must dress in an immaculate manner. Crisp, sharp, clean, and polished are the indicators that point to a professional officer who will execute his/her protection obligations in a proficient manner and will be a credit to the profession.

Law Enforcement Liaison

It is the responsibility of each officer to make every effort to encourage and enhance positive relations with members of public law enforcement. Seek assistance when a genuine need exists and offer assistance whenever possible.

Strive to Learn

To become professionally competent, each officer must constantly strive to be knowledgeable about all aspects of his/her chosen career. How to protect people, assets and information must always be a learning priority for every officer.

Develop Rapport

It is necessary to be constantly aware of the image that our profession projects. All officers can enhance the image of the industry, their employer, and themselves. Recognize and respect peers and security leaders throughout the industry.

Honesty

By virtue of the duties and responsibilities of all officers, honest behavior is absolutely essential at all times. Each officer occupies a position of trust that must not be violated. Dishonesty can never be tolerated by the security profession.

Prejudice

The job of protecting means that the officer must impose restrictions upon people that frequent the security workplace. All human beings must be treated equally, with dignity and respect, regardless of color, race, religion, or political beliefs.

Self-Discipline

With the position of trust comes the responsibility to diligently protect life and property. These duties can only be discharged effectively when the officer understands the gravity of his/her position. Self-discipline means trying harder and caring more.

CONCLUSION

The job of protecting life and property focuses much attention on the individual security officer. Hence, it is essential to be aware of the need for professional conduct at all times. By strictly adhering to each section in this code of ethics, it may be expected that we as individuals and the industry as a whole will enjoy a good reputation and gain even more acceptance from the public as well as private and government corporations. You as the individual officer must be a principle in this process.

Chapter Summary Review

PURPOSE AND SCOPE

For the convenience of readers of this manual, each unit and chapter have been summarized. An abbreviated narrative of the contents is set forth in a manner that offers a quick and concise reference to the core material.

There are 12 units, containing 43 regular chapters and one separate Miscellaneous section. Pages are numbered by unit, chapter, and page — for example, Unit 5, Chapter 2, Page 7 would appear PROTECTION OFFICER TRAINING MANUAL: Unit 5-2-7.

Protection Officer Ethics

The security industry has not developed a recognized code of ethics or standard of conduct for security personnel. Senior management in large corporations, both private and public, has often been remiss for failing to develop a code of ethics for all employees to be used as a guide to encourage integrity-based behavior.

Leaders must not only produce a code of ethics but demonstrate by exemplary personal and business conduct that rules are for everyone in the organization. Because of the nature of the duties performed by protection officers, it is imperative that a code of ethics be readily available for constant reference and application to duties performed.

The matter of professional ethics for protection officers is a topic that is seldom discussed but is of vital importance to the entire profession. These ethics provide not only a guide for the officer, but also for the various levels of security management and the user of security services.

UNIT ONE

The Evolution of Asset Protection and Security

The study of history is essential to understanding present and future events. Asset protection (the more all-inclusive term denoting protection from a variety of threats) and security (the traditional term focusing on threats posed by malevolent humans) is rich and varied. Generally private initiatives to control crime and fire preceded public ones. Class struggles between the upper and lower classes of society are a large part of the history of both security and law enforcement (note that security and policing are inextricably intertwined in many instances). Commerce, marketing considerations, and demographics play a major role in the evolution of assets and threats posed to those assets. Military forces are often involved in protection against foreign invaders, riots, and international terrorists. Security efforts are usually a step behind the actions of criminals.

The development of control forces (contract security, state, and city police), the insurance industry, and the discipline of physical security can all be traced to the presence of serious security problems and a need for mutual protection. So, too, does the development of fire protection measures. Similarly, the development of law mirrors social changes and new threats from malevolent humans. Careers in asset protection and security continue to develop both in terms of numbers of jobs and the diversity and specialization of those positions.

UNIT TWO

Field Notes and Report Writing

This chapter begins by stressing the importance of the written word, particularly as it relates to the role of the protection officer. The notebook is described as a "tool of the trade." The reader is given guidance in selection of a suitable notebook, proper note taking, notebook maintenance, notes for future reference, and utilizing the notebook as an aid in giving evidence.

The best methods of transferring information from the notebook to the report format are discussed in detail. The importance of a well-written report is underscored as the most effective means by which the work of the protection officer may be evaluated by fellow officers, supervisors, the courts, and other departments and organizations, both private and public.

The chapter discusses the various kinds of reports that may be encountered by the protection officer and how these reports form an integral part of the security organization's administration process. Finally, the chapter spells out how the written report conveys to the reader how competent the officer really is in terms of effective task completion.

Observation Skills and Memory

The modern protection officer must improve memory skills, as do security supervisors and managers. This is a popular and useful chapter for all security personnel. What the professional protection officer observes during a normal tour of duty after studying this chapter and what the officer who has not read the chapter observes will probably be quite different.

By using the methods of observation suggested in this chapter, readers will discover that there is an opportunity to detect, observe, and report more information than was previously thought possible.

This chapter will enhance the opportunity for the protection officer to be more resourceful, observant, and provide more in-depth and meaningful reports. By combining learning skills, study habits, and memory and observation techniques, a much higher level of information retention will result, as well as improved performance.

Patrol Principles

The patrol function can be significantly improved by applying some of the awareness, observation, memory, and preventive skills covered in Unit One of this manual. This is one of the most important functions of the modern protection officer.

Results of effective patrolling can enhance the overall protection of personnel, assets, and information. Protection officers are advised as to the kind of facility violations to be expected, a description of potential perpetrators, and the danger signals that can alert the officer.

This chapter gives the reader information on patrol preparation, execution, and reporting. It clearly illustrates the most effective methods of patrolling and provides excellent cautionary guidelines to promote officer safety. The importance of the connection between the patrol, field notes, and the finished report is reiterated in this chapter.

Safety and the Protection Officer

There has always been a close link between safety and security. For example, the title "Public Safety Officer" frequently replaces a more traditional security-oriented rank description. And some organizations have attempted to incorporate a total "Loss Control Concept" by including safety, security, and fire protection into one organizational job description.

The protection officer is in an ideal position to combine safety responsibilities with regular security duties. This chapter gives the reader a clear picture of the overall organizational safety structure, individual responsibilities, and how the protection officer can bring safety hazards to light. By close scrutiny of potential safety risks and effective reporting, the protection officer can make beneficial contributions to organizational safety.

Traffic Control

Vehicular movement, at every location that is protected by security, becomes a responsibility of the protection officer. This chapter first discusses the need for proper preparation for duty by describing the physical items required to get the job done. The importance of "good attitude" is explained and the need for full officer attention to safety is emphasized.

Signs and automatic signals are discussed, as well as a careful description of hand gestures and the officer's position when directing traffic. The use of the whistle can maximize effective traffic movement and control. Reference is made to pedestrian traffic; an officer can assist police in the execution of this important security function.

The chapter concludes by providing some useful tips on traffic control and site locations from which the protection officer may be expected to perform traffic control duties.

Crowd Control

The effective management of large groups of people is becoming a major role of the protection officer. Failure to understand or execute correct procedures can lead to disastrous consequences. Effective crowd control is the difference between a smooth flow of pedestrian traffic and a hysterical mob of uncontrollable individuals who can cause serious injury or death to innocent people and severe damage to property.

This chapter describes the kinds of gatherings that can be defined as a crowd, demonstration, riot, or disaster. The reader is made to understand the causes of crowd formation, such as casual, social, political, or economic. It discusses countermeasures that can be employed to neutralize a crowd that has become unruly.

Manpower considerations are covered as well as liaison with local law enforcement personnel. Additional methods of crowd management, such as isolating individuals, removing leaders, diverting attention, and other effective tactics, are covered in detail. The chapter concludes with a crowd control planning checklist and shows illustrations that indicate effective personnel deployment.

UNIT THREE

Physical Security Applications

This facet of security is vitally important to the protection officer. Every facility requires various forms of physical security. This can range from a simple access control system, such as key control, to various sophisticated, integrated control access methods, such as magnetic strip cards, voice prints, laser readers, and new technology, such as retina scan (eye readers), advanced hi-tech access control systems, closed circuit TV, robots, and alarms systems that monitor unauthorized and authorized movement of personnel, as well as the environment, are becoming common methods designed to improve physical security.

At the top of the list of physical security measures is the trained protection officer. Adding integrated security systems to any facility means more effective deployment of security personnel. Personnel, hardware, and software are part of the protection link.

This chapter discusses physical security in depth, and it is essential that officers fully understand the connection between the human and technical aspects of physical security. This chapter discusses the five steps that are involved with physical security, such as the following:

Identification of assets: Asset protection includes safeguarding personnel, information, and all corporate possessions that can be classified and protected. Corporate assets must be accurately inventoried so that effective measures of protection can be implemented to preserve these assets. Failure to develop and maintain productive asset protection can most certainly result in business failure.

Loss events: Threats to organizational assets must be identified. Considering the potential consequences of the threat, the likelihood of the loss event actually occurring, and the effects that such a loss event would have on the organization is a vital exercise in physical security planning. The protection officer can be an integral part of the system that monitors the effectiveness of physical security measures.

Occurrence probability: There are a number of methods that will assist in determining, with reasonable accuracy, the likelihood of the loss event actually occurring. This condition has significant bearing on the level of physical security that must be placed on assets that are affected. Gathering intelligence from past, present, and anticipated events is a function that can be enhanced by effective officer observations and reports.

Impact of occurrence: The effects that a loss event may have on an organization are critical in the overall loss control planning process. For example, a disaster, manmade or by act of God, could require numerous contingency plans, ranging from auxiliary power to such considerations as mutual aid from other corporations. When a loss event occurs, the protection officer is often first on the scene and must take immediate remedial action.

Countermeasures: There are a wide range of countermeasures that must be considered in the physical security planning process. Asset identification, potential loss events, the probability of an occurrence, and the impact this occurrence (event) would have on the organization are all actors that influence the level of physical security. Readers should relate Emergency, Disaster Planning Techniques covered separately in Unit Four of this manual when considering physical security countermeasures.

Alarm System Fundamentals

An understanding of basic alarm systems should be considered a "core knowledge" requirement for anyone responsible for the protection of people, property, profits, and information. This chapter provides the fundamental information today's protection officer needs to know to be successful at her/his job. The material includes a discussion about different types of monitoring systems, the importance of an effective operator interface, and a description of the most commonly used alarm sensors.

This chapter also includes coverage of "false alarms" and their various causes. Finally, this section concludes with an important discussion of alarm response procedures and the importance of officer safety when investigating alarm events. General in nature, this material must be supplemented with specific information as it applies to the alarm systems at the reader's duty location.

Central Alarm Stations and Dispatch Centers

This chapter explains the role of the control room in security operations and details the physical location, staffing, equipment, and training.

The first major topic is the ergonomics of the dispatch center, which includes computer monitor and keyboard location, heating and cooling, and access control to authorized personnel.

The next topic is staffing, based partially on studies done by the National Burglar and Fire Alarm Association, Underwriters Laboratories, and APCO.

Communications tools, such as the phone and radio, are examined, along with the logging computer, the alarm receiver, audio recorder, and video surveillance. In addition, electronic access control is further defined as well as mechanical keys and locks.

Finally, the education of security operators via in-house, distance, and seminar programs is presented. Formal certifications, such as the IPFO protection officer and CSAA Central Station Dispatcher, are defined as well.

In general, the chapter underscores that the security control center is the focal point of any protection function, ranging from a one-man post at the front desk of an office building to a fully staffed central alarm station that receives worldwide signals.

Access Control

This chapter is an overview of the function of access control from its most simple form to the use of complex access control systems. Emphasis is placed not only on the common function of granting and denying access, but also the value of audit trails and the need to follow and enforce policy with diplomacy.

Access control does not only apply to the security officer stationed at a desk checking facility occupants in and denying those trying to breach security. The function of access control can range from the control of users on a corporate network to the facial recognition systems in use at border crossings and airport customs.

The following chapter describes the various forms of controlling access and describes the "tools of the trade" in the world of controlling access.

UNIT FOUR

Introduction to Computer Security

This chapter begins with a discussion of the growth of computer crime. As computers become almost universal, the protection officer must increase his or her awareness of computer security issues. Presented in a nontechnical manner, the chapter provides key definitions as they apply to computer and information security issues. Also included are various types of security threats, different kinds of hackers and crackers, and recommended security policies.

Information is the lifeblood of most organizations. Although computer security has become a highly technical specialty, today's protection officer is increasingly expected to support the organization's computer security program and understand its important relationship to traditional protective tasks.

Information Security

This chapter begins by explaining the growing importance of protecting information as the focus of industry progresses in its development of technical concepts. The identification of critical information is discussed as it relates to the value it represents to the rightful owner. Basic methods of initiating an information security plan are explored, including identification of proper users, the nature of the information, and in what form it is retained. The basic idea of physical security is also highlighted. The proper use of policy and procedure controls is discussed, inclusive of obtaining "Trade Secret" status, and the benefits and limitations of that status. Confidentiality agreements are also discussed. Potential sources of threats are explored, and the differing levels of threat and goals of the threat are discussed.

UNIT FIVE

Explosive Devices, Bomb Threats, and Search Procedures

Legitimate uses of explosives are explained, as well as possible motivations for unlawful uses. The potential scale and scope of damage are discussed as they relate to size and composition of the device. A definition of explosives is provided with further classification as "high" or "low" explosives. Triggering and detonation methods are also discussed. Development of an action plan is discussed, as well as threat checklists and coordination with outside agencies. The nature of bomb threats is discussed, as well as response phases. The initiation and execution of a search is discussed, including methods of searching, identification of persons involved in the search process, and response to device discovery. Responses to explosions are explored, including the need to be aware of possible secondary devices. Deterrence and designing to mitigate blast effects are explained, with possible action steps provided.

Fire Prevention, Detection, and Response

The basic nature of fire threats is explained in the beginning of the chapter with an emphasis on the benefits of prevention, as opposed to response. The basics of fire are explored, including the Fire Triangle and some common fire source areas. Methods of detection are explained, inclusive of human observation, electronic systems, and automated sprinkler systems. A definition of the basic types of fire is provided with an explanation of the corresponding portable extinguishers. Permanent extinguisher and suppression hardware is also described with the methods of operation explored. Concepts related to containment are listed, referencing fire doors, construction materials, and the importance of monitoring for proper upkeep of the structural aspects. The critical importance of development of a realistic fire plan is stressed with basic components explained. The possibility of arson and the related hazards are also explained.

Hazardous Materials

Considerably more attention has been focused on the topic of hazardous materials in recent years. The day-to-day and long-term management of these kinds of materials is becoming a part of everyday life, particularly in the industrial world. The protection officer is now called upon not only to have a good understanding of what constitutes a hazardous material, but what has to be done to ensure that the same substance does not pose a risk to employees and the public. While the types of materials are not discussed in detail, there are numerous suggestions as to how these materials can be identified.

People play a key role in the misuse and abuse of hazardous materials. The protection officer plays a key role in enforcing the rules and procedures that are designed to safeguard a contaminated area. Numerous location and facilities, both public and private, industrial, commercial, and recreational, may be adversely affected by improperly stored, handled, or transported hazardous materials. By developing a broad knowledge base about this topic, the protection officer can do a great deal to protect people and the environment.

This chapter begins by discussing the response methods to deal with the uncontrolled release of hazardous materials. The statement "Dilution was the solution to pollution" does not necessarily hold true today. Diluted hazardous solutions can have long-term devastating effects on the environment. In years past, the job of dealing with these situations was primarily a fire department responsibility. Today specialized hazardous material (HazMat) response teams have been developed to respond to uncontrolled releases of hazardous substances. This chapter deals with the necessary response needed to deal with the risk of uncontrolled hazardous materials which includes the following:

- Activate the contingency plan
- Identify the substance released
- Determine the quantity of the released substance
- Determine the extent of the damage
- Perform "site security"

This chapter provides details of each of the necessary steps to manage uncontrolled hazardous materials that pose an immediate threat to life and property.

While each of the five steps is of vital importance, the final step, "site security," is of primary importance to the protection officer. This relates to keeping onlookers and bystanders out of the contaminated area. Coworkers, the public, and even the media, can all pose serious security problems. They must be kept clear of the affected area for their own safety. The HazMat response team has a big job to do and can't be burdened with the task of dealing with unwanted onlookers.

An excellent illustration depicts how the security function can be implemented. It describes the three critical zones: hot, warm, and cold. All nonessential personnel must be kept clear of the contaminated area and restricted to the cold zone area where the command post is established and controlled by the incident commander.

Once the contamination has been cleaned up or safely controlled (decontaminated on DECONed), the incident commander will make a decision about further security measures. Only once the area has been classified as safe will the strict security procedures be relaxed.

Protection Officers and Emergency Response
Legal and Operational Considerations

The protection officer's responsibilities increase as each day passes. Fire prevention, asset protection, and policy enforcement are among the tasks charged to security officers. Along with these are many everyday duties like access control, maintaining general safety, and the monitoring of properties. Security operations are moving toward response to medical emergencies, too. With areas and properties getting larger, security patrols are the only link between a sick or injured person and help. Security is beginning to encounter legal issues when dealing with first response to medical emergencies. What are the legal repercussions of first response for security officers? What can the company or department do to protect itself from legal actions?

One such statute that has an effect on everyone, not just security officers, is the Good Samaritan Law. This law appears in one form or another in most states and can be referred to as the "Good Samaritan Rule" or the "Firemen's Rule." This law is in effect in most states and protects emergency care providers from civil liability. The law basically states, "Any individual who gives emergency care at the scene of an emergency shall not be held liable to that same person acting in 'good faith' as a result of any actions except those that prove intentionally harmful or grossly negligent."

Throughout this chapter, recommendations are made as to what sort of recommended training should be provided to the security officers in terms of responding to emergency medical needs. Additional information is provided in this chapter as it relates to the automated external defibrillator (AED).

This chapter also reviews medical emergencies, fire safety and hazardous or biohazardous materials.

UNIT SIX

Strikes, Lockouts, and Labor Relations

Wildcat strikes, lawful strikes, and lockouts are frequent occurrences on the labor scene. When any of these conditions are anticipated by management, extensive contingency plans are developed with a view to protecting nonstriking employees, and the physical aspects of the struck facility. The roles of the protection officer in labor disputes include but are not limited to the following:

- Access control
- Escorts
- Chain of command (security)
- Police liaison
- Communication
- Prestrike vandalism
- Fire safety
- Building security
- Security lighting
- Supply acquisitions
- Threatening phone calls
- Crossing picket lines
- Picket line surveillance

Other strike conditions that are discussed in this chapter are searches, employee misconduct and dishonesty, employee discipline, types of discipline, arbitration, and interviews. It must be remembered that the protection officer's role in matters of labor unrest is one of neutrality. It is important that strikers do not perceive security as an extension of management.

By maintaining a friendly, cooperative attitude, it is possible to reduce much of the friction that is normally present during strike or lockout conditions. However, disgruntled strikers will resort to numerous tactics designed to intimidate nonstriking employees and cause management hardships.

While maintaining good relations is very important, sometimes it is necessary to compel strikers to adhere to company strike policy. In the absence of court injunctions, the employee has all of the legal powers necessary to protect the property and the people having legal access to the facility.

Workplace Violence

Violence is pervasive in our world and has been a part of the human society since its earliest recorded time. Violence in society, in one form or another, is unfortunate and is simply unavoidable. According to the National Institute for Occupational Safety and Health (NIOSH), it is clear from the available data that workplace violence is a public health problem of significant proportion. In a report that covered the years 1980–1985, it was reported that homicide was the third largest cause of occupational injury death in the workplace. Workplace violence is a specialized problem and one that security professionals must deal with in their day-to-day work lives. The cost of a workplace violence incident is exhorbitant. Therefore, it is incumbent on the organizational leadership to do all they can, at all levels, to prevent a workplace violence incident from occurring. Upon investigation of incidents after they occurred, it was apparent that people who have perpetrated workplace violence incidents displayed warning signs prior to the incident occurring. Also, employees who committed workplace violence often started out being rude to coworkers. There was an escalation that occurred, culminating in homicide. Security officers will likely be among the first ones to be on the scene if an incident occurs. Thus, it is essential that security officers possess the personal demeanor and professional skills necessary to respond to and successfully manage a workplace violence incident. The primary purpose of this chapter is to provide protection officers with the tools and knowledge they need to successfully recognize and respond to workplace violence.

Employee Dishonesty and Crime in Business

Employee theft is not uncommon. In fact, it has been said that the level of controls and the threat of punishment are directly linked to the amount of dishonest behavior that can be expected in an organization.

Preventive security and security awareness programs have a definite relationship with increased loss control resulting from dishonesty in the workplace.

This chapter discusses the WAECUP acronym, which is pronounced "Wake up." These are the key terms that relate to employee theft in the WAECUP program.

W   Waste
A   Accident
E   Error
C   Crime
UP   Unethical Practices

Each term in this model is discussed, and the connection between each portion of the acronym is explained as it relates to losses resulting from a criminal act committed within the organization.

Not all internal (employee) theft is preventable. We will learn in this chapter some ways in which to minimize, moderate, and control criminal activity. This will enhance our ability to be effective protection officers. The protection officer can have a significant impact on theft prevention. They can deter and displace theft. When security is tight, thieves look for another place to steal.

Employees will recognize that effective professional security is in place and generally avoid the risk of detection that would precede an illegal act directed against the organization.

This chapter gives tips on observation techniques that enhance effective theft prevention. It explains the importance of effective reports and the correlation between information related to management and increased security. It will provide a number of suggested actions in theft prevention. It also provides the officer with cautionary practices that, if followed, will reduce the opportunity for unfavorable publicity or even possible lawsuits for acts or omissions on the part of the officer(s). It is essential to understand the protection officer's authority to search and seize. It is also necessary to fully understand company policy and the organization's expectations of security.

Substance Abuse

Substance abuse is one of the leading social problems of our time. It adversely affects the health and creative potential of individual abusers, and, therefore, deteriorates the stability of institutions under individual control. One such institution is the workplace.

Throughout this chapter, the protection officer will develop an awareness for the issues related to an individual's motive to abuse drugs, why they continue using drugs in spite of deteriorating physical and mental health, and how they become dependent. Also, the protection officer will become familiar with the meaning of substance abuse and a variety of terms associated with the prevention and treatment of the problem.

Specific workplace issues are discussed and the cost associated with substance abuse is identified. To effectively address substance abuse in the workplace, there should be a comprehensive drug-free workplace program. Such a program consists of several components. These components, including the security function, will be reviewed.

The security response is a critical component of any drug-free workplace program. As such, the protection officer is presented with information about the various techniques available to respond to criminality and major policy violations.

Finally, this chapter reviews the most prevalent drugs of abuse and their signs and symptoms. A chart graphically displaying this information and more is presented.

By carefully reviewing this chapter, the protection officer will gain sufficient insight into the general nature of substance abuse and drug dependence and a specific awareness regarding workplace issues, the security response, and the officer's responsibility.

UNIT SEVEN

Effective Communications

The chapter points out that risk analysis, vulnerability assessments, integrated countermeasure designs, security officer practice and procedure, and emergency response and contingency planning could not exist without "effective" written and verbal communications. This chapter places great emphasis on the fact that effective communications is not "effective" if a mutual "understanding" between the sender and receiver of the message is missing. We should be sending messages using words that are on a level that will be understood by the new recruit and/or the least knowledgeable person on the team.

It reminds us of the obvious: that effective communications become critical when communicating with public assistance personnel, such as fire, police, and emergency medical personnel. The author places the burden for clear and concise communications squarely on the **message sender**. **Message receivers** should never have to decipher a message. Messages sent should be so clear that anyone with a seventh-grade education could understand the message with little or no effort.

The chapter also breaks down myths and misconceptions regarding the use of abbreviations, shorthand, and brevity. Being brief many times is *not* an important goal of writing. Saying as few words as possible and speaking in code are *not* always the best ways to communicate verbally.

The chapter ends with suggestions for use of communications devices, including the use of telephone systems, two-way radios, pagers, and intercoms.

Crisis Intervention

The personal safety of protection officers has to be of paramount importance because each officer working in security today is frequently exposed to conflict oriented situations. Crisis intervention/management is a technique of communicating in a nonthreatening manner with individual(s) who are behaving in a disruptive or violent manner.

This chapter deals with the causes that lead to disruptive behavior such as illness, injury, emotional problems, substance abuse, stress, or anger. To cope with individuals exhibiting these kinds of characteristics, the protection officer must develop a plan of action that is designed to reduce the risk, not only to the distraught individual, but also to employees and, of course, the officer.

Each situation must be evaluated—in other words, "What is going on here?" Once it has been determined what is actually happening, there has to be a plan of action. This deals with ensuring that necessary personnel and other resources are available to manage the situation. The next step is to implement the plan. The action taken must be appropriate and designed to sustain the safety of the officer(s) and subject(s). After the appropriate action has been taken, it is necessary to carefully document the entire crisis situation. Finally, a review process must take place that includes all of the personnel involved. This gives everyone the opportunity to openly discuss what happened. It is a positive critiquing exercise.

The writer of this chapter encourages effective listening techniques. Listening in an empathetic manner tends to reduce anxiety on the part of the subject. By projecting a caring attitude, there is a greater opportunity to gain the confidence of the individual. Past prejudices and biases must be put aside, and the protection officer has to be objective. A person suffering from distress, frustration, anger, or dismay can easily detect insincerity. Be genuine and never ignore the principal of the conflict. Listen carefully to clarify any messages. Reinforce in the subject's mind what has been said so that he/she knows that you really do understand.

The chapter also deals in some length with nonverbal communications. Almost 85 percent of messages are conveyed without words, so it is vitally important to watch for body language that will give clues as to the emotional state of the principal(s) to a conflict. Honor the personal space of the subject and be aware of posture that may be interpreted as threatening. Maintain a position/stance that is nonthreatening while rendering maximum personal safety.

The "team approach" is suggested in dealing with crisis situations. It offers more personal safety to other team members while maintaining a stronger deterrent. Team members do not feel that aggression is directed at them personally but rather at the team. A team should remain small, and backup personnel should avoid the scene unless the situation requires support personnel. Avoid a mass convergence. Preincident training is extremely important. Team drills are performed to ensure that each player fully understands his/her role.

In extreme situations of emotional turmoil that has been initiated by an individual(s) that is suffering from severe stress or behaving in a violent manner, the action taken by the first officer on the scene is critical to successfully resolve the situation. By carefully analyzing the threat, keeping calm, being objective, and listening in a sympathetic manner, the potentially violent situation can usually be diffused. The author cautions all officers to first ensure that there are sufficient backup personnel before taking a corrective action.

Security Awareness

This chapter begins by explaining the benefits of having the involvement of all persons in the security efforts. Methods of creating a team mentality are introduced, as well as the possible levels of involvement that others may have. The creation of a clearly communicated plan is described as essential in the development of the proper environment, as is an understanding of the nature of the target audience. Some additional ideas to increase involvement and awareness are explained and keyed to the various phases of contact that each person moves through over time.

Environmental Crime Control Theory

While the average reader, in reviewing existing security literature, will read about crime prevention through Environmental Design, or CPTED, as it is more commonly referred to, there are a host of other theories that offer as much or more insight into crime control. If one is considering the implementation of a host of new security applications, one should start by asking, "Why?" Learning and applying these theories will not provide the magic answer, but they will allow one to make informed decisions as to why or why not security precautions should or should not be carried out. Once a deeper understanding of why a person chose to carry out the activity in a particular area can be made or just as importantly why an act was not carried out, then understanding and further applications can be instituted.

This section will go into detail and explain the various crime control theories that can both help explain and prevent criminal activity. It starts with an explanation of the evolution of crime prevention through environmental design before discussing the differences between social crime prevention and environmental theory. Following this is an explanation of the various theories including rational choice theory along with the corresponding 16 situational crime prevention techniques, parts I and II. Following this is an explanation of both displacement and diffusion of benefits. Routine activity and crime pattern theory are also discussed. Crime prevention through environmental design and defensible space are also highlighted and reviewed.

UNIT EIGHT

Operational Risk

The primary function of security professionals is to protect the safety and security of the people, property, and information that they are entrusted with protecting. Security officers need to understand the basic concepts of risk and risk management to be effective in their positions as security professionals. To the extent that organizational safety and security risks can be identified through proper risk analysis, they can be mitigated. One tool that security managers, as well as all others in the security department, can use to reduce losses and minimize risk is to institute an Operational Risk Management (ORM) program in the organization. In its most elemental form, an ORM process will cause security personnel at all levels to answer three questions about any obvious or potential incident. These questions are What can hurt my organization or me? How bad can it hurt me or my organization? What (if anything) can I do about it? While traditional ORM was originally developed and used in conjunction with military planning and operations, it is equally effective when used in day-to-day security operations. ORM, as developed, is a five-step decision-making process that is designed to enable individuals to identify hazards, assess risks, and implement controls to reduce risk associated with any action or operation. The ORM process exists on three levels: time-critical (an "on the run" mental or oral review); deliberate (application of the complete five-step process); and in-depth (a deliberate process with a more thorough risk assessment involving research of available data, use of a diagram and analysis tools, formal testing, or long-term tracking of the hazards associated with the operation to identify and assess the hazards). ORM incorporates the four principles of (1) accepting risk when benefits outweigh the cost, (2) accepting no unnecessary risk, (3) anticipating and managing risk by planning (risks are more easily controlled when they are identified early in the planning process), and (4) making risk decisions at the proper level in the organization. Protection officers are responsible for continually assessing risk and looking for ways to mitigate risk. An organizational Operational Risk Management program is an essential part of the risk identification and mitigation process.

Emergency Planning and Disaster Control

Advanced planning is the key to controlling emergencies and disasters in any workplace. For this reason, such a plan should be a basic part of every safety and accident prevention program.

This chapter presents general guidelines for setting up a disaster control plan and then provides a step-by-step outline of specific actions to be taken, including an organizational chart showing how to assign individual responsibilities for each step of the plan. Prominent in the emergency plan is the protection officer, who once again is often the first officer available to take action.

These are some of the manmade or act-of-God disasters discussed in this chapter.

- Fire
- Explosion
- Civil disturbance
- Hazardous chemical or gas leaks and spills
- Earthquake
- Building collapse
- Hurricane
- Tornado
- Flood
- Nuclear holocaust, radiation accident

Once the type of disaster has been identified, it is essential that the correct group(s) or individuals be identified and located to render all possible and necessary assistance. Protection officers must be aware of the signs and effects that will assist in determining the kind of disaster that has occurred.

The next step is to have available a list of personnel and organizations that have been designated to cope with the disaster. Home telephone numbers, as well as alternately designated personnel who are trained to deal with disasters, must be known to the officer, so as to limit the time consumed in summoning assistance. Other considerations that involve security personnel are as follows:

- Plant warning and communication systems
- Transportation
- Medical services
- Employee training—first aid, firefighting, and rescue
- Emergency power sources
- Mutual aid programs
- Availability of facility plans, maps, and diagrams

Security personnel must assume a major responsibility in such crisis conditions. It is essential that each officer carefully studies the Emergency Disaster plan and understands how his/her responsibilities interface with other designated employees named in the plan. Protecting life and property is a major concern of the protection officer, and it is important to restore full security as quickly as possible. This means gaining control of access points, providing direction to emergency response units, and encouraging an atmosphere that will reduce panic.

Terrorism

Terrorism can seem like a "big picture" problem only. That is, it can seem like only military forces and to a lesser degree, civilian public safety agencies are the only ones that deal with terrorism. While these are vital forces in the war on terrorism, the notion that terrorism is only fought by military and public safety personnel is off-base and could not be more incorrect. The ever-increasing frequency and severity of terrorist acts in the past few years, culminating in the horrific events that occurred on September 11, 2001, affected everyone. Those particularly affected are those who work in the public safety profession. The role of the protection officer has changed since September 11, 2001. Private security professionals now have a key role to play in the fight against terrorism. This chapter provides the reader with an understanding of what terrorism is, why it exists, and what security professionals can expect of terrorists in the future. This chapter defines terrorism and provides readers with information about the two types of terrorist groups that exist. The best way for protection officers to prepare for a terrorist attack is to have a systemwide emphasis on emergency planning and incident response. In many ways, preparing for a terrorist attack is no different from planning for other disasters. As with any security plan, it is critical to conduct ongoing training and to conduct drills to test the security plans.

Counter-terrorism and VIP Protection

This chapter begins by explaining the current state of terrorism. Terrorism is a strategy employing the use or threat of force to achieve political or social objectives. It is a form of coercion designed to manipulate an opponent (government or private organization). The chapter describes a terrorist as having the following characteristics:

- 21 to 40 years old
- Often female
- Having no criminal record
- Well educated
- Skilled in military techniques
- Dedicated to a cause

This chapter explains the structure of terrorist groups by geographical location and provides details on the methods of operation employed by the various terrorist groups. Counterterrorist security personnel are given excellent information as to the tactics that are employed by terrorists. Foremost in terrorist groups are advanced intelligence and careful planning. They will only attempt a mission if they believe that it has an excellent opportunity to succeed.

Terrorist plans include the manipulation of existing security systems, including the recruitment of personnel from within the organization. They most frequently have inside sources of information that provide them with the ability to strike at a time and a place when they are least expected. Frequently, they will kidnap an employee or employee's family prior to an attack or they will seize a hostage during the attack.

Prior to the attack, they will embark upon such measures as isolating the facility by eliminating power or communication. They are either experts at detonating explosive devices, or they recruit sympathetic groups or individuals to assist in the deployment of explosives. They will rehearse their plan at length and usually implement an attack under adverse weather conditions.

The thrust of this chapter is to point out that effective physical security measures are frequently one of the best means of countering terrorism. The chapter lists more than 25 tactical procedures that can reduce the threat of terrorism.

The author suggests that a well-trained security force, conversant with terrorist tactics and trained in all security areas ranging from physical fitness to recognizing ploys that are utilized by terrorists, is necessary to protect against terrorism.

This chapter also offers readers excellent information on current strategies that may be employed to enhance VIP protection. The matter of hostage-taking is discussed at length and techniques that are essential to improve the chance of hostage survival are dealt with in considerable detail. Hostage negotiation and release measures are also integral parts of this excellent guide to life-threatening facets of crisis management.

Weapons of Mass Destruction: The NBC Threats

The chapter begins by defining the nature of Weapons of Mass Destruction, including the definition found in the U.S. Code. The nature of each type of potential threat is discussed to identify them individually. Device detection and incident prevention are also discussed, inclusive of the challenges of identifying these threats, as they can be easily disguised. The immediate response to an incident is explained, as is a listing of some common indicators of chemical weapon effects. The fact that nuclear and biological threats have varied effects is discussed. The treatment and long-term response are also explored, with emphasis placed on the responsibility of outside agencies in determining the actual nature of the threat, the decontamination of the area, and the return of control to the rightful owners.

UNIT NINE

Crime Scene Procedures

How successfully the protection officer is able to protect the crime scene and preserve evidence has considerable impact on the outcome of a criminal investigation, either by the police or senior members of the security organization.

The protection officer who encounters a crime scene must first take measures that will afford officer safety. Criminal apprehension is less important than reducing the chance of injury or death to protection personnel.

Once it has been established that a crime has taken place and in fact a crime scene does exist, the officer must then seek backup personnel. The boundaries of the crime scene must be determined and declared a sterile area. No one without authorization from the senior security or police officials may be allowed into the restricted area.

The protection officer has specific responsibilities, foremost of which is properly preparing notes that may later be helpful in crime detection activities. This chapter explains what the protection officer might expect to find at a crime scene. It also provides information as to how the protection officer can best render assistance to investigating officers on the scene. The chapter concludes with a caution to the protection officer: "Don't touch—preserve and protect."

Foundations for Surveillance

The basic goal of surveillance is explained in the beginning of the chapter as being the obtaining of information through focused efforts. The subtypes of surveillance operations are explored, with the basic four being explained in detail. Equipment requirements are also explored as they relate to the nature and scope of each type of operation. The importance of understanding privacy laws and similar restrictions are emphasized. The importance of recording and retention of recordings is explained.

Interviewing Techniques

The protection officer has been described a number of times in this manual as the first officer on the scene. First officer at a fire, emergency, accident, crime scene, alarm response, a labor dispute—you name it—the officer *must be there*. Interviewing is no exception.

The officer must carefully record initial remarks made by witnesses or suspects, record what occurred at a crime or accident scene, and take statements given under conditions of distress. This is not an easy task because how well this information is obtained and recorded will frequently have a major impact on the action taken by affected parties and individuals.

Readers should review the Field Note and Report Writing chapter in conjunction with this part of the manual.

The basic difference between note taking and interviewing is that the interviewer must take charge of the situation. There are a number of proven methods that will assist the officer in assuming the command position in these circumstances. There are several stages that should be followed when interviewing.

- Getting acquainted
- Developing a rapport
- Motivating the subject
- Keeping the subject talking
- Listening to what is said

Many times it is not possible to conduct a structured interview, so it is doubly important to carefully record all information that is seen or heard. If the formal interview is conducted by a senior member of the guard force, the preliminary information obtained by the field officer will prove invaluable to the supervisor.

This chapter discusses obstacles that can be encountered in an interview and gives the interviewer helpful tips to avoid losing the lead role. Such tactics as initially avoiding specific questions, avoiding yes or no answers, not using leading questions, avoiding rapid-fire questions, not using open-ended questions, avoiding a long pause if necessary, and not taking the nondirect approach are all useful interviewing techniques. The chapter concludes with helpful suggestions on how to successfully conclude the interview.

Investigations: Concepts and Practices for Security Professionals

Protection officers sometimes have misconceptions about what constitutes white-collar crime. Because the protection officer is an adjunct member of the management team, it is his/her duty to provide management with information.

The officer reports this information after conducting some basic types of investigative activity such as searching, interviews, attending an accident or crime scene, interven-

ing in a conflict situation, or any number of the routine occurrences that involve security on a regular basis.

Generally, the protection officer becomes involved in the preliminary investigation. This is an important facet of the entire investigation process because initial information must be factual and accurately recorded. These are the initial investigation steps.

- Attending to injured persons
- Detaining suspects known to have committed a crime
- Finding and questioning witnesses
- Preserving the crime/accident scene
- Forwarding information to dispatch
- Completing a preliminary report

The chapter goes on to discuss follow-up investigations, auditing, interviews, interrogations, informants, undercover investigations, and testifying in court. The role of the protection officer is often limited to the preliminary investigation, but officers should have an overall understanding of the entire investigative process.

With fewer law enforcement personnel available to private and government organizations, and more crime, corporations are becoming more dependent on professional security personnel to provide organizational protection. An informed officer who understands the entire investigative process is a valuable asset to any security organization.

UNIT TEN

Legal Aspects of Security

Protection officer discretion is the fundamental message that should be derived from this chapter. The law is a complex and changing field, and the members of the security community cannot be expected to be totally conversant with all facets of the administration of justice. It is, however, of vital importance to understand the rights and duties that are exercised in the everyday security role.

This section will examine what law is, the sources of our laws, and the differences between some of the more important parts of the legal framework. The powers of the protection officer are examined, including arrest and search. When the term "arrest" is mentioned, it is essential that cautionary remarks accompany any reference to this aspect of security and the law.

Two types of arrest are covered in this chapter: arrest with a warrant and arrest without a warrant. Arrests with a warrant are generally a matter for police authorities, and the only involvement on the part of security personnel would be a supportive role.

Arresting a person without a warrant is a very serious undertaking, which could have far-reaching civil and criminal legal repercussions if complete adherence to the law is not observed. A protection officer, who is in lawful possession of real property, may arrest a person without a warrant found committing a criminal offense on or in relation to the property that is being protected.

If it is essential to execute an arrest, there must be absolutely no doubt in the mind of the protection officer that the offense was committed. The officer protecting the property must have found the offense being committed.

Before effecting an arrest, every other possible means of detaining the person should be explored. It is inherently dangerous to take away the liberties of a person. Every possible effort should be made to detain the individual on a voluntary basis. An arrest should only be made if there are no other courses of action available and there is a serious threat to life or property.

If every other course of action has been explored and an arrest must be effected, support personnel are the prime consideration. Officer safety and the safety of others are essential.

If a person responsible for committing a criminal offense is arrested, there are several important procedures that are followed. The arrested person(s) must be advised of the following:

- The reason for the arrest
- The right to legal counsel
- That the person under arrest is not required to say anything

Once arrested, the protection officer is responsible for the safety of the individual(s). The protection officer has a legal responsibility to deliver the arrested person(s) to a police officer as soon as practically possible.

This chapter provides readers with general information on common law, criminal and civil law, search authority, use of force, evidence, confessions, and gives the reader an overview of legal aspects in security.

The objective of the section is to help members of the security community to understand the authority that is available to them and how it can be applied to the protection of life and property. The protection officer who understands the nature and extent of their personal authority does the best job for his/her employer without unnecessary exposure to liability.

Court actions for false arrest and illegal searches can be costly in terms of legal fees and damages if the case is lost. It is the duty of every protection officer to keep current and understand the administration of justice as it relates to security in the particular jurisdiction concerned.

UNIT ELEVEN

Use of Force

In this chapter, the use of force is thoroughly discussed particularly with respect to its legal implications for the security officer. Ultimately, the use of force should be considered as an absolute last resort. Rather, the security officer is encouraged to develop his/her abilities in the use of verbal deescalation techniques, such as slowing down the action of, and actively listening to, the perpetrator and ask-

ing the perpetrator's friends and/or relatives to assist in the negotiation by speaking directly to the perpetrator.

The key to effecting calmness in a potentially aggressive situation is for the security officer to maintain self-control at all times. The formula for self-control is presented: control = I/E, where I and E represent intellect and emotion, respectively. While fear and stress may have the effect of altering the officer's physical state, such as inducing sweating, rapid heartbeat, shortness of breath, and ultimately lowering his/her capacity for self-control, intensive professional training will allow the officer to quickly regain his/her confidence and self-control in these threatening situations.

Recognizing potentially dangerous situations before they start is a very important skill for the security guard to master. Several indicators, or "red flags," are discussed, such as the posture and hand movements of the subject.

Finally, the writing of reports is considered with specific reference to a use of force incident. The goal of the report is to clearly show that, under identical circumstances, anyone would have done exactly the same things as the attending officer. However, because of the potential legal and social hazards associated with the use of force, it is portrayed throughout this chapter as something to be avoided with verbal deescalation the much more favored method of dealing with potentially violent situations. Successful verbal deescalation depends on impeccable self-control, which is considered to be one of the primary goals of every security professional.

Defensive Tactics and Officer Safety

This chapter begins by stressing the importance of maintaining awareness in order to best provide for their own safety. The concept of "observe and report" is stressed, as opposed to involvement in confrontation. Officers are directed to use caution, call for assistance when needed, properly utilize lighting to their advantage, and utilize all senses. A basic description of combat is given, including the concepts of control of space, timing, and damage. Officers are encouraged to gain an understanding of their own limitations to better understand their own responses. Officers are also directed to research local laws as they relate to use of force and self-defense. Stroberger's Rule of Seven is discussed as they relate to firearm exchanges, use of OC sprays, and minimum safe reaction gaps. The use of force is explored with an explanation of the continuum and the levels of force in sequential order. Officers are directed to deescalate levels of aggression and to maintain a level of force that is reasonable based on the perceived level of threat. Training concepts are explored as they relate to realism, environment, and probable attacker types. The idea of formal martial arts training is discussed and the limits and advantages explored. The application of weapons is also discussed with a focus on training, proper application, and legal implications. The expectation of injury is explained to prepare the officer to more effectively manage the physical and psychological effects. Basic tips are given.

Apprehension and Detention Procedures

There is probably no topic in the security profession that generates as much discussion, and misunderstanding, as apprehension and detention. It is not only the source of many complaints by the clients we serve, it can also be the beginning of a very lengthy and costly legal action. For these two reasons alone, it is worth a long look by people in the business. But, that is not where it ends. We also have to look at the possibility of injury, and even death, that could result in a misunderstanding of just how much authority a security officer really has to control the movements of another person.

Arrest procedures are covered in this chapter as is the different powers of arrest, what constitutes an arrest, and the different authorities bestowed to certain individuals. In addition to this, the author looks at what gets a security officer in trouble and keys to avoiding criminal and civil liability. Topics that are included in this include, assault, battery, false arrest, false imprisonment, malicious prosecution, and invasion of privacy.

Additionally, there is a very concise section on detention and apprehension methodology and use of force.

UNIT TWELVE

Public Relations

The security officer is often the first person that a member of the public will encounter when approaching a particular private company or institution. As such, the security professional must be well versed in the "art" of maintaining good public relations. This is because the security officer is the direct, out-front representative of his/her company, and by maintaining favorable relationships with the public and the community as a whole, the criminal element may be subdued. Good public relations are, in effect, good loss control tactics.

Security professionals should consider themselves to be "salespeople." They should always present a professional image to the public by dress code, posture, demeanor, and by their eagerness to genuinely volunteer assistance to anyone who approaches them.

Special emphasis is given to the methods by which good public relations may be maintained with respect to the media. Again, the emphasis is always on the attending security officer being as helpful and courteous as possible without volunteering specific information. That job is always handled by the public information officer (PIO). The skill with which a security professional can guide the interests of the media to the PIO is an invaluable asset to his/her company.

Finally, specific tactics regarding public relations and the occurrence of an emergency within the parent organization are discussed. Two strategies, creating a plant emergency organization and contacting an external security contingent, are outlined. The "bottom line" is that the security profes-sional must become skilled at managing situations so that good public and media relations are maintained at all times.

Police and Security Liaison

This chapter takes an in-depth look at some of the past and present problems that have hampered the relationship between law enforcement and private security personnel. It also discusses some of the findings of various studies that have been conducted on the relationship between the two professions (Hallcrest I and II).

Later sections of the chapter discuss the differences between the two professions and the common ground that the two professions share (personal protection, crime prevention, and order maintenance). Growth trends of industry and privatization are also discussed.

The chapter closes by giving some general recommendations for improving relationships between police and security personnel. The following recommendations are discussed:

- Establishing credibility with local law enforcement
- Establishing and/or following a code of ethics
- Maintaining the highest levels of professionalism
- Increasing police knowledge of private security
- Establishing mutual agreements between security and law enforcement personnel
- Developing cooperative programs
- Nurturing professional growth and development

Ethics and Professionalism

Private security is rapidly becoming a profession in its own right. As such, it is necessary for security officers to abide by a code of ethics and present themselves in professional ways. Ten items are presented and discussed as the International Foundation for Protection Officers, Code of Ethics. These include exhibiting exemplary conduct, encouraging liaison with public officers, and maintaining a safe and secure workplace.

Continued education and training are key issues to obtaining and maintaining professional status. Several acronyms are presented in order to more clearly illustrate the important points about portraying a professional image, such as P for precise, exact, detailed, and F for factual in all reporting processes, honest, for example. The personal deportment of individual officers is also discussed with the use of the acronym, placing particular emphasis on a dress code, professionalism, and high self-esteem.

Understanding why unethical behavior occurs is presented as an important skill for the security officer to obtain as it relates to controlling losses for the organization with which he/she is employed. Only when ethical behavior is truly understood and adopted as the required norm for security professionals, can unethical behavior be clearly recognized for its potential dangers to the companies and institutions that will be hiring professional protection officers.

Unit One

Evolution of Asset Protection and Security

The Evolution of Asset Protection and Security

By John Christman, CPP
Christopher A. Hertig, CPP, CPOI
Philip P. Purpura, CPP
Jill Segraves, CPO

INTRODUCTION

History is illustrative for many reasons; there are trends and themes that run throughout the march of time and which repeat themselves—to a degree. P. T. Barnum said, "All history is bunk," and he was right—to a degree. History is a *perspective*. In many cases, that perspective gets distorted, or lost over time.

Studying history is important as it gives us perspective on where things were, where they are now, and where they may be in the future. Historical analysis can provide insight into how certain issues were dealt with. This may give guidance in contemporary or future problem solving.

Finally, history provides a laboratory for the testing of theory. Solutions that were developed in response to certain problems had positive or negative effects in addressing the problems. A commonly used example is the Era of Prohibition which began in the United States with the passage of the Volstead Act in 1919. Alcoholic beverage distribution or possession was against the law. As a result, huge criminal enterprises sprang up in response to consumer demand. A black market economy was formed with gangsters seeking to profit. Some people feel that the current legal prohibition against drugs is analogous to Prohibition. This is an arguable point: drugs don't taste good and are not as socially accepted as the drinking of alcohol was in 1920s American society. Nonetheless, the emergence of black markets due to extensive consumer demand for illegal goods or services is something that all students of Asset Protection should appreciate.

THE CYCLE OF HISTORY

The security industry has a rich and varied background! "Security" implies protection: safety from attack, espionage, or sabotage. It means being able to live, work, or play free from harm in a stable environment. Organizations must take measures to minimize disruption. These measures are dependent on a variety of factors, such as threat probability, criticality, culture of the organization, financial resources available, and so on. The measures taken have changed through "the march of time."

The historical development of "asset protection" (the broader, more contemporary term encompassing safety and fire protection) and "security" (the older, more crime/espionage/terrorism-oriented term) reveals several trends. These trends appear to be cyclical in nature.

1. Private initiatives generally precede public. In many cases, private protective measures are initiated to fill a void in services offered by governments.
2. Control forces are involved in class struggles. Control forces—military, police, security—work to keep the underclass, the "have nots," in line.
3. There is a strong relationship between commerce and protective needs. The amount and type of commerce (ships, trains, Internet, and so on.) determine the threats or risks posed to the commerce system. Each risk demands differing protective strategies and tactics. This changes with technological development.
4. Demographics—population size, density, age distribution—plays a key role in crime control and safety measures. Large numbers of recent immigrants who do not understand the language or customs of their newly adopted country create safety and security challenges. American college students living in dormitories create a different set of challenges. High-rise office buildings with business tenants have different protection needs than two-story apartment complexes for low-income families. The list goes on. Security measures must be relevant to the environment in which they are implemented.
5. Military forces and concepts are intimately involved in protection. Threats to a country from foreign invaders, riots that have to be contained by soldiers, and international terrorists are all addressed by military forces. Contemporary protective forces often operate on a military organizational structure; they have a paramilitary chain-of-command with sergeants, lieutenants, and captains. The military has clearly exerted an influence over police, security, and fire departments.
6. Security efforts generally are a step behind the latest methods of criminal attack. The saying "*As one hole in the net is mended, the fish swim toward another*" seems particularly relevant.
7. Protective efforts are usually initiated after serious problems have occurred. The September 11, 2001, attacks on the Pentagon and World Trade Center initiated

substantial reforms in the federal government such as the Transportation Security Administration.

8. Protective efforts often are spawned by the need for mutual protection. Homeland Security is one example with governmental units at all levels coming together in partnership with private organizations to protect against terrorism. Another example was fire societies where society members helped each other to salvage goods after fires was established in Boston in 1718 (Cote & Bugbee, 1988, p. 5).

KEY TERMS

"Assets" are tangibles or intangibles that have value. If assets are stolen, lost, destroyed, or damaged, the entity (organization or individual) owning them suffers a loss. There are four (4) basic classifications of assets.

1. People—employees, visitors, clients, patients, students, and so on.
2. Property—real estate, buildings, raw materials, equipment, merchandise, and so on.
3. Information—vital information that is necessary for an organization's survival such as employee and vendor lists, organizational plans, and other items without which the organization could not operate; confidential information such as patient records; proprietary information such as trade secrets, customer lists, and marketing plans; classified information that is essential to national defense.
4. Image—the image cultivated through years of public relations and advertising that an organization or individual (celebrity) has established. Customer goodwill is an asset. So, too, is a positive image that will not attract the ire of extremist groups or individuals.

"Security" is concerned with those threats that are posed by humans. Espionage, sabotage, theft, and assault are examples.

"Crime Prevention Through Environmental Design" is a theory of crime deterrence based on environmental design. Facilities are constructed—or arranged—in such a way that criminals feel uncomfortable and refrain from committing crimes.

"Physical security" is a system to minimize the threats posed by humans. It incorporates locks, barriers, access control systems, lighting, alarms, and security officers. Physical security is a vast field of study! It can be said that it is the "heart" of security. It encompasses Crime Prevention Through Environmental Design (CPTED) as well as procedural controls.

"Personnel security" is designed to screen out undesirable employees. It is done to protect both the employer and other employees. The screening, or *vetting,* of employees to prevent probes by foreign intelligence agents originated within the "military-industrial complex" of the 1950s to 1980s. The old term "industrial security" (as in "American society for Industrial Security") referred to Department of Defense (DOD) contractor firms who made munitions, tanks, airplanes, and so on for military usage. While espionage—in particular economic espionage—is a major issue, contemporary personnel security also deals with concerns, such as workplace violence, the prevention of internal theft, and terrorism.

"Asset protection" encompasses those threats posed by nature, accident, market, and economic factors as well as those posed strictly by humans. Asset protection incorporates fire protection, HAZMAT, and safety within the discipline. It seeks to identify and manage all risks posed to an organization and incorporates many concepts of *risk management.* Asset protection is the approach used in addressing problems by many organizations. In some cases, the term "loss prevention" is used. This has been particularly common in the retail security sector.

As threats change over time and involve different environments, asset protection is a dynamic undertaking! The history of security/asset protection is formulated in a variety of areas.

PHYSICAL SECURITY

Physical security planning was originally based upon response to a military threat. A traditional reference for physical security is *FM 19-30 Physical Security*, published by the United States Army.

The process used to plan physical security measures is as follows:

1. Identify assets. These generally include *personnel*, *property, information,* and *image*.
2. Loss events are exposed. Risks are identified. This involves research rather than "seat of the pants" reasoning!
3. Probability of the loss events occurring is calculated.
4. Impact of occurrence is assessed for each loss event. This means the effect the loss event will have in terms of *direct*, *indirect,* and *extra-expense* costs.
5. Countermeasures are selected. There can be a vast array of interventions; generally physical security utilizes target hardening techniques, such as patrols, access control, lighting, intrusion detection, surveillance, weapons detection, and so on.
6. Countermeasures are implemented.
7. Countermeasures are evaluated as to their effectiveness. Traditionally, this step has been avoided by practitioners in physical security and crime prevention.

Note: See simon.net for information on physical security products; securitysolutions.com and securitymagazine.com for products and applications.

Patrols are a key part of a physical security system. They serve as catalysts for the system, bringing all parts together. Patrols have been traditionally used by military forces to scout out the location and disposition of an enemy force. They are used today by police and security forces. While still endeavoring to locate hostile individuals (felons), modern police patrols are used to assess community environments. In a contemporary asset protection scheme, patrols are not only concerned with criminal acts, but with unauthorized activities, safety and fire protection issues, and the performance of auxiliary services. These can include delivering the company mail, checking gauges, conducting lighting surveys, assessing crowd and customer behavior, enforcing lease agreements, and assisting customers. Note that a *community policing* or *problem-oriented policing* strategy that public police have adopted is very similar to what security practitioners have been doing for decades!

CRIME PREVENTION THROUGH ENVIRONMENTAL DESIGN

Crime Prevention Through Environmental Design (CPTED) is a system whereby territoriality reinforcement is established via barriers, access control, and surveillance. Its genesis may have been in the construction of castles and forts. The contemporary beginnings of it were through the writings of Oscar Newman *(Defensible Space)* and C. Ray Jeffery (**Crime Prevention Through Environmental Design**). CPTED theory consists of these various components.

Territoriality: Boundaries and property lines are marked. This can be the placement of barriers, shrubbery, and the use of different colors of walkways to mark areas. *Psychological* deterrents to trespass are erected to establish territoriality.

Surveillance: Observing areas makes detection and deterrence of criminal behavior more likely. There are several types of deterrence.

Natural—keeping areas open to observation, such as by clearing bushes near access points, having windows facing out into a common courtyard, or placing a picnic area near a basketball court. All of these make observation of the area to be protected easier. They facilitate detection of criminal or unauthorized activity.

Electronic—technological aids are used, such as closed circuit television (CCTV), and volumetric intrusion detection systems, such as passive infrared (PIR)

Organized—patrols by security personnel, police, or citizen crime watches.

Access control: Maintaining boundaries by restricting access to an area. Access is controlled via the use of locks, biometric systems, cardkeys, and other methods. Access control is a *physical* deterrent to trespass.

Positive activity support: In a significant departure from physical security, CPTED uses activities that divert people in the environment from involvement in crime. This may take the form of recreation, entertainment, or volunteer efforts that help society (volunteer fire companies for youth).

Maintenance: The repair of "broken windows." An environment that is not kept up properly may degenerate further. People see broken windows and believe it is acceptable to break other windows. A "snowballing" or "rolling ball" effect occurs. Prompt repair and cleaning of damage or graffiti is an essential part of CPTED.

THE WARTIME GROWTH OF SECURITY

Military defense is often discussed in the literature on the history of security. Ortmeier (1999) reveals that in prehistoric times, cavedwellers stacked rocks around perimeters in front of their caves to both mark this space and warn off intruders (p. 98). The Praetorian Guard in ancient Rome were military personnel. Military threats employ military approaches. Such approaches often utilize military personnel and incorporate ***military culture.***

"Defense-in-depth" is a military concept wherein assets are protected by successive lines of defense. This includes clear zones, outer perimeters, inner perimeters, and soldiers or protection officers. This is a key element of physical security plans. Contemporary facility models of defense-in-depth incorporate safes and vaults, alarm systems, and insurance coverage into the protection plan.

Military threats and organizations are easily seen from reviewing history. There are numerous examples! The Texas Rangers—established as a light cavalry unit during the Texan Revolution and later used to repel Indians and control the borders; the RCMP, which played a key security role during World War II, and the ***Pennsylvania State Police,*** which was formed after the Great Anthracite Strike of 1903–1904. The strike lasted nine months and cost Pennsylvania over a million dollars to pay for the National Guard. The governor of Pennsylvania realized that calling out the National Guard was not an effective means of handling strikes. The head of the Philadelphia City Cavalry—which was used during the strike—was recruited by the governor to start the Pennsylvania State Police. State police officers in Pennsylvania are "troopers" organized in troops—based on the organizational design of a cavalry unit.

A review of some events in history that created security problems is outlined here.

July 1916—an explosion at Black Tom Island, a munitions storage facility in New Jersey, was set off by a German saboteur. This increased War Department security measures. The potential for problems caused by saboteurs, foreign intelligence agents (spies), and terrorists who are state-sponsored creates a need for increased security measures during all military conflicts.

World War II—U.S. Department of War established internal security division and swore in 200,000 security officers as military police auxiliary. State National Guard units were also activated. In some cases, states had Home Guard organizations that enabled the National Guard to engage in combat or combat support activities while the Home Guard maintained a domestic security posture.

Korean War—The "Cold War" era began with heightened tensions between the United States and Russia. *The Industrial Security Manual* was published in 1952. This was considered the Bible of Department Of Defense contractor security procedures. It established information protection, personnel security, and physical security measures for DOD contractors. Since the United States was in a wartime economy until about 1975, there was lots of activity in this sector. Many security personnel worked in "industrial security."

POLICING

Police in Ancient Rome consisted of the Praetorian Guards which were a military unit. There were also cohorts who kept peace. The vigiles were civilian freemen who controlled fires and assisted in controlling crime and riots. It is interesting to note that urban mob violence was one reason why municipal police were formed in both England and the United States.

With the Norman Conquest of England in 1066, there were several significant governmental developments.

1. The introduction of feudalism, a contractual relationship between lords of the manor, and their tenants or vassals
2. The centralization of government
3. The reorganization of the church

One protection development that was established was a community-based system of policing called the *frankpledge*. The frankpledge system required every male over the age of 12 to form into a group of 10 with his neighbors called a "tithing." The tithing was sworn to help protect fellow citizens and apprehend and deliver persons who committed crimes. Ten tithings were grouped into hundreds who were directed by a constable. The constable was appointed by a nobleman and was, in effect, the first police officer (Peak, 1997, p. 6).

Note that early Roman and English—and later American—policing functions were dependent on citizen involvement. The need for mutual assistance spawns protective efforts.

In the early 19th century, London continued to have a large population with crime and disorder problems. As few organizational models were available at this time, the military model was adopted for the London Metropolitan Police (Ortmeier, 1999, p. 53). What Robert Peel established in 1829 in London served as an organizational model for police in American cities. These cities began to develop uniformed police forces in the mid-1800s which were similar to what we have today. Peel set forth a series of principles upon which a police force could be established and administered. While his specific frame of reference was public law enforcement, the principles are generally adaptable to uniformed private protection forces.

1. The police must be stable, efficient, and organized along military lines.
2. The police must be under government control.
3. The absence of crime will best prove the efficiency of police.
4. The distribution of crime news is absolutely essential.
5. The deployment of police strength both by time and by area is essential.

6. No quality is more indispensable to a police officer than a perfect command of temper; a quiet, determined manner has more effect than violent action.
7. Good appearance commands respect.
8. The securing and training of proper persons is at the root of efficiency.
9. Public security demands that every police officer be given a number.
10. Police headquarters should be centrally located.
11. Police officers should be hired on a probationary basis.
12. Police records are necessary to the correct distribution of police strength.

In the mid-19th century major American cities began to develop police departments. The following cities initiated police departments in the 1840s to the 1860s: Boston, New York, Chicago, New Orleans, Cincinnati, Philadelphia, Baltimore, and Newark. These forces began to evolve out of earlier night watch systems that utilized volunteers or civilians. Some of these forces only operated at night, and they were no longer effective at controlling crime in burgeoning urban environments. Organized, paid, full-time police operating under the principles established by Robert Peel began to take shape.

State police forces also developed. The first of these was the Pennsylvania State Police. This is generally regarded as the first modern state police department. While Texas and Massachusetts had state police forces, these were vastly different from the organizations we think of as "state police." The Pennsylvania State Police have full law enforcement authority. They also are responsible for traffic control on state highways such as the Pennsylvania Turnpike. In some states, there are separate highway patrol forces that specialize in traffic law enforcement (California Highway Patrol, Ohio Highway Patrol).

"PRIVATE SECURITY" OR "PUBLIC POLICE"?

Policing is both public *and* private. Public policing as we know it is relatively recent. Private police forces are older in most cases. Private policing preceded public policing with merchant, parish, and dock police forces in England. Public and private were difficult to distinguish from each other. The **Railroad Police** were, and still are, a privately employed police force with full law enforcement authority. The **Coal and Iron Police in Pennsylvania** were also privately employed and had law enforcement powers.

Current policing in the United States was greatly influenced by the **Omnibus Crime Control** and **Safe Streets Act of 1968**. This created the **Law Enforcement Assistance Administration**, which funded training and education for police. Police by the thousands began to acquire college educations. Criminal justice programs were spawned at colleges across the country. The LEAA also provided grant monies for equipment and crime analysis. One could argue that modern policing in America began in 1968!

Fees were used to pay for early police services. The Parliamentary Reward System in England paid a fee of 40 English pounds to private persons who captured felons. Both Jonathan Wild and the Bow Street Runners were early private detectives who worked under the Parliamentary Reward System. Similarly, constables in Pennsylvania are private citizens with arrest powers who serve warrants and perform various court functions on a fee basis. The constable system was imported from England and is an elected office. In the 19th century, there were private detectives who received rewards for recovering stolen property. These detectives worked for the rich and were associated with the unseemly criminal underworld. Their aim was to receive the fee, not work toward the ends of justice! Over time these private detectives were replaced by public police. This occurred because of criticism of their methods as well as the entry of insurance companies. Once there were insurance policies to compensate policyholders for their losses, the incentive to recover stolen property subsided (Kukendall, 1986). This change was gradual; U.S. police often worked for rewards. One of the notable contributions of Allan Pinkerton was that he established a code of ethics and forbade the acceptance of rewards by his men.

Some other examples of "private security" or "public law enforcement" include the following:

1. Police in major cities serve as "ambassadors" of the city, a role assumed by private protection officers in hotels, resorts, casinos, and shopping centers. Note that tourism = municipal revenue!

2. Contract security personnel patrol apartment complexes, housing developments, and shopping centers in a form of "community-oriented policing." Some firms specialize in "weeding" out the criminal element via surveillance and apprehension of drug dealers and other criminals. Once the area has been "weeded," it can be "seeded." The contract officers then assume a "community-oriented" policing role. They help neighborhood children, organize community activities, and so on.

3. College campuses often have campus police who conduct more asset protection and security work than law enforcement functions. Some colleges have both police and security divisions. Almost all have some type of student patrols.

4. Federal agencies such as the Secret Service and U.S. Marshals are really more concerned with security than law enforcement functions.

5. Government agencies often have either proprietary or contract security departments. Housing bureaus, school systems, parks departments, reservoirs, and so on. are protected by security personnel. Some cities and counties have their own proprietary security departments.

6. Military and federal installations have security forces. These may be either proprietary government employees or private contract officers.

7. Shopping centers are private properties open to the public for business. They usually have private security forces. Some have police substations within so that close cooperation between mall management, security department, and police department is facilitated.

8. Commissioned security officers are used in some environments. These are privately employed protection officers who have police commissions. This enables them to make arrests under certain circumstances, for certain types of offenses and/or within a specified area. Large hospitals and resorts located in remote locations, and some private colleges use this model.

The term "private security" has limited meaning when one considers the array of public-private protection and enforcement arrangements!

The **blending** of police and security was very great in the 19th century and, it is probably safe to say, within the last 30 years or so. It will probably continue as our society becomes increasingly complex and we utilize resources on a contractual/outsourcing or task force basis more and more. Computer crimes will necessitate contracting out for investigative expertise by government agencies. So, too, will cost considerations as police are extremely expensive employees to maintain (screening, training, equipment, and health benefits). Functions that do not absolutely require a sworn law enforcement officer can be performed by a civilian. This can be a proprietary municipal or contract employee. Additional factors are retirement plans and an aging population. Retired police do not make enough money to cease working. Employing them as security officers or investigators may utilize their skills in a mutually beneficial manner to both employer and officer.

An area of concern is police "moonlighting" in security. This can create numerous problems, such as determining whether the off-duty police officer is a police officer or security officer when making apprehensions, and so on. There may be a temptation to use official databases for the benefit of a private employer. Preferential treatment of the employer (store, mall, theater, restaurant, hotel, and so on.) may occur. The off-duty work may also begin to take precedence over the full-time job. The officer may spend too many hours working off-duty and be tired. Officer survival concerns are greatly expanded with off-duty police! Employers of off-duty police will also have a hard time in controlling them, as terminating their employment can create intense hostility from local police departments!

For more information on the history of policing, visit the Police Heritage Museum in York, PA. See policeheritage-museum.com or call 717/845-COPS.

THE "WILD WEST"

The American West in the latter 19th century had its share of security problems in the form of outlaws and hostile **Indians**. Western outlaws were prevalent in the frontier areas. With the California gold rush of 1849 and the latter discovery of gold and silver in various areas, mining and railroad towns emerged. There were lots of immigrants and alcohol abuse was common—conditions not unlike those in London during the Industrial Revolution. Railroads and cattlemen had extensive assets to protect over long stretches of territory.

Outlaws flourished in the Wild West for the following reasons:

1. Poor coordination/communication between law enforcement agencies. There was no Internet or Interpol!
2. Jurisdictional limitations of lawmen who could not cross state, territorial, or national borders in the pursuit of criminals.
3. Popular "hero" status of outlaws. In the aftermath of the American Civil War, many outlaws who had participated in military operations against the Union remained as raiders. Some citizens regarded them as heroes because they preyed on banks and trains—the institutions most closely associated with the Union government.
4. Violent personal background of outlaws. The Civil War was often the cauldron within which violence was developed in men.
5. Charisma of outlaws. Some outlaws were charismatic charmers. They were popular and well liked by people in their area of operations so that they were given shelter, information, food, and so on.
6. Psychopathic personalities. Jesse James may have been psychopathic. John Wesley Hardin and others were also virulently antisocial.

In the American West, there were various control forces operating:

Pinkerton agents who investigated crimes and pursued criminals across the United States as well as in foreign countries. The Wild Bunch—popularized by the film *Butch Cassidy and the Sundance Kid*—were pursued to Bolivia. Frank Reno of the infamous Reno Gang was apprehended by Pinkerton agents in Windsor, Ontario, and later extradited from Canada. Pinkerton also did work in Cuba for the Spanish government. The Pinkerton Agency filled the void that not having a Federal Bureau of Investigation created.

Railroad police. Railroads had police, which numbered 14,000 by 1914 (Purpura, 1991, p.12) as well as hired security personnel such as the famous Bat Masterson. Their contribution to law and order must have been significant, since there were large numbers of them. Unfortunately, many history sections of criminal justice and security books do not discuss them in any great detail.

Deputy U.S. Marshals in the American West were public police but were not on a career track like today's civil servants. They received rewards/fees for services (similar to PA's constables). They drifted from job to job in many cases, as did town and county sheriffs and marshals. Contemporary U.S. Marshals transport prisoners, protect federal courthouses, and enforce federal court orders. They are more closely related to county sheriffs, who perform the same functions at the county level.

Vigilantes were citizens who took legal matters into their own hands. Lynching of outlaws was not uncommon in some locations.

Town marshals who were hired by municipalities to enforce the law and keep the peace. These marshals often drifted from job to job. Some drifted back and forth between being lawmen and being criminals! See the film *Wyatt Earp* with Kevin Costner for some treatment of this.

Texas Rangers, who protected the borders of Texas from Indians and worked to control rustlers. Founded in 1836 during the Texas Revolution, they were a light cavalry unit. Later, toward the end of the 19th century, Arizona and New Mexico also established rangers.

The U.S. Army provided security from Indian attacks and pursued hostile natives. **The Union Army** numbered about 27,000 men immediately after the Civil War. Many were deployed in the West with roughly one-fifth of the Army dedicated to railroad protection. With the railroad becoming transcontinental in 1869, the lines moved through Indian territory and created friction between natives and railroad workers.

The Royal Canadian Mounted Police enforced laws throughout Canada. The "Mounties" were established in 1873. They enforce federal statutes, maintain national security, and frequently provide assistance to other government departments. The RCMP first started with 300 men; the contemporary force has increased to approximately 20,000 people.

FIRE PROTECTION

Fire Protection is a major issue in Asset Protection! Fire can destroy almost anything. It is a chemical process whereby heat, fuel, and oxygen combine in a chemical chain reaction to turn a solid or liquid into a gas. **With adequate amounts of heat and oxygen, virtually anything can become fuel for a fire.**

The first known attempt to control a fire according to history books was about 300 BC in Rome. A form of a watch service, which was called the Corps of Vigiles, was created to watch for any fires that might have started. The Corps of Vigils could have been the first municipal-type fire department. Cote and Bugbee (1988) maintain that they were the first organized form of fire protection. Each vigil was assigned a specific task such as carrying water. The threat of fire varies with the environment. The *perception* of that threat also changes. Prior to the Civil War, fire insurance executives generally viewed fire as good for business (Purpura, 1991, p. 10). Fires were similar to airplane crashes in that they were relatively improbable events that created hysteria and spurred the purchase of insurance policies. Insurance companies made money on these policies until excessive fires—in heavily populated areas where buildings were constructed of wood—caused enormous amounts of claims to be paid.

Here is a brief overview of some major events in the development of fire protection.

1631 A disastrous fire in Boston resulted in the first fire ordinance in the United States. This ordinance prohibited wooden chimneys and thatched roofs (Ortmeier, 1999, p. 103). Wooden chimneys were banned in London in 1647 (Cote & Bugbee, 1988, p. 3). Wooden chimneys were often used in American soldiers' winter quarters and the cabins of slaves.

1666 The Great Fire of London spread due to closely situated wooden buildings, wind, and dry weather. The fire initiated some interest in fire prevention by insurance companies. A complete code of building regulations was adopted but not made effective, since commissioners to enforce the regulations were not appointed until 1774 (Cote & Bugbee, 1988, p. 3). It also destroyed the environment that rats lived in so that the Black Plague was eliminated.

1667 Phoenix Fire Office—a private firefighting service that suppressed fires on subscribers property. Subscribers had a crest on their buildings to mark them. Other private fire companies also formed. Today some industrial complexes and other facilities have their own proprietary fire brigades. Some of these are well equipped and can suppress small fires. In most cases, fire departments are paid public professionals. Volunteer firemen are also used and play an important role in providing firefighting to many areas.

1871 Peshtigo Fire—a logging community in Wisconsin; Peshtigo had very dry weather and this created a forest fire that burned vast acres of land. A massive firestorm formed where the fire consumed oxygen at such a rate that it created significant draft. This was probably the worst fire in U.S. history. It is relatively unknown because the Chicago Fire, which occurred a few days later, received more attention from the news media.

1871 Chicago Fire. As in the Great Fire of London, closely situated wooden buildings caught fire in dry weather. The wind whipped the fire through Chicago, and the city was destroyed. We commemorate the Chicago Fire with Fire Prevention Week. Fire Prevention Week is held each year in the week in October containing October 9.

1894 Underwriter's Laboratories was formed. UL is an independent testing laboratory. It subjects products to extensive tests to see if they work as they are supposed to and if they are safe.

1896 The National Fire Protection Administration development of *standards* for fire protection. These standards are used throughout industry and are the basis for many municipal fire codes.

1948 The National Burglar and Fire Alarm Association was formed. NBFAA offers membership, publications, seminars, and professional certification programs for alarm installers.

1965 National Board of Fire Underwriters was merged with the American Insurance Association. This resulted in the development of the National Building Code for municipalities (Purpura, 1991, p. 10).

For more information on fire protection, visit the National Fire Protection Association at nfpa.org.

SAFETY

Safety ushers in the more contemporary emphasis on Asset Protection and incorporates the **WAECUP Theory of Loss Control** developed by Bottom and Kostanoski in *Security and Loss Control* (first published by MacMillan in 1983).

W – Waste of time, resources, man-hours, space
A – Accident that causes injury, downtime, increased workman's compensation costs, and so on
E – Error in planning or execution, which results in lost funds
C – Crime that causes loss and/or injury
UP – Unethical/unprofessional practices, such as misrepresentation, discrimination, conflict of interest, and so on

Accidents cost extensive amounts of *direct loss* (cost of replacement and repair) as well as indirect *loss* (downtime, investigative costs, lowered morale, legal fees, and so on.) and *extra-expense loss* (advertising, rental of new rooms or equipment). Note that there are also extensive administrative law requirements under OSHA and state agencies (CALOSHA and PA Department of Labor and Industry), which organizations must comply with. Safety is a major concern to organizations for all of these reasons. Many persons in charge of security are also in charge of safety. Director of Safety and Security is a not uncommon title in healthcare, college campuses, and hotel environments.

COMMERCE

Commerce has a tremendous relationship to Asset Protection. Professional security personnel must understand the marketing of their employer's goods and services in order to be effective. A retail Loss Prevention Agent must understand that selling merchandise is the reason for the existence of the store, not the apprehension of shoplifters! *Marketing must be balanced with security.* They are "both different sides of the same coin." It can be said, in both a theoretical and practical sense, that "marketing is the 'flip side' of security."

From the beginning of the 19th century until the development of the railroads, massive canal networks were constructed in the eastern United States. Mules pulled barges along towpaths to ship freight long distances. Canals were replaced by railroads beginning in about the 1850s. During their heyday, canals had asset protection concerns with accidents and labor shortages. Workers were sometimes injured and barges and canals damaged. Getting qualified workers to construct canals was a problem.

Railroad expansion during the 19th century was dramatic. Railroads were necessary to ship goods and raw materials in large quantities. Railroads had, and still have, a variety of security—and safety—issues. Nineteenth-century American railroads faced Indian attacks and sabotage of tracks and telegraph lines. In one instance, Indian warriors attempted to capture a locomotive by using lariats stretched across the track attached to their saddles. When the engine hit the rawhide, warriors were swung into the locomotive and dismembered (Constable, 1990, p. 198). There were also buffalo stampedes, wrecks, and labor difficulties, which included both shortages of workers and strikes. An external control force—the Union Army—was also employed with nearly 5,000 soldiers patrolling along and around the tracks in 1868 (Mattthews, 1990, p. 101). Brigadier General John Stephen Casement, construction manager for the Union Pacific under Major General Grenville Dodge, utilized a varied labor supply of Irish immigrants, discharged soldiers, fed-up farmers, disillusioned prospectors, and a few Indian women. He trained them as a quasi-military force to lay tracks in a quick, efficient fashion and at the same time repel Indian raiders with Spencer repeating rifles that were kept nearby (Constable, 1990, p. 195). Such human resource management problems (recruitment of quality personnel), safety issues, and external threats (Indian raids) parallel the challenges facing contemporary asset protection managers. Today's manager is concerned with personnel recruitment (hiring) and retention (keeping workers), OSHA compliance, and external threats, such as sabotage by terrorists.

Air transport is vulnerable to theft, safety problems, terrorists, and "air rage" by emotionally disturbed passengers. In 1969, numerous airplane hijackings occurred, and in 1974, the Anti-Hijacking and Air Transportation Security Act was passed, establishing security programs at airports. "Air rage" and the September 11 hijackings as well as the shoe bombs possessed by Richard Reid are more current issues.

Shipping on the high seas has historically presented problems with piracy and labor/human resource management (HRM) issues. Contemporary cruise ships face issues such as drunken, assaultive passengers and lawsuits due to cases of sexual harassment and rapes. The threat of terrorism by Islamic fundamentalists is also very real be it through the commandeering of a cruise ship, the smuggling of weapons of mass destruction aboard freighters, or attacks on ports such as detonating an explosive-laden ship within a harbor. Piracy—the robbery or hijacking of ships—continues to be a problem in some areas.

Telephone communication and Internet commerce are the new fronts for security issues relating to commerce. *Disinformation* (the deliberate dissemination of false information such as "urban legends"), theft of communications services, and so on are major concerns.

ECONOMIC AND MARKETING TRENDS AND ASSET PROTECTION

The desirability of an asset has an effect on the probability of it being stolen. A fundamental component of protection is to assign a monetary value to something. Historically, the "robber barons" of the late 19th century needed protection of their railroads, coal mines, and steel mills. They also needed personal protection due to their vast wealth, as do current celebrities such as rock stars, film stars, and corporate executives.

With the availability of retail store outlets and self-service shopping, shoplifting has become a major issue. It is a low-tech crime that can be carried out by juveniles, drug addicts, and so on. With the high value of some store merchandise, sophisticated professional thieves and even terrorist groups engage in retail theft. Organized Retail Theft (ORT) incorporates theft, repackaging, and distribution of the stolen product. It is a sophisticated operation involving various entities and warehouses to store the merchandise.

See lpjobs.com or *Loss Prevention* magazine for more on retail security. Also see the books available through the ASIS bookstore at asisonline.org.

Contemporary loss problems include the counterfeiting of name brand items. This is particularly acute in certain areas of the world with emerging markets such as Russia. Cigarettes are also a prime black market item because of their cost due to tax increases. Criminal enterprises that respond to these black markets are becoming more sophisticated. The theft of information concerning the development of new toys and drugs are major issues. "Competitive intelligence" and counterintelligence are key asset protection functions today. Internet crimes ranging from harassing e-mail to viruses, diversion of funds, and espionage are also problems. The theft of phone service and credit (identity theft or credit card theft) is also a major problem. Identity theft creates large amounts of indirect loss to the victim as investigating and cleaning up the problem takes enormous amounts of time. Employers of identity theft victims are also affected by a loss of productivity.

All of these criminal targets change as rapidly as economics and markets dictate. Understanding markets is crucial to comprehending—and planning—protective measures. "Marketing is the 'flip side' of security" in more ways than one.

Technological innovations also help to keep protection professionals from being bored! Generally speaking criminals outpace the efforts of police and security professionals. Historically they are able to create loss by being one step ahead of protective measures.

DEMOGRAPHICS

Demographics plays a major role in asset protection. *Demographic* theories of crime causation focus on the changing composition of the population. *Urbanization* theories of crime causation focus on the changing of a society from rural ety from rural to urban and *cultural-difference* theories focus on cultural conflict within a society (Ortmeier, 1999, p. 14).

Population shifts in London during the Industrial Revolution brought in large numbers of shop workers who had previously worked in farming. There were cultural conflicts, drunkenness, overpopulation, and rampant crime. Riots were common and police action needed to be concerted and organized ("along military lines"). American cities such as New York during the 1850s experienced similar crime and social problems.

Immigration causes increases in crime due to cultural conflicts. The rapid expansion of Irish immigration in America during the period 1845 to 1852 in response to the Potato Famine of 1847 ("Black 47"). Coleman (1969) cites Census Statistics from 1870 as stating that there were 8,641 Irish immigrants to the United States in 1845; 29,540 in 1847; and 157,548 in 1852 (p. 21). As the coal mines provided, on their face, lucrative offers of employment, numerous Irish immigrants became employed as coal miners. Irish miners who felt exploited struck back at the mine bosses and railroad owners through organized criminal activities.

PRACTICAL EXERCISE: List an ethnic group that is largely employed in a certain industry. Do their employers exploit that group? How? What types of actions could they take to exact revenge on their employers?

The Mollie Maguires were an underground organization of Irish miners who perpetrated assaults and homicides against those they didn't like. They also engaged in acts of sabotage against the railroads. They were thugs in the eyes of Allan Pinkerton, labor union activists according to revisionist historians in the 1970s, and, perhaps, to a degree, terrorists. The Mollies were investigated by a Pinkerton operative in a three-year undercover operation. Interestingly enough, the operative, James MacParland, had owned a tavern that burned during the Chicago Fire. Many of the Mollie Maguires were hanged in the mid-1870s. The Mollie Maguires took their name from Irish activists/criminals who dressed as women and fought the landlords in Ireland (a class struggle). See *The Mollie Maguires* with Sean Connery and Richard Harris for a 1969—and perhaps "revisionist"—perspective on this.

The Mollie Maguires case was important as it was probably the first use of a task force (Pinkerton men teamed with Coal and Iron Police) as well as the first major undercover investigation.

Invariably there are criminals among immigrant groups who exploit their fellow countrymen. Organized criminal activity and immigration go hand-in-hand. In most cases, the organized crime activity dissipates after the immigrant group becomes assimilated into the dominant culture. Common examples of this are slave trading, prostitution, gambling, narcotics, and smuggling. Extortion via protection rackets as well as criminal group infiltration of organized labor also occur. See the films *Goodfellas* and *Once*

Upon a Time in America for some perspective on organized crime infiltration.

Current immigrant criminal enterprises are from Russian organized crime groups, South Korean groups, and so on. With the breakup of the Soviet Union, many of these immigrant groups have turned to criminal enterprises. A new wrinkle is that some organized crime today is *transnational* and crosses international borders. The more traditional organized crime groups have stayed within their own ethnic group and preyed upon the members.

Population density, culture, age, gender, and other factors also play heavily in terms of safety issues. Elder care requires certain aspects of asset protection. Government requirements for long-term care facilities and patients suffering with Alzheimer's create daily challenges. Emergency planning for a population that is not ambulatory and has failing hearing and sight is also an issue. In school security, managers must focus on drug dealing, evacuation plans, active shooters, parking, and crowd management at special events. Hotel security must be concerned with a transitory population. Issues include disorderly guests, dishonest employees, sexual assault, and fire and guest services. Each population has unique safety and security needs.

CLASS STRUGGLES AND TERRORISM

A recurrent theme concerning the history of security is that it involves class struggles. Class struggles have been apparent with the French Revolution and the development of terrorism as a significant security/law enforcement problem. It also relates, to some degree, the problems encountered with the organized labor movement in America. The following discussion on terrorism relates to left-wing and right-wing terrorism that is politically and economically inspired. There are, however, numerous other types of terrorist activities; not all are politically inspired. In the United States many are the acts of crazed individuals. Each terrorist threat requires both a pro-active and a reactive response to it.

Terrorism can perhaps be understood by looking at a few significant events.

1848 *The Communist Manifesto* was written by Karl Marx and Friedrich Engels. This established the political theory of Marxism—often called "Communism." The bourgeoisie (ruling class of capitalists) exploit the proletariat (laborers). The proletariat should rise up and overthrow the bourgeoisie and establish a utopian society, a "dictatorship of the proletariat" where everyone shares equally. Propaganda is used to educate the masses and inspire them to revolt. Marxism was born in 1848 and left-wing terrorist groups throughout the world followed it.

1886 The Haymarket Riot in Chicago was instigated by anarchists during a rally against McCormick Harvester. A bomb exploded, and a policeman was killed. Anarchists believed in the abolition of governments.

This movement utilized terror tactics such as assassination (William McKinley and six other heads of state) and bombings. They were very active in France, Russia, and the United States during the latter 19th and early 20th centuries. There are still anarchists in contemporary American society, but their violent activities have subsided greatly since the 1880s–1920s. After the Haymarket Riot, local industrialists donated land to the federal government so that troops could be stationed nearby. Fort Sheridan was built for this purpose.

1969 There were numerous hijackings of airliners to Cuba by dissident individuals. There were also bombings of federal buildings. See the film *1969* with Kiefer Sutherland for a treatment of the antigovernment sentiment of the times. In the Munich Massacre, Israeli athletes at the Olympics were killed by Palestinian terrorists. The Munich Massacre showed the world that terrorism was indeed a problem. It brought terrorism via TV to the living rooms of the world.

1972 Patty Hearst and the Symbionese Liberation Army (SLA)—a left-wing antigovernment group. The granddaughter of newspaper magnate William Randolph Hearst was kidnapped by the SLA and later joined them. She was underground for 20 months, having traveled across the country. The Patty Hearst case showed that fugitives could remain underground for extensive periods of time in the United States. See the film *The Patty Hearst Story* for an excellent treatment of how left-wing radicals operated in the United States during the early 1970s.

1973 Nyack Incident—Several left-wing terrorist groups thought to be long dormant collaborated on a "fundraiser" (armored car robbery) in Nyack, NY. This showed that groups thought to be long dormant were still active. Note that the Vietnam War created intense antigovernment feelings in the United States. After the U.S. involvement in Vietnam ended in 1973, much of the left-wing sentiment faded. The Nyack Incident showed that there were still some virulent left-wing terrorist groups operating. Note that occasionally 1970s terrorists are still being caught. The film *Running on Empty* with Judd Hirsch and River Phoenix portrays the parents of a teenage son who are still fugitives after being terrorists in the 1970s. The Nyack Incident also showed that left-wing groups were working in concert with one another. This is a major concern with terrorism as "the enemy of my enemy is my friend." Alliances can easily and quickly form between groups.

In the 1980s and 1990s, right-wing terrorism became more of an issue than left-wing, Marxist-inspired terrorist activity. Economically disenfranchised males in rural America often believed that they were being subjugated economically by Jewish bankers and a federal government that raised their taxes and took away their gun ownership rights. Minority groups were seen as taking their jobs. In urban areas, the Skinheads formed. American Skinheads are based on a working-class movement in the United Kingdom during the early 1970s. The British Skinheads wore Doc Marten boots and close-cropped hair, and they targeted minority group members and immigrants for taking their jobs. The right-wing groups gain followers during economically depressed times. They are also inspired by government control over gun ownership and increased taxes.

See the film *Dead Bang* with Don Johnson for a good treatment of right-wing terrorist activity as well as *American History X* with Edward Norton for its portrayal of right-wing hate groups.

In the 1990s and into the early 21st century, terrorism perpetrated by right-wing extremists was largely overshadowed by the activities of radical Islamic fundamentalists.

A series of terrorist events within the United States' borders in the 1990s and early 21st century include the following:

- The 1993 World Trade Center bombing by Isamic fundamentalists who planted an explosives-laden vehicle in the parking garage and detonated it.
- The 1995 Oklahoma CitybBombing by right-wing terrorists who used a massive truck bomb to demolish the Murrah Federal Building.
- The September 11, 2001, World Trade Center and Pentagon attacks by Islamic fundamentalists associated with Al-Quaida. The attackers hijacked four airliners and crashed two of them into the World Trade Center and one into the Pentagon. One airliner was crashed in a field near Somerset, PA after passengers overpowered the hijackers. This alerted the United States that it had a serious problem with radical followers of Islam.

To better understand the forces driving radical Islamic fundamentalists, consider the following:

Old vs. New—There is a "clash of cultures" between traditional ideals and new, Western values. There is also a power shift away from religious leaders who formerly had much more control over their followers.

Class struggles—Large numbers of unemployed or underemployed persons living in poverty.

Demographics—Undereducated or *miseducated* young men who have been taught that the United States is **"The Great Satan."** Massive numbers of them exist in the Middle East as well as in places such as Indonesia. These impressionable young men can become an army of destruction if the right conditions are met.

Culture of warfare—Some areas of the world have experienced warfare – low, medium, or high intensity–over a period of years. In some cases, entire generations of people have been immersed in wars. Afghanistan, Palestine, and Bosnia are examples of this.

Religion—A perversion of Islam that emphasizes traditional values and demonizes the West has occurred. Religion is a powerful influence on people. Persons who are living in poverty or feel discriminated against may turn to religion as an answer to their problems. Religion also gives legitimacy to the exhortations of leaders. If a leader advocates deviant behavior—violence—it may be acceptable to his impressionable followers.

Charismatic leaders—all dynamic groups have charismatic leaders. Extremist groups thrive on them. A charismatic leader can exploit—as did Adolph Hitler—cultural, social, and economic forces in a negative way.

Note: for more information on terrorism in the United States, view the Professional Security Training Network video *The Threat of Terrorism in the U.S.* (pstn.com).

PRACTICAL EXERCISE: Develop a list of specific threat actions posed by terrorists, such as bombings, assassinations, cyber attacks, kidnapping, and so on. Next, list a proactive countermeasure to be used before the attack is launched. Finally, list a reactive countermeasure to be employed as the attack is taking place or after the attack has occurred.

Terrorist Threat Action	Proactive	Reactive

LABOR RELATIONS

Labor relations have played a very large role in the history of both policing and security in America. It is also important for understanding the development of society as a whole. Organized labor brought together people of different ethnic groups. It established numerous changes in the workplace, such as benefit plans for employees and the establishment of disciplinary procedures based on the concept of due process.

While union membership is declining at present, many of the contemporary approaches to labor relations, physical security, contingency planning, and personnel security are a result of earlier labor issues. One must understand the historical context of "labor relations" in American society to fully appreciate the development of both labor unions and control forces.

"Labor relations" during "the mean years" of 1866–1937 (Calder, 1985) consisted of some tactics employed by management that would be unacceptable by contemporary society. These included the intimidation of labor leaders, spies, and "agent provocateurs" (persons who instigate illegal activity and then work to have the participants arrested for violating the law) in unions; assaults with machine guns; the importation of strike breakers (workers who replace those who are on strike); the subversion of attempts by workers to organize by the promotion of interethnic conflict; and the use of thugs to intimidate workers.

Note: See *Matewan* with James Earl Jones, Chris Cooper, and Mary MacDonald for an excellent treatment of this topic based on the 1920 Matewan Massacre. The Matewan Massacre was a gun battle waged between striking miners and the Baldwin-Felts Detective Agency in Matewan, WV.

These are some of the key events in the struggle of organized labor.

1866 National Labor Union was formed in Baltimore —a national union was now in place rather than the previous groups. These were local or trade-specific small groups with little power. A national union could mobilize large numbers of workers. These workers could organize massive strikes and shut down factories, mines, and railroads.

1892 Homestead Strike—a labor dispute between the Carnegie Steel Company and the Amalgamated Association of Iron and Steel workers resulted in a lockout. Henry Clay Frick, Carnegie's general manager, tried to get the workers to accept a wage cut. He then locked the workers out of the plant so that they could not work. The workers assumed that Frick would do this and reopen the plant using strikebreakers (employees who replace striking workers). Three hundred Pinkerton detectives came by barge up the Monongahela River and tried to secure the plant. A battle ensued which lasted all day. The workers used a small cannon to try and sink the barges and set them on fire by pouring oil into the river and lighting it. The Pinkertons were defeated and had to surrender (Fossum, 1982, p. 24). The militia were called in by the governor. Interestingly enough, Frick was later shot by an anarchist.

1894 Pullman Strike—the Pullman Palace Car Company laid off half of their employees and forced the rest to take a 40 percent wage cut. Workers were required to live in company housing. After the wage reductions, there was no reduction in the rent for the housing. The local strike became a sympathy strike as American Railway Union members refused to handle trains with Pullman cars. Trains were stopped and Pullman cars were uncoupled. The rail owners assembled trains so that if Pullman cars were uncoupled, mail cars would also be cut off. Interfering with the mail was a federal offense. Eugene Debs, the ARU leader was sent to jail for conspiring to obstruct the mails. President Grover Cleveland called out the Army so that the mail could be delivered and the strike was broken (Fossum, 1982, p. 24, 25).

1900 Latimer Massacre—large numbers of Serbian miners were killed by sheriffs' deputies during a strike in Latimer, PA. The United States offered an official apology to the government of Serbia after this incident.

1905 PA State Police—first modern state police force. Formed from the Philadelphia City Cavalry after the Great Anthracite Strike in 1903–1904.

1933 National Industrial Recovery Act insured collective bargaining rights. Wagner Act (National Labor Relations Act) created the National Labor Relations Board in 1935 giving a real enforcement function to the National Industrial Recovery Act.

1937 Battle of the Overpass. During a strike against Ford Motor Company, labor leader, Walter Reuther, and a companion were severely beaten by Ford Service security officers while not doing anything illegal. This beating was not unusual except that it was photographed by newspaper reporters. The American public was not sympathetic toward unions as they were regarded as "communist" or "anarchist." In this instance, the public was outraged at the actions of Dearborn, MI police and Bennett's Ford Service men—the end of "the mean years" of "labor relations."

1947 In 1946, there were a large number of strikes; organized labor reached its zenith in this period. Congress passed the Taft-Hartley Act. One of the provisions of the Act is that the U.S. president, through the attorney general, can obtain an injunction against a strike or lockout if a substantial area is affected or national security is threatened.

Today, there are specialized contract security firms that have strike security forces. Vance International and Special Response Corporation are well-known examples.

These specialized firms are able to manage volatile labor disputes with minimal harm to persons or property. Additionally, the collective bargaining rights of workers are upheld.

PRACTICAL EXERCISE: It is 1920. The Great War is over and you are a military veteran with service in WWI. You are out of work and have several children to feed. The best employment prospect is with a private security firm that is doing strike security work. How do you feel about this?

RISK MANAGEMENT AND INSURANCE

"Risk management" is a term closely associated with the insurance industry. It is similar conceptually to the Physical Security Planning Process in its implementation, but it deals with risks other than "security" threats caused by humans. It is not limited to "target hardening" (*risk reduction*) approaches, such as the use of locks, barriers, intrusion alarms, and so on. Strategies for managing risk include the following:

Risk avoidance—completely avoiding the risk of earthquake by not being in a geographic area where there are active fault lines. Staying out of countries that are known to kidnap people for ransom. Not making products that are dangerous, such as explosives.

Risk transfer—transferring the financial impact of loss to another organization or entity. Insurance coverage is the usual means of risk transfer. Outsourcing hazardous operations to other organizations is another example.

Risk assumption—or risk retention—is accepting the risk as it has a very low probability of occurring or is extremely difficult to protect against. It is extremely unlikely that an asteroid will strike. It is also impractical to defend against it.

Risk spreading—redundant systems of communication, power, or information storage.

Risk reduction—reducing the probability of a loss-causing event through the adoption of preventive measures. Physical security and crime deterrence would be considered risk reduction. So, too, would the use of safety equipment.

PRACTICAL EXERCISE: Pick some assets such as vital information that an organization needs to operate: people, works, art, and so on. Place these assets in the boxes to the left. Next place the primary threats that may face those assets such as fire, terrorism, theft, and so on. In the column on the right, list a risk management approach, such as transfer, avoidance, or acceptance that would be most appropriate for dealing with the threat.

ASSET	THREAT	RISK STRATEGY

Insurance can be thought of as the "last line of defense" in a physical security system. It provides the policyholder with financial compensation from the insurance company after a loss has occurred. According to Purpura (1991), loss prevention originated within the insurance industry (p. 10). Note that the term "loss prevention" is utilized primarily within the retail sector; it is gradually being replaced with the more representative term "asset protection."

Insurance policies provided by an insurance company are driven by the probability of a loss event occurring based on actuarial tables. The premiums and deductibles are adjusted according to the loss event probability; so, too, is the availability of insurance if insurance carriers deem a risk to be too high and refuse to write a policy. In these cases, organizations must *self-insure* or join an *insurance pool* of other organizations that pool their funds in a liquid account set aside in the event of a loss. There are also government insurance programs for crime and floods on the federal level and worker's compensation on the state level.

Various types of insurance coverage have evolved, such as the following:

Business interruption—of use for losses incurred after a disaster, accident, or fire while a business is not operating. Business interruption insurance helps to control indirect losses stemming from lost productivity.

Kidnap and ransom (K & R)—for firms who have had executives abducted by criminals or terrorists. This coverage became popular in the early 1980s in response to left-wing terrorist kidnappings in Latin America. The film *Proof of Life* with Russell Crowe portrays K & R coverage.

Workman's Compensation—required by state laws to compensate workers injured on the job from the results of work-related accidents and occupational diseases (Purpura, 1991, p. 265). Rates paid for premiums by employers are based in part on an employer's record of accidents.

Liability insurance—to cover legal costs and *compensatory* damage awards (punitive damages are not generally covered). Attorney's fees and associated costs can become quite high during civil litigation regardless of whether the case is settled or goes before a court.

Fire insurance—one of the first types of insurance developed; some policies mandate that the insured conduct periodic patrols of various areas on the property—the use of watch tour systems had developed as a result of this.

Burglary insurance—for losses associated with unlawful intrusion. Burglary insurance policies generally require evidence of forced entry.

Robbery insurance—coverage for forcible thefts committed in the presence of another.

Theft insurance—policies cover losses from theft; may include burglary and robbery losses.

Bonds—*fidelity* bonds require investigation of the covered employee by the bonding company (the insurer); these bonds indemnify the holder against dishonest acts committed by the employee. The holder of the bonds is exempt from financial responsibility for the dishonest acts of the employee.

Employment Practices Liability (EPL)—insures against legal costs due to unlawful employment practices such as sexual harassment, discrimination, and so on. Contemporary liability exposure for ongoing illegal employment practices is substantial with awards and settlements running into the multi-millions.

LAW

The first codification of law in Western civilization is generally attributed to Hammurabi who served as king of Babylon from 1792–1750 B.C. The Code of Hammurabi specified offenses and punishments for each. While the popular view is that the Code consisted of "an eye for an eye," this may not be completely true. There were differing punishments based on the social class standing of the victim and offender.

Another major legal development occurred in 1215 with the Magna Carta ("Great Charter") in England. The Magna Carta established the concept of *due process*. This means that everyone should be treated fairly and according to uniform procedures. It is the basis for most law and disciplinary procedures. Due process was incorporated into the Fifth Amendment of the United States Constitution: "no person shall be deprived of life, liberty or property without due process of law." Perhaps most importantly, the Magna Carta implied that the King was not above the law.

Law can be divided into *statutory*—established by legislative statute, *case law*—established by a court decision, and *common law*—passed down through tradition. All relate heavily to asset protection. Protection professionals must be well versed in legal concepts! In many cases, security managers, safety directors, and consultants develop policies and procedures based on legal obligations. Protection managers are also occasionally asked to give upper management advice on general legal issues (specific legal concerns should *only* be addressed by an attorney after careful research of similar cases). Protection officers and investigators must also make legal determinations during the course of their duties. Protection officers must be "legal consultants" well versed in legal standards relating to privacy, property rights, and governmental mandates.

Laws are authored in response to social changes, which apply political pressure. Areas of the law relating to asset protection/security include the following:

1. Criminal law with offenses such as trespassing, various types of thefts (retail theft, theft of trade secrets, and so on.), vandalism, assault, burglary, robbery, rape, and so on. Criminal offenses that an environment is most likely to encounter vary with that environment. Schools have different legal challenges than shopping centers; manufacturing facilities face their own unique legal issues, as do hotels. Protection officers should become

familiar with the criminal laws that are most commonly violated in the environment they are assigned to protect. *Note:* See looseleaflaw.com or gouldlaw.com for state criminal codes in the United States.

2. Civil law relates to legal standards, which govern the conduct between individuals. Civil law relates to contracts that include the following.

   a) Contract security service
   b) Private investigative service
   c) Armored car service
   d) Personal protection/executive protection service
   e) Alarm monitoring
   f) Alarm response
   g) Employment contracts for management and labor
   h) Nondisclosure pacts—agreements not to disclose proprietary information, such as trade secrets
   i) Noncompetitive agreements or pacts—agreements not to seek employment with competing firms within a specific time frame and/or geographic area after termination of employment
   j) Leases between landlords and tenants—these can be individuals who rent apartments or businesses, such as in shopping centers

Civil law also involves asset forfeiture and civil demand or civil recovery. The former is a civil process used by law enforcement officials to obtain property used to commit crimes; the latter is used by merchants to obtain monetary fees from shoplifters. As the processes for forfeiture and civil recovery are not encumbered by constitutional protections to the accused (as in criminal law) and the burden of proof is a preponderance (majority such as 60 percent) of the evidence as opposed to proof beyond a reasonable doubt (99 percent certainty), civil laws are being used increasingly to combat criminal activity.

Civil law also covers torts or private wrongs committed against another, such as defamation, invasion of privacy, assault, battery, and so on.

Negligence is a failure to exercise reasonable and due care (such as not following a recognized standard) by doing something dangerous or not doing something, which is necessary for safety. In order to prove negligence, the plaintiff (party bringing the action or suit) must show the following:

- The existence of a duty
- A failure to perform that duty
- Injury or harm occurring to a party to whom the duty was owed
- The harm was reasonably foreseeable
- The harm was caused by the failure of the defendant to perform the duty

(Hertig, Fennelly & Tyska, 1998)

Note: For more information on civil liability see *Civil Liability for Security Personnel* (International Foundation for Protection Officers); various chapters of *Security Supervision: Theory and Practice of Asset Protection* (Elsevier). See also straffordpub.com, which offers a variety of newsletters related to civil liability.

3. Administrative or regulatory law is established to regulate technical aspects of society. Administrative or regulatory agencies are created, which have the authority to create rules and regulations, investigate and enforce compliance, adjudicate violations, and **mete out** punishments. These agencies are very powerful! Complying with their regulations is extremely important; so, too, is complying with them and remaining in business. Federal administrative agencies in the United States include the following:

   a) Occupational Safety and Health Administration
   b) National Labor Relations Board
   c) Environmental Protection Agency
   d) Federal Aviation Administration
   e) Nuclear Regulatory Commission
   f) Federal Communications Commission
   g) Equal Employment Opportunity Commission

Agencies also exist on the state level, such as California OSHA or the Pennsylvania Department of Labor and Industry, Human Relations Commission, Alcoholic Beverage Commissions, and so on. There are also city or municipal boards of health, building inspection, zoning, and so on. These latter regulate food handling in public kitchens, fire escapes and fire detection equipment, the number of parking spaces required, set-back rules from property lines, building permits, and so on. For information on state security licensing, see the International Association of Security and Investigative Regulators (iasir.org).

The 1990 Campus Security and Student Right to Know Act passed in the United States requires colleges to report all crimes committed on their campuses. They must also publish crime statistics. The Act is enforced by the U.S. Department of Education, which can levy monetary penalties for noncompliance. Another important regulatory law is the Bank Protection Act of 1968. This law established security standards to be used in banks that are insured by the Federal Deposit Insurance Corporation (FDIC). Portions of the Act are enforced by different federal agencies.

4. Labor or employment law consists of statutory laws, court decisions, and administrative agency regulations (Equal Employment Opportunity Commission, National Labor Relations Board, and so on.) that regulate the employer-employee relationship. Labor law also consists of contracts between employees and employers and privacy issues. *Note:* For information on privacy and links into employment law sources, see privacyrights.com. Also see *Security Supervision: Theory and Practice of Assets Protection* for chapters on employee screening, contracts, legal issues, liability, and so on.

HISTORY OF SECURITY SERVICES

Security services or contract security agencies have played a large role in both public and private protection. Outsourcing for security makes economic sense, since flat hourly rates are charged and clients do not have to worry about benefit costs and associated human resource management issues. The client can hire as many personnel as desired for as long as desired. This provides for flexibility in protection. Additionally, contract service firms may have specialized expertise that the client does not.

There are career opportunities here for those who are adept at sales, client relations, and human resource management (HRM). Security services are growing and will continue to do so. In addition to standard "guard service" (it may be advisable to avoid using as the "g" word, since it demeans protection officers), there are alarm response, alarm monitoring, armored car, personal protection (PPS), and private investigation. There will always be a need to understand the dynamics of the outsourcing process for both contractors *and* clients. Visits to the Web sites of Wackenhut (wackenhut.com) or Pinkerton (pinkertons.com) can provide more detail on these services.

While contract security firms usually offer private investigative services, most firms specialize in one or the other. Early security service firms began by offering investigative services and later transitioned into primarily providing contract security officers on client property. This happened because there were greater markets—and profits—in providing security service. In some cases, this continues to occur although the growth in demand for private investigation is robust enough to allow companies to be profitable while keeping investigation as their sole service. Wicklander-Zulewski at w-z.com gives a good description of investigative services.

1855 Allan Pinkerton, a Scottish immigrant, became involved in investigation by accident. While searching for wood to make barrels, the young cooper discovered a gang of counterfeiters. His business grew through work with the railroads (George McClellan was president of the Illinois Central Railroad; the legal counsel was a man named Abraham Lincoln). During the Civil War, Pinkerton performed intelligence services for General McClellan and protected President Lincoln. Pinkerton established the largest protective and investigative agency in the world with branch offices in many countries. By the mid-1990s, Pinkerton's had 250 offices worldwide with over 50,000 employees (Mackay, 1996, p. 239). Pinkerton had extensive centralized records, a code of ethics, used undercover investigation, employed the first female detective (Kate Warne—50 years before the first female police officer!) and used wanted posters. Pinkerton is credited with being the first to start a security service; in actuality there were other services started before him, but none have become as well-known as his was.

1858 Edwin Holmes started the first "central office" (central station) for alarm monitoring and response. Today we use the term "central alarm station" or "central station" to describe this. Many central stations are contract, off-premises facilities that monitor intrusion, fire and process (temperature or pressure gauges), or emergency medical or robbery (duress) alarms. Customers pay for the monitoring services. Holmes Protection provides monitoring and alarm response services.

1874 ADT—American District Telegraph was founded. ADT became the largest alarm company in the world. Their main product was magnetic contact switches (the little gray boxes above doors and windows in restaurants and stores). Today they provide an array of electronic security equipment. ADT bought Holmes Protection in the late 1990s.

1891 Brinks Armored became the largest armored car company in the world. Founded by Washington Perry Brinks, the firm transports cash and other valuables.

1909 William J. Burns—Burns was the original head of the "Bureau of Investigation", which later became the Federal Bureau of Investigation under J. Edgar Hoover in 1932. William J. Burns founded the William J. Burns Detective Agency in 1909. He was virulently antianarchist and anti-communist, believing that unions were being controlled by subversives and that unions were fronts for anarchists and communists. Burns was known for his ability to use evidence collection at the scene of crimes to capture suspects. In 1910, he apprehended the McNamara brothers, who were president and secretary of the United Iron Worker's Union for an attempted bombing of the Los Angeles Times building. He traced them from parts of the unexploded bomb. The McNamaras were supposedly avowed anarchists. In the 1970s and 1980s, Burns International Security Services, Inc. became one of the largest contract security firms in the world. It has since been acquired by Securitas.

1954 George Wackenhut founded the Wackenhut Corporation (wackenhut.com—see the job info on the Custom Protection Officer program). The firm provided security services in over 55 different countries backed by a staff of 70,000 employees. In addition, Wackenhut is a major "player" in the private prison market.

1955 Wackenhut was acquired by the Danish firm Group4falck in 2002.

THE PATH TO PROFESSIONALISM

There have been some significant developments along the path toward professionalism for the Security Industry.

1955 The American Society for Industrial Security was formed in Washington, D.C. ASIS consisted of security directors for Department of Defense contractor firms. Over the passage of time, ASIS International has grown to over 33,000 members in over 100 different countries. Members have a diverse range of positions within private industry, law enforcement, government and security service, and supply firms. ASIS has numerous councils on such topics as health care, retail, campus, banking, economic crime, commercial real estate, gaming and wagering protection, and so on.

1971 *The Rand Report on Private Police in America*— This was a private research study by the Rand Corporation. It was important as the security industry had not been studied. The *Rand Report* found that the security industry was large, growing, and unregulated. The average security officer was an aging white male with a limited education who was usually untrained and who worked a lot of hours to make ends meet. The *Rand Report* was useful as a reference point for the *Report of the Task Force on Private Security* in 1975.

1975 The *Report of the Task Force on Private Security* conducted by the National Advisory Committee on Criminal Justice Standards and Goals was published in 1976. The committee found a lack of training, regulation, and job descriptions within the security industry. The report advocated minimum training standards; these have been used as guides by some states in setting up mandated training and licensing requirements.

1977 Certified Protection Professional (CPP) Program established by ASIS. First envisioned during the 1950s, the CPP Program acknowledged that managers must be competent in a variety of generic subjects such as physical security, personnel security, legal aspects, management, investigations, and so on. As of 2002, there have been over 9,500 persons designated as Certified Protection Professionals.

1985 *The Private Security and Police in America: The Hallcrest Report* was published. This report was written by Hallcrest Systems under funding from the Department of Justice. The report studied the contributions of police and security to control crime as well as the relationship between the public and private sector. The report also found that the average security officer was younger and better educated than the "aging white male" in the *Rand Report* of 1971.

1988 International Foundation for Protection Officers— formed to upgrade the professional status of public and private protection officers. The IFPO has membership, publications, an Article Archives on their Web site, and several professional certification programs. Over 14,000 persons in over 45 different countries have become Certified Protection Officers. There is a also a Certified Security Supervisor (CSS) designation. In 2001, the Foundation launched the Certified Protection Officer Instructor (CPOI) designation for those individuals who may instruct the CPO Program in a traditional classroom environment. Certified Protection Officer Instructors must be CPOs with several years security and teaching experience.

CONTEMPORARY CAREERS IN ASSET PROTECTION

There are numerous career fields open to persons seeking a challenging and rewarding career in asset protection. Every organization employs some type of protective measures. Many —if not most—have security personnel. A sampling of positions available and functions that persons holding those positions perform is outlined here. Note that information on careers in law, public safety, and security can be obtained by visiting careerclusters.org.

Fixed posts: Many protection officers work at fixed posts. These may include baggage screening at airports, vehicle gates at manufacturing facilities, emergency rooms in hospitals, access control points at concerts, in museums or the lobbies of high-rise buildings. Generally fixed post duties are more rudimentary and are assigned to new officers. Once the officers master the post assignment, they may be given duties at other posts. Often fixed post functions are contracted out to security service firms as it is cheaper to do so. Additionally, the contract agencies can supply the required number of personnel when manpower requirements fluctuate, such as at special events, emergencies, or when facilities close for the evening. College students, retirees, homemakers, or active duty military personnel may begin their careers performing fixed post duties. *A key point in career development is to master the fixed post duties.* Persons who have not done that will probably not get additional duties assigned to them. There are generally extensive opportunities for promotion available to those who are willing to work hard, grow, and develop professionally.

Patrol officer: A patrol officer must be able to observe and report discrepancies in the protected environment. They must collect intelligence on changes, unusual situations, or suspicious persons (intelligence agent role). Patrol officers must be adept at interacting with the public in the environment be that visitors, employees, students, patients, or guests (management representative role). Patrol officers must effectively maintain compliance with organizational policies (enforcement agent role). In doing so, they must know the rules of the facility as well as legal issues relating to privacy, search and seizure, property rights, and the rights of employees (legal consultant role). Patrol officers must also be able to respond to problems that may occur, such as slippery walkways, blocked emergency exits, hazardous materials spills, fires, fights, or crimes in progress. Obviously, patrol officers need a variety of skill sets. They must be competent in many things.

Retail Loss Prevention Agent positions are available with many large firms. These jobs offer persons the ability to learn valuable investigative skills, such as surveillance and interrogation. They are readily available and often accept part-time employees. There are extensive opportunities for advancement within retail security!

Central alarm station operator/dispatcher: Security officers in many environments will act as dispatchers or central alarm station operators. They will monitor alarm panels, CCTV screens, and electronic access control systems. As technology expands, so does the job of the central alarm station operator. These central alarm stations may be either proprietary or contract. In a proprietary "in-house" setting, central alarm stations evolve over time. Many facilities develop central alarm stations in an incremental manner. They often start with a security office that has a desk, a telephone, and a radio. After a while, the organization will add additional monitoring systems. First, there is a camera observing the lobby. Next, there is a camera on the parking area. Then there may be intrusion detection systems in sensitive areas which annunciate (terminate) at the central office. Fire alarm panels may also be located there. Finally, an electronic access control system is added which has a monitor in the central office.

There are access control systems and alarm systems. The reader must bear in mind today we have various types of alarms.

1. Intrusion alarms which are *point protection* (on a specific point, such as door or window) *perimeter protection* (fence protection, such as those that detect vibration on a chain link fence or beam type systems, such as microwave placed along a perimeter line) or *area protection* (volumetric intrusion detection for an area such as passive infrared or PIR or ultrasonic).
2. Fire alarms that may be ionization detectors (responding to the products of combustion in the earliest phase of a fire).
3. Emergency, panic, or duress alarms which are activated by someone in distress.
4. Process alarms that monitor equipment or utilities (temperature, water pressure, air pressure, power).

What began as a security office is now a central alarm station/dispatch center! Obviously, facility managers must plan for the eventual expansion of their security offices. Similarly, there must be serious thought given to alarm response. If alarms notify property managers of problems, there must be a rapid, effective response to resolving those problems. Contract alarm response or patrol car service is one option: what Edwin Holmes started in 1858 needs to be integrated into a contemporary asset protection system. Persons beginning careers in asset protection should seek to understand the central alarm/dispatch operation. It is "the brain' of the security operation, serving as a **command, control,** and **communications** center.

Auditor/investigator: Auditors check on things such as financial records (financial audits) or procedures (procedural or operational audits) to see if conditions are what they are supposed to be. Audits seek to uncover deviations from procedure, errors, or criminal behavior (Purpura, 2002). A deviation from a procedure might be documenting something that the writer did not verify occurred—taking a "shortcut." Audits may also uncover errors such as mistakes made in pricing merchandise or forgetting to record required information. Criminal behavior may include falsifying employee attendance records or removing raw materials from the workplace.

Private investigators work for companies, individuals, or governments on a fee basis. They contract out to perform various types of investigative activity. Criminal investigation done by private investigators includes undercover investigation of workplace theft, sabotage, or drug abuse. Surveillance of suspected employees may also be conducted. Some private investigators are forensic accountants, trained to investigate fraudulent accounting and present a case in court. Fraud examination is a large and growing concern of all types of organizations, not just insurance carriers. Visit the Association of Certified Fraud Examiners at acfe.net for more on fraud examination.

Specialized security functions such as K-9 handlers, crowd management specialists who work concerts in arenas, strike security personnel, and information technology (IT) specialists also exist. These persons are specialists with unique skill sets. They have prior experience, training, and education that qualifies them for their positions. They have "paid their dues" and evolved in their careers.

Educational opportunities are available both online and in traditional college programs. Persons wishing to move up the ranks of management will need higher education. Asisonline.org has information on careers and academic programs. There is an extensive listing of colleges that offer academic coursework in security. In addition, ASIS offers full-time college students membership at greatly reduced rates. There is also a Student Paper Competition for both undergraduate and graduate students. Winning papers are eligible for cash prizes.

The International Foundation for Protection officers also features links to colleges on their Website (ifpo.org). The Foundation has also provided scholarships to faculty who teach Security courses.

Networking is crucial to career success in security or investigation. Few, if any, good jobs are advertised publicly. Almost all are obtained through personal contacts. There is an old saying:

"If you don't know nobody, nobody knows you."

This saying makes up for in accuracy what it lacks in English! Professional contacts can be gained through organizational membership, such as ASIS International, IFPO, or the International Foundation for Cultural Property Protection (ifcpp.org). Professional organizations usually have job placement services and membership directories. They provide members with the opportunity to meet others in their field and discuss matters of mutual concern. Attendance at seminars sponsored by professional organizations is another way to network. Management level personnel can participate in the International Association of Healthcare Security & Safety (iahss.org) or the International Association of Campus Law Enforcement Administrators (iaclea.org).

Professional development can be obtained through a variety of sources. Professional organizations offer seminars and online programs. Some offer certification programs such as the International Foundation for Cultural Property (ifcpp.org) that offers both the Certified Institutional Protection Specialist (CIPS) and Certified Institutional Protection Manager (CIPM) designations.

Training courses online can be obtained through AST Corporation (astcorp.com). There are a wide variety of courses! Specialized topics can be studied so that new assignments or jobs can be prepared for. These courses can be used to target individual career interests and earn recertification credits for Certified Protection Officer designates. Other courses are available through ASIS International (asisonline.org) and lpjobs.com.

"Learning never ceases."

This chapter discussed the past and present.

The future belongs to those who reach out and grasp it.

REFERENCES

Calder, J.D. (1985). "Industrial Guards in the Nineteenth and Twentieth Centuries; The Mean Years." *Journal of Security Administration*, Vol. 8., No. 2.

Coleman, J.W. (1969). *The Molly Maguire Riots: Industrial Conflict in the Pennsylvania Coal Region.* New York, NY: Arno & The New York Times.

Constable, G. (Ed.). (1990). *The Old West.* New York, NY: Time-Life Books.

Cote, A. & Bugbee, P. (1988). *Principles of Fire Protection.* Quincy, MA: National Fire Protection Association.

Fiems. R. & Hertig, C. (2001). *Protection Officer Guidebook.* Naples, FL: International Foundation for Protection Officers.

Fossum, J. (1982). *Labor Relations: Development, Structure, Process.* Dallas, TX: Business Publications, Inc.

Gilbride, B.P. (1999). "Sexual Harassment" in Davies, S.J. & Minion, R.R. (Eds.) *Security Supervision: Theory and Practive of Asset Protection.* Woburn, MA: Butterworth-Heinemann.

Johnson, T. (2002). *Retail Loss Prevention Management Models.* Unpublished paper. York College of Pennsylvania.

Hertig, C.A. (2002). *Investigative Concepts.* Unpublished paper. York College of Pennsylvania.

Hertig, C.A., Fennelly, L. J. & Tyska, L. A. (1998). *Civil Liability for Security Personnel.* Naples, FL: International Foundation for Protection Officers.

Kuykendall, J. (1986). "The Municipal Police Detective: An Historical Analysis." *Criminology.* Vol. 24., No. 1.

Matthews, L.J. (1990). *Pioneers and Trailblazers: Adventures of the Old West.* New York, NY: Derrydale.

Mackay, J. (1996). *Allan Pinkerton: The First Private Eye.* New York, NY: John Wiley & Sons.

Nalla, M. & Newman, G. (1990). *A Primer in Private Security.* Albany, NY: Harrow & Heston.

National Advisory Committee on Criminal Justice Standards and Goals (1976). *Report of the Task Force on Private Security.* Washington, D.C.

Peak, K.J. (1997). *Policing in America: Methods, Issues, Challenges.* Upper Saddle River, N.J.: Prentice-Hall.

Purpura, P.P. (2002). *Security and Loss Prevention: An Introduction.* Stoneham, MA: Butterworth-Heinemann.

SECURITY QUIZ
The Evolution of Asset Protection and Security

1. List five (5) reasons why outlaws were prominent in the American West.

    A _____

    B _____

    C _____

    D _____

    E _____

2. Identify five (5) types of insurance policies.

    A _____

    B _____

    C _____

D _____

E _____

3. List the three (3) control forces used in Ancient Rome. Next, specify what each one did.

CONTROL FORCE	FUNCTIONS

4. Match the year with the event in the table below.

YEAR	SIGNIFICANT EVENT
1215 in England	
1855 in America	
1968 in America	
1988 in America	
1066 in England	
1892 in America	
1792–1750 B.C. in Babylon	

5. List three (3) reasons why Islamic fundamentalist terror groups are growing.

A _____

B _____

C _____

6. List in the box at right the importance of the event in the box at the left.

EVENT	IMPORTANCE

7. List three (3) of the important studies done of the security industry.

A _____

B _____

C _____

8. List five (5) of the lessons learned from studying the history of security.

A _____

B _____

C _____

D _____

E _____

9. List three (3) of the innovations of Allan Pinkerton.

A _____

B _____

C _____

10. List three (3) organizations that offer memberships to protection officers.

A _____

B _____

C _____

Unit Two

Field Notes and Report Writing
Observation Skills and Memory
Patrol Principles
Safety and the Protection Officer
Traffic Control
Crowd Control

FIELD NOTES AND REPORT WRITING

By Martin A. Fawcett, CPO

Consider for a moment what our world would be like without newspapers, magazines, books, or any other kind of written material. How would we learn about things that were happening in other parts of the world? How would we learn new skills, become educated, or pass what we have learned on to others?

The only source of knowledge that we would be able to obtain would be that which was readily at hand to us through other people, providing they were willing and able to pass along this information. Without the written word for us to read and to learn, we would still believe that the world was flat, there wouldn't be the advances in technology that we have become accustomed to over the years, such as television, radio, automobiles—and the list goes on and on.

In order for man to advance as he has and to continue to advance, there must be a written word that can be passed on to future generations in order that they will learn through our mistakes and our successes.

As you may now appreciate, the written word is an important and integral part of our personal and professional lives. There is not one part of our culture that is not affected directly or indirectly by the written word. It is the foundation upon which we build our knowledge, our experience, and our life.

In the security industry, like other professions, the written word is an important "tool of the trade." It is the means by which detailed, factual reports of events or incidents are recorded so that others may learn what has occurred and if necessary, take action.

A protection officer in the course of duties may encounter a myriad of events or incidents that will require the passing of factual information to person(s) who were not present at the event or incident. In order to effect this duty, the protection officer must be able to accurately observe the event and then take those observations and put them on paper in a clear, concise, and logical manner.

This passing of information takes the form of notes and reports. Unfortunately, experience has shown us that many people lack appreciation of the value of taking good notes and preparing proper reports. There are no prerequisites set by employers on notes and reports in most instances, and the matter of notebooks and the manner of report writing is often left up to the individual protection officer or his immediate supervisor's discretion.

Experience has also shown us that many inaccurate reports are the direct result of inaccurate or incomplete notes. This has led to losses in assets, information, statistical data, and convictions in court.

As you can see, both notes and reports are very important and that it becomes incumbent on the protection officer to become as proficient and as professional in his/her use of these valuable tools.

FIELD NOTE-TAKING

A protection officer's notes may be defined simply as "a quick and accurate method of recording that what you saw, did, and heard."

Let's take a closer look at what the notebook is. A notebook should have the following features.

1. Small enough to carry easily in your clothing
2. Large enough for easy writing
3. Clothbound with no looseleaf pages
4. Pages numbered sequentially
5. Protected by adequate cover

Before looking at what should go into the notebook and how it should be put in, let's look first at why we need them.

There are five main areas of consideration when determining the purpose of keeping a notebook.

1. Assist in preparing reports
2. Detecting contradictions in statements
3. Refresh your memory
4. Investigative aid
5. Reflect officer ability

ASSIST IN PREPARING REPORTS

The protection officer, during the course of a tour of duty, may have occasion to investigate a number of events, incidents, and people. In most instances, some form of report will have to be submitted. Some of the events that will be looked at will not necessarily be investigated at a place that is convenient to the protection officer.

As a result, report forms, desks, office areas, and so on will not be available. Notes will be made in the officer's notebook and a full report will be made at some point in time after the investigation is completed. It now becomes necessary for the protection officer to ensure that he has all the facts, details, names, addresses, and so on, that will be required when it comes time to complete his report.

The protection officer cannot trust these facts and details to memory. The tendency to forget details and events with the passage of time is a well-known fact. Notes, properly made at the time, are seldom forgotten, will never change with the passage of time, and will ensure that accuracy and detail are not lost.

DETECT CONTRADICTIONS IN STATEMENTS

During any investigation, certain facts are made known by witnesses and suspects, and certain statements may be made by those persons involved. If the protection officer has conscientiously made good notes regarding the events, then any contradictions or changes in facts or details will be found and further questioning may result in the apprehension of the culprit or the recovery of assets or information.

If proper notes have not been made, then the officer must rely on memory, which may or may not be accurate. The proper use of notes in this instance makes for a more professional investigation and more credibility when questioning people regarding conflicting facts.

REFRESH MEMORY AT LATER DATE

As discussed earlier, man's memory is far from infallible. Notes made at the time of an event will not change and form a permanent record of events as they occurred or were observed by the protection officer.

They become an invaluable aid when trying to recall an incident or specific detail of an investigation at a later date. The notes will remind you of what you actually saw, did, and heard.

This in turn assists you in report preparation, giving evidence in court, or in apprising a supervisor of what occurred. The courts have long recognized the value of the written word over memory.

INVESTIGATIVE AID

In some instances, an investigation into an event or incident may take many days and many hours to complete. During the investigation, notes are being made of each step in the investigation and subsequent reports are being filed as they are completed.

Should you become involved in this type of investigation, then it becomes apparent that it is most cumbersome to carry around a briefcase filled with reports concerning the event.

The use of a notebook in these instances makes the investigator's job that much easier, as he has much greater freedom in packing around a notebook filled with facts than in carrying around a briefcase filled with numerous reports.

REFLECT OFFICER ABILITY

Many times during his career, the protection officer may be required to show his notebook to any number of different people. He may be required to show it to his supervisor on a regular basis; he may be asked to produce it in court as part of his evidence.

In any of these circumstances, the protection officer's abilities may be judged solely on the basis of what is presented in his notes. (*Note:* While the protection officer may not be directly involved in the investigation or interrogation process, what he/she saw, did or heard is vital to the information-gathering process.)

Tips on the Use of Notebooks

While most of the rules governing the preparation and content of report writing apply to note taking, here are a few items worthy of mention.

1. Prepare your notes in a legible manner

This means that you are able to go back anytime in the future and be able to understand what you have written. Many people are unable to go back to their notes even a week later and be able to remember what has occurred because they are unable to make accurate observations from their own notes.

2. Keep your notes complete

If your notes are legible and you are able to go back and read them and understand them, you must also ensure that there is enough detail in your notes to give you a complete picture of the event that you are detailing. Again, many people will jot down some basic facts regarding an incident, but if asked to relate what actually occurred, they are at a loss because their notes are incomplete.

3. Be systematic

Record your observations in chronological order; don't bounce around in your story because this becomes confusing when refreshing your memory at a later date. Also, keep the day-to-day details pertaining to your tours of duty in proper sequence. It does no good to have to look back through an entire notebook to find one day's events. If your notes are kept in proper order, it becomes easy to find specific information no matter when it occurred.

4. Abbreviations

As long as you can remember what word or phrase you are abbreviating, then go ahead and use them. If you will be unable to remember what the abbreviation means, then use the full form of the word or phrase.

5. Use all pages and spaces

Use all spaces and all pages in your notebook. By leaving spaces, you are not only wasting space, but you are leaving yourself open to questioning regarding the accuracy of your notes at some future time. The courts, especially, view the leaving of blank pages and spaces with extreme skepticism, believing that you may have added or deleted vital information. Don't fall into this trap. Always fill in every line, even if you must draw a line as a filler.

6. Develop your own style

Remember that these are your notes. Develop a style that is comfortable for you to use. Everyone will have a slightly different style of using a notebook, and no one way is better than another. Try different methods and use those that will be of benefit to you and discard the rest.

7. As soon as possible

Get into the habit of making your notes as soon as possible after an event or incident. The longer you wait to record your observations, the less you will remember. The best method is to write down your observations as you make them and to note details provided by witnesses as they give them. If this is not practical, then at the earliest possible moment, take the time, stop what you are doing, and make your notes.

8.   Ripping out pages

Whenever possible, avoid ripping out pages from your notebook. Should the occasion arise that you must do this, take a page from the back of the notebook and use it. When this is done, you should note the time and date on the stub that is left.

9.   Errors

Should you make an error while making an entry, do not attempt to erase it. Draw a single line through the error and initial it, then continue. Any other method is unacceptable in a court of law.

10. Personal notes

Personal notes have no place in your notebook. If you find that you need to jot something down and do not have any extra paper to write on, tear out a piece from the back of your notebook as discussed earlier. Never leave any personal notes in your notebook.

11. Opinions

Opinions have no place in your notebook. Remember that your notebook is a "diary" of what you saw, did, and heard—not your opinion.

12. Review

Always try to take your notes with the idea that you will, at some point in the future, have to re-read them and be able to understand all that occurred. After you have completed your notes on an event, review them and see if they make sense, and if they tell the entire story and represent the event as it actually occurred.

Remember, there is no better way to ensure accuracy than properly prepared, properly preserved, and properly presented notes. This information will be invaluable to the protection officer in bridging the gap between the "first occurrence" and their "later use."

"The dullest pencil has a better memory than the sharpest mind."

REPORT WRITING

The basic elements of report writing are taught in the elementary and high school years. All protection officers have had a certain level of education and must know how to lay out and write an account of their actions.

They should understand singular and plural persons; past, present, and future tenses; and masculine, feminine, and neuter gender. They should have a good vocabulary and know how to spell. In general, before they even become a protection officer, they should have a reasonable education.

A dictionary should be within reach at all times. The report requirements of a protection officer today are much more rigid than in past years—therefore, standards must be higher.

You must combine your prior learning with knowledge of security work, experience, and common sense for better

security reports. Remember, your written work is the mirror of your mind at the time of writing. Even more important, it may well be a permanent reflection of your thinking.

A well-written report by an efficient protection officer displays not only their proper application to duty in the field, but their completeness as a competent individual in applying their academic side to their vocation. Today both qualities are not only desired but imperative.

Progressive protection officers who recognize a weakness in themselves in the field will attempt to improve. A recognized weakness in written work must be treated likewise.

Do not become one of the smug individuals who say to themselves, "I'm as good as, or better than, other officers. I just can't put it on paper." Do something to improve this self-acknowledged weakness. It will be easier for you to eliminate the problem than to live with it.

Who Security Reports Are For

1. The security supervisor
2. The security organization
3. The client
4. Various civic organizations
5. Various segments of Industry
6. The courts (criminal and civil)
7. Anyone who may request and is entitled to proprietary information

Security reports are prepared by the protection officer in order to pass on information to those concerned parties who are not present at the time of the incident or event. The report must be complete and accurate and answer all possible questions the reader might have.

The security report that is incomplete or inaccurate will have to be sent back to the writer for clarification, which is not only a waste of valuable time, but shows a lack of professionalism on the part of the writer.

Many reports are copied and sent on the other organizations or individuals. Depending on the type of event, some reports end up being read by lawyers who may be defending or prosecuting a case based on the event reported.

Many of these people will have little if any experience with security work, and the only information available to them will be the security report. As a result, you, your company, and other protection officers may be judged solely on the basis of the security report.

Remember this point each time you set out to write a report: Your report must be clear and concise, accurate and complete. The reader of the security report must be able to understand what has occurred based on the contents of the report.

Types of Security Reports:

There are a large number of different types of security forms and reports, and each client or company will have some that are unique. These are some of the more common varieties that you may encounter.

1.   Daily occurrence

2. Weekly summary
3. Motor vehicle accident
4. Department memorandums
5. Visitor access logs
6. Administrative policy
7. Employee evaluations
8. Event occurrence
9. Post orders

Planning the Security Report

Before writing a security report, particularly a lengthy one, the protection officer should plan how he is going to write it before starting. All the relevant facts should have been obtained and should be readily available.

All relevant reference material, post orders, directives, dictionary, and so on. should be readily available for quick and accurate reference.

You should not be rushed in compiling your information into the written format of the security report. The most common error made by protection officers is that they rush through their reports believing that they have done a satisfactory job and that their time is of more value in the field than in writing the report.

In fact, the opposite is true. The protection officer who takes the extra time to properly write a complete and accurate report is of more benefit to his/her employer than the one who races through reports and makes mistakes.

Reports should be completed as soon as possible after an event has occurred and never later than the end of the tour of duty. Leaving reports to pile up only encourages the protection officer to hurry through the reports. Remember that report writing is just as important as patrolling and should be given the same thoroughness and attention to detail.

Avoid distractions; be thorough. Go to the area that has been set aside for writing your reports, place all your materials down, make sure that you have everything you will need, and then you will be ready to start your report.

Before beginning to write, arrange all your facts into chronological order so that the reader can progressively follow you through the sequence of events.

Refer to your notes and other reference material to verify that you have the correct information. Absolute accuracy is essential; do not trust your memory in relating facts. Check facts before committing them to paper.

Vital facts such as names, addresses, company names, vocations, times, occurrences, and so on should be emphasized in the report. This can be done in a number of different ways. Block lettering is useful in a written report, as is underlining. Choose a method that makes these facts stand out from the rest of the information in the report.

First-person conversation, when used, should be in quotation marks. A word of caution about direct conversation —if you are not absolutely accurate in reporting what was said, word for word, don't use quotation marks. Start off saying that what was spoken was "words to the effect" and then write down what you believe was said. Using quotation marks at the wrong time has been the scourge of many a protection officer and could result in misleading the report reader.

Avoid abbreviations, unless they are in common use. The writer must clearly indicate which facts are attributable to their own actions or observations and which were the actions or observations of others.

If certain facts are not available at the time you write your report, then these facts must be clearly spelled out along with what action has been taken or will be taken in order to complete the report.

Never leave a report incomplete at the end of your tour of duty without authorization and without attaching a memo to indicate the date you expect to have it completed.

To ensure that your reports are submitted in the proper manner, they must be kept in a safe and secure place away from any unauthorized personnel. Confidentiality is a key component in the report writing process.

THE SIX ESSENTIAL INGREDIENTS

There are six main essential ingredients that must be included in most security reports. Not all security reports will contain these ingredients. Some, such as access logs, will only contain a minimum of information; however, whenever an event occurs or an incident requires reporting, then all six ingredients will be present and **must be** included in the report. These six ingredients are **Who, What, When, Where, Why,** and **How**.

1. Who relates to who was involved in the event, the name of the complainant, client, witnesses, suspects, accused parties or officers.

2. What relates to the type of incident or event, what actually occurred.

3. When is the time and date that the event occurred.

4. Where is the location that the event took place, or subsequent locations, depending on the type of incident.

5. Why is the motive. It can frequently be determined by proper investigation. It may explain the reason for the occurrence, but can't be officer speculation or unfounded opinion.

6. How is how the event came to your attention, how it occurred. This means the complete details about how the event happened from start to finish.

In a normal occurrence report outlining even the simplest event, all six ingredients will be present. Unfortunately, most protection officers fail to include all six ingredients as some of the details seem unimportant at the time.

This results in lost information that may prove valuable at some later time and may also lead to the embarrassment of having to explain a sloppy report to an irate client or supervisor.

Always ensure that all six ingredients are properly explained in your report.

SECURITY REPORTS ARE IMPORTANT

We have been stressing the importance of submitting complete, accurate security reports, but before we go further into how to write useful reports, let's examine just what it is about reports that makes them so important.

1. Accurate and permanent record (memory bank)— Reports that are submitted become part of the "paper flow" of your organization. Every business, no matter how large or small, requires a certain amount of paper flow.

With proper record-keeping, this paper flow will allow you and every other member of your security team to instantly access information that has been stored. If proper security reports are written and filed, this storehouse of information can be priceless. This includes manual and electronic filing.

2. Detecting problem areas—We have already examined the reasons that the passing of information is a vital tool in our everyday lives, but in security it becomes even more important. The submission of reports allows every other officer access to your experiences while on the job. Everything that has occurred while on duty has been properly submitted in the prescribed report format.

You are now able to access that information as far back as your file/data system allows. This can become a useful tool to the effective protection officer who sees from many reports various patterns forming regarding a problem area in the security of the facility.

It may be something as innocuous as a side door being constantly left unlocked. You may only have noticed it once and not thought much about it.

But if a number of reports pointing to the same event are filed, if suddenly becomes a serious matter, a breach in security that may indicate an employee is testing the security.

3. Statistical data—From the security reports that are generated, it is possible to compile statistics that may eventually assist in justification of existing or future expenditures in the areas of personnel, equipment, and facilities.

4. Indication of work—This means that there is a simple and effective way to check on the amount of work and the type of work each officer has been doing.

REPORT ORGANIZATION

The security report detailing a specific occurrence should contain an introduction, a body, and a conclusion.

INTRODUCTION
The introduction should let the reader know in the briefest manner what basically occurred. It should include the date and time, the location, people involved, and what happened.

BODY
The body will include a detailed chronological narrative of what actually occurred, observations made, and subsequent interviews and inquiries, witnesses' names, statements, and descriptions.

CONCLUSION
The conclusion will show what follow-up actions are still required and expected time of completion, preventative

action taken, and a brief summary of any points that are not completely answered in the body of the report.

All reports, no matter how seemingly insignificant, have value. The value is the information contained. It must be remembered that information is our greatest asset in security work. We must have it to operate effectively. It is of little value if it is retained by one individual. Through reports, this information is recorded and is disseminated to the security personnel.

Every person who writes a report, fills out a form or makes a memorandum must question in their minds what essential ingredients are required. They must ask themselves this question: "Is my work clear, concise, accurate, and complete?"

Every security report must be self-explanatory. It must clearly paint a word picture for the reader. If it does not, then the report has failed to serve its purpose. A well-written report must contain the following properties:

1. Clear—The language and format must be simple and to the point; facts must follow a logical sequence.

2. Legible—When handwritten or printed, the reader must be able to understand what is written; it must be easily read by others.

3.   Complete—All available information will have been included in the report covering all six essential ingredients.

4. Accurate—All facts presented in the report must be accurate. To ensure accuracy, the officer must make the effort to check and double-check facts before committing them to writing.

5. Brief—Keep the report as brief as possible by eliminating excess words. The report needs to have all essential ingredients, with nothing more.

6. Re-read—Before submitting a report, re-read it and be sure that all the questions that could possibly be asked have been answered in the report. Do not assume that the report is complete until you have proofread it. If necessary, rewrite the report.

7. Prompt—Reports must be completed as soon as possible and never later than the end of the tour of duty. All reports must be handed in to the appropriate person as soon as possible in order that the information contained in the report can be acted upon quickly.

Remember, you must satisfy the questioning mind of your supervisor, who does not see you at work, and the judgment of your abilities will come from reading your reports. Your personal evaluation is often based largely on the type of report you submit, so take care in the preparation of your security reports.

A shift properly conducted, but inadequately reported, not only fails to provide the administration with the products needed for proper record-keeping, but reflects on the protection officer's total job performance. On the other hand, reports alone do not equate to an effective protection officer.

SECURITY QUIZ
Field Notes and Report Writing

1. Notes and reports can be considered tools of the _____ to the protection officer. (Fill in the blank.)

2. An officer's notes are a quick and accurate method of recording what he _____, _____, and _____. (Fill in the blanks.)

3. Properly made notes will ensure that _____ and _____ are not lost. (Fill in the blanks.)

4. It is important to double-check and _____ all facts before committing them to a report. (Fill in the blank.)

5. When choosing a notebook, which of the following should be considered?
   ☐ (a) Small enough to carry easily in clothing
   ☐ (b) Pages numbered sequentially
   ☐ (c) Durable cover
   ☐ (d) All of the above
   ☐ (e) None of the above

6. Notes will assist the officer in:
   ☐ (a) preparing reports
   ☐ (b) refreshing memory
   ☐ (c) reflecting officer ability
   ☐ (d) All of the above
   ☐ (e) None of the above

7. Notes are important in ensuring that:
   ☐ (a) facts will not be forgotten
   ☐ (b) your supervisor knows you are doing a good job
   ☐ (c) you will remember what shift you are working
   ☐ (d) All the above
   ☐ (e) None of the above

8. The protection officer must be able to observe accurately and record observations on paper in a clear, concise, and logical manner.
   ☐ T ☐ F

9. Accurate reports can be traced back to poor notes.
   ☐ T ☐ F

10. Detecting contradictions in statements results from a protection officer's interrogation.
    ☐ T ☐ F

OBSERVATION SKILLS AND MEMORY

By R. Lorne Brennan, CPO

In the profession of security, as in other professions, you develop various skills which make your job easier. Observations as well as memory are skills such as these.

You will find that as your **observation and memory** skills improve, all aspects of your job become easier. This will show from the way you handle situations right through to the written report you will complete after—from the way you conduct your patrols to the way your peers and supervisors see you.

One of the differences between a professional security officer and other security officers is that the professional can and does utilize his senses, through observation and memory, in all aspects of the job.

The professional security officer will do the following:

- Be able to see a problem situation forming and be able to take appropriate action before the situation erupts.
- Be able to give more accurate descriptions of people, places, and things he encounters.
- Be able to see signs of untruths when interviewing people.
- Be able to conduct more effective patrols, both inside and outside.
- Be able to say with full confidence that he has conducted his tour of duty in the best possible manner.

Observation is the act of noticing and noting the information we gather through our senses. The degree to which we observe is what this chapter is all about. The following pages will assist you in understanding your senses as related to security and in developing your skills of observation as well as your memory.

Most people feel that our five senses and our memory are automatic and some people just have better senses and memories than others. This idea is wrong. Your five senses and your memory, although somewhat automatic in function, are skills. You can build these skills just as one would build muscles, through use and "awareness."

As a professional security officer, you will rely on these skills; the better you can use them, the more effective a job you can do. You need to be able to **see, hear, smell, touch,** and **taste** with accuracy and be able to **remember** this information for your notes, reports, and discussions with fellow guards.

YOUR FIVE SENSES

Your five senses are the basis for effective observation. The information these senses gather is the information you use, through your memory, in every aspect of security work.

Your ability to gather information through your senses depends fully on your awareness.

Example 1

You are on a floor patrol and you enter the lobby of the building on your way back to the security office. There are many people and much movement. After you make your way to the office and your supervisor asks what is happening in the lobby, could you say:

- How many people were in the lobby?
- Did they all seem to belong?
- Was all the fire safety equipment in place and good working order?
- Did anyone need assistance or directions?

Example 2

You are now sitting at your desk, the phone rings, and the caller tells you a bomb has been placed in your building. After the caller hangs up, do you know:

- If the caller was disguising his voice?
- If the caller was calling from a phone booth?
- The approximate age of the caller?
- Did you note anything else, or were you not aware and now can't remember?

You can think back to a time, probably not that long ago, when you were confronted with a similar situation. A situation we all fall into, when we look without seeing, listen without hearing, touch without feeling, not knowing what we smell, or not knowing what we taste.

The difference is in "thinking" about out surroundings and being "aware" of what is happening around us.

Sight

What can we do about sight? There are a few things we should know about seeing and perception that will improve the information our eyes are giving us.

Visibility

The visibility of an object depends on three things.

1. The **distance** from the observer.

A person who has distinctive features will be recognized by friends or relatives in daylight up to 100 yards away, whereas a person who is not known by the observer can only be recognized in daylight up to 30 yards away. In contrast, a person can rarely be recognized beyond 10–12 yards under a full moon.

2. The **size** of object.

A large object can be recognized at a further distance because its features are more distinctive. The larger the object is, the further away the observer will be able to recognize it.

3. The **illumination** of object.

The amount of light that reflects from an object to the observer's eye determines how easily the observer will recognize the object. The observer can recognize an object easier by sunlight than by street lights.

The direction of illumination is also a factor. The observer can see much better if the light is on the object and away from the observer, than toward the observer.

The observer must also remember that the color of illumination can change the color of the object to the observer's eye.

Problems Related to Sight in Observation

1. Night vision

At night you use the periphery of the retina to receive light. The problem you run into is that if you look directly at an object at night, it tends to fade away because the image strikes a "dead spot" in the eye.

To solve this, look slightly above, below or to one side of the object, thus the image will not strike the "dead spot" of the eye.

2. Position of the observer

The position of the observer in relation to the object can alter the observer's perception of the object.

A seated person will often overestimate the height of a person standing nearby. Keep this factor in mind when recording descriptions.

This problem also works in reverse. It is hard to estimate the height of a person seated close by a standing observer.

Hearing

This is an important aid in identifying persons, places of events, and things—especially at night when sight is limited.

You must be aware of the different sounds which are normal at your worksite.

The following are sounds that you should learn to recognize and be able to differentiate:

1. Activity noises—animal calls, footsteps, glass breaking, and so on
2. Voices—volume, pitch, accents, intonation, and so on
3. Motors—drills, saws, foreign vehicles, domestic vehicles, and so on
4. Firearms—pistols, rifles, shotguns, automobile backfires

Smell

The professional security officer must be able to distinguish potentially dangerous odors, as this may assist emergency personnel, as well as cut down the extent of loss through life and property.

The following are substances you should know and be able to distinguish:

- gasoline
- natural gas
- gunpowder
- gas fumes that endanger life and health, such as chlorine gas
- smoke: wood, electric, or rubber

Remember that certain substances such as gas and ether, may diminish your sense of smell temporarily. The longer you are exposed to any smell, the less distinguishable it will be.

Touch

This sense can give you vital information which would be difficult to obtain in any other way.

The following are some of the ways touch can assist you in your job:

1. Feeling walls or glass for heat from an unseen fire. For vibrations created by sound, movement, or tools in a burglary.
2. Check the pulse or heartbeat of an unconscious crime or accident victim.
3. Examine doors and windows in the dark for signs of forced entry.
4. Check tires, engines, or mufflers for warmth to see if a car has been running recently.
5. To identify types of cloth or paper.

Taste

This sense should never be used on the job by anyone who has not received extensive training and then only with extreme caution.

Never taste any substance that could be narcotic or poison. You won't like the trip.

Memory

Memory is the act of recalling information. You need this skill, and it is a skill, in order to be effective in the security field. You may have developed your senses to their peak, but if you can't recall the information they give you for your notes and later your reports for your superiors, you are not fulfilling your responsibilities.

Your memory skills, like your muscles, grow the more they are used. Therefore, you should incorporate memory tests into your everyday life.

These memory tests need not be complicated and take a lot of time, but can be extremely simple and can be done at any time of the day or night, in any atmosphere.

Here are some simple tests to assist you in improving this skill.

1. During your patrols or even when out shopping, examine a pedestrian who walks by you and mentally record his or her appearance. Then double back and determine how close your mental record was to the person's appearance. As you progress, cut back on the time you take to study the person and lengthen the time you take to double back to re-examine them.
2. Use this same technique on display cases in stores or other locations which have a variety of objects.
3. Study photographs, set them aside, write lists of your observations; then compare. You can also do this with objects in a box.
4. Discuss with other guards what events or characteristics arouse their suspicions about situations or persons. More than increase your memory capacity, this will give you a chance to relay information you remember

about specific situations and allow you to see others' views about what they remember.

HOW TO IMPROVE YOUR SENSES

1.   Sight

Ensure that your vision has been tested and that it is in peak medical condition. (If you require glasses or contacts, ensure that you wear them.)

Make a conscious effort to see instead of just look. Be "aware" of what you look at. This can't be stressed enough.

Ensure that you understand the various factors that affect your vision and learn how to compensate for them.

2.   Hearing

Ensure that your hearing is in peak medical various condition.

Know and be able to distinguish various sounds sometimes associated with crime and also those sounds that are normal for your job site.

Know your limits. Don't state that your heard a particular sound unless you are 100 percent sure that is the sound you heard.

When making your rounds, take time to stop and just listen. It's amazing how many sounds you'll hear that you're not consciously aware of.

3.   Smell

Know when this sense is limited, through a cold or other sinus condition. Guard against this happening to you.

Know the various dangerous smells, and be able to distinguish them.

Be aware of what you smell; take time to give this sense justice.

4.   Touch

Don't hamper this sense by covering it with other materials.

Know when and how to use it—for example, for feeling doors when there is a possible fire in the area.

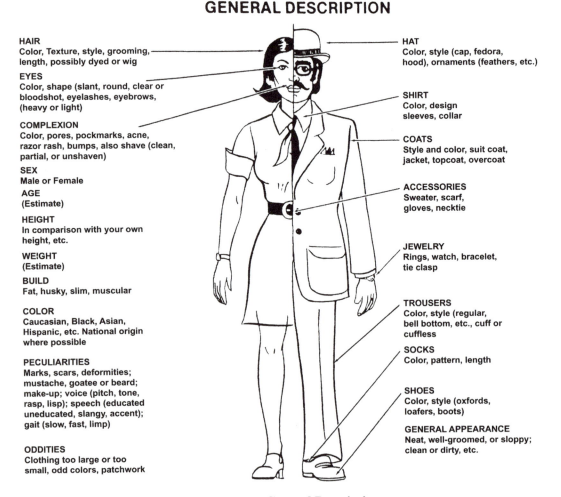

GENERAL DESCRIPTION

HAIR
Color, Texture, style, grooming, length, possibly dyed or wig

EYES
Color, shape (slant, round, clear or bloodshot, eyelashes, eyebrows, (heavy or light)

COMPLEXION
Color, pores, pockmarks, acne, razor rash, bumps, also shave (clean, partial, or unshaven)

SEX
Male or Female

AGE
(Estimate)

HEIGHT
In comparison with your own height, etc.

WEIGHT
(Estimate)

BUILD
Fat, husky, slim, muscular

COLOR
Caucasian, Black, Asian, Hispanic, etc. National origin where possible

PECULIARITIES
Marks, scars, deformities; mustache, goatee or beard; make-up; voice (pitch, tone, rasp, lisp); speech (educated uneducated, slangy, accent); gait (slow, fast, limp)

ODDITIES
Clothing too large or too small, odd colors, patchwork

HAT
Color, style (cap, fedora, hood), ornaments (feathers, etc.)

SHIRT
Color, design sleeves, collar

COATS
Style and color, suit coat, jacket, topcoat, overcoat

ACCESSORIES
Sweater, scarf, gloves, necktie

JEWELRY
Rings, watch, bracelet, tie clasp

TROUSERS
Color, style (regular, bell bottom, etc., cuff or cuffless

SOCKS
Color, pattern, length

SHOES
Color, style (oxfords, loafers, boots)

GENERAL APPEARANCE
Neat, well-groomed, or sloppy; clean or dirty, etc.

Figure 2-1   General Description

Know the feel of different material. This may assist city police in identification of suspects you encounter.

5. Taste

Know the taste of the drinking water at your worksite. This will assist you in case of possible additives being placed in the drinking water.

Other than in this case, the sense of taste should never be used.

As you can see, the skills that have been discussed in this chapter will serve you in all aspects of your work. You, your peers, and your supervisors will notice improve-ments in all aspects of your job the more you work on these skills.

The more exercises you do, the easier these skills will become. Use the diagrams in this chapter to assist in your training. The more aware you become, the easier the exercises will become.

Remember to always be aware of the senses you are using at any given time, and make a point of utilizing them to their fullest capabilities. Consider at all times which of the senses will give you the most and the best information and then remember that information.

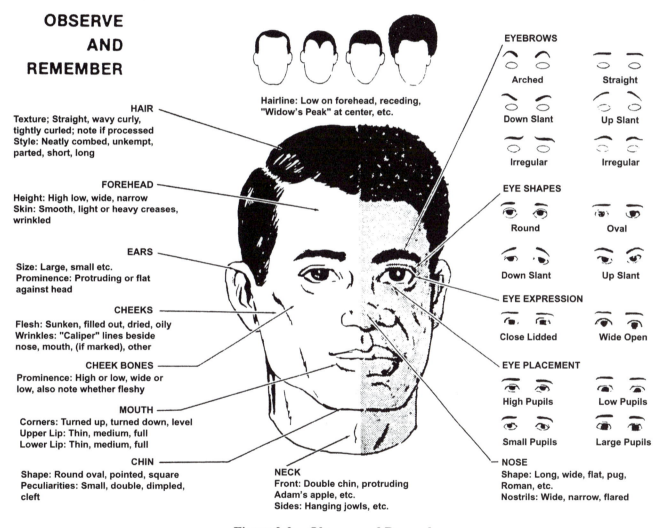

Figure 2-2   Observe and Remember

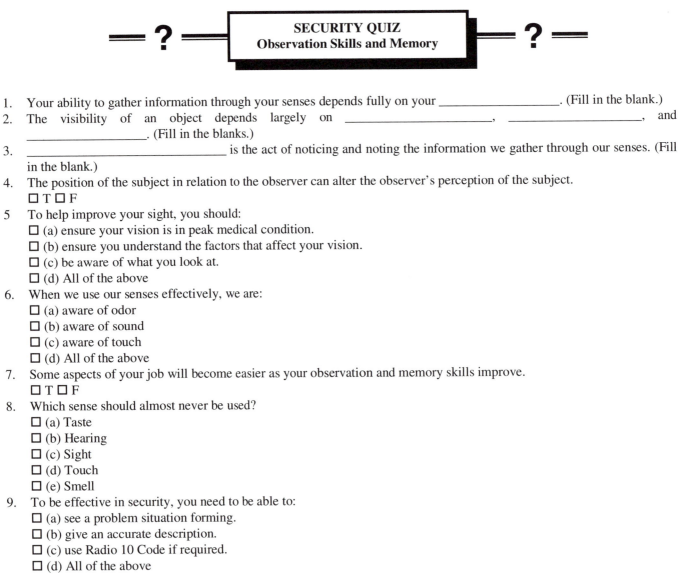

SECURITY QUIZ
Observation Skills and Memory

1. Your ability to gather information through your senses depends fully on your _____. (Fill in the blank.)
2. The visibility of an object depends largely on _____, _____, and _____. (Fill in the blanks.)
3. _____ is the act of noticing and noting the information we gather through our senses. (Fill in the blank.)
4. The position of the subject in relation to the observer can alter the observer's perception of the subject.
    □ T □ F
5   To help improve your sight, you should:
    □ (a) ensure your vision is in peak medical condition.
    □ (b) ensure you understand the factors that affect your vision.
    □ (c) be aware of what you look at.
    □ (d) All of the above
6. When we use our senses effectively, we are:
    □ (a) aware of odor
    □ (b) aware of sound
    □ (c) aware of touch
    □ (d) All of the above
7. Some aspects of your job will become easier as your observation and memory skills improve.
    □ T □ F
8. Which sense should almost never be used?
    □ (a) Taste
    □ (b) Hearing
    □ (c) Sight
    □ (d) Touch
    □ (e) Smell
9. To be effective in security, you need to be able to:
    □ (a) see a problem situation forming.
    □ (b) give an accurate description.
    □ (c) use Radio 10 Code if required.
    □ (d) All of the above
10. There is no need to know the "normal" sounds at your worksite.
    □ T □ F

PATROL PRINCIPLES

Christopher L. Vail

HISTORY OF PATROL

Security work encompasses many different and various functions; however, there is one function that is common to all security agencies – the job of patrol. In order to understand the technical aspects of patrol, it is important to see how this function came about, how it developed, and how it changes over time. Eugene O'Neill, a famous writer, once said, "The past is the present, isn't it? It's the future, too." Therefore, to gain more insight and understanding of the patrol function today, it's necessary to see its genesis. The very word "patrol" is thought to be derived from the French work *patrouiller,* which originally meant "to tramp in the mud." To many, this translation may well reflect what may be described as a function that is "arduous, tiring, difficult, and performed in conditions other than ideal."

Patrol has roots that go back to the days of the caveman. The caveman moved from the solitude of the cave to small family groups that became clans or tribes. Tribal customs developed and informal codes of conduct evolved, although laws did not follow until written records were kept. The people were the police. The chief of the tribe or clan exercised all executive, legislative, and judicial powers. Eventually, the tribe or clan chief appointed members to perform such duties as bodyguard or enforcer of his edicts. Crimes against a member of the tribe or clan were handled by the person injured or by his family. Crimes against the clan or tribe were handled by the group itself. This led to rather harsh, barbaric, and retaliatory punishments often known as the concept of "an eye for an eye, and a tooth for a tooth."

Around 2100 B.C., the first codification of customs was written by Hammurabi, King of Babylon. Under these laws of Hammurabi, it is believed that messengers were appointed to carry out the commands of the law—the first form of patrol duty. About 1400 B.C., Amenhotep, king of Egypt, developed a marine patrol on the coast of Egypt, the first recorded history of a patrol unit.

In early Greece, guard systems were established to protect the tower, highways, and the person of Pisistratus, ruler of Athens. Ancient Rome saw the establishment of quaestores (inquirers; also basically judicial officers) who would go to the house of the accused and blow a trumpet or horn as an indication of his arrest. In 27 B.C., under Augustus, emperor of Rome, the Praetorian Guards were formed to protect the life and property of the emperor, and urban cohorts were established to keep the peace of the city. The vigiles (from which the word vigilantes comes) were formed to patrol the streets and act as enforcement officers.

While they were non-military, they were armed with staves and the traditional shortswords. These patrolmen were also assigned to patrol geographical precincts.

The Romans began to move north toward England, leaving Europe in a terrible state of turmoil and strife for about five centuries after the fall of the Roman Empire. Little is known of policing and law enforcement during this time. Between A.D. 450–650, the Anglo-Saxons in England developed small groups of people known as tuns (from which the word town comes). A form of individual and group responsibility for policing began to emerge through the concept of local self-government. Around A.D. 700 tithings (groups of ten families) were formed for the purpose of maintaining the peace and protecting the community. Tithingmen were elected by the group, and their responsibilities included raising the hue and cry upon learning of a crime in the group and dispensing out punishment. Ten tithings were called a hundred and the head man was called a reeve. Several hundreds within the same geographical area were collectively called a shire (the equivalent of our county) and the chief law enforcement officer was called a shire-reeve (what we now call the sheriff).

William, the duke of Normandy, introduced a highly repressive police system in A.D. 1066., in which collective security was deemed far more important than individual freedom in England. He divided England into 55 separate military districts and appointed an officer of his choice to be the shire-reeve in each shire, or military district. The state assumed the responsibility for keeping the peace in this system. England lived under this system until the Magna Carta (Great Charter) was written in A.D. 1215, guaranteeing civil and political rights to individuals and restoring local control to the communities.

In 1252 in England, the watch system was established. People appointed to the duty of watchman had the responsibility for keeping the peace. They were unpaid and the dregs of society—the old, infirm, sick, and criminally inclined. After 1285, some watches grouped together for the purpose of safety, forming a "marching watch," which may be considered the first form of patrol organization found in our present-day system. The only paid watchmen were those paid by merchants, parishioners, and householders. In 1737, the Elizabethan Act of 1585 was enlarged to allow cities to levy taxes to pay for the night watch.

In 1748, Henry Fielding suggested that policing was a municipal function and that some form of mobile patrol was needed to protect the highways. The Bow Street Runners were formed, with a foot patrol to operate in the inner areas of London, and a horse patrol to operate in the outer areas.

In 1829, the Home Secretary, Sir Robert Peel, introduced "An Act for Improving the Police In and Near the Metropolis"—the Metropolitan Police Act. This legislation forms the basis for law enforcement organizational structure in America. Setting the stage for organized patrol activity, one of the 12 fundamental principles of the Act stated that "the deployment of police strength by time and area is essential." By the end of 1830, the metropolitan area of London was organized into 17 divisions and superintendents were appointed. Patrol sections were created, and each section was broken down into beat areas.

Basically, Peel replaced the patchwork of private law enforcement systems then in existence, with an organized and regular police structure that would serve the state and not local interests. He believed that deterrence of criminal activity should be accomplished by preventive patrol officers trained to prevent crime by their presence in the community. Hence, modern patrol was born.

America was founded along the Atlantic coast and many English systems and beliefs became the basis for our social, political, legal, and governmental systems. The New England part of America was built and developed basically under a system of commerce and industry. Communities were formed around towns and villages, which relied on constables to provide protection and keep the peace by using the watch system. The south developed differently. It was more rural and agricultural with smaller communities. The county was the primary form of government, in which the sheriff system was the prominent form of law enforcement. As the country developed further to the midwest and west, law enforcement organizations combined the functions and roles of constable and sheriff.

Patrol activity in America can be traced to Boston in 1636, when a night watch was formed. In 1658, New York City formed a "rattle watch," so named because they used a rattle to communicate their presence and signal each other. Philadelphia formed a night watch in 1700. Just as in England, these early watchmen were lazy and inept. Often times, people who committed minor crimes were sentenced to serve on the watch as punishment. As can well be imagined, order discipline was a major problem, leading New Haven to create a regulation that said "no watchman will have the liberty to sleep." A 1750 Boston rule said that "watchman will walk their rounds slowly and now and then stand and listen."

Following this rule—as well as making sure to look up, down, and all around—are good procedures for contemporary protection officers to follow.

Uniformed and paid police did not come about until the early to mid-1800s. In 1833, Philadelphia began paying police officers and the New York City Police started wearing uniforms around 1855. Politics and corruption permeated police departments as America grew during the 1800s. In 1855 Allan Pinkerton founded the Pinkerton Detective Agency in Chicago, which became the forerunner of the U.S. Secret Service. As America grew, policing took on new shapes and challenges, with the addition of technological advances, new organizational and political structures, new laws requiring more police officers, societal reliance on law enforcement, and the slow growth of private police and security agencies. However, the patrol function of police and security remains the same, and is considered "the back-bone" of security and police agencies.

Security patrols may be routine and boring to some; however, the patrol activity of today is much more than "tramping in the mud," sounding the hue and cry, or shaking a rattle. The officer of today who protects a facility is responsible for the safety and security of physical—and often intellectual—assets of tremendously high value. He/she is responsible for the safety and security of a workforce consisting of people who are educated, well-trained, and professional—a huge investment of human worth and productivity. Today's security officer has the availability of training, equipment, and technology heretofore unheard of. We now live in an age of more random violent criminal activity, much of which is directed toward innocent victims; of drug related crime; of juvenile crime involving senseless violence; of overloaded legal systems; and of more and more civil litigation. At the same time, there is more being demanded from property and organizational managers in terms of protection from fire, disaster, and accident. Administrative agencies at the federal, state, and local level continue to enact new regulations that employers must follow. **Security officers have more responsibility now than they have ever had before.** In fact, the patrol function is more than just the backbone of security; it is also the heart and soul of a total loss control approach.

PURPOSE OF PATROL

The function of security is to prevent and control loss. As a means of accomplishing this, patrol officers make periodic checks around a facility. Therefore, patrol can be defined as the act of moving about an area to provide protection and to conduct observation. That is a fairly simplistic definition, since while protection and observation may be the major elements of patrol, there are numerous other functions that the officer may be called on to perform during his or her tour of duty. Based on organizational needs, there are several major purposes of patrol.

1. Detection of criminal or unauthorized activity. Contingent upon organizations' needs; this could include trespassing, noise violations, safety violations, lease violations by tenants, alcohol violations, parking violations, and so on. In order to be effective at this, officers must be intimately familiar with organizational rules, laws, and patterns of criminal behavior, all of which are constantly changing.

2. Prevention and deterrence of crime and unauthorized activity. This includes projecting a security presence into the environment. Making the security program visible will at least temporarily suppress criminal/unauthorized activity.

3. Ensure compliance with organizational policy. At the same time this is done, public/community relations are maintained by interacting with persons in the work environment. Relations with tenants, vendors, neighboring security departments, and local law enforcement certainly come into play here! Additionally, officers may help ensure compliance with administrative agency regulations such as OSHA, EPA, or Labor Department mandates.

4. Assess, report, and record loss causing situations or circumstances. This could include any type of fire, safety, or health hazard, such as chemical spills, overcrowding of rooms/area, radiation leaks, coffee pots left on, leaking pipes, unsanitary conditions, congested areas, mechanical failures, and so on.

5. Investigate as directed by the central alarm station (CAS), dispatch, or supervisor in charge. There are a host of possible lines of inquiry which can be requested of the patrol officer by management.

6. Test and inspect the physical security system. This includes alarms, locks, lights, CCTV, access points, and physical barriers such as fence lines. While assuming greater importance in high security installations, this is a function of patrols in all environments to some degree or other.

7. Act as a compensatory measure during system outages. Should there be an outage or malfunction of a physical security system component, the patrolling officer will stand by and assume a fixed post at the affected point/area until the situation is remedied. This may simply involve calling maintenance and standing by until a lock is fixed, or it may require continuous posting out in a high security facility with an alarm or power outage.

8. Respond to emergencies. This is where security patrol has traditionally varied from police patrol; while security emphasizes prevention, law enforcement emphasizes response to problems. Unfortunately security departments must be able to respond professionally to accidents, fights, fires, intrusions, assaults, thefts, HASMAT problems, or other reasonably foreseeable emergencies. Staffing levels, response times, training, and equipment must all support the requirement for emergency response.

9. Performance of other services required by management. This can include opening up areas and making them ready for visitors. It could also include dispensing literature, conduction of formal or informal surveys of visitors, testing equipment, finding lost children, or acting as an escort.

Obviously, the needs of all organizations/facilities are unique. Shopping centers have different loss control needs than warehouses. Hospitals are different from power plants. Hotels are different from amusement parks. Military installations are different from college campuses. What activities occur and what activities are unauthorized vary considerably. Patrol may involve taking action against unauthorized personnel, suspicious persons, illegal activities, and suspicious automobiles. Pertinent state and local laws, and company policies will dictate what security officers are to do in these situations. Depending on the officer's employer, he or she may also be required to conduct an investigation of criminal activity. The catch-all phrase of "performance of

other services" may include a multitude of functions as requested by the officer's employer, the client, and/or as needed by others such as visitors, vendors, and employees. In any event, patrol is the "eyes and ears of security."

The provision of security services is not an "afterthought"; it is a business necessity. Organizations that don't take steps to protect their assets will lose them! Employers also have a legal and moral responsibility to provide a safe and secure workplace for their employees, and those who visit their organization. Insurance companies require that certain security measures be enacted. There are court decisions affecting security, particularly relating to the commission of wrongful acts or the omission of required acts. Federal, state and local laws, rules, and regulations dictate that certain security measures be placed in effect. Security, therefore, is a part of management in any company or organization. Patrol is the essence of providing those security measures.

TYPES OF PATROL

There are two basic types of patrol: foot and mobile. Within each type of patrol, different methods may be used, depending on many factors that will be discussed. Mobile patrols include the use of automobiles, bicycles, mopeds, and golf carts. Helicopters and horses are other means of mobile patrol, but are not all that common.

Foot patrols are conducted normally by one officer "walking a beat." Areas to be patrolled are both indoors and outdoors. The major advantage to this type of patrol is that officers can really learn their assigned areas well. While this is not an all-inclusive list of what a foot patrolman can learn, he or she will learn what doors and windows are normally locked or unlocked, what lights are normally left on at night, what personnel are authorized in certain areas, where emergency equipment is located, and what potential hazards exist. Such knowledge and information will assist the officer in determining if anything is amiss. It is also a good opportunity for the officers to become known to the employees and to establish a positive professional relationship with everyone they contact. One way to accomplish this is by discussing the above-mentioned items, or any other official matter, with the people involved. Another advantage of foot patrol is that an officer could place himself or herself at or near high security risk areas on a frequent and random basis, making it difficult for one with criminal intent to penetrate that area. Officers on foot patrol also have as much use of their five senses—sight, smell, taste, feel, and hearing, as their physical condition allows. If they are in excellent health, this is very advantageous, and they can actually "patrol" a larger area using one or more of these senses.

Major drawbacks to foot patrols are the small size of the area that can effectively be patrolled, the amount of time taken to conduct one round while carefully checking everything, and getting from one part of the area to another. Other drawbacks include access to emergency equipment if needed and personnel costs involved—it takes a lot of protection officers to provide adequate protection. Inclement weather conditions also sometimes restrict foot patrol activity.

Patrol officers can use a number of different methods of mobile patrol. The automobile is the most common form of patrol; however, many agencies find it economical, while providing other benefits, to patrol with golf carts, bicycles, or mopeds. The advantage of mobile patrol includes the very fact that it is mobile. The officer can patrol a much larger area. Depending on which type of vehicle is used, the officer has access to emergency equipment, and he/she can carry different amounts and types of equipment. Obviously, a car can carry a lot more than a bicycle, and this is a bona fide consideration when determining what type of mobile patrol to use. While a bicycle can't carry as much equipment as a car can, it can get to places a car can't, and can do it much more quietly. These are some other factors to consider in selecting what type of mobile patrol to use.

1. The initial cost of purchase
2. Ongoing maintenance costs
3. Size of the area to be patrolled
4. The need to access emergency and other equipment, such as first-aid kits, traffic control equipment, extra rain ponchos, additional radios, and so on
5. The type of facility being protected, and the organizational image and culture of the facility
6. The threat model, and degree of vulnerability of the facility

Depending on the size of the patrol area, a car, or in some cases where golf carts are used, the officer can also carry patrol dogs. Dogs enable the officer to search a large and/or complex environment very quickly with minimal manpower. In very large areas, aerial patrols may be conducted by helicopter. In rugged terrain, horses or ATVs may be used. Each of these methods has some capacity to carry equipment.

PREPARATION FOR PATROL

Preparation for going on patrol duty is not only the physical act of putting on a uniform; it also requires mental and psychological preparation. Security officers should act and look professional not only while on duty, but also while going to work. This not only produces a positive impression on the people they serve, but it helps the officer to perform better. When they look and act like professional security officers, such demeanor demands more respect from others. This respect generates a positive attitude in the officer, and he or she becomes more confident and more competent in his or her work.

While people should not "judge a book by its cover," the fact remains that people do judge protection officers based on their first impression. Clothes "do make the man," so one's personal appearance is important. The officer's uniform should be properly tailored and in good condition—neat, clean, and pressed. There should be no holes, patches, or loose threads dangling from it. Shoes and leather equipment should be polished. Male officers should be clean

shaven. Hair and fingernails should be clean. No items not authorized by the employing organization should be attached to the uniform.

The officer should have a positive attitude when going to work—his or her mind should be focused on the job ahead. No personal problems, hobbies, or business should be carried to work with the officer.

There should be absolutely no ingestion of alcoholic beverages or other psychoactive substances at least eight hours before going on duty. The officer should have had ample rest before going to work, as he or she will need to be both mentally and physically alert on duty. Officers should have a positive attitude and an accompanying bearing that reflects courtesy, politeness, and a willingness to serve. These are basic qualities of professionalism, which instill confidence in a department.

All personal and company equipment issued or used while on duty should be checked to ensure that they are in working order. For example, an officer conducting an interview or investigation while away from the office may be embarrassed to find his or her pen has dried up. Or, the officer's radio may not receive or transmit because the battery is dead. Without having checked beforehand to see if it worked, the officer could also be dead. Officers need to know all policies, rules, and regulations that pertain to the security of the facility, and particularly, the assigned patrol post. While proper procedures for performing the job should be known, many officers have their own procedures for accomplishing a task. If used, they should be in compliance with accepted practices of the security agency, the client, and certainly, the law.

It is important when preparing to go on patrol, that the officer knows the property he or she is protecting "like the back of his/her hand."

The location and condition of emergency equipment, water shut-off valves, electrical controls, fire alarms, and telephones should be known, as the patrol officer may be the first responder to a situation requiring their use. The location of any hazardous materials, or places where hazardous materials are worked with, should be firmly implanted in the officer's mind. All doors and windows, and the condition they're normally found in, should be well known. This includes the knowledge of existing scratches or other marks that, if not known about in advance might be a sign of forcible entry. Also, some doors and windows are frequently left open, some partially open, and some should never be open. Knowledge of the state of these exits and entrances is very valuable to the patrolman.

The alert patrol officer will know what type of conduct, organizational behavior in this case, is considered acceptable or normal at his or her facility. Conduct which is considered abnormal in one area or section may be very commonplace in another. Examples of this conduct include such things as what doors are normally left ajar; what vendors or service personnel use what doors regularly; what computers are left on; what certain smells or odors are normal; and what types of people frequent the facility. The officer must first be able to determine what is customary for his or her patrol area, and then look for actions, conditions, or patterns that are unusual. Each officer must decide in his or her own mind, and to his or her own satisfaction what is suspicious. This will vary her experience, background, training, attitude, and type of environment in which he or she works. A successful officer is one who is able to combine a logical suspicion with being a skillful observer and has enough natural curiosity to investigate those conditions that he or she feels are unusual.

If an officer works the night shift, it's advisable to visit the work site during the day. This will give the officer a fresh and clearer perspective of his/her responsibilities. For example, the officer might discover the existence of doors or windows that he or she didn't even know were there. He or she might discover that a part of the facility thought to be empty or unused is really full of expensive equipment. Or the officer might find that an area thought to contain valuable equipment or materials is actually empty or full of items to be discarded. It also gives the officer the opportunity to talk with and discuss security issues about the facility with other officers whom he or she normally doesn't meet.

These are some techniques that enhance an officer's ability to detect unusual situations.

- Getting to know people in the patrol environment. Maintain a professional—not personal—relationship with them. Have some idea what their jobs and/or functions are. Most people will gladly elaborate on what they do if asked in a tactful manner.
- Inspecting equipment. Get in the habit of checking maintenance tags on equipment. Know what the equipment does.
- Getting to know maintenance personnel and procedures. Consider taking an orientation tour with the maintenance department.
- Visiting the central alarm station, if possible. Become familiar with the alarms and CCTV in each protected point and area.

There are many different sorts of incidents that could occur to an officer on patrol that may require immediate action on his or her part or on the part of others. As the first responding authority to such incidents, the officer should be mentally and physically alert and able to respond to these incidents, making correct decisions as to what needs to be done. The officer may have to take immediate action using his or her own professional knowledge, skills and abilities, or he or she may have to direct others such as the police, EMS, fire, or maintenance personnel to the scene via the most expedient way.

In some circumstances, the officer may have to control a gathering group of onlookers and it is essential to know how to isolate them from the crisis point (problem area). Being able to block off an area quickly and efficiently is obviously important in emergencies. Since anything could happen at any time, the effective security officer knows his or her patrol area very well.

When arriving for duty, an officer should be briefed by a supervisor or check with the previous shift for any unusual events or occurrences; suspicious activities or persons; facility problems dealing with security, fire, or safety; orders, directives, and policies; and any expected VIPs, vendors, contractors, and so on. Determine if there are any communication "dead areas" and where they are. In other words, to be fully prepared to go on patrol, an officer must know what has happened, what is happening, and what is likely to happen.

One area of preparation often overlooked by many officers and departments is that of continuing training and education. With the many and increased demands being placed on security personnel today, it is essential for the officer to stay abreast of the latest laws, equipment, products, services, and procedures in security. This information is gained only through education or training. Companies who contract out for their security services, proprietary security departments, and security companies themselves, should provide basic and ongoing training for their security officers. Companies can establish internal training programs, send officers or require officers to attend local colleges that have security educational programs, or have their officers take home-study courses.

There are also private vendors who specialize in conducting security training programs. If a local police department has a "ride-along" program, this can provide excellent training for the security officer. Another way for an officer to gain new information and knowledge is by reading security and law enforcement related professional journals and magazines. *Protection News, Security, Police and Security News, FBI Law Enforcement Bulletin,* and *Security Management* are all excellent sources of up-to-date professional information.

TECHNIQUES OF PATROL

As stated earlier, patrol is defined as the act of moving about an area to provide protection and conduct observation. In the security world, the majority of patrol activity is focused on the prevention of criminal behavior. A crime cannot occur unless three elements are present: the opportunity, the desire, and the tools. Patrol officers have a direct influence over the first one and some influence over the second. An effective patrol officer, by following accepted patrol procedures, can and will hinder the first element—the opportunity to commit a criminal act. By ensuring all doors and windows are properly closed and locked, by ensuring there is adequate lighting in vulnerable areas such as where safes or valuables are kept and around the building(s) proper, and by making access difficult to possible targets for criminal activity, opportunities for the criminal are reduced or eliminated. This is the very essence of loss prevention.

While the patrol officer may not be able to directly influence the desire of a person to commit a crime, that desire is greatly hampered by the very presence of a security officer performing his or her patrol duties in a professional way. It is indeed a rare criminal who will commit a crime in the presence of a patrol officer (although it has happened), especially one who is visible, alert, and showing confidence. The third element is not a controllable one by security personnel; however, security officers should know what tools are generally used by criminals. Guns are obviously a tool, but some people have the authority and permission to carry weapons. Screwdrivers and pry bars are common everywhere, but in the hands of a criminal, they become burglar tools. Information gathering equipment, such as photographic or recording devices, may be used to steal information. Radio transmitting or monitoring devices may also be used by terrorists and sophisticated professional criminals.

Patrol is never routine; anything is liable to happen at any time. Therefore, there are two major principles of patrol that guide the effective patrol officer. **The first principle of patrol is that it should always be done in a random fashion.** Never patrol by driving or walking in the same direction. Alter routes; change the pace occasionally; walk or drive for a while then stop to look and listen. Sometimes, turn around and backtrack your route. If someone is trying to figure out where the patrol officer will be at any given time so that they may conduct some illegal act, random patrolling will keep them off guard.

The second principle of patrol ties in with randomness: The frequency of patrol should be random. Do not go on patrol the same time each time; the officer's patrol schedule should always vary. Depending on the vulnerability of the facility being protected, the officer may want to patrol the area once every few hours, once every two hours, once an hour or more each hour. At the very least, every facility or area should be patrolled when going on duty and just before going off-duty. Patrol should never be conducted the same way each time by timing or route; there should be nothing predictable about a patrol officer's schedule as the officer should not patrol by a set routine or pattern.

With the use of automatic monitoring systems or barcode technology, patrols are documented. These systems generally require that officers patrol in a set sequence within an established time period. Using a random patrol route with a bar-code unit is still possible by approaching each patrol point from a different direction. Times may also be varied to some degree.

Another principle of patrol is communication. Patrol officers should always keep the command post, supervisor, backup officer, or central alarm station advised of where they are and what the situation is. They must follow the following proper radio procedures:

1. Listening before speaking into the radio
2. Depressing the microphone a split second before and after speaking to ensure that all syllables are transmitted
3. Speaking clearly and slightly slower than normal into the microphone

4. Not broadcasting when not necessary.
5. Avoiding the use of profanity, horseplay, or confidential information on the radio. Scanners abound — especially with reporters

Patrol officers must also thoroughly document their observations. There should be detailed notes taken on any unusual, suspicious or potential loss causing situation. Notes must be kept professionally and observations reported up the chain of command to the appropriate management personnel. Forms designed specifically for each environment should be on hand. Whether there is a predesigned form or not, the important thing is to report all situations where there is any doubt as to their importance.

Although it is not a patrol technique in the true sense of the word, officer survival is a major consideration when on patrol. One way to survive patrol is to use "sensible" patrol methods—that is, use all five natural senses—sight, hearing, smell, touch, and sometimes, although rarely, the sense of taste on patrol. The two strongest senses the officer will use are that of sight and hearing. If riding in a motorized vehicle, an officer should keep the windows opened a little, allowing him or her to detect the sound of breaking glass or other noises of suspicious origin. He or she should not play a commercial radio loudly if the car is equipped with one as it could drown out noises that require investigation. An open window will also allow the officer to use his or her sense of smell to detect the smell of smoke or other odor that should be investigated.

Often a person is known to have a "sixth sense." This means that they seem to know "when something just isn't right," or they get a "feeling" about a person or a situation. This sense is called intuition. It develops from experience, and it permits a person to sense what is abnormal or unusual. While an officer cannot testify in court that he or she performed a certain duty by using his or her "sixth sense," it can be very accurate in determining when something needs further investigation. While it can be used as a guide to determine which action or actions are appropriate, it should never be used as the sole determining factor.

Another means of patrol survival is the use of the mental "what if? game." This game (also known as creative daydreaming or mental rehearsal) is played as an officer patrols his or her area by thinking of any possible incident, remote as it might be, that could occur at any place or time. For instance, the officer could think of what to do if someone came running out of an office or building that is supposed to be closed and locked, just as he or she gets there. The officer could think about what actions to take if he or she heard a loud explosion, or gunshots in the area. What would an officer do if it he or she smelled smoke in the area, or if the officer saw a fire in progress? What would an officer do if he or she saw a chemical leak in progress? The list goes on and on. "If this happened, what would I do?" is the question asked by security officers playing this game. It might uncover a potential loss event that has occurred or is occurring. It will also keep an officer up-to-date on company rules, regulations, policies, and procedures. It is a form of self-training, as the officer can determine his or her own needs for improvement and take the appropriate steps to correct any deficiencies in his or her professional life. Finally, it makes response to the event more efficient should it occur. It may save the life of an officer or the life of another.

Light and noise discipline should be practiced when on patrol. This means that patrolling officers should avoid making any more noise than is necessary. They should keep the radio turned down somewhat, keep keys and equipment from jangling, and so on. They should be able to "hear others before they hear you." Note that radio net discipline is also important: Overuse of the radio ties up the net and depletes the battery. Extended conversations should be carried out by landline methods, such as telephones or fax phones. Note too that backup means of communication should always be considered when on patrol or fixed post duty: Always have a contingency plan if the primary means of communication doesn't work.

Similarly, light discipline should be practiced. This means to avoid being silhouetted. Never sit with lights behind you or stay in a car with the dome light on. Use a clipboard light or flashlight. If there is a glare from lights, use it to your advantage if necessary! Use flashlights judiciously; don't have them turned on more than necessary (although for walking safety they should be used if other light sources are not available). "See others before they see you."

FACTORS THAT INFLUENCE PATROL EFFECTIVENESS

As patrol is an expensive loss control technique, it only makes sense to have the officer detect the greatest number of loss causing situations as possible. The WAECUP Theory of loss control can be applied here.

Waste—Patrol officers check scraps being thrown away, look for lights, heat, and water turned on needlessly.

Accident—Officers look for spills and other slippery walking conditions. Always observe all around patrol points for fire hazards, materials stacked too high, and so on. "Look up, down, and all around."

Error—Patrol officers should be thoroughly briefed prior to their shift as to what activities are occurring in their patrol environment. They should check and double-check schedules of building openings and shipments of personnel arrivals. In many cases, the Security department functions as "the grease in the machine," making things run smoothly between different departments. In most organizations, Security makes sure that things don't "fall through the cracks." This is particularly true. Patrol officers can play a key role here in alleviating problems caused by simple human error.

Crime—Become familiar with criminal behaviors in the local area. Also, keep up to date on criminal trends within the industry. Speaking with local police and reading industry specific management literature are good ways to maintain one's professional education. Also, patrol in a random

manner and develop professional relationships with people in the patrol area so that you are approachable. If people observe something that doesn't quite seem right, and they are comfortable talking with a security officer about it, they will! This can uncover numerous potential crimes.

UNETHICAL/UNPROFESSIONAL PRACTICES

Patrol officers should be wary of fraternizing with employees ("Familiarity breeds contempt"). They should also be on guard for possible indications of collusion between employees, employees who constantly work when no one else is around, gambling between employees, racist graffiti in bathrooms and elevators, employees conducting competing businesses using company resources, and so on.

Since observation and perception are key to effective patrol techniques, the officer should be aware of certain internal factors that can influence his/her ability to perform on patrol effectively. While the officer may not be able to control all of these factors, the very realization that they exist can help the officer be more effective. Internal factors include:

• **Fatigue:** Feeling tired or worn out can affect the way an officer perceives things (with the use of all five senses).

• **Boredom:** The more often a task is performed, the more it becomes routine and boring. Boredom leads to stress; stress leads to hasty, improper decisions being made. This can be a deadly distraction if not kept under control.

• **Personal problems:** Preoccupation with personal problems distracts from keeping one's mind on the job at hand and should not be brought to work with the officer.

• **Known facts:** Officers with security or law enforcement experience will recognize things such as burglary tool marks or the smell of marijuana more quickly than an inexperienced officer.

• **Variety of activities:** Officers do many various things, many of which don't even appear to be connected, and things can happen very quickly. Other employment, such as an extra job, can influence an officer's work performance (see *fatigue* above).

• **Failing senses:** Age or illness affect an officer's senses; the older or sicker he or she becomes, the less quickly the body is able to respond to stimuli. Obviously keeping in good health aids in being more discerning on patrol. It also makes for better interactions with others; something that is critical to the success —and job survival —of the officer.

There are also external factors that can affect the ability to perform the patrol function effectively, including the following.

• **Environmental conditions:** These can be weather, highway traffic and conditions, lighting (day patrol vs. night patrol, interior patrol and exterior patrol).

• **Distance:** Things that are closer to us are easier to perceive, and things more distant are harder to identify clearly.

• **Time:** The more intense a person's involvement in an activity, the faster time seems to go. Also, security officers may work shift hours and often an officer needs to adjust his or her "internal clock" both at work and at home.

• **Duration of the Input:** The longer a stimulus is received, the more accurate the interpretation will be.

FIXED POSTS

While not patrols in the strict sense of the word, fixed posts manned by security personnel are a part of almost every facility. In some cases, these are in designated structures like those manufactured by commercial suppliers. In others, they may consist of manning a desk in the lobby during evening hours. Many situations support the use of temporarily fixed posts such as at public events, at traffic control points during rush hour, or during heightened periods of security, such as strikes.

Regardless of the employment, fixed posts represent a substantial amount of man-hours and cost. Fixed post duties should be performed in a professional manner, bearing in mind the following:

1.   The mission or objective of the post must be clearly understood. The reason for the existence of the post should be specified in written post orders. These orders should be readily available to the officer manning the post.

2.   Duties as mandated by the post orders should be read and understood. A supervisor or auditor who inspects the post should be favorably impressed with how well the officer knows his or her duties.

3.   Post orders should be kept neat, orderly, and secure. Persons without a "need to know" should not be told what the orders of the post are.

4.   Light discipline—the avoidance of being silhouetted should be maintained just as on patrol. "See others before they see you."

5.   All equipment, especially communications equipment, should be checked when first manning the post. Simple tests of detection equipment (X-ray, metal detectors, explosive detectors, and so on) should be conducted as early in the shift as is practical. Manuals for the use of the equipment should be readily available. Officers must be accountable for the presence and condition of all equipment on post.

6.   Officers being relieved on post should brief their relief officer. A predesigned form can be made for this in large, complex operations, or a simple list of things to advise the relief of can be made up by the officer being relieved.

7.   In high-threat situations such as strikes, civil disturbances, or crowds that could trample an officer, a route of retreat should always be open to the officer manning the post. There may also be justification for concealing the post or building cover into it. Whatever the situation, safety of the officer must be the paramount value.

8.   Comfort—reasonable comfort—should always be afforded to officers on post. Care should be taken to ensure that guard booths are not so hot as to induce sleepiness.

9.   Fixed posts should be visible from other posts, patrolling officers (on foot or in a vehicle), or CCTV. This helps to ensure safety of officers, and provides overlapping visual coverage of the area being secured.

10.   Officers should not leave the post until properly relieved. This is of critical importance in high security installations or where a contract firm is billing a client for a fixed post officer. Officers should stay in the immediate vicinity of the post. They should check out the area near the post for unusual or unacceptable conditions, prior to assuming it.

CONCLUSION

The need for security is not a modern requirement. The caveman was initially concerned only for his personal well-being, and then he became responsible for his immediate family's safety and security. Eventually, families became clans or tribes which evolved into communities. Security became a social responsibility. Within this responsibility, the patrol function with designated people to conduct the patrols dates to early Egypt. Despite political, legal, and other changes, the patrol function has remained the primary means of providing security services to communities, regardless of whether they are public or private entities.

Protective services in America are based on English precedents. Modern-day patrol techniques can be traced to Sir Robert Peel's reforms in 1829 in England. While there have been tremendous changes in technology, society, word political scenes, economies, and the work forces themselves, the purpose of patrol today remains as it has always been: the protection of property and lives, the prevention and detection of crime, and the performance of other services. Today's security officer has many more duties and responsibilities than his predecessors. Because of that, today's officer cannot be from the lowest level of society. He or she must be technically competent in patrol techniques; the laws, rules, and regulations pertaining to security; and numerous other areas of responsibility, such as fire fighting and medical emergencies. Embracing the WAECUP theory, and putting it into practice, will go a long way towards making patrols more cost-effective and professional.

Proper training and preparation for patrol, professional work habits, and attentive patrolling techniques will enhance the patrol officer's skill and abilities. What was once considered a punishment for minor criminal offenses, or a job with little or no responsibility for the "down and out," is rapidly becoming a profession.

In conclusion, professional patrol performance may be considered using the following acronym:

P   **Preparation**
A   **Alertness**
T   **Thoroughness**
R   **Reports**
O   **Observations**
L   **Language (communication)**

REFERENCES

Bopp, William J. and Schultz, Donald O. *Principles of American Law Enforcement and Criminal Justice*, Springfield, IL: Charles C. Thomas, 1972.

Bottom, Norman R. Jr. and Kostanoski, John I. *Security and Loss Control*, New York, NY: Macmillan, 1983.

Brisline, Ralph F. *The Effective Security Officer's Training Manual*, Boston: Butterworth-Heinemann, 1995.

Cole, George F. *The American System of Criminal Justice*, 7th Edition. Belmont, CA: Wadsworth, 1995.

German, A.C., Day, Frank D. and Gallati, Robert J. *Introduction to Law Enforcement and Criminal Justice*, Springfield, IL: Charles C. Thomas,

Purpura, Philip P. *Security and Loss Prevention: An Introduction*, Stoneham, MA: Butterworth-Heinemann, 1991.

United States Nuclear Regulatory Commission. *ITE Security Personnel Training Manual*, Springfield, VA National Technical Information Service, U.S. Department of Commerce, 1978.

RESOURCES

Butterworth-Heinemann, an imprint of Elsevier Science, has books on physical security, alarms, report writing, and security in schools, hotels, colleges, office buildings and retail stores. http://stbooks.elsevier.com/security. (800-545-2522), 200 Wheeler Road, 6th Floor Burlington, MA 01803.

Professional Training Resources has books and videos on patrol, and a multitude of other security topics. (800-998-9400), P.O. Box 439, Shaftsbury, VT 05262.

Performance Dimensions Publishing provides patrol books, videos, and equipment. (800-877-7453), Powers Lake, WI 53159-0502.

1. List five of the purposes of patrol.
    (a) _____
    (b) _____
    (c) _____
    (d) _____
    (e) _____
2. An officer who works an evening shift should visit the site during the _____ to see the change in activities there.
3. Patrolling officers should check their equipment _____ to going on patrol.
4. Patrolling officers should play the "_____ game" to both discover and prepare for possible emergencies.
5. While patrolling in a vehicle, the officer should keep the _____ opened so as to be able to hear and smell better outside the vehicle.
6. Patrolling officers should look _____, _____, and all around their patrol areas.
7. Embracing the WAECUP theory and putting it into practice will go a long way toward making patrols more cost-effective and professional.
    ☐ T ☐ F
8. Avoid silhouetting and "_____ others before they _____ you."
9. Officers on post should always _____ their relief officer.
10. Patrols should occur at the same time every day.
    ☐ T ☐ F

SAFETY AND THE PROTECTION OFFICER

By David J. DeLong, CPP

The disciplines of safety and security share the same common objectives: conservation of the company's assets, human life, and property alike. Each approaches the goal of providing a safe and secure physical environment utilizing the same methods, eliminating, segregating, or protecting against potential hazards.

Many companies combine the disciplines of safety, security, and fire protection into one single department because of their common objectives. This department is usually referred to as the loss control department or the loss prevention department usually directed by a manager or administrator.

The protection officer by nature of his duties is in a position to observe and correct unsafe conditions, unsafe acts and potential hazards. The protection officer can play a significant role in accident prevention and safety awareness.

BASIC ELEMENTS OF A SAFETY PROGRAM

The protection officer should be familiar with the basic elements of the safety program at his company because his activities may have an influence on the program.

1.   Company Safety Policy

A company safety policy provides a guide outlining the responsibilities of all employees whether they are hourly workers, supervisors, or managers in the prevention of accidents, injuries, and illnesses on and off the job site. Without a formal safety policy, the reduction or elimination of accidents is extremely difficult.

2.   Safety Committees

Safety committees are a vital component of a successful company safety program. Safety committees carry out the following basic functions which enhance the overall safety program.

- Discover unsafe conditions and unsafe practices, identify hazards, and make recommendations to control or eliminate them. Discuss safety policies and procedures with recommendations for management.
- Teach safety to committee members who will in turn teach safety to all employees.
- Review accident reports recommending appropriate changes.

3.   Safety Audits or Inspections

The protection officer should be familiar with safety audits or inspections because this procedure is a principal method of discovering accident causes. The safety audit or inspection uncovers unsafe conditions and work practices by means of inspection and provides the means of promptly correcting these unsafe conditions and work practices.

A safety program that initiates regular safety inspections or audits demonstrates to employees, management's interest and sincerity in accident prevention. Also, inspections enable the individual worker to make contact with loss control personnel on a one-to-one basis. The worker can point out unsafe work conditions unique to his work area that would otherwise go undetected. When a worker's suggestions are acted upon, he realizes that he has made a contribution to the safety program and his viewpoints are taken seriously.

Normally, when safety inspections are conducted, checklists are used. Each company, plant or department usually develops its own checklist. Items usually included on an inspection report are as follows: housekeeping, material handling, material piling and storage, aisles and walkways, machinery and equipment, electrical and welding equipment, tools, ladders and stairs, floors, platforms and railings, exits, lighting, ventilation, overhead valves, protective clothing and equipment, dust, fumes, gases and vapors, explosion hazards, unsafe practices, hand and power-driven trucks, fire fighting equipment, vehicles, guards and safety devices, horseplay, and maintenance.

The protection officer should remember that the safety inspection is one of the best methods to prevent accidents and safeguard employees.

4.   Safety Training

An effective company safety program is based on proper job performance. When employees are trained to do their jobs properly, they will do them safely. Supervisors should know how to train an employee in the safe and proper method of doing a job. The immediate job of accident prevention falls upon the supervisor, thus the need for supervisor safety training. Most companies give extensive supervisor safety training programs.

5.   Safety Awareness and Motivation

Safety requires constant and skillful promotion. Some methods of awareness and motivation that are common in the industry that the protection officer should be aware of include the following.

- On-the-job safety discussion and safety meetings
- Safety contests with awards are effective in increasing employee safety awareness and motivation, stimulating pride among departmental employees, and improving the safety record.
- Posters and displays

- Safety campaigns serve to focus the attention of the entire plant on one specific accident problem (i.e., campaign may be undertaken to promote use of safety glasses).
- Educational materials (films, newsletters, booklets, leaflets, and so on)

6.   Motor Vehicle or Fleet Safety Program

Depending on the nature and type of company, the loss control or loss prevention department may organize a complete program for motor vehicle/fleet accident prevention and operator education.

7.   Accident Investigation

Accident investigation is essential in the prevention of future accidents. An effective investigation should produce information that will lead to the development of counter-measures which will prevent or reduce the number of accidents.

Obviously, serious injuries and fatalities should be investigated. The near accident or incident should also be investigated to determine cause to prevent the possibility of a future accident. Near accidents usually indicate deficiencies in the system. The investigation can bring out these problems. Thorough investigations will bring out contributory causes of supervision and management.

For purposes of accident prevention, investigations should be fact-finding and not fault-finding. The investigation should be concerned only with the facts. The investigating officer, who may be the protection officer, is best kept free from involvement with the discipline aspects of their investigation.

KEY FACTS IN ACCIDENTS

The protection officer must be knowledgeable of the key facts in accidents. Whether or not all the key facts are present in an accident will depend upon the particular case.

Key facts are taken from "Accident Prevention Manual for Industrial Operations," p. 154, National Safety Council 1980.

- a)   nature of injury—the type of physical injury
- b)   part of body—the part of the injured person's body affected by the injury
- c)   source of injury—the object, substance, exposure, or bodily motion that directly produced the injury
- d)   accident type—the event which directly resulted in the injury
- e)   hazardous condition—the physical condition or circumstance that permitted the occurrence of the accident type
- f)   agency of accident—the object, substance, or part of the premises in which the hazardous condition existed
- g)   agency of accident part—the specific part of the agency of accident that was hazardous

- h)   unsafe act—the violation of a commonly accepted safe procedure that directly permitted the occurrence of the accident event

Other items of information closely related to the key facts that the protection officer should be aware of include age, sex, type of occupation, and type of work.

Remember: The protection officer must be knowledgeable of the eight basic elements of a safety program.

1. Company safety policy
2. Safe rules
3. Safety committees
4. Safety audits or inspections
5. Safety training
6. Safety awareness and motivation
7. Motor vehicle or fleet safety
8. Accident investigation

ACCIDENTS

The protection officer should have some basic knowledge of accident types and accident causes because he may be involved in accident investigation.

Definition—An accident is an unexpected event in which physical contact is made between a worker and some object or exposure to a substance that interrupts work.

These are the three elements to remember about accidents:

- a)   An accident is an unexpected event.
- b)   Contact is made.
- c)   Work is stopped or delayed.

Accident Types

Accidents normally involve a physical contact between the worker and some object, substance or exposure. With this in mind, accidents are categorized into the following basic types:

struck by	example: struck by a falling tool
contacted by	example: contacted by hot steam
struck against	example: banging your head against a low beam
contact with	example: touching a hot pipe
trapped in	example: trapped in a tank
caught on	example: pant cuff caught on a board, causing a fall
caught between	example: finger caught in a car door
different level fall	example: falling down stairs
same level fall	example: slipping or tripping
exposure	example: exposure to toxic gasses
overexertion	example: back strain

Accident Causes

Generally speaking, there are four major causes of accidents.

1. Unsafe acts—Action(s) by the worker that deviate from the accepted safe work procedure that cause or contribute to an accident. (Examples: horseplay or worker not wearing proper personal protective equipment)

2. Personal factor causes—Any personal characteristic or conditions that may cause or influence a worker to act unsafely. (examples: physical or mental conditions, extreme fatigue, intoxication, attitudes)
3. Unsafe conditions—Any condition of structures, materials, tools, equipment, machinery, or other conditions of a worker's environment that cause or contribute to an accident. (Examples: inadequate lighting, poor housekeeping, or lack of warning systems)
4. Source causes—Any unsafe condition has a source cause. A source cause can contribute or cause an unsafe condition that could lead to an accident. (Examples: normal wear and tear, pipes corroding from within, ropes becoming rotted creating an unsafe condition, or lack of preventive maintenance)

THE ROLE OF THE PROTECTION OFFICER IN SAFETY

The protection officer is trained to observe and identify potential hazards. The majority of large companies maintain a loss prevention department with protection officers on duty 24 hours a day, seven days a week. The protection officer is in a position to report and correct unsafe acts, unsafe conditions, and potential hazards while conducting routine patrols.

The protection officer who observes a safety violation by a worker should do the following:

*   Record the worker's name and advise the worker of the safety violation committed.
*   Notify the worker's supervisor advising him of the safety violation committed.
*   Document the safety violation and forward a report to appropriate management.

The protection officer who observes an unsafe act, unsafe condition, or a safety hazard should do the following:

*   Correct the condition or report it to someone who can correct the condition.
*   Mark off the condition as a hazard where immediate corrective action is not possible.
*   Document the unsafe hazard or condition and the action taken forwarding the report for appropriate action.

Common Safety Hazards

There are numerous safety hazards that the protection officer should be made aware. Some of the frequently encountered safety hazards or conditions include the following:
1. Fire protection
    -   violation of no smoking regulations
    -   unusual odors, especially smoke
    -   obstructed passageways and fire door
    -   inadequate exit signs
    -   obstructions in front of hydrants, alarm boxes, extinguishers

    -   electrical heaters, coffee pots left turned on
    -   improper disposal of waste
    -   flammable gasses and liquids which are uncontrolled in areas where they may pose a hazard
    -   paint or painting areas poorly ventilated and not properly secured
    -   gas pumping areas close to operations where an open flame may be used
    -   use of flame or spark-producing equipment near flammable substances
    -   missing fire protection equipment
2. Housekeeping
    -   missing handrails on stairways
    -   debris on grounds
    -   inadequate containers for trash
    -   broken glass
    -   obstructions on walkways, such as snow and ice
    -   oil spills or slippery substances that may cause slipping and tripping
    -   cables, pipe, electrical wires across aisles
    -   aisle obstructions
    -   litter accumulation on shop floors
    -   cracks, holes, breaks in parking lots, roadways, and sidewalks
3. Doors and emergency exits
    -   burned out or missing emergency lights
    -   doors that don't fit properly that would hinder emergency exit
    -   improper fitting door frames
    -   equipment or debris blocking emergency doors
    -   improper panic hardware for doors
4. Vehicle and fleet safety
    -   improper audible warning devices for backing up
    -   improper wheel chocking for parked vehicles
    -   speeding violations
    -   improper preventive maintenance procedures
    -   vehicles parked in fire lane or blocking emergency exit
    -   vehicles without proper signaling devices or lights
    -   improper tires for road conditions
5. Personal protective equipment
    -   improper personal protective equipment for the job
    -   protective eye goggles not worn
    -   safety-toed boots not worn
    -   protective gloves not worn
    -   hearing protection not utilized
    -   respiratory protective equipment not maintained
    -   proper protective clothing not worn.
6. Machinery maintenance
    -   lack of adequate guarding
    -   worn belts, pulleys, gears, and so on.
    -   frayed electrical wiring that may result in short-circuiting
    -   workers operating machinery with loose-fitting clothing
    -   dangerous machinery lacking automatic shut-off devices

7. Other hazards
   - first aid supply improperly stored and maintained
   - emergency routes not adequately marked
   - improper labeling of dangerous goods
   - broken or damaged equipment not adequately tagged

These are the more common safety hazards encountered by the protection officer on routine patrol. The protection officer should devote one complete patrol during his shift for the observation and reporting of unsafe acts, unsafe conditions, and safety hazards.

SECURITY QUIZ
Safety and the Protection Officer

1. The disciplines of safety and_____ share the same common objectives in terms of the overall protection process. (Fill in the blank.)
2. The protection officer can play a significant role in _____ prevention. (Fill in the blank.)
3. A company safety _____ provides a guide outlining the responsibilities of all employees in terms of accident prevention. (Fill in the blank.)
4. One aspect of a formal safety policy is to prevent accidents and illness on and off the job.
   ☐ T ☐ F
5. One of the main functions of a safety committee is to administer effective rescue training programs.
   ☐ T ☐ F
6. The safety committee has the authority to make safety recommendations to management.
   ☐ T ☐ F
7. The protection officer should carefully inspect the work habits of members of the workforce and report deficiencies detected.
   ☐ T ☐ F
8. A safety program that initiates regular safety inspections (audits), demonstrates to employees: (Check correct answer.)
   ☐ (a) Management's concern for improved productivity
   ☐ (b) Management's interest in accident prevention
   ☐ (c) Management's concern for the off-duty worker
   ☐ (d) Management's concern for an unsafe workplace
9. When a safety recommendation made by an employee is acted upon, (Check the two best answers.)
   ☐ (a) Management recognizes the employee's contribution to the safety program.
   ☐ (b) The employee is likely to become a member of the safety committee.
   ☐ (c) The employee is likely to become even more safety conscious.
   ☐ (d) Management perceives this kind of action as interfering with the safety committee.
10. A safety checklist is useful because: (Check best answers.)
   ☐ (a) It makes employees aware of safety hazards.
   ☐ (b) It can be used by various departments to audit general safety procedures.
   ☐ (c) It can be incorporated into security patrol procedures.
   ☐ (d) It enhances corporate proprietary information retention.

TRAFFIC CONTROL

By Arthur A. Holm, CPO

An officer directing traffic at a busy site provides the most frequent contact between citizens and security personnel. The importance of bearing, appearance, and attitude cannot be over-emphasized. Likewise, the skillful handling of what citizens recognize to be a difficult and hazardous job can generate and maintain public respect.

SIGNS AND AUTOMATIC SIGNALS

If you hold a driver's license, then your knowledge and awareness of most traffic signs can be assumed. The STOP sign is without a doubt the most important sign in use today. These three functions of a STOP sign are taken for granted.

1. Regulates traffic flow
2. Clarifies the question of right-of-way at intersections;
3. Reduces motor vehicle accidents at intersections

Generally speaking, there are two main types of automatic traffic signals.

1. Traffic lights of three colors, sometimes with an arrow for easy turning
2. Visual and audio warning signals commonly seen at railway crossings

Automatic traffic signals normally provide adequate intersectional control. However, there are numerous situations that must be directed by a "point control" officer, to assure safe and efficient vehicular and pedestrian movements. Construction sites, accidents, rush hour periods, special events, or any other condition that causes congestion of traffic must receive immediate attention.

Traffic duty consists of directing and supervising traffic at gates, intersections, and patrolling parking areas. These duties are performed in order that traffic can be kept moving with a minimum of delay and maximum of safety.

Since traffic control duty may require an officer to remain at his post for hours in all kinds of weather, protective clothing must be readily available. Proper protection against the elements is an important factor in maintaining efficient traffic control. It has been observed that a wet or cold officer presents a hazard to himself as well as to motorists.

Proper clothing should also include high visibility potential to increase the safety value during nighttime assignments whether the intersection is well lit or not.

ROADWAY POSITIONS

The position selected to direct traffic must be suited to the particular intersection and expected traffic patterns. It must command a full view of the intersection and its approaches.

In turn, the officer must be completely visible to the motorists and pedestrians. In many instances, disobedience to gestures or whistle signals is caused by the inability of the motorist to see the officer. Usually, officers assigned to traffic control will select a position in the centre of the intersection or at one of the corners.

1. The center of the intersection: This position affords the greatest visibility, but it is also the most hazardous. This location is usually selected when traffic signals are inoperative, traffic is not moving at a high rate of speed, and where there is little pedestrian traffic.
2. The corner position: Intersections having heavy pedestrian or vehicular turns can be controlled by an officer standing a few feet off the curb line at one of the corners having the greatest personal safety and better pedestrian control.

Posture serves to communicate the fact that the officer is in command of the situation. He must therefore assume a military bearing, with his weight evenly distributed on both feet.

When not engaged in signaling motorists, he must stand at the "at ease" position, facing traffic, and with his hands at his sides. When directing traffic, his shoulders must be in line with the flow of traffic and his attention must be directed to the vehicular movements.

HAND SIGNALS

Prompt compliance to hand signals is dependent on the officer's ability to use uniform, clearly defined, and understandable gestures. Intersectional control does not call for complicated choreography or wild arm movements.

Improper hand signals, although highly entertaining to bystanders, cause confusion, hesitation, and lead to violations and accidents. Unusual movements undermine the purpose of traffic control and direction.

Stopping traffic: Two clearly defined motions are required to stop traffic. First, select the vehicle to be stopped. Look directly at the driver, and point in his direction with the arm fully extended. The position is held until you are observed by the driver. Then raise your hand so that the palm is extended. The position is held until you are observed by the driver. Then raise your hand so that the palm is toward the driver and the arm is slightly bent at the elbow.

Maintain this position until the oncoming traffic has stopped. With the one arm still raised, turn your head and repeat the procedure with your other hand to stop the traffic moving in the other direction. The arms are now lowered until all traffic has stopped.

Figure 2-3   Stopping Traffic

Starting traffic: To start vehicular movement on the cross street, pivot a quarter turn to place your shoulders parallel with the vehicles waiting to move. When the intersection is cleared, turn your head to one side facing the waiting traffic. Attract attention by pointing to the lead car. Then, turning the palm inward, bring the hand up and over to the chin, bending the arm at the elbow.

If the driver's attention has been properly obtained, it will only be necessary to make a few motions. After traffic begins to move, the arm is dropped to the side. The opposing traffic is then started in the same manner, but with the other arm.

Slow or timid drivers may be urged to speed up by increasing the rapidity of the arm movements. However, flailing the air with wild arm gestures and shouting at the slow-moving vehicles is unnecessary and only confuses nervous drivers and may lead to greater traffic congestion or accidents.

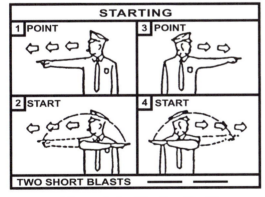

Figure 2-4   Starting Traffic

THE WHISTLE

The whistle, when properly used, attracts the attention of motorists and pedestrians and facilitates compliance with hand signals. Improperly used, it becomes a meaningless distraction which adds to the confusion.

To be effective, the whistle must be used in moderation. It then becomes an invaluable aid to assist in the control of the various road users. The whistle should be blown loudly and not tooted lightly. It is a means of communicating rather than a musical instrument.

One long blast is used to attract the motorist's attention to the officer's hand signals to stop. **Two short blasts** are used to give warning of unusual or dangerous conditions — turning vehicles, improper crossing, and the like. The number of warning sounds should be limited as it is in this area that most improper whistle usage occurs. Normally, **three short blasts** will suffice to warn any motorist or pedestrian.

TRAFFIC CONTROL

For responsibility of traffic direction, you will be assigned to control for the purpose of obtaining maximum vehicular movement by preventing congestion and by safely expediting the flow of traffic. The following responsibilities must be fulfilled in order to properly carry out this assignment:

1. *Regulate the flow of traffic.* Give priority of movement to the most heavily travelled areas by allowing longer periods of running time. Traffic movements must be of equal and adequate time, if the intersecting streets carry an equal traffic volume. Long runs are preferable as they reduce the loss of time from frequent changes of traffic directions.

2. *Control and assist turning vehicles.* Supervise all vehicular turns. If traffic is exceptionally heavy or a spillback is caused by another intersection, determine the preference of traffic direction. If turning vehicles increase the amount of congestion, direct traffic to continue straight ahead during the period of the backup.

Prevent improper turns; right turns from the left lane or a left turn from the right lane must be prohibited. Not only are they illegal, but increase the potential of congestion and accidents.

Traffic backups or accidents may be caused by motorists waiting to turn left or cutting in front of oncoming automobiles. Assist vehicles wishing to turn left. Direct the waiting motorists to enter the intersection on the left turn lane. Allow approaching vehicles that present an immediate hazard to pass. Stop the other oncoming traffic and motion the vehicles turning left through the intersection.

Figure 2-5   Directing a Left Turn

Priority of movements is determined by the amount of traffic flow in each direction. If the number of vehicles turning left is greater than the opposing traffic flow, the turning traffic is given preference. If the oncoming traffic is heavy and there are only a few vehicles waiting to turn, these vehicles are held up until a sufficient amount of traffic has been permitted to pass through. The cross traffic is not started until the intersection has been cleared.

In heavily congested situations when a large number of motorists are making right turns, hold back pedestrians to give precedence to the vehicular traffic.

3. *Coordinate the flow of traffic with the adjacent intersections.* Whenever applicable, allow the movement of traffic at the adjoining intersections to serve as a guide. If the vehicular movement is not coordinated, traffic spillbacks may occur by reason of traffic being stopped at the next intersection.

4. *Protect pedestrians.* Immediate motorist responses cannot be assured when traffic is signalled to stop. Mechanical failure, inattentiveness, or other reasons may cause failure to obey the signal. Pedestrians can then be protected only if they are held back at the curb until all moving traffic is completely stopped. Pay particular attention to children, blind or handicapped persons, and the elderly. Escort these people across the street if necessary.

5. *Assist people seeking information.* Carry a street guide or a map of the local area to assist out-of-towners or local citizens seeking directions. If an enquiry can be quickly answered, there is no need to leave the intersection. However, if a detailed explanation is necessary, direct the citizen to the curb where the answer may be given in safety. Don't leave your post unless traffic conditions permit.

6. *Assisting emergency vehicles.* Stop all vehicles and pedestrian traffic when an emergency vehicle is approaching. Give the driver a "Go" signal indicating the intersection is clear. If the driver of the emergency vehicle signals for a turn, acknowledge by motioning in the proper direction, indicating that the way is clear.

There is no written, legal authorization that allows private citizens (security officers) to direct traffic on public land or thoroughfares. However, should you be requested or ordered by a police officer to assist him, you are obligated to do so. This includes directing traffic if necessary.

On private property, the safe movement of traffic is the responsibility of the owner or someone delegated by the owner. In most cases, the delegated authority is the security officer.

On construction sites, assistance is required to get traffic in and out of the site quickly and safely. Highway flagmen are required for the safety of the workers and for an even flow of traffic around building or repair sites.

GATE DUTY

Directing traffic from or at a gate would include such duties as—checking passes, checking trip tickets, and regulating special types of traffic flow.

The position you take at a gate is determined by the design of the gate, traffic characteristics, whether daylight or night conditions, and the degree of control required. In taking up your position, keep these factors in mind.

a) Be visible to approaching traffic.
b) Be in a position to see approaching traffic.
c) Do not interfere unnecessarily with the flow of traffic.

EQUIPMENT

It is essential that you have the proper equipment when on traffic control.

1. Clothing—You must dress properly according to the weather conditions. If you are uncomfortable because you are cold or wet, you cannot perform at peak efficiency.

2. Reflective body vests and armlets—These aids help the motorist to see you and help protect your safety.

3. Flashlight—Use a flashlight with a red or orange cone on the end of it at night. This makes you more visible to the motorist and also aids in giving directions.

4. Whistle—The whistle is used to attract the attention of the motorist and is used in conjunction with hand signals.

5. Radio—The radio provides a means of communication with your supervisor or other security officers.

6. Signs—Stop and Go signs and flags are most commonly used on construction sites and highways.

7. Pass or badge—In some situations, you are required to have a pass or a badge to allow you to perform your duties at a gate, crosswalk, building or highway construction site.

GENERAL RULES FOR TRAFFIC DIRECTION

1. Select a position best suited for the intersection.
2. Use uniform signals and gestures.
3. Keep stragglers alert and rolling in their proper traffic lanes.
4. If a spill-back begins to form, look immediately for the source of the trouble and take action.
5. Be cheerful, but firm. Do not shout or argue with motorists or pedestrians.

As a general rule, protection officers are assigned to control private parking and traffic scenes. Examples are shopping centers, parking lots, sporting events, construction sites, resort areas, and so on.

Each area is different and the protection officer must exhibit sound judgment in selecting his position. For example, when an extremely heavy flow of traffic is expected at a football game, a pregame plan should be formulated.

Vehicles should be allotted space by sections ensuring one section is filled in an orderly fashion before rotating to another section. The signals to start and stop traffic are extremely important. **Practice them.**

1. The _____ sign is without doubt the most important sign in use today. (Fill in the blank.)
2. Directing traffic from or at a gate would include such duties as checking _____. (Fill in the blank.)
3. On private property, the safe movement of traffic is the responsibility of the _____ or someone delegated by the owner, such as a security officer. (Fill in the blank.)
4. When signaling a driver to stop, your hand should be:
    - ☐ (a) closed.
    - ☐ (b) palm open.
    - ☐ (c) finger pointed.
    - ☐ (d) fist clenched.
5. Slow or timid drivers should not be urged forward with increased rapidity of arm motion because they may over-react and cause an accident.
    ☐ T ☐ F
6. Directing traffic from the corner position is safer than a center-of-the-intersection position.
    ☐ T ☐ F
7. Proper protection against the elements is an important factor in maintaining efficient traffic control.
    ☐ T ☐ F
8. The primary use of the traffic whistle is to attract the police.
    ☐ T ☐ F
9. General rules for traffic direction are:
    - ☐ (a) select a position best suited for the intersection.
    - ☐ (b) use uniform signals and gestures.
    - ☐ (c) be cheerful, but firm.
    - ☐ (d) All of the above
10. When on traffic control, proper equipment includes:
    - ☐ (a) proper clothin.g
    - ☐ (b) flashlight.
    - ☐ (c) radio.
    - ☐ (d) All of the above

CROWD CONTROL

By Patrick C. Bishop, CPP

Whenever people gather together in large numbers, such as at athletic events, parades, strikes, peaceful demonstrations, protest rallies, and so on, there exists a potential threat for mass discord.

When disturbances do occur, it becomes the responsibility of the police, and in some instances, that of security forces to restore order. Once a crowd has been allowed to get out of hand through inadequate supervision or in spite of the best efforts by security personnel to prevent a disturbance, the task of restoring any semblance of order, protecting life and property, and the eventual disbursement of the crowd or mob is a tremendous one.

It is important therefore, that police and security forces be able to quickly determine if a gathering will become uncontrollable and must be able to take immediate steps to prevent disorder. The only way this will be successfully accomplished is for the personnel of all control groups to have a good understanding of the types of crowd formations that are likely to be encountered. Also, these personnel should note the different responsibilities of security office, police, and riot control forces.

DEFINITIONS

1. **Crowd**—A concentration of people whose present or anticipated behavior is such that it requires police action for the maintenance of order.
2. **Demonstration**—A crowd that is exhibiting sympathy for or against authority, or some political, economical or social condition.
3. **Riot**—A breach of the peace committed to violence by three or more persons in furtherance of a common purpose to execute some enterprise by concerted action against anyone who may oppose them.
4. **Disaster**—A disaster means any extreme or catastrophic condition which imperils or results in loss of life and/or property.

FORMATION OF CROWDS

A crowd may exist as a causal or temporary assembly having no cohesive group behavior. It may consist of curious onlookers at a construction site, spectators at the scene of a fatal accident, or curious citizens who are attracted to a soapbox orator. Such a crowd has a common interest for only a short time. It has no organization, no unity of purpose beyond mere curiosity, and its members come and go. Such a group will normally respond without resentment to the urgings of a police officer to "stand back," "move on," or "keep moving." There is no emotional unity and they offer little concern.

However, even in this most ordinary and routine situation, the person in authority who is lacking in good judgment and discretion may meet with resistance. Derogatory remarks, unnecessary shoving and the like cause immediate resentment in people and become self-defeating. Impartiality, courtesy, and fair play hold the key to any situation involving people.

When you instruct a crowd to "move on," it must mean everyone. If you make exceptions and allow some persons to remain, strong objections may be raised. This glaring partiality may cause some of the people to defy you. Incidents such as these can rapidly change crowd attitudes, and if nothing else, impart a very poor impression of the security officer.

A crowd may also assemble for a deliberate purpose — spectators at a football game, a rally of some sort, or it may be a disgruntled citizen or group of citizens willing to be led into lawlessness if their demands are not met.

Members of these crowds have little dependence on each other, but they do have a unity of purpose; they are drawn together to share a common experience. If outside influences interfere with their purpose or enjoyment, it is possible for some individuals in the group to become unruly and aggressive. There are numerous instances of riots occurring during, or immediately following, a sporting event or rally in which emotions run high.

CAUSES OF CROWD FORMATIONS

1. **Basic cause**—The basic reason for the formation of any crowd is the occurrence of an event that is of common interest to each individual. The nature of the crowd is largely governed by the nature of the event.
2. **Casual causes**—A large and comparatively orderly "casual crowd" may gather in a shopping area or at a sporting event. This casually formed crowd is characterized by the fact that its members think and act as individuals. There is an absence of cohesion or organization. This type of crowd is easily controlled in its formative stages, but it may develop otherwise if the event becomes alarming, or if something occurs which causes severe emotional upset to its members.
3. **Emotional causes**—Crowds that are formed due to events that have incited the emotions of the individual are almost invariably unruly and troublesome simply because emotion makes them blind to reason. These are the most frequently encountered emotional causes.
   a) **Social**—Crowd disturbances resulting from racial or religious differences, or excitement stemming from a celebration, sports, or other similar event.

b) **Political**—A common political cause may result in attempts by large groups to gain political power or settle political disputes by other than lawful means.

c) **Economic**—Economic cause of disturbances arise from conditions such as disagreements between labor and management, or from such extreme conditions of poverty that people resort to violence to obtain the necessities of life.

d) **Absence of authority**—The absence of authority or the failure of authorities to carry out their responsibilities may cause people to believe they can violate the law without fear of reprisal or hindrance.

e) **Disaster**—Disaster conditions may result in violent emotional disturbances among people in the area due to fear, hunger, loss of shelter, or injury and death of loved ones.

PSYCHOLOGICAL FACTORS

In addition to the factors that cause crowds to form and turn peaceful groups into disorderly mobs, it is important that people dealing with crowds understand that a small crowd often attracts a great many initially disinterested people, thereby rapidly increasing its size; this snowballing effect is caused by certain psychological factors.

1. **Security**—Certain individuals may be attracted to a crowd due to the feeling of security and safety it provides while associating with large numbers. This situation is most likely to arise during periods of civil unrest where large gangs are roaming the streets looting and threatening the safety and peaceful existence of the citizens who become fearful for their well-being and join with the gang for the security it may afford them.

2. **Suggestion**—Persons joining a crowd tend to accept the ideas of a dominant member without realization or conscious objection. If the dominant member is sufficiently forceful with their words and ideas, they are able to sway the good judgment and commonsense reasoning of those about them; there is a tendency to accept even the wildest of ideas, thus they transform the susceptible into unthinking followers.

3. **Novelty**—An individual may join a crowd as a welcome break in their normal routine and through persuasion and suggestion react enthusiastically to what they consider proper form under these new circumstances.

4. **Loss of identity**—Similar to that of the "security" factor. The individual tends to lose self-consciousness and identity in a crowd. Consequently, they may feel safe that they can be neither detected nor punished for any wrong-doing they may take part in.

5. **Release of emotions**—The prejudices and unsatisfied desires of the individual that are normally held in restraint may be released in an emotional crowd. This temporary release of emotions is a strong incentive to an individual to participate in the activities of the crowd. It provides the opportunity to do things he or she was inwardly desirous of doing, but hitherto, has not dared.

TYPES OF CROWDS

The behavior of crowds varies widely depending on its motivation interest. Crowds are classified in accordance with their behavior patterns and it is essential that any security measures are based on recognition and in understanding of the type of crowd they must deal with. The following outline is representative of most of the crowd types that might be encountered in this country.

1. **Acquisitive**—The members of an acquisitive crowd are motivated by the desire to get something. They are best illustrated in a crowd of shoppers seeking items in short supply or at an auction sale. They have no leaders, little in common, and each member is concerned with his or her own interest.

2. **Expressive**—In this type of crowd, the members gather to express their feelings such as at a convention or political rally. The expressive crowd is usually well-behaved; however, some persons in it may feel that slight disorders and unscheduled demonstrations should be condoned by the officials. When they are thwarted or restrained, resentment occurs and their otherwise cheerful enthusiasm may be replaced by hostility.

3. **Spectator**—This crowd gathers to watch out of interest, curiosity, instruction, or entertainment. It is invariably well behaved and good-humored initially, but since spectator sporting events, parades, and so on tend to stir the emotions rapidly, this kind of crowd can quickly become unruly and very violent.

4. **Hostile**—Crowds of this nature are generally motivated by feelings of hate and fear to the extent they are prepared to fight for what they want. The most prominent types are strikes, political demonstrations, and hoodlums or rival mobs. Hostile crowds may have leaders who direct and maintain a high degree of hostility in their followers, but not always.

5. **Escape**—An escape crowd is one that is attempting to flee from something it fears. It is leaderless and completely disorganized, but it is homogenous in that each person is motivated by the same desire, which is to escape. Once an escape crowd reaches safety, it will lose its homogeneity and its members must then be handled as refugees.

CROWD ACTIONS AND SUGGESTED COUNTERMEASURES

The majority of crowds do not, as a rule, resort to violence; however, any crowd is potentially dangerous or at the least, aggressive. The mood of a peaceful crowd—that is, "acquisitive," "spectator," or "expressive" may change quickly to that of a "hostile" or "escape" crowd. Since most concern is caused by a "hostile" crowd, as opposed to the other types mentioned, a more thorough study should be made of it.

A hostile crowd is usually noisy and threatening, and its individual members may harass security personnel. This kind of crowd will hesitate to participate in planned lawlessness because it generally lacks organization and leadership in its early stages. However, it may provide the seedbed for "mob" action when it is aroused by the more forceful persons who assume leadership. It may also be triggered into violence by the undesirable actions of individual protective personnel.

Aroused crowds will often vent their resentment and hostility on those assigned to maintain order. Some individuals may try to bait security officers into committing errors of judgment or displays of unnecessary force in order to discredit authorities or to further incite crowd members to commit acts of lawlessness or to oppose efforts in regaining control. Such crowd actions are usually directed toward one or two individual officers in the nature of taunts, curses, and other minor annoyances. Verbal abuses must be ignored, no matter how aggressive they may become. On the other hand, immediate action must be taken to those who assault, throw rocks, or attempt in any way to interfere with protective units.

In controlling a hostile crowd, sufficient manpower is basic to your success. If it appears that a peaceful demonstration or other large crowd gathering is showing hostile tendencies, do not hesitate to report and call for immediate assistance. This does not, however, mean you may or should resort to the use of unnecessary force. Such action is never justified. Potentially dangerous crowds can usually be controlled by the following methods:

1. *Removing or isolating individuals involved in precipitating an incident before the crowd can achieve unity of purpose.* This may cause temporary resentment in a very small portion of the crowd members. It is important, therefore, to immediately remove the subject from the area. Elimination of the cause of irritation will prevent an ugly incident. Remember that the injudicious use of force can well defeat your purpose and turn the entire crowd against you.

2. *Fragmentizing the crowd into small isolated groups.* The police often arrive at the scene of an incident or hastily conceived demonstration after a crowd has assembled and achieved a degree of unity. The close contact of the crowd members and the emotionalism of the situation cause the individuals in the crowd to become group-influenced and directed. Individual controls disappear and each person is swayed by the mood and feelings of the crowd. This collective excitement is communicated to each member of the group in what is known as the "milling process."

The presence of an adequate force of men to disperse the crowd and break it into small isolated groups before it becomes hysterical and aggressive is an effective method of coping with the "milling process." It is necessary for security to make a show of force, which does not necessarily mean the use of force. The mere presence of an adequate number of well-disciplined and well-trained control forces often suffices.

3. *Removing the crowd leaders.* The most excited and vocal members of a crowd establish themselves as the informal leaders. Removing or isolating the agitators contributes greatly to eventual crowd dispersal. Isolating the more boisterous individuals should only be attempted if sufficient manpower is available. A crowd is not impressed with inadequate manpower and violence may result. Individual heroics are not only foolhardy, but dangerous as well.

4. *Diverting the attention of the crowd.* The use of a public address system on the fringe of a crowd, urging the people to "break up and go home" is a successful crowd dispersal tactic. Amplifying the authoritative tone of the command attracts the attention of individuals in the crowd and breaks the spell cast by the more excited crowd members.

5. *A crowd that grows in hostility and defies orders to disperse can also be controlled by forcing the individuals to focus attention on themselves rather than the objectives of the group.* Instead of making a direct assault on the crowd, a series of random arrests is made of individuals situated on the edge of a crowd. The crowd will soon recognize that a greater number of persons are being arrested. But the fact that arrest is threatened through haphazard selection causes them to fear for their safety and a spontaneous dispersal results.

6. *Using a recognized leader.* An effective method of counteracting the developing leadership in a crowd is by using someone having greater appeal to the crowd. A trusted labor leader, a member of the clergy, a well-known sports figure or a well-known civil rights leader can often successfully plead for order and reason. Depending on the origin and cause of the crowd formation, an appropriate public figure or official may greatly assist in calming the excitement and emotions of the crowd.

7. *Try to prevent panic from developing in a crowd.* Panic is caused by fear and is most often found in the "escape" crowd fleeing from disaster or the threat of disaster or violence. The primary cause of panic is blockage of the escape route. Security actions should aim at providing an escape route, directing and controlling the progress of the crowd along the route, and at the same time dividing the crowd into small groups if possible. The following control techniques might be implemented:

a) Displaying a helpful, calm, and confident attitude. Loudspeakers should be used to give directions and helpful information.

b) Use of rational members of the crowd to assist in calming or isolating hysterical persons.

c) By providing first aid and medical attention to the injured and weak, particularly women and children.

d) The use of security to block off routes so as to channel movement in the desired direction. Care must be taken to ensure that the police forces do not panic a crowd by hasty action, arrogance, or thoughtlessness.

8. *Using women and children.* Crowds and demonstrators may resort to having women or children wheeling baby carriages at the head of their advance. If the marchers must be stopped, an attempt should be made to divert the women and children or let them pass through the ranks and then close rapidly behind them.

SECURITY AND DEMONSTRATIONS

Security organizations assigned to supervise demonstrations have a twofold responsibility. Regardless of individual convictions, they must protect the peaceful demonstrators who are exercising their right to protest.

Spectators not in sympathy with the demonstration constitute a potential threat of violence. This is often aggravated by counterdemonstration whether they are organized or spontaneous.

Control forces must also protect the general public from demonstrators who infringe upon the rights of others. The more common problems occur when demonstrators engage in "sit-ins," and so on, and violate property rights of others. Fanatical members may even lie down in the path of vehicles and refuse to move. They must be picked up and carried away at once. Use of tear gas in this situation is not generally recommended in view of the passive nature of the gathering and their relatively few numbers.

Such groups may attempt to discredit security by harassment during removal, by resorting to shouts of "brutality," raising their hands as if to ward off blows, and emitting cries of pain when they are aware of the presence of news media. Such encounters will tax the patience and control of individual security officers, who must ignore all such verbal attacks.

FORMATION OF A MOB

The crowd or demonstration will deteriorate into a mob if it has been preconditioned by irritating events, aroused by rumors, and inflamed by professional agitators who appeal to emotional levels rather than to reason. Hostility prevails and unity replaces confusion and disorganization.

The early frustrations engendered by agitation and rumor require a climactic incident to unleash the mob. It may come about for any number of reasons. It may often be influenced by the apparent weakening of the strength and attitudes of security groups assigned to preserve the peace.

RESPONSIBILITY AND BEHAVIOR OF PROTECTIVE GROUPS

Protection must extend to all people. This means fair and equal treatment to all. Observe a position of neutrality—act with firmness—this is not belligerence or unreasonable force. After an order is given, it must be enforced for the preservation of the public peace and the carrying out of the traditional mission of protecting life and property of citizens to assure the basic rights of all people.

If you observe a hostile crowd gathering, never hesitate to request assistance. In these instances, it is definitely safer to overstate the number of men needed to restore order than to attempt to act alone or underestimate your requirements. A show of force not only has a restraining effect on the crowd, but it will also provide the necessary manpower.

Order must be established. Approaching the more vocal individuals in a crowd is an effective method of dealing with a group. When addressing these persons, be firm and carefully phrase your commands. Do not become involved in an argument. Use simple language and inform the people of the violations they are or may be committing. Request that the violations stop and that the groups disperse. Allow the crowd the opportunity to withdraw peacefully without interference. If the throng defies authority and the apparent leaders make no efforts to disperse the crowd, arrests should be made, or police assistance sought.

Whenever you are dealing with an excited or hostile crowd, remember that it is potentially dangerous and may require only a slight incident to turn it into a mob—your example and your ability to maintain order are the best deterrents to mob action.

PLANNING CONSIDERATIONS

From time-to-time, security personnel have the opportunity to plan for large crowd control events. An example of this may be political rallies, sporting events, parades, and planned shopping mall events. As there is always some form of advance notice for these expected large crowd events, the following considerations should form part of the contingency procedure.

1. Is police involvement required?
2. Barriers (this includes metal fencing, ropes and stanchions, people)
3. Communications (radio and telephone, PA system)
4. First aid staff
5. Ambulance or first aid rooms
6. Doctors
7. Location of event
8. Fire procedures, equipment, personnel
9. Communication center
10. Media observation area
11. Entry and exit location for VIP
12. Parking
13. Lavatories
14. Food concessions
15. Disabled person's areas (wheelchairs)
16. Entertainment before or after event
17. Signing
18. Timings
19. Number of security personnel and degree of expertise required
20. News releases and media precoverage

21. Time of year and type of environment
22. Alternate power sources
23. Size of crowd expected
24. Vehicles for movement of VIPs, and so on

As you can see, when a large crowd control event is known and sufficient time is available for preplanning, the event should be able to take place with minimal problems for both Security staff and participants alike.

PERSONAL BEHAVIOR

1. Stand your ground without yielding. Your job is to maintain order and protect life and property.
    a) Avoid all unnecessary conversation.
    b) Do not exchange pleasantries with the crowd or apologize for your actions.
    c) Do not give the impression you will not enforce orders to disperse or arrest individuals defying such an order.
2. Place lawbreakers under arrest.
3. Use reasonable force to enforce the law.
    a) Do not overlook violations or defiance of lawful orders.
    b) The use of unreasonable force often incites a crowd which normally would be passive or curious.
    c) Charges of brutality are often made in an attempt to discredit the security force, they will have little basis in fact if discretion is used.
4. Remain on the fringe of the crowd. Do not close or mix with a hostile crowd. Remain out of reach and observant of crowd and individual activities, pending the arrival of reinforcements.
5. Assist fellow officers who may be in trouble. If one of your members situated near you is physically attacked, go to his immediate assistance. Arrest the assailant. To permit such a person to escape will encourage others to assault or try to overpower individual security personnel.
6. Refrain from participating in crowd activities.
    a) An aggressive crowd will invariably throw a barrage of rocks, sticks, bottles, and so on at opposing forces. DO NOT throw them back at the crowd! This will only precipitate greater hostility and supplies the crowd with a further supply of missiles.
    b) Withdraw to a safe distance until dispersal operations can be commenced.

RIOT CONTROL FORCE DEPLOYMENT PROCEDURES

Basic riot and crowd control formations used by control forces exist in the following forms.
1. **Arrowhead**—This is used to strike into and split a crowd or mob, to provide an escort for a person(s) to a given point through a friendly or disorganized crowd. The use of an additional inverted arrowhead at rear of the formation will give all-round protection.
2. **Left flanking and right flanking**—Used to move a crowd or mob to the right or left, or to turn a crowd away from the front of a building, fence, and so on.
3. **Line**—Used to move a crowd or mob straight back up the street.

PERSONNEL EMPLOYMENT

BASIC RIOT AND CROWD CONTROL FORMATIONS USED BY CONTROL FORCES EXIST IN THE FOLLOWING FORMS:

a) ARROWHEAD

THIS IS USED TO STRIKE INTO AND SPLIT A CROWD OR MOB, TO PROVIDE AN ESCORT FOR A PERSON (S) TO A GIVEN POINT THROUGH A FRIENDLY OR DIS - ORGANIZED CROWD. THE USE OF AN ADDITIONAL INVERTED ARROWHEAD AT REAR OF THE FORMATION WILL GIVE ALL AROUND PROTECTION.

b) LEFT FLANKING   AND   RIGHT FLANKING

USED TO MOVE A CROWD OR MOB TO THE RIGHT OR LEFT, OR TO TURN A CROWD AWAY FROM THE FRONT OF A BUILDING, FENCE, ETC.

c) LINE

USED TO MOVE A CROWD OR MOB STRAIGHT BACK UP THE STREET.

Figure 2-6   Riot and Crowd Control Formations

SECURITY QUIZ
Crowd Control

1. The majority of crowds do not as a rule resort to _____. However, any crowd is potentially dangerous. (Fill in the blank.)

2. In controlling a hostile crowd, sufficient _____ is basic to your success. (Fill in the blank.)

3. The protection officer should attempt to isolate or _____ an individual trouble-maker. (Fill in the blank.)

4. If you observe a hostile crowd gathering, never hesitate to request additional _____. (Fill in the blank.)

5. A demonstration is a crowd that is exhibiting sympathy for or against authority, or some political, economical, or social condition.
   ☐ T ☐ F

6. A riot means any extreme or catastrophic condition that imperils or results in loss of life and/or property.
   ☐ T ☐F

7. The basic reason for the formation of any crowd is the occurrence of an event that is of common interest to each individual.
   ☐ T ☐ F

8. Some psychological factors in crowd formation are:
   ☐ (a) security
   ☐ (b) novelty
   ☐ (c) loss of identity
   ☐ (d) None of the above
   ☐ (e) All the above

9. The protection officer when dealing with crowds should:
   ☐ (a) exchange pleasantries with the crowd
   ☐ (b) give the impression you will enforce orders
   ☐ (c) apologize for your actions
   ☐ (d) All the above
   ☐ (e) None of the above

10. Some riot control, force deployment procedures are:
    ☐ (a) arrowhead, left and right flanking, line
    ☐ (b) right flanking, bullet, left flanking
    ☐ (c) line, bow, arrowhead
    ☐ (d) arrowhead, bullet, left flanking

Unit Three

Physical Security Applications
Alarm System Fundamentals
Central Alarm Stations and Dispatch Centers
Access Control

PHYSICAL SECURITY APPLICATIONS

By Denis A. O'Sullivan, CPP, CPO

What is "physical security planning"? It is a recognized security process that, if followed, will result in the selection of physical countermeasures based on appropriateness. The countermeasures selected should also be justifiable from a cost point of view.

The process consists of the following five steps:

1. Assets are identified.
2. Loss events are exposed.
3. Occurrence probability factors are assigned.
4. Impact of occurrence is assessed.
5. Countermeasures are selected.

Let's look at each of these steps.

1. Assets are identified

At first glance, this step would appear easy; however, this is not necessarily the case. Have you ever attempted to take inventory of your personal property? The major problem seems to be "how to": Do we include every nut and bolt? For the purpose of following the security process, this is not necessary. It should suffice to group assets according to category except where an item is especially attractive (from the point of view of a thief) and valuable. The following categories should include most assets for most companies:

- land	- buildings
- heavy machinery	- production equipment
- office equipment	- office furniture
- vehicles	- cash or other negotiables
- goodwill	- public image
- raw material	- finished product

Depending on the nature of the company's activities, there may be other categories. In any event, there is one asset I have not mentioned primarily because it is controversial: employees being a company's most valuable asset; however, some people do not like to group employees with all the other assets.

2. Loss events are exposed

This step consists of exposing all possible threats to the assets that we have identified. Similarly to the way we grouped assets, we will group threats according to their nature. All threats can be grouped under the following headings: industrial disaster, natural disaster, civil disturbance, crime, and other risks.

Industrial disaster—These should be easy to identify, associated threats related to on-site or adjacent activity. The following are typical industrial disasters that might affect most companies: explosions, fire, major accident, and struc-

tural collapse. To correctly assess the threat, you must know intimately the nature of company activity, the nature of activity on adjacent properties, dangerous routes, flight paths, and the existence of nearby major oil or gas pipelines.

Natural disaster—The potential to become the victim of a natural disaster largely rests with the geographic location of the company property. If property is located in the southeast of the United States, it is reasonable to identify hurricanes as possible loss events. Similarly, if the property is in California, it would be reasonable to plan for earthquakes. Other areas may suggest the need to identify flood or tornados as threats.

Civil disturbance—Most companies either directly or indirectly can be threatened by actions that can be categorized as civil disturbances. If your company is engaged in weapons technology, or indeed any activity that might be viewed as threatening the environment, it is reasonable to expect that the company might become the target of demonstrators. All labor disputes can be categorized under this heading.

Crime—It is relatively easy to identify the crimes that might effect company operations. Any or all of the following will affect most companies: arson, assault, bomb threats, breaking and entering, theft, and vandalism. If a company is engaged in high-tech, it would be reasonable to also identify espionage, extortion, and sabotage as likely threats.

Other risks—This is meant to be a catchall for those threats that do not neatly fit the above categories. Two examples are disturbed persons and loss of utilities.

3. Occurrence probability factors are assigned

Having identified assets and exposed the threats to those assets, the next step is to quantify the possibility that the threat will occur. This is probably the most difficult step in the process. Information must be collected and carefully analyzed to determine its affect on the probability for occurrence. The following all affect probability:

*   The physical composition of structures—for example, wood frame, or concrete block.
*   The climatic history of the area, such as number and frequency of tornados, hurricanes, earthquakes, and so on.
*   The nature of activity at the property to be protected. For example, if the products being produced are televisions and related products, then the probability for theft will likely be high.
*   The criminal history for the immediate and adjacent areas.

• Is there community conflict in the area?

An analysis of the foregoing, coupled with a review of the activity and organization of the company to be protected, will enable a determination with reasonable accuracy to be made regarding the probability for a loss relative to specific assets or groups of assets.

The probability for occurrence will not be the same for all loss events. For this reason and to facilitate later correlation with impact factors, we must assign probability ratings. While the actual wording is not important, the following are suggested:

• Certain
• Highly probable
• Moderately probable
• Improbable

To make these words more meaningful, we can assign percentage weights to each: certain 75 to 100 percent, highly probable 50 to 75 percent, moderately probable 25 to 50 percent, and improbable 0 to 25 percent.

4. Impact of occurrence is assessed

This step is not as difficult or as uncertain as determining probability. Impact for almost all organizations has a bottom line of dollars and cents. The most important thing to remember is that dollar losses may be either direct or indirect and that they may be so high as to be crippling.

Direct costs are those that can be directly assigned as the value of the asset that has been lost or damaged. Indirect losses are those costs associated with the loss that would not have been incurred if the loss event had not occurred. An example is downtime.

The final task in relation to impact is to assign levels or classifications that will allow for correlation with the four degrees of probability. Again the actual words are not important; however, the following are suggested:

• Very serious
• Serious
• Moderately serious
• Unimportant

Shortly we will see the importance of these ratings. Before we go on to the final step, let's recap. We have taken inventory of our assets, identified the threats to those assets, assessed the probability that any one of these threats will actually occur, and if one of these threats were to occur, we have assessed the potential impact on company operations.

5. Countermeasures are selected

This is the final step in the planning process. We now have to use all the data that we have collected to use to protect our property. The initial step is to decide on the level of protection needed; the level can range from low to very high.

The simplest method to use to ascertain the desired levels of protection is a matrix as illustrated in Figure 3-1. For example, let's look at the threat of fire. The probability of a fire can be rated as "moderately probable" for most types of

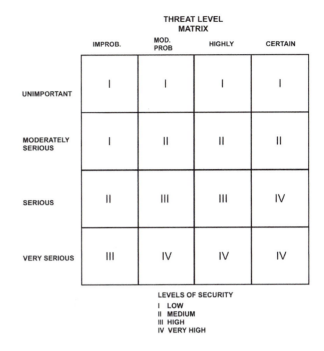

Figure 3-1   Threat Level Matrix

businesses; from a criticality point of view we must consider fire as potentially "very serious." Referring to our matrix, we can quickly see that the recommended level of protection is "level IV," or to put it another way, the highest level possible. This would suggest using an effective detection system coupled with an efficient suppression system.

The large number and variety of assets and associated threats mean that we will end up with a complex pattern of different levels of protection. This is not as confusing as we might expect, particularly if we think in terms of security-in-depth.

Security-in-depth is a military concept that means placing a series of progressively more difficult obstacles in the path of an aggressor. These obstacles are often referred to as "lines of defense."

The **first line of defense** is at the property line. Methods of defense at this point may be either natural, such as a river, or man made, such as a fence. Additionally the barrier may be psychological or physical. At a very minimum, the property boundary must be defined in some way that separates it from its neighbors. Psychological barriers, such as property definition, do not impede would-be trespassers; however, they do play an important role in the rights of the property owner.

The **second line of defense** is the exterior of buildings. Controls at this point should be difficult to overcome. It is important to remember that all six sides of structures (roof, floor, and walls) often present weaknesses that must be strengthened. Special attention must be given to the usual points of break and enters; doors, windows, and skylights. In fact, any opening greater than 96 square inches in area and less than 18 feet from grade must be protected. It is usually at this line of defense that most use is made of electronic intrusion detection devices and electronic access controls.

The **third line of defense** is interior controls or object protection. Controls at this line of defense include electronic motion and intruder detection devices, access controls, safes, vaults, document storage cabinets, quality locking devices, and fire protection.

The application of the concept **"security-in-depth"** means more than simply establishing three lines of defense that will meet all your needs. Ideally, we would apply the principle first to the property in general terms as described above, and then to each and every asset separately. For example, an industrial complex and an asset such as information.

The complex itself will be protected probably by a perimeter fence. Each building within will be properly secure and there will be an electronic intrusion detection system within the buildings. In addition to this general protection, we should attempt to establish protective rings around the information. Working backwards, the information should be stored in a safe (third line of defense), the safe should be in a room that has interior motion detection (second line of defense), and access to the room should be via a door equipped with proper locking hardware and possibly with a card access system (the first line of defense).

Selecting appropriate countermeasures is a difficult task requiring considerable practical experience and extensive knowledge of the various controls and their strengths and weaknesses. Effective planning will result in a cost justifiable, integrated protection program.

An integrated protection program results from a systems approach to selecting controls. The following are two important points in relation to using a systems approach:

1. The whole rather than its individual parts must be considered.
2. Design should allow for an acceptable level of redundancy, without any unnecessary duplication of effort.

A systems approach is often referred to as systems engineering.

The remainder of this chapter will concentrate on the physical components of a protection program. While space will not permit great detail, we will attempt to explain the major points relative to security lighting, security glazing, alarm systems, card access systems, locks and keying, closed circuit television, safes and vaults, and fencing.

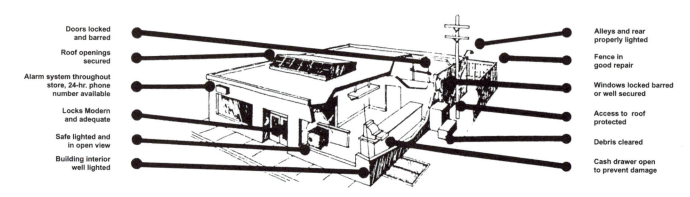

Figure 3-2   Defense Around Exterior of Building

SECURITY LIGHTING

Security lighting has three primary objectives.

1. It must act as a deterrent to intruders.
2. If an intrusion is attempted, it must make detection likely.
3. It should not unnecessarily expose patrolling personnel.

Lighting systems are often referred to as either: "continuous," "standby," and "movable" or "emergency."

Continuous lighting is the type most commonly used. Lamps are mounted on fixed luminaries and are normally lit during the hours of darkness.

Standby lighting is different from continuous lighting in that the lamps are only lit as required.

Movable or emergency lighting is portable lighting that may be used to supplement either continuous or standby lighting. Light sources may be either incandescent, gaseous

discharge, or quartz lamps. The common lightbulb emits incandescent light.

Gaseous discharge lamps are street-type lighting and may be either mercury vapor or sodium vapor lamps. Mercury vapor lamps emit a strong light with a bluish cast. Sodium vapor lamps emit a soft yellow light. Both types of gaseous discharge lamps take two to five minutes to reach maximum intensity. They are very effective in areas where fog is prevalent. A word of caution in relation to gaseous discharge lamps is that they make color identification unreliable.

Quartz lamps emit a very bright white light. Lighting may be classified as floodlights, searchlights, fresnels, and street lighting.

The difference between floodlights and searchlights is that searchlights project a highly focused beam of light, whereas floodlights project a concentrated beam.

Fresnels produce a rectangular beam of light and are particularly suitable for illuminating the exterior of buildings.

Streetlights produce a diffused light and are suitable for use in parking areas and driveways.

Certain lighting intensities are recommended for specific situations.

perimeter or property boundary	0.15 to 0.4 fc
vehicle entrances	1.0 fc
pedestrian entrances	2.0 fc
exterior of buildings	1.0 fc
open yards	0.2 fc

The foregoing are suggested lighting intensities only; specific circumstances may dictate different lighting intensities. To place some perspective on the intensities suggested, it is necessary to explain "fc": "fc" means footcandle and simply refers to the amount of light emitted within one square foot from a lit standard candle.

APPLICATION CONSIDERATIONS

1. When designing a protective lighting system, consider approaching the task from the point of view of "three lines of defense," the perimeter, open yards, and building exteriors.

2. All accessible exterior lamp enclosures should be in tamper- or vandal-resistive housing. This means that the receptacle and lens should be constructed of a material that will resist damage if attacked and that the mounting screws or bolts be tamper-resistant.

3. If protective lighting is to be located in an area that may be subject to explosions, then the housings should be explosive-resistant.

4. Before finalizing any decision on the installation of lighting, consider the impact that additional lighting will have on your neighbors. Failure to consult with a neighbor prior to an installation may result in costly re-design.

The foregoing is a presentation of the basics of security lighting. Prior to utilizing any of the suggested standards, please check local codes or ordinances.

GLAZING

The various uses, methods of fabrication, and the over-abundance of trade names make the selection of an appropriate glazing material appear very confusing. In an effort to simplify the process, we will address the subject under the following headings.

- Safety/fire
- Burglar/vandal-resistive
- Bullet resistive
- Special purpose

Safety/fire: Under this heading, we are basically looking at two types of glass: tempered and wired.

Tempered glass can be considered safety glass as it is several times stronger than ordinary glass. It is especially resistive to accidental breakage. If it does break, it will dis-integrate into small pieces will dull edges, thereby minimizing risk of injury. Tempered glass is available in different thicknesses to suit different purposes.

Wired glass in glass with a wire mesh built into it. The wire is embedded in the glass when it is still in its molten state. Wire glass resists impact because of its strength. It is also listed by Underwriter's Laboratories as a fire retardant material.

Here are some suggested uses for safety/fire-retardant glass.

- Along passageways
- Entrance doors and adjacent panels
- Sliding glass doors
- Bathtub enclosures and shower doors

Burglar/vandal-resistive: Several types of burglar/vandal-resistive glazing materials are available, including laminated glass, wired glass and acrylic, and polycarbonate plastics.

Laminated glass will resist degrees of impact proportionate to its thickness. This type of glass is particularly valuable where the quality of transparency is important and where other types of impact-resistant material may be subject to vandalism.

Wired glass provides resistance of a limited nature; it will not resist prolonged attack.

Acrylic plastic is particularly resistive to forced attack; however, it is not as resistive as polycarbonate. It is, however, much more transparent than polycarbonate.

Polycarbonate plastic is 20 to 30 times stronger than acrylic of comparable thickness.

Bullet resistive: Bullet-resistive material is available in the form of laminated glass or acrylic and polycarbonate plastics.

Bullet-resistant laminated glass consists of multiple plies of glass and plastic material laminated together.

Highly transparent bullet resistant acrylic material is suitable for many cash handling situations, such as in banks.

Polycarbonate consisting of several sheets of plastic laminated together is highly resistive to ballistics; however, visibility is somewhat impaired.

Special purpose: Under this heading, we will look at transparent mirror glass, coated glass, heated glass, and rough or patterned glass.

Transparent mirror glass may be installed in a door or in a wall. From one side, it is functionally a mirror and from the other, it permits an unobstructed view through the mirror. The primary purpose of transparent glass is for surreptitious surveillance.

Flow-on or cement-on plastic coating is available for application to existing installed glass. This material may serve well as an interim measure until a more appropriate vandal-resistive material can be installed.

Rough or patterned glass is available with many different designs that make it range from practically opaque to practically transparent. This type of glazing is most appropriate where there is a conflict between the need for privacy and natural light.

INTRUSION DETECTION

Every intrusion detection system is meant to detect the following:

    a)   Unauthorized entry
    b)   Unauthorized movement within
    c)   Unauthorized access to controlled areas or objects

There are three components to an intrusion detection system

    a)   Detectors/sensors
    b)   System controls
    c)   Signal transmission

DETECTORS/SENSORS

Selection of the appropriate detector, from the numerous and varied options available, is a difficult task. An end user is well advised to become familiar with the different types of detectors/sensors available. If reliance for proper selection is placed on advice from a vendor, then it is essential that the end user be able to describe accurately his objective and to make the vendor contractually responsible for meeting the stated objective.

In the following paragraphs, we will look at different types of detectors: magnetic switches, metallic foil, audio, vibration, ultrasonic, photoelectric, passive infrared, and microwave.

Magnetic switches: These are often referred to as door contacts. They may be either surface-mounted or recessed. The choice is largely an aesthetic one; however, the recessed ones do afford more protection from tampering. Switches are commonly "unbalanced," which means that they may be defeated by substitution of a secondary magnetic field to keep the contacts in the open position while the detector magnet is moved away from the housing containing the contacts.

For high security application, a "balanced" switch is available. This switch is designed to withstand defeat by creation of a secondary magnetic field. Magnetic switches have many potential uses in addition to their traditional use on doors and windows. They may be used on desk or file cabinet drawers or to secure equipment to a fixed position.

Metallic foil: A narrow strip of very thin metal foil designed to break if the surface to which it is attached is attacked. It is mostly used as a glass breakage detector and is commonly seen on storefront windows and glass doors. It may also be used as a barrier penetration detector, such as in a wall under gyprock. If properly installed, it should do its job well. A major detractor is that it is not considered aesthetically pleasing; this can also be overcome to some extent by the experienced installer.

Vibration: Vibration detectors are shock sensors. They may be used to detect persons climbing chain-link fencing, breaking through walls, or attacking safes or other containers. As glass breakage detectors, they are very effective and not too expensive.

Ultrasonic: These are motion detectors. A protected area is flooded with an oval pattern of sound waves. As the sound waves bounce off objects, they reflect a signal back to a receiver. Any movement in the protected area will cause a change in the reflected pattern, which will result in an alarm. Ultrasonic sound waves are in a frequency range that is above the capacity of the human ear. These detectors are particularly susceptible to false alarm due to air turbulence.

Photoelectric: A beam of light is transmitted to a receiver. The transmitter and receiver may be in one housing with the beam being reflected. Any interruption of the beam causes an alarm. These devices are commonly used as automatic door openers or in stores to warn off a customer from entering. When used for security purposes, different methods are used to make the beam invisible to the naked eye. Either an infrared light-emitting diode is used or an infrared filter is simply placed over the light source. Either method effectively makes the beam invisible.

Infrared: These are probably the most versatile detectors currently available. Patterns of coverage are available that will protect practically any configuration of space. They can be used effectively to protect long narrow corridors, portions of rooms, or entire large rooms. Infrared detectors are often referred to as passive detectors because they are the only detector that does not monitor an environment that has been created by the detector. Infrared detectors measure radiated energy. When activated, they simply establish the ambient temperature. From that point on any significant deviation will result in an alarm.

Microwave: Microwave detectors use high frequency radio waves to establish a protected area. They are particularly suitable for use in areas where air turbulence or changing air temperatures may prohibit the use of ultrasonic or infrared detectors. A major weakness with microwave is that it can penetrate beyond a protected area. Microwaves will penetrate practically all surfaces except concrete and metal.

SYSTEM CONTROLS

System controls consist of components that transform individual sensors/detectors into a network of intelligence-gathering devices. System controls include data processing equipment, signal transmission equipment, on/off and reset controls, backup power supply, LED system status indicators, and any other equipment specific to a particular system.

The data processing equipment basically acts as a receiver and interpreter of signals from the sensors/detectors and reacts to these signals in accordance with preprogrammed instructions.

The signal transmission equipment is the means by which an alarm is raised. This equipment may simply activate a local siren or it may send a signal over telephone wires to a remote monitoring location. The telephone wires may be either dedicated (the most secure system) or via the normal telephone network by use of a digital dialer transmitting to a special type of receiver/decoder.

The on/off and reset controls are either keys, toggle switches, or digital key pads. The digital key pad is recommended.

The backup power supply is essential in case the electrical power supply fails or is sabotaged.

The LED (light-emitting diode) system status indicators indicate by different colors whether the system is on or off, or if there is trouble in the system. The usual colors are red for system okay, but in the off mode, yellow signifies trouble somewhere in the system and green usually signifies that the system is armed and functioning correctly.

SYSTEM MONITORING

There are basically three options.

1. Local
2. Proprietary
3. Commercial

The local system is just that, a siren or bell on the outside of the protected premises. This system is not recommended due to its reliance on a passerby to actually call the police.

The proprietary system is similar to a local system in that the system is monitored on-site or remotely by employees of the owner of the protected premises. If this system is used, it is advisable to have a link from the proprietary station to a commercial station in the event of a holdup of the monitoring personnel.

The commercial monitoring falls into two categories: monitoring stations or answering services. The answering services are useful for the economical monitoring of signals transmitted by telephone dialers; however, this is not for high security systems. Commercial monitoring stations are either Underwriters Laboratories of Canada (ULC) approved or they are not. The ULC approved is the best guarantee of quality service.

Note: An initial step in planning an intrusion detection system is through a thorough understanding of building operations to identify zones of protection that will create a series of independent sub-systems. Each subsystem should (1) be compatible with normal operations and (2) allow for prompt response to a specific problem area.

When the functional requirements of a system have been identified, the system engineering should be left to experts.

CARD ACCESS

The decision to use, or not to use, a card access system should be based on the perceived need for accountability and the accompanying financial considerations.

An objective statement for a card access system might read:

"To economically eliminate the inherent security weaknesses in key access systems by electronically supervising and documenting the activities or persons authorized to access the property."

To be useful, a card access system should have the following minimum capabilities to do the following:

- Restrict access by authorized persons to certain times and/or days of the week.
- Allow controlled after-hours access to selected areas within.
- Control after-hours access to a parkade.
- Selectively control after-hours use of elevators.
- Maintain a record of all valid and invalid use of cards.
- Provide an audit trail permitting a printout of persons on the property at any one time.

There are numerous types of cards.

- Magnetic coded
- Magnetic strip coded
- Proximity coded
- Weigand coded
- Hollerith
- Optical coded

The magnetic coded contains a sheet of flexible magnetic material on which an array of spots have been permanently magnetized. The code is determined by the polarity of the magnetized spots.

The magnetic strip encoding is widely used in commercial credit cards.

The proximity card is a badge into which electronically tuned circuits are laminated. The badge gets its name from the fact that it only has to be held near the reader for authorized access to be granted. The reader for this card is concealed in the wall behind drywall or paneling.

The weigand coded badge contains a series of parallel wires embedded in the bottom half of the badge. Each wire can be assigned a logic "O" or "1"; the combination reveals the ID number.

The hollerith badge is easy to recognize because the card has small rectangular holes punched in it. It cannot be considered a high security badge.

The optical coded badge is easy to recognize if it utilizes the "bar" code as its encoding device. The "bar" code is commonly used on retail goods to assist the cashier with pricing.

All of the commonly used coded cards are reliable and with the exception of the hollerith badge, are reasonably resistive to compromise.

Although it is not recommended, many organizations like to use their access cards as both an access card and an identification badge. The information contained in the normal employee ID card can easily be incorporated into any access card.

- Company name and logo
- Details or cardholder
- Name
- Department
- Date of birth

- Signature
- Photograph
- Condition of use (restrictions)

This is not recommended, however, because if the card is lost, it will be obvious to a finder that it is owned by a particular organization, which may lead to unauthorized use of the card. There are many different card readers. However, the significant difference is the addition of a secondary method of verification or confirmation such as the requirement for insertion of a personal identification number (PIN) via a numerical key pad.

The use of a numerical key pad usually offers the very valuable option of an ability to allow a user to signal that he is operating under duress.

Figure 3-3 shows the functional operation of a card access system.

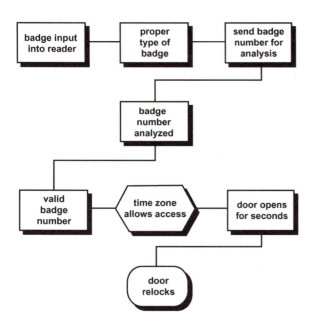

Figure 3-3   Functional Operation of a Card Access System

LOCKING HARDWARE

Locking hardware can be categorized as either mechanical, electrical, or electromagnetic, and as either security or non-security.

Quality mechanical security locks should be used for all of the following.

- Perimeter openings
- Doors that control/restrict internal movement
- Doors to sensitive/restricted areas

Only deadbolt locks should be considered. The bolt should offer a minimum of 1-inch throw. If the door is a glass metal-framed door, the bolt should be of the pivotal type to ensure maximum throw.

Electric locks are particularly suitable for the following:

- Remote control of the after-hours pedestrian entrance door
- Grade level emergency exit doors
- Exit doors from stairwells to grade level
- All stairwell doors

Electric locks are available where the strike is normally in the locked or the unlocked position.

Electromagnetic locks are particularly suitable for use on emergency exit doors as there is no moving parts that can accidentally become jammed. Several conditions must be met before this type of lock can be used on an emergency exit door:

- A 24-hour proprietary control center must exist in the protected property.
- An activation/deactivation capability must exist from the control center.
- Activation of the fire alarm system automatically deactivates the locking device.
- Each location must have a fire pull station in its vicinity and the fact that its activation will automatically deactivate the lock.

Note: It is essential that the fire department be consulted prior to any final decision on the use of locks on any door that may be considered an emergency exit. Get their decision in writing and carefully consider before compliance.

Emergency exit devices that are normally used on emergency exit doors cause justifiable security concern.

If permitted, only quality electric or electromagnetic locks should be used.

If electric or magnetic locks cannot be used, great care should be taken to ensure the emergency devices use such features as the following:

- Deadbolts
- Deadlocking latches
- Vertical locking bars for pairs of doors

Remember that emergency exit devices can be connected to a proprietary or commercially monitored alarm system. Loud local alarms are also an effective way to protect emergency exits.

CLOSED CIRCUIT TELEVISION

If used selectively, CCTV can be very effective and has the potential to significantly reduce security manpower costs.

An objective statement for a CCTV system might read:

"To avoid costly manpower requirements by using CCTV to monitor several sensitive/critical areas simultaneously, thereby ensuring the safety/security of property and occupants."

Great care must be exercised in designing a CCTV system to ensure that the objective statement is achieved. Caution is also necessary to ensure that costs do not get out of hand. This is a common problem when the system is not designed by a security expert.

The following are suggested practical applications for CCTV:

- Parkade areas, entrances/exits shuttle elevator lobbies stairwells, and elevators
- Shipping/receiving areas
- Main floor elevator lobbies
- Cross-over floors
- Cash handling areas

All CCTV systems are made up of several components that an end user should be, at the very least, familiar with. The following is a brief description of each component

Cameras—The primary consideration in relation to camera selection is the available light coupled with required image quality. The two most common cameras are the "vidicon" and "newvicon." The big difference is that one performs better than the other in adverse conditions. The vidicon is only suitable if the area is well lighted and if the quality of lighting, during the time it is expected that the camera will be required to operate, is stable. Naturally, it follows that the newvicon is significantly more costly.

Housings—Several types of housings are available. They fall into two categories: aesthetic and environmental. Housings can also effectively disguise the existence of a camera.

Monitors—Monitors are available in different sizes and in color or monochrome. When a quality image is required, it is necessary to use a high-resolution screen.

Sequential switches—It is not necessary, or usually desirable, to have a monitor for every camera. By using a sequential switcher, the image from two or more cameras can be routinely rotated for viewing on one monitor. When required, an operator can lock on the image from one particular camera for select viewing.

Motion Detectors—Cameras are available with a built-in motion detection capability. If movement occurs within the field of view of the camera lens, an alarm will sound at the control center or a video recorder will be activated to record the activity that caused the alarm. This feature is very valuable when a large number of monitors are used.

Pan/tilt/zoom—The need to use several cameras to cover an area or activity can be avoided by careful positioning of one camera and providing pan/tilt/zoom features.

Controls—In addition to the normal television controls, controls will be required for whatever special features that are built into the system.

Consoles—The design of a control center console that houses a CCTV system is definitely an engineering task. Care must be exercised to ensure operator comfort, particularly in relation to viewing angles and ease of accessibility of controls.

Video recorders—A CCTV system should be considered incomplete if it does not have the ability to selectively record events.

Day/time generators —This feature has potential benefits in specific circumstances—for example, where no immediate incident response capability is available, or if the recording may be required as evidence in court.

For an example of a typical system diagram, see Figure 3-4.

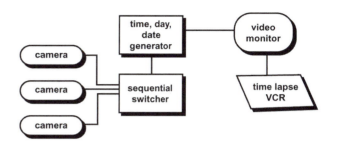

Figure 3-4   Typical Closed Circuit Television System

SAFES AND VAULTS

Safes and vaults are designed to offer varying levels of protection from specific risks, namely burglary, robbery, and fire.

Burglary-Resistive Safes

In addition to their actual construction, burglary resistive safes have a number of protective features that we should be familiar with.

- Locks
- Interior design
- Depository
- Time locks
- Time delay locks
- Relocking device
- Extra weight
- Floor anchoring
- Counterspy dials

Locks

Safes are available with three types of locking systems.

- A single combination
- A single key lock combination
- Dual combination locks

With the single combination option, an unaccompanied person with the combination can access the contents at any time.

The second option is that a key lock combination requires two persons to be in attendance to open the safe. One person has the key to unlock the combination-turning mechanism and the other has the combination to unlock the safe.

The third option is similar to option two in that two persons must be in attendance to open the safe. Each person only has one of the combinations.

Interiors

Sufficient options are available in interior configurations so that the need for customizing may be avoided. Features available include fixed or adjustable shelving and enclosed compartments that may be either key or combination-locked. Available options increase proportionately to the size and cost of the safe.

Depository

This feature permits the inserting of property, most often cash, without allowing access to the safe contents. The depository is usually fitted with an antifish device to inhibit retrieval of deposited property.

Time locks

Time locks prevent access to the safe contents for predetermined time frames by persons normally authorized for access. For example, when a bank safe is locked at the close of the business day, it cannot be opened again until the following morning. Should the bank manager be forcibly taken from his home, he cannot be forced to open the safe.

Time-delay locks

This feature is designed to protect against a holdup. To open a safe equipped with this feature requires keying the lock, followed by predetermined waiting period before the locking mechanism will unlock. A safe with this feature is often used at late night convenience stores or 24-hour gas stations.

Relocking devices

These devices are designed to act as a secondary locking feature if the normal one is attacked. For example, if someone attacks the combination dial with a sledgehammer, the relocking device will activate. After this happens, only a qualified safe expert can open the safe.

Extra weight

To prevent thieves simply walking away with a safe, it is recommended that a safe weigh a minimum of 340 kg or 750 lbs. Most large safes do weigh 340 kgs, and smaller ones can be ordered with extra weight added.

Floor anchoring

An acceptable alternative to extra weight, where extra weight may present problems for structural reasons, is floor anchoring—provided a concrete slab is available.

Counterspy dials

It is not uncommon for thieves to note the combination of a safe while surreptitiously viewing it being unlocked. This is often done from a building across the street. A counterspy dial prohibits anyone other than the person immediately in front of the dial to see the numbers and only one number is visible at a time.

Apart from the foregoing, obvious security features, we can tell little about a safe by looking at it; nowhere can appearances be more deceptive. For this reason, a purchaser has to rely on a particular vendor or on independent appraisal. Independent appraisal is available from Underwriters Laboratories Inc. (UL).

If a manufacturer submits a product sample to UL, they will conduct various tests and issue authority to the manufacturer to affix a specific label to the protect line. The following UL labels are available:

UL Labels	Resistant to Attack From:
T.L. - 15	Ordinary household tools for 15 minutes
T.L. - 30	Ordinary household tools for 30 minutes
T.R.T.L. - 30	Oxyacetylene torch or ordinary household tools for 30 minutes
T.R.T.L. - 30x6	Torch and tools for 30 minutes, six sides
X - 60	Explosives for 60 minutes
T.R.T.L. - 60	Oxyacetylene torch for 60 minutes
T.X. - 60	Torch and explosives for 60 minutes
T.X.T.L. - 60	Torch, explosives and tools for 60 minutes

Safe manufacturers sometimes assign their own rating to a safe. An assigned rating will usually mean that the safe offers a level of protection that compares to what UL would say if they had the opportunity to test. A concern exists, however, that without an independently assigned rating or classification, a purchaser has no way of verifying the expected level of protection.

Burglary-Resistive Vaults

Any storage container specifically designed to resist forcible entry and large enough to permit a person to enter and move around within while remaining upright can be considered a vault.

Vault construction consists of reinforced concrete walls, floor and ceiling, and a specially constructed vault door.

Any consideration to build/purchase (a prefabricated vault is available from most large safe manufacturers) must be carefully assessed to ensure cost effectiveness. The evaluation to determine need must recognize that the value of the asset to be stored in the vault will likely attract the professionally competent thief. The impact of this is that regardless of construction, the vault will only delay penetration.

In addition to applicable features as mentioned for "burglary-resistive safes," the possibility that an employee(s) may be locked into the vault accidentally or deliberately in a robbery situation must be considered. To ensure safety of employees, all vaults should be equipped with approved vault ventilators and a method of communicating to outside the vault.

Fire-Resistive Containers

Insulated safes, filing cabinets, and record containers are available that offer varying degrees of protection to contents from exposure to heat.

The appearance of fire-resistive containers can be particularly deceptive—it must be remembered that, of necessity, the construction material is totally different from burglary safes. The insulation material used in fire-resistive containers offers little protection from physical assault.

Two very important points in relation to fire-resistive containers are:

- Paper records will destruct at temperatures in excess of 350°F (159°C).
- Computer tapes/disks will destruct at temperatures in excess of 150°F (66°C).

Underwriters Laboratories tests fire-resistive containers for their ability to protect contents when exposed to heat. Tests are also conducted to determine the container's ability to survive a drop as might happen when a floor collapses in a fire situation.

Note: It is of the utmost importance to remember that safes and vaults are only designed to delay entry when attacked; they are not impenetrable. For this reason, safes and vaults should always be protected by a burglary alarm system. Similarly, alarm systems should be used to protect the contents of record safes from theft.

FENCING

The subject of fencing is a much more interesting and important topic than most people at first realize. Fencing has been used throughout history as a defense against enemies — the walled city of Pompeii dates back to 800 B.C., and it was not uncommon for the complete frontiers of kingdoms in China to be walled (origin of the Great Wall of China). Closer to home, the old city of Quebec remains the only enclosed city in Canada and the U.S.A.

Modern acts of terrorism and civil disturbance have resulted in innovations in the types and usage of fencing. Barbed tape (razor ribbon), a modern version of barbed wire, is a very effective (if not vicious) defensive, or should we say, offensive material. Its use is rarely justified except where the highest standards of security are necessary—for example, in a federal penitentiary.

The use of barbed tape in industrial facilities is not common in North America. Barbed tape can be used in coils along the top of fences instead of the conventional barbed wire overhang. In very high-risk situations, coils of barbed tape stacked in a pyramid configuration between a double conventional fence will provide a very effective defense.

Another product of modern terrorism is the freely rotating barbed wire fence topping recently developed in Ireland. When a would-be intruder grabs the overhang in an attempt to gain leverage, a second overhang simply rotates into place. This is more effective than the conventional overhang and much more acceptable for routine application than coils of barbed tape.

Fencing as used in most applications is the common chain-link type with a barbed wire, outward facing overhang. A major weakness with the chain-link fence is the ease with which it can be climbed. To overcome this problem, the British developed the "welded mesh fence." Compared to the 4-square-inch opening in chain-link fence fabric, the welded mesh fence has openings of 1.5 square inches. The openings are 3" × ½" and run vertically. The narrowness of the openings makes it almost impossible for a climber to gain purchase. The width of the openings also inhibits the use of wire or bolt cutters.

Prior to making any decision on the location and type of fencing, it is necessary to conduct a risk assessment. It is also necessary to gain a thorough understanding of the enterprise's operation. For the purpose of this article, we will discuss the fencing requirements for a typical manufacturing plant located in an industrial area of a large city. The objective of the fencing program is twofold—to control movement to and from the property and to minimize the need for costly manpower at control points. The latter is to be attained by keeping the number of perimeter openings to a minimum.

While it is true that industry is becoming ever-more security conscious, it is also true that the owners of industrial facilities do not want their property to look like a prison compound or armed camp. With this in mind, the first objective is to define the boundary of the property. Most often, this will require a combination of structural and psychological barriers.

From a psychological point of view, we are only concerned with defining the boundary—mostly for legal reasons, prevention of trespass, and liability law suits. Property definition may be simply a change in landscaping, or indeed anything that distinguishes the property from its neighbor.

Somewhere between the property line and the area of company activity, it will be necessary to install a structural barrier that will act as a physical deterrence to the would-be intruder. Usually this barrier will be chain-link fence and it should be topped with a barbed wire overhang. The following are suggested minimum specifications:

1. 7" in height excluding top overhang.
2. Wire must be 9-gauge or heavier.
3. Mesh openings must not be larger than 4 square inches.
4. Fabric must be fastened securely to rigid metal or reinforced concrete posts set in concrete.
5. There should be no more than two inches between the bottom of the fence and the ground.
6. Where the ground is soft or sandy, the fence fabric should extend below the surface.
7. Top overhang should face outward and upwards at a 45-degree angle.
8. The overhang supporting arms should be firmly affixed to the top of the fence posts.
9. The overhang should increase the overall height of the fence by one foot.
10. Three strands of barbed wire, spaced 6" apart, should be installed on the supporting arms.
11. A clear zone of 20 feet or more should exist between the perimeter and exterior structures.
12. Where possible, a clear zone of 50 feet or more should exist between the perimeter barrier and structures within the protected area.

Vehicular and pedestrian gates in the perimeter fence should be kept to a minimum—ideally only one common entry point for employees and business visitors. Depending on the size and layout of the site, it may be necessary to install a secondary entry point for emergency use, such as access by the fire department. However, this entry point should normally remain closed and locked.

All openings in the perimeter fence should be equipped with gates. Even if these gates are not to be electronically controlled initially, planning should provide for power to each gate location with provision for a remote control capability from the control/security center.

Typically, security control is provided at the first defensible point; however, numerous facilities allow free access beyond this point to an inner control location. This may be beneficial for many reasons, especially in large, heavy traffic plants. Once inside the initial perimeter, signs would direct employees to the employee car park, visitors to an information center and truck traffic to shipping/receiving areas. Beyond these points, a secondary secure perimeter would be established.

The employee car park should be completely enclosed; access to the area would ideally be controlled by a card access system. Access from the car park to the plant would be through a control point (manned during shift changes).

In addition to the possible need for a secondary line of defense, there may also be a need for fenced areas to provide secure overnight storage for company vehicles, secure storage for bulk raw materials, or for the storage of large finished products. Waste awaiting disposal should also be stored within a fenced area. Fencing may also be required to segregate operational areas, such as stores, tool crib, and so on.

It is important to remember that fencing is first and foremost a barrier and that as a barrier it does not have to be chain-link fencing. If we also remember that fencing will only delay the determined would-be intruder, it should be easy to be flexible regarding the material used. Hedging, poured concrete, solid concrete blocks, and decorative concrete blocks are all suitable fencing material.

If fencing is required to provide a very high level of protection, its use should be supplemented by the use of fence disturbance detectors, motion detectors, and patrolling guards or surveillance by closed circuit television.

SECURITY QUIZ
Physical Security Applications

1. What is "physical security planning"? It is a recognized security process that if followed will result in the selection of _____ based on appropriateness. (Fill in the blank.)
2. Effective security lighting acts as a _____ to intruders. (Fill in the blank.)
3. Polycarbonate plastic is _____ and _____ resistive. (Fill in the blanks.)
4. There are three components to an intrusion detection system: detectors/sensors, systems controls, and _____ devices. (Fill in the blank.)
5. Microwave detectors use high-frequency sound waves to establish a protected area.
    □ T □ F
6. Deadbolt locks should have a minimum of a ½" throw.
    □ T □ F
7. Card access systems permit accountability.
    □ T □ F
8. The most commonly used security fencing material is:
    □ (a) barbed wire
    □ (b) barbed tape
    □ (c) chain-link
    □ (d) welded wire mesh
9. The minimum height of a security fence should be:
    □ (a) 7 feet
    □ (b) 6 feet
    □ (c) 8 feet
    □ (d) 9 feet
10. Which of the following types of lighting are only lit on an as-required basis?
    □ (a) Continuous
    □ (b) Standby
    □ (c) Movable
    □ (d) Emergency

ALARM SYSTEMS FUNDAMENTALS

By Cole Morris, CPP, CFE, CPO

In many cases, alarm systems form the backbone of a facility's physical protection program. Universally used, alarms are very likely to be encountered by the protection officer or security specialist as they perform their daily duties. In fact, regardless of your industry, employer, shift schedule, or geographic location, the chances are good that you will have some involvement with alarm systems.

An understanding of basic alarm systems should be considered a "core knowledge" requirement for anyone responsible for the protection of people, property, profits, and information. This chapter provides the fundamental information you need to know to be successful at your job. It is important to point out that this material must be supplemented with specific information as it applies to the alarm systems at your duty location.

Starting with the basics, a definition of an alarm system is in order. Quite simply, an alarm system is used to provide early warning of an intruder. The "system" can consist of a relatively simple switch that activates a local audible device (i.e. a horn or siren). It can also be quite complex, consisting of hardware and software elements that require considerable skill and training of assigned security staff.

The most effective physical security is "layered." An alarm system should be designed to provide one or more layers of detection around an asset. Each layer is made up of a series of detection zones designed to isolate the protected property and to control the entry and exit of authorized personnel and materials.

In more sophisticated systems, sensors are interfaced with electronic entry-control devices, CCTV, alarm reporting displays (both visual and audible), and security lighting. As you can see, the alarm system can serve as a crucial "layer" in any physical security plan.

ALARM MONITORING

Your involvement with an alarm system will depend largely on how it is monitored. There are four methods of monitoring.

1. Local Monitoring

This is the simplest form of alarm monitoring. It consists of a bell or horn located near the protected door or window. In the event of an attempted penetration, the resulting sound is intended to alert nearby police, security personnel, neighbors, or company employees.

A major drawback of this approach is the fact that many people will not bother to investigate a blaring alarm. Furthermore, manpower shortages often make a security or police response impractical. Although relatively inexpensive to install, this form of alarm monitoring does not provide an adequate level of protection for most situations. Also, a potential criminal can disable these alarms relatively easily.

When activated, the audible alert tells the intruder his activities have been noticed. In many cases, this will scare the criminal off before the crime can be completed. However, in other instances, a seasoned criminal may realize a response is dependent on someone in the local area not only hearing the alarm, but also taking action to investigate it. In short, the criminal may be well aware that he has a certain amount of time to "work" despite the activation of the alarm.

2. Central Station Monitoring

This is a popular method of alarm monitoring. It consists of a company that is paid to provide monitoring services for a variety of clients. Typically, these alarm companies charge a one-time installation fee and then bill monthly for monitoring services.

When an alarm signal is received, an employee of the alarm company is responsible for notifying the police so they can respond. In most cases, a company's security officers are also notified so they can respond also.

Despite its popularity, central station monitoring is not without problems. There have been several documented cases where the alarm company "dropped the ball" and failed to make the proper notifications. In these cases, significant property losses have occurred.

Some alarm companies will provide their own security officers to respond to and investigate alarm conditions. In these instances, the alarm company's employees must be given keys to the protected premises in order to investigate alarms. From a security and business viewpoint, this should be considered an additional risk.

3. Direct Fire or Police Monitoring

This is no longer a common method of alarm monitoring. However, in some jurisdictions the local police or fire station will monitor alarms from their headquarters. When used, this method tends to be a relatively reliable way to monitor alarms.

4. Proprietary Monitoring

In this approach, alarms are monitored by the company's security staff. In most cases, a security control center is on the premises and serves as a focal point for all security operations.

During an alarm event, the situation can be assessed by dispatching security staff to the alarm location or by using CCTV to "check things out."

In a proprietary monitoring approach, the alarm system is operated and controlled by the property owner. In most cases this means assigned security specialists are adequately trained and are very familiar with their property and its various security systems. They have a vested interest because they are protecting "their" company.

A drawback, however, is that proprietary monitoring can be very expensive. This is because the company not only must buy the required monitoring equipment; it must also pay people to operate it. Likewise, a proprietary system may provide inferior results if it is not designed for the specific needs of a building and its occupants.

Regardless of the type of monitoring being used at your location, the alarm system must be resistant to tampering or system failure. For instance, systems should have at least 24 hours of battery backup. The phone lines that carry the alarm signal to an off-site central monitoring station should be fully supervised, as should all circuits within the building. That way, any attempt to cut or disrupt the alarm signal as it leaves the building will be immediately detected.

OPERATOR INTERFACE

Regardless of the type of alarm monitoring used at your current location, eventually the system's operation will come down to a human being. This person might be a monitor in a central station hundreds of miles away, or it could be one of your coworkers assigned to the security control system on the first floor of corporate headquarters. In all cases, the operator interfaces with the alarm. He or she interacts with the alarm system through devices that can be seen, heard, or touched and manipulated. In most modern systems, visual displays and printers can be used to inform the operator of an alarm or the equipment's status. Likewise, audible devices are frequently used to alert an operator to an alarm or the equipment's failure. Devices such as push buttons and keyboards permit an operator to acknowledge and reset alarms.

Visual displays. The type of display used to inform the operator visually of the system's status is determined mostly by the system's complexity. Today, status information is usually displayed on monitors.

Monitors provide great flexibility in the type and format of alarm information that may be displayed. Both text and graphic information can be presented in a variety of colors. Multiple alarms may also be displayed. If alarms are prioritized, higher-priority alarms may be highlighted by blinking, changing colors, or by using bold print, and so on. To assist the operator in determining the correct response, alarm-specific instructions may be displayed adjacent to the alarm information.

Audible alarm devices. In conjunction with the visual display of an alarm, the system must also generate an audible alarm. The audible alarm may be produced by the ringing of a bell or by the generation of a steady or pulsating tone from an electronic device. In any case, the audible alarm serves to attract the operator's attention to the visual-alarm display. Most systems have a switch to silence the audible signal before the operator resets the alarm.

Logging devices. All alarm-system activity (such as arming the system, de-arming, maintenance, and system faults) should be logged and recorded. Logged information is important not only for security personnel investigating an event, but also for maintenance personnel checking equipment. This is especially important when trying to troubleshoot nuisance or "false" alarms.

Alarm printers. Alarm printers are typically of the high-speed, continuous-feed variety. The printer provides a hard-copy record of all alarm events and system activity.

Report printers. Many modern systems include a separate printer for printing reports using information stored by the central computer.

Operator control. A means is required to transmit information from the operator to the system. The type of controls provided usually depends on the type of display provided. The following are commonly used control devices:

- Keypads consist of a numeric display system that will generally be provided with a 12-digit keypad and several function keys. These allow the operator to perform such actions as to secure, access, acknowledge, and reset alarms.

- Monitor-based systems are usually provided with a typewriter-type keyboard that enables an operator to enter more information using a combination of alphanumeric characters and function keys. The keyboard is usually identical to that used by desktop computers.

- Not surprisingly, most alarm systems include devices to help the operator enter information or execute commands quickly. A mouse or a trackball are typical examples.

ALARM SENSORS

A basic alarm system is divided into three layers: perimeter protection, area protection, and spot protection. Perimeter protection is the first line of defense to detect a potential intruder. Alarm sensors on the perimeter are typically mounted on doors, windows, vents, and skylights. Since a vast majority of burglaries are committed using such openings, it is important they be a priority for protection. Commonly used perimeter sensors include the following.

Glass-break sensors. These detect the breaking of glass. The noise from breaking glass consists of frequencies in both the audible and ultrasonic range. Glass-breakage sensors use microphone transducers to detect the glass breakage. The sensors are designed to respond to specific frequencies only, thus minimizing such false alarms as may be caused by banging on the glass.

Balanced magnetic switch. Balanced magnetic switches (BMSs) are typically used to detect the opening of a door, window, gate, vent skylight, and so on. Usually, the BMS switch is mounted on the doorframe and the actuating magnet is installed on the door. The BMS has a three-position reed switch and an additional magnet (called the bias magnet) located adjacent to the switch. When the door is closed, the reed switch is held in the balanced or center position by interacting magnetic fields. If the door is opened or an external magnet is brought near the sensor in an attempt to defeat it, the switch becomes unbalanced and generates an alarm.

Grid-Wire sensor. This consists of a continuous electrical wire arranged in a grid pattern. The wire maintains an electrical current. An alarm is generated when the wire is broken. The sensor detects forced entry through walls, floors, ceilings, doors, windows, and other barriers. The grid wire can be installed directly on the barrier, in a grille or screen that is mounted on the barrier, or over any opening that requires protection. The wire can be stapled directly to barriers made of wood or wallboard. Wood panels should be installed over the grid to protect it from day-to-day abuse and to provide concealment.

Area protection is also sometimes called volumetric protection. The sensors used for this purpose protect the interior spaces of a business or residence. These devices provide coverage whether or not the perimeter is penetrated and are especially useful in detecting the "stay-behind" criminal. As a general rule, area sensors may be active or passive. Active sensors (such as microwave) fill the protected area with an energy pattern and recognize a disturbance in the pattern when anything moves within the detection zone.

On the other hand, active sensors generate their own energy pattern to detect an intruder. Also, some sensors, known as dual-technology sensors, use a combination of two different technologies, usually one active and one passive, within the same unit.

Sensors used for area protection include the following:

Microwave motion sensors. With microwave motion sensors, high-frequency electromagnetic energy is used to detect an intruder's motion within the protected area.

Passive infra-red (PIR). These motion sensors detect a change in the thermal energy pattern caused by a moving intruder and initiate an alarm when the change in energy satisfies the detector's alarm criteria. These sensors are passive devices because they do not transmit energy; they monitor the energy radiated by the surrounding environment.

Dual-technology sensors. To minimize the generation of alarms caused by sources other than intruders, dual-technology sensors combine two different technologies in one unit. Ideally, this is achieved by combining two sensors that individually have high reliability and do not respond to common sources of false alarms. Available dual-technology sensors combine an active ultrasonic or microwave sensor with a PIR sensor.

Video motion sensors. A video motion sensor generates an alarm when an intruder enters a selected portion of a CCTV camera's field of view. The sensor processes and compares successive images between the images against predefined alarm criteria. There are two categories of video motion detectors—analog and digital. Analog detectors generate an alarm in response to changes in a picture's contrast. Digital devices convert selected portions of the analog video signal into digital data that are compared with data converted previously; if differences exceed preset limits, an alarm is generated.

Spot protection is used to detect unauthorized activity at a specific location. It serves as the final protective layer of a typical alarm system. Assets most commonly secured with spot protection include safes, vaults, filing cabinets, art objects, jewelry, firearms, and other high-value property. These sensors (sometimes referred to as proximity sensors) detect an intruder coming in close proximity to, touching, or lifting an object. Several different types are available, including capacitance sensors, pressure mats, and pressure switches.

Capacitance sensors. These detect an intruder approaching or touching a metal object by sensing a change in capacitance between the object and the ground. A capacitor consists of two metallic plates separated by a dielectric medium. A change in the dielectric medium or electrical charge results in a change in capacitance, and thus an alarm.

Pressure mats. Pressure mats generate an alarm when pressure is applied to any part of the mat's surface. For example, an alarm is triggered when someone steps on a mat. Pressure mats can be used to detect an intruder approaching a protected object, or they can be placed by doors or windows to detect entry. Because pressure mats are easy to bridge, they should be well concealed, such as hidden beneath carpeting.

Pressure switches. Mechanically activated contact switches can be used as pressure switches. Objects that require protection can be placed on top of the switch. When the object is moved, the switch actuates and generates an alarm. Naturally, in such applications, the switch must be well concealed. The interface between the switch and the protected object should be designed so that an intruder cannot slide a thin piece of material under the object to override the switch while the object is removed.

DURESS ALARMS

In addition to perimeter, area, and spot protection, alarms can also be used for specialized applications. For example, duress alarms (sometimes called "panic buttons") are frequently encountered in many business settings. They are often concealed under a desk or countertop. Duress alarms are often used by receptionists, cashiers, bank tellers, security officers, and customer service employees engaged in transactions with the general public. In short, anyone who may encounter a threatening, hostile individual in the course of his or her work may find a duress device of value.

Duress alarm devices may be fixed or portable. Operations and security personnel use them to signal a life-threatening emergency. Activation of a duress device will generate an alarm at the alarm-monitoring station. Police or security personnel are then dispatched to render assistance.

Fixed duress devices are mechanical switches permanently mounted in an inconspicuous location. They can be simple push-button switches activated by the touch of a finger or hand or foot-operated switches attached to the floor.

Portable duress devices are wireless units consisting of a transmitter and a receiver. The transmitter is portable and small enough to be conveniently carried by a person. The receiver is mounted in a fixed location within the facility. Either ultrasonic or RF energy can be used as the communication medium. When activated, the transmitter generates an alarm that is detected (within range) by the receiver. The receiver then activates a relay that is hardwired to the alarm-monitoring system.

NUISANCE ALARMS

A vast majority of alarms are nuisance or "false" alarms. In many jurisdictions this places a great deal of stress on local law enforcement agencies. Each time a police officer is dispatched to investigate an alarm, valuable resources are being consumed. To make matters worse, most faulty alarms are generated by the following:

- User incompetence
- Poor installation
- Poor maintenance
- Substandard materials
- Employee indifference

Security officers and business owners must learn as much as possible about their alarm systems. Where are the sensors located? What type are they? Who monitors the system? Awareness is the first step in effective alarm management. There is simply no excuse for arming a security system only to have alarms activated because people are still in the building.

Similarly, at some larger facilities, people sometimes simply forget to turn the alarm system on. Checklists should be used to arm and de-arm various parts of the alarm system as required during the business day. This will also provide documentation of who did what and will minimize the chances for oversights between shift changes.

When it comes to installation, many alarms are the result of inappropriate sensor selection or placement. Alarm installations and equipment selection are not jobs for amateurs.

Alarms are electrical/mechanical devices. As such they require periodic maintenance. Routine operational checks should be included to ensure sensors and related components are working properly. For example, security staff should walk-test every motion detector each day. This involves physically ensuring that each detector is functioning properly.

Likewise, there is considerable truth in the old saying, "you get what you pay for." Substandard materials can in-clude sensors, mounting hardware, wiring, and even software. There is nothing wrong with going for the lowest bid on an alarm installation. However, make sure you are not chasing false economy by using inadequate materials which will break and require continual replacement and repair.

Many nonsecurity employees have little understanding of security issues. This includes even the most basic awareness of the company's alarm system. Often, employees will think nothing of coming into work early, stay late, or visit the office on a holiday. There is usually nothing wrong with such activity. However, if it results in continuous alarm activations, an employee awareness program is probably in order.

Nuisance alarms consume security and law enforcement resources which could be more usefully employed in other activities. And for those coming to the attention of the police, they can also be expensive. The nuisance alarm rate has become so bad in many areas that local governments are now assessing businesses and residences fines. These can run into the thousands of dollars.

As you might imagine, your organization's ability to operate its alarm system may not only protect property, it can also help protect hard-earned profits as well.

ALARM RESPONSE

Earlier, the various types of alarm monitoring were discussed. In some cases, the protection officer or security specialist will be dispatched to investigate an alarm event. The alarm might be the result of an employee entering his office before the alarm is deactivated. It could be a stray cat wandering the interior of a warehouse. It might even be a cluster of birthday balloons that activate a motion detector.

Then again, it could be something much more dangerous.

One of the major problems with nuisance alarms is that they invariably reinforce a mindset that every alarm is a nuisance alarm. For both public law enforcement and private security, this leads to complacent attitudes and poor officer safety procedures. For the private sector protection officer, the following alarm response tactics are recommended:

- Never assume an alarm event is "nothing." Assume you are responding to an intrusion until proven otherwise.
- Maintain radio contact with fellow officers and your security control center.
- Maintain sound discipline. Keep radio volume low. Secure noisy keys and other equipment.
- If upon arrival to the scene you detect broken glass or other indications of an intrusion, do NOT proceed into the building. Call the police and assume a position from where you can "be a good witness."
- Evaluate all alarm information. Has there been just one alarm? Is there a series of alarms which might indicate someone is actually moving around the interior of the building? The professional evaluation of all alarms can assist you in determining where the in-

truder is. Relay this information to responding police units.

- Know your company's policy for alarm response. Use common sense and avoid complacency that can lead to tragic consequences.

Any alarm system is only as good as the people who operate, monitor, and respond to it. Protection officers must be properly trained to respond to alarms. They must understand how their system works and the need to treat every alarm seriously.

SECURITY QUIZ
Alarm System Fundamentals

1. In many cases, _____ _____ form the backbone of a facility's physical protection program.
   - ☐ (a) Alarm systems
   - ☐ (b) Covert surveillance
   - ☐ (c) Report writing
   - ☐ (d) Physical force

2. The primary purpose of an alarm system is:
   - ☐ (a) to conduct area surveillance
   - ☐ (b) to serve as a physical barrier
   - ☐ (c) to provide early warning of an intruder
   - ☐ (d) lower insurance rates

3. According to the text material, the most effective security is provided with a:
   - ☐ (a) technical approach
   - ☐ (b) layered approach
   - ☐ (c) large security force
   - ☐ (d) key and lock program

4. In more sophisticated alarm systems, sensors are interfaced with electronic entry-control devices, CCTV, alarm reporting displays (both visual and audible), and _____ _____.
   - ☐ (a) police patrols
   - ☐ (b) aerial units
   - ☐ (c) sniper teams
   - ☐ (d) security lighting

5. How many different types of alarm monitoring were examined in the text?
   - ☐ (a) Two
   - ☐ (b) Three
   - ☐ (c) Four
   - ☐ (d) Six

6. Which of the following is *not* a type of alarm monitoring?
   - ☐ (a) Central station
   - ☐ (b) Direct fire and police
   - ☐ (c) Satellite
   - ☐ (d) Proprietary

7. Logging devices are used for:
   - ☐ (a) recording system activities and faults
   - ☐ (b) controlling CCTV cameras
   - ☐ (c) recording time and attendance of security staff
   - ☐ (d) access control to computer networks

8. Alarm printers are typically:

☐ (a) of the color laser type
☐ (b) of the high-speed, continuous feed type
☐ (c) black and white and medium speed
☐ (d) extremely expensive

9. A glass-break sensor is an example of:

☐ (a) a perimeter sensor
☐ (b) a spot sensor
☐ (c) an area sensor
☐ (d) a volumetric device

10. A duress alarm is also sometimes called:

☐ (a) a reset button
☐ (b) a panic button
☐ (c) an activation switch
☐ (d) a silent partner

CENTRAL ALARM STATIONS AND DISPATCH CENTERS

By Rich Abrams

The control room is the nerve center of any safety and security department. It is the usually the first recipient of any requests for assistance, and provides the documentation for all assigned calls. In addition, it is the "eyes and ears" of the protected location, utilizing both audio and video surveillance. All communications, from patrol officers as well as the public, are relayed and recorded by the dispatcher. Furthermore, owing to the 24-hour 7-day availability of the operation, the monitoring of nonsecurity tasks such as temperature, power, elevators, and parking gates is possible.

The dispatch center should be located in an easily accessible area, such as a building lobby, or management office. This allows easy access to a complaint window for occupants and visitors, but also assures separation from the direct pedestrian path. Comfortable heating, ventilating, and air conditioning are required for the 8- to 12-hour shifts spent at the console. The main door should be controlled by card access to allow authorized staff to enter and limit visitors. Lighting should be adjustable and focused to avoid glare and eye strain from computers.

Another important design variation is the equipment console itself and the chairs that employees use during the shift. The radio controls and auxiliary buttons should be installed with the dispatcher's easy grasp, and computer terminals necessitate a slight angled mounting and measured distance from the seat. Long phone cords or headsets will prevent stretching and possible neck strain. In short, the control center is the second home of the security dispatcher and thus ergonomics and creature comforts are warranted.

Staffing requirements for the alarm room depend on a few key concerns. As an example, both Underwriters Laboratories and the National Burglar and Fire Alarm Association have standards. They suggest at least two operators. (One employee may also perform "runner tasks.") This allows personal breaks, coverage during busy periods, relief from one function to another to avoid boredom (One officer takes the radio and phone while the other receives alarms and greets any walk-up complaints), and the "quiet time" necessary to perform logging or filing duties. If your security department is smaller, the supervisor should arrange for a trained patrol unit to be detailed to the dispatch area for relief. There are additional details on manpower specifications from 911 organizations such as APCO and NENA as well as the Central Station Alarm Association.

Now that we've discussed the room and the operators, it's time to examine the equipment that is found in most security offices. The two most important tools are the telephone and the radio. Today, digital phones are equipped with speakers, last-number dialed command, a bank of important numbers that can be speed-dialed, caller ID display, and cordless headsets. Pre-programmed voicemail and automatic transfer ensure that calls are answered promptly, with the designated emergency number (911, 111, 555 or whatever your agency uses for security access) taking priority. Radio base stations are also digital, which allows user-friendly adjustments for volume, channel, unit display, and other accessories. Many newer consoles have touch-screen command from a computer terminal, which eliminates the knobs and buttons found on earlier apparatus. The speaker and microphone, as with any device, need to be located within easy reach of the dispatcher. A good working relationship with your radio and telephone vendor is essential.

Another vital element is the alarm receiver and associated displays. All signals, including fire, burglar, and auxiliary (temperature or AC power), are collected here. Each building or floor, as well as each room, is given a numeric code for easy identification. Here is an example: 1-10003 (account number); 350 Commerce Parkway (building); 2nd Floor Research (floor and designation); Lab 227 (room). The computer screen may also contain specific dispatch instructions: Fire Alarm-Call 911 and notify the building manager; Burglar Alarm-Call Midvale Police and advise the Research Building patrol officer; Elevator Alarm-Notify Acme Elevator and page the on-call custodian. Many alarm systems also have a graphic map display with color-coded details to assist the dispatcher when identifying a specific activation's location. Ease of operation and speedy alarm verification are both requirements for life and property safety.

A computer assisted dispatch logging program provides instant display of patrol unit status, up-to-date information about alarms out of service or special events, a history of past incidents organized by location, and an accurate accounting of all events occurring during the shift. There is space provided for comments or supervisor notification, and routine details such as officer patrol times (rounds) or parking lot activity can be promptly transcribed. The logging software also supplies written reports, activity charts, officer appraisal, and vehicle or bicycle operation. This replaces the time clock, which once manually stamped paper cards for all records. In addition, a digital audio recorder receives signals from radios and phones.

This serves two purposes: All events during the shift are taped for a permanent record of the conversations that took place. Secondarily, the Instant Play Back function gives the dispatcher the opportunity to repeat all or part of an episode for clarification. (Example: **Spruce Hall** and **Bruce Hall** may sound alike when an excited caller is reporting an emergency.)

Video surveillance monitors, linked by cable to remote cameras, give the dispatcher a "window on the world." A CCTV controller allows the security officer to select cameras, focus on a particular location with pan, tilt, and zoom functions, choose a display monitor and send the resulting picture to a VCR recorder. Some cameras are permanently assigned in a parking lot or building lobby. Others are mounted atop buildings for a panoramic view. Special lenses and infrared light sources pierce the night, and for special investigations, covert locations with miniature cameras are used. Another link between the dispatcher and the public is the intercom or callbox. These special weather-proof phones, activated by a "big red button," are located at entrance gates, garage stairwells, loading docks, and other after-hour destinations. They can be used for entry requests, emergency assistance, security officer response, or delivery notification. Some phones are equipped with a blue or green light to emphasize their location.

Alarm rooms are also equipped with direct-dial "Hot Line" phones, special radio channels, or digital paging terminals. These are utilized to alert other agencies, from local police departments to the corporate headquarters (in another city) of a building tenant. Whatever the incident requires, the dispatcher transmits some basic information: What occurred? Where did it take place? When did it happen? How can the person (on the other side of the message) assist? Who is taking command?

Another function that security control centers are tasked with is access control and oversight of door keys. Most modern buildings are secured with electronic access card readers, which are programmed by a computer for specific entry and schedules. Some have key fob transmitters, which function similarly to a garage door opener. The newest door controls are wireless, allowing the occupant to waive the access card near the door with the same technology used in Speed Pass for bridges and tunnels. The dis-

patcher has the ability to remotely lock or unlock a door via the keyboard.

Keys are readily available for maintenance staff, emergency responders, part-time employees, and building management through a device called a Key Safe. It works like a bank vault, storing master keys in a locked drawer and maintaining a list of authorized users. Each key is logged in and out, and missing master key rings are immediately identified by a time-out alarm. In many locations, the security officer is dispatched from the office with a designated key to assist someone who is locked out.

The final ingredient in a control room is proper training. IFPO sponsors a protection officer and supervisor program, which provides an excellent understanding of the functions and tools of a security employee.

Additionally, the manufacturers of most communications equipment offer in-service instruction, which covers operation and troubleshooting. Private seminar workshops, held in major cities, give assistance with general topics such as customer service, telephone techniques, stress management, and group dynamics. Dispatch organizations, including APCO and NENA, specialize in telecommunications education from 911 to emergency management. ASIS has workshops in video surveillance, access control, and false alarm reduction. NBFAA and CSAA have a central alarm operator certification program, which is required by many private alarm companies.

Local police and fire departments have workshops in crime prevention, fire alarm response, and occupant safety. Security center management should provide ongoing education for the operators, including cross training.

The control center remains at the heart of any security agency, ranging from the one-man post in a small corporate building to the ten-man fully automated alarm station in a nationwide location. The basic equipment remains the same, with radios and phones still being the primary tools. In addition, computers and digital electronic devices have made the dispatcher's tasks easier. Records are kept in the CAD computer and the tape recorder. Intercoms and video cameras link the operator to the public. Fire, burglar, and auxiliary alarms protect lives and properties. Buildings are secured via electronic access control and Key Safes. Most importantly, trained dispatchers operate the apparatus and notify the responders. A well-designed and appropriately equipped control room is an integral component of any security and loss prevention department.

```
 =  ? =  ┌─────────────────────────┐  = ? =
          │     SECURITY QUIZ       │
          │   Central Alarm Stations │
          │   and Dispatch Centers  │
          └─────────────────────────┘
```

1. The main door to the dispatch center should be unlocked at all times.
   ☐ T ☐ F

2. What is the minimum number of operators suggested by the Underwriters' Labs and the NBFAA for any dispatch center?
   _____

3. The two most important tools in a dispatch center are the _____ and the
   _____.

4. All types of alarm signals are collected by the receiver in the dispatch center.
   ☐ T ☐ F

5. The time clock was replaced by the _____ in modern dispatch centers.

6. Some call boxes are equipped with a red light.
   ☐ T ☐ F

7. The _____ is a special telephone that connects the dispatch center with other agencies.

8. The access card reader can be remotely controlled by the dispatch center.
   ☐ T ☐ F

9. Name two organizations that provide training for dispatchers.
   _____

   _____

10. The _____ is at the heart of any security agency.

ACCESS CONTROL

By Colin Best, CPO

INTRODUCTION

The concept of access control is relatively simple. Access control is essentially what the wording implies, the control of access to property, services, events, or information. A large part of the protection of assets, personnel, and information begins with controlling access to them and the facilities where they exist. The function of access control is fundamental to the protection officer in his or her duties. The security officer will almost certainly be expected to perform a duty relative to access control during the course of their employment. Access control is usually more than just the face at the front door. Access control is a combination of several things including control, record keeping, and careful planning. In many instances, access to a given area may be by patrol and identifying any people in the area being patrolled. Other forms may be by monitoring large-scale access control, alarms, and CCTV systems.

One typical example of access control begins at the desk of the security officer at the front entrance of an office building, industrial facility, or other property. This area is often called a "checkpoint" or "guard station." This checkpoint is often a fixed post, meaning the officer is posted permanently until relieved or when policy and/or post orders dictate. The presence of the officer in the key location of common access is a deterrent to those who may be unauthorized to enter the protected area or structure. In addition to the deterrent function, an officer familiar with the protected property and its frequent occupants will recognize those who are common to the property and can challenge those who are unauthorized. This form of aiding control of access is common in large apartment complexes. Recognition of regular occupants by the security officer is a very reliable form of controlling access.

Achieving the task of controlling access may be considered somewhat difficult if an officer were for example, assigned the task to control access to a property consisting of acres of land with no fences or physical boundaries. Access control might only be achieved by frequent patrols of the protected area, challenging those unfamiliar caught on the property. In this example, it may be the accepted form of access control and no further control may be necessary. Most facilities require additional forms of controlling access, such as our national borders, waste sites, storage yards, and many other facilities.

It is this reason that it usually becomes necessary to utilize various forms of physical security in order to achieve access control suitable to the facility or property being protected. Fences may be erected around a property to control access and to force or "funnel" visitors or employees to a common entrance, or checkpoint manned by the protection officer. Appropriate signage indicating a no trespassing order will aid in controlling access with the understanding that anyone trying to breach security and access the forbidden area risks arrest and charges. In situations where it is expected that the protection officer arrest anyone caught trespassing, it is crucial that signage is in accordance with the laws concerning the trespass act. It is also extremely important that it is within the legal rights of the protection officer to perform the arrest. The addition of locks to alternate entrances to the facility or property will further control access. Other forms of additional physical security, such as CCTV and alarm systems, will further assist in the prevention of unauthorized access, though physical security must not interrupt safe egress from the property or site in the event of an emergency.

EMERGENCY ACCESS CONTROL

One must take caution in controlling access that egress in the event of an emergency is not sacrificed. Local and national fire codes often present challenges to controlling access to many facilities and it is imperative that there is no sacrifice to the safety of the occupants of a facility in order to achieve better security. In most instances, policies are drastically altered for access in an emergency. Where policy dictates, a fixed post may become a roaming position for the officer to facilitate an escort for emergency medical services or the fire department. The opposite may be true in where a roaming officer will be called from a patrol to fixed position at the entrance of the protected facility to provide speedy access for emergency service dispatched.

Generally, an emergency, such as fire, medical, hazardous spill, or gas release, should result in the halt of all work in the facility to help facilitate access. Elevators and other conveyances and facilities designated for emergency use should be immediately surrendered from casual use for use by the emergency service dispatched. Parking control at a facility entrance or loading dock can be considered an access control duty where entrances are kept clear to make way for emergency personnel.

EXAMPLES OF ACCESS CONTROL

Now that a given facility or property has been equipped with fences, locks, and other barriers, access can be controlled at one focal point. Visitors and workers can be directed to one common point of access, but still one question remains unanswered. What prevents those unauthorized to simply access the facility by way of the front entrance where the security officer is stationed? This is the reason for a policy for access control. The policy should outline a clear definition of the requirements for access to the property. For instance, a facility such as a nightclub may only permit access to those of a consenting age, so it may be required to present a valid operator's license to gain access. Some facilities may require the presentation of an invitation or ticket for a public venue or private function, such as concerts, large weddings, or other events. Sometimes the officer will be assigned access control to a parking garage and handling of cash becomes part of the assignment. The protection officer may control access to other services. For example, the officer may control access to a conveyance such as managing elevator bookings or to a loading area or entrance. The issue of visitor and contractor badges may accomplish control of access by temporary contractors. Office and industrial facilities may require the presentation of company identification.

The identification industry is becoming more and more advanced and many large corporations are implementing identification systems as corporate standards for all employees. Unfortunately, the tools to replicate identification are becoming more available to the criminal population. Dye-sublimation card printers are readily available and are compatible with most personal computers and graphics programs. It is this reason that many companies are adding modern security features to their corporate IDs. The use of holograms and watermarking making replication of a well designed identification card difficult by unauthorized persons. Company identification can be combined or integrated

Figure 3-5   Corporate ID Card
Source: Hughes Identification Devices

with an access card for the facility. In addition, the security officer may be provided with a list or permits for authorized personnel. Those appearing on permits or lists will be the only persons allowed access.

AUDIT AND RECORD KEEPING

Signing in a security register or muster is a common form of controlling access. The necessity to sign in the security register can be considered a valid deterrent to unauthorized visitors even if the visitor needs not present any other credential. This form of controlling access can be applied to many facilities and areas. The security register can have two functions. The register can be used as an audit trail of who accessed the facilities at any given time. The register can also be used for reference by the fire department to obtain a list of who's in during a facility emergency such as a fire. A register commonly contains information such as the name, employee number, work location, and phone number, as well as the time in and time out, and signature or initials of the individual requiring access. The officer assigned to maintaining the security register should be prepared to assist those unfamiliar with the process in order to keep neat and consistent files. Records of this nature should be archived for retrieval according to the policies outlined by your employer or the client. Once expired, their contents must be considered confidential and should be destroyed prior to disposal. Control of confidentiality of these files can be considered part of the access control duty.

ACCESS AUTHORIZATION

During the course of performing the function of access control, it may become necessary to deny access to those without proper credentials. The person wishing to gain access may very well have legitimate business on the protected property and outright denial could create losses for the facility or property being protected. It is this reason that a clear policy for the denial of access for individuals without proper credential needs to exist.

There are some facilities that may employ a strict "No Authorization, No Access" policy that will dictate that the person requesting access without proper credentials is denied. Many facilities will have a "backup" procedure to obtain the proper authorization for access. One example may be that a facility manager or supervisor could be called to provide verbal authority for access. Another may dictate that a visitor needing access would be required to call an authorized occupant in the facility to provide an escort.

When the security officer is left with the decision whether or not to allow access, it is usually best that the officer acts on the side of caution and denies access tentatively until a fair approval or compromise is reached. Advising the person that he or she has to be denied access is an act best accomplished with diplomacy and respect. The event of the denial should also be documented on a report suitable for the employer or client. Policies for granting and denying access should comprise part of the protection officer's post orders.

APPLYING PHYSICAL SECURITY IN ACCESS CONTROL

For many facilities, the control of access at one point may not be practical, particularly in large facilities with many areas, such as industrial and office buildings, where it may be necessary to control access to areas within the facilities. Posting officers at these various checkpoints to control access would be an effective form of access control; however, in most circumstances that would not be a cost-effective long-term solution. These areas may consist of executive offices, chemical rooms, file rooms, and any other area that may require the limiting or curtailing access. Rather than posting an officer at every area, most often access is controlled by way of applying physical security barriers such as doors, locks, CCTV, alarms, and electronic access control. The effectiveness of physical security is further enhanced by strict key control, effective monitoring of CCTV and alarm systems by the security officer, and accurate database management in electronic access control systems. One important tool used in aiding access control is intercom, telephone, and other voice communications systems. Requests for access can be requested from remote points within the facility, allowing an officer to be dispatched or grant access remotely from an electronic access system, given proper authorization.

Locks and Key Control

Locks and keys have been around for literally thousands of years and are definitely the standard for controlling access in many areas. Since their invention, the durability and security of locks and keys have greatly increased along with the use of them. Today, they help control access to almost every structure imaginable. Generally speaking, the lock is a mechanical device consisting of a cylinder, springs, and several pins or 'tumblers' preventing the rotation of the lock cylinder without the insertion of a correctly cut brass key. Higher security locks manufactured today make unauthorized replication virtually impossible. Proprietary key blanks can have a restricted issue to one distributor. A restricted proprietary keyway combined with strict key control is an effective form of controlling access. Permanent keys should not be issued without signature or receipt. Identical keys should each have unique control numbers permanently stamped on the key to identify issue. Temporary issue of keys should be accompanied by signature on a register or key sign out form indicating a return time. All codes and control numbers appearing on the keys should be documented on all documentation for key sign out. All key control documentation should be considered confidential and subject to similar record keeping procedures as the security register.

Electronic Access Control Systems

With the addition of electronic access control to a facility, the officer can gain control by many individuals to different

Figure 3-6   Lock and Key
Source: Schlage

areas of the facility at different times in great volumes. Most access systems installed today provide ease of access for authorized parties to come and go to their authorized destinations. Access is gained by presentation of a card or other physical medium to a "reader." The reader is usually connected electronically to an "interface" or "controller," which in turn is usually connected to a host computer system. Modern systems usually will have a technology present where the controller will make local decisions for access control and retain history transactions locally in the event of a host computer failure or scheduled maintenance. This feature is usually called distributed technology and the activation of this feature is often referred to as "degraded mode'" When access is granted to a given area, the access transaction is usually stored electronically on disk, tape, or printed media for future retrieval as part of a "history." The attempt of a person to gain access where it is not permitted can usually be reported as an alarm on a computer screen directing the security officer to take a predetermined action. Specifics as to the name, ID number, time of transaction, and type of denial are also recorded electronically to histories as well as other alarms. Histories and other system reports can be customized in various ways and can be a valuable aid in the investigation of various incidents as well as controlling time and attendance.

The industry of electronic access systems is continually expanding in terms of technologies, manufacturers, and installations. The majority of these systems are becoming more affordable and easier to use, whereas the technology that makes the systems work is becoming more and more advanced. The compiling of modern, easy to use graphical interface software has made the management of "enterprise" scale systems a much easier task than just a few years ago. Older enterprise scale systems use operating systems and software that consist mostly of typed command line interfaces that are less user friendly than the more recent Windows-based technology. Front-end computers on these earlier systems usually require more frequent maintenance and are more costly to repair than the modern systems being installed today. Installation of an electronic access control system will also contribute to the control of keys. Master keys need only be issued in certain circumstances and may be signed out only when necessary. A daily sign out control policy can ensure that master keys need never leave the property. Most access systems installed use a card or similar medium to provide access in place of the key. If lost, the card can easily be voided by the operator of the system. This compared to the loss of a master key resulting in the changing of many locks and reissue of keys to all keyholders. The access card has a numeric or binary code that is verified by a computer host ensuring validity. These are the three most common card technologies.

- Magnetic strip
- Proximity
- Wiegand

Magnetic strip technology usually consists of a ferrite strip affixed to a vinyl card. The strip may have several 'tracks' containing binary data to a length of up to 128 bits. The magnetic strip has been the most popular form of card access for years, but is quickly being replaced by the proximity technology. Proximity cards usually work on radio frequencies to provide contactless badging by merely holding the card in proximity of the card reader, hence the name. Convenience and low maintenance are the advantages of proximity. Wiegand is also a popular format due to their durability, low maintenance, and high security. Specially wound wires that are embedded in the access card in certain patterns cause a unique pulse effect when passed through a wiegand reader. There are many other technologies in electronic access control, including the following:

- Hollerith
- Barium ferrite
- Dallas Touch memory
- Smart technology
- Bar code

Use of bar codes as a form of physical security access control is not common due to the lack of security it presents. Most barcodes can easily be copied using a conventional photocopier making it more suitable as an inventory control technology. Any of these technologies can usually be combined with a keypad entry to combine the entry of a PIN in conjunction with the use of the card for a higher level of security.

Modern electronic access systems have many features to enhance the level of access control to a facility, area, or room. Turnstiles, interlocking mantraps, and parkade gates are combined with access readers to prevent passback and "piggybacking" in parking garages and high security areas. Cards may only allow one badge in and one badge out to track the time in and out of the facility or area. Some systems have enhancements such as the addition of "mobility impaired" added to the access system database record to allow the extended opening time of a door. In the event of a stolen card, the card can often be "tagged" with an alarm upon use alerting the operator at the monitoring station to

Figure 3-7   Keypad for Entering Code
Source: Hughes Identification Devices

dispatch security personnel to the location of the cardholder. Meanwhile the card remains active and permits access as not to alert the unauthorized holder of the card.

Systems can be interfaced or integrated with other systems such as building automation, fire systems, and human resources computer databases to name a few. This would allow the access holder to gain access and turn on lights and air conditioning to his or her work area with the use of the access system. With the activation of a fire alarm, an access card could be automatically validated for use by the fire department. The interfacing of electromagnetic locks (Mag Locks) and other specialty electric locking devices to release upon a fire alarm is necessary by most national and local fire codes and is usually subject to verification by an engineer.

ACCESS SYSTEM DATABASE MANAGEMENT

Controlling the access system should have similar strict procedures to that of the key systems. Issue should be controlled by consistent and appropriate documentation. All information should be kept in a cardholder's file where a history of changes and authorizations should be maintained. Typically these files should remain easily accessible until a time has elapsed since termination of the cardholder. This not only assists in audit, but can also control costs as a card with picture identification can be kept on file in the event that the cardholder returns to work in the near future. Returned, damaged, or defective cards should be destroyed and documented in the system database so identical cards can be reissued in the future. Equal attention should be paid to the management of the electronic databases. Spelling and pattern consistency are vital to good database management. Frequent software backups may one day pay off in the event of host server failure.

BIOMETRIC TECHNOLOGIES

Another form of electronic access control does not use a form of card or PIN entry at all. The unique "signature" embedded genetically in parts of our own human bodies are used to provide us access. Hand geometry, finger and thumbprint, and retinal scan readers can often be interfaced with modern access control systems to provide a high security level of access control. This technology is called "biometrics." Biometric readers are usually installed as access control for high security vaults, file rooms, and other high security areas where access is limited to few authorized persons. Security is further heightened when combined with another card type of access technology. The technology still has some drawbacks. The necessary scanning of large databases of authorized personnel is time consuming, even for today's fastest computers, making the technology more suited for smaller areas with limited access. Frequent rescanning of the human feature necessary for access is common too, due to injury or surgery to those using the technology for access.

Figure 3-8   Biometrics Using Hand Geometry
Source: Hughes Identification Devices

Figure 3-9   Computer Password
Source: 100 MEGS Web Hosting

Biometric technology is slowly becoming more commonly used in airports and other immigration checkpoints. Facial recognition technology is integrated in CCTV systems to identify individuals who are either wanted by law enforcement or may not be permitted travel to a given country. Facial recognition technology is fast becoming an important tool in the prevention of international terrorism, smuggling of contraband, and child abduction on an international basis at the point of entry into countries around the world.

ACCESS CONTROL IN THE INFORMATION AGE

Now, there is another form of access control, which has only recently become a necessity on a large scale in the past decade or so. The controlling of access to information in computers comprises a large part of computer security since the mid-1990s brought us the Internet and most large corporate networks became part of the "global handshake." Audit and control of user access to systems is often dedicated to one individual. Most networks have an automatic update feature that will 'force' the end user of the network to regularly change their authentication password on a regular basis to prevent unauthorized entry to a network. Access is curtailed in the form of user "privilege" limiting access to view and edit certain data. Barriers within a computer network called Firewalls prevent access from the network Internet connection.

Another large part of controlling access is security awareness. Identifying and reporting lapses in security can prevent unauthorized access. Closing blinds in a locked office prevents access to some of the visible information held within. Paying extra attention to weaknesses in physical security, policy, and facility design can play a large part of access control. As with many processes, the policies and procedures for controlling access in facilities are sometimes subject to flaws or 'room for improvements' and should be scrutinized by management. Some ideas for change and improvements can be made at the level of the protection officer and discussion with fellow officers concerning problems should be encouraged at shift exchanges during officer briefing and at staff meetings. Tightening security should not be the only criteria for continuous improvement. In many instances, the need for faster authentication of authorized personnel may be considered essential as losses may occur due to the unauthorized person being held up by security.

RESOURCES

Figure 3-5: http://www.recogsyscom/products/hk/pi_handkey_2.htm
Figure 3-6: http://www.schlagelock.com
Figures 3-7 & 3-8: http:// www.hidcorp.com/pages/media.html
Figure 3-9: http://support.100megswebhosting.com/docs/index.htm

1. The point of entry where security is posted to control access is often referred to as a:
   - ☐ (a) storage yard
   - ☐ (b) lunch room
   - ☐ (c) checkpoint
   - ☐ (d) physical security

2. The policy for granting access should be kept:
   - ☐ (a) in a secure file cabinet inaccessible by security personnel
   - ☐ (b) in the site post orders
   - ☐ (c) in a fire resistant waste receptacle
   - ☐ (d) posted in the facility lounge

3. The use of _____ and watermarking make the replication of company identification more difficult.

4. Signing in a security _____ at the front desk of a facility is a common form of controlling access.
   - ☐ (a) control
   - ☐ (b) guard
   - ☐ (c) garage
   - ☐ (d) register

5. Access control records should be kept:
   - ☐ (a) until end of shift, then destroyed
   - ☐ (b) 7 years
   - ☐ (c) a period determined by your employer or the client
   - ☐ (d) 30 days

6. Advising the person that he or she has to be denied access is an act best accomplished with diplomacy and _____.

7. Besides its use as an audit trail, the register can be used by _____ in a facility emergency as a muster of who is inside.
   - ☐ (a) emergency services (Fire, EMS)
   - ☐ (b) security management
   - ☐ (c) facility management
   - ☐ (d) the criminal population

8. The three most popular access card technologies are _____, proximity, and wiegand cards.

9. _____ of regular occupants in a facility by the security officer is considered a very reliable form of controlling access.
   ☐ (a) Arrest
   ☐ (b) Recognition
   ☐ (c) Search
   ☐ (d) Control

10. _____ recognition technology is integrated in CCTV systems to identify individuals who are wanted by law enforcement.

Unit 4

Introduction to Computer Security
Information Security

INTRODUCTION TO COMPUTER SECURITY

By Cole Morris, CPP, CFE, CPO

Today's security officer must work in an increasingly technological environment. When it comes to computer security, a basic awareness of issues, potential threats, and recommended procedures is rapidly becoming a job requirement for those charged with the protection of people and property.

Computers and networks originally were built to ease the exchange of information. Early information technology (IT) systems were focused on central computers or large mainframe systems. In those days, security was a relatively straightforward affair. The computer users were limited in number. Likewise, the machines were kept in a few locked rooms. However, with the advent of the personal computer and information networks, new security issues arise. What some thought impossible has become reality and today businesses are being driven by the power of the personal computer. These computers are often accessed with little more than a password.

The information age has also opened new horizons for crime. Today, attackers are using the information revolution to steal passwords and gain access to information or to create disastrous effects on networks and computers.

THE GROWING PROBLEM

In 2002 the Computer Security Institute (CSI) announced the results of its seventh annual "Computer Crime and Security Survey." The survey provides an excellent idea of the threats facing computer users.

The survey was conducted by CSI with the participation of the San Francisco Federal Bureau of Investigation's (FBI) Computer Intrusion Squad. Based on responses from 503 computer security practitioners in U.S. corporations, government agencies, financial institutions, medical institutions, and universities, the report provided the following highlights:

- Ninety percent of respondents (primarily large corporations and government agencies) detected computer security breaches within the last 12 months.
- Eighty percent acknowledged financial losses due to computer breaches.
- Forty-four percent (223 respondents) were willing and/or able to quantify their financial losses. These 223 respondents reported $455,848,000 in financial losses.
- As in previous years, the most serious financial losses occurred through theft of proprietary information (26

respondents reported $170,827,000) and financial fraud (25 respondents reported $115,753,000).
- For the fifth year in a row, more respondents (74 percent) cited their Internet connection as a frequent point of attack than cited their internal systems as a frequent point of attack (33 percent).
- Thirty-four percent reported the intrusions to law enforcement. (In 1996, only 16 percent acknowledged reporting intrusions to law enforcement.)
- Forty percent detected system penetration from the outside.
- Forty percent detected denial of service attacks.
- Seventy-eight percent detected employee abuse of Internet access privileges (for example, downloading pornography or pirated software, or inappropriate use of e-mail systems).
- Eighty-five percent detected computer viruses.

The growth of the Internet and electronic commerce is also having an impact, For example, the survey reported the following:
- Ninety-eight percent of respondents have WWW sites.
- Fifty-two percent conduct electronic commerce on their sites.
- Thirty-eight percent suffered unauthorized access or misuse on their Web sites within the last 12 months. Twenty-one percent said that they didn't know if there had been unauthorized access or misuse.
- Twenty-five percent of those acknowledging attacks reported from two to five incidents. Thirty-nine percent reported ten or more incidents.
- Seventy percent of those attacked reported vandalism (only 64 percent in 2000).
- Fifty-five percent reported denial of service (only 60 percent in 2000).
- Twelve percent reported theft of transaction information.
- Six percent reported financial fraud (only 3 percent in 2000).

WHAT IS COMPUTER SECURITY?

Computer security means to protect information. It deals with the prevention and detection of unauthorized actions by users of a computer. In recent years, computer security has been expanded to include issues such as privacy, confidentiality, and information integrity.

Today's security specialist must understand that information has value. Protective measures must be developed and enforced to protect it. Measures designed to protect information should consist of three components.

Prevention: An organization must take actions to protect its information. This includes measures to prevent information from being lost, stolen, damaged, or altered. Preventive measures can include basic physical security practices such as locking the sever room door or checking for company identification cards.

Detection: An information protection plan must include actions that permit an organization to detect when information has been stolen, altered, or damaged. It should allow you to determine who committed the unauthorized act. There are many tools on the market that can help the computer security specialist detect electronic intrusions, alterations, damage, and viruses.

Reaction: A plan should also include actions that enable the recovery of electronic information, even if information is damaged or lost.

Each of these three components contributes to the protection of information as it is stored in computer systems. However, to be effective, the protection officer must also understand how information may be compromised. As with other aspects of security, you cannot take protective measures unless you understand the nature of the threat. Information has several characteristics, each of which provide a possible avenue for compromise.

Confidentiality: This is the cornerstone of many computer security programs. It is the prevention of unauthorized disclosure of information. Confidentiality can be lost as a result of poor security measures or information leaks by personnel. An example of poor security measures would be to allow an unauthorized person access to sensitive company or personal information.

Integrity: This is the prevention of erroneous modification of information. Computer security experts report *authorized* computer users are probably the biggest cause of mistakes and the inaccurate changing of data. Storing incorrect information can have grave consequences. In fact, in many situations, storing incorrect information can be as disastrous as losing information.

Availability: This includes the prevention of unauthorized withholding of information or computer resources. Information should be as freely available as possible to *authorized* users. In other words, computer data is of little value if people cannot get to it.

Authentication: This is the process of verifying that users are who they claim to be when logging onto a computer system. Generally, the use of user names and passwords accomplishes this. More sophisticated systems use various biometric technologies. It is important to note authentication does not grant the user access rights to resources. Instead, this occurs during the *authorization* process.

Authorization: This is the process of allowing only authorized users access to sensitive information. An authorization process uses the appropriate security policies and procedures to determine whether a computer user should have access to specific resources.

THREATS

In today's world, information is a crucial asset in most organizations. Companies gain a competitive advantage by knowing how to use information. A common threat includes others who would like to acquire your organization's information or limit business opportunities by interfering with normal business processes.

The object of computer security is to protect sensitive organizational information while making it readily available to the people who need it. Attackers trying to harm a system or disrupt normal business operations exploit vulnerabilities by using various tactics.

Like anyone else, people who attack computer systems generally have motives or goals. For example, they may want to disrupt normal business operations or steal information. They may be motivated by revenge, monetary gain, or business advantage. Others may be attracted simply by the technical challenge. In all cases, these individuals use various methods to take advantage of vulnerabilities in a computer system or an organization's security practices.

Threats can come in many forms. Natural phenomena can impact a computer system just as seriously as a human attack. For instance, earthquakes, hurricanes, floods, lightning, and fire can cause severe damage to computer systems. Information can be lost, downtime or loss of productivity can occur, and damage to hardware can disrupt other essential services. Few safeguards can be implemented against natural disasters. Obviously, your organization's disaster response plan must include information systems and computer security issues. Such contingency plans should also include hostile action such as riots, wars, and terrorist attacks.

Human Threats

Since there is little you can do to defend against natural disasters and social unrest, it is prudent to consider potential threats you *can* control.

For example, *malicious threats* include inside attacks by disgruntled or malicious employees and outside attacks by non-employees just looking to harm and disrupt an organization. A malicious attacker uses a *method* to exploit *vulnerabilities* in order to achieve a *goal*.

Vulnerabilities are weak points or loopholes in security that an attacker exploits in order to gain access to the network or to resources on the network.

Experience tells us the most dangerous attackers are usually insiders (or former insiders), because they know many of the computer procedures, systems, programs, and security measures that are used by the organization. Insiders are likely to have specific goals and objectives, and have legitimate access to the system. These people are likely to cause the most damage to a computer system. Insiders can plant viruses, Trojan horses, or worms. Likewise, they often know where the most valuable information is stored in the computer system.

The insider attack can affect all components of computer security. By browsing through a system, confidential information can be acquired. Trojan horses are a threat to both the integrity and confidentiality of information in the system. Insider attacks can affect availability by overloading the system's processing or storage capacity, or by causing the system to crash.

Hackers and Crackers

People who "break in" to computer systems are often called "crackers" or "hackers." The definition of *hacker* has changed over the years. A hacker was once any individual who enjoyed getting the most out of the computer he or she was using. A hacker would use a system extensively and study it until they became proficient in all its capabilities. These individuals were respected and served as a resource for local computer users, groups, clubs, and software developers.

Today, however, the term *hacker* refers to people who either break in to systems for which they have no authorization or intentionally overstep their bounds on systems for which they do not have legitimate access.

The correct term to use for someone who breaks in to systems is a *cracker*. Common methods for gaining access to a system include password cracking, exploiting known security weaknesses, network spoofing, and social engineering.

Malicious attackers normally will have a specific goal, objective, or motive for an attack on a system. These goals could be to disrupt services and the continuity of business operations by using denial-of-service (DoS) attack software packages. They might also want to steal information or even hardware such as laptop computers. Hackers can sell information that can be useful to competitors.

Nonmalicious threats usually come from employees who are untrained in computers and are unaware of security threats and vulnerabilities. You should realize that poorly trained employees usually have no motives and goals for causing damage. The damage is accidental. In many cases, malicious attackers can deceive poorly trained employees by using "social engineering" to gain entry to a computer system. For example, the intruder can claim to be a system administrator and ask for passwords and user names. Employees who are not well trained and are not security aware often fall victim to this tactic.

MOTIVATIONS

There is a strong overlap between physical security and data privacy and integrity. Indeed, the goal of some attacks is not the physical destruction of the computer system but the penetration and removal or copying of company information. Types of attacks can include the following:

Committing information theft and fraud: Information technology is increasingly used to commit fraud and theft. Computer systems are exploited in numerous ways, both by automating traditional methods of fraud and by using new methods. Financial systems are not the only ones subject to fraud. Other targets are systems that control access to any resources, such as time and attendance systems, inventory systems, school-grading systems, or long-distance telephone systems.

Disrupting normal business operations: Attackers may want to disrupt normal business operations. In any circumstance like this, the attacker has a specific goal to achieve.

Deleting and altering information: Malicious attackers who delete or alter information normally do this to prove a point or take revenge. Inside attackers normally do this to spite the organization. Outside attackers might want to do this to prove that they can get in to the system. They are motivated by the technical challenge.

ATTACK METHODS

Malicious attackers can gain access and interfere in your company's computer in several different ways:

Viruses: Attackers can develop harmful computer code known as viruses. Using hacking techniques, they can break into systems and plant viruses. Viruses come in different forms and although not always malicious, they always take up time. Viruses can also be spread via e-mail and floppy disks.

Denial-of-service attacks: This attack exploits the need to have a service available. It is a growing trend on the Internet because Web sites in general are open doors that often invite an attack.

Trojan horses: These are malicious programs or software code hidden inside what looks like a normal program. When a user runs the normal program, the hidden code runs as well. It can then start deleting files and causing other damage to the computer. Trojan horses are normally spread by e-mail attachments.

Worms: These are programs that run independently and travel from computer to computer across network connections. Worms may have portions of themselves running on many different computers. Worms do not change other programs, although they may carry other code that does.

Password cracking: Attackers use this tactic to secretly gain system access through another user's account. This is possible because users often select weak passwords. The two major problems with passwords are when they are easy to guess based on knowledge of the user (for example, a favorite sports team) and when they are vulnerable to dictionary attacks (that is, using a computerized dictionary as the source of guesses).

E-mail hacking: With access to Internet e-mail, someone can potentially correspond with anyone of millions of people worldwide. These are some of the threats associated with e-mail.

Impersonation: The sender address on Internet e-mail cannot be trusted because the sender can create a false return address. For instance, an e-mail might appear to come from a company executive directing the sale of company assets. In fact, the e-mail might have originated from someone totally outside the organization.

Eavesdropping: E-mail headers and contents that are transmitted in the clear text without encryption can be intercepted and read by unauthorized individuals. E-mail can also be altered in transit or redirected to an unintended audience.

Social engineering: This is a common form of cracking. It can be used by outsiders and by people within an organization. Social engineering is a hacker term for tricking people into revealing their password or some form of security information.

Network spoofing: In network spoofing, a computer system presents itself to the network as though it were a different system (computer A impersonates computer B by sending B's address instead of its own). This allows an unauthorized computer to join a network and thus, have access to an organization's information.

SECURITY POLICIES

Policies can be defined for any area of security. It is up to the security manager or IT manager to classify what policies need to be defined and who should plan the policies. As a protection officer you should be aware of these policies and be prepared to help enforce them. Keep in mind, there could be policies for the whole company or policies for various sections within the company. The various types of policies you may encounter include the following:

- Password policies
- Administrative responsibilities
- User responsibilities
- E-mail policies
- Internet policies
- Backup and restore policies

Password policies: The security provided by a password system depends on the passwords being kept secret at all times. Thus, a password is vulnerable to compromise whenever it is used, stored, or even known. When it comes to passwords, the security specialist or protection officer should realize the following:

1. A password must be initially assigned to a user when enrolled on the system.
2. A user's password must be changed periodically.
3. Users must remember their passwords.
4. Users must enter their passwords into the system at authentication time.
5. Employees may not disclose their passwords to anyone. This includes administrators and IT managers.

Administrative responsibilities Many computer systems and software programs come from the manufacturer with a few standard user logins already enrolled in the system. The IT staff should change the passwords for all standard user logins before allowing the general user population to access the system. For example, change administrator password when installing the system.

The system administrator is responsible for generating and assigning the initial password for each user login. The user must then be informed of this password. Individual users should then change their issued password to a personalized, confidential password.

When a user's initial password must be exposed to the administrator, having the user immediately change the password will minimize this exposure.

Occasionally, a user will forget the password or the administrator may determine that a user's password may have been compromised. To be able to correct these problems, it is recommended that the administrator be permitted to change the password of any user by generating a new one. The administrator should not have to know the user's password in order to do this, but should follow the same rules for distributing the new password that apply to initial password assignment. Positive identification of the user by the administrator is required when a forgotten password must be replaced.

User responsibilities: Users should understand their responsibility to keep passwords private and to report changes in their user status, suspected security violations, and so forth. To assure security awareness among the user population, each user should be required to sign a statement to acknowledge understanding these responsibilities.

The simplest way to recover from the compromise of a password is to change it. Therefore, passwords should be changed on a periodic basis to counter the possibility of undetected password compromise. They should be changed often enough so that there is an acceptably low probability of compromise during a password's lifetime. To avoid needless exposure of users' passwords to the administrator, users should be able to change their passwords without intervention by the administrator.

E-mail policies: E-mail is increasingly critical to the normal conduct of business. Organizations need policies for e-mail to help employees use e-mail properly, to reduce the risk of intentional or inadvertent misuse, and to ensure that official records transferred via e-mail are properly handled. As with other company requirements, you may be required to enforce e-mail policies as a routine part of your job. These policies typically include guidance regarding the following:

- The use of e-mail to conduct official business
- The use of e-mail for personal business
- Access control and confidential protection of messages
- The management and retention of e-mail messages

Internet policies: The World Wide Web has a body of software and a set of protocols and conventions used to traverse and find information over the Internet. The Web is easy for anyone to roam, browse, and contribute to. The important thing to understand is that an employee's access to the Internet also provides a potential gateway into your company's network. This exposure can be minimized with the installation of firewalls and other solutions. Nonetheless, organizational policies must clearly define appropriate use of the Internet. As with e-mail policies, such guidance is very similar to that published regarding the use of company telephones, credit cards, and copier machines.

Backup and restore policies: Backups are important only if the information stored on the system is of value. Backups are important for a number of reasons.

- Computer hardware failure
- Software failure
- User error
- Administrator error
- Hacking and vandalism
- Theft
- Natural disasters
- Unforeseeable problems

Information that should be backed up includes important information that is sensitive to the organization and to the continuity of operations. This includes databases, mail servers, and any user files. System databases, such as registries and user account databases, should also be backed-up.

The backup polices should include plans for the following:

- Regularly scheduled backups
- Types of backups. Most backup systems support normal backups, incremental backups, and differential backups
- A schedule for backups. The schedule should normally be during the night when the company has the least amount of users.
- The information to be backed up
- Type of media used for backups: tapes, CD-ROMs, other hard drives, and so on
- The type of backup devices: tape devices, CD writers, hard drives, and so on

Onsite storage: Store backups in a fireproof safe. Backups should not be stored in the drawer of the table on which the computer sits. Secure storage protects against natural disaster, theft, and sabotage of critical data. All software including operating system software, service packs, and other critical application software should also be safely stored.

Offsite storage: Important data should also be stored offsite. Several firms specialize in storing data. An alternative solution could be using a safe deposit box and a bank.

Information is the lifeblood of most organizations. Your awareness of its importance and value is crucial if you are to perform your duties properly. By understanding potential threats and by complying with sound security policies, the modern protection practitioner plays a key role in the continued success of his or her organization.

COMPUTER SECURITY TERMINOLOGY

When dealing with computer security topics, the protection officer will quickly discover a multitude of new terminol-ogy and specialized jargon. Although the following is certainly not an all-inclusive glossary, these terms are commonly used when considering computer security issues.

back door: a potential weakness intentionally left in the security of a computer system or its software by its designers

biometrics: the use of a computer user's unique physical characteristics—such as voice, fingerprints, retinal and iris scans, or facial geometry—to identify that user

Computer Emergency Response Team (CERT): organizations or computer specialists that collect and distribute information about security breaches

countermeasure: any measure or device that reduces a computer system's vulnerability

cracker: a term occasionally used to refer to a hacker who breaks into a system with the intent of causing damage or stealing information

cybercrime: crime related to technology, computers, and the Internet

denial of service (DoS): an attack that causes the targeted system to be unable to fulfill its intended function

e-mail: an application that allows the sending of messages between computer users via a network

encryption: the process of protecting information or hiding its meaning by converting it into a code

firewall: a device designed to enforce the boundary between two or more networks, limiting access

hacker: a term sometimes used to describe a person who pursues knowledge of computer and security systems for its own sake; sometimes used to describe a person who breaks into computer systems for the purpose of stealing or destroying data

information security: a system of procedures and policies designed to protect and control information

intranet: a private network used within a company or organization that is not connected to the Internet

intrusion detection: techniques designed to detect breaches into a computer system or network

malicious code: any code that is intentionally included in software or hardware for an unauthorized purpose

phreaker: a person who hacks telephone systems, usually for the purpose of making free phone calls

Trojan horse: an apparently innocuous program that contains code designed to surreptitiously access information or computer systems without the user's knowledge

virus: a computer program designed to make copies of itself and spread itself from one machine to another without the help of the user

worm: a computer program that copies itself across a network

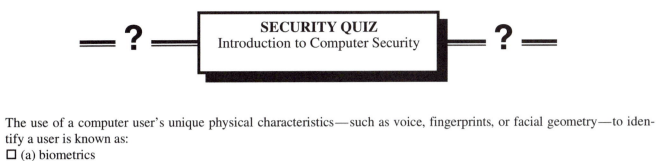

SECURITY QUIZ
Introduction to Computer Security

1. The use of a computer user's unique physical characteristics—such as voice, fingerprints, or facial geometry—to identify a user is known as:
   - ☐ (a) biometrics
   - ☐ (b) encryption
   - ☐ (c) digital security
   - ☐ (d) phreaking

2. What type of attack causes the targeted system to be unable to fulfill its intended function?
   - ☐ (a) Covert
   - ☐ (b) Denial of Service (DoS)
   - ☐ (c) Encrypted
   - ☐ (d) Modem assault

3. "IT" stands for:
   - ☐ (a) information technology
   - ☐ (b) interactive technology
   - ☐ (c) intelligent translation
   - ☐ (d) internet technology

4. In recent years, computer security has been expanded to include issues such as:
   - ☐ (a) privacy
   - ☐ (b) information integrity
   - ☐ (c) confidentiality
   - ☐ (d) All of the above

5. Measures designed to protect information should consist of three components. Which of the following is not one of these components?
   - ☐ (a) Prevention
   - ☐ (b) Reaction
   - ☐ (c) Retention
   - ☐ (d) Detection

6. This is the prevention of unauthorized disclosure of information. It can be lost as a result of poor security measures or information leaks by personnel.
   - ☐ (a) Integrity
   - ☐ (b) Confidentiality
   - ☐ (c) Availability
   - ☐ (d) Liability

7. This includes the prevention of unauthorized withholding of information or computer resources.
   - ☐ (a) Confidentiality
   - ☐ (b) Availability
   - ☐ (c) Integrity
   - ☐ (d) Compatibility

8. A malicious attacker uses a method to exploit _____ in order to achieve a goal.
   - ☐ (a) back doors
   - ☐ (b) vulnerabilities
   - ☐ (c) people
   - ☐ (d) software

9. The correct term to use for someone who breaks into systems is a:
   - ☐ (a) "cracker"
   - ☐ (b) "hacker"
   - ☐ (c) administrator
   - ☐ (d) "user"

10. These are malicious programs or software code hidden inside what looks like a normal program.
    ☐ (a) Malicious e-mail
    ☐ (b) Virus
    ☐ (c) Biometric
    ☐ (d) Trojan horse

READINGS

The following readings are recommended if the student wishes to gain a more in-depth knowledge of the topic.

Computer Security

Enger, Norman L. and Paul W. Howerton. *Computer Security: A Management Audit Approach.* New York: AMACOM, 1980.

Freedman, Warren. *The Right of Privacy in the Computer Age.* New York: Quorum, 1987.

Hoffman, Lance J. *Modern Methods for Computer Security and Privacy.* Englewood Cliffs: Prentice-Hall, 1977.

Martin, James. *Security, Accuracy, and Privacy in Computer Systems.* Englewood Cliffs: Prentice-Hall, 1973.

Rullo, Thomas A., ed. *Advances in Computer Security Management, Vol. I.* Philadelphia: Heyden, 1980.

Schweitzer, James A. *Managing Information Security: A Program for the Electronic Information Age.* Boston: Butterworth, 1982.

Trainor, Timothy N. and Diane Krasnewich. *Computers!* Santa Cruz: Mitchell, 1987.

Data Security/Cryptography

Denning, Dorothy Elizabeth Robling. *Cryptography and Data Security.* Reading: Addison-Wesley, 1982.

Katzan, Harry, Jr. *Computer Data Security.* New York: Van Norstrand Reinhold, 1973.

U.S. Department of Commerce. *Computer Science and Technology: Computer Security and the Data Encryption Standard.* NS Special Publication 500-27. National Bureau of Standards, 1978.

U.S. Department of Commerce. *Computer Science and Technology: The Network Security Center: A System Level Approach to Computer Network Security.* NS Special Publication 500-21, Vol. 2, 1978.

BIBLIOGRAPHY

"ATM Card Rip-offs: Who Pays?" *Money,* November 1985, p. 13.

Baier, Kurt and Nicholas Rescher, eds. *Values and the Future.* New York: Free Press, 1971.

Bequai, A. "The Rise of Cashless Crimes (electronic funds transfer systems)." *USA Today,* January 1986, pp. 83–85.

Berney, K. "The Cutting Edge." *Nation's Business,* April 1986, p. 57.

Comer, J.P. "Computer Ethics." *Parents,* September 1985, p. 158.

DeGeorge, Richard T. *Business Ethics.* New York: MacMillan, 1982.

Denning, Dorothy Elizabeth Robling. *Cryptography and Data Security.* Reading: Addison-Wesley, 1982.

Elmer-Dewitt, P. "Cracking Down." *Time,* 14 May 1984, p. 83.

Elmer-Dewitt, P. "The Great Satellite Caper (arrest of New Jersey teenage hackers)." *Time,* 29 July 1985, p. 65.

Elmer-Dewitt, P. "Surveying the Data Diddlers" (Study released by National Center for Computer Crime Data). *Time,* 17 February, 1986, p. 95.

Enger, Norman L. and Paul W. Howerton. *Computer Security: A Management Audit Approach.* New York: AMACOM, 1980.

Eskow, D. and L. Green. "Catching Computer Crooks." *Popular Mechanics,* June 1984, pp. 63–65+.

Filepski, A. and J. Hanko. "Making Unix Secure." *BYTE,* April 1986, pp. 113–114+.

Freedman, Warren. The Right of Privacy in the Computer Age. New York: Quorum, 1987.

Hoffman, Lance J. *Modern Methods for Computer Security and Privacy.* Englewood Cliffs: Prentice-Hall, 1977.

Johnson, D.W. "Computer Ethics." *Futurist,* August 1984, pp. 68–69.

Katzan, Harry, Jr. *Computer Data Security.* New York: Van Nostrand Reinhold, 1973.

Lewis, M. "Computer Crime: Theft in Bits and Bytes." *Nation's Business,* February 1985, pp. 57–58.

Lewis, M. "Scuttling Software Pirates (Association of Data Processing Service Organizations)." *Nation's Business,* March 1985, p. 28.

Mano, D.K. "Computer Crime." *National Review,* 27 July 1984, pp. 51–52.

Martin, James. *Security, Accuracy, and Privacy in Computer Systems.* Englewood Cliffs: Prentice-Hall, 1973.

Morrison, P.R. "Computer Parasites." *Futurist,* March/April 1986, pp. 36–38.

Ognibene, P.J. "Computer Saboteurs." *Science Digest,* July 1984, pp. 58–61.

Peterson, I. "New Data Increase Computer Crime Concerns (report by the American Bar Association)." *Science News,* 23 June 1984, p 390.

Reilly, A. "Computer Crackdown." *Fortune,* 17 September 1984, pp. 141–142.

Rokeach, Milton. *The Nature of Human Values.* New York: Free Press, 1973.

Rullo, Thomas A., ed. *Advances in Computer Security Management, Vol. I.* Philadelphia: Heyden, 1980.

Sandza, R. "The Night of the Hackers." *Newsweek,* 12 November 1984, pp. 17–18.

Sandza, R. "The Revenge of the Hackers (animosity directed at *Newsweek* writer for anti-hacker story)." *Newsweek,* 10 December 1984, p 81.

Schiffres, M. "The Struggle to Thwart Software Pirates." *U.S. News and World Report,* 25 March 1985, p. 72.

Schweitzer, James A. *Managing Information Security: A Program for the Electronic Information Age.* Boston: Butterworth, 1982.

Sterne, R.G. and P.J. Saidman. "Copying Mass-Marketed Software (Lotus lawsuits)." *BYTE,* February 1985, pp. 387–390.

Steward, G. "Computer Sabotage (disgruntled employee at Calgary Herald)." *Macleans,* 23 April 1984, pp. 59–60.

"Three Teenage Hackers Arrested in Computer Scam." *York Daily Record,* 26 July 1987, p. 2A.

Tracey, E.J. "Selling Software on the Honor System (combating piracy by giving programs away)." *Fortune,* 15 October 1984, p. 146.

Trainor, Timothy N. and Diane Krasnewich. *Computers!* Santa Cruz: Mitchell, 1987.

U.S. Department of Commerce. *Computer Science and Technology: Computer Security and the Data Encryption Standard.* NS Special Publication 500-27. National Bureau of Standards, 1978.

U.S. Department of Commerce. *Computer Science and Technology: The Network Security Center: A System Level Approach to Computer Network Security.* NS Special Publication 500-21, Vol. 2. National Bureau of Standards, 1978.

Weberman, B. "Book-entry Blues" (Potential for computerized securities fraud). *Forbes,* 5 May 1986, p. 104.

"When Thieves Sit Down at Computers" (Study by American Bar Association). *U.S. News and World Report,* 25 June 1984, p. 8.

Wyden, R. "Curbing the Keyboard Criminal." *USA Today,* January 1984, pp. 68–70.

"Youths Charged in Computer Crime Ring." *York Daily Record,* 23 July 1987, p 6A.

INFORMATION SECURITY

By Michael Stroberger, CPO, CSS, CPOI, CLSD, CPP

Information security is becoming more important as we continue to progress in technology and business. It is the defending of such information as design documents, formulae, financial information, legal communications, and other data that is critical to the operation and survival of its rightful owner. This is done through certain legal steps, proper physical security, internal confidentiality agreements, and other prudent measures, which will be explored in detail in the following sections.

The protection of such information is not just a game of "Spy vs. Spy," it is often the critical balance that can determine the course of a company's future. Take for example the automotive industry. How well would one company do if its innovative designs for the next market year had been obtained by a competitor who could put production models on the street using the plans that the rightful owner had spent millions in researching? They would appear to have "scooped the competition," and the rightful owners could appear to be, instead of the innovative design leaders, simply following the lead of their competitor.

CRITICAL INFORMATION

In many companies, there is a small percentage of retained information that could either positively or negatively alter the course of that company's future dramatically. How it actually impacts that company depends on exactly how it is used. Here are some examples.

- Design plans
- Research and development program records
- Legal strategies and briefs
- Mailing and client lists
- Budget proposals and forecasts
- Expansion and acquisition plans
- Product formulae
- Personal information, related to employees

Some information is available to those who know where to look and how to look for it. In other cases, persons must go well out of their way and beyond the boundaries of what is legally permissible to obtain it. In every case, if a specific piece of information could have an impact on a business or person, it should be protected in a manner appropriate and proportionate to its potential usefulness.

It is also important to note that, based upon the nature of the actual information, it does not always have to be taken or to be used against its rightful owner. Often, it is seen as a better alternative to simply copy it without the owner being aware that it has been compromised or destroy it altogether. A good example of the first option would be a football coach obtaining a copy of the opponent's playbook. In the early stages, he would get the most benefit from this if the rightful owner were not immediately aware that their plays were known to the opposition. In the latter case, take a moment to imagine the impact of a company suddenly discovering that the original and backup copies of a product design that required six years of work to create had been lost in what appeared to be an accidental erasure of the storage media. In either case, the impact could cripple their effort.

METHODS OF SECURING INFORMATION

The securing of information relies on two key points.

- Who should have access to it?
- In what form is it kept?

Need to Know

The first thing that one must determine when deciding how a certain piece of information will be secured is who actually needs to have access to it. This also relates to how critical it actually is.

If everyone in the company needs to have access to it, it should not be critical to operations, or should not be of a nature that it could be used against the company. The more people that have access to information, the more probable it is that it will be leaked or compromised. Determine who actually has a functional need to know the information, then design the defenses in such a manner that they can still access it, but others cannot.

Form of the Information

The actual methods of securing information may vary largely according to the nature in which it exists. Files on a computer require a very specific type of security programs, while paper files would not benefit from these at all. Some key concepts, based on the nature of the method of storage, should be explored to better understand this.

Paper Documents

Paper documents can be one of the simplest forms to secure, given proper space. They have the benefit of not being sensitive to loss of power, magnetic fields, or being detectable from remote locations while in transit.

Unfortunately, they can become very cumbersome, disorganized, and require large amounts of storage space.

Your best initial line of defense is simply a good physical security program. If unauthorized persons cannot access the room, they cannot access the contents of the room. Access control is critical. To prevent compromise through destruction, fire vaults might be a consideration also. High-quality fire suppression systems used with document containers that reduce the likelihood of the suppression equipment damaging the documents as they activate are also highly recommended.

Try to keep critical paper documentation in defined areas, and require that persons gaining access to it be properly authorized, their identity confirmed, and the limits of movement clearly understood.

Electronic Information

More and more frequently, critical information is being stored and maintained in electronic form. This has brought into being storage programs designed to protect that form of information from unauthorized users. The actual storage hardware and the password and authorization software that limits access to that stored information are best determined based on the cost and potential impact of the uses of that information. Obviously, if you have a formula that is essential to the creation of a product that is only likely to make a profit of $10,000 during its useful lifetime, you would not spend $10,000 on the hardware and software to protect it. All defensive expenditures must be in line with the value of that which it is intended to protect.

Networked systems present additional issues. As they are, by their nature, designed to allow access from multiple locations, you must take care to ensure that the system screens request for critical information based upon the actual location requesting it, the identity of the person requesting it, and the manner in which it would be delivered to that physical location. In many cases, the most critical information can only be accessed from a small number of very specific locations, by a very small number of people.

Information in an electronic form is also potentially compromised while it is in transit. Such methods as faxing, emailing, and even transfer over a network, when the line of communication is accessible, can result in the transmitted information being intercepted. Encryption software should be seriously considered, and again, this should be based upon the actual value or use impact of the information that will be transmitted. Phone lines, fax lines, data lines, and certain wireless transmission systems must all be assessed to determine how vulnerable they are. In the case of wireless systems, it is most alarming that the information could be intercepted without any evidence of this occurring. In the case of other methods, there is usually some form of connection that could be identified in a physical inspection.

Physical Security Aspects

As previously mentioned, the physical security program is a primary resource in the protection of information. If a building is difficult to enter, the offices even more difficult, and the terminal, which can access the storage location, is secured within a hardened container when not in use, the chances of unauthorized access are minimal. Nothing is ever guaranteed, though, and regular audits should be performed.

Communication equipment, carrier lines, and other routes of monitoring transmissions should also be inspected regularly for signs of tampering. In some cases, wiretaps have been found, which appeared to have been in place for a considerable period of time, providing those receiving the signal from them with duplicate copies of each piece of information that had been transmitted over the compromised carrier line.

Physical access of the area should be considered with identity of those attempting to access the storage area being confirmed, possibly at multiple points, as they pass through progressive layers of security.

POLICY AND PROCEDURE FACTORS

Two of the more recognized methods of protecting information from compromise are classification as a "Trade Secret" and use of confidentiality agreements. Both should be considered supporting measures acting in cooperation with physical and electronic methods of protection. These steps provide a psychological deterrent, which dissuades most casual considerations of compromising information.

Trade Secret Status

For any item to be classified as a trade secret, it must meet a set of defined criteria.

- It must be owned and created by those seeking this status.
- It must be effectively controlled, by the owner, through:
  properly labeling the documents / information as "confidential."
  limiting access to only those with a need to know.
  releasing the information to individuals only after they have signed a confidentiality and nondisclosure agreement.

While the first requirement is fairly clear in its intent, the second is often where problems arise. This stipulation simply means that even if the information is produced by the owner, if it is regularly left in unsecured areas, if it fails to bear any form of marking that indicates the sensitive nature of the contents, or if it is carelessly compromised in similar manner, the owner has failed to uphold the Trade Secret status. In such a case, any attempt to pursue individuals who might have compromised that information would prove difficult at best.

Trade Secret status gives the holder of that information certain rights and protections in order to defend the competitive edge it provides in the marketplace. Unlike copyrights or patents, a Trade Secret retains this status until such time as the information becomes generally known to the industry through independent development by other parties, or the holder fails to keep it secret.

Confidentiality Agreements

These agreements entered into between employers and employees, as well as contractors and clients, are written documentation of the fact that one party is expected to become aware of sensitive or secret information, and is agreeing to hold that information in strict confidence. Failure to abide by these agreements, once entered into, usually results in a civil suit and/or internal discipline based upon the status of the party that violated the agreement. In most cases, for a given piece of information to be recognized as being within the protected information covered by such an agreement, it must bear some indication of its sensitive nature. Most commonly, "Confidential" is clearly indicated on these documents, but similar references also can be found.

Threat Sources

The source of these types of threats can be varied and depend to some degree on the nature of the information, sector of industry, and market value. In general, the sources can be categorized as one of the following three types:

- Disgruntled employees
- Corporate espionage
- Malicious outsiders

Within each grouping, there are different types of threats based upon their level of sophistication and long-term intent.

Disgruntled Employees

These individuals, turned against their employer for any of a vast number of real or perceived reasons, can have the potential to do vast amounts of damage. Based upon their position and level of access, it is possible that an insider could compromise all of the critical information of a given company under the right circumstances. Imagine the potential if the vice president of a company, responsible for Information Systems, were to decide to damage the storage media of the home office. The damage could effectively destroy the business.

This is one reason to limit the number of people that have access to any given piece of information. The fewer people who have access, the lower the likelihood of someone with access to it becoming a liability.

Corporate Espionage

In our modern world, there are almost no lines of business that have not had cases of this nature. Be it a client list found in a dumpster or R&D plans intercepted from communications lines that were thought to be secure, anything of value to one company must also be of value to another. Unfortunately, there are some that do not want to work for their advantage and turn to their competitors as unwilling providers of the needed information.

Although most such cases, which make it into the media, are purely wars between rival companies, there is another disturbing trend resulting from the collapse of the Soviet Union. Following the end of the Cold War, many international intelligence services found themselves struggling to justify the size and scope of their previous existence. In some cases, the result was well-trained and experienced intelligence officers finding themselves looking for work in the private sector as the organization reduced its ranks. In other cases, the organizations redirected their efforts, to support their nation's major industries. In either case, the persons involved tend to be extremely effective and technically superior to the typical insider due to extensive training.

Malicious Outsiders

The ranks of this group include hackers, pranksters, and others who do not understand the value of what they take or damage, or the implications for the lives of those that the victimized company supports. These persons range in expertise from those completely unaware of technical aspects, to the brilliant, yet misdirected personalities. The type and volume of damage they inflict is usually related to the level of sophistication they command, but there are occasions where less skilled intruders have caused considerable damage to electronic storage media.

CONCLUSION

Any information that is of value to one company, or even individual, is probably of value to another and should be protected in a manner that is dictated by that information's own value or importance. The secrecy of any information must never be taken for granted. Without actively securing it and regularly confirming that it remains secure, there is no guarantee that it will not be compromised.

SECURITY QUIZ
Information Security

1. Trade Secret status expires after 7 years.
   ☐ T ☐ F
2. Anything that is of value to one company is probably of value to its competitors.
   ☐ T ☐ F
3. Disgruntled employees pose little threat because they are easy to identify and control.
   ☐ T ☐ F
4. Limiting the number of people who have access to information generally reduces the chances of it being compromised.
   ☐ T ☐ F

5. Some information that could be considered critical would include:
   - ☐ (a) design plans
   - ☐ (b) product formulae
   - ☐ (c) client lLists
   - ☐ (d) All of the above
6. When securing electronic information, some points to consider might be:
   - ☐ (a) communications lines
   - ☐ (b) wireless transmission and reception
   - ☐ (c) internal network access
   - ☐ (d) All of the above
7. When securing paper documents, some points of consideration might be:
   - ☐ (a) magnetic field effects on ink
   - ☐ (b) fire protection
   - ☐ (c) inordinately low temperatures
   - ☐ (d) None of the above
8. Physical security concepts will aid and support:
   - ☐ (a) paper document protection
   - ☐ (b) electronic media protection
   - ☐ (c) area surveillance prevention
   - ☐ (d) All of the above
9. A form that states that a person will protect the information made known to them for business purposes, would be called a
   "_____   _____."
10. One company obtaining information owned by another company through unauthorized means is generally referred to as
   "_____   _____."

Unit Five

Explosive Devices, Bomb Threats, and Search Procedures
Fire Prevention, Detection, and Response
Hazardous Materials
Protection Officers and Emergency Response: Legal and
Operational Considerations

EXPLOSIVE DEVICES, BOMB THREATS, AND SEARCH PROCEDURES

By Michael Stroberger, CPO, CSS, CPOI, CLSD, CPP

Explosives are an essential part of our modern world and play a critical role in many industries. When used properly, they are an exceptional tool and greatly reduce the amount of manual labor required to perform certain tasks.

In areas such as highway construction, mining, quarrying, and the military, explosives can be some of the most critical tools available.

Unfortunately, this valuable tool can also be misused. In various forms, explosive devices have been used to cause loss of life, damage to property, and to hinder components of infrastructures in almost every part of the world. Each year, the number of explosive device attacks is well beyond what the media usually reports. In many cases, these attacks are on such a small scale that they are rarely reported beyond the local media outlets. Despite this, explosives are real and potentially deadly threats, and should always be taken seriously.

The misuse of explosives can be the result of any number of lines of thought. Some of the more common motivations have included:

1. Broken interpersonal relationships
2. Revenge for perceived wrongs
3. Attempts at financial gains through Insurance
4. Theological disputes
5. Ideological disputes
6. Territorial disputes
7. Mental instability

In each case, the scale of the device may vary widely based on availability of materials, financial considerations, and the actual intent of the parties involved. In many cases, in the United States, explosives have been used to harm specific individuals, such as in vehicle bombs, and have been small enough to harm only one person. Not all bombs cause major damage, although the possibilities can be staggering. The other end of the scale would be such attacks as the Murrah Federal Building in Oklahoma City, the Marine Barrack attack in Beirut, and the damaging of the USS *Cole*. Although far less common, such attacks can be overwhelming in their damage, loss of life, and in the emotional impact on the survivors, witnesses, and world observers.

Despite the potential harm that these can cause, it is a fact that explosive materials are more available than most would think. Explosives can be obtained through direct purchase (given certain permits), theft, personal manufacturer, or even through sources willing to ship them. In some cases, the permits and identification to purchase these have been forged. In others cases, they have been obtained under false pretenses. The theft of explosives, military and commercial grade, is a continuing issue and occurs with alarming frequency. One government report indicated that in a single year, 3,999 pounds of military/commercial grade explosives were stolen from various locations in a single state. The explosive formulae are available in many cases and on the Internet as well.

WHAT IS AN EXPLOSIVE?

An explosive compounds is typically classified as either "low explosive" or "high explosive," based on the speed at which it reacts and converts to a gas. It is this change that results in the generation of force. As the substance reacts, its form changes from a solid to a gaseous cloud that then expands to occupy a larger area. As this cloud expands, it creates pressure by rapidly pushing outward on the atmosphere and solid objects in its path. Low explosives, those with a slower reaction speed, tend to create a pushing effect as the pressure wave expands. This can result in the "Hollywood" effect of seeming to "throw" objects away from the point of origin (as this pressure wave has more time of contact with the object to accelerate it in the same direction). High explosives, on the other hand, create a pressure wave that expands so quickly that it is more likely to shatter objects as it impacts upon them. This wave moves so quickly that it does not have time to impart momentum, but it does impact the surface with great force. It is because of this shattering or cutting effect that High Explosives are utilized in demolitions and most military ordinance, as they are more likely to cause structural damage by shattering or shearing building supports, pavement, or other solid objects.

The actual compounds utilized in an explosive device vary widely. In some cases, it is very simple and easily obtained, in others very complex and difficult to obtain or manufacture. One of the earlier devices utilized by the "Unibomber," reportedly contained shavings of the heads of matches as its charge. Typically, the more simple the compound, the slower the rate of reaction. Consequently, using the more common source materials, and the simpler the design and manufacture, the less powerful the final device will usually be.

Two things that all explosive devices have in common are some form of triggering mechanism and a method if initiating detonation. In some cases, this is nothing more than a burning fuse that will suffice for both parts given the right charge. In other cases, the trigger and detonator can be extremely complicated with components based upon the following methods:

1. Electronic—Devices with digital timers, radio controls, light sensors, sound sensors, motion detectors, and even attempts to tamper with the mechanism itself are all possible.
2. Chemical reaction—Two or more substances may require a certain amount of time to fully react, creating a crude timed delay.
3. Mechanical—Devices using impact, such as ammunition primers, or mechanized clocks, rolling metal bearings, and wire release mechanisms may be utilized.

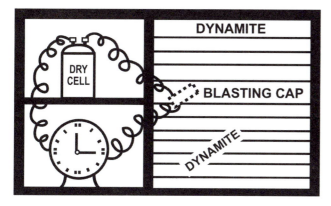

Figure 5-1.   Alarm Clock Time Bomb

In truth, just about any device that can be made to create a spark, an impact, or the generation of sufficient heat could be used to activate an explosive device. In some cases, the intended compound requires an exceptional amount of force to cause it to react. In these situations, a smaller charge, sometimes large enough to be considered a very hazardous device, may be used to cause detonation. In these designs, known as "explosive trains," the smaller charge is referred to as the "booster," and the larger as the "primary."

In addition to the use of compounds to fabricate devices, there are numerous pre-fabricated explosives, both commercial and military, which could find their way into the wrong hands. Items such grenades, rockets, and mines (although uncommon) have been found in the hands of criminals and extremists.

The one rule to remember when identifying an explosive device is that they do not always look like an explosive device. Most people who are intent on causing damage or loss of life will make an attempt to disguise or conceal the device.

Explosive devices can vary widely in shape, size, and the location in which one might place them. As such, it would be nearly impossible to completely prevent the threat. A good physical security program might cause the intended perpetrator to reconsider the choice of location, but a dedicated individual could eventually find a method of delivery.

When attempting to reduce potential damage from explosives and bomb threats, these are some steps to consider.

1. Create a formal, detailed plan of action to address the issues of bomb threats, actual devices, and the response to an explosion.
2. Ensure that the overall plan is properly documented, that the participants are effectively trained, and that drills are regularly conducted to ensure that every member is fully aware of his or her responsibilities.
3. Distribute a "Threat Checklist" to all areas. This is used to record information related to threats received at that location. The ATF has a standard checklist, available through their Web site, which provides a good basic model. Ensure that all personnel are trained in the use of the checklist and have copies available within reach of any telephone where a threat might be received.
4. Develop a strong liaison with your law enforcement representatives. Get their input into the local crime trends; reports that might suggest a threat to your location. They may even assist in training those that might be called upon to conduct a bomb search.
5. Create a search program in which people familiar with the area are trained in identifying basic devices. It is essential that people familiar with the area be used in this capacity, since they are the most likely to be able to identify items that are out of place, altered, or new to the area.

As in all facets of our industry, preplanning is essential if the program is to be effective and properly executed. Develop lines of communication with similar facilities and operations in order to pool resources. In many cases, extra details that are identified in the process of developing such a plan have already been thought through and addressed by other groups.

BOMB THREATS

Bomb threats, actual or hoaxes, are the most common explosive-related events. These are the communicated warnings of an impending explosion delivered by those responsible for the alleged placement of the device. In most cases, these do turn out to be malicious calls that are intended simply to instill fear, disrupt normal activities, or to provide the caller with some form of "thrill." Despite this, every such threat should be handled in a timely and professional manner. The potential for damage and loss of life, if there is an actual device, is too high to be set aside. The plan for responding to such incidents, as in the other areas of this subject, must be well defined and known by those responsible for its execution and documented. Every second counts when responding to these incidents!

When responding to specific threats, some basic steps will help to provide a reasonable level of safety and security, while also assisting in the follow-up investigation.

Written Threats

1. Retain all packing, shipping, and content materials. Once an item is recognized as a threat, it should be put down on the nearest dry and flat surface and not touched again, except by the proper authorities. This will help to preserve any physical and trace evidence that may be present. All packing and shipping materials should also be left untouched from that point forward.
2. Report the threat to the proper authorities and advise them of the specifics of the threat, as well as the current location of the threat materials.
3. If a specific time, location, or other reference was noted, advise the authorities of this information when making the initial call.

Telephone Threats

Record all possible information on a Threat Checklist.

1. Keep the caller on the line as long as possible.
2. Get the attention of a nearby coworker, and draw that attention to the fact that you are filling out a "Threat Checklist" so that they can call the authorities on another phone while you continue to keep the caller on the line.
3. If no coworkers are in the area, or the caller does not stay on the line, call the authorities immediately after the end of that call.
4. When completing the checklist, or while trying to keep the caller on the line, tell them that any detonation may cause loss of life. In many cases, callers want the threat to result in an evacuation so that the detonation will only cause property damage. Advising them that evacuation may not be completed in time may prompt them to provide additional information.
5. Make note of any distinct background noises, speech patterns, accents, repeated phrases, or similar unique aspects of the call.
6. Try to obtain the exact time of detonation, location, and type of explosive if possible.

Although most received threats eventually turn out to be a hoax, the possible damage and loss of life clearly indicates that all such threats be handled with a serious, committed, and organized response until such time as it can be reasonably confirmed to be a hoax. In all cases, the following should be part of your written response plan and should occur, unless advised otherwise by the responding law enforcement authorities:

1. Advise local law enforcement.
2. Designate and activate your Incident Command Center. Ensure that critical leaders and decision makers move to that area, and direct the responding public agency commanders to this area as well.

3. Evacuate all personnel from the area in an orderly and safe manner.
4. Cease all use of two-way communications devices! Such equipment may cause some types of detonators or triggers to activate under certain circumstances.
5. Assign and dispatch search teams with the cooperation of the public agency commanders if possible. Although each search team should include a person familiar with the area, each team should also have an officer from the Explosive Ordinance Disposal Team ("EOD Team" or "Bomb Squad") with them to take command if a suspicious item should be discovered.
6. Searches should continue until such time as all areas have been inspected or the senior EOD commander, or ranking law enforcement officer, determines the scene to be safe.

SEARCH PHASE

At some point, unless directed to the contrary by your senior responding law enforcement officer, a search will have to be conducted to determine if a device or suspicious object can be located. The execution of this phase must also be trained for in advance to ensure that all parties involved understand their role.

In defining search teams, it should be standard practice to group them in sets of at least two or three people to provide a reasonably fast rate of inspection. It is important that the groups not be so large that they cannot move freely in a small room. As indicated elsewhere, a member of the responding law enforcement agency should be with each search team if possible.

The search itself should be orderly, systematic, and thorough. No area should be ignored or believed to be safe without inspection. Look for any object that appears to be unusual, tampered with, or in an odd or unexpected position.

Utilize a rising search pattern to ensure thoroughness. This involves checking all possible locations on the floor before you step into that area. Once the floor has been inspected from one side to the other, all areas below hip level (roughly 3') should be inspected. This includes in and around furniture. Once this lower band has been checked, look at all areas in the height range of hips to shoulder (3' to 5'). Again, sweep from an identified starting point in a continuous flow around the area until you return to that starting point. Finally, all areas above shoulder level (5') should be checked. It is important to obtain and utilize a short ladder when performing this final phase as objects placed on top of taller furniture, in air vents, above suspended ceilings, and within hanging light fixtures often go undiscovered due to being inconvenient. Do not let any area go uninspected!

Here are some additional guidelines when performing a search.

1. Do not carry any devices that transmit a signal. Turn off all cellular telephones, radios, and even pagers, which are capable of sending responses to messages.
2. Do not touch any suspicious object. Report it to the proper authorities and secure the area.
3. Do not alter the energy state in any area. Do not turn anything on or off. If you find lights on, leave them on. If you find lights off, leave them off.
4. Use all of your senses! Objects may give off unusual smells, make new sounds, or have other indicators that could be missed.
5. Check all sealed or closed areas for signs of tampering. As an example, electrical outlets should be inspected to see if the cover screws have been recently removed and replaced. This could indicate a device or trigger has been placed behind the plug cover.
6. Utilize any additional support offered by law enforcement and fire personnel, but ensure that all others remain out of the area.
7. Monitor the time to ensure that the building is fully evacuated as the reported time of detonation approaches if this is known.

Thoroughness is absolutely essential! In many cases, people who place such devices understand that the average person does not "look up" as much as they "look down." They may use this and other basic understandings of human behavior to place the device in a location that is more likely to be overlooked.

EXPLOSIONS

Of course, in some cases, there is no warning. Should an explosion occur, the response must be swift, organized, and aimed at the preservation of life. Emergency services should be called immediately, and those found to be injured should be given care consistent with the training and abilities of those available to assist them. The area of the explosion should be completely evacuated and entry by people other than law enforcement and fire department officials refused. This is now a crime scene and must be preserved. All people should be kept a considerable distance away and not in the immediate area of the responding public agencies unless they require medical aid. There is always the possibility of secondary devices designed to detonate at a time when the fire, EMS, and law enforcement personnel can be harmed. If one device has already detonated, the individual(s) who placed it have already demonstrated that they have little value for human life.

PREVENTION AND MITIGATION

As indicated earlier, a dedicated person is probably not going to be prevented from placing an explosive device. The options for placement, delivery, shape, and size are too numerous to be completely prevented. There are, however,

some steps that can be taken in the right environment to lessen the chances of this type of incident, or to minimize the damage of their actual use.

Deterrence. If the nature and design of the location permits such steps, the active enforcement of tightened security practices can discourage a large percentage of potential crimes, including explosive incidents. Some steps to consider might be the following:

1. Well-defined entrance/exit routes, with officers performing container inspections of all purses, bags, backpacks, or other objects which might contain suspicious items before they enter the main portion of the property;
2. Securing all equipment and storage rooms when not actually in use; and
3. CCTV monitoring to document arrival, departure, and movement of persons on property.

In addition, there are some design and use considerations that might lessen the damage of an explosive device activating. Although some of these require additional expense, others are simply alterations to the way in which space is utilized. Some examples might include:

1. Utilizing the concept of a "standoff" space. This involves designing the routes of vehicles, unsearched containers, and arriving freight, such that it is not brought within a predetermined distance of the building, people, or critical equipment that you intend to protect. This distance is usually determined by the level of perceived threat, the level of expected sophistication in the possible attacks, and the value or criticality of the potential target.
2. Utilizing retrofit materials and equipment that is blast and ballistic resistant. In many cases, the addition of window film, designed to reduce the spray of broken glass and penetration of flying debris, will offer significantly improved survivability to the occupants of the attacked room. Care should be taken, though, to ensure that the window frame and the supporting wall can also withstand the pressure and impact, or the window might also become a projectile.

Although explosives do make many valuable contributions to our modern life, they can be a highly effective method of creating pain and damage as well. All such cases, threats, or discovered devices must be handled with extreme care and caution. Although most private sector protection officers do not have the training of an EOD technician, they do have a valuable knowledge of the location, the people, and the operation. All of these can aid in the process of resolving the incident. Proper planning, training, and coordination are the keys to the smooth and effective response that will greatly increase the probability of a safe and successful outcome.

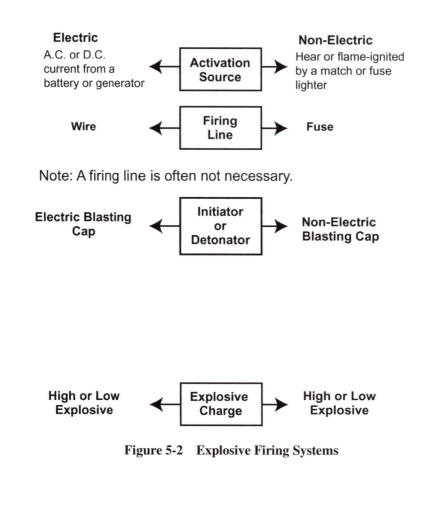

Figure 5-2   Explosive Firing Systems

SECURITY QUIZ
Explosive Devices, Bomb Threats and
Search Procedures

1. The terms "low explosive" and "high explosive" are references to the cost of obtaining the substance.
    ☐ T ☐ F
2. Due to technological advances, there are no legitimate, nonmilitary uses for explosives.
    ☐ T ☐ F
3. "Explosive train" is a term used exclusively to describe the transportation of explosive materials.
    ☐ T ☐ F
4. Explosive devices are easy to identify once found.
    ☐ T ☐ F
5. Some potential motivations for explosive attacks might be:
    ☐ (a) interpersonal relationships
    ☐ (b) insurance fraud
    ☐ (c) ideological disputes
    ☐ (d) All of the above
6. The response to the bomb threat received through the mail should include:
    ☐ (a) delivering the letter to the police department for testing
    ☐ (b) an immediate and thorough search of the inside and outside of the shipping container
    ☐ (c) placing of the letter in water to prevent possible contamination threats
    ☐ (d) reporting of the threat to police immediately

7. Telephone threats should be responded to by:
   ☐ (a) completing a "Threat Checklist"
   ☐ (b) contacting the police
   ☐ (c) keeping the caller on the line as long as possible
   ☐ (d) All of the above
8. Search guidelines might include which of the following?
   ☐ (a) Turn off everything electrical
   ☐ (b) Do not use a radio
   ☐ (c) Remove all suspicious objects for further examination
   ☐ (d) None of the above
9. "_____ explosive" compounds are more likely to produce the effect of "throwing" objects, as the pressure wave expands.
10. "_____ explosive" compounds are more likely to produce the effect of "shattering" objects, as the pressure wave expands.

FIRE PREVENTION, DETECTION, AND RESPONSE

By Michael Stroberger, CPO, CSS, CPOI, CLSD, CPP

Fire has long held a position as one of the most feared threats to life and property. Fires not only destroy homes and buildings, but they can consume vast expanses of wilderness or entire neighborhoods and take the lives of people within their area of effect. Once initiated, fires spread rapidly and become extremely hard to control or extinguish with alarming speed.

Our best defense is the prevention of fire situations before they begin. Through effective controls and inspection, this threat can be significantly reduced to the benefit of everyone.

In all fire situations, the protection of human lives must be the most important factor. Property can be replaced, information recompiled, and other materials remade. This must be the overriding consideration in every prevention and response plan.

FIRE BASICS

Fire is, in its basic mechanics, nothing more than an extremely rapid conversion from one state to another. This reaction requires three components to occur and must continue to utilize these three components to be sustained. As such, in looking at the prevention and response to fires, it is essential that everyone understand these parts known as the Fire Triangle.

1. Fuel—For a fire to exist, there must be some materials available that are capable of combustion. This could be as simple as paper or wood, or as complex as magnesium. In every case, this fuel is the component that undergoes the conversion from its current state to a different state. In most cases, this conversion is from a solid to a gas with some solid materials remaining.

2. Oxygen—The conversion of states in a fire situation requires an interaction with available oxygen. In most cases, fires are entirely dependent on the oxygen in the surrounding air; in other, fairly rare, cases, the material that is being consumed may produce oxygen as a result of this process.

3. Heat—The final component required to cause the fuel in an oxygenated environment to begin the process of conversion is some source of heat.

Without the presence of all three components, a fire cannot begin or be sustained. This leads us to the basic concept of cleanliness being a major contributor to the prevention of accidental fires. If all available fuels are stored in a manner consistent with fire prevention practices, they will be sufficiently removed from identified sources of heat and the chance of combustion is almost eliminated. This means that all identified sources of fuel must be watched for and properly utilized and stored to prevent exposure to heat.

Figure 5-3   The Fire Tetrahedron

As an example, one of the more common fire locations in the hospitality industry is the laundry area. The operation of industrial dryers requires the production of heat. When processing cloth, there is a certain amount of lint that is produced. As a result, there is a ready supply of fuel (lint is very combustible) in close proximity to a heat source. The prevention practice is extremely simple; remove and clean the lint filter after each load, or at least on a regular frequency.

Other typical hazard areas to inspect for could include the following:

- Boilers, heaters, and furnaces
- Cooking areas
- Electrical equipment and breaker rooms
- Storage areas for flammable liquids
- Vehicle storage areas
- Work areas that utilize oils, paint thinners, and other combustible liquids
- Smoking areas

As a general rule, areas that are cluttered tend to have an increased chance of fire hazards, and should be frequently inspected until such time as it is properly cleaned.

When inspecting for fire hazards, which should be a constant aspect of every patrol, it is also essential that identified hazards be corrected, documented, and prevented from reoccurring.

DETECTION METHODS

If prevention methods fail and a fire begins, it becomes a matter of being able to detect the hazard so that the response program can be effective. The two methods of fire detection are human observation and electronic systems.

Human observation is often more effective, since it allows for the use of reasoning and judgment to determine the nature of the actual situation. In this case, however, there must be people present to make this discovery. Patrol officers have excellent opportunities to identify potential fires through smell, sight, and even sound and touch. In some cases, officers observe fires in such an early stage of development that they are able to effectively extinguish them without outside assistance. In addition, by obtaining the cooperation of other people in the environment, the chances of human observation can be increased. Often, these other observers must be given some form of basic training to identify hazards or early stage fire threats, so that they can be more effective.

Electronic detection can also be highly effective, especially in areas where chances of observation by people is relatively low due to infrequent travel through them or visual obstructions. Electronic systems of detection can include sensors that watch for smoke, rapid increases in temperature, temperatures above certain levels (regardless of how quickly that temperature is reached), and even early combustion airborne particles. Unfortunately, electronic sensors can also trigger alarms as a result of situations other than fires. It is because of this that all alarms must be investigated to determine the actual cause.

The ideal detection program is, of course, a combination of human observation and electronic monitoring. By thoroughly training the protective force and offering basic training to all other people that will be in the area and utilizing an electronic system as a backup to these components, you greatly increase the likelihood of identifying fire situations. As previously stated, it is essential that fires be identified at the earliest possible moment, so that they have not had a chance to grow too large to be contained and extinguished.

FIRE TYPES

Although based upon the same concept, fires can be divided into four basic types determined by the nature of the Fuel component of their Fire Triangle. It is important to know these types and the differences in their fuels, as it can make a difference in how the fire is contained and extinguished. The basic types are:

A. Type A fires generally have common solid combustible materials as their fuel. This would include such fuels as wood, paper, and cloth. This is a very common form of fire and the most basic.
B. This is a fire that is fueled by liquid or gaseous fuels, such as gasoline, kerosene, and compressed gas tanks like propane.
C. This represents fires that are initiated by, or now contain an element of, electrical involvement. Fires in a breaker box, power strip, frayed extension cord, or item of powered equipment would fall into this category.
D. Burning metals, such as magnesium, fall into this category. Often extremely intense and requiring special equipment to handle.

Once the nature of a fire is understood, it becomes a determining factor in how to handle that situation. For the most part, class A, B, or C fires of sufficiently small size can be contained and extinguished by a person utilizing an appropriate extinguisher. Class D fires require such specialized equipment that most responders will not be able to effectively handle them, and should be cautioned to maintain a safe distance, in the process of evacuating the immediate area.

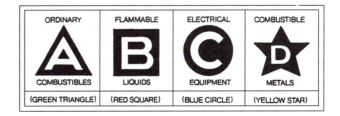

Figure 5-4 Fire Classifications

EXTINGUISHERS

The most critical aspect of deciding if you are going to attempt to extinguish a fire is determining if you can do so without serious risk to your own safety or the safety of others. Make no mistake: Fighting a fire is dangerous. By its very nature, this activity requires that you intentionally remain within, or move within, close proximity to a highly hazardous environment. Care should be taken to ensure that the responding person understands the dangers, the equipment to be used, as well as its limitations. The purpose of fighting a fire is to save lives and property, not to risk them needlessly.

When working in an environment with extinguishers that you may have not used before, it is recommended that a test unit be obtained, even in a group setting, so that the area of effect, and limits of range and duration of use, can be explored.

When deciding if it is appropriate to attempt to extinguish a fire, it is important that the equipment you select matches the fire type. Mismatching the extinguisher and fire types may result in a marked increase in the level of personal danger to which the responder is exposed.

With this in mind, some of the more common extinguisher types, and the class of fires they are intended to be used on, are as follows.

- Dry chemical—These utilize a powder that is expelled from the nozzle in a stream of pressurized, nonflammable gas. Dry chemical extinguishers are usually classified as usable on Class A, B, and C fires, as it will be both effective and relatively safe in those applications. These extinguish the fire by coating the fuel of the fire, making it unavailable for combustion.
- Carbon dioxide—These units produce a cloud of "snow-like" particles that quickly evaporate into a carbon dioxide layer. This layer reduces the available oxygen and cools the area, breaking the Fire Triangle. Commonly classified as B and C type extinguishers.
- Water-based—Water is a good extinguishing agent for Class A fires, but can aggravate other types. If used on burning liquids, Class B, it can spread the fuel enlarging the fire area. If used on electrical fires, Class C, it can cause serious harm to the responder, as it may conduct that electrical charge causing an electrical shock to be delivered to the holder of the unit, or others standing in the runoff from it.
- Halogenated units—These are referred to as "clean agent" extinguishers because they contain a chemical that leaves no residue upon evaporation. They cool and smother fires making them typically usable on Class A, B, and C fires. These are the ideal type of unit if responding to fires in computer and other delicate electrical equipment, as they are far less likely to cause damage to that equipment in the process of extinguishing the fire.
- Foaming agents—These units produce a foam layer that blocks the flow of oxygen to the fire area. As such, this is very effective against Class A and B fires. Unfortunately, these often utilize a water-based agent, and should not be used on Class C fires as a result.

In the past, there were extinguishers that had to be inverted to cause a reaction between the main tank contents and a bicarbonate material resulting in a development of pressure through this reaction. It has been recognized that this motion, the inversion of a heavy extinguisher, may not be within the capabilities of persons with disabilities, and their use has been largely discontinued. In the United States, such extinguishers do not comply with the Americans with Disabilities Act and should not be present in the workplace.

Extinguishers should also be checked and inspected on an appropriate basis. If there is high traffic in a given area, especially open to the public, checking these daily, or even on each 8-hour shift, might be in order. Ensure that they have not been discharged or tampered with so that they will be available for use if a fire is discovered.

PERMANENT EXTINGUISHING HARDWARE

In addition to extinguishers, which may be carried by possible responders, there are also some more elaborate extinguishing devices that are installed into buildings.

- Automatic sprinklers—These operate through a spring-loaded valve that opens when exposed to certain minimum temperatures. These valves, called "sprinkler heads," are located at regular intervals throughout the entire building. Once the valve opens, the feed pipe that it is attached to it will continue to supply it with water until the control valve for that area is closed or the sprinkler head is replaced. In most systems, the feed pipe has a sensor added to it to activate the alarm system if the water begins to flow toward an activated sprinkler head.
- Range-hood systems—In kitchen areas, there are often specialized systems designed to blanket the entire working area with a special chemical agent. This is designed to be highly effective on grease fires and other common kitchen fires yet still be relatively easy and sanitary to clean up. These systems are triggered manually by persons who observe a fire.
- Stand pipes—Based on application of fire codes, most buildings have a stand pipe system that allows for the connection and supply of fire hoses. Like an extension of a fire hydrant, these allow the fire department, or in-house fire brigade, with an available source of water.

It is widely accepted that, even under the best of circumstances, these types of automatic or large-scale systems usually slow or contain a fire but often do not extinguish them. As a result, it is essential that each activation is investigated and the fire department becomes involved to ensure that the hazard is eliminated properly.

CONTAINMENT

In addition to the actions of responders, and the utilization of various systems and equipment, there are usually design limitations that aid in the containment of a fire. In most jurisdictions, and within many companies, there are specific design and construction requirements with regard to the use of fire resistant building materials. Such items as fire resistant doors, designed to resist the spread of a fire for certain periods of time, aid greatly in the containment of a fire. However, to be effective, they must be in their proper position and working in accordance with their original design. As part of every officer's patrol, confirming that fire doors are in proper condition and not propped or wedged open should be a constant component.

FIRE PLANS

Designing a Fire Plan, prior to an actual event, is the most effective step in any fire prevention, fire detection, and fire response program. It is through this plan that all of these factors would be addressed and provided structure and detail.

Developing such a plan must be cooperative in nature with those expected to execute the plan involved from the beginning. Without this, it is possible that aspects of the final plan my be unrealistic and could prevent an effective program from being implemented.

The written plan should include the following as a basic guide:

- Emergency contact names and telephone numbers
- A formal chain of command
- Detailed explanations of the responsibilities of each person or department in prevention aspects
- Detailed explanations of the responsibilities of each person or department in response aspects
- An explanation of the equipment available, the frequency of inspection, and method of documentation
- An explanation of the training that personnel receive, the frequency of retraining, and the specific responsibilities bestowed as a result of this training
- Charts and diagrams of the property detailing equipment locations, routes of egress, evacuation meeting locations, and similar fixed points

It is essential that senior management review this program and support it. It is also essential, and in some areas required, that the fire marshal have a chance to review the Fire Plan and approve it prior to implementation.

As part of a formal plan, alarm systems should be regularly inspected and tested to ensure that the components are functioning properly. This should include activation of every sensor through cooperation with a qualified/certified inspector or installer and the presence or approval of the fire marshal.

Above all, the response portion of a Fire Plan must be realistic in its assignments and expectations. It should be written with the following limits in mind:

- Assign duties only to people or positions that will always be present. If you work in an area where the patrol officer is the only position that is staffed at all times, the response plan should assume that this will be the only person present for its critical aspects. It is easier to assign an extra person to a new duty than it is to find an extra person for a vacant function.
- Write each phase with the protection of lives as the primary focus and property concerns as a secondary motivation.
- Write the plan based on existing equipment and supplies only. Do not count on having time to obtain other items before the plan must be put into action.

The most important point about Fire Plans is that *they must be put into effect!* What good is a plan that is exhaustively researched, designed by a broadly scoped committee, approved by every member of the team, and then put on a shelf and never utilized?

ARSON

Fires are not always accidents or acts of nature. An alarming number of cases are thought to be intentionally set fires resulting from any of a vast number of reasons. In some cases, insurance fraud is believed to be the motivator; in others it is psychological disorders. Whatever the motive, arson fires are some of the most dangerous. Often, accelerants are utilized to cause the fire to grow rapidly beyond the containment and extinguishing capabilities of the responding fire department. In some tragic cases, this reduces the time available for those within the structure to a point where they cannot escape before falling victim to smoke inhalation. In even more sinister cases, arsonists have been known to block or lock doors closed preventing escape from the flames.

Your best protection against arson is a combination of highly visible patrols, to deter the attempt, and effective securing of unused rooms and flammables. These steps will reduce the areas of concealment, which the arsonist often relies on to prepare for the incident, and also cause them to have to bring their own materials, which could draw attention to them. Much like other crimes, a motivated and dedicated arsonist will eventually find a way to attempt to carry out their crime, but you can create an environment where the arsonist looking for a random place to start a fire will be less likely to feel comfortable.

CONCLUSION

Know the basics and apply them to every patrol. Train each member of the team that is supposed to respond to fire situations so that they are not hesitant when that time comes. Train everyone in how to prevent fires and respond to discovering them for their own safety. Fire can be a devastating event, especially if the response is uncoordinated or slow. Check and inspect equipment, regularly, to ensure that it is in usable condition if the need should arise.

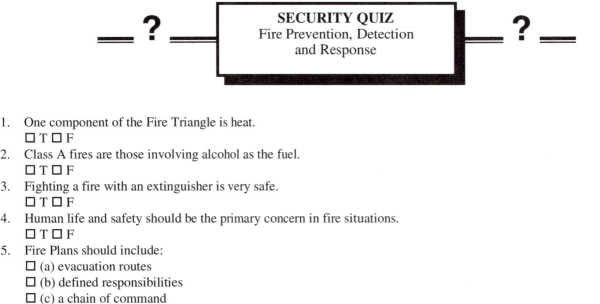

SECURITY QUIZ
Fire Prevention, Detection
and Response

1. One component of the Fire Triangle is heat.
    ☐ T ☐ F
2. Class A fires are those involving alcohol as the fuel.
    ☐ T ☐ F
3. Fighting a fire with an extinguisher is very safe.
    ☐ T ☐ F
4. Human life and safety should be the primary concern in fire situations.
    ☐ T ☐ F
5. Fire Plans should include:
    ☐ (a) evacuation routes
    ☐ (b) defined responsibilities
    ☐ (c) a chain of command
    ☐ (d) All of the above
6. The detection of fires can be broken into:
    ☐ (a) electronic methods
    ☐ (b) human methods
    ☐ (c) Both of the above
    ☐ (d) Neither of the above
7. Arson fires are:
    ☐ (a) intentionally started
    ☐ (b) often made more dangerous through the use of accelerants
    ☐ (c) sometimes part of insurance fraud attempts
    ☐ (d) All of the above
8. Typical hazard areas include:
    ☐ (a) boilers, heaters, and furnaces
    ☐ (b) cooking areas
    ☐ (c) smoking areas
    ☐ (d) vehicle storage areas
    ☐ (e) All of the above
9. Dry chemical hand extinguishers are usually considered Class _____. (Fill in the blank.)
10. A magnesium fire is an example of a Class _____ fire. (Fill in the blank.)

HAZARDOUS MATERIALS

By Thomas E. Koll, CPP

Chemical substances have been used by mankind for thousands of years. From the paints used by ancient cave dwellers to the secret potions of the alchemists, we have always found ways to use chemicals to make our life better. With the birth of our present technological age came an explosion in the number and type of chemicals in common use. There are now more than 500,000 different chemical compounds in use, with hundreds of new compounds being created every month. Chemicals are here to stay, and to a large extent, they have made our modern civilization possible.

Chemicals can be viewed as being similar to fire in that when their use is safely controlled, they are a benefit to civilization: however, if allowed to get out of control they can cause damage and destruction.

It should be said here that the majority of chemicals and other substances considered "hazardous materials" are not inherently dangerous in and of themselves. So what are hazardous chemicals or hazardous materials? Hazardous material definitions range from a few sentences to several hundred words in length. For the purpose of our discussion a hazardous material is any substance that has the potential to cause people, or the environment (plants, animals, and waterways) harm if allowed to be released in an uncontrolled manner.

Some common examples of hazardous materials include acids, cyanide, cleaning solvents, propane gas, and even gasoline. These and many other hazardous materials are commonly used on a daily basis throughout industry and commerce. When their use is strictly controlled, through piping systems, storage tanks, and safety devices, they present no danger; however, if an uncontrolled release of the substance is allowed to occur, the results can range from stoppage of work to fires and explosions that can destroy a facility. Ultimately, all uncontrolled releases can be traced to one or a series of human failures that lead up to the release. Whether it's a machine operator who wasn't paying attention to safety procedures, a faulty maintenance program that didn't provide for proper equipment inspections, or willful negligence as in the case of so called illegal toxic dumps, the results are always the same. Human error caused the release of the toxic material.

METHODS OF RESPONSE

There are several methods of possible response to an uncontrolled release of a hazardous material. For decades hazardous materials have been used with little or no training provided to the end users or those individuals charged with responding to a hazardous material release.

The common point of view was that dilution was the solution to pollution. This theory held that no matter how hazardous a substance was, if you were able to dilute it enough (usually with water), it would be rendered harmless. In the event of a hazard release, the common response was to call the local fire department or plant fire brigade, who would then wash the contaminated area down in an effort to decontaminate the area. In the process, the contaminated water was usually washed into the sewer systems and surrounding ground, and ultimately into the environment.

To a limited degree this method worked for a while. The problem is that after diluting so many hazardous materials into the environment for so many years, the environment has become saturated and, as a result, traces of those same substances are appearing in our food and water supplies today—to say nothing of the risk that untrained firefighters were placed in.

Today government and industry agree that, just as firefighting requires specialized training, also, response to hazardous materials requires specialized knowledge and training to be handled in the safest manner possible.

Today specialized hazardous materials (HazMat) response teams are used to respond to the uncontrolled release of a hazardous substance. Usually, though not always, these teams are part of the local fire department or industrial fire brigade.

THE INITIAL RESPONSE

Whether or not a facility has a HazMat Response Team in place, there are some basic steps that must be followed.

1. Activate the contingency plan.
2. Identify the substance released.
3. Determine the quantity of the released substance.
4. Determine the extent of the damage.
5. Perform "site security."

ACTIVATE THE CONTINGENCY PLAN

In many countries, facilities are required by law to have a HazMat Contingency Plan in place that would be activated in the event of an uncontrolled release of a hazardous material. In the United States, this is covered by the Occupational Safety and Health Administration (OSHA), Hazardous Waste Operations, and Emergency Response (Hazwoper) Standard!

If there is no legal requirement for a Contingency Plan or for another reason your facility does not have one, notify the public agency involved in handling HazMat incidents for your area. This will usually be the local fire department. When they arrive on the scene, they take command and control of the situation. You would then be directed by incident commander.

IDENTIFY THE SUBSTANCE AND QUANTITY RELEASED

The first thing that you must do is to determine what the released substance is and how much of it has been released. To illustrate the uncontrolled release of 8 oz. (1 cup full) of acetone, while requiring caution in cleanup, does not necessitate response from a HazMat Team. The same quantity of cyanide or a high explosive would. By determining what substance has been released as soon as possible, more time is bought for the HazMat Team to decide what course of action they must take.

There are several ways you can safely determine what has been released. The easiest way is to ask the person who was using it in the case of an employee-related spill. This may not always be possible, since the employee in question may have been injured. So how can you identify the substance? There are several safe ways to determine what a released substance is.

If the release is a liquid or solid and has occurred in a more or less open area, it may be possible for you to see where the substance is leaking from. Under no circumstances are you to go near the area unless you have been properly trained and have the proper personal protection equipment or PPE; otherwise you may become another victim of the incident.

Hazardous materials, when transported, are identified on their containers by the International Classification System. Under this multinational system, chemical containers have a diamond-shaped placard label placed on them that can be used to identify the basis, type, and class of chemical. It may be possible to read the placard from a safe distance with or without the use of binoculars. The placards may either name the class, such as "Poison Gas" and may have the class or division number or both. These classes, while not all inclusive, will give the Hazardous Material Response Team a valuable guide as to what they are dealing with.

DETERMINE THE DAMAGE

Now that you have determined what has been released and how much has been released, you need to make a basic evaluation as to the extent of any damage that may have been caused. You need to know if there are any fires or fumes being spread by the release.

It is extremely important to keep clear of the area and to keep others clear until this determination has been made. The smoke produced by a fire can carry the contaminating substance for hundreds of feet and sometimes even for miles. Try to determine what path any fumes or smoke is taking from a safe distance. HazMat Response Teams, even if composed of employees, are often not familiar with areas

Figure 5-5   Types of Gas Masks

of the facility outside of their normal work area. As a protection officer, you are in the unique position of routinely patrolling all areas of your facility. Your knowledge can be invaluable to the HazMat Team in helping to direct their response properly.

Any injured people should be treated by qualified first aid or medical personnel as soon as they are safely removed from the contaminated area. A word of caution is needed here, though: The injured person, if contaminated, will need to be decontaminated before treatment can be rendered.

PERFORM "SITE SECURITY"

What we mean by site security in this context is simply keeping onlookers and bystanders out of the contaminated area. This can be a bigger challenge than it sounds.

No matter how well you communicate to your coworkers or to the general public that there is a hazardous area, and that they must keep away for their own good and the good of others, people seem to have a strong belief that no matter what they do, no harm will come to them.

The logic is simple yet flawed: "Accidents don't happen to me; that's something that happens to someone else." Invariably the people with this logic eventually end up getting hurt. Often they are the ones who get seriously hurt and force rescue workers to jeopardize their own safety to save these poor fools.

The most notorious abusers of this type of behavior are the news media. Reporters and camera crews will take risks that most normal people would never dream of just to "get that scoop" on their competition. Reporters have been known to cross barricades and sneak past security to get a close shot of the incident area.

This poses several problems of which you should be aware. First of all, they interfere with the HazMat Team's operation by attempting to talk to them and generally get in their way.

Second, they will tend not to follow any type of safety precautions and risk becoming exposed themselves. When this happens, the news crew becomes part of the list of victims and must be treated themselves. This has the effect of putting an even heavier workload on response personnel who may already be strained to adequately handle the situation. Another problem is that their entering restricted areas encourages curiosity seekers to also go beyond safety barricades.

For some unknown reason, people like to watch others dealing with problems. Whether it is a sales clerk dealing with a boisterous, irate customer, a fireman at a fire, or even someone changing a flat tire on the side of the road, we love to watch others deal with their problems. Perhaps it helps us forget about our own or perhaps deep down it makes us feel better to know that other people have troubles of their own. It has always amazed me how on a crowded highway, drivers will also slow down to take a closer look at a car along the side of the road with its hood open, as though they had never seen such a sight before! This same compulsion draws onlookers to the scene of a hazardous materials incident.

Figure 5-6 shows a typical layout for site security around a hazardous material–contaminated site. At the top left of the diagram is the area of highest contamination, also called the *Hot Zone*, which ends at the *Hotline*. From the Hotline there is an area called the *Contamination Reduction Zone (CRZ),* or *Warm Zone.* The Contamination Reduction Zone ends at a line known as the *Contamination Control Line.*

Beyond the Contamination Control Line is the area known as the *Cold Zone.* The Cold Zone is where all of the incident activities are directed from. Every effort should be made to keep all nonessential personnel clear of the contamination control zone and the command post where the incident commander directs all of the operations.

The specific distances from one zone boundary to another are determined by the Incident Commander and vary from incident to incident due to specific conditions such as wind speed and direction. Whether the incident is contained indoors or not, there is potential for fire or explosion.

Once the release has been safely controlled, contained, and cleaned up (decontaminated or DECONed for short), the incident commander will make the determination that the incident has been resolved and the area may be reentered without the use of personal protective equipment (PPE). This entire process may take anywhere from a few hours to several days. By the time the incident is completed, the HazMat Team will have followed most or all of the steps diagrammed in Figure 5-7. The important thing to remember is that if all activities are conducted with safety in mind, almost any incident can be resolved with little or no injury.

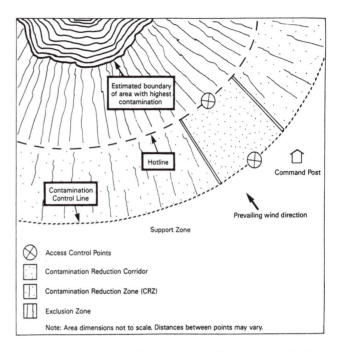

Figure 5-6   Security Around a Contaminated Site

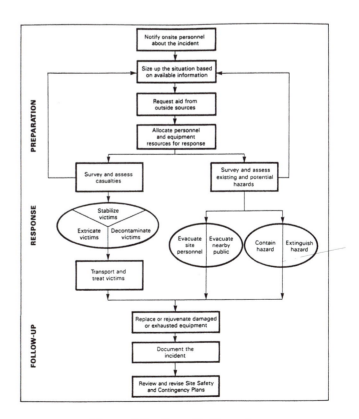

Figure 5-7   Security Procedure

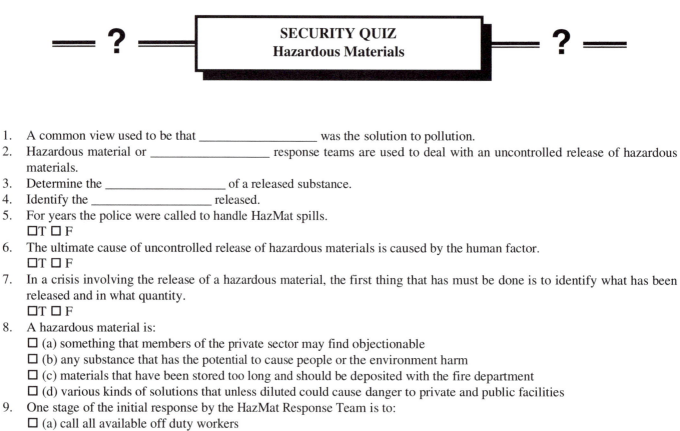

1. A common view used to be that _____ was the solution to pollution.
2. Hazardous material or _____ response teams are used to deal with an uncontrolled release of hazardous materials.
3. Determine the _____ of a released substance.
4. Identify the _____ released.
5. For years the police were called to handle HazMat spills.
   □T □ F
6. The ultimate cause of uncontrolled release of hazardous materials is caused by the human factor.
   □T □ F
7. In a crisis involving the release of a hazardous material, the first thing that has must be done is to identify what has been released and in what quantity.
   □T □ F
8. A hazardous material is:
   □ (a) something that members of the private sector may find objectionable
   □ (b) any substance that has the potential to cause people or the environment harm
   □ (c) materials that have been stored too long and should be deposited with the fire department
   □ (d) various kinds of solutions that unless diluted could cause danger to private and public facilities
9. One stage of the initial response by the HazMat Response Team is to:
   □ (a) call all available off duty workers
   □ (b) alert local civil defense personnel
   □ (c) determine the extent of the damage
   □ (d) develop the contingency plan
10. There are several ways that you can determine what hazardous substance has been released in an employee related spill, but the best way is to:
    □ (a) ask bystanders and onlookers
    □ (b) contact the local fire department as quickly and practically as possible
    □ (c) assemble members of the HazMat Response Team
    □ (d) ask the person who was using it

PROTECTION OFFICERS AND EMERGENCY RESPONSE: LEGAL AND OPERATIONAL CONSIDERATIONS

By John Ryan, CPO

The protection officer's responsibilities increase as each day passes. Fire prevention, asset protection, and policy enforcement are among the tasks charged to security officers. Along with these are many everyday duties like access control, maintaining general safety, and the monitoring of properties. Security operations are moving toward response to medical emergencies, too. With areas and properties getting larger, security patrols are the only link between a sick or injured person and help. Security is beginning to encounter legal issues when dealing with first response to medical emergencies. What are the legal repercussions of first response for security officers? What can the company or department do to protect itself from legal actions?

One such statute that has an effect on everyone, not just security officers, is the Good Samaritan Law. This law appears in one form or another in most states and can be referred to as the Good Samaritan Rule or the Firemen's Rule. This law is in effect in most states and protects emergency care providers from civil liability. This law basically states that "any individual who gives emergency care at the scene of an emergency shall not be held liable to that same person, acting in "good faith," as a result of any actions except those which prove intentionally harmful or grossly negligent.

Negligence is defined in *West's Encyclopedia of American Law* as "conduct that falls below the standards of behavior established by law for the protection of others against unreasonable risk of harm. A person has acted negligently if he or she has departed from the conduct expected of a reasonably prudent person acting under similar circumstances. This implies that the acting person breached their duty by failing to conform to the required standard of conduct and conduct was the cause of the harm." This means that the training a security officer has received is what that officer can—and should—apply to an injured person.

The officer must hold a current certificate, which indicates the successful completion of a class in first aid, cardiopulmonary resuscitation (CPR), or basic life support. The American National Red Cross, the American Heart Association, or an equivalent class, which is approved by that state's Department of Health, must sponsor these classes. CPR, in most areas, is taught in conjunction with the automated external defibrillator (AED).

Similar circumstances apply to the use of the AED as the Good Samaritan Law covers its use. A person who is trained to use an AED and who in good faith uses that AED in an emergency shall not be liable for any civil liability. Good faith can be defined in the law to designate the mental and moral state of honesty. If a person is deemed to be acting in a truthful way, even if wrong in procedure, that person will not be held liable. Good faith is a great protection to those who mean to do the right thing but unfortunately did not execute that desire to do right in a proper way. This, at the same time, allows the individual(s) who act wrongly and injure an individual more than they had been to be held liable.

Those liabilities include any acts or omissions by such a person in using the AED. The Good Samaritan Law does not cover any acts or errors that are purposely designed to harm or any grossly negligent acts. It does not cover the user of an AED from civil damages when that user hinders or impedes the care and treatment provided by emergency medical services (EMS) personnel or a health professional (doctors and nurses).

This contingency must include that the AED users (the officers) receive proper training from an accredited certifying agency.

- The officers or the company must maintain and test the AED in accordance with the manufacturer's specifications for operation.
- The company must have a policy for the officers in which that policy provides guidelines requiring the user of the AED to make use of all available options to activate EMS right away.
- The policy must include that all known information is made available to EMS personnel or other health care providers as they request it.

All these items indicate that the company must make a policy providing for the training of the officers in first aid and AED operation, maintenance of the AED, an assurance that the officers contact EMS, and that the responding officers gather all the available information about the injured person.

Since the Good Samaritan Law protects the officers from civil liability when they act properly in an emergency, it does not even have to be the best thing for the injured person, just as long as it is not intentionally harmful or negligent.

The important fact about the Good Samaritan Law is that any person who lacks the proper AED training but who has access to one and, in good faith, uses that AED in an appropriate emergency as an ordinary person would do under the same conditions should receive immunity from civil damages as covered by the statute.

With this law in effect across most states, security departments should not be fearful of training their officers to provide medical assistance to workers in the company or to visitors on the property.

It's also a good idea for protection officers to have first aid training as they could prove life saving should an emergency arise at their place of employment. Medical training is also an excellent form of public relations. If an officer can provide assistance to a person visiting or working for the organization, the actions taken leave that person with a good impression that someone was willing and able to help.

With all the positive impacts of proper emergency response for security officers, it proves that it is better to have those officers trained then to not and roll the dice with liability. If all the untrained officers just stand around and someone is injured or worse, what is the liability issue there?

The standard of care (also referred to as "duty of care" in some legal dictionaries) is another major issue in this topic. The standard of care is defined in the following excerpt from *West's Encyclopedia of American Law:* "The law recognizes that even a reasonable person can make errors in judgment in emergency situations. Therefore, a person's conduct in an emergency is evaluated in light of whether it was a reasonable response under the circumstances, even though, in hindsight, another course of action might have avoided the injury."

This definition means that a failure of a company to anticipate possible safety issues where injuries could result may be constituted as negligence. Precautions must be taken to limit this negligence through the marking of exits as an example. Emergency response trained security officers are the best way to limit this liability. Injuries can happen, but the response is the key to the lawsuit. If proper precautions were taken, and security officers maintain safety, it becomes more difficult to sue the company where the injury took place.

With all these factors in mind, it is clear that your security agency should have the officers trained in emergency response. This is especially valuable when you provide these services and a competitor does not. The officers cannot only provide the company with security, they can also provide emergency response, and limit possible lawsuits against the company. It is obvious that security departments should move towards getting their officers trained for emergency response on their properties.

With the legal issues defined, responding to emergencies becomes the focus. Security officers arriving on an emergent scene taking place on their property should be prepared for medical, fire, and hazardous materials emergencies.

MEDICAL EMERGENCIES

The key to quick emergency medical response is **Check, Call, Care**.

- **Check** the scene for dangers to the responding security officer. These dangers would consist of any instance when the officer's life could be placed in jeopardy. These dangers could consist of downed power lines, traffic, a crime scene, falling objects, hostility of the victim or crowd, smoke or fire, dangerous fumes, or weather events. The responding officer cannot provide help if they *become* a victim themselves. While checking the scene, look for additional victims and or clues to the event that caused the emergency. When the scene is determined as safe, the officer should check the victim(s) for injuries. Try not to move the victim, unless hazardous situations develop and movement is unavoidable (as listed earlier). If immediate life threatening injuries are present, immediately call 911 or your local emergency number. Life threatening injuries are: absent or decreased breathing, unconsciousness, no signs of circulation, or severe bleeding. The next step is to get consent to assist the victim. This is accomplished by informing the victim that you are a security officer with the company, your level of training, and your intentions for their treatment.

- **Call** for assistance. Relaying the emergency to 911 or your local emergency number in order to get Emergency Medical Services (EMS) workers to the victim. Call for EMS when the victim is unconscious; is having difficulty or not breathing; has chest pain; has no signs of circulation; bleeding severely; has severe burns; is vomiting blood or passing blood through feces or urine; is having a seizure; has a severe headache or slurred speech; has injuries involving the head, neck, or back; or has broken or suspected broken bones. When calling for help, tell the dispatcher the incident address, number the officer is calling from, the officer's name, the nature of the emergency, the number of victims and their condition, and the care being provided.

- **Care** for the victim. Only after 911 or your local number has been called and the appropriate agencies alerted should the officer begin to assist the victim with treatment. The officer would focus on trouble breathing over a leg injury. The officer should look for any changes in the victim's condition until EMS arrives. The officer could use a form like this to fill out the victim's information to aid EMS and to enhance report writing.

Name		Date of Birth	
Address		Social Security Number	

Chief Complaint:

TIME		B/P	
RESP		02	
PULSE			

HISTORY:

PUPILS	EDEMA	OTHER:
NECK VEINS	LUNGS	
SKIN		

MEDS:	ALLERGIES:

*** These items are in accordance with the American Red Cross First Aid program. For First Aid, CPR, or AED classes contact the Red Cross at www.redcross.org or your local hospital, Emergency Medical Services agency, fire department, or police department.

FIRE SAFETY

The key to fire safety is the **R.A.C.E.** method.

- **R**escue—The officer should remove people in immediate danger of fire or smoke to safe areas.
- **A**larm—The officer should pull the nearest fire alarm box. Dialing 911 or the local emergency number will alert fire service personnel. People near the fire should also be alerted.
- **C**onfine—Closing all the windows and doors will act to contain the fire and smoke. Closing doors is the single most important element to saving lives in the event of a fire.
- **E**xtinguish or **E**vacuate—Use the proper fire extinguisher only if the alarm has been sounded, only if the officer has been trained, and only if it is safe to do so. If safety becomes an issue, assist in the evacuation procedures as specified in fire escape plans.

The officer should remain available to assist the fire service personnel with location of the fire, access control, and account for all of the workers located in the affected area or building. The fire should then be properly documented and should include the location of the fire, the actions taken by the officer, the times of those actions, and of the responding agencies to the location. The incident should then be critiqued in order to improve response and to develop additional procedures in the event of potential occurrences. The analysis should also serve in developing successful and efficient inter-agency relationships.

HAZARDOUS OR BIO-HAZARDOUS MATERIALS

The key to hazardous or bio-hazardous materials (HAZMAT) incidents is to contact the proper agencies and containing the effected area.

- Realize that a HAZMAT incident exists.
- Contact proper agencies—911 or the local emergency number.
- Isolate the area—evacuate the area or building quickly while closing doors and windows.
- Retrieve the Materials Safety Data Sheets (MSDS) for the materials located on the property.
- Secure the area around the item or building.
- Meet responders at main entrance and give them the information that the officer has collected.

- Guide the responders to the location of the incident.
- Keep back and let the responders do their jobs, but be on hand to assist in a support role. The officer can offer assistance to the fire personnel if needed.
- Properly document the incident
- Critique the incident afterwards to enhance response and develop new procedures in case of future incidents. The critique can also aid in developing effective interagency liaison.

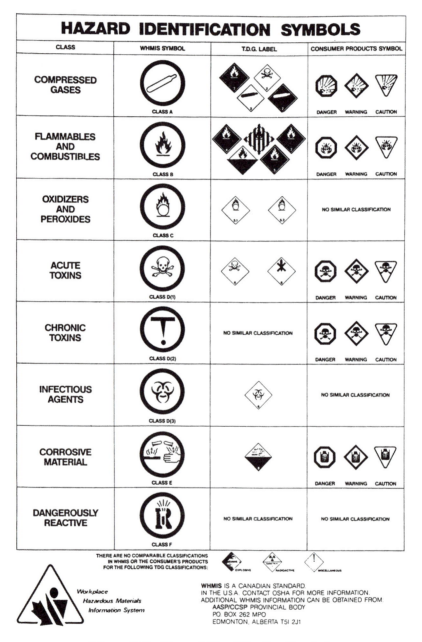

Figure 5-8   Hazard Identification Symbols

WORKS CONSULTED

1. Carr, Robert. Lieutenant - Bordentown Township Fire District 2. Personal Interview. 26 October 2002. www.btfd2.com.

2. Code of Virginia- Section 8.01-225. <u>Virginia "Good Samaritan" Law.</u> Approved 7 April 2002 <http://www.vdh.state.va.us/oems/GoodSam99.PDF>

3. *Emergency Response to Terrorism: Basic Concepts.* Published by the Federal Emergency Management Agency. 18 August 1997.

4. *First Aid: Responding to Emergencies 3rd edition.* Published by the American Red Cross. 2001.

5. Fresco, Joseph. Emergency Medical Services Coordinator - Bordentown Township Fire District 2. Personal Interview. 27 October 2002. www.btfd2.com.

6. Gillespie, Keith. Director of Safety and Security—Memorial Hospital of York, Pennsylvania. Personal Interview. 20 October 2002.

7. "Good faith." Wikipedia Online Encyclopedia. Updated 26 October 2002. http://www.wikipedia.org/wiki/Good_faith.

8. Hertig, Christopher. Asset Protection Instructor—York College of Pennsylvania. Personal Interview. 10 October 2002.

9. Illinois Compiled Statutes: Civil Immunities. Good Samaritan Act: 745 ILCS 49. 1 January 1997. <http://www.legis.state.il.us/ilcs/ch745/ch745act49.htm>

10. Massa, Patrick. First Aid/CPR/AED Instructor - York College of Pennsylvania. Personal Interview. 24 October 2002.

11. Medical Malpractice Laws In Florida. <u>768.13 Good Samaritan Act: Immunity from civil liability.</u> Updated 2000 version. <http://www.floridamalpractice.com/statgoodsamact.htm>

12. Pennsylvania Emergency Health Services Council. *Non-Medical Good Samaritan Civil Immunity.* 30 April 2002. <http://www.pehsc.org/goodsam.htm>

13. Premack, Paul "Good Samaritan Law Is a Liability Shield." Inside the Law Column, San Antonio Express News. 25 July 1996.

14. "Standard of Care" and "negligence." *West's Encyclopedia of American Law,* Minneapolis/St. Paul: West Publishing, 1998.

15. Texas Charitable Immunity and Liability Act. <u>Chapter 84 of the Texas Civil Practice and Remedies Code.</u> Copyright 1999, Paul Premack. http://www.premack.com/cil-sem.htm.

SECURITY QUIZ
Protection Officers and Emergency Response:
Legal and Operational Considerations

1. What does MSDS stand for? _____
2. Does inaction constitute negligence?
   ☐ Yes ☐ No
3. What does R.A.C.E. stand for? _____
4. Why is it important to critique after an incident? _____
5. Who is able to use an AED? _____
6. What is the first step in medical emergency response? _____
7. When should the alarm be pulled in a fire? _____
8. What are life-threatening conditions? _____
9. What is the best way to limit liability? _____
10. What is the last step in a HAZMAT response? _____

Unit Six

Strikes, Lockouts, and Labor Relations
Workplace Violence
Employee Dishonesty and Crime in Business
Substance Abuse

STRIKES, LOCKOUTS AND LABOR RELATIONS

By David J. DeLong, CPP

The protection officer should have a thorough knowledge of the security practices and producers in existence at his place of employment and their role in the labor relations process. Labor relations are a subsection of industrial relations in existence at any company, particularly those with unionized employees. Labor relations include the employer/employee relations dealing with matters connected with collective bargaining and associated activities.

The role of the protection officer and his activities can have a major influence on labor relations at any given company. Security's role in the following activities can have a major influence on labor relations: strikes, searches, employee discipline, employee misconduct and dishonesty, arbitrations, and interviews.

STRIKES

Strikes are a part of carrying on business. It is an almost inevitable occurrence for many unionized companies. Indeed, it may be argued that for such companies, strike costs are an integral part of the *labor* costs to maintain the operation.

Work stoppages as a result of labor relation activities and difficulties will arise primarily in three instances.

1. *Wildcat strike or illegal walkout*—This type of strike is an unauthorized work stoppage that is in violation of the law and/or a collective agreement in existence.

   The most common reason for a wildcat strike is the result of what a union considers unjust cause or reason.

2. *Lawful strike*—This type of strike takes place in accordance with applicable laws and the collective agreement in existence.

   The lawful strike usually occurs as a result of terms and conditions of employment. For example, at the expiry of an existing collective agreement, a strike may result after a strike vote has been taken. Wages or certain aspects of the collective agreement, such as health and safety, may not be satisfactory to members of the union with a resulting strike.

3. *Lockout*—This type of work stoppage takes place in accordance with applicable laws and the collective agreement in existence.

   The lockout refers to the refusal by management to allow members of the bargaining union onto company property. The purpose of a lockout by management is to put economic pressure on members of the union to

cause a behavior change that members of the union are not willing to accept.

The protection officer should be familiar with the company strike plan and manual that are in place. The strike plan will highlight and provide guidelines for the protection officer to follow. Normally, the strike plan is designed and updated to eliminate problems that occur during a strike and provide guidance for security and management.

The protection officer should be aware of the following security procedures during or prior to a strike, whether they are covered in a strike manual or not.

1. Access Control

Will locks be changed on all gates surrounding the property? How will premise access be handled? Normally, the majority of company vehicles are left within the plant main gate. The fewer the number of company vehicles crossing the picket line, the better. Nonunion employees who travel to work should travel in a fleet and cross the picket line at the same time.

Besides those nonunion people working, who else may desire access to the property?

2. Escorts

Any union member desiring access onto the property should be escorted by a protection officer at all times. An employee may want access to the property for a variety of reasons (i.e., employee has quit and wants to remove tools, and so on).

Any visitors who have authorization to access the property should be escorted by a protection officer from the property line to their contact on the property, and escorted off the property once business has been conducted.

3. Chain of command

The protection officer should be fully conversant with the chain of command in existence during a strike. Normally, the site security supervisor or the security chief will be responsible for all security and fire watch responsibilities.

4. Police assistance

The security department should notify the police ahead of time of the labor situation should a strike appear inevitable. Arrangements should be made for the police to be present at the picket during shift changes to avoid problems.

5. Communications

The main security gatehouse is normally designated as the command post because of its rapid response capabilities.

This command post is occupied 24 hours a day by a protection officer.

6. Prestrike Vandalism

Employees may attempt to sabotage operations just prior to the strike commencing, especially if they know the company intends to continue production. The protection officer must be especially alert on patrol rounds for any indications of sabotage.

7. Fire Safety

The protection officer may have fire responsibilities in the absence of a fire crew or maintenance crew during a strike. These responsibilities may include inspecting extinguishers, testing sprinkler systems, and inspecting fire alarms, hoses, and fire equipment.

8. Building Security

The security department recovers keys from all but essential persons prior to the strike commencing. If there is any reason to believe that strikers have keys for exterior doors, then the locks should be changed. It is common for strikers to make locks nonfunctional by driving spikes into keyholes or filling the lock with glue. Plenty of spare locks should be available.

9. Security Lighting

All security lighting should be checked prior to a strike. All perimeter and yard lighting should be available.

10. Purchasing

The purchasing department ensures that there is an adequate supply of raw materials available for any work that is to be continued during a strike. Constant communications exist between purchasing and security in the event that special shipments may need access to the property.

11. Threatening Phone Calls

Frequently strikers or their sympathizers will telephone threats to the company or to officials' homes. The protection officer should record such phone calls and be prepared to be part of a security investigation.

12. Crossing the Picket Line

The protection officer may be required to cross the picket line for a variety of reasons. The protection officer should keep in mind the following points when crossing a picket line.

- a) Cross the line only if necessary.
- b) Do not cross on foot.
- c) Try not to cross the line alone. Two witnesses to an incident are better than one.
- d) Move slowly and steadily in your vehicle, trying not to stop.
- e) Only stop when directly confronted by picketers who are in front of your vehicle.
- f) Don't leave the vehicle if stopped.
- g) Keep vehicle windows up and doors locked.
- h) Be cautious about verbal exchange with picketers. Be aware of the mood of the picketers.
- i) Observe and report any picket line infractions.

13. Picket Line Surveillance and Documentary Coverage

Surveillance of picket line activity is crucial during a strike to monitor and gather appropriate evidence that may be used in supporting company discipline imposed on an employee, supporting criminal charges, supporting or defending complaints about unfair labor practices, and supporting obtaining an injunction, which is a court order requiring a party to do or refrain from doing a particular act. For example, a company may obtain an injunction to try and limit the number of pickets on a picket line.

One of the primary functions of the protection officer during a strike is picket line surveillance. The surveillance on the picket line should continue 24 hours a day for all or part of the strike. The protection officer should be trained in the use of both still and movie cameras with telescopic lenses. Pictures don't lie, and they are difficult to contradict. The protection officer should also have a tape recorder to keep a running verbal account of picket line activity. If a tape recorder is not available, then a detailed written diary of events should be kept on at least an hour-by-hour basis. The following should be documented.

- a) Location of pickets (attach plan showing pickets by company property lines and gates) and whether pickets are on company property
- b) Number of pickets, location (i.e., whether spread out or in a group) and description of their conduct
- c) Time and place that picketing commenced and ended
- d) Identity of pickets and union affiliation. License numbers of any vehicles at or near the picket line.
- e) Number, size, wording of placards, and general description
- f) Conversations with pickets: Caution should be used. It is quite proper to ask the pickets their names, who sent them, how long the picket line will last, and its purpose. Relate conversations overheard between pickets or between pickets and other persons. Make notes of all conversations.
- g) Behavior of picket lines: Provide details of whether pickets are stationary or walking, whether talking to employees or other persons. Note any threats, threatening behavior, damage to property, acts of violence, and so on, and make notes. Provide details if any vehicles have been unable to enter or leave company property.
- h) Photographs: It is recommended that color photographs be taken with a Polaroid camera. Each should be marked on the reverse side with the name of the photographer and the date and time, with a brief explanation.
- i) Witnesses: Full names, addresses, and occupations of other people who have witnessed any illegal activity on the picket line should be recorded.

The role of the protection officer is essential prior to and during a strike. His role can be vital to the protection of company assets, especially during a strike.

SEARCHES

There is not much literature available on searches and labor relations for the protection officer. The protection officer should only conduct searches under the following conditions:

1. If an employee consents, a search can be conducted of his effects.
2. The employer or his representative, who is usually the protection officer, can conduct a search of an employee or his effects if there is an expressed term in the collective agreement. Also a search can be conducted of an employee or his effects if there is an implied agreement or implied term. An implied term can be derived by the company developing a formal search policy that is practiced regularly, consistently, and in a nondiscriminatory manner.
3. If no expressed or implied term exists on employee searches in a collective agreement, the protection officer should have reasonable and probable grounds before conducting a search.

The protection officer may ask himself why he must conduct searches at every shift change at his plant or facility. **Remember, every company has a right to protect its assets.** A protection officer conducting searches of employees and their effects on a regular basis can help a company protect its assets in the following manner.

1. May reduce accident rates (alcohol and drug related).
2. May reduce company material loss through theft and through employees hoarding materials in their lockers.
3. May reduce the use or possession of contraband on company property.
4. May increase employee morale because employees will feel that the company is concerned about maintaining a safe and secure physical environment.
5. May develop employee awareness about theft. Regular searches conducted by protection officers deter employees from taking material off a property. Remember, the key to a good security is prevention, not apprehension.

EMPLOYEE MISCONDUCT AND DISHONESTY

There are many types of dishonesty and employee misconduct at the workplace that the protection officer should be involved in. The protection officer should be aware of these types of dishonesty and employee misconduct.

1. Employee theft
2. Employee fraud—falsification of employment records, falsification of time cards and employee rebates, or falsification of workers' compensation insurance claims
3. Sabotage
4. Conflict of interest—kickbacks, selling information
5. Fighting, assault
6. Alcohol and drug use
7. Insubordination
8. Sleeping on the job
9. Safety violations
10. Leaving work early
11. Horseplay

All of the above types of dishonesty and employee misconduct may merit some form of discipline. The protection officer should be aware of the variety of discipline available to his employer.

EMPLOYEE DISCIPLINE

The protection officer should be aware of the types of discipline available to his employer for these reasons.

- The type and severity of discipline imposed may depend on how thorough the protection officer's investigation is.
- The protection officer may be in a position to recommend the type of discipline to be imposed.
- Discipline is an effective deterrent in the assets protection program.

Types of Discipline

1. Verbal—This type of discipline is given by an immediate supervisor where normally there is no documentation of the conversation.
2. Written warning—A formal warning is given by the immediate supervisor and placed in the employee's file as a record of discipline.
3. Suspension—This type of discipline is normally the first steps toward discharge. The time off provides the employee an opportunity to think about the infraction(s) committed and whether the employee wishes to pursue employment with the company.
4. Demotion—This type of discipline is used infrequently. An employee may be removed from the job for discipline reasons or because of physical or emotional difficulties in performing the job.
5. Termination or discharge—This type of discipline is the most severe available. Before terminating an employee, a company must consider the following factors.
   a) The age of the employee
   b) Company seniority
   c) The marital status of the employee
   d) The previous work record of the employee with the company
   e) The severity of the offense (i.e., extent of damage to equipment in case of negligence)
   f) The willingness of the employee to cooperate with the company investigators
   g) Whether or not the employee shows remorse
   h) Whether or not the offense was premeditated or a spur of the moment act.
   i) Whether the discipline is in accordance with past practice (i.e., do all employees receive the same discipline for the same act?)

ARBITRATION

The protection officer may find himself involved in an arbitration case as a witness of a breach of a company rule of policy where discipline has been given. The union representing the penalized employee may feel that the discipline is too severe or unjust, thus taking the case to arbitration.

An arbitrator acts as an impartial third party to determine whether the discipline was just. Both the company and the union reach agreement in choosing an arbitrator.

The arbitrator is not bound by formal rules of evidence so the arbitration is less formal than courtroom proceedings. In an arbitration hearing, it is a principle of common law that the onus is on the company to establish the existence of just cause. In other words, the company has to show good reason why an employee may have received the type and nature of discipline.

Remember: The protection officer could find himself going to court and going to arbitration over the same employee offense.

INTERVIEWS

The protection officer should keep in mind that a union representative should be provided if a witness or a suspect makes such a request. The protection officer may face accusations of harassment or unfair labor practices should a union representative not be provided.

SUMMARY

The protection officer must be aware of the union in existence at his plant or facility and the influence it may have on the following security functions: strikes, searches, employee misconduct and dishonesty, employee discipline, arbitration, and interviews.

SECURITY QUIZ
Strikes, Lockouts and
Labor Relations

1. Labor relations include the employee/employer relations dealing with matters pertaining to _____ bargaining and associated activities. (Fill in the blank.)
2. The role of the protection officer has an influence on the labor _____ climate at any given company. (Fill in the blank.)
3. A _____ by management is a form of legal work stoppage. (Fill in the blank.)
4. A wildcat strike is a legal strike.
    ☐ T ☐ F
5. Work stoppages as a result of labor relations difficulties will arise when union officials order production limitations.
    ☐ T ☐ F
6. The protection officer should be aware of the types of discipline available to his employer because:
    ☐ (a) the protection officer may hand out discipline
    ☐ (b) the protection officer will be disciplined if he doesn't know the types of discipline
    ☐ (c) discipline is an effective deterrent
    ☐ (d) the protection officer should know what is going on
    ☐ (e) None of the above
7. Which of the following is not illegal during a legal strike?
    ☐ (a) Picketing of residences
    ☐ (b) Obstructing highways
    ☐ (c) Carrying placards
    ☐ (d) Picketing within the premises
8. An incident of theft whereby an employee is discharged can become an issue in:
    ☐ (a) civil court
    ☐ (b) criminal court
    ☐ (c) an arbitration hearing
    ☐ (d) All of the above
    ☐ (e) b and c only
9. The strike plan is designed and updated to eliminate problems that occur during a strike and provide guidelines for security and management.
    ☐ T ☐ F

10. When stopped at a picket line in your vehicle, you should:
    ☐ (a) cross the picket line on foot
    ☐ (b) roll down the window and demand that you be let through
    ☐ (c) remain in the vehicle and proceed with caution
    ☐ (d) unlock the windows and doors
    ☐ (e) None of the above

WORKPLACE VIOLENCE

By Tom M. Conley, MA, CPP, CFE, CPO

Violence is pervasive in our world and has been a part of the human society since its earliest recorded time. Violence in society, in one form or another, is unfortunate and is simply unavoidable. Workplace violence is a specialized problem and one that security professionals must deal with in their day-to-day work lives. Whether it is at a large governmental facility, a retail store, or a private small professional business, there is no industry, profession, or organization that is immune from the threat of workplace violence. There are many definitions of workplace violence. The U.S. Department of Labor, Occupational Safety and Health Administration (OSHA) states, "Workplace violence is violence or the threat of violence against workers. Violence can occur at the physical workplace or outside the workplace (such as a taxi cab driver) and can range from threats and verbal abuse to physical assaults and homicide, one of the leading causes of job-related deaths [in the United States]. However it manifests itself, workplace violence is a growing concern for employers and employees nationwide" (OSHA, 2002).

The generally recognized primary objective of a security program, and the priority hierarchy, is the protection of people, property, and information. Of this protection hierarchy, people always come first, and a workplace violence incident always affects the people of the affected organization, including friends and family, in one way or another. Suffice it to say that the cost of a workplace violence incident is, at minimum, exhorbitant. Therefore, it is incumbent on the organizational leadership to do all they can, at all levels, to prevent a workplace violence incident from occurring. All individuals in the security department, including all security officers, must be an integral part of this prevention process to achieve the maximum level of success. The fact is that workplace violence *is* the business of the security department and all those in that department because security officers will likely be among the first ones to be on the scene if an incident occurs. Thus, it is essential that security officers possess the personal demeanor and professional skills necessary to respond to and successfully manage a workplace violence incident.

While we intuitively know that workplace violence has been occurring in organizations for as long as organizations have existed, only in recent decades has the U.S. government measured and statistically reported on the topic of workplace violence incidents in the United States. One of the first workshops held on the topic of workplace violence was a workshop on occupational homicide prevention that occurred on July 23 and July 24, 1990, in Washington, D.C. This workshop, which was sponsored by the National Insti-

tute for Occupational Safety and Health (NIOSH), concluded, in part, that "it is clear from the available data that workplace violence is a public health problem of significant proportion" (Bell & Jenkins, 1992). In that report, which covered the years 1980–1985, it was reported that homicide was the third largest cause of occupational injury death in the workplace. The workplace homicide rate in the private sector during this period was 0.8 deaths per 100,000. Employees working in the retail trade accounted for 33 percent of the workplace homicides, those working in the service industry comprised 19 percent of workplace homicides, and 11 percent in public administration (government services). Public administration services were the category with the highest rate of workplace homicide, which were 2.1 deaths per 100,000. Law enforcement officers comprised 83 percent of public administration services workplace homicides. The study also found that local passenger transportation was one of the occupations with the highest probability of workplace homicide, with a rate of 3.5 for every 100,000. Taxicab drivers accounted for 47 percent of these deaths. Retail workers suffered 2.2 deaths for every 100,000 workers during this period. In December 2001, the Department of Justice, Bureau of Justice Statistics reported that 1.7 million victimizations were committed per year during the period of 1993 to 1999 (Duhart, D.T., 2001, December). According to this report, workplace violence accounted for 18 percent of all crime during this 7-year period. Of the occupations examined in this study, police officers experienced the highest rate of workplace violence (261 deaths per 1,000 people) and college and university teachers experienced the lowest rate of workplace violence (2 deaths per 1,000 people). Finally, most workplace crime is not coworker-to-coworker crime. According to the Office of Safety, Health, and working Conditions, Bureau of Labor Statistics, contrary to popular belief, the majority of these incidents are not crimes of passion committed by disgruntled coworkers and spouses, but rather result from robberies (Sygnatur, E.F. & Toscano, G.A., 2000).

Some practical conclusions can be deduced from these statistics. First, a workplace violence incident can be perpetrated by either an internal or external source. An external source typically refers to those individuals who are not employed with an organization, whereas an internal source is most often used to identify an employee of a particular organization. Statistically speaking, most workplace violence incidents are committed by individuals who are external to the organization (nonemployees). An example would be an armed robbery of a convenience store clerk. An example of

Occupations with the highest work-related homicide rates, 1998				
Occupation[1]	**Homicide**		**Relative standard error**[3] **(percent)**	**Annual average employment**[4] **(thousands)**
	Number	**Rate**[2]		
All occupations	709	0.5	0.1	131,463
Taxi drivers and chauffeurs	49	17.9	6.2	273
Police and detectives, public	52	4.4	3.0	1,180
Guards and police, except public	39	4.1	3.3	946
Supervisors and proprietors, sales	117	2.5	1.5	4,719
Executive, administrative, managerial	102	.5	7.0	19,054
Managers, food and lodging	36	2.5	2.7	1,453
Cashiers	45	1.5	1.8	3,025
Truck drivers	22	.7	1.9	3,012

[1]Occupations with more than 20 homicides and employment exceeding 100,000 workers.

[2]The fatality rate is an experimental measure that represents the number of fatal occupational injuries per 100,000 workers and was calculated as Rate=(N/W) x 100,000 workers where:

    N = the number of fatal work injuries, in this case homicides, and

    W = the number of workers 16 years of age and older

[3]Relative standard errors of the Current Population Survey employment estimates can be used to approximate confidence ranges for the fatality rates. For example, a confidence range for the taxi drivers' and chauffeurs' rate can be approximated as follows: (Rate) x (Relative standard error) x (Multiplication factor for 9 observations at the 95-percent confidence level) = 17.9 x 0.062 x 2.77 = 3.1. The confidence range for this rate is (17.9) +/- 3.1 or 14.8 to 21.0

[4]Annual average employment estimates of employed civilians 16 years of age and older are based on the 1998 Current Population Survey.

    SOURCE: U.S. Department of Labor, Bureau of Labor Statistics, Census of Fatal Occupational Injuries

a workplace violence incident being committed by an internal source (employees, contractors, and so on) would be one employee physically assaulting another employee while at work. Second, most workplace violence incidents occur in occupations that are *somewhat* predictable, such as taxi drivers and retail workers. This means that if a security officer works in any of the known "high probability of violence occurring" professions, then he or she knows that there is inherently greater probability of an incident occurring than if an office professional works in a profession with reduced exposure to a workplace violence incident occurring. Third, when we have an idea of what workplace violence threats our workers are likely to encounter, we can implement precautions that can reduce the probability of an incident occurring. Lastly, just because most workplace violence incidents occur in occupations that are somewhat predictable, this does not, in any way, mean that a workplace violence incident cannot occur in any business or organization at any time. It is imperative that both security managers and security officers understand this reality and that they must be prepared for such an incident in their particular organization should one occur.

Preparation for a likely incident, especially one involving an external threat, is much easier than preparing for any eventuality involving an internal incident that might occur. This is especially true when it comes to identifying internal threats that could pose a workplace violence threat to the organization. Of all the workplace violence threats, there is little question that internal workplace violence threats cause organizational leaders the most significant level of anxiety. This is because of the uncertainty of when and how a threat can emerge within the organization.

The good news is that only a very small percentage of employees who have violent propensities will actually perform a violent crime. Additionally, most potential workplace violence incidents are preventable if proper intervention is achieved early in the escalation process. The difficulty and challenge, from both a business and a security perspective, is knowing which threats will turn into violence before they occur. This is why adequate preparations must be made to effectively deal with threats before they become an actual workplace violence incident. As is the case with most of the security function, prevention is the key.

Upon investigation of incidents after they occurred, it was apparent that people who have perpetrated workplace violence incidents displayed warning signs prior to the incident. Also, employees who committed workplace violence often started out being rude to coworkers. There was an escalation that occurred, culminating in homicide.

The *Hierarchy Escalation Model* is as follows:
- Level 1: Rude manners
- Level 2: Harassment
- Level 3: Verbal abuse
- Level 4: Threats of violence
- Level 5: Use of physical force
- Level 6: Weapons use/indicates acts of finality

Security professionals knowing the warning signs of a person who is a potential workplace violence threat is crucial. These are some general warning signs and clues.

- Has little tolerance of others.
- Intimidates others around them, including verbal threats.
- Gets away with overinflated and unearned performance evaluations.
- Has a history of family problems.
- A history of alcohol and/or drug abuse.
- Frequently talks about or is obsessed with violence or killings.
- Is fond of violent films and television shows.
- Has a fascination with weapons (guns/knives/others).
- Has a history of job losses.
- Is depressed, feels desperate; has mood swings.
- Displays feelings of job dissatisfaction.
- Frequently complains and appeals—always seems to be the victim.
- Has a history of violent episodes or criminal acts.
- Does not have a communicative personality.
- Has a chemical imbalance.
- Known as "crazy," "wound up tight," "strange," or "a time bomb."
- Has extreme reactions to new policies or procedures.
- Has a hard time with persons of authority and may challenge authority.
- Is very neat or very sloppy.
- Has a history of lying or exaggerating.
- Is self-centered.
- Seems aloof, distant, and detached.
- Has withdrawn all funds from bank account for no apparent reason.

- Lacks little or no social skills.
- Overreacts to small changes on a regular basis.
- Tolerates attitudes of violence.
- Has a history of continuous stressors in life.
- Ties their self-esteem and self-worth to their job.

Even though they may appear normal or somewhat normal, security officers should remember that individuals who commit a workplace violence incident are not mentally stable. The reality is that there is not one warning sign or clue that indicates mental instability. Thus it is important to "read the big picture" and not focus in on specific actions and then draw broad-based conclusions from those acts.

It is also essential that every organization provides meaningful training on the topic of workplace violence to all employees within the organization. If employees are not educated about the workplace violence warning signs, then the probability is greater than not that management will find out about a workplace violence incident as it is occurring or after it occurs. According to the United States Office of Personnel Management's Office of Workforce Relations, "[Employee] Training is a critical component of any prevention strategy. Training is necessary for employees, supervisors, and the staff members of each office that may be involved in responding to an incident of workplace violence" (Office of Personnel Management, 1998, February). Employee training is one of the best and lowest cost measures organizations can take to help combat workplace violence. And, all organizations should have a zero-tolerance policy to violence and threats of violence.

The purpose of this chapter has been to identify what workplace violence is, to identify steps that an organization can take to prevent a workplace violence incident from occurring, and to better prepare the security officer so they will recognize a potential threat and take appropriate action to prevent an injurious incident from occurring or properly react to an incident if it is occurring or has occurred. There is not one response plan or program that fits all needs of all organizations. In fact, the opposite is true. Every organization has its inherent risks and those risks must be identified and mitigated by the organization's leadership. The security team should be a significant part of this planning and mitigation effort. If an organization fails to plan, then it is planning to fail.

REFERENCES

Bell, C.A., & Jenkins, E.L. (1992 September) *Homicide in U.S. Workplaces: A Strategy for Prevention and Research.* Morgantown, WV.: United States Department of Health and Human Services.

Duhart, D.T. (December 2001) *Violence in the Workplace 1993–99.* (NCJ Publication No. 190076). Washington, D.C.: United States Department of Justice.

Occupational Safety and Health Administration. (2002) Workplace Violence Fact Sheet, United States Department of Labor, 2002.

United States Office of Personnel Management. (February 1998) Dealing with Workplace Violence. (OWR-09).

Sygnatur, E.F., & Toscano, G.A. (Spring 2000) *Work-Related Homicides: The Facts.* United States Bureau of Justice Statistics.

SECURITY QUIZ
Workplace Violence

1. Workplace violence is defined as the use of violence against workers.
    ☐ T ☐ F
2. According to the National Institute for Occupational Safety and Health (NIOSH), workplace violence is a public health problem:
    ☐ (a) of concern
    ☐ (b) that is cause for worry
    ☐ (c) of significant proportion
    ☐ (d) of great concern
3. An employee who exhibits rude manners toward his or her fellow workers is a definite workplace violence threat.
    ☐ T ☐ F
4. Workplace violence situations normally occur as a result of
    ☐ (a) one worker's aggression toward his or her fellow employees in the workplace
    ☐ (b) an armed robbery of a taxicab driver
    ☐ (c) criminal activity involving personal injury to a worker
    ☐ (d) All of the above
5. According to this chapter, the generally recognized primary objective of a security program is the protection of:
    ☐ (a) property and the organization's employees
    ☐ (b) people, property, and information
    ☐ (c) fire, property, and information
    ☐ (d) people, property, and money
6. According to this chapter, a very small percentage of employees who have violent propensities will actually perform a violent crime.
    ☐ T ☐ F
7. According to the United States Office of Personnel Management's Office of Workforce Relations, employee training is _____ component of any prevention strategy.
    ☐ (a) a critical
    ☐ (b) a very important
    ☐ (c) a low-priority
    ☐ (d) an important
8. All organizations should have a zero-tolerance policy to violence and threats of violence.
    ☐ T ☐ F
9. According to this chapter, most potential workplace violence incidents are preventable if:
    ☐ (a) workers who display warning signs of workplace violence are immediately fired.
    ☐ (b) employees with violent tendencies are never hired.
    ☐ (c) workers who have displayed personal problems are ignored because you never know what will set them off.
    ☐ (d) proper intervention is achieved early in the escalation process.
10. According to the National Institute for Occupational Safety and Health (NIOSH), during the years of 1980–1985, it was reported that homicide was the _____ largest cause of occupational injury death in the workplace.
    ☐ (a) first
    ☐ (b) second
    ☐ (c) third
    ☐ (d) fourth

EMPLOYEE DISHONESTY AND CRIME IN BUSINESS

By Dr. Norman R. Bottom, CPP, CPO, CST

Some employees will steal. The more opportunity we allow for theft, the more theft. Dishonest employees tend to steal what is most available to them. Computer people steal computer time. Cashiers steal cash. Warehouse employees take merchandise passing through their hands. Office personnel steal office supplies.

Managers steal, supervisors steal, and line employees steal. Protection officers have been known to steal, too. Many times, dishonest employees use external accomplices such as family members and friends to help them steal. An employee can steal on his own, or several employees may conspire to commit theft for their mutual benefit.

People steal from their employers for many reasons. Criminologists study the causes of crime. You and I do not need to know the competing theories of employee crime causation. It is our job to prevent as much theft as possible. (If you are interested, I personally think people steal from employers on purely economic ground—in other words, they are greedy!)

Opportunities for employee theft come about because of waste, accident, error, crime, and unethical or unprofessional practices. The first letters of these opportunities (threats, really) come together to form the acronym "WAECUP." (WAECUP is pronounced "wake up.") Below is a list of WAECUP loss threats with several examples of each.

A. Waste
1. Protection officers who waste time create opportunity for employees to steal.
2. Waste containers are favorite stash places for employees who steal.

B. Accident
1. The confusion that surrounds an accident scene may be used to screen an employee theft.
2. Arson has been used by employees to cover up theft. (What seems to be an accident can actually be a crime.)

C. Error
1. Protection officers who err in following procedures, such as in failure to make an assigned round, create opportunity for undetected theft.
2. Other (nonsecurity) employees who fail to follow security-related instructions, such as failing to lock up storage areas or exterior doors, create opportunity for theft.

D. Crime
1. If protection officers allow employee theft, other employees will get the idea that it is all right to steal and commit other crimes.
2. Failure to recognize valuable merchandise allows more crime. (You will not be watching the right stuff.)

E. Unethical/Unprofessional Practices
1. A general feeling among employees that it is okay to pilfer (steal) will result in more theft.
2. Unprofessional practices by management create resentment among other employees leading to deviant acts like theft.

WHAT SOCIETY THINKS ABOUT THE THIEF

Employee theft is a crime repugnant to society as a whole and to the employer as an individual. Property rights are fundamental to our way of life. We want to keep what belongs to us. So does the businessman.

Theft is a violation of property rights and universally condemned by right-thinking persons. Stealing from an employer is simply an ungrateful, criminal act. It is not a right. It is a wrong.

THE REALITIES OF THEFT PREVENTION

Not all internal (employee) theft is preventable. We will learn below some ways to minimize, moderate, and control this criminal activity. Thus we become better protection officers.

Protection offers can have an impact. They can prevent theft. They can deter and displace theft. When security is tight, thieves look for another place to steal. We can make theft so difficult and so much trouble that the would-be thief will decide against it.

Theft prevention is a good idea at any time. Today it is even more important. Many business enterprises teeter on the verge of going out of business. Times are tough. Preventing theft can save many jobs, and that includes your own.

OBJECTIVE

Protection officers *must* reduce employee theft. This chapter focuses on practical methods to reduce this theft. However, it takes more than your presence, standing around in a sharp uniform, or strutting through an area. You must know what to look for, what to report, and what actions to take. You must know, also, what actions not to take.

Thieves can be clever, and new opportunities for employee theft will develop. This chapter is only a beginning. You must continue to study employee-theft prevention as long as you are a protection officer. The objective of this chapter is to whet your appetite on the scope of employee theft prevention and widen your knowledge.

This chapter will give you some tips on observation. For example, employees who bring in empty or almost empty shopping bags, then leave with bags bulging should be viewed with suspicion. Those bulging bags may contain company property. As a general rule, always look for the unusual and out-of-place; then investigate discreetly.

Also this section will explain some things about reporting and discuss what to report and to whom. For example, doors propped open (that are normally locked) may be used by thieves as access points to sneak company property outside. Such things should be reported and written up.

Also, this will be a discussion of actions to take and actions not to take. For example, managers and other executives often work at home during the evening. They are usually permitted to take company property home to do this. Hourly workers (shift workers) seldom have the right to take company property home. Know company rules before you act or accuse.

DEFINITION OF EMPLOYEE DISHONESTY

What is employee dishonesty? It is theft. It is cheating customers. It is committing industrial espionage. It is lying on employment applications and falsifying time records. It is claiming sick leave when there is no sickness. Anything that can be moved, or taken apart and the pieces moved, is a candidate for employee theft.

We are going to learn some things about **theft prevention** in this chapter. Other types of employee dishonesty will be covered elsewhere in this manual or in later supplements. Theft of visible items is our theme. Illegal computer access or electronic data intercepts will not be discussed.

Protection officers can reduce the theft of *visible* items of company property. They can catch thieves, of course. But it is better to reduce *opportunity* for theft to catch thieves.

Each company has its own types of property. That property includes personal (movable property) and fixed (real property). Real property, such as permanent buildings and land, cannot be carried off. In this chapter, we need to worry only about personal property.

Personal property, in business usage, is not what you or I mean by our "personal effects." Business tries to protect the machinery or means of production. The materials or equipment used for production (or sale) of goods and services need protection. And those goods, services, products, and so on offered to the public must be guarded.

Business wants to protect and keep its reward: the income received for selling its products, of course. Those categories are what we mean by business personal property.

Some business is devoted to manufacturing. Here the threat of employee theft takes place at several stages. Those stages occur from the time that machines are installed and raw materials purchased, through the entire production process— and until the finishing goods are delivered.

Other companies specialize in storage and transportation. They warehouse and distribute manufactured products. These companies worry while goods are stored. Every time goods are handled by employees causes theft concern, too. Goods in transit present additional possibilities for theft.

We all shop at the malls and other retail stores. Retail is certainly a familiar business to all. There are also wholesale outlets that specialize in selling quantities to the trade. Each retail store, and each wholesaler, worries about losing that property they hope to sell. Employee theft is one way the property can be lost to these owners.

Institutions like hospitals have special employee theft problems. These include the unauthorized use or taking of narcotics and theft of patient's property. Banking institutions worry about their cash, naturally. The point to remember is that all business needs protection against employee theft. That protection need demands proper security and loss control effort by protection officers.

FIRST STEPS

The first step in employee theft prevention is to learn what can be stolen. A list of property categories is useful for reference. All protection officers need such a list to help them identify company property.

Sample List—Retail Establishment

Office Area
1.   Paper products
2.   Typewriters, calculators, computers, telephones
3.   Desks, chairs, bookcase, file cabinets
4.   Rugs, paintings
5.   Petty cash

Stock Room
1.   Sales merchandise of various types
2.   Shelving
3.   Materials, handling equipment
4.   Some office supplies

Sales Area
1.   Merchandise to be sold
2.   Shelving and cabinets
3.   Cash registers/computerized sales terminals
4.   Product displays
5.   Sales receipts (cash, checks, etc.)

Parking Areas and Outbuildings
1.   Exterior merchandise displays
2.   Equipment stored outside (in the open or in outbuildings)
3.   Company vehicles
4.   Trash and refuse containers

A similar category list can be drawn up for any work environment. Buy a notebook and make your own list, especially if there is no master list available. Test your powers of observation by comparing your list with those of other protection officers. Update your list as new property arrives and old property is replaced.

It is good to know as much as is possible about all company property including value. More valuable items, especially if easily moved (portable), deserve special theft prevention effort.

MARKINGS

Life becomes difficult if company property is not marked to indicate ownership. Learn what marking system, if any, is used to mark all equipment. That includes office typewriters, computer equipment, and so on. Sale merchandise should be marked, too, with special tags.

Some marking systems use stick-on labels. Other marking systems involve stamping numbers on metal. Paint and stencil are used by some companies for identification purposes. There are chemical compounds that can be painted (or sprayed) on. These compounds leave markings visible only in certain light.

If valuable items are not marked, you should ask "Why not?" Your supervisor might give you a good explanation. He may commend you for an idea whose time has come. A good protection officer learns how to recognize company property.

A general reminder: Learn, learn, learn—continue to ask good questions. Keep written records of the answers. In that way you will not have to ask the same question twice. And you will have a ready reference when there is no supervisor available.

CONCEALMENT

Hide and sSeek is a children's game familiar to most of us. The basic instructions call for someone blindfolded to count while other children hide. Then the counter opens his eyes and tries to find the others. It may help to think of employee thieves as the other children who have the time to take and hide your company's property. The protection officer should not, of course, have his eyes closed while this theft and concealment go on.

Trash and garbage containers are time-honored hiding places for employee thieves. Plastic garbage bags are another useful item for thieves. Modern garbage bags are sturdy and unaffected by moisture, and they are opaque—that is, you cannot see through them. The protection officer should look for garbage bags in containers, both inside and outside the building. And garbage bags will be found in corners and adjacent to doorways.

Periodically check all garbage cans, dumpsters, and sealed garbage bags for stolen merchandise. Be especially alert to those employees who take garbage and trash outside. That activity is a critical junction. It is critical because stolen merchandise can be hidden in the trash. It is junction because the merchandise is leaving the premises. Normally, only a few trusted employees are allowed to take trash outside. Know who those are.

Another trick of the employee thief is to take a particular item and hide it for later pickup. Remember that everything has its place. And everything should be in its place. Be alert to the out-of-place item concealed in a strange or unusual location. That may be an indication of employee theft in progress. Look behind shelved merchandise. Examine storage rooms and broom closets.

Examples
- Valuables, like watches, normally under lock and key, found on open shelves tucked behind cheap items.
- Office equipment and/or office supplies stashed in an area where there is no desk or clerical work performed.
- Valuable merchandise found in areas set aside for employees to leave their purses and other personal belongings. The same goes for employee locker area.
- Sheds, lean-tos, truck courts, and other locations outside main buildings but on company property. Company property found at these locations should be appropriate to the area. For example, office typewriters do not belong in a garden shed.

Briefcases, lunchboxes, purses, shopping bags, and even stranger containers will be carried to work by employees. Thieves use these containers to remove company property from the side. You realize, of course, that such personal items are entitled to reasonable privacy. You had better remember this, or your search will only cause trouble to you. Always check with a supervisor before searching an employee or his property.

Many companies have rules about what type of items can be brought onto company property. Know these rules. You may prevent a theft by advising an employee that the gunny sack in his hand cannot be brought in.

Vehicle parking is another factor in concealment. The personal vehicle of an employee should not be parked next to the storeroom door, for example. In fact, employee parking should be at some distance from buildings and doorways. Company policy establishes the parking rules. But you should point out parking hazards that make employee theft easier.

Employee thieves may use their own car or truck. They may also use a company vehicle to haul away the stolen merchandise. For example, a driver may load a few extra cases on the truck, cases not listed on the manifest. These will be sold for his personal profit and the company's loss.

Some thieves are very bold. They will attempt to walk out with stolen merchandise in their hands. Employees who attempt to remove company property from the premises should have a pass or other authorizing document. Since pass forms may be stolen or counterfeited, it is important to know and recognize authorized signatures. When in doubt, check with your supervisor. And make sure that the pass covers each and every item. If the pass says "six" items, do not let the employee remove seven.

REPORTING

All suspicious activity observed, and especially that involving employees, should be immediately reported.

Remember that all observations and concealment findings are a waste of time unless your results are promptly reported. Along with the need for *timely reporting,* there is a second thing to remember. *Get report results to the right individual(s).* The right person or persons will be able to take the necessary action.

So far, we have three main points to remember. First, reporting must follow observation. Observation may involve the sight of suspicious activity on the part of employees. Observation may involve threat potential such as open doors. Or the protection officer may have discovered concealed company property. **First observe, then report.**

The second main point is timely reporting. If you wait too long to report suspicious activity, the theft will take place. If you wait too long to report a suspicious open door, stolen items will exit through that door. If you wait too long to report a concealed item, it will be removed by the thief.

The third main point is reporting to the right people. The right person will be able to react properly to the threat you observed. The right person will authorize or take corrective action in timely fashion. The right person will see that your work is not wasted. **Who is the right person(s)?**

Your supervisor, if available, is the right person. The nonsecurity supervisor in the hazard area is another right person. Each company and each business will have a chain of command or leadership tree. Protection officers must know the responsibilities of various managers. They must know how to reach managers in case of an emergency. Emergencies include a serious threat of employee theft.

Reports about employee theft should be both verbal and written. The need for verbal reporting often increases with rapidly unfolding events. The need for written reports is twofold. First, *clarity.* Verbal information often becomes distorted when relayed from one person to another.

Second, *recordkeeping.* Written reports serve as the basis for planning by the security and loss control staff. History tends to repeat itself, and hazards repeat unless records are kept and used.

Written reports from protection officers are sometimes hastily read by management, if read at all. This is especially true of shift reports. It is hard to say why these reports are not properly used. Sometimes it is the protection officer's fault.

Reports are not valuable if poorly written or have illegible handwriting. Other problems relate to forms that are poorly designed. At other times, the boss means well but just cannot seem to get around to reading activity reports until they are stale.

A protection officer may develop a negative attitude about reporting his observations (to include employee theft hazards). Perhaps nobody asked for an explanation of important observations. No pats on the back or "attaboys." Or nothing seems to have been done to reduce the reported threat. Many protection officers, especially those working the night shift, never see the protection boss or his deputies. That shift especially may wonder if their reports are ever read.

What can be done? Report suspicious activity, and other employee theft potentials, verbally. Discuss your written reports with supervisors whenever you can. Once in a while, take some initiative and call the protection office when you are off-duty and the boss is in. Show your concern for your duties and for your reports. That is dedication often rewarded.

The protection officer bears responsibility for his observations on employee theft or the potential for that theft. They must be understood by the top ranks. No excuses or moaning about lack of communications will help the situation.

PREVENTIVE ACTIONS

Observation and reporting are crucial in employee theft prevention, as we have seen. Preventive action is also important. But, actions can be hazardous. The wrong action can bring unnecessary embarrassment to an employee, the protection manager, and to the individual protection officer.

Wrongful action can expose you and your company to civil suit. For example, an employee falsely accused of theft can bring suit for monetary damages. Some wrongful actions lead to criminal prosecution and jailing of the protection officer. Be careful in accusations. Be especially careful in conducting searches. Search actions are the most troublesome preventive actions.

Preventive actions do not always mean trouble. Many preventive actions are pleasant. They involve heading off employee theft at an early stage. Never forget, the essence of protection is prevention of employee theft. Cultivate a good liaison with as many senior employees as you can. Let these employees be additional eyes and ears.

SEARCH POLICY

You may feel it necessary to search a lunch bucket or purse. You may decide an employee locker contains stolen merchandise. There may be an excellent reason to suspect company property is in an employee's personal vehicle. Before you take action, before you search, know your company policy. And, always follow policy.

Do not take actions in conflict with company policy. Policy may state that employee packages or vehicles can be inspected on demand. Or, policy may authorize periodic and random searches of employee parcels, briefcases, and purses. A company without a written and well-communicated policy is buying trouble for itself and the protection staff. When in doubt about search policy, ask your supervisor. Remember that an error on your part could result in your termination and court action.

Searching a company vehicle is less hazardous, but company policy still rules. It may be necessary to break a door seal. A search could delay delivery of overdue merchandise.

The union contract may set limitations or requirements. For example, rules may require the presence of a union steward or a supervisor during the search. **Know the rules and follow them.**

Searching other areas, such as storage sheds, or checking trash containers and garbage bags is normally simple. But it is wise to ask your supervisor if such routine checks can be done without giving prior notice to the protection office or some supervisor. Routine searches should be done at different times, of course. If you always check a trash container at 4:00 P.M., employee thieves will wait until 4:10 to stash the stolen goods.

Protection officers may not be allowed in some areas unless invited. Such areas often include the research laboratory and executive offices. Barging into a research laboratory could ruin experiments in progress. And remember that company executives do not want protection officers poking around when important business is under way.

Public relations are the key to almost everything the protection officer does. This is never more true than in searching an employee's bag, briefcase, or vehicle. Your attitude during a search must be professional and non-threatening. Remember that you must work tomorrow with the same employees you search today. An overbearing or nasty attitude will make enemies you cannot afford.

EMPLOYEE LIAISON

No protection officer can be successful without help. Help will come from the protection staff of course. There is another type of help. That comes from the nonsecurity employee. It is necessary to cultivate the respect of those employees who can assist you to estimate employee theft threats.

Morale is a good indicator of theft potential. When overall morale is high, there tends to be less employee theft. When moral is low, more theft is likely. The protection officer needs to keep his finger on the pulse of employee morale. This can best be done through contacts in the work place.

Often, nonsecurity employees will witness an employee theft, but fail to report it. That can go on for a long, long time. If the protection officer has the respect of key employees, hints will be forthcoming about the deviant activities of employees. These hints are golden.

Liaison with nonsecurity employees has other benefits. A roving protection officer will never know an area or the activities taking place as well as employees who work there. Changes in the workplace—for example, getting a shipment of new, valuable items, opening a formerly sealed door, or hiring temporary help—can raise the potential for employee theft.

New merchandise represents something additional to observe. Opening a previously sealed door means another access route to remove stolen merchandise. Temporary staff may themselves steal or be blamed as regular employees attempt theft.

SUMMARY

This chapter presented some lessons about controlling employee dishonesty. Employees at all levels may steal from their employers. Most employees steal what is immediately available to them. Opportunities for theft come about because of waste, accident, error, crime, and unethical/unprofessional practices (WAECUP).

Society is against theft on principle. Protection officers cannot prevent all employee theft, but they can have a positive impact. Theft prevention is a good idea at any time. Today it is especially important due to the economic climate.

Practical methods to prevent theft were explained. These include tips on what to look for, what to report, and what actions to take. As a general rule, always look for the unusual and out of place. But be prudent in taking action. An employee may have permission to take company property off premises.

Theft of visible items is the focus of this chapter. Protection officers can reduce the theft of visible items, but it is better to reduce opportunity for theft than to catch thieves. Theft reduction requires knowledge of company property, how it is marked, and its value. Make a property list to aid your memory.

Concealment often comes before removal of company property by the employee thief. Trash and garbage containers and bags are favorite hiding places. The thief may conceal valuable merchandise behind less valuable items. Everything should be in its place. Look behind shelved merchandise; examine storage rooms and brooms closets.

Know the rules about what employees may bring onto company property. You may be able to prevent a theft simply by advising an employee not to bring a container in. Vehicle parking is another factor. Point out parking hazards which make employee theft easier.

Suspicious activity should be reported. There should be a verbal report and a written report. Timely observation is critical to the right person or persons. Know who the right person is. Follow up your reporting in discussions with protection supervisors.

Preventive actions are important to employee theft prevention. Wrongful actions by protection officers can lead to civil and criminal problems. Care is needed in making searches and in making accusations. Some preventive actions are pleasant. Employee liaison is an excellent way to prevent employee theft. Liaison with senior employees means additional eyes and ears.

Company search policy must be understood and applied. Know whether policy allows random searches or searches on demand. A written search policy is essential. Search of company vehicles may be easier. But complications can arise with respect to seals, delays, or contract provisions. Always follow the rules.

Search of trash or storage areas is usually without complication. These searches should be done at staggered times.

Some areas, such as research labs and executive offices, need prior permission to enter—even by the protection officer. There are valid reasons for these restrictions.

Public relations are always an important skill. This skill is important during any search involving an employee. Remember, you must work tomorrow with the employee you search today. Cultivate the respect of senior employees who can help you recognize employee theft potential. Morale is a good indicator of theft potential. Low morale is likely to mean more employee theft problems.

Sometimes employees witness theft, but do not report it. If the protection officer develops the respect of key employees, hints to employee deviancy will be given. Liaison with nonsecurity employees has other benefits. Changes in the workplace environment can raise the potential for employee theft. Good liaison will keep you up-to-date on such changes.

The protection officer can do a good job in preventing employee theft but only if he follows the methods outlined and company policy.

SECURITY QUIZ
Employee Dishonesty,
Crime in Business

1. The more _____ we allow for theft, the more theft. (Fill in the blank)
2. WAECUP   stands   for: _____   _____   _____   _____
   _____ (Fill in the blanks.)
3. As a ground rule, always look for the _____. (Fill in the blank.)
4. The activity of removing trash and garbage is a critical _____. (Fill in the blank.)
5. What step must immediately follow observation of suspicious activity? (Check correct answer.)
   ☐ (a) Marking
   ☐ (b) Concealment
   ☐ (c) Reporting
   ☐ (d) Liaison
6. Liaison with nonsecurity employees has many benefits to the protection officer.
   ☐ T ☐ F
7. Protection officers may visit any office or activity without notice and at the officer's convenience.
   ☐ T ☐ F
8. Employee package policies usually include:
   ☐ (a) search on demand
   ☐ (b) periodic or random search
   ☐ (c) Neither of the above
   ☐ (d) Either a or b
9. Suspicious activity should be reported only in writing.
   ☐ T ☐ F
10. Reporting observations to the right person or persons is vital.
    ☐ T ☐ F

SUBSTANCE ABUSE

By Francis J. Elliott, CPP

Today, we live and work in a society where substance abuse is omnipresent. It is a major domestic problem confronting the United States and the leading cause of crime, health problems, and child abuse. Substance abuse adversely affects our schools and the education of our children; it divides and destroys families, drains the economy of entire communities, and jeopardizes the ability of business and industry to be competitive. Substance abuse is a threat to our society and public safety. It destroys the human will and denies dreams. Substance abuse does not discriminate. It favors no race, age group, intelligence level, social or economic status, or sex. It consumes anyone who dares to embrace its false promises for perpetual self-gratification and well-being.

This chapter is aimed at elevating the protection officer's awareness about substance abuse in the workplace, and about psychoactive drugs and the behaviors resulting from their use and/or abuse. This chapter also identifies the risks that these behaviors pose for employees and the employer, and the methods by which to prevent or confront these risks. As a security professional, you must be prepared to deal with substance abuse on the job and effectively communicate your observations and information to your supervisor. Because of your daily interaction with employees and others who visit your workplace, you must be able to recognize conditions that may point to a security risk or vulnerability

For purposes of this chapter, the phrase "substance abuse" refers to the use, usually self-administered, of any psychoactive drug in a manner that deviates from the approved legal, medical, or social patterns within a given culture. A drug is defined as any substance that by its chemical nature alters the structure or function of the living organism. A psychoactive drug is one which alters the structure or function of the brain. Psychoactive drugs alter mood, perception, or consciousness. Examples include nicotine, alcohol, marijuana, cocaine, biphetamine, LSD, and many others, which will be described later in this chapter.

Because our focus is on drugs that directly impact performance and behavior on the job, nicotine will not be a focus of this chapter. However, it is important to note that nicotine consumption produces classic drug dependence characteristics. Along with alcohol, it is considered a gateway drug for those who ultimately use other dependence-producing drugs, such as marijuana and cocaine. Finally, nicotine has been clearly identified as an insidious substance responsible for hundreds of thousands of deaths annually.

IMPACT ON BUSINESS AND INDUSTRY

Recent studies reveal that 74 percent of illicit drug users and 90 percent of alcoholics are employed in the American workplace. Many of these employees are poly-drug abusers. They abuse more than one drug in the course of their drug-taking behavior. Employees with alcohol and other drug problems represent 10 percent to 20 percent of any given workforce. Within this workforce, the highest concentration of abusers is within the 18- to 25-year-old age group. A recent study shows that 20 percent of workers age 18 to 25 use drugs on the job, while the rate for 27- to 34-year-olds is 13 percent. The economics cost of this extensive involvement with mind-altering drugs is in excess of $1 billion annually to the American business community. The annual cost for a single employee with a substance abuse problem is $7,621.00. Aside from the substance abuser population, there exist an unspecified number of employees who are codependent. These employees to not abuse drugs. However, they share a common thread. They are the spouses, children, and significant others who arrive for work each day preoccupied with the physical and emotional condition of their loved ones.

These are some of the tangible costs generated by the substance abuser.

1. **Decreased productivity**—They are 25 percent less productive.
2. **Accidents**—They are three to four times more likely to have an accident on the job. Fifty percent of all accidents are attributable to substance abusers. Forty percent of industrial accidents resulting in fatality are linked to alcohol consumption and alcoholism.
3. **Absenteeism**—They are absent four times more often. Also, they are more likely to be away from their assigned locations during regular work hours.
4. **Theft**—They are responsible for 50 percent to 80 percent of employee thefts.
5. **Workers' compensation**—They are five times more likely to file a workers' compensation claim.
6. **Health care costs**—They use medical benefits five times more often, and the family members of substance abusers generally have higher than average health care claims.

Aside from the tangible costs of substance abuse, many hidden costs exist for which a dollar figure cannot be assigned, such as the following:

- Morale problems
- Intimidation of managers and employees

- Wasted supervisory time
- Overtime costs
- Grievance costs
- Training and replacement costs
- Decrease quality of products and services

To successfully address the adverse consequences of substance abuse in the workplace, we must elevate awareness and change existing attitudes and procedures that enable the problem to perpetuate itself. There is no single solution. The greatest success will come through the selection of various prevention and remedial components that complement a company's particular philosophy and culture. These components include policy development, training and education, employee assistance programs, the security function, and drug testing measures.

SUBSTANCE ABUSE: WHAT IS THE MOTIVATION?

Time and again the question is asked, "Why do people abuse drugs?" The reasons are usually complex. Early drug use, at any age, may be a result of peer pressure, low self-esteem, insecurity, or various other social, environmental, psychological, and biological factors that induce stress and anxiety. In all likelihood some combination of these variables stimulates the initial use and abuse of psychoactive drugs. Initial use is usually re-enforced as a result of (1) their pleasant effects, (2) a perceived control over the drug, (3) peer acceptance and recognition, and (4) myth and misinformation. What we know is that drugs can quickly relieve unpleasant feelings. Mind altering drugs quickly affect the pleasure centers of the brain so that the user who is feeling good will feel better, and those feeling badly will feel good. The result is nearly immediate self-gratification, but it is only temporary. In reality, sooner or later, the user and others always pay the price.

Continued use of a psychoactive drug will most often result in problematic behavior such as drinking and driving, job jeopardy, or splitting with the family. Ultimately, repeated use can lead to physical and/or psychological dependence. As use continues, there are usually three anticipated outcomes.

1. Return to a drug-free lifestyle.
2. Continue to abuse drugs, avoiding dependence but exhibiting problematic behavior at work, home, or the community.
3. Continue to abuse drugs to the point of dependence and most likely die from his/her disease.

How each substance abuser will land is unpredictable, and is often guided by circumstance beyond anyone's control.

HOW PROBLEMATIC BEHAVIOR AND DEPENDENCE DEVELOP

Today, drug dependency is viewed as a disease with identifiable causes, signs, and symptoms. It follows a predictable course and outcome, and it is treatable. The disease of drug dependence can be the following.

- **Primary**—it is not simply the symptom of some other problem(s), it is in itself the problem.
- **Contagious**—it attracts others who are vulnerable.
- **A family disease**—it affects their families, and not just the individual abuser.
- **Chronic**—it is difficult to control, is quite often recurring, and although treatable, it is incurable.
- **Fatal**—it takes hundreds of thousands of lives annually.

Drug dependence may be physical or psychological, and it represents an individual's loss of control. Physical dependence occurs when a person cannot function normally without the repeated use of a drug. If the use of the drug is abruptly discontinued, the person experiences severe physical and psychic disturbance, known as withdrawal. Psychological dependence provides a strong psychological desire to continue the self-administration of drugs for a sense of improved well-being.

A great number of programs and treatment approaches exist for the treatment of drug dependencies. What we do know about these various programs is that no single approach or program is effective for every drug dependent person. We also know that there are not enough of these programs to meet the needs of the afflicted. In spite of the various programs and models, we know that recidivism rates are high. So, for all that is known, the experts still have much to learn and continue to do so each day. There is, however, a solid body of evidence pertaining to the stages of dependency and associated behaviors which the protection officer should know. An understanding of the process is critical to prevention and rehabilitation efforts.

Drug dependence follows a predictable course of action which, most often, begins with experimentation. This may be the result of curiosity, peer pressure, or a variety of other variables or combination of variables. Everyone is susceptible to the abuse of drugs; some, more so than others, due to a host of social, environmental, psychological and biological issues, or in some cases, heredity. What is significant is that each incidence of use makes the user more susceptible to continue use, up to and including dependence. Further, the earlier drug use begins, the more likely it is to progress to abuse and dependence.

Another facet of dependence is recovery. The individual user has a greater opportunity for a full recovery if treatment begins before dependence sets in. The longer one uses a drug(s), the more complex the physical and psychological symptoms become. As a result, recovery for the dependent person, or daily user, is a greater challenge in most instances than recovery from occasional use of experimentation. This is why early intervention is significant.

Whether an intervention occurs at home, work, school, or in the community, it is certain that the earlier the intervention takes place the greater the opportunity is for recovery.

HOW IS SUBSTANCE ABUSE PERPETUATED?

There are essentially five reasons why substance abuse continues to be a problem in the workplace.

1. Denial
2. Mixed messages
3. The "harmless" theory
4. Drug use is controllable by the user
5. The problem is viewed as controllable through attrition

Denial provides the biggest single roadblock to successfully addressing the problem of substance abuse in society or the workplace. Parents, teachers, husbands, wives, managers, and users themselves all tend to deny the problem exists, even in light of hard evidence. Some familiar phrases illustrate the point: "Not *my* kid," "What is wrong with a few drinks?" "Not in *my* company," "Not Joe—he's just a good-natured guy," "It must have been entrapment."

Mixed messages are heard daily, and are confusing to the layperson. Some insist the use of certain drugs for "recreational" purposes is harmless. Others say that the same drugs contribute to many individual, social, and occupational ills. For instance, some marijuana advocates say that this drug is harmless and does not interfere with one's work. Others claim that the drug has a negative impact on education, motivation, and the ability to remember and perform complex or new tasks. Hence, marijuana use may contribute to industrial accidents.

The "harmless" theory contends that the use of drugs such as marijuana, cocaine, and alcohol is considered by many to be an innocuous activity, on or off the job. In fact, some forces are aggressively moving to legalize all psychoactive drugs. In reality, no drug can ever be considered harmless. Any drug is harmful when taken in excess, even aspirin and, of course, alcohol. Some drugs can also be harmful if taken in dangerous combinations, such as barbiturates and alcohol. Some drugs, like over-the-counter medications, can be harmful in therapeutic doses if alertness is diminished or drowsiness results. Finally, certain drugs taken by hypersensitive people can be lethal—for example, Penicillin. Given the potential harmfulness of some legal, prescription, and over-the-counter drugs, one must realize the increased potential for harm, impairment, and death with illegal street drugs, whose composition is never truly known.

Controllable use is some people's belief that drug use can be "recreational" providing one controls his/her intake of a given psychoactive drug. However, this arrangement is academic because even so-called "social," "recreational," or "controlled use" of psychoactive drugs on the job often leads to impairment, which in turn leads to diminished performance, accidents, and other adverse consequences. Everyone pays a price for his/her drug use. Some pay earlier than others, and all too often innocent people suffer first.

Attrition in industry is often seen as a solution to the drug problem. Unfortunately, tomorrow's workforce is intimately involved with drugs today. Consider the following:

After several years of declining abuse among high-school-aged children, the rate of abuse in the United States for 12- to 17-year-olds rose 78 percent between 1992 and 1995, and it continues to rise.

The data clearly shows that tomorrow's workforce is intimately involved with the use and abuse of alcohol and other drugs today. Unless we heed the warning of history we will once again be confronted with a new generation of young people predisposed to tolerating the use and abuse of psychoactive drugs. For this reason, the business community must gather its resources to establish sound drug-free workplace programs that will meet this challenge.

CONDITIONS ADVERSELY AFFECTING THE WORKPLACE

As substance abusers arrive for work each day, they generally fit into one or more of these categories that present threatening conditions for employees and their employer.

1. Appear for work under the influence of drugs and will be openly and obviously impaired, or intoxicated and unfit for duty.
2. Possess and use drugs on the job. Although they are impaired, it will not be evident.
3. Sell or otherwise distribute, or transfer illegal drugs or legal drugs illegally, while on the job.
4. Display impairment due to the residual effects of drugs taken hours or even days prior to coming to work. These effects may include emotional outbursts, personality changes, irritability, combativeness, memory problems, and the inability to complete assignments.
5. Have codependent loved ones working at jobs where they will be less productive.

Keeping in mind that the protection officer is not a diagnostician, recognizing impairment due to sustained low dosages and residual effects, or codependence, will be unlikely unless he/she is informed of this information by a third party. If third-party information is received, then the protection officer should bring this intelligence to his/her supervisors immediately. These conditions are best left to supervisors and managers who can evaluate these issues as a matter of job performance and make the necessary referrals, or take disciplinary action when performance is considered to be deteriorating. However, the protection officer should be alert for the outward signs of drug possession, use, and distribution, that are often overlooked by the layperson. These signs include the following:

1. Observation of drugs and/or drug paraphernalia in the workplace.
2. Observation of suspicious activity especially in secluded areas of the facility or parking lots. Whenever suspicious activity is observed, you should immediately contact your supervisor and request backup before approaching. However, immediate action may be necessary if a threat to personal safety exists.

3. Scent of chemical odors not commonly present in the workplace.
4. Observation of abnormal behavior including the signs of intoxication. Keep in mind that not all abnormal behavior is an indication of substance abuse. Some employees may have legitimate medical problems that can result in behavior similar to intoxication. Regardless of the cause, immediate action is required to protect the employee, coworkers, and the company's property and interest.

HOW MUST INDUSTRY RESPOND?

The workplace plays an integral part in the fight against substance abuse. When continued employment is conditional upon being drug-free, then employment becomes a powerful incentive in support of a drug-free workplace. When a company demonstrates commitment to a comprehensive program in support of a drug-free workplace, then the opportunity to affect attitudes, behavior, and the lifestyles of employees is significant. Through the influence of these programs employees are likely to make healthier choices. Employees who are educated and committed to a drug-free lifestyle convey this attitude to their families and friends. In effect, the employee not only serves to reduce substance abuse at work, but he/she serves to improve the health of his/her family and community.

Until now, the workplace has been underutilized in the fight against substance abuse. Recently, however, government mandates and current trends are requiring aggressive action. To respond effectively, a multidimensional approach is necessary. A company should consider five components in the development of a comprehensive drug-free workplace program.

1. Policy development
2. Training and education
3. Employee assistance
4. Drug testing
5. Security measures

A company policy is the first step on which to build an effective drug-free workplace program. It must clearly state the company's purpose, what will and will not be tolerated, how the company will respond to violations, and what training and treatment support are available. It should also describe the company's drug testing policy, if they chose to conduct these tests.

Training and education should be provided at all levels of employment, especially supervisors and manager, for they represent a company's first line of defense. Training and education should focus on a review of the company's policy, and provide a clear understanding of the nature and scope of substance abuse and the required response to prevent and properly address the problem.

Employee Assistance Programs (EAP) are most often a resource offered by large companies. However, more and more smaller-sized companies are forming consortiums and thereby making the availability of EAP services cost effec-tive. An EAP may be an in-house function or contracted out through an independent service. These programs assist employees and their families in addressing a wide range of personal problems, including substance abuse. In addition, they offer training programs, consult on matters pertaining to troubled employees, assess employee problems, make referrals for treatment and counseling, and in some instances, oversee drug testing programs. Current data reveals that each dollar invested in an EAP can save a company $5.00–$16.00 in the long run. Where an EAP is not available, a company may provide insurance coverage that will allow an employee to seek community resources.

Drug testing programs like the EAP have traditionally been employed by large companies. One of the restrictive factors for a small company is, of course, cost. As with EAPs, smaller companies are banding together to form consortiums in order to make drug testing more cost effective. The purpose of drug testing is to deter substance abuse, prevent the hiring of substance abusers, and provide for the early identification and referral to treatment of employees with a substance abuse problem.

Several types of testing can be performed by a company, depending on their needs and collective bargaining or legal restrictions. These include preemployment, postaccident, follow-up to treatment or counseling, reasonable suspicion, and random. Urinalysis has been the predominant method used to test for the presence of controlled substances. However, other testing materials being evaluated and/or used include blood, hair, and saliva.

Each of the components discussed above plays an integral part in a drug-free workplace strategy. However, these components cannot address all situations. Sometimes a security response is required. This is true when reckless and wanton behavior places the safety of employees and the interest of the company at great risk. Protection officers should clearly understand why and when the security response is necessary.

There is a small percentage of substance abusing employees, perhaps 4 percent to 10 percent, who will not accept or benefit from an offer to assistance in the way of treatment or counseling. These individuals include drug dealers who may or may not use drugs on the job, and users who are not interested in or ready for recovery, because they are in denial. Employees who deal drugs are engaged in criminal activity that cannot be tolerated. They make available the supplies on which troubled employees depend and they establish new opportunities for other types of criminal activity such as gambling, prostitution, and theft. A survey conducted with substance abusing employees revealed that 44 percent had sold drugs on the job. They sell their drugs in bathrooms, parking lots, vehicles, and secluded areas.

In some cases, major drug trafficking organizations have directed dealers to secure jobs in industry and to develop a clientele. Why? Because (1) there is low police visibility, (2) security forces are well known and predictable, and (3) there is a ready-made clientele. These types of employees create morale and safety problems and, in many cases, create a great deal of intimidation for employees and managers alike.

Theft is a major problem for both employers and employees. Employees who use drugs on or off the job need to support that use. In many cases the cost of drugs is very high. For instance, the average weekly expenditure for cocaine may be as high as $637.00. To support this need, the theft of valuables such as equipment, money, and trade secrets, are a few methods that have been exploited. On the other hand, a person who spends $20.00–$40.00 a week for marijuana and/or other drugs can effectively supplement their income by removing valuable equipment or money from the employer or other employees.

To counteract the activities of drug dealers, the company's security department or independent contractor may have to employ certain investigative techniques. For the most part, these techniques include interviews with employees, undercover operations, covert surveillance, or searches conducted by drug-sniffing dogs or chemical process.

Interviews are conducted for the purpose of gathering intelligence that may dictate future action, such as policy changes or the selection of an investigative technique. Employees quite often possess critical information, but may not recognize its significance unless questioned by a trained investigator.

An undercover operation is a specialized investigative technique. It is employed for the purpose of covertly infiltrating a workforce in order to identify violations of company policies or law. These investigations are usually initiated when there is a suspicion or clear knowledge that dug dealing is taking place, but the source and the degree are unknown. Even if a source was identified, in many instances an undercover operation may be necessary to gather the required evidence to take disciplinary or legal action.

Covert surveillance or hidden cameras are used when the activity in question is confined to an individual or specific location. When these circumstances exist, a special surveillance camera can be covertly secreted inside a ceiling, wall, fixture, or a variety of other areas restricted only by one's imagination. The greatest advantage to the hidden camera is the undisputed nature of the evidence, a picture of the event, and those responsible.

The act of searching a work area or entire workplace is not a common practice in most industries. When a search is performed it is usually carried out by drug-sniffing dogs or by chemical analysis. Most employers reject searches by dogs, based on the perceived negative impact it would have on employee morale. However, these searches can and do detect the presence of controlled substances in the workplace. Once detected, a host of questions are raised regarding what legal or disciplinary action may be justified or taken. The action to be taken can only be determined, on a case by a basis, after analyzing a variety of factors.

The second type of search is less intrusive and much more discrete. The chemical analysis search involves sweeping an area and analyzing the contents for the presence of a controlled substance. The chemical analysis is, however, restricted to the identification of a limited number of drugs. The same legal and disciplinary issues apply, as mentioned above.

DRUGS OF ABUSE, PARAPHERNALIA, AND DEFINITIONS

Although there are many drugs that will fall within the psychoactive classification, it is important that protection officers have an awareness of those that are most prevalent in the workplace The following are in order of significance:

1. Alcohol
2. Cannabis
3. Stimulants
4. Depressants (other than alcohol)
5. Narcotics
6. Hallucinogens

To facilitate a review of the most popular drugs of abuse within each class, a controlled substance chart is provided that identifies specific drugs, trade or other names, medical uses if any, its potential for producing dependence and tolerance, duration of effects, routes of administration, and possible effects of abuse, overdoses, and withdrawal.

Before continuing, it will be helpful to review the following definitions:

Tolerance: Refers to a state in which the body's tissue cells become accustomed to the presence of a drug at a given dosage and eventually fail to respond to this ordinarily effective dosage. Hence, increasingly larger dosages are necessary to produce the desired effect.

Physical dependence: Often referred to as addiction, this occurs when a person cannot function normally without the repeated use of a drug. If the drug is withdrawn, the person has mild to severe physical and psychic disturbance, known as withdrawal.

Withdrawal: This is characterized by symptoms that occur after drug use is abruptly discontinued. Symptoms may be mild or severe and include seizures, restlessness, irritability, nausea, depression and more. In some cases, as with alcohol and other depressants, withdrawal can be life threatening.

Psychological dependence: This is the result of repeated consumption of a drug that produces psychological but not physical dependence. Psychological dependence produces a strong desire to continue taking drugs for the sense of improved well-being. Psychological dependence is the most difficult to treat.

Potentiation: This is concurrent use of two or more depressant drugs with the same action that produce a multiple effect greater than the sum of either drug when taken alone. For example, use of barbiturates/alcohol. Potentiation can result in unexpected lethal overdose.

Lookalike drugs: Drugs (tablets, capsules, and powders) that are manufactured to closely resemble the appearance of well-known, brand name drugs, such as Dexedrine (dexies), and Biphetamine (black beauties). They generally contain drugs found on over-the-counter medications, but usually in larger amounts to provide greater potency.

A WORD OF CAUTION: You should never taste, smell, or directly touch an unknown substance. IT COULD BE HAZARDOUS TO YOUR HEALTH!

INDICATORS AND COMMON SIGNS OF ABUSE

There are various indicators that suggest or positively identify drug involvement in any environment, including the following:

- Presence of a drug and/or drug paraphernalia
- Physical signs (needle marks, dilated pupils)
- Behavioral signs (slurred speech, irritability, personality changes)
- Analytical tests (saliva, urine, blood, hair)

There are many signs of substance abuse that can be identified by the protection officer. However, keep in mind that some people have legitimate reasons for possessing a syringe and needle (diabetics), or having capsules and tablets (valid prescriptions). Having the sniffles and running eyes and nose may be due to a head cold or allergy, and not cocaine use. Unusual and odd behavior may not be connected in any way with drug use. For these reasons protection officers cannot and should not view themselves as a diagnostician. The protection officer's role is to observe and report suspicious conduct or behavior to the appropriate supervisory contact within the company, so that they can evaluate each incident and follow through in the appropriate manner.

SIGNS AND SYMPTOMS: CONTROLLED SUBSTANCES

The following are specific characteristics attributable to each drug class:

Cannabis: Marijuana, Hashish, Hashish Oil

1. Initially, the person may appear animated with rapid loud talking and bursts of laughter. In later stages, he/she may be sleepy.
2. Pupils may be dilated and the eyes bloodshot.
3. Use results in distortion of depth and time perception making driving or the operation of machinery hazardous.
4. Smokers may be impaired for as long as 24 hours following intoxication, which may last 1–2 hours.
5. Short-term memory is impaired.
6. Long-term use of marijuana is associated with mental deterioration in some users and presents a significant health risk to adolescents, the unborn, diabetics, the emotionally disturbed, and those with respiratory problems.

Marijuana is the most commonly used illicit drug in the workplace, because it is easily concealed and use can be accomplished quickly.

This drug is often a brown, herbaceous substance, but may be shades of brown, red, green, or yellow depending on its origins. Marijuana is smoked as a "joint" (cigarette) or through various types of pipes. When the joint is reduced to a butt and can no longer be held with the fingers, it is referred to as a "roach" and held with a "roach clip" for continued smoking. Another method used to smoke marijuana is to hollow out a cigar and fill it with the marijuana. This preparation is referred to as a "blunt."

Marijuana may also be taken orally when used in the preparation of food or drink. However, smoking is the preferred route of administration.

Cost is based in large degree on availability and/or its potency, which is determined by the percentage content of the psychoactive chemical called THC (Delta 9 Tetrahydrocannabinol). It is often packaged in clear plastic baggies, but any type of container may be used.

Marijuana users attempt to avoid detection on the job by smoking small amounts of marijuana, called "sustained low dosages," throughout the workday. This enables the user to avoid intoxication and therefore detection, because the euphoria or impairment is not outwardly obvious. The user experiences mild effects along with a level of impairment that can adversely affect one's fitness for duty and safety on the job.

Hashish and hashish oil contain concentrated levels of THC, which result in increased potency over marijuana. These forms of cannabis are generally not consumed at work because of the preparation required, but they are readily distributed.

Stimulants: Cocaine, Amphetamines, Lookalikes

1. The user may be excessively active, irritable, argumentative, nervous, or restless.
2. The user generally shows signs of excitation, euphoria, talkativeness, and hyperactivity.
3. May perform the same tasks repeatedly.
4. Dilated pupils and dry mouth are common.
5. Regular users can go long periods without sleeping or eating. This can result in fatigue, depression, and weight loss.
6. Long term heavy use can produce delusions, psychosis, paranoia, or death.
7. Specific to cocaine—the user may exhibit runny nose, sniffles, watery eyes (symptoms similar to the common cold), and ulcerations of the nasal passage.
8. Paraphernalia consists of razor blades and mirrors for chopping cocaine into fine particles. Straws and small spoons are then used for snorting.

Cocaine is a drug produced by chemically processing the leaves of the coca bush, which is indigenous to South America.

Cocaine is usually a white, crystalline substance that looks like snow. When sold and used as "crack," it takes the form of solid matter and resembles small rocks or pebbles. Various containers are used to conceal or store the drug, such as tin foil, paper, and small glass vials.

Cocaine is taken by various routes of administration, including snorting (the most popular route), injection, and smoked as crack. On-the-job use is usually confined to snorting, which can be accomplished quickly and surreptitiously.

Cocaine can be snorted with the use of a coke spoon, a straw, the corner of a matchbook cover, or the tip of a long fingernail. When using a straw, which might be a rolled-up piece of currency, the user refers to this as "snorting a line" of cocaine. In addition, there is paraphernalia available today that is disguised as common sinus inhalers but is used to dupe unsuspecting employers into believing the user is treating a cold. In some cases employees have been dismissed on sick leave to address their symptoms!

Although traces of cocaine remain in the body for up to a week, its mind-altering effects, which users seek, last only 15–30 minutes. This is important because following this brief drugged state, the user experiences varying degrees of depression, exhaustion, and dullness, due to chemical disturbances in the brain that reinforce readministration of the drug. This may lead to continued or compulsive use and quite often to new routes of administration to achieve a more potent effect. The high cost is a powerful force that can lead to theft, drug dealing, and other criminal activity in the workplace.

Amphetamines are produced by both legitimate pharmaceutical companies for medical purposes and by clandestine laboratory operators (drug traffickers) in makeshift laboratories located in bathrooms or garages, or in elaborate facilities including workplace laboratories. Their effects are similar to cocaine with one important exception: They last for hours rather than minutes. When these drugs are used for nonmedical reasons, they are commonly obtained through (1) pharmacy theft, (2) clandestine manufacturers, or (3) unscrupulous doctors who write illegal prescriptions for monetary gain.

Some of the more popular amphetamines are Methamphetamine (Speed), Biphetamine (Black Beauties), Dexedrine (Dexies), and Benzedrine (Pink Hearts). Ritalin and Preludin are amphetamine-like substances that are also popular.

Amphetamines are taken orally as tablets or capsules that vary in color, shape, and size. Some, like Methamphetamine or Methcathinone (CAT), are available in powder form and are injected, snorted, or taken orally.

Aside from the drugs listed above, a whole new class of substances referred to as "lookalike" drugs have become problematic. Initially utilized by truck drivers and students, these substances have now infiltrated the workplace and are taking their toll. These substances can be distributed legally. They consist of capsules, tablets, and powders that contain legal, over-the-counter stimulants such as caffeine and ephedrine. They are marketed as "stay awake" and "stay alert" drugs. However, their use can cause irritability and fatigue that in turn has contributed to morale problems within the workforce.

The use of stimulants, often referred to as "uppers" or "speed," on the job poses three serious problems. First, being under the influence of these drugs gives one a false sense that they are capable of achieving any task or conquering any challenge. In this condition, employees may use poor judgment or attempt tasks that are beyond their training and knowledge, resulting in wasted time, property or personal damage, safety infractions, and accidents. Second, in a stimulated, talkative and hyperactive condition, users often disrupt co-workers, thereby creating employee morale problems. Finally, stimulant users tend to repeat tasks. This reduces productivity and quality control, and can affect morale in an environment dependent upon a team effort.

Note: Many precursor chemicals necessary to manufacture illegal drugs are legitimately used in private industry. To avoid theft of these chemicals by drug traffickers, a company should establish safeguards. Also, the workplace has been used to manufacture illegal drugs. This not only creates an image problem, but also a safety problem, because many of the necessary precursor chemicals are highly flammable and/or explosive.

Depressants: Alcohol, Barbiturates, Tranquilizers, Rohypnol
1. Behavior like that of alcohol intoxication, but without the odor of alcohol on the breath
2. Staggering, stumbling, or decreased reaction time
3. Falling asleep while at work
4. Slurred speech
5. Constricted pupils
6. Difficulty concentrating and impaired thinking
7. Limited attention span

These drugs, with the exception of alcohol, are produced and obtained in the same manner as amphetamines.

The most commonly abused drugs in this group, aside from alcohol, are the barbiturates, such as Second (Red Devils), Tuinal (Rainbows), and Nembutal (Yellow Jackets), and the benzodiazepines, such as Valium and Librium. Another popular drug in this classification is Rohypnol.

The depressants possess two important characteristics that bear mentioning. First, as stated in the definitions at the beginning of this section, they are potentiating when combined with other depressant drugs. Second, the withdrawal from alcohol and other depressants is life threatening, and should always be done under medically supervised conditions.

Valium and Librium are the most widely prescribed and abused tranquilizers. They are also potentiating when combined with alcohol, barbiturates, or other tranquilizers.

"Lookalike" substances containing antihistamines and analgesics like acetaminophen are also available as described for the stimulants.

Rohypnol is one of the latest fad drugs of the 1990s, which is becoming increasingly popular with young people. It has Valium-like effects and is referred to as "Roofies."

Depressants are taken orally and no specific form of packaging is outstanding.

The use of depressants diminishes alertness and impairs judgment, making the operation of machinery difficult. Manipulative skills and coordination are also affected. This type of impairment can lead to accidents and poor quality control, as well as diminished work performance.

The depressants are frequently referred to as dry alcohol, and alcoholics routinely substitute these drugs for alcohol during the work day in order to avoid detection from alcohol's odor.

Narcotics: Heroin, Dilaudid, Percodan

1. Scars (tracks) on the arms or on the backs of the hands, caused by repeated injections
2. Pupils constricted and fixed
3. Scratches oneself frequently
4. Loss of appetite
5. May have sniffles, red watering eyes and a cough that disappears when the user gets a "fix" (injection)
6. User often leaves paraphernalia such a syringes, bent spoons, cotton balls, needles, metal bottle caps, eye droppers, and glassine bags in lockers or desk drawers They may also be discarded in stairwells, remote areas of a parking lot, or a secluded location within the workplace.
7. Users, when under the influence, may appear lethargic, drowsy, and may go on the "nod" (i.e., an alternating cycle of dosing and awakening.

Natural narcotics (opium, morphine, codeine) are a product of the opium poppy, which is cultivated for the purpose of extracting these powerful drugs for medical use. Major growing areas include Southeast Asia, Southwest Asia, Middle East, South America, and Mexico. In addition, semisynthetics like Heroin and Dilaudid, and synthetics like Demerol, Percodan, and Fentanyl, are popular.

Narcotics are usually available in tablet, capsule, or powder form, and can be injected, smoked, snorted, or taken orally. In addition, capsules may be used to conceal heroin in powder form to produce a legitimate appearance. Heroin is generally packaged much like cocaine in tin foil, paper, balloons, baggies, and vials. Heroin is usually white, brown, or black ("black tar"), or in shades of these colors. Synthetic and semi-synthetic tablets and capsules appear in various colors, shapes, and sizes.

The narcotics are not popular drugs of abuse in the workplace, because their use suggests a long history of abuse, which contributes to unemployment and criminal careers. The time required to prepare an injection is another factor discouraging heroin use on the job. However, the administration of heroin by the method of snorting is becoming more popular. If this trend continues then heroin may become as popular as cocaine. Aside from the issue of use, the narcotics are quite often encountered for sale and distribution on the job.

Hallucinogens: LSD, PCP, DMT

1. Behavior and mood vary widely. The user may sit or recline quietly in a trance-like state or may appear fearful or even terrified.
2. Rapid eye movement, drooling, flushed and sweaty appearance, trembling hands, and dizziness.
3. There may be changes in sense of light, hearing, touch, smell, and time.

Hallucinogens are rarely utilized by employees on the job because of their long duration of effects (2–12 hours) and their unpredictable nature. Also, impairment is total, therefore obviating any degree of productivity. Hallucinogenic drugs are especially popular with 18- to 25-year-olds, and are frequently available at the workplace for distribution in their various forms. The most popular hallucinogens include LSD and PCP.

Hallucinogens, often called psychedelics, are a group of drugs that alter perception and awareness. Their effects are generally unpredictable and in some cases, bizarre. The nature and intensity of the drug experience is determined by the potency and amount taken, the user's personality, mood expectation, and the social and environmental setting.

The LSD experience is labeled a "trip" that is characterized as "good" or "bad." The nature of the trip can only be determined after ingestion, and can last as long as 10–12 hours. The "good trip" is characterized by a passive trance-like state with pleasant hallucinations, perhaps a kaleidoscope of colors and altered sensations. Senses sometimes cross so that the user sees sounds and hears colors. These characteristics result in the hallucinations being touted as mind expanding drugs. The "bad trip" is characterized by unpleasant experiences including terrifying hallucinations, panic, and irrational acts, which have resulted in injury and death.

LSD is sold on the street in tablet and blotter form. As tablets, they are commonly referred to as "microdot acid," and are sold in variety of colors, shapes, and sizes. When liquid LSD is dabbed on blotter paper it is called "blotter acid." Because of LSD's negative reputation as an unpredictable and bizarre drug, it is commonly sold to unsuspecting buyers as THC or Mescaline.

Mescaline (Mesc), PCP, Psilocybin (mushrooms), and DMT (Dimethyltryptamine) are other commonly used hallucinogens.

Inhalants: Glue, Gasoline, Erasing Fluid

1. Odor of substance inhaled on breath and clothes
2. Excessive nasal secretions and watering of the eyes
3. Poor muscular control
4. Drowsiness or unconsciousness
5. Presence of plastic or paper bags or rags containing saturated quantities of the inhalant
6. Slurred speech

Inhalants represent a diverse group of psychoactive chemicals composed of organic solvents and volatile substances. These chemicals like glues, paint products, gasoline, and white erasing fluid, can be readily found in the home and workplace. Their easy accessibility, low cost, and ease of concealment make inhalants, for many, one of the first substances abused.

Inhalants are usually sniffed directly from an open container or from a rag soaked in the substance and held to the face. This is usually referred to as "huffing." Some users have been known to place open containers or soaked rags inside a bag, where the vapors can concentrate, before being inhaled. These substances are rapidly transported to the brain, and can result in unconsciousness or death.

These substances are not widely abused in the workplace. However, incidents of abuse in the workplace have been reported. Many of the chemicals used by some businesses can and are diverted for the purpose of inhalation. In some cases, the diversion and subsequent use has resulted in death on company property.

For further information on drugs of abuse, a comprehensive description and colorful photographic collection of drugs and paraphernalia can be found in "Drugs of Abuse," published by the U.S. Department of Justice, Drug Enforcement Administration. Edition 1996.

Protecting People and Assets

The role of any protection officer is that of protecting people and assets. The protection officer accomplishes this responsibility by observing and reporting incidents or situations which present a threat to the people and assets he/she has a duty to protect. Substance abuse is one such threat, and the protection officer represents a critical component in a company's effort to combat this threat and maintain a drug-free workplace. By understanding the scope and nature of this problem, along with the specific security related concerns, the protection officer will be prepared to recognize and report substance abuse situations that undermine safety and security.

Finally, every protection officer should communicate his/her knowledge about the causes and effects of substance abuse beyond the confines of the workplace. By sharing this vital information about the perils of abuse, the protection officer can influence his/her family and community in a most positive way.

1. Drug dependence is a primary disease.
     □ T □ F
2. Which of the following applies to drug dependence?
     □ (a) It is fatal.
     □ (b) It is a family disease.
     □ (c) It is contagious.
     □ (d) All of the above
3. The biggest single roadblock to addressing a person's substance abuse problem is _____.
4. A company can effectively fight substance abuse by just starting a drug testing program.
     □ T □ F
5. A person who does not use drugs, but is preoccupied with a loved one who does, is said to be _____.
6. The first step in developing a Drug-Free Workplace Program is to:
     □ (a) provide education
     □ (b) start an employee assistance program
     □ (c) write a policy
     □ (d) start drug testing
7. The most widely used drug testing material in use today is:
     □ (a) blood
     □ (b) saliva
     □ (c) urine
     □ (d) hair
8. Psychoactive drugs affect the _____.
9. Nicotine and _____ are referred to as gateway drugs.
10. Your job as a protection officer is to observe and _____ substance abuse behavior activity.

Controlled Substances: Uses and Effects

	Drugs	Trade or Other Names	Medical Uses	Dependence Potential Physical	Dependence Potential Psychological	Tolerance	Duration of Effects (in hours)	Usual Method of Administration	Possible Effects of Abuse	Effects of Overdose	Withdrawal Symptoms
Narcotics	Fentanyl	Innovar, Sublimaze	Analgesic anesthetic	High	High	Yes	10 to 72	Injected	Euphoria, drowsiness, respiratory depression, constricted pupils, nausea	Slow and shallow breathing, clammy skin, convulsions, coma, possible death.	Watery eyes, runny noses, yawning, loss of appetite, irritability, tremors, panic, chills, and sweating, cramps, nausea
	Morphine	Morphine	Analgesic, antitussive	High	High	Yes	3 to 6	Oral, Smoked, Injected			
	Codeine	Codeine	Analgesic, antitussive	Moderate	Moderate	Yes	3 to 6	Oral, Injected			
	Heroin	Diacetylmorphine, Horse, Smack	None in U.S.	High	High	Yes	3 to 6	Injected, Snorted			
	Methadone	Dolophine, Methadone, Methadose	Analgesic, Heroine substitute	High	High	Yes	12 to 24	Oral, Injected			
	Other Narcotics	Dilaudid, Darvon, Demerol, Percodan	Analgesic, antidiarrheal, antitussive	High	High	Yes	3 to 6	Oral, Injected			
Depressants	Chloral Hydrate	Noctec, Sommos	Hypnotic	Moderate	Moderate	Yes	5 to 8	Oral	Slurred speech, disorientation, drunken behavior, stubling.	Shallow respiration, cold and clammy skin, dilated pupils, weak and rapid pulse, coma, possible death.	Anxiety, insomnia, tremors, delerium, convulsions, possible death.
	Barbiturates	Amytal, Nembutal, Phenobarbital, Seconal, Tuinal	Anesthetic, anti-convulsant, sedation, sleep	High-Moderate	High-Moderate	Yes	1 to 16	Oral, Injected			
	Glutethimide	Doriden	Sedation, sleep	High	Moderate	Yes	4 to 8	Oral			
	Alcohol	Ethyl Alcohol, Ethanol	Ingredient in some medicines	Moderate	Moderate	Yes	2 to 8	Oral			
	Benzodiazepines	Ativan, Halcion, Equanil, Librium, Miltown, Serax, Tranxene, Valium, Verstran	Anti-anxiety, sedation, sleep	Moderate	Moderate	Yes	4 to 8	Oral, Injected			
	Other Depressants	Equanil, Dormate, Nobudar, Placidyl, Faimid	Anti-anxiety, sedation, sleep	Moderate	Moderate	Yes	4 to 8	Oral			
Stimulants	Cocaine	Coke, Snow, Flake, Crack	Local anesthetic	Possible	High	Yes	1 to 2	Injected, Snorted, Smoked	Increased alertness, excitation, euphoria, dilated pupils, increased pulse rate and blood pressure, insomnia, loss of appltite.	Agitation, Increase in body temperature, hallucinations, convulsions, possible death.	Apathy, long periods of sleep, irritability, depression, disorientation.
	Amphetamines	Biphetamine, Ice, Desoxyn, Dexedrine,	narcolepsy, weight control	Possible	High	Yes	2 to 4	Oral, Injected, Smoked			
	Phenmetrazine	preludin	Weight control	Possible	High	Yes	2 to 4	Oral			
	Methylphenidate	Ritalin	Hyperkinesis, narcolepsy	Possible	High	Yes	2 to 4	Oral, Injected			
	Other Stimulants	Plegine, Sadorex, Adipex	Weight control	Possible	High	Yes	2 to 4	Oral, Injected			
Hallucinogens	LSD	Acid, Microdot	None	None	Degree Unknown	Yes	8 to 12	Oral	Illusions and hallucinations (with exception of MDA); poor perception of time and distance.	Longer, and more intense "trip" episodes, psychosis, possible death.	Withdrawal symptoms not reported.
	Mescaline and Peyote	Mescal, Buttons, MESC	None	None	Degree Unknown	Yes	8 to 12	Oral			
	Amphetamine Variants	MDA STP, Ecstasy, COM, MDMA	None	Degree Unknown	Degree Unknown	Yes	Variable	Oral, injected			
	Phencyclidine	PCP, Hog, Angel Dust	None	Degree Unknown	High	Yes	Days	Oral, Smoked, Injected			
	Other Hallucinogens	DMT, DET, Psilocybin	None	None	Degree Unknown	Possible	Variable	Oral, Injected, Smoked, Snorted			
Cannabis	Marijuana	Pot, Frass, Sinsemilla, Thai Sticks, Marinol (Synthetic THC)	Marijuana - None, THC - Antiemetic	Degree Unknown	Moderate	Yes	2 to 4	Oral, Smoked	Euphorial, relaxed inhibitions, increased appetite, depth and time perceion distorted.	Fatigue, paranoia, possible psychosis.	Insomnia, nervousness and decreased appetite.
	Hashish & Hashish Oil	Hash, Hash Oil	Hashish - None	Degree Unknown	Moderate	Yes	2 to 4	Oral, Smoked			
Steroids	Testosterone	Depo-Testosterone, Delatestryl	Hypogonadism	Degree Unknown	Degree Unknown	Degree Unknown	14 to 28 days	Injected	Virilization, acne, edema, aggressive behavior, testicular atrphy, Gynecomastia	Unknown	Possible depression
	Nandrolone	Nortestosterone, DECA	Anemia, Breast Cancer	Degree Unknown	Degree Unknown	Degree Unknown	14 to 21 days	Injected			
	Oxymetholone	Adadrol - 50	Anemia	Degree Unknown	Degree Unknown	Degree Unknown	24	Oral			

Figure 6-1   Controlled Substances: Uses and Effects
Source: National Drug Institute

Unit Seven

Effective Communications
Crisis Intervention
Security Awareness
Environmental Crime Control Theory

EFFECTIVE COMMUNICATIONS

By Charles T. Thibodeau, M.Ed, CPP, CSS

EFFECTIVE COMMUNICATIONS DEFINED

"Effective communications," is the faithful reproduction of a thought, idea, observation, instruction, request, greeting, or warning, expressed in a verbal, written, electronic alarm annunciation, or pictorial media, originated by and transmitted by a communicator or communicating device to a specifically targeted receiver or receiver group. The term "faithful reproduction" means that whatever was contained in the original message that left the communicator is both received by and understood by the targeted receiver or receiver group. The element of understanding the message is the central focus of this definition for without that element, communications are blocked. Put another way, effective communications simply are nonexistent without a two-way, mutual understanding of the message being communicated.

DUE DILIGENCE BASED ON EFFECTIVE COMMUNICATIONS

Businesses are required by law to establish and maintain what is called "due diligence." In layman's terms that means operating their affairs by paying particular attention to the best welfare and interest of their visitor's safety and security needs. To meet this "due diligence" requirement, businesses must focus on foreseeability of real and perceived threats. Next the law expects businesses to warn people of danger and then avoid or mitigate those threats that have a chance of materializing and causing a substantial loss of assets, damage to property, and/or injury to people.

To comply with this mandate, businesses must conduct perpetual risk analysis, vulnerability assessments, integrated countermeasure designs, security officer training, employee security awareness training, and contingency planning. However, without "effective" communications, none of these practices and procedures could exist. Thus, effective communications are a key element in assisting businesses in meeting their mandate to provide proof of compliance with required levels of due diligence.

CHANNELS OF COMMUNICATIONS

There are four channels of communications in any organization or company: top-down, bottom-up, horizontal, and the grapevine. The first three are essential for information to flow in every direction. These are the formal and official forms of communications. The fourth form of communications found in most organizations is the grapevine, which consists of an outgrowth of informal and casual groupings of employees. Effective communications in any security department requires all four of these forms. They provide maximum performance both during stable and predictable periods and during times of stress.

THE SIX ESSENTIALS OF EFFECTIVE COMMUNICATIONS

Effective communications must be timely, complete, clear, concise, factual, and accurate. This is a bare bones list of requirements. Certainly the complete list includes other attributes, but if these six factors are present, communications will be extremely effective.

CONSIDER THE AUDIENCE

Everyone communicates at different levels. If you are communicating with someone who is many levels below your communication level, the message you are sending stands a good chance of being misunderstood. Also, assuming that everyone speaks and understands on your level is almost a guarantee that you will be an ineffective communicator. The midpoint between talking above your audience and talking below your audience is currently the seventh-grade level. If you want perfect clarity in your communications, then speak slowly, carefully choosing your words, using no more than five- or six-letter words, and choosing words that are commonly known. In many cases, when asked to repeat a message, the receiving person uses different words. It is very likely that the receiver's vocabulary is lacking. Thus, each time you are requested to repeat a message, say it in different words.

This seventh-grade level is the midpoint in the year 2002 when this chapter was written, but this midpoint level will be adjusted lower in future years as our nation's schools continue to turn out functionally illiterate students with poor math and English skills. Every indication is that failing progressive teaching methodologies, coupled with many changing social morays, will continue this downward spiral into illiteracy far into the future. We may see in our lifetime our nation's high school graduates communicating at the fourth-grade level. Many are at that level now.

The security officer's communications must also accommodate the language difficulties of an ever-growing ESL (English as a second language) population. Spanish and French are the two predominate languages at this time in year 2002. However, there is an ever-growing population of Asian-speaking people in the public domain that English-speaking Americans will have to contend with. The security officer of the future will almost have to be bilingual. Then there are the medically afflicted people with communication impediments and there may be nothing you can do to breach their difficulties with communicating. When dealing with the deaf, blind, or MS-afflicted people, patience is your greatest asset, and a strong commitment to help these people will get you through it. Just be persistent until you can find the way each one communicates.

VERIFYING COMMUNICATIONS WITH FEEDBACK

It is of the utmost importance that the receiver of a message gives you some kind of indication that he or she received the message and the message they received is the same one you sent. What I am alluding to here is the use of feedback to confirm that the receiver did in fact receive the message and understood the message. The initial communicator who sent the message is responsible for assuring that the message was not only received, but was the same message that was sent. The communicator has a right to believe the message was received and understood if a confirmation message is returned. Acceptable confirmation messages would be any of the following: "10-4," "roger," "good copy," or a very short verbal message repeating your message.

MYTHS AND MISCONCEPTIONS IN COMMUNICATIONS

There is one misconception that causes more errors than any other in the communications field and that is something called brevity, or keeping each and every communication as brief as possible. In their attempt to accomplish this one goal, the communicator uses abbreviations, personal shorthand, partial words or partial sentences, poor grammar, and a message that requires deciphering. Being brief many times is *not* an important goal of writing. Saying as few words as possible and speaking in code is *not* always the best choice of content for verbal communications. The above list of six essentials must be present to have a clear and concise message.

The length of the message is important in many situations, such as sending duress codes or using a two-way radio. However, brevity is one of the least important factors and most destructive factors to the attempt to be "effective" with your communications. A much better question to ask, when finished preparing a message is "Does this message have all six essentials of effective communications?" If not, fix it before the message is sent. If that fix extends the message length, it is better to violate the brevity rule than the antidecipher rule.

Abbreviations are only valuable to the receiver who can decipher them. Shorthand is usually only valuable to the sender of the message and in many cases cannot be deciphered readily by the receiver of the message. If there is any absolute in effective message sending, it is this: **No message other than a crypto-message should have to be deciphered by any receiver of the message.**

PROPER USE OF COMMUNICATIONS DEVICES

Telephone Systems

The telephone is one of the most important tools that any security officer can have at his or her disposal. At the same time, if the telephone equipment is not properly designed for a security or emergency setting, it can be a great problem, hampering effective communications. The telephone equipment in a security program must be simple to use with the least probability of failing during an emergency.

In modern leading edge security control centers, there will be a ten-button phone with a caller ID on it for day-to-day business. It will be a part of the facility PBX or electronic phone system, and, like all phones will have the ability to call outside the facility as well as within the facility. It will also be tied into a tape recording device to record all incoming and outgoing calls.

Separate and apart from the ten-button phone there will be a red phone used exclusively for emergencies with a caller ID and tape recording device on it as well. This red phone may have a strobe light connected to it to distinguish the ringing sound from all the other phones in the room. This phone will have no dial out capability; in fact, the face of the phone will have no dialing keyboard.

The reason for having a separate red phone for emergencies is that the security operator or dispatcher will at some point need to communicate over the regular phone lines to call for fire, police, or emergency medical assistance and for other assistance. If the emergency phone is tied into the ten-button phone, the emergency event caller at the scene of the emergency must be put on hold while public assistance is being called. Never hang up on the emergency event caller or put the emergency event caller on hold during an actual emergency. The caller under the stress of an emergency may hang up whenever they can't hear the sounds of your voice or noise in the control center.

In addition, each security station in the facility should be equipped with a red phone as well as a regular phone. When an emergency call comes in, each red phone should be picked up with the remote stations just listening in to the conversation between the dispatcher and emergency event caller.

Then, before hanging up, each station will confirm that they have received the message heard over the red phone. The emergency telephone system is not a place to skimp on cost or design when so much depends on effective communications during emergencies. In fact, just in case you lose your connection with the emergency event caller, it is best to jot down that person's name and phone number immediately at the outset of the call.

A third phone, a yellow phone, would be a single analog line separate and apart from the facility PBX or electronic telephone system. This phone will have a hardwired four lead telephone cable inside of a conduit from the wall jack in the room where the phone is located to the street level mainframe. The conduit will lesson the threat of the line being cut or burned through during an emergency. This line will tie directly to the mainframe of the local telephone office and it will operate on its own power. Therefore, this direct tie to the outside world will be somewhat protected from numerous threats. The conduit encased phone line would almost assure an outside line during any power outage or computer failure that could cripple the facility's PBX or electronic telephone system.

A fourth phone in some facilities, a black phone, is physically identical to the red phone. It cannot be dialed. This phone is dedicated to panic alarm annunciation. If there is a threat on executive row, or a robbery in the credit union, certain designated employees are trained to use the black phone for "duress code" messages.

The cell phone is the newest addition to the phone systems available for security officers. In many locations, security departments are investing in cell phones that double as two-way radios. At this point, for most security departments, these telephone-radio combination units are too costly. In other locations, cell phones are used as back up units to the two-way radios for communications where two-way radio signals are blocked by dead spots. Cell phones play an important part during patrol duties to allow emergency calls to be made from the scene, back to the control center when the two-way radio is ineffective. The cell phone can also be used for calls directly to the 911 emergency response center.

Two-Way Radios
The two-way radio is the primary mobile communications device that almost all security officers use to communicate with the control center and between other officers, supervisors, and management. There are some problems with most two-way radio systems and that trouble includes, but is not limited to, failure to operate in dead spots, being susceptible to operator error, and having short battery life. In addition, an adequate two-way radio system is expensive; the units are bulky and take up space on a crowded utility belt. Some of these radios break down regularly and are costly to maintain. But all of these shortcomings aside, we could not do the security job as well as we do without effective communications devices like the two-way radios.

Two-way radios are miniature radio stations and as such something called "ground-wave propagation" makes the difference between effective communications and either broken communications with static or no communications at all. Ground-wave propagations are the scientific explanation that explains how a radio signal travels from the source antenna to the receiving antenna. It also explains that if anywhere along that path, there is an object that is so well grounded, like an I-beam or other metal object, the signal will be short circuited and driven into the ground before the message reaches the receiver's antenna. Because the transmission antenna sends out many pear-shaped signals, not just one, to overcome this signal interference problem, the officer needs only to walk a few feet from where the transmission is garbled and the signal may be reestablished.

The two-way radio is most effective, with the antenna 90 degrees perpendicular to the ground. The antenna should be pointing straight up in the air during use. By tipping the antenna sideways or horizontal to the ground, the unit becomes somewhat directional and the strongest transmission will be along the line where the antenna is pointing. If a two-way radio antenna is pointing away from the receiving antenna, then the radio is being used in a very ineffective manner.

In many systems, signal strength gets a boost by use of a repeater. A repeater is a great help but it brings with it one major problem. The way it works makes it somewhat user-unfriendly. The repeater receives the signal, turns it around, and sends it back out as a more powerful signal. That process takes time. Thus, the two-way radio communicator must hold the transmission switch down for two seconds before talking to engage the repeater and then the communicator must hold the switch down for two seconds after the message is finished to allow for processing. If this is not done, your message will be clipped at both ends. Then there is the way one should talk into the transceiver. When holding the transceiver up to talk, hold it to the side of your mouth and speak across the microphone. Do not speak directly into the microphone or you may speak too loudly and cause distortion of the transmitted message.

The frequency of the radio also has an impact on effective communications. Most radios used by security are FM transceivers. They are either VHF or UHF. Two-way radios that are called VHF transceivers, work on what is known as very high frequency. The UHF radios operate on ultra high frequency. Science explains the differences between these two transmission levels. The lower the frequency, the longer the wavelength. That means the VHF signal will travel a long way, but a VHF signal is a relatively weak signal and does not work as well in tall buildings with lots of steel. The UHF transceiver on the other hand is a stronger signal but has a much shorter wavelength. That means it packs a wallop and works well in tall buildings with lots of steel, but it can't travel too far. A UHF system with a repeater in line is possibly the most effective two-way radio communications system.

Pagers
The pager takes a telephone call to respond to unless it is a voice pager or a text pager that displays messages. Pagers are nice because they are small and work just about everywhere. However, they do not allow the message receiver to respond with a message and they do not allow for verification that the signal was received and understood. Pagers should be used for back up only. Two-way radios and cell phones are the best communications devices for portable operations.

Intercoms
In a retail setting or a hospital setting emergency, codes are sent over the intercom. We all know that "code blue" means cardiovascular problems complicated by respiratory failure. We know that "code red" means fire. In some retail compa-

nies a call over the intercom such as "Mr. Jones, please come to the front of the store" means that security is needed at the front of the store. The intercom is useful when it is working, but traditionally the intercom system is a weak link in the communications systems of any facility. There are problems with volume and static, and they seem to have more than their fair share of maintenance needs. If the intended receiver of the message is out of the area where there are no speakers, the message will not be received. In addition, there usually are no procedures to inform the communicator that the message was received and understood. However, we still need the intercom and it is advised that we fix it as soon as it breaks down. Extra speakers should be placed in remote and hard-to-hear-in areas all over the facility to assure emergency messages reach everyone. If you work in a facility and you even think that a message might have been transmitted over an intercom, call dispatch and check out your suspicion.

The greatest mistake that a communicator can make using the intercom is to speak too loud into the microphone. Many systems will distort if the input signal exceeds maximum input voltage. You do not have to speak loud when announcing over an intercom. They all have an amplifier in them that takes care of sound level.

BIBLIOGRAPHY

Fay, J.J., *Encyclopedia of Security Management*, Boston, Butterworth-Heinemman, 1993, pp. 748–750, *Upward Feedback.*

Fischer, R.J., and Green, G., *Introduction to Security*, 5th Edition, Boston, Butterworth-Heinemman, 1992, p. 238, *Elements of the Emergency Plan.*

Hess, K.M., and Wrobleski, H.M., *Introduction to Private Security*, 4th Edition, St. Paul MN, 1996, pp. 358–368, *The Communications Process.*

Hilgert, R.L., and Leonard, E.C., *Supervision, Concepts and Practices of Management*, 6th Edition, South Western College Publishing, 1995, pp. 52–69, *The Need for Effective Communications.*

Daughtrey, A.S., and Ricks, B.R., *Contemporary Supervision, Managing People and Technology*, 1989, Pages Chapter 12, *Communicating Effectively.*

SECURITY QUIZ
Effective Communications

1. Which of the following best describes effective communications?
   - ☐ (a) A faithful reproduction of a message directed to a target audience that is clearly understood by that target audience
   - ☐ (b) A message sent by a communicator who expects the receiver to understand it
   - ☐ (c) A message that is sent to a person or persons with hope that it will be understood by all
   - ☐ (d) All the above
2. Tort law expects every business to actively pursue the following.
   - ☐ (a) Employee background checks
   - ☐ (b) Due diligence
   - ☐ (c) Adequate training
   - ☐ (d) Employee benefits
3. There are four channels of communications in most companies; which of the following is not a channel?
   - ☐ (a) Top-down communications
   - ☐ (b) Bottom-up communications
   - ☐ (c) Grapevine communications
   - ☐ (d) Reverse-horizontal communications
4. There are six essentials of effective communications; which of the following is not an essential?
   - ☐ (a) The communications must be complete.
   - ☐ (b) The communications must be clear.
   - ☐ (c) The communications must be consistent.
   - ☐ (d) The communications must be concise.

5. Effective communications has built in flexibility to facilitate the needs of the receiver or receiver groups. Which of the following characteristic is important to take into consideration?
    □ (a) Communications grade level remembering the seventh-grade midpoint rule
    □ (b) English as a second language (ESL), people with poor understanding of English
    □ (c) Medical condition causing speech impediment, hearing loss, or poor sight
    □ (d) All the above

6. A very important part of effective communications is that the communicator must be able to tell which of the following? Choose the best.
    □ (a) That the communications were necessary
    □ (b) That the communications were timely
    □ (c) That the message was received
    □ (d) That the message has been received and understood

7. There is one misconception that causes more errors than any other in the communications field, and that is:
    □ (a) every message must be brief.
    □ (b) every message requires some interpretation.
    □ (c) every message must be clear and concise.
    □ (d) None of the above

8. The telephone equipment in a security program must be which of the following? (Choose the best answer)
    □ (a) It must be technologically rugged and capable of working under severe conditions.
    □ (b) It must be simple to use with the least probability of failing during an emergency.
    □ (c) It must be available on a 24/7 basis.
    □ (d) None of the above

9. In the security office, separate and apart from the general use telephone, there will be a red phone used exclusively for emergencies.. That phone will have the following attachments to make it more effective.. Which of the following is not a part of that phone?
    □ (a) Ringer
    □ (b) Strobe
    □ (c) Tape recording device
    □ (d) Beeping sound every three seconds

10. During some emergency situations, the phone system will be destroyed, especially where there is a building collapse.. What can we do to protect that phone line?
    □ (a) Use a separate single-cable phone line not part of the building's main phone system.
    □ (b) Place the telephone cable inside of a metal conduit
    □ (c) Have the cable enter/exit the building at the lowest level of the building
    □ (d) All the above

CRISIS INTERVENTION

By Michael A. Hannigan, CPO

INTRODUCTION

Over one hundred years ago, Walter Bagehot, a British journalist wrote, "Violence heads the list of inherent fears that are experienced by mankind." It is safe to say that the risk that violence may be perpetrated against individuals in our moderate workplaces has to be a major security/loss control concern.

The protection officer, by the nature of his/her job function, must deal with individuals that present the threat of violent behavior for reasons such as involvement with alcohol or drugs, being a victim of a crime, suffering from an accident, illness, an argument with their spouse, or even the loss of a loved one. These individuals not only pose a serious threat to themselves, but most certainly to employees, the public, and of course, protection personnel.

There is a technique that can be used to allow more control of the outcome of a situation that involves a person who is behaving in a violent manner. A positive outcome can be achieved by suggesting certain proactive behavior to these individuals by actions or what you say and how the message is verbally or nonverbally communicated. This technique is *behavioral management,* or perhaps better known as *crisis intervention.* Crisis intervention is a relatively safe technique designed to aid in maintaining the best possible care and welfare of agitated or out of control individuals while lending maximum safety to protection personnel.

CAUSES OF DISRUPTIVE BEHAVIOR

The reasons people become violent or disruptive vary greatly but most frequently fall into at least one of the following categories:

1.   Illness or Injury
People who are suffering from insulin shock, have severe breathing problems, or are in need of a particular medication can become physically violent until they receive medical attention. Sustaining a head injury, for example, could cause a person to become aggravated. In all of these situations, the affected individual may not have control over their actions or even remember what they have done.

2.   Emotional Problems or Mental Illness
People with these types of problems may become physically violent or verbally affronting. They could be suffering from severe depression, psychosis, or schizophrenia. These individuals require prompt professional attention. The psychiatric or medical professional may order medication or a change in medication.

3.   Substance/Alcohol Abuse or Medication Reaction
Those who abuse alcohol or other substances such as PCP (animal tranquilizers), cocaine, LSD, heroin, the list goes on, are prime candidates for violence. It is not possible to predict behavior patterns without having some indication of the kind of substance involved.

4.   Stress
Stress is often referred to as the "silent killer." Everyone suffers from various levels of stress from time to time. Stress more frequently leads to depression that remains a personal matter. However, individuals who are not able to manage personal stress may be susceptible to severe aggravation, which can precede violence directed against others.

5.   Anger/Frustration
These conditions are often exhibited by individuals who lack the common decency to behave in a manner that is socially acceptable. Often the level of individual maturity will dictate the extent of objectionable conduct. But in some cases, the anger and lack of emotional control can lead to any number of violent reactions on the part of the subject.

STAGES OF MANAGEMENT OF DISRUPTIVE BEHAVIOR

The management of disruptive or violent behavior consists of five states which are conditions a protection officer must learn to recognize.

1.   Evaluation
What is going on? Why? Who is involved? Is the protection officer, disruptive person, or others in immediate danger? Is support needed from fellow officers or resource personnel such as supervisory staff, social worker, medical personnel, or police?

2.   Planning
Now that I know what is going on, what do I need to do? How do I do it? Do I have the resources available, such as people or equipment? Remember that situations usually start out one-on-one, but should never be permitted to stay that way for long, no longer than it takes to get back-up personnel. Once you have determined your plan of action, whether it be to continue talking, containment, restraint, removal of the person(s), referral or arrest, communicate your decision to team members. When planning, seek input from others when possible.

3.   Implement
Put your plan into action. At this state, things may not go the way you anticipated, but regardless, remain calm. A

contingency plan can be activated that may be more fitting for the circumstances. In all crisis situations, your personal safety is of prime importance. Your actions should be dictated accordingly. Do not attempt to resolve a volatile situation alone. Observe exactly what is happening and position yourself with personal safety in mind and await support staff.

4. Document

Effective documentation of a crisis incident is vital for future reference and guidance. A well documented report will also serve to provide litigation protection should legal actions result from actions or inactions on the part of crisis respondents. The final report should include the standard who, what, where, when, how, and why. Address each of these questions carefully so that the report can be read and understood by all individuals and organizations involved.

5. Review

This is the final stage of the crisis management phase, but by no means any less important. This is when you critique the entire crisis event. Carefully examine all documentation. It is imperative to openly discuss exactly what happened. It gives all protection personnel involved the opportunity to vent feelings and frustrations and gain the needed confidence to deal with future similar situations. Talk openly about what happened, why it happened, and if it could have been prevented. Could it have been handled more effectively, if so how? This is the reconstruction state that must be managed in a positive manner. It is not a "fault finding mission," rather a time to reflect positively on the actions taken and develop safeguards for future occurrences.

CRISIS DEVELOPMENT BEHAVIOR MODULES

During a crisis development situation, there are four distinct and identifiable behavior levels.

1. Anxiety
2. Defensive
3. Anger/frustration
4. Tension reduction

For each level there is a demand for a specific response to provide the maximum chance of defusing the crisis.

1. Supportive
2. Directive
3. Nonviolent physical crisis intervention
4. Therapeutic rapport

It is important to relate each behavior level to a specific response.

Behavior Level

1. Anxiety: A notable state of dismay/torment.
2. Defensive: Beginning stage of loss of rationality. Unreasonable and challenging.
3. Anger/frustration: Loss of control, physically acting out.

4. Tension reduction: Regaining of rationality after physically acting out.

Response

1. Supportive: Active, friendly, emphatic attempts to alleviate observed behavior.
2. Directive: Set limits, suggest expected outcomes.
3. Nonviolent crisis intervention: Safe, prudent control, and restraint techniques.
4. Therapeutic rapport: Communication with individual during reduction.

PROTECTION OFFICER GUIDELINES

Written policy and procedures will vary from one organization to another, but there are three basic guidelines that are applicable for any situation.

- Remain calm
- Act appropriately
- Be objective

Do not allow the subject to make you angry or to act inappropriately. Losing your composure will most certainly intensify the situation. Don't become complacent and take anything for granted. Always be alert. In terms of personal protection, never stand directly in front of the individual; this could make them feel threatened. Stand just off to the side, at an angle; this is considered a nonthreatening position. Use the person's name, treating him/her with respect. Keep a minimum of three feet distance between yourself and the subject. This serves two purposes. First, it will preserve the individual's personal space, and second, it will give you time to react if the individual begins to physically act out. Remember the amount of personal space may vary according to the individual and the situation. For example, if the person is highly agitated, he/she may need more room and coming closer may intensify the crisis. On the other hand, a troubled person may want to have you closer; your presence may be reassuring. Identify the amount of space needed to develop a calming effect.

How to react and how quickly to react will depend on the nature of the disturbance and if there is an immediate threat constituting a safety hazard. If you do not perceive such a threat, use the time to attempt to calm the subject and to continue your evaluation of the situation. If you have an audience, move them or move the situation. Only people who could provide probable support should be allowed to remain in the area—not spectators.

It is important to know how and why the situation started and always make sure help is available.

VERBAL AND PHYSICAL DISRUPTIVE BEHAVIOR

When a person is verbally acting out, they may or may not be fully aware of what they are saying or doing. They may express anxiety or defensiveness, make demands or threats, or use abusive language. This is especially true when the subject is in insulin shock, having severe breathing difficulties (lack of oxygen to the brain), or has suffered a head injury. These individuals are not usually able to control their actions and may suffer memory loss.

Subjects that are physically violent and require preventative measures can be easily detected by the protection officer. Typically, they throw objects or use them as weapons, kick, or attempt to grab or strike other individuals. These physically out of control persons may even try to barricade themselves in a room or a particular area.

Protection officers need to be aware of the indistinct signs of physical acting-out (violence). Certain signs are likely to precede more combative behavior. Watch for indicators such as gritting teeth, closing and opening hands, and tensing. These are strong indicators of a possible outbreak of physical aggression.

EMPATIC LISTENING

Empatic listening is an active process to see through what the person is saying. There are five measures that will enhance the listening and understanding process.

1. Don't be judgmental. Never come on with the attitude that the other person "caused his/her own problem." Don't adapt the position that the subject's actions have been carefully thought out with a view to inflict pain or injury to others.
2. Don't fake attention or ignore. If you do ignore the individual, you will not only make them upset, but you will experience difficulty in learning what is really happening. Encourage free-flowing communications.
3. Carefully listen to what the subject is really saying. This gives you the opportunity to gain accurate insight into what is actually happening and what may have caused the crisis to develop. Listen for verbal clues that may be used to help defuse the situation.
4. Use silence and listen carefully to clarify message. This technique serves two useful purposes. First, it provides you with the opportunity to better understand what the subject is actually trying to say, and second, it indicates that you are genuinely concerned.
5. Reflection can be used to reinforce. When the individual completes his/her statement, simply communicate words that leave no doubt in the subject's mind that you understand his/her message. Simply convey to the person that you understand what they have said.

NONVERBAL COMMUNICATIONS

Nonverbal communication deals with body language—a message that is conveyed to someone without words. Subtle or obvious body movements or gestures that can provide clear indications as to what another person might be thinking. Only 15 percent of what is said is conveyed by the use of words, whereas at least 85 percent of interpersonal communications are nonverbal. Individuals that are functioning under a stressful or emotional state of mind will often communicate even more useful information in a nonverbal

manner. Practice identifying what people are saying without words. Here are some useful points to consider.

Proxemics or personal space—Respect the subject's personal space, which is considered to be 1½ to 3 feet in distance.

Kinesics—Body posture and movement is critical in a crisis situation. Avoid toe-to-toe or eye-to-eye gestures that can be considered challenging.

Supportive stance—Approximately one leg length away, on an angle, and slightly to the side of the individual. This avoids any feelings of encroachment, invasion of personal space, and enhances officer safety.

CONTROLLING DISRUPTIVE OR VIOLENT BEHAVIOR

There are a number of useful methods that can be applied to control violent or aggressive behavior, such as verbal communications, use of chemicals, physical force, or a combination of all three.

Verbally—Assume a neutral body stance, let the individual talk and listen to what they are saying. Do not argue or threaten. Acknowledge feelings and thoughts. This can be achieved without agreeing or disagreeing. Consider voice tone, volume, and rate when communicating verbally. Use the person's name and maintain eye contact. It may be necessary to make the subject aware that his/her actions are inappropriate, and he/she will be held accountable for his/her actions and responsible for the outcome of the situation.

Chemically—In most crisis situations that occur, the protection officer seldom had the use of chemicals as a viable option. The decision to chemically control an individual can only be made by qualified medical or psychiatric personnel. Medications that could be used in these instances are generally depressants such as valium, thorazine, or haldol. There are other medications to choose from and the qualified medical professional will use what is felt to be most effective after evaluating the behavior of the individual.

Physically—Physical control techniques are used to prevent harm or injury to the individual or others in the immediate vicinity of the incident. Application of physical force should be considered only if no other feasible options are possible. If an individual has to be restrained, nonviolent techniques are the logical choice. These techniques are intended for personal safety and self defense and must be taught by a qualified instructor. The primary focus is to protect employees and clients from injury.

Other—Whether or not to use such devices as chemical mace, stun devices, or lasers is a question to be addressed by local laws, ordinances, and organizational policy. Intensive training is a must before any consideration can be given to the use of these kinds of protective equipment.

TEAM INTERVENTION

Team intervention is considered to be the best approach to be used during crisis development. Personnel should use the least restrictive method to control aggressive/disruptive individual(s). The objective, as in almost all volatile conditions that require security intervention, is to defuse the situation in a manner that reduces the risk of guilt, pain, or injury.

POSITIVE FACTORS RESULTING FROM TEAM APPROACH

The team should consist of no more than five people who are capable of dealing with a crisis situation. More than five members tend to lead to confusion and a lack of unit cohesiveness. When team action seems inevitable, reserve/resource members should remain out of sight, nearby and ready. These are some of the advantages of the team approach.

1. Team members enjoy more personal safety and a feeling of security resulting from the presence of fellow officers or other support staff.
2. Team members are able to maintain a professional profile because of the support and reliance that results from team member interactions.
3. Team members do not feel that the violence or unruly behavior is directed against them personally, rather the team as a whole.
4. Team members can provide verification of actions and inactions which tend to support a legal position in the event of later litigation proceeding being initiated by affected individual(s).

The manner in which you get the team to the scene is vitally important. A mass convergence of staff will be perceived as a show of force and have an unsettling effect on the disruptive individual(s). Try to avoid the attraction of a crowd. Protection officers should carry two-way radios that facilitate effective communication with other team members.

Resource staff that is involved in deployment to the scene must receive preincident training and instruction in all facets of the intervention process, particularly methods of communications.

LEADERSHIP IN THE TEAM APPROACH

As in any kind of teamwork approach, there has to be a leader/captain. The team leader can be anyone that has special skills, training, or expertise that will lend strength and unity to the team. When the leader arrives at the scene, he/she must be prepared to "take over." Here are some additional points to consider when selecting a team leader.

1. The leader will likely be the first person on the scene. Accessibility to the scene is an important consideration.
2. The leader must be confident.
3. The leader must be familiar with personnel that occupy the facility or facilities that may be a target for a crisis.
4. The leader must be familiar with the physical layout of the facility.

When the event occurs and team action is called for, the team leader must take charge and ensure that the following measures/steps are taken as quickly and prudently as possible:

1. Assess the situation, and then determine what action will be taken.
2. Formulate the action plan and put it into play as quickly and effectively as conditions allow.
3. Apprise the team of what is happening. Each team member must know his/her responsibilities. In the event practice/drills have not been conducted, the leader must improvise.
4. Begin the communication process. Assess the situation. Take whatever remedial actions are warranted. Activate contingency plan(s) as required. Keep team members appraised.

SAFETY CONSIDERATIONS IN CRISIS INTERVENTION

The goal in any crisis situation is to neutralize the threat/risk while maintaining the safety and welfare of everyone involved. Mentally deranged or violent individuals will often resort to throwing objects or try to grab or strike the person they envision as a threat, usually the person in charge, most often the protection officer. In these instances, be resourceful, protect yourself with a pillow, chair back cushions, or any object that is readily available. A blanket or coat can be used to help restrain an individual while distracting their attention.

Note the location of windows, doors, and furniture in the area. Normally you would not want to block a door with your body, nor would you want the disruptive person between you and the door that may be your only escape route. Stay away from windows. Try to keep the subject away from things that can be used as weapons; chairs, water pitcher, phone, glass, desk accessories, and any kind of blunt or sharp objects.

CONCLUSION

Disruptive individuals can have a serious adverse effect on organizational operations. If such incidents are perceived as a threat by employees, it will reduce productivity, lower morale, and instill a sense of fear. The presence of a capable, confident protection officer, willing and able to effectively communicate with employees, will have a stabilizing effect in the workplace.

In a post crisis intervention situation, you, the protection officer, may experience anger, fear, or frustration; this is a natural reaction that must be controlled. It is not uncommon for the officer to feel that he/she has been the victim. This can result from a real or perceived lack of management support during and after the crisis or being exposed to the crisis for a prolonged period of time. Do everything possible to resolve the crisis in an expeditious manner which will reduce team frustration and apprehension.

Waste no time in committing your thoughts to paper. By promptly composing a well-written report, you can vividly recall what exactly has happened. Documenting the report will provide a vehicle to vent frustration. Discuss the matter with other team members and most of all, do not get discouraged and maintain a positive attitude.

Remember, when crisis intervention is required, stay calm, be objective, and act appropriately. Let common sense prevail. Remember the plan for success: EVALUATE, IMPLEMENT, DOCUMENT, and REVIEW. For more information, visit crisisprevention.com.

SECURITY QUIZ
Crisis Intervention

1. Crisis intervention is a technique of behavioral management that is done by suggesting certain _____ _____, whether by action or what you say.
2. Persons suffering from insulin shock may physically act out and may not have _____ of their actions.
3. Illness or _____ may cause an individual to behave in a disruptive manner.
4. Being complacent during a crisis situation is good; it allows the individual not to know what you are thinking.
   ☐ T ☐ F
5. The best stance during a crisis situation is just off to the side at an angle.
   ☐ T ☐ F
6. Indistinct signs of possible physical acting out, such as gritting teeth, closing and opening of hands, and tensing, may precede more combative behavior.
   ☐ T ☐ F
7. Experts say that 50 percent to 65 percent of the messages we convey are nonverbal.
   ☐ T ☐ F
8. Paraverbal communications—how we deliver our words or verbal intervention— includes which of the following?
   ☐ (a) Tone
   ☐ (b) Volume
   ☐ (c) Rate
   ☐ (d) All of the above
9. Persons who are behaving in a physically violent manner may be controlled in all of the following ways except:
   ☐ (a) verbally
   ☐ (b) challenged
   ☐ (c) physically
   ☐ (d) chemically
10. When involved in a one-on-one situation, your first action taken should be:
   ☐ (a) make a plan of action
   ☐ (b) do not block the doorway
   ☐ (c) communicate with the individual
   ☐ (d) be sure assistance is en route

SECURITY AWARENESS

By Michael Stroberger, CPO, CSS, CPOI, CLSD, CPP

The best teams are those that know when to ask for help in achieving their goals. The goal of providing a reasonably safe and secure environment requires the support of every person, not just the designated protective force or department. The concept of security awareness has been around for some time and continues to be refined.

In its most basic form, security awareness means that persons not directly responsible for the security program are aware of that program, the goal of the program, the methods by which they can support the program, and are actively acting to provide that support. It is an expansion of the team that carries out the policies and procedures that are in place to protect the identified assets. In addition, security awareness, instilled in persons outside of the company, can be one of the strongest deterrents to crime. Outside of special circumstances, criminals tend to look for targets that are poorly defended as a method if reducing their chances of being observed, caught, or prevented from achieving their goal. If it is clearly obvious that a given location is well organized, and the majority of persons present are active participants in the protective program, they are likely to move on to another possible target.

EXPANDING THE TEAM

The outward perception of security comes from an internal embracing of the policies and procedures that have been developed to create a secure environment. This can only come from a team effort, where even those not directly responsible for that protection are contributing to the overall effort.

The contribution of others does not have to be in the form of actively playing a role in the operation of the protective program. It can be as simple as being conscious of policies, consistently abiding by those policies, and encouraging those around them to do the same. This supportive, team-oriented effort creates an environment where accidental or careless exposures are not typically present. It is often these exposures that create the gap that results in a criminal act being easier to perform or an accident occurring.

Through a team involvement, the senses, intellect, and experience of every person is brought to bear on the issues at hand. Often, those outside of the protective force have expertise, which that protective force might lack. In many cases, the average employee, working for no more than a week in a given position, has a better understanding of that specific job, working environment, and the fellow employees of that area than anyone on the protective force. It is a matter of contact hours and a focus on a single environment which can give them that edge.

A high level of familiarity with a certain environment allows one to more quickly recognize potential threats such as the following:

- Electrical equipment that is beginning to show signs of wear—a potential *fire hazard*
- Unknown individuals in the area—a potential *crime hazard*
- Mechanical wear and tear—a potential *safety hazard*

The officer patrolling this area might catch these as well but has a lower probability of success because he/she does not have constant contact with the area. The perspective and experience of each person make them uniquely qualified to observe changes in their immediate environment. Such support should be sought actively.

Another positive aspect of involving everyone in the program is that they often find these activities new and exciting. An employee in a kitchen, well aware of his/her own direct responsibilities, may take great pride in having identified and corrected a safety hazard. It is something out of the ordinary and a break from the usual daily pattern of work. In some cases, this eagerness might result in identifying the need to correct a situation that might have existed, uncorrected, for an extended period of time. Because of their personal perspective and the interest in pursuing something outside of their daily activities, they might move to correct something which others have, over time, come to ignore.

DEVELOPING THE TEAM MENTALITY

By now, it is obvious that this development of security awareness is highly beneficial. The only question now is: How is this accomplished? It is not something that simply happens of its own accord. There are some basic tactics that can be applied, as well as some underlying foundations that must be present if these efforts are to continue to be effective.

FOUNDATIONS

The basic environment, essential to the attempt to develop positive awareness, are absolutely critical. If these are absent or create a negative image or impact, awareness programs will be ineffective, possibly counterproductive.

- The formal program must be visibly active. If officers are utilized, they must be visible and performing their designated functions with professionalism. Officers poorly representing the protective efforts send a non-verbal message that the program is not worth supporting.

- The policies and procedures must be well designed, known, available to any person operating within their restrictions, and enforced fairly. No one wants to support a program that could act against him/her in an unfair or discriminatory manner.
- The benefits must be understood. When educating people about safety issues, they should be told exactly what type of damage or injury is to be avoided by following a given plan of execution. This brings them into the "inner circle," allowing them to see the reasoning behind the policy or procedure. In many cases, people have resisted otherwise positive efforts simply because they were told they "had to do it," rather than told why it would be a good idea.

UNDERSTAND THE INTENDED AUDIENCE

Once a solid foundation has been created, it is time to bring others into the program. In many cases, those outside of the protective force can be categorized into one of three groups.

- Supporters—those who think this is a great idea and will follow the directives no matter what anyone else tells them
- Neutrals—those willing to support the program as long as it makes sense, and the value is clearly understood. They may not go out of their way to ensure others follow the program, but they will do it themselves;
- Opposers—those who think any protective program is "out to get them," designed to make their lives more difficult, or even those intending to act in a manner that is contrary to the program. This often includes persons currently engaged in activities that are illegal or unethical, those who have done so in the past, or those thinking of doing so in the future.

For the most part, active supporters will not question later changes, modifications, or additions to the program, because they have accepted that the original plan made sense. Neutrals may have to be shown that the new aspects also make positive contributions. The opposers may be wholly resistive to any new aspects and often claim such excuses as "the original plan was too much to handle, already!" The goal, then, is to bring as many people as possible into the ranks of the supporters, and make as many opposers as possible move into at least the ranks of the neutrals.

TACTICS FOR DEVELOPING AWARENESS AND TEAM THINKING

Once the foundation is in place, the next phase is to ensure that the concepts are communicated to the audience. This takes on many forms and must be continuous in nature. Here are some examples.

- *First moment of contact.* For employees, this would be the hiring process. Ensure that the application clearly indicates that, if these are part of the program, criminal background checks, drug testing, and reference checks are conducted as part of every persons hiring process. For nonemployees, the first point of contact may be the property perimeter, the entry doors, or even a telephone call. In these cases, it should be clear that an effective protective program is utilized as evidenced by well-maintained signs, security hardware, or similar equipment. Refusal to provide sensitive or personal information is a method of demonstrating good security policies over the telephone.
- *Continuation of contact.* For employees, this would be in the orientation/training phase. Security and safety should be part of every employee orientation to begin instilling these concepts from the first moment of employment. Previous successes, as well as potential hazards and proactive prevention concepts, must be explained. For nonemployees, this would equate to encountering continued security measures throughout the contact with the facility and people. Such examples as not observing people in violation of posted orders (smoking within sight of a "No Smoking" sign) make a strong impression.
- *Newsletters.* Congratulate those that make significant contributions in a manner in which they are individually comfortable. Make it known that they have supported the efforts, and show the benefit it has had for the company, coworkers, and others. For employees, these could be circulated as a periodical, attached to paychecks, or posted in work areas. For nonemployees, observing plaques that congratulate individuals or departments for contributions to the safety or security efforts will add to the perception that these practices are encouraged.
- *Meetings and seminars.* Have a speaker address groups of employees. Bring in a well-respected professional, and have him/her speak about the importance of a given aspect of the program, the benefits it has, and how the individual can contribute to those efforts. Outside of the employee population, have your internal success stories relayed to others. Have one of your star performers speak to a group in another location, and show that the applied concept is of benefit to others as well.
- *Visual aids.* Use posters, videos, and similar media to continually promote the security and safety efforts in a wide variety of area. Care should be taken to avoid presenting this information in a forceful manner as opposed to simply demonstrating the benefits. In addition, such materials may be seen as intrusive if put in areas where people expect some level of privacy or a break from the working environment. Make these items interesting, vary the appearance occasionally, and ensure that you are telling them why it would be good to act in the described manner rather than simply telling them they "have to."

Developing security awareness is not complicated if a basic understanding of these concepts is achieved. Most people do not actively oppose security or safety measures and look for some guidance in how to prevent incidents from occurring. By providing a guide and being supportive of those efforts, this sense of employee ownership will grow. Once this occurs, those seeing the program from the outside will easily recognize that the security and safety program is very active, supported by the entire team and continually vigilant. This is the type of environment that criminals dislike, and where accidents are rare. This is a "security aware" team.

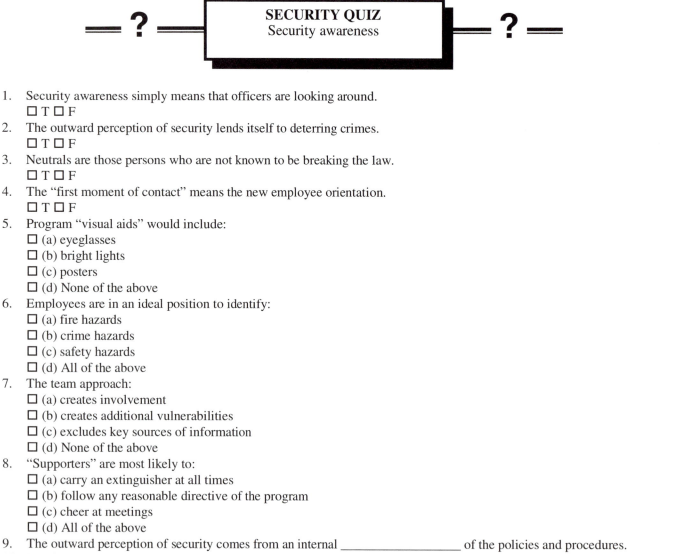

SECURITY QUIZ
Security awareness

1. Security awareness simply means that officers are looking around.
    ☐ T ☐ F
2. The outward perception of security lends itself to deterring crimes.
    ☐ T ☐ F
3. Neutrals are those persons who are not known to be breaking the law.
    ☐ T ☐ F
4. The "first moment of contact" means the new employee orientation.
    ☐ T ☐ F
5. Program "visual aids" would include:
    ☐ (a) eyeglasses
    ☐ (b) bright lights
    ☐ (c) posters
    ☐ (d) None of the above
6. Employees are in an ideal position to identify:
    ☐ (a) fire hazards
    ☐ (b) crime hazards
    ☐ (c) safety hazards
    ☐ (d) All of the above
7. The team approach:
    ☐ (a) creates involvement
    ☐ (b) creates additional vulnerabilities
    ☐ (c) excludes key sources of information
    ☐ (d) None of the above
8. "Supporters" are most likely to:
    ☐ (a) carry an extinguisher at all times
    ☐ (b) follow any reasonable directive of the program
    ☐ (c) cheer at meetings
    ☐ (d) All of the above
9. The outward perception of security comes from an internal _____ of the policies and procedures.
10. Employees working in a given area typically have a _____ understanding of that area then the security officers.

ENVIRONMENTAL CRIME CONTROL THEORY

By Glen Kitteringham, MSc., CPP, CPOI, CSS, CPO

INTRODUCTION

The security industry has come a long way in the past 150 years. One can argue that it took a giant step forward in the middle of the 19th century when Alan Pinkerton created his world famous Pinkerton's Detective Agency. In the intervening one and one half centuries, there has been a great deal of activity. Giant steps have been taken in lock and key systems, access control hardware, the increasing ingenuity of vaults and safes, fencing systems, CCTV, increasing professionalism and training of security officers, and a host of other physical security enhancements. What has not been given the proper attention is the crime control theory behind why all this human, hardware, and software is being deployed.

While the average reader in reviewing existing security literature will read about Crime Prevention Through Environmental Design or CPTED as it is more commonly referred to, there are a host of other theories that offer as much or more insight into crime control. But again, back to the focus of this section, why should security practitioners know not only the applications but also the theory behind it? If you are going to implement a host of new security applications, you should start with why! Learning and applying these theories will not provide the magic answer but they will allow you to make informed decisions as to why or why not security precautions should or should not be carried out. Once a deeper understanding of why a person chose to carry out the activity in a particular area can be made or just as importantly why an act was not carried out, then understanding and further applications can be instituted. Was there an absence of a capable guardian as Felson and Cohen theorize? Did rational choice on behalf of the offender play a role as Cornish and Clarke believe take place? A deeper understanding of the offense allows the responding security professional to make keener and more analytical choices about how to respond.

The short and simple is that once a criminal act has occurred, it becomes a problem or mathematical equation in an abstract way. This is not to take away from the other issues around it. This is not to minimize the activity. There are very real victims that are created from this act. Pain and suffering are not minimized. However, as stated, the criminal act could be viewed as a mathematical equation waiting to be solved. There is a danger in doing this as this may lead some to believe that once the equation is figured out, there could be an assumption that there will never again be a crime in this same location. This may be true, but the ef-

fects of displacement and diffusion of benefits kick in and the equation changes. This forces the security officer to continually review the situation from many different angles. Has new technology made the old security solutions moot? Will an attack come from a different direction and time of day; will the attacker be forced to try new methods? Continual awareness and review is necessary.

ENVIRONMENTAL CRIME PREVENTION vs. SOCIAL CRIME PREVENTION

A short and simple explanation of environmental crime prevention is that crime control practitioners focus their attention and energies upon potential locations of criminal activity. Locks, doors and other barriers, CCTV equipment, and patrolling security officers are all examples of environmental crime control. On the other side of the coin is social crime prevention. This area focuses upon social programs, education, employment creation, welfare, unemployment insurance, police, corrections, and other after the fact follow-up programs. While the intent of this chapter is not to argue the pros and cons of one theory over the other, one comment will be made. While all the programs and money spent upon social crime control can be considered laudable, it would be a foolish security manager who donated his or her security budget to a social crime control program regardless of how noble it may seem. Government and big business have already spent billions of dollars on this issue for many years, but physical security is required more than ever.

Regarding environmental crime control theory, as the proceeding theoretical model indicates, this is an area that has not been relegated the same attention and respect as the social crime control model. Social crime control has been practised in one form or another for hundreds of years. Environmental crime control in contrast grew from work completed at the University of Chicago in the 1920s. It was there that attention was paid not to the people who committed the criminal acts, but the areas in which the crime was being committed. However, this area grew dormant for several decades. The idea was given a re-birth by the influential writer and social commentator, Jane Jacobs, when she wrote *The Death and Life of Great American Cities* in 1961. Her work inspired both C. Ray Jeffery and Oscar Newman, both of who took off in new directions; Jeffery with his book *Crime Prevention Through Environmental Design* and Newman and his *Defensible Space*. In turn, both researchers inspired others such as Paul and Patricia

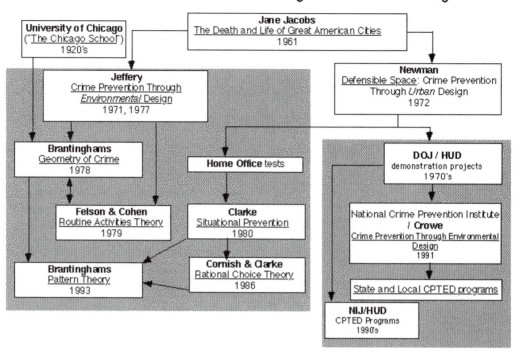

Figure 7-1
Evolution of Crime Prevention Through
Environmental Design

Brantingham, Tim Crowe, Ronald V. Clarke, Marcus Felson, and others. What follows is an overview of the various environmental crime control theories.

THEORIES

Rational Choice Theory

Rational Choice Theory was first fully presented by Ronald V. Clarke and Derek B. Cornish in 1986 in *The Reasoning Criminal: Rational Choice Perspectives on Offending*. As Tayler (1997: 293) states, the rationale behind the theory is that people will commit a crime if it is in their own best interests. Basically the offender uses a decision making process whereby the positive and negative aspects of committing a particular act are weighed. If the perception is that there are more reasons for proceeding, regardless of the existing security barriers, then at the very least an attempt will be made. If an opportunity presents itself, there is a benefit and there is little likelihood of being apprehended, then they will commit the crime. Further, Pease quotes Clarke and Cornish (1985), who claims that "the underlying assumption is that offenders seek to benefit themselves by their criminal behavior. This entails making decisions and choices, however rudimentary their rationality might be, being constrained by limits of time, ability, and the availability of relevant information" (1997: 967).

Following this rationalization, it is up to the security personnel to convince the potential offender that it is not in his or her best interests to carry out the act. This is carried out by target hardening. The application of situational crime prevention techniques are the results of this theory. As rational choice is the theoretical element, what follows are situational crime prevention techniques that are the practical efforts used to reduce criminal opportunities. These techniques (Clarke, 1997: 18) involve increasing efforts, increasing risks, removing anticipating rewards, and removing excuses. These four techniques are further subdivided into four categories to help eliminate opportunities for criminals. They can range from physical access control devices to the use of psychology to deter people's criminal tendencies. One final statement must be made regarding situationalism and that it must be directed at highly specific forms of crime.

The techniques for doing so are laid out in Figure 7-2.

To sum up the principles of rational choice theory there are a number of observations to be made.

Criminals are opportunistic. These opportunistic criminals are average everyday people. If the reward is high enough, deterrents will not work. People will weigh the pros and cons of committing the crime and it is centered on the specifics of the target. Finally, situational crime prevention works best with the amateur and least with the professional. Bearing in mind that there are different classifications of criminals, primarily amateur and professional, the more the security precautions taken, the more likely all

16 Situational Crime Prevention Techniques:

Increasing Perceived Effort	Increasing Perceived Risks	Reducing Anticipated Rewards	Removing Excuses
1. **Target Hardening** Slug rejecter device Steering locks Bandit screens	5. **Entry/Exit Screening** Automatic ticket gates Baggage screening Merchandise tags	9. **Target Removal** Removable car radio Women's refuges Phonecard	13. **Rule Setting** Customs declaration Harassment codes Hotel registration
2. **Access Control** Parking lot barriers Fenced yards Entry phones	6. **Formal Surveillance** Red light cameras Burglar alarms Security guards	10. **Identifying Property** Property marking Vehicle licensing Cattle branding	14. **Stimulating Conscience** Roadside speedometers "Shoplifting is stealing" "Idiots drink and drive"
3 .**Deflecting Offenders** Bus stop placement Tavern location Street closures	7. **Surveillance by Employees** Pay phone location Park attendants CCTV systems	11. **Reducing Temptation** Gender neutral listings Off-street parking Rapid repair	15. **Controlling Disinhibitors** Drinking age laws Ignition interlock V-chip
4 . **Controlling Facilitators** Credit card photo Gun controls Caller-ID	8. **Natural Surveillance** Defensible space Street lighting Cab Driver ID	12. **Denying Benefits** Ink merchandise tags PIN for car Radios Graffiti cleaning	16. **Facility Compliance** Easy library checkout Public lavatories Trash bins

These techniques were developed by R. V. Clarke and R. Homel (Clarke, 1997, p.18).

Figure 7-2   Situational Crime Prevention Techniques

but the most determined attacker will be stopped. Other factors come into play as well. Two that will be discussed are displacement and diffusion of benefits.

DISPLACEMENT OF CRIME

Displacement states that a determined attack, if stymied with one method, location, and so on, will keep trying until successful. Diffusion of benefits states that security precautions taken in one place will overlap onto others and crime will be reduced overall.

There are five aspects of displacement, bounded by time of day or activity, location of target, technique of criminal, type of victim or property, and target of criminal (Tyska and Fennelly, 1998: 49). Displacement claims that regardless of whether a specific crime is committed at a particular location the criminal will simply move onto a more "criminal user-friendly" locale where the crime is then carried out. This results in a zero sum gain for rational choice theory and society.

METHODS OF DISPLACEMENT

1. The time in which it was committed
2. The method in which is used
3. The type of target which is attacked
4. The location of the act
5. The type of offense

Each of these characteristics provides varying means in which to commit a criminal act. For example, if bank robbers find it impossible to break into a vault after hours, they may choose to rob the bank when it is serving the public. If one bank is too difficult to break into, the offender may choose to go down the street where a review of the location shows weaknesses that convince the criminal to break into that one. One should explore the concept of displacement further as there are arguments for and against it.

DIFFUSION OF BENEFITS

Diffusion of benefits is the opposite side of the coin in discussing displacement. Just as it is assumed by critics of Rationalism that crime is simply moved to another location, there is also a belief that the benefits of situational crime prevention techniques are also moved to other locations, thereby resulting in a decrease in crime. Pease states the following in reference to both issues.

> The fact that displacement has been long debated, and that diffusion of benefits has been neglected suggests that displacement is dominant not because it reflects a real attempt to understand crime flux, but because it serves as a convenient excuse for doing nothing ('Why bother? It will only get displaced'). (1997: 978)

A further somewhat controversial point to displacement is that there may be a benefit to displacing certain kinds of crime. For example, drug and prostitution control may be made easier or more tolerable when it is away from residential neighborhoods or concentrated in one locale (Pease, 1997: 979).

Following up on the heels of the situational crime prevention techniques, Wortly introduced a further 16 techniques in a second-generation review: "The new classification is based upon the argument that there are two distinct situational forces acting upon potential offenders—the perceived costs and benefits of intended criminal acts (the basis for Clarke's classification) and factors that may induce individuals to commit crimes that they would not have otherwise considered (the basis of the present classification)" (Wortley, 2001, 63).

Routine activity theory, developed by Cohen and Felson, revolves around three things, those being a "potential offender, a suitable target and the absence of a capable guardian" (Bottoms and Wiles, 1997, 320). All three must come together in order for criminal activity to be realized. Routine activities theory uses the same rational choice methodology and situational crime prevention techniques as a basis. As in any theory, routine activities theory has its criticisms. One of the prime criticisms is that criminals are irrational in their decision making. They may not use the same rationale as the person implementing the security measures. They may not even be aware of the situational crime prevention techniques put in place in the first place, they may be under the influence of drugs or alcohol, or for whatever reason, they may simply not care about the security measures.

Crime pattern theory, developed by Paul and Patricia Brantingham, crime pattern theory is a rather complex amalgamation of both rational choice and routine activity, and a further introduction of sociocultural, economic, legal, and the physical environmental cues. The premise is that crime does not occur randomly in time, place, social group cohesiveness, or a host of other aspects. Acknowledging the complexity of the theory, a response to prevent crime can come from no other area. Instead, a multidisciplinary approach must be taken where responses must be tailored for the situation. One must consider the criminal opportunity, the individual offender and his or her readiness and willingness to commit crime, and the combination of the previous three aspects as they impact upon the sociocultural, economic, legal, and environmental cues. Granted, this is not an easy theory to deal with either from a theoretical or practical perspective. Some of the issues discussed here are certainly out of the reach of security practitioners to respond to but knowing that a detailed examination at the environment is required, practitioners may be able to see things in a new light. Knowing that often decisions to conduct criminal activity may be carried out for entirely different reasons than previously suspected, gives the security officer a chance to view things in a new light.

Four Components of Situational Crime Prevention, Part II. with 16 Opportunity Reducing Techniques

Controlling Prompts	Controlling Pressures	Reducing Permissibility	Reducing Provocations
Controlling Triggers Gun control Pornography restrictions Environmental self-management	**Reducing Inappropriate Conformity** Dispersing gang members Screening children's associates Bolstering independence	**Rule Setting** Harassment codes Staff inductions "Shoplifting is stealing" signs	**Reducing Frustrations** Inmate control of comfort settings Improved wet playtimes Efficient road design
Providing Reminders Warning signs Symbolic territorial markers Litter bins	**Reducing Inappropriate Obedience** Support for whistle blowers Participatory management Semi-independent units	**Clarifying Responsibility** Server intervention Assigning discrete tasks Encouraging sense of ownership	**Reducing Crowding** Limiting nightclub patron density Regulating nightclub patron overflow Use of colour, windows, light, etc.
Reducing Inappropriate Imitation Rapid Repair of vandalism Controls on television content Supervisors as exemplars	**Encouraging Compliance** Persuasive signs Fairness of request Participation in rule making	**Clarifying Consequences** Copyright messages Public posting Vandalism information brochures	**Respecting Territory** Identifiable territories for residents Privacy rooms for residents Avoiding intrusions into inmates' cells
Setting Positive Expectations Pub gentrification Domestic prison furniture Fixing "broken windows"	**Reducing Anonymity** Restricting uniform use (perpetrators) School dress code Low-profile crowd management	**Personalizing Victims** Victim cooperation Humanizing conditions for prisoners Concern for employee welfare	**Controlling Environmental Irritants** Smoke-free nightclubs Air conditioning Noise control

Figure 7-3   Four Components of Situational Crime Prevention

CRIME PREVENTION THROUGH ENVIRONMENTAL DESIGN (CPTED)

Probably the most well known of the environmental crime control theories, the theories of CPTED were first expounded upon by Dr. C. Ray Jeffery in 1971. To quote Tim Crowe, a proponent, CPTED "expands upon the assumption that the proper design and effective use of the built environment can lead to a reduction in the fear of crime and the incidence of crime, and to an improvement in the quality of life" (Crowe, 1991, p: 1).

There are three key concepts specific to CPTED.

The Use of Natural Surveillance

Natural surveillance is obtained through increasing the ability of legitimate place users to see further and wider and decreasing the ability of illegitimate place users to hide awaiting for the time to carry out their activity. An example of the use of natural surveillance would be in an underground parking lot as users leave their cars and head towards either an elevator lobby or staircase. Often it is difficult to see what lies inside. By using glass partition instead of cinderblock, the property manager increases the natural surveillance whereby legitimate users can see directly into the vestibule area instead of guessing what lies ahead. Also, it is difficult for an illegitimate user to stay for long in this area as they are subject to increased scrutiny.

The Use of Natural Access Control

This falls under the definition of spatial definition. An example of natural access control may be normal place users are encouraged to use the area for legitimate purposes and illegitimate users are encouraged to not remain in the area. However this is accomplished is up to the particular location and imagination of the property manager. For example, if unwanted visitors are remaining in an area because of a design feature such as wall or barrier, a recommendation is that the feature unless required could be removed or changed to make it less attractive thereby reducing the attractiveness of the area. Another example is that if skateboarders are using a particular plaza because of the many attractive flat wooden benches, then pop up seat on the benches could be installed making it difficult if not impossible for them to be utilized.

Territorial Behavior

This concept is key to reclaiming an area if it has been taken over by illegitimate users. If design features have made a haven for illegitimate users and have frightened off legitimate users, then one of the most important actions that is required is for this space to be reclaimed. Initially this may take the form of enhanced security patrols to keep illegitimate users away until the area is seen as a desirable area once again for legitimate users. This, in turn, will keep the illegitimate users away because the high numbers of normal space users will deter abnormal space users. A prime example based upon the previous example of skateboarders. In one example, an area had practically been taken over by illegitimate users making it a dangerous area to come to.

Several CPTED strategies were made including making design changes and enhanced security officer presence. Eventually, a large number of legitimate users returned to the area, which in turn further decreased the skateboarders from coming back in large numbers. While the problem has not completely gone away, it has decreased noticeably to the extent that the quality of life for legitimate users has increased.

Further, CPTED planners should classify security strategies into three categories. The first is through the use of organized strategies. This encompasses the use of human resources to increase security. Such examples are security or police officers, or some other type of official guardian. The second strategy is to incorporate mechanical methods into enhanced security. This is achieved through the use of hardware such as CCTV, locking mechanisms, access control systems, fences, and other barriers. Finally, the third strategy, probably the most important, is to use a natural enhancement to enhance security awareness. This may take the form of increased usage by legitimate place users, the proper use of windows to increase surveillance, making all users responsible for security, and so on. It is important to start with the natural methods of enhancing security then augmenting through organized and mechanical methods.

DEFENSIBLE SPACE: CRIME PREVENTION THROUGH URBAN DESIGN
(Oscar Newman)

This revolves around the public housing environment and seeks to reduce crime through the use of natural surveillance, natural access control, and territorial concern.

History of Defensible Space

While Oscar Newman has written many influential pieces on this important concept over the past 30 plus years, two of his most important works are *Architectural Design for Crime Prevention,* published in 1971 through the U.S. Department of Justice, and *Defensible Space*, published in 1972. Further work such as *Creating Defensible Space* from 1996, published through the U.S. Department of Housing and Urban Development, adds to his significant body of work.

Concept and Strategies

While there will not be a detailed analysis of all the concepts that encompass the theory of defensible space, a general overview will be made. The writer encourages interested parties who seek a deeper understanding to access the aforementioned books for an in-depth analysis. Basically defensible space calls for proprietors and legitimate users of residential space to act as guardians of their living areas. In *Architectural Design*, Newman states the following.

Physical mechanisms for achieving defensible space are as follows:
- Those that serve to define spheres of influence of territorial influence that occupants can easily adopt proprietary attitudes.

- Those that improve the natural capability of residents to survey both the interior and exterior of the residential space.
- Those that enhance the safety of adjoining areas such as communal facilities.
- Finally, through the judicious use of building materials to reduce the perception of peculiarity, such as vulnerability, isolation, and stigma of housing projects and their residents. (p. 2)

Practical Applications

As one can see, there are some similarities between Defensible Space and CPTED applications. The important concept of legitimate users verses illegitimate users, the proper and effective utilization of surveillance, both natural and man-made, and creating safe havens for normal users are common to both. Knowing and understanding who belongs and who does not in an area (legitimate users verses illegitimate users of space), the importance of various types of surveillance, and encouraging legitimate users of space to use or reclaim areas for activities are issues that security practitioners can understand and appreciate.

SUMMARY

While the previous discussion has not detailed each and every theory or practice as detailed in the Evolution of Crime Prevention Through Environmental Design as outlined in Figure 7-1, there has been attention to the main existing environmental crime theories. The reader is encouraged to consider further detailed examinations of the theories outlined here, since they are an important aspect of crime control. They are certainly not the only ones, but rational choice, routine activities, CPTED, Defensible Space, Crime Pattern Theory, and Situational Crime Prevention Techniques are an important basis for explaining some the root causes of why certain crimes may occur over and over in specific locations. Not all the answers are contained here, and while every situation can be considered unique, the security practitioner should understand that there are some basic explanations and rationale behind criminal activity. Consideration for implementing security enhancements should not be made in a vacuum. Hence, a detailed study of the criminal area with the accompanying rationale should make for reduced criminal opportunity.

CHAPTER REFERENCES AND ADDITIONAL SOURCES OF INFORMATION
http://www.arch.vt.edu/crimeprev/pages/hdevbody.html

Bottoms, A. and Wiles, P. (1997) "Environmental Criminology," in M. Maguire, R. Morgan, and R. Reiner (Eds), *The Oxford Handbook of Criminology, 2nd Ed., Oxford: Clarendon Press: 305–359.*

Clarke, Ronald V. (1997, 2nd Ed.) *Situational Crime Prevention: Successful Case Studies,* Albany: Harrow and Heston.

Crowe, Timothy D. (1991) *Crime Prevention Through Environmental Design,* Boston: Butterworth-Heinemann.

Module 1 (1999) *Criminological Theory 2: Rational Choice Theory*: 277–304, The Scarman Center for Public Order: University of Leicester.

Module 1 (1999) *Crime Prevention 2: The "Situational Approach"*: 305–344, The Scarman Center for Public Order: University of Leicester.

Module 5 (2000) *Applied Crime Management: Unit 3: Crime Pattern Analysis*: 113–168, The Scarman Center for Public Order: University of Leicester.

Newman, O. (1971) *Architectural Design for Crime Prevention,* National Institute of Law Enforcement and Criminal Justice.

Pease, Ken (1997) 'Crime Prevention,' in M. Maguire, R. Morgan and R. Reiner (Eds), *The Oxford Handbook of Criminology, 2nd Ed., Oxford: Clarendon Press: 963–995.*

Tayler, Ian. (1997) 'The Political Economy of Crime,' in M. Maguire, R. Morgan, and R. Reiner (Eds), *The Oxford Handbook of Criminology, 2nd Ed., Oxford: Clarendon Press: 265–303.*

Tyska, Louis A. and Fennelly, Lawrence J. (1998) *150 Things That You Should KnowAabout Security,* Boston: Butterworth-Heinemann.

Wortly, Richard (2001) "A Classification of Techniques for Controlling Situational Precipitators of Crime," in B. Fisher and M. Gill (Eds.) *Security Journal, Perpetuity Press, Vol. Fourteen Number 4: 36–82.*

OTHER SOURCES

Applied Crime Analysis by Karim Vellani and Joel Nahoun published by Butterworth-Heinemann, 2001.

Creating Defensible Space by Oscar Newman published by U.S. Department of Housing and Urban Development, 1996.

Defensible Space: Crime Prevention Through Urban Design by Oscar Newman published by The MacMillan Company, 1972.

Spotlight on Security for Real Estate Managers by Laurence J. Fennelly and John H. Lombardi, published by the Institute for Real Estate Management, 1997.

The Death and Life of Great American Cities by Jane Jacobs, published by Vintage, 1992.

Understanding Crime Prevention, Second Edition by the National Crime Prevention Institute (NCPI) published by Butterworth-Heinemann, 2001.

```
═ ? ═    ┌─────────────────────┐    ═ ? ═
         │  SECURITY QUIZ      │
         │  Environmental Crime │
         │  Control Theory     │
         └─────────────────────┘
```

1. The two differing crime prevention theories discussed here are _____ and
    _____.

2. _____ crime control theory focuses on the _____ of the criminal act, which is opposed to what
    traditionally has been the focus of crime reduction attempts, the _____.

3. A short and simple explanation of environmental crime prevention is that crime control practitioners focus their attention
    and energies on _____ locations of _____ activity.

4. _____ states that a determined attacker, if stymied with one method, location, and so on, will keep trying until
    successful.

5. _____ of benefits states that _____ precautions taken in once place will overlap onto others and crime will be
    reduced overall.

6. Environmental crime control theory focuses on the _____ of the criminal act.
    ☐ (a) time
    ☐ (b) location
    ☐ (c) perpetrator
    ☐ (d) victim

7. Basically the offender uses a decision making process whereby the positive and negative aspects of committing a particu-
    lar act is weighed. This is an example of_____.
    ☐ (a) CPTED (Crime Prevention Through Environmental Design)
    ☐ (b) Routine Activities Theory
    ☐ (c) Rational Choice Theory
    ☐ (d) defensible space

8. The application of situational crime prevention techniques are the results of this theory.
    ☐ (a) Rational Choice Theory
    ☐ (b) Routine Activity Theory
    ☐ (c) Crime Pattern Theory
    ☐ (d) Defensible space

9. There are _____ aspects of displacement.
    ☐ (a) three
    ☐ (b) four
    ☐ (c) five
    ☐ (d) six

10. There are three key concepts specific to CPTED. Which of the following is not one?
    ☐ (a) Natural surveillance
    ☐ (b) Defensible space
    ☐ (c) Natural access control
    ☐ (d) Territorial behavior

Unit 8

Operational Risk
Emergency Planning and Disaster Control
Terrorism
Counterterrorism and VIP Protection
Weapons of Mass Destruction: The NBC Threats

OPERATIONAL RISK MANAGEMENT

By Tom M. Conley, MA, CPP, CFE, CPO

The primary function of security professionals is to protect the safety and security of the people, property, and information that they are entrusted with protecting. Thus, true security professionals are highly committed to do the best job that they can to reduce the probability of a loss occurring. Even with the best security program, including the best-trained security people, there is no way that a security officer can protect their customer against all losses; there is simply no solution or combination of solutions that results in 100 percent success at all times. However, just because all losses cannot be avoided, it does not mean that risks cannot be reduced through proper planning. The fact is that there must be a combination of people and systems that work together to reduce the probability of loss. To the extent that organizational safety and security risks can be identified through proper risk analysis, they can be mitigated. While the organization's chief security officer, security director, or security manager is primarily the person who is responsible for conducting the risk analysis and security survey in their organizations, the reality is that reducing loss and the probability of loss in the organization are every person's business—and every person's responsibility. In a message to all personnel, the Honorable Gordon England, secretary of the United States Navy stated, "Simply put, every one of us [in the U.S. Navy and U.S. Marine Corps] must ensure the safety of ourselves [and others]" (England, 2001). Protection officers are no different in that our safety, and the safety of the people whom we protect, are the primary concern.

Security officers need to understand the basic concepts of risk and risk management to be effective in their positions as security professionals. Typically, when conducting a risk analysis and security survey, the primary objectives of the person or persons who are conducting the survey and analysis are to identify the organization's overall risks, determine how susceptible the assets are to loss (vulnerability), and then determine how important the assets are to an organization (criticality). Finally, the person or persons conducting the survey and analysis will employ a concept known as the Principles of Probability. This process will quantify the potential losses to the organization in terms of actual dollars. "Risk is the possible happening of an undesirable event. An event is something that can occur, a definable occurrence. When the event happens, it can be described. Protection is designed to protect against harmful events." For this reason, as Alan Krull [IBM Information Systems] has stated, "The question, Is a system secure? is meaningless. What should be asked is, Is the system protected against events which will be harmful" (Broder, 1984)?

The quantitative approach of assigning a financial loss to the lack of risk controls is essential because it justifies the security program's budget and its existence. Without some type of justification, there would be little or no reason for an organization's upper-level managers to authorize funding for a security program. One tool that security managers, as well as all others in the security department, can use to reduce losses and minimizing risk is to institute an Operational Risk Management (ORM) program in the organization. In its most elemental form, an ORM process will cause security personnel at all levels to answer three questions about any obvious or potential incident. These questions are: What can hurt me or my organization, how bad can it hurt me or my organization, and what (if anything) can I do about it?

The original ORM program was developed by the U.S. Army in 1989 and was adopted by the U.S. Navy and other U.S. Department of Defense service branches shortly thereafter. ORM, as developed, is a five-step decision-making process that is designed to enable individuals to identify hazards, assess risks, and implement controls to reduce risk associated with any action or operation. The ORM process exists on three levels: **time-critical** (an "on the run" mental or oral review); **deliberate** (application of the complete five-step process); and **in-depth** (a deliberate process with a more thorough risk assessment involving research of available data, use of a diagram and analysis tools, and formal testing or long term tracking of the hazards associated with the operation to identify and assess the hazards). ORM incorporates the four principles of (1) accepting risk when benefits outweigh the cost, (2) accepting no unnecessary risk, (3) anticipating and managing risk by planning (risks are more easily controlled when they are identified early in the planning process), and (4) make risk decisions at the proper level in the organization.

While traditional ORM was originally developed and used in conjunction with military planning and operations, it is equally effective when used in day-to-day security operations. ORM does not have to be complex to be effective. In fact, implementing ORM at a basic level within organizations is the key to a successful ORM program. Like most systems, ORM uses "tools" as a part of the process. These tools include a risk assessment matrix, loss severity categories, the loss probability, and the use of risk assessment codes.

An ORM Risk Assessment Matrix (RAM) is used to accomplish the second step of the five-step ORM process.

Using the RAM to quantify and prioritize the risk(s) does not lessen the inherently subjective nature of risk assessment. However, the RAM does provide a consistent framework for evaluating risk. Although different matrices may be used for various applications, any risk assessment tool should include the elements of hazard severity and mishap probability. The Loss Severity is an assessment of the worst credible consequence that can occur as a result of an incident. Severity is defined by potential degree of injury, illness, property damage, loss of assets (time, money, and personnel), or potential to affect a mission. The combination of two or more incidents may increase the overall level of risk. Loss probability is a degree of how likely an event is to occur. Loss severity categories are assigned as Roman numerals according to the following criteria:

- **Category I**—The incident may cause death, loss of a facility/asset, or result in grave damage.
- **Category II**—The incident may cause severe injury, illness, property damage, or degradation to efficient use of assets.

- **Category III**—The incident may cause minor injury, illness, property damage, or degradation to efficient use of assets.
- **Category IV**—The incident presents a minimal threat to personal safety or health, property, or efficient use of assets, affected populations, experiences, or previously established statistical information.

Loss probability is assigned an English letter according to the following criteria:

- Subcategory A—Likely to occur immediately or within a short period of time. Expected to occur frequently to an individual item or person or continuously to a group or an organization.
- Subcategory B—Probably will occur in time. Expected to occur several times to an individual item or person or frequently to a group or an organization.
- Subcategory C—May occur in time. Can reasonably be expected to occur some time to an individual item or person or several times to a group or an organization.
- Subcategory D—Unlikely to occur.

Risk Assessment Matrix

Hazard Severity:

Category I: The hazard may cause death, loss, of facility/asset or result in grave damage
Category II: The hazard may cause severe injury, illness, or property damage
Category III: The hazard may cause minor injury, illness, or property damage
Category IV: The hazard presents minimal threat to personal and equipment

Probability:

Category A: Likely to occur Immediately
Category B: Probably will occur in time
Category C: May occur in time
Category D: Unlikely to occur

	Probability			
Severity	A	B	C	D
I	1	1	2	3
II	1	2	3	4
III	2	3	4	5
IV	3	4	5	5

RAC Definitions:
1. Critical
2. Serious
3. Moderate
4. Minor
5. Negligible

Never except Unnecessary Risk!
If it looks like a hazard it probably is!
Use Common Sense at all times!

Operational Risk Management

Purpose: ORM is a decision making tool used by people at all levels to increase operational effectiveness by anticipating hazards and reducing the potential for loss, thereby, increasing the probability of a successful mission

Process:

1. Identify the Hazards:
   a. Outline the major steps in the operation
   b. List all of the hazards in each step
   c. List possible causes of each hazard

2. Assess the Hazard:
   a. For each hazard determine probability and severity
   b. Assign each RAC (see reverse side)

3. Make Risk Decisions:
   a. Start with most serious risk and select controls
   b. Make decisions at the appropriate level
   c. With the controls in place, decide if the benefit outweighs the risk
   d. If more controls are needed to outweigh the risk, communicate with higher authority

4. Implement Controls:
   a. Engineering Controls: Remove hazard before a person comes in contact with it
   b. Admin Controls: Training, SOP's, warnings, limit the exposure
   c. Personal Protective Equipment (PPE)

5. Supervise:
   a. Conduct follow-up evaluations of plan
   b. Stay flexible
   c. Take corrective action when needed

Figure 8-1   Risk Assessment Matrix

The Risk Assessment Code (RAC) is used to define the degree of risk associated with a risk and considers incident severity and incident probability. The RAC is derived by using the RAM. RAC definitions are 1—Critical Risk, 2—Serious Risk, 3—Moderate Risk, 4—Minor Risk, and 5—Negligible Risk.

The components of an ORM program have been developed to minimize the risk of injury and death of people, the devaluation or loss of property, and the loss of information. Developing and measuring a successful organizational ORM program is based on the following assumptions:

- ORM is vital to the protection of people, property, and information.
- While ORM is not a safety program, ORM and safety are mutually inclusive.
- To achieve success, the ORM program and concepts must be understandable and achievable, and must be embraced by all personnel in the organization. ORM, if implemented, will effectively reduce the likelihood of adverse events occurring.
- In order to reduce the probability of adverse events occurring, an ORM program must be implemented and maintained.
- Initial and periodic training of all affected personnel on the topic of ORM and on the organization's ORM program is essential to mitigating risk.
- The ORM program must be periodically assessed to ensure the ongoing validity of the ORM program and to assure compliance with the program's objectives, policies, and procedures.

- If ORM is to be successful, it must be fully integrated into the organization's culture as a standard way of doing business. While ORM is, by definition, a program, a "program approach" to ORM will not produce the results needed to realize the benefits of ORM.

On August 23, 2001, the U.S. Secretary of Defense, the Honorable Donald H. Rumsfeld, asked the military services to better balance the risks of today and tomorrow. "We have established some defense planning guidance which will set forth to the services and the components areas that we feel need to be addressed in a priority manner," Rumsfeld told reporters at the Pentagon. He said, "Those areas would balance the risks of not modernizing, of not transforming, of not taking care of the force, and operational risk. The defense establishment has done a good job in terms of balancing operational risks, but, we have not done a good job on balancing risks with respect to the damage to the force, and the damage to the infrastructure, and the slow modernization and the slow transformation." All the risks are to be "put up on the table," he added (Gilmore, 2001). Secretary Rumsfeld's comments are an example of a leader's tasking for all his personnel to employ in-depth risk assessment and risk management processes that will lead to intelligent analytical choices during the planning process. Our organizations are no different in our responsibility to continually assess risk and look for ways to mitigate risk. An organizational Operational Risk Management program is an essential part of the risk identification and mitigation process.

		PROBABILITY				RAC's
		LIKELY to occur very soon	PROBABLY will occur in time	MAY occur in time	UNLIKELY to occur in time	
		A	B	C	D	
Catastrophic	I	1	1	2	3	1 = CRITICAL
Critical	II	1	2	3	4	2 = SERIOUS
Moderate	III	2	3	4	5	3 = MODERATE
Negligible	V	3	4	5	5	4 = MINOR
		RISK ASSESSMENT CODES				5 = NEGLIGIBLE

Figure 8-2   Risk Assessment Codes

REFERENCES

Broder, J. (1984). *Risk Analysis and The Security Survey* (p. 24). Stoneham, MA: Butterworth Publishers.

England, G. (2001, August). *Navy Administrative Message.* ALNAV 081/01. DTG R 091747Z AUG 01.

Gilmore, G.J. (2001, August 24). *Services Need to Balance Risks Better, Rumsfeld Says.* The American Forces Information Service. Washington, D.C.

SECURITY QUIZ
Operational Risk Management

1. Reducing loss and the probability of loss in the organization is whose responsibility?
   - ☐ (a) The organization's chief security officer
   - ☐ (b) The organization's president or chief executive officer
   - ☐ (c) All personnel in the security department
   - ☐ (d) Everyone in the organization

2. Operational Risk Management incorporates the four principles of (1) accepting risk when benefits outweigh the cost, (2) accepting no unnecessary risk, (3) anticipating and managing risk by planning (risks are more easily controlled when they are identified early in the planning process), and (4) make risk decisions at the proper level in the organization.
   ☐ T ☐ F

3. The Operational Risk Management Risk Assessment Matrix provides a consistent framework for evaluating risk.
   ☐ T ☐ F

4. The Operational Risk Management loss probability is a degree of how likely an event is to occur. According to this chapter, Loss severity Category III describes an incident that:
   - ☐ (a) presents a minimal threat to personal safety or health, property, or efficient use of assets, affected populations, experiences, or previously established statistical information.
   - ☐ (b) may cause minor injury, illness, property damage, or degradation to efficient use of assets.
   - ☐ (c) may cause death, loss of a facility/asset, or result in grave damage.
   - ☐ (d) may cause severe injury, illness, property damage, or degradation to efficient use of assets.

5. Operational Risk Management, as developed, is a four-step decision-making process that is designed to enable individuals to identify hazards, assess risks, and implement controls to reduce risk associated with any action or operation.
   ☐ T ☐ F

6. In its most elemental form, an Operational Risk Management process will cause security personnel at all levels to answer _____ question(s) about any obvious or potential incident.
   - ☐ (a) one
   - ☐ (b) two
   - ☐ (c) three
   - ☐ (d) four

7. True security professionals, working in the best security program, can protect their customers against all losses.
   ☐ T ☐ F

8. The Operational Risk Management process exists on three levels. The level that describes the application of an "on the run" mental or oral review is the _____ level.
   - ☐ (a) in -depth
   - ☐ (b) time-critical
   - ☐ (c) non-time-critical
   - ☐ (d) deliberate

9. An organizational Operational Risk Management program is an essential part of the risk identification and mitigation process.
   ☐ T ☐ F

10. According to the chapter, an Operational Risk Management program is a _____ that security managers, as well as all others in the security department, can use to reduce losses and minimizing risk is to institute in the organization.

☐ (a) tool
☐ (b) program
☐ (c) strategy
☐ (d) approach

EMERGENCY PLANNING AND DISASTER CONTROL

By Michael Krikorian, CPP

INTRODUCTION

A basic necessity for every loss prevention program is the provision made for emergency and disaster planning. No plant or workplace should be without such a plan. There will be no time for plans or details when the emergency occurs.

The lessons taught by the adverse experiences over the years, and repeated much frequently as of late, emphasize the importance of a well-planned program that encompasses all of the aspects of an adequate emergency plan. Advance planning is the key.

"Emergency plan" means more than providing a first-aid kit, a fire extinguisher, a stretcher, an emergency shower and eye-wash fountain, and a fire blanket. Instead, there should be a written plan of action for every facility detailing (to the extent possible) those actions that will be taken when an emergency occurs, so that an effective response will be insured when it becomes necessary to face an extraordinary circumstance.

The effectiveness of any of these plans will usually be proportionate to the thoroughness and soundness of the planning effort. One of the management's major responsibilities today is to plan ahead of time for as many as possible of the actions to be taken for the different kinds of emergencies.

The time devoted by security professionals and others to the preparation of an adequate plan will enhance speedy decisions and actions at the time of an emergency and can result in lives saved and limits to the extent of damage. It will also provide the means for those responsible for the direction of these plans to concentrate on the solution of major problems and not be required to spend an undue amount of time attempting to bring some organization out of chaos.

Justification for emergency planning and disaster control becomes readily apparent with a study of the statistical evidence of fires, explosions, floods, and social disorders that produce riots, civil disturbances, and other hostile and destructive acts.

The dollar losses from these occurrences are counted in the billions of dollars, whereas in term of lives lost and individuals injured, the numbers are substantial.

The information here is an outline of those items considered important to the establishment of emergency plans. It will prove of value to anyone who is involved with emergency disaster conditions. The security practitioner should assume leadership and actively participate in the development of these programs.

GENERAL GUIDELINES

1. It is recommended that every facility have an emergency plan in writing.
   a) These plans should be developed locally.
   b) They should be comprehensive enough to cope with all eventualities, and
   c) It must be an effective plan.
2. The emergency plan must provide for the following:
   a) The protection and safeguarding of company employees on company properties
   b) The protection and safeguarding of company customers, members of the public, and others on company premises at the time of an emergency
   c) The protection and safeguarding of company property, while keeping damage and loss to absolute minimum
   d) Periodic review and updating as necessary
   e) Resumption of partial or complete business activity
   f) Rehearsal of plan as necessary
   g) A basis for orderly actions and decisions to control damage and loss

Keep in mind that management has the responsibility to take all possible and practical steps to protect the interests of employees, customers, members of the public, and the property under its control.

3. The emergency plan and disaster control program must be flexible enough to meet a variety of complex emergency situations, either those that are manmade or acts of God, such as the following:
   a) Fire
   b) Explosion
   c) Civil disturbance (riot or labor strife)
   d) Hazardous chemical and gas leaks or spills
   e) Earthquake
   f) Building collapse
   g) Hurricane
   h) Tornado
   i) Flood
   j) Nuclear holocaust, radiation accident, and so forth
   k) Terrorist act
   l) Bomb threats

Emergency action plans are generally basically similar for all exposures. Details depend not only on the anticipated disaster, but also to a certain extent, on the size of the facility, its geographic location, and the nature of its operation. An important consideration when developing an emergency action plan is that it has to work under disaster conditions. Many commonplace conveniences—such as water, telephones, light, power, or normal transportation methods—may be nonexistent.

OUTLINE OF ACTION

In approaching the problems of disaster control and plant security, the following outline of recommended action should be considered.

It is essential that security personnel have an integral role in the development and maintenance of the emergency and disaster plan. Security officers will be key players in any emergency situation; therefore, it is essential that each officer fully understand the overall emergency response process and their individual contributions to plan implementations.

Contacting the Authorities

Liaison should be established and maintained by security officers. Get in touch with the local law enforcement agency, fire department, Red Cross, and civil defense director.

1. Determine extent and direction of emergency planning.

2. Determine ability of those groups to cope with a serious disturbance and the degree of cooperation, and the extent of protection that can be expected.
3. Maintain liaison with these groups.
4. Utilize their intelligence for a better evaluation of potential problems and to ensure proper coordination.
5. Wherever possible, utilize these groups for advice and guidance on your individual emergency plan.
6. Routinely communicate essential plans to the employees.

Base your plan on as much self-help as possible, keeping in mind that government units may not be available during certain types of emergencies. Assign individuals to specific responsibilities. Select alternates for every position (see Figure 8-3).

Delegating Responsibilities

Establish responsibility and authority for implementing the plan so that action can be immediately taken by local management, as follows.

1. Prepare a policy statement assigning final authority for physical security of the location and for arranging appropriate delegations to insure that a single individual in authority will be available under any circumstance to place the plan in action. Select also a competent individual to serve as plan coordinator or director. Always provide alternates for backup to assure continuity of operations.

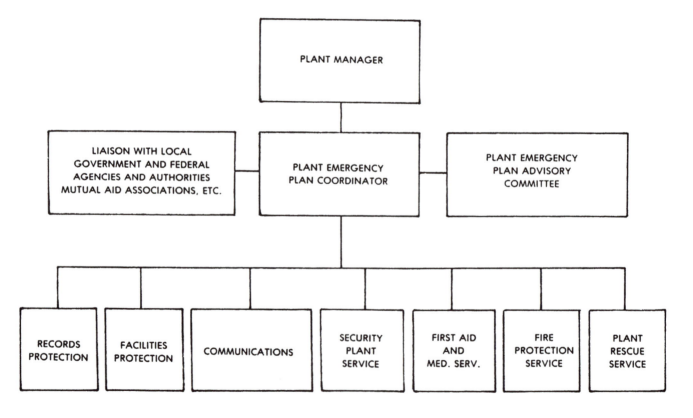

Figure 8-3 Organization Chart

2. Appoint disaster advisory committees representing various departments of the plant to assist the emergency plan coordinator in the development of the various phases of the program.

3. Wherever possible, utilize to the maximum present departments and key management employees—such as plant protection, fire and emergency brigades, maintenance, engineering, safety, medical, personnel, and so on as an organization framework.

4. Inventory skills of employees and of available emergency supplies.

5. Provide for a plan of action that designates what conditions the plan is to be put into effect. Furnish procedures for advising employees of the decision to activate the plan.

6. Provide for the orderly termination of the emergency measures after cessation of the disturbance or emergency.

Limiting Facility Operations

Provide specific criteria for determining at the time of the emergency whether the location will be (to be determined by type of emergency).

1. Operated on a normal basis (possible with some modification to guard and protect tours)

2. Operated on a limited basis (designate those functions that will operate)

3. Closed down and manned by supervisory and plant protection personnel

4. Closed down and unmanned for the duration of the emergency (with or without plant protection personnel) These are some of the factors to consider in making these determinations.
   a) Extent of damage to facility, utilities, declaration by government officials of state of emergency, and so on.
   b) Location's proximity to or distance from the center of a serious disturbance
   c) Anticipated emergency service demands on the location
   d) Availability of the workforce
   e) Extent of protection to be supplied by enforcement authorities
   f) Availability of security or plant protection personnel and type of guard protection
   g) Labor, political, and moral climate in the area
   h) Possible involvement of identified employees

Plant Warning and Communications System

1. Arrangements with suitable alternatives should be made to quickly communicate a warning or alarm to employees, police and fire department officials, and others as necessary.

2. Every facility should insure that the internal alarm or warning system is adequate to meet all needs. They should also be sure that they have a means to receive an alarm from outside the facility.

3. Communicate the warning plan in writing to all employees; be sure they understand it, what it means, and what action is to be taken if the warning signal is given. If an emergency occurs during, before, or after normal working hours, employees not assigned to emergency service should receive prior instruction on actions they are to take.

4. Maintain a roster with current telephone numbers of key company personnel, union officials, law enforcement, hospitals, civil defense, and fire department contacts to minimize any delay in making emergency contacts. Keep in mind that during emergencies, telephone switchboards are likely to be overloaded. Make plans for unlisted numbers and for alternate means of communications.

5. Here are some other points to consider.
   a) Use of plant public address system.
   b) Use of internal emergency telephone numbers and use of switchboard.
   c) Warnings to remote or field operations.
   d) Use of local radio or TV station (spot announcement at designated times).
   e) Telephone committees.
   f) Key employee list: maintenance, plant protection, engineering, services, and so forth

Establish Facility and Perimeter Security and Guard Force Preparation

1. Select and designate entrance and parking facilities to be used by personnel expected.

2. Arrange for police protection at designated entrances and/or roadways where possible. It may be desirable to solicit the advice of the police department before selection of an entrance is made.

3. Secure all entrances that will not be used; if property is fenced, each entrance that will not be used should be closed and securely locked, as should doors, windows, and other openings. Master key should be located centrally for emergency use by authorized personnel.

4. Determine the availability and the total number of security officers that may be needed. This could involve round-the-clock tours which may require the services of additional personnel.

5. All security officers should be thoroughly briefed regarding their emergency assignments, tours, behavior, and responsibilities. Discuss especially their scope of responsibility during riots or civil disturbances. If security officers normally carry firearms, the practice is to be continued; if on the other hand they do not, then we recommend that they do not be given firearms. Security officers must be instructed to stay on company property and not go onto public property.

6. Location of security officers should be considered for maximum enforcement; the presence of a guard at a strategic point may prevent trouble.

7. Where the location is not fenced, security officer's activities should be confined to the inside of the buildings.

8. Arrangements may have to be made for living-in by security officers and other personnel, should local conditions warrant.

Some other Points to Consider in Local Plans

1. Photographic equipment to compile photographic evidence of conditions during the emergency. Thorough documentation in both video and still photography is recommended. Since the appearance of a camera could incite additional trouble, it is recommended that, where possible, photographers operate from protected positions.
2. Provide for an alternate operating location away from the disturbance area—for use by key management personnel.
3. Transportation service: provide for the protection of incoming and outgoing truck and rail shipments. Provide for the diversion of incoming shipments to locations outside the disturbance area should this be warranted by local conditions.
4. Medical service: provide for in-plant emergency medical services or suitable alternates which would be capable of treating personnel casualties in the event of any emergency.
5. Employee training: provides for first-aid, medical self-help, firefighting, rescue, etc. of employees.
6. Review and update employee identification program as may be necessary.
7. As necessary, conduct disaster-control drills: practice evacuation of facility, extinguishing fires, emergency rescue techniques, and so on. Make necessary revisions in plans as indicated by tests and to meet changing local or national conditions.
8. Maintain a record of all conversation with government officials, requests for assistance and others, including a complete record of all emergency actions taken.

9. Provide for emergency lighting of aisles, exits, special processes, and so on., in the event of power loss or failure during regular working hours.
10. Investigate mutual-aid programs with other industries in your area.
11. Have available at the facility and in a remote location up-to-date maps, layouts, specifications, and similar essential data on utilities, hazardous processes, and underground installations.

Protecting Propriety and Classified Company and Government Documents

1. Establish a records-protection program; duplicate vital records and store in a remote location. Essential records such as account payable and receivables, process data, models, blueprints, payroll accounts, propriety data on machine designs, and processes should be microfilmed and placed in storage in a safe location. Secondary or off-site data storage is essential.
2. Plants with government contracts should follow the recommendations of the cognizant government contracting agency for necessary security procedures.

Legal Aspects and Requirements

1. It is primarily the responsibility and function of the local law-enforcement agency to maintain law and order, to protect life and property, and to protect civil rights in the public interest.
2. Local management should ascertain if local statutes have been passed concerning plant-protection requirements.
3. Conduct a review of property and liability insurance against potential loss of obligations resulting from riots and other acts of civil disobedience.

REFERENCES

1. National Association of Manufacturers; "A Checklist for Plant Security," Washington D.C. 1968.
2. Machinery and Allied Product Institute; "Company Planning with Respect to Riots or Other Civil Disorder," Washington D.C. 1968.
3. American Association of Industrial Management/NMTA; "How to Cope with a Crisis," Melrose Park, PA. 1968.
4. U.S. Departmental of Commerce in cooperation with the Department of Defense/Office of Civil Defense; "Preparedness in the Chemical and Allied Industries," Washington D.C. 1968.
5. Healy Richard J. *Emergency and Disaster Planning.* John Wiley and Sons, Inc., New York, NY 1968.

1. A basic necessity for everyday safety and accident prevention programs is the provision made for emergency and _____. (Fill in the blank.)

2. Lessons taught by adverse experiences over the years emphasize the importance of advanced _____ in the development of an emergency plan. (Fill in the blank.)

3. A management responsibility is to plan ahead of time for as many as possible of the actions to be taken for different kinds of _____. (Fill in the blank.)

4. The dollar loss from such disasters as fires, floods, explosion, riots, civil disturbances, and other hostile acts runs in:
    ☐ (a) thousands
    ☐ (b) millions
    ☐ (c) billions
    ☐ (d) trillions

5. It is recommended that every facility have an emergency plan in writing and: (Choose incorrect answer)
    ☐ (a) these plans should be developed locally
    ☐ (b) these plans must be confidential
    ☐ (c) these plans should be comprehensive enough to cope with all eventualities
    ☐ (d) these plans must be effective

6. The emergency plan must provide for: (Choose incorrect answer)
    ☐ (a) continual corporate executive rehearsal
    ☐ (b) the protection of company employees and property
    ☐ (c) periodical updating and review
    ☐ (d) resumption of partial or complete business activity

7. Management has a responsibility to include the protection of certain groups and individuals when developing the plan. (List priority group)
    ☐ (a) Executive families
    ☐ (b) Nonaffected individuals
    ☐ (c) Employees
    ☐ (d) Visitors to facility

8. Emergencies can be man-created or be acts of God.
    ☐ T ☐ F

9. Explosions are invariably described as "acts of God" types of emergency situations.
    ☐ T ☐ F

10. If disaster strikes a facility, it may not be uncommon to expect to be required to function without water, telephones, power, and transportation.
    ☐ T ☐ F

TERRORISM

By Tom M. Conley, MA, CPP, CFE, CPO

The seventh edition printing of this manual is the first version to contain a chapter on the topic of terrorism. Why? The answer is the ever-increasing frequency and severity of terrorist acts in the past few years, culminating in the horrific events that occurred on September 11, 2001. The cowardly terrorist attacks that occurred on September 11, 2001 were not only attacks against the United States of America but were an attack on the world. On October 11, 2001, President George Bush said, "The attack(s) [on September 11, 2001] took place on American soil, but it was an attack on the heart and soul of the civilized world. And the world has come together to fight a new and different war, the first, and we hope the only one, of the 21st century. A war against all those who seek to export terror and a war against those governments that support or shelter them" (Congressional Report, 2001). Moreover, the attacks were an attack on the very ideals that those in the military services, public service, and private security profession are charged with upholding. Therefore, as private security professionals, we have a role to play in the fight against terrorism. In fact, there is little question that terrorism has fundamentally changed the way organizations view security, safety, and risk management. The role of the protection officer has also changed since September 11, 2001. However, before protection officers can be truly effective in the war on terrorism, they must gain a firm understanding of what terrorism is, why it exists, and what we as a collective society and security professionals can expect of terrorists in the future.

WHAT IS TERRORISM?

The United States Federal Bureau of Investigation has defined terrorism as "the unlawful use of force or violence against persons or property to intimidate or coerce a government, the civilian population, or any segment thereof, in furtherance of political or social objectives" (FBI, 1999). And, there are many more definitions that exist. Within the general definition of terrorism, there are two types of terrorist groups; left-wing terrorist groups and right-wing terrorist groups. Although the end-result of both groups' activities frequently end in criminal activity, these two types of groups have different reasons for existing as groups and for committing the types of terrorist acts they commit.

Left-wing terrorist groups, also known as *international* terrorist groups, include, but certainly are not limited to, the Abu Nidal Organization, Al-Qaeda, Hamas, Hizballah, Kahane Chai, Mujahedine-E-Khalq, National Liberation Army, Palestine Islamic Jihad, Red Army, and the Shining Path. Right-wing terrorist groups, also known as *domestic* terrorist groups, tend to be either single-issue groups or hate groups. Single-issue terrorist groups in the United States are frequently eco-terrorists or extremist animal rights groups. These groups include the Animal Liberation Front (ALF), Greenpeace, Stop Huntingdon Animal Cruelty (SHAC), and members of the People for the Ethical Treatment of Animals (PETA) group. On a Web site devoted to providing information to extremist animal rights groups in case they are taken into custody by the police, it states, "Our aim is to show that ploys used by the police are predetermined and well practiced; that you are not the exception to the rule; but most of all with knowledge of the interrogator's games comes a massive psychological advantage to help you through your time in police custody" (Geocities, 2002). Hate groups, also known as militia groups, have been operating in the United States, some for many decades. They include, but are not limited to, the Klu Klux Klan (KKK), Arian Nations, Neo Nazis, Christian Patriots Defense League, Posse' Comitatus, and The Order. In the United Kingdom, the Irish Republican Army (IRA) is an example of a domestic terrorist organization.

State sponsorship (supported by a government) of terrorist organizations is important to note. In fact, one of the major differences in these two types of terrorist groups is that left-wing terrorist organizations (International Terrorists) tend to be state sponsored, whereas right-wing terrorist organizations (Domestic Terrorists) tend not to be state sponsored.

The United States first encountered the first incident of modern-day left-wing terrorism on May 1, 1961. On that date, Puerto Rican-born Antuilo Ramierez Ortiz forced at gunpoint a National Airlines plane to fly to Havana, Cuba, where he was given asylum. Since that date, there have been more than 150 major terrorism events that have occurred around the world (Bureau of Public Affairs, 2001).

Domestic terrorist groups, in their many forms, have been in the United States and other countries for many years. Most right-wing domestic terrorist groups do not pose the same threat level as do international terrorists. However, that does not mean that they should not be taken seriously. They absolutely should be taken seriously. The most horrific example of domestic terrorism occurred in Oklahoma City, Oklahoma. On April 19, 1995, at 9:03 A.M., a truck bomb shattered the Alfred P Murrah Federal Building in downtown Oklahoma City, killing 168 people —including children playing in the building's day care center. The worst terrorist bombing in U.S. history reminded us that America is no longer a sanctuary from her enemies. The bombing also reminded us that some of those enemies might be from within our borders (Terrorism Research

	Left-wing groups	Right-wing groups
Ideology	Communist/socialist orientation. Seek to overthrow governments.	Nazi/fascist. May seek isolation from government rather than overthrow.
Gender	Male or female members.	Predominantly male.
Age	Young, generally under 45. Leaders may be older.	Older, including retirees, although may be involved in youth hate groups.
Education	Usually college educated to some degree. Literate.	High school education or less. May have technical or computer skills. Some are former military.
Religion	Religion often not a large factor. Agnostic or atheist belief systems are common in North America.	Christian fundamentalist. Protestant. Often anti-Semitic.
Social and Economic Class	Upper class or upper middle class.	Working class, blue collar. Often economically disenfranchised.

Figure 8-4   Extremist Groups

Center, 1996–2000). Timothy McVeigh, the individual convicted of activating the bomb, was put to death for his crime on June 11, 2001.

What the protection officer really needs to know is, one, regardless of the act, both international and domestic terrorism are crimes and, two, there is a very real possibility that protection officers will have to deal with either or both in his or her career.

WHY DOES TERRORISM EXIST?

Put simply, terrorism is an ***illegal*** method that both individuals and groups use to change the way something is to the way they would like it to be. The Terrorism Research Center lists the main cause for terrorism as "dissatisfaction with a political or social system or policy, and an inability to change it through 'mainstream' or nonviolent means" (Terrorism Research Center, 1996–2000). This definition is appropriate for both domestic and international terrorists and terrorism groups. For law-biding people, the philosophy of committing criminal acts to bring about political changes is simply illogical. We accept and abide by the law as it is written. While some may not like certain existing laws, or think laws should be different, law-abiding people

certainly do not use crime in an attempt to make changes. This philosophy is the primary difference in how terrorists think and what they believe, versus what we think and believe. These differences in our thoughts and beliefs are what separate us from the bad guys. It is particularly important to note that many Islamic fundamentalist groups use "religion" as a cover to perpetuate terrorist activities. And, they are not the only groups who use religion as the primary justification for perpetrating terrorist acts. Many domestic groups use religion as a hook to ensure followers' compliance. The Branch Davidian cult is an example of this type of dogmatic deception. By understanding why terrorism exists, we can be better prepared to recognize terrorist activity and be able to take appropriate action that may help stop a terrorist event from occurring.

THE PROTECTION OFFICER'S ROLE

Terrorism can seem like a "big picture" problem only. That is, it can seem like only military forces, and to a lesser degree, civilian public safety agencies are the only ones who deal with terrorism. While these are vital forces in the war on terrorism, the notion that terrorism is only fought by military and public safety personnel is off-base and could not be more incorrect. The fact is that protection officers have as much or more of an impact on terrorism than many public safety officials. The primary reason for this is that terrorists, especially international terrorist groups, operate in a "cell" configuration. The cell configuration, often referred to as sleeper cells, is a term used to define what occurs when there are small clusters of terrorists placed throughout the United States and other countries. Members of these terrorist sleeper cells, which are estimated to number in the hundreds, work and live among us. They work where we work, shop where we shop, and live where we live. The terrorists have spent many years literally blending into our society. They are masquerading as normal people and are simply waiting for orders to commit a terrorist incident. This is what makes detecting terrorists so difficult for public safety and military personnel. The United States Government, as well as other governments, knows that sleeper cells exist and are concerned about what future acts of terror they may propagate. When discussing the possibility of future attacks, Vice President Dick Cheney said, "There's no reason for us to operate on the assumption that it was a one-off event that's never going to happen again... we have to assume it will happen again, and that's the only safe way for us to proceed" (Cheney, 2001).

The fact that terrorists work and live among us is the precise advantage that the protection officer has, and will be a key asset in fighting terrorism. Law enforcement officials seldom, if ever, come into a private organization's workplace. When they do come, they are often called there and are responding to a call for service. Perhaps an employee's car was broken into or there might be company property that is suspected stolen. Therefore, security officers work full time in environments that law enforcement personnel rarely go. Terrorists who live among us know this. Therefore, they will often feel safe from the law when on the job. This is where the security officer has a unique opportunity. Because they work where others live and work, they have an excellent opportunity to observe conditions that could lead to illegal activity. If terrorists use their place of work for planning or otherwise discussing terrorism or terrorist activity, it is the security officer who is on the front line. If the security officer fails to observe and report suspicious behavior, it will probably go unchecked and unreported. The key is for protection officers to know their area of responsibility, be able to distinguish what is "normal" for the area, and understand the warning signs of activity that could be deemed suspicious.

In the final analysis, the best way for protection officers to prepare for a terrorist attack is to have a systemwide emphasis on emergency planning and incident response. In many ways, preparing for a terrorist attack is no different from planning for other disasters. As with any security plan, it is critical to conduct ongoing training and conduct drills to test the security plans. Protection officers should always remember that the probability of a protection officer being involved in a terrorist incident is low. However, if a terrorist incident does occur, it's probably going to be really bad.

A couple of words of caution apply when discussing the topic of terrorism and the protection officer. First, protection officers should not become so preoccupied and focused on a possible terrorist event occurring that they lose sight of their fundamental security and risk management duties. Ignoring other threats that have a much higher probability of occurring, such as natural disasters, crimes, theft, and so on will negatively impact the effectiveness of the overall security program. Second, there is a danger for protection officers to engage in racial profiling. While we are naturally more suspicious of individuals who look like what we believe to be terrorists, the reality is that we cannot determine if a person is or is not a terrorist by their ethnicity, religion, or manner of dress. Rather than focus on profiling, the protection officer must be observant for suspicious or out of the ordinary behavior.

It is imperative that protection officers operate in cooperation with law enforcement, fire and EMS personnel, HAZMAT personnel, emergency and disaster personnel, and homeland security personnel. It is prudent to develop strong relationships with public safety officials before their help is needed. Protection officers should, to the extent possible, participate in professional meetings and conferences. Protection officers should always be professional when dealing with public safety officials. Those protection officers who are deemed as "unprofessional" by public safety officials have no credibility, and thus, will be ineffective and may even hurt the organization that they represent. Cooperation and collaboration between public and private protective organizations are a must. Protection officers can and should share resources and information without divulging confidential or propriety information about their company. Likewise, while law enforcement officials cannot provide protection officers with much information at times, it is critical for the protection officer to establish a relationship that enables law enforcement officials to share intelligence information with security personnel. This cooperation can and is being accomplished today between the public and private sectors. The key is collaborating while knowing, respecting, and not crossing the boundaries.

CONCLUSION

Protection officers, now more than at any time in our history, must be professionally competent. This means officers must be able to not only detect abnormal or suspicious behavior, but they need to be able to properly articulate that abnormal or suspicious behavior to their supervisors and the law enforcement. Protection officers must understand that terrorism can happen where they work. They must consider and plan for a terrorist attack the same as they would address any other disaster or threat. The best advice I can give protection officers is to not obsess about a terrorist event occurring where they work or live. However, as we learned from the 15 security officers and managers who died in the World Trade Centers on September 11, 2001, one must be ready in case it does occur.

REFERENCES

Bush, G.W. (2001, October 11). "The War on Terrorism—The First 100 Days" report to Congress. Washington, D.C.: The White House.

Cheney, D. (2001, October 15). View from the VP's Office. Newshour Extra [Online]. Available: http://www.pbs.org/ newshour/extra/features/july-dec01/terrorism10-15.html.

Federal Bureau of Investigation. (1999). *Terrorism in the United States 1999* Washington, D.C.: United States Department of Justice.

Office of the Historian, Bureau of Public Affairs. (2001, October 31). *Significant Terrorist Incidents, 1961–-2001.* Washington, D.C.: United States Department of State.

Police Interrogation. A Guide for Extremist Animal Rights Groups [Online]. Available: http://www.geocities.com/CapitolHill/ Lobby/6423/interog.html (2002).

Terrorism Research Center. Next Generation Terrorism Analysis [Online]. Available: http://www.terrorism.com/terrorism/ okc.shtml (1996-2000).

Terrorism Research Center. FAQ [Online]. Available: http://www.terrorism.com/FAQ.shtml (1996-2000).

SECURITY QUIZ
Terrorism

1. The United States Federal Bureau of Investigation has defined terrorism as:
   - ☐ (a) the unlawful use of violence against persons or property to intimidate or coerce a government, the civilian population, or any segment thereof, in furtherance of political or social objectives.
   - ☐ (b) the unlawful use of force or violence against persons or property to intimidate or coerce a government, the civilian population, or any segment thereof, in furtherance of political or social objectives.
   - ☐ (c) the unlawful use of force or violence against any person or persons to intimidate or coerce a government, the civilian population, or any segment thereof, in furtherance of political or social objectives.
   - ☐ (d) the unlawful use of force or violence against persons or property to intimidate or coerce a civilian population, or any segment thereof, in furtherance of political or social objectives.

2. Protection officers can and should share resources and information with law enforcement sources without divulging confidential or propriety information about their company.
   ☐ T ☐ F

3. "State-sponsored" terrorists organizations refer to terrorist organizations that are:
   - ☐ (a) supported by a state within the United States
   - ☐ (b) prosecuted by members of national governments
   - ☐ (c) supported by the citizens within a state in the United States
   - ☐ (d) supported by a national government

4. There are two types of terrorist groups, left-wing terrorist groups and right-wing terrorist groups, who have the same reasons for existing as groups and for committing the types of terrorist acts they commit.
   ☐ T ☐ F

5. Many Islamic fundamentalist groups use religion to perpetuate terrorist activities. Because of this, security officers need to pay particular attention to anyone who they suspect is a member of the Muslim religion because they might be a terrorist.
   ☐ T ☐ F

6. Protection officers should always remember that the probability of a protection officer being involved in a terrorist incident is high. And, if a terrorist incident does occur, it's probably going to be really bad.
   ☐ T ☐ F

7. An example of a "single-issue" terrorist group is:
   - ☐ (a) eco-terrorists or extremist
   - ☐ (b) animal rights groups
   - ☐ (c) hate groups
   - ☐ (d) All of the above

8. In many ways, preparing for a terrorist attack _____ different from planning for other disasters.
    ☐ (a) is
    ☐ (b) is not

9. The Ku Klux Klan (KKK), Arian Nations, Neo Nazis, and the Christian Patriots Defense League are examples of what type of domestic terrorist organization?
    ☐ (a) Extremist
    ☐ (b) Animal rights groups and extremist
    ☐ (c) Hate groups and Militia groups
    ☐ (d) Eco-terrorists and hate groups

10. While protection officers may know that terrorists work and live among them, fighting terrorism is strictly the job of law enforcement officials and the military.
    ☐ T ☐ F

COUNTERTERRORISM AND VIP PROTECTION

By Christopher A. Hertig, CPP, CPOI

Concerns with terrorism and workplace violence have been growing over the past several decades. We have seen spectacular terrorist acts such as the airline attack on the World Trade Center. We have also seen disgruntled current or former employees opening fire in their workplaces. We have seen assaults on staff at abortion centers and we have seen acts of violence perpetrated in our courthouses.

Protection officers play an important role here as they are often the ones controlling access to facilities, guard payrolls and armored trucks, drive executives to the airport, escort VIPs through crowds at public affairs, and maintain the physical security at airports, courthouses, power plants, corporate headquarters, and military bases. In order to play this role safely and professionally, they must have a basic understanding of the threat(s) confronting their work environments. They also need to be competent in crucial job tasks such as operating detection equipment, searching personnel and vehicles, driving vehicles, and so on.

TERRORIST ACTIONS AND ACTIVITIES

Terrorist activities are contingent upon the capabilities of the terrorist organization, the philosophy of that organization, and the area in which the action takes place. Whereas Middle-Eastern terrorists drive car bombs into target areas, European groups may attack police stations, airports, and so on, and North American terrorists may plant bombs, murder members of certain ethnic or professional groups (police, doctors at abortion clinics), and rob banks or armored cars.

One cannot assume what terrorists will or will not do, but counterterrorist security personnel should be familiar with the groups in their particular area. This will provide them with sufficient indication from which a more accurate assessment of their activities can be made.

Task b, Element D in "Nuclear Security Personnel for Power Plants: Content and Review Procedures for a Security Training and Qualification Program" (NUREG 0219) lists the following characteristics involved in the planning and execution phases of a terrorist attack.

1. Terrorists will learn as much as possible beforehand about the engineering details of a facility.
2. They will assess power plant security ahead of time by observing the plant, talking to plant personnel, talking to an insider, and intercepting radio transmissions.
3. They will attempt to recruit an accomplice on the security force.
4. Terrorists will also try to recruit nonsecurity employees as accomplices.
5. They will consider kidnapping an employee or an employee's family member prior to an attack.
6. They may take hostages during the attack to force cooperation.
7. Terrorists will isolate the target site by cutting off communications and power supplies.
8. The group will assemble the necessary weapons and equipment to use in the attack (this can include firearms, military issue shoulder weapons, SMGs, antitank rockets, high explosives, radio jamming or monitoring devices, power tools, construction equipment, and incapacitating agents).
9. The terrorists may use diversionary tactics such as sniping or detonating explosives.
10. They will try to intercept, delay, or destroy responding police forces so that security personnel should not rely on local law enforcement assistance.
11. They may use unknowing personnel as part of an attack plan such as duping truck drivers into carrying explosives.
12. Terrorists will take advantage of periods when security performance is lowered such as adverse weather (rain, snow, fog) or when there are workers onsite.
13. The terrorists will plan and rehearse the attack.
14. The attack will be planned to take the fire objective in less than three minutes.
15. Terrorists will not attack unless they are 100 percent confident that they will be successful.

While the foregoing was written with nuclear power plants in mind, the concepts are applicable to virtually any fixed site facility such as a bank, airport, or residence. Attacks against vehicles for the purpose of securing hostages also utilize the elements of surprise, speed, diversions, and, ultimately, violence. What can be gleaned from this is as follows.

1. **Communications and computer security is paramount.** Communications security protects against the compromise of information to terrorist/adversary groups. It also plays a key role in maintaining an effective physical security posture. Disgruntled employees/customers/terrorists will undoubtedly target computer systems more in the coming decade than they have previously.

2. **Confidentiality of information is essential!** The less a terrorist or other adversary can learn about an organization and its defenses, the less likely that an attack will be planned. An organization's information protection

program can be a cornerstone of a terrorism defense strategy.

3. **Personnel security**—the protection of the workforce from infiltration by terrorists, foreign agents, criminals, and competitors who wish to steal proprietary business information is important. Much of the workplace violence issue revolves around the screening and management of employees.

4. **Access control**—over both personnel and vehicles—must be designed into the physical security system and maintained through the efforts of protection officers. Terrorists can be deterred from selecting a facility as a potential target if they perceive that target as being too well protected.

Personnel security, physical security, and information security all work cohesively to protect against terrorist threats.

Personnel Security
Physical Security
Information Security +
TERRORISM PROTECTION

COUNTERTERRORIST STRATEGY

In essence, defending against terrorism is no different from defense against other types of threats. Even though terrorism is complex insofar as assessing the threat is concerned, the physical security planning process is the same as would be used with any other threat or situation. Physical security must always be planned in several stages.

1. **Assets are identified.** What has value to the organization? What has value, either *strategic, monetary,* or *symbolic* to threat groups/individuals?

2. **Loss events are exposed.** These include bombing/arson as these are easily employed tactics that can be performed by a single individual and which have a substantial impact on the organization. Assassination, kidnapping for "fund-raising" or publicity, sabotage of machinery, implantation of computer viruses, or product tampering.

3. **Occurrence probability factors are assigned,** such as *certain, highly probable,* *moderately probable,* and *improbable.*

4. **Impact of occurrence is assessed.** Direct (replacement), indirect (loss of business), and extra expense (added advertising fees, room rentals) costs are identified.

5. **Countermeasures are selected.** This can include the following Risk Management approaches:

   Risk avoidance, such as not operating in a hostile country or having a business operation that is prone to attack.

   Risk reduction includes target hardening by patrols, locks, lights, barriers, and so on. *It is usually the most expensive means of risk management. It is also inconvenient to employees, customers, and so forth. As such it should not be employed without first considering alternative approaches to addressing the risk!*

   Risk spreading would be having several facilities in different areas so that if one facility—or key executive—is destroyed, the entire organization is not crippled.

   Risk transfer means transferring the financial risk of the loss event to another entity. Generally, this is via insurance coverage. Kidnap insurance policies have been used for the past two decades by major corporations. All organizations must assess the potential costs of extended business interruption, civil litigation in the event of a death and negative publicity. Once this is done, various modifications to existing insurance coverage can be made.

TERRORISM DEFENSIVE STRATEGIES

National	Corporate/Organizational
Diplomacy/projecting a positive image to the world community	Public and media relations/projecting a positive image in the operating environment
Intelligence efforts	Intelligence efforts
Investigation of suspected activities	Investigation of suspect activities
Target hardening/physical security	Target hardening/physical security
Tactical /emergency planning	Emergency planning

Obviously *liaison* with various organizations is important to strategies designed for defense against terrorism. This is important for both nations and corporations. Liaison is important when planning for public events (Olympics, concerts, speeches, etc.), responding to incidents (fires, floods, bombings, power outages, etc.), and planning for terrorist attacks. There are some specific things that can be done by both public and private entities regarding counterterrorism:

Government Agencies	Private Organizations
Provide and share intelligence on the macro environment; the city, state, or nation	Provide and share intelligence on the micro environment; the facility, other branches
Offer extra seats in training classes to security personnel	Offer public employees extra seats in corporate training programs
Provide consultation on terrorism, threat response, HAZMAT, etc.	Provide facilities for conducting training such as drills in buildings that are closed
Provide instruction on terrorism, hostage negotiation, WMD response	Provide facilities for incident command when a crisis arises
Share equipment obtained through government grant monies or military giveaways	Provide funds for equipment purchase such as robots, bomb suits, dogs, vehicles, etc.

COUNTERTERRORIST TECHNIQUES BY ORGANIZATIONS/FACILITIES

Using the physical security concepts of deter, delay, deny, and detect in regard to terrorist attack includes:

1. Techniques used to **deter** terrorist activity include hardening the target so that the terrorists do not have a 100 percent chance of success. Checking IDs, packages, and vehicles before they enter a secured area; making patrols or routes of travel unpredictable; and maintaining confidentiality are all target-hardening approaches.

2. Terrorists can be **delayed** by the use of barriers, locks, and response forces. Vehicular access to potential targets should also be controlled as much as is practical under the circumstances. This can be via barriers as well as access/parking arrangements that don't allow quick and easy access to the target.

3. **Denial** of terrorist objectives can be accomplished through the use of contingency plans for dealing with the media and negotiating for hostages. These deny the terrorists the use of widespread panic and media leverage which they attempt to exploit.

4. **Detection** of terrorist activity can be accomplished through the analysis of threat intelligence. It can also occur by conducting entry searches, using detection equipment (x-ray, metal, explosive), CCTV, alarm systems, lights, patrols, and access control systems. Detection equipment deserves special consideration. The use of this equipment was limited to metal detectors in nuclear power plants, airports, and prisons a decade or so ago. There were also the Electronic Article Surveillance Systems (EAS) in use in retail establishments. Today this has expanded to include metal detectors in night clubs and schools. EAS systems are used in long term care facilities, pediatric units of hospitals, libraries, and for the protection of high value merchandise and discs. September 11 has ushered in a wave of new technologies for explosive detection and the detection of WMDs manufactured with biological, chemical, and radioactive agents. The use of dogs has also expanded in regards to explosive detection. Obviously there will be additional uses of detection equipment in the future.

These are a few key points to consider when purchasing and using the equipment.

- Initial cost
- Volume of traffic to be screened
- Single or progressively higher levels of screening, such as with layered access control
- The time needed to scan—delays, man-hours of searches and operators
- Aesthetic interface with the environment
- Response to alarm/detection—there should be a systematic process in place for investigation, isolation of the person/area being screened who emits an alarm, communication with the cover officer/access controller/floor detectives, etc., and control over the person who is causing the detector to respond.
- Ease of use—"idiot proof" and amount of training required (note that hand searches are usually necessary with metal detectors and x-rays).
- Cultural fit with the environment—it must be accepted by management and users such as employees, students, visitors, and so on.
- Durability—how long the equipment will last is key.
- Reliability/pick rate/false alarm rate—consideration should be given to independent testing or endorsement by a regulatory agency (TSA, NRC).
- Routine maintenance needed—cleaning, start of shift tests, and so on.
- Service contracts to maintain the equipment, possibly conduct in-depth performance tests, and repaid the equipment.
- Education of searchees so that they cooperate with the search effort.
- Training of users such as preemployment training, in-service instruction, and audits/inspections or drills/scenarios to insure competency on the job.

SPECIFIC TECHNIQUES FOR COUNTERTERRORIST SECURITY

Some specific techniques that counterterrorist security personnel (personal protection specialists, airport, power plant, military security officers) may utilize include the following:

1. **Become thoroughly familiar with any and all security equipment.** While this sounds overly simple, routine audits at airports and nuclear facilities commonly reveal that equipment is not being properly used for any one of a number of reasons.

2. **Check and test equipment frequently.** Develop overlapping auditing systems for the equipment, such as having technicians, officers, and supervisors all performing their own tests. Protection officers must be familiar with equipment manuals for equipment and perform tests of the equipment at the start of their shift. Operational tests using standard test items must also be conducted at prescribed intervals.

3. **Rotate personnel assignments** as often as practical, take notes and perform communication checks to maintain and insure personnel alertness.

4. **Check all areas** that the person or materials being protected are about to enter before they enter.

5. **Maintain weapons and other emergency equipment in position** so that they can be employed instantaneously. If it can't be, something is seriously deficient.

6. **Ascertain the legal implications of carrying or using weapons before they are carried.** Never assume something is legal; check it out first.

7. **Be familiar with what belongs in an area and what doesn't**, so that explosives, weapons, and surveillance devices can be detected.

8. **Use cover and concealment to their utmost.** Stand behind objects which can shield you from bullets (cover) and have the protectee do the same whenever possible. Hide movements via darkness, tinted glass, or drawn blinds (concealment). Maintain light and noise discipline at appropriate times such as on patrol. *"See others before they see you; hear others before they hear you."*

9. **Select positions that provide the greatest visual vantage point.** This may be a corner of a room or an elevated position.

10. **Stay close enough to persons who are being protected so that effective defensive actions can always be taken, yet not so close as to intrude on the principal's personal space.**

11. **Plan for communications failures** and develop alternate means of communications. There should always be at least two means of communication available to the PPS.

12. **Practice duress codes** (verbal and nonverbal) so that secret, emergency messages can be transmitted at all times.

13. **Take appropriate action in a tactful manner to ensure that counterterrorist security personnel (airport or nuclear plant protection officers; personal protection specialists) do not become occupied and burdened with nonsecurity duties.** Auxiliary duties are important; *they are nice to do*. Security duties are the most important; *they must be done*.

14. **Vehicles should be driven so that there is always room to maneuver** in case escape is necessary. Drive on the left side of the road to prevent the vehicle from being forced off the shoulder. Protective services personnel who drive should have specialized training!

15. **Always keep parked vehicles locked and secured** as much as possible with alarms, guards, or other techniques.

16. **Check out the vehicle prior to departure** for basic mechanical soundness (gas in the tank, fan belts, and tires in good condition). Have a detailed check done regularly by a mechanic.

17. **Check vehicles for the presence of unauthorized personnel in or around them, attempts at tampering with the engine, gas tank, doors, tires, or undercarriage before departure.**

18. **Assess the security of the route and location being traveled to prior to departure.**

19. **Establish and maintain positive working relationships with agencies or departments that can provide support services.** Be friendly, polite, and tactfully inquisitive enough to find out how much and what type of assistance they can and will provide.

20. **As searching is almost always part of the security function, keep in mind and practice the *principles* of searching which can be applied to any type of search.**

    a) **Identify the search object; know what is being looked for.** The more known, the better! Protection officers must know what weapons or explosives look like! Continuous professional education is key here.

    b) **Establish parameters for the search; know boundaries for the search.** Determine how *thorough* and *intrusive* the search effort must be.

    c) **Assess the environment to be searched for obvious items, as well as the development of a search system.** A general scan of the area (visual, audio, olfactory) should always be used.

    d) **Devise a systematic method for conducting the search such as top to bottom, front to rear, (with bomb searches, go bottom to top) after analyzing the search environment.** Each pattern or system must be based upon the complexity and time necessary to conduct the search. How large an area/person; how complex—how much stuff to search—and how much time is available will determine the type of pattern used. In many cases, a priority search is used. This means that the most obvious or accessible areas are searched first. Lobbies and rest rooms of buildings for explosives would be an example. Another would be searching the hand area, ankle area, and waist area of a person for weapons—the weapons are most likely to be hidden there and are most accessible to the person carrying them. Alternatively, priority searches can be of areas that are most vulnerable such as the computer center or power or heat center of a building. An explosive placed there would do the most damage. Nuclear, biological, or chemical WMDs would be most damaging near air intake systems. In the event of a threat, these areas might be searched first. Other than priority searches, search patterns uses should incorporate *overlap*. There is a slight degree of *overlap* so that no area is missed during the search.

e) **Search thoroughly using *visual assessment*, touch, hearing, and aids such as detection equipment, dogs, flashlights, and mirrors.** "Look before touching" is always good advice! One technique is to use visual angles. Walk around the object, vehicle, or person to be searched. Look at them from various angles to see if there is anything hidden. Do this before actually moving in to conduct a search.

f) **Spread out or open up the person, package, or vehicle to be searched.** If a vehicle is searched with all the doors, etc., open it is easier to see items that don't belong. The same is true with baggage or persons. Have the baggage opened up with the contents carefully removed and stacked. Have the person assume a posture with his/her arms outstretched.

g) **Continue searching until the entire area has been searched—don't stop after finding one item (or person if it is a building search).** Terrorists have planted secondary explosives. Don't become a secondary victim! And don't call in a bomb squad until the entire area has been searched and the technicians know precisely what the problem is. They do not like surprises!

h) **Disturb the environment as little as possible during the search, try to observe before you touch something.** *"Look before touching."* This is important for safety as well as human relations concerns—nobody wants their persons, personal effects, vehicles, or offices to be rummaged through.

i) **Be as polite, considerate, and courteous as possible.** Professional conversations with searchees make the search more efficient. ***Interview the searchee*** to learn more about what is being looked for. This is part of the assessment of the search environment.

j) **Search with appropriate personnel such as a searcher and a cover officer/access controller.** The searcher conducts the search while the cover officer or access controller oversees it so that it is done properly. The cover officer also acts to insure that everything is done safely. He/she intervenes appropriately if there is an imminent threat against the search officer.

k) **Evaluate the search effort.** This is done with an observer such as a cover officer/access controller. The search must be done properly and completely. The final part of evaluation is to determine when the search is finished.

PROFESSIONAL DEVELOPMENT FOR PERSONAL PROTECTION SPECIALISTS

Counterterrorist security personnel must have highly developed professional knowledge and skills in order to be effective. They must think in terms of the various areas of **competency** required. By focusing on these competencies, the protection officer can better chart a course for continuous professional development. In general, the following areas of proficiency must be present in counterterrorist security personnel operating in any environment (i.e., personal protection specialists, nuclear security officers, airport security officers, etc.).

1. **Knowledge of physical security concepts and techniques.** A personal protection specialist or other counterterrorist security person should be a physical security specialist first and foremost. An understanding of the theory of physical security and risk management including various responses to risk and the physical security planning process are crucial to the success of his/her mission.

2. **Knowledge of terrorism, especially of terrorists operating in the immediate work area.** Reading various newspapers is essential! So, too, is keeping in contact with professional groups such as local chapter of the American Society for Industrial Security or state crime prevention officers associations.

3. **Public relations skills so that security can be maintained unobtrusively.** Manners, etiquette, and public speaking are all essential.

4. **Sufficient (college) education to communicate, understand, and record information that is learned during training or encountered on the job.**

5. **Physically fit so as to be able to perform strenuous tasks during emergencies and so that martial skills can be learned (one must be fit to fight).**

6. **Martial skills such as the *practical* use of weapons and defensive tactics.** Training for the "5-second fight," where the adversary is neutralized as quickly as possible, or as a means of low-key, almost invisible control over a disruptive person who is approaching a principal are important.

7. **Familiarity with explosives and the weapons of terrorists so as to be able to identify dangerous items.** This means knowing standard military and commercial explosives as a start. It also means being able to recognize improvised explosives and keeping abreast of the latest means of employing them.

8. **Knowledge of security equipment**. The application of technology can be a great asset, but only when done correctly. Attending professional meetings and trade shows can help a great deal. This is a key area of competency in counterterrorist security. Unfortunately, it is often ignored. Counterterrorist security personnel should read a lot of equipment manuals!

9. **Searching skills used for bomb, personnel, building, package, and vehicle searches.** This is usually a sorely neglected area; often times officers conduct searches to conduct searches. They do them simply to follow procedures. *Searches are to find things.*

10. **Professional dedication to enable one to put up with boredom, long hours, and uncooperative persons.**

PERSONAL PROTECTION SPECIALISTS (PPS)

Many people still conceptualize of the "bodyguard" as being a physically tough individual who has an imposing appearance and/or highly developed martial skills (martial arts, firearms, other weapons). While there may be a need for such an individual, and martial skills have practical application, there is a whole lot more to the makeup of a Personal Protection Specialist. Like other counterterrorist security personnel, the Personal Protection Specialist must be a security practitioner first and a "trained killer" second. Of even greater importance to the PPS is to have highly developed communications and human relations abilities. He or she must be highly polished. Etiquette and the ability to blend in with the protectee is more important than being able to destroy all opposition.

Few people perform PPS duties on a regular full-time basis. Those who do have generally proven themselves through a series of assignments. They usually obtain their positions through networking. Organizations such as Nine Lives Associates are invaluable in this regard.

What generally happens is that a protection professional is called upon to protect a principal for a short period of time. It may be during a speech, a concert, a meeting, and so on. A typical example would be a police department that deploys a few officers to VIP duty while a celebrity is in the city. For this reason, PPS functions are probably important in the repertoire of professional competency for virtually all protection officers.

Knowledge of the protectee's business and personal habits is very important. Personal Protection Specialists must be able to plan out security measures in accordance with the principal's business and personal lifestyle. He or she must be able to devise protective strategies that are reasonable and unobtrusive. Embarrassment of the principle is a major threat; the PPS should not do anything to cause this!

Driving skills and knowledge of vehicles are especially important to the Personal Protection Specialist. Much of the time spent guarding executives and other VIPs is while those persons are traveling. Specialized driving classes should be attended. Knowledge of airline customs and regu-lations should be acquired and kept up to date. In effect, Personal Protection Specialists should be "**travel consultants**"!

Personal security from crime must be studied and mastered. In many areas, attacks from local criminals are the most probable threat. A PPS should be adept at performing home security surveys. They should be able to set up security systems at residences, hotel rooms, and apartments.

Emergency medical skills must be developed. Every PPS should be certified in first aid and CPR. They should be aware of and plan for any medical problems that the protectee might have. Advanced emergency medical training is a real plus for Personal Protection Specialists as medical emergencies can arise at any time.

Martial skills are important. These skills must be practiced and refined. In order to learn them adequately and safely, security personnel must be in good physical condition. In order to use these skills in an emergency, Personal Protection Specialists must be in excellent physical condition. Here are some tips on physical training.

- Develop endurance and stamina through running, swimming, or sport activity.
- Develop explosive power by sprinting, lifting light-weights rapidly, lifting heavy weights, and maintaining flexibility. Plyometrics are often used by athletes and can certainly be adapted to emergency skill development.
- Static strength or the ability to apply force for an extended period of time can be developed by practicing holding weights up or remaining in push-up or pull-up position for a period of time.
- Hand strength—which is important for grabbing and using any type of weapon—can be developed in any one of a number of ways. Squeezing a rubber ball is the most effective. Crumbling up newspaper pages with one hand, doing fingertip push-ups, pull-ups, and virtually any type of weightlifting involving a pulling type of motion are other approaches.
- Flexibility is important not only because speed is increased, but because injuries are prevented and body tension caused by stress may be reduced. Stretch first thing in the morning! This "sets" your body's range of motion for the rest of the day. Stretching should be done after a warm-up that gets blood flowing to the muscles. During all workouts, stretch and contract muscles. Once the muscles have been contracted, stretch them. Rhythmic stretching is a fast, effective method of stretching. It involves ten repetitions of a stretch. Taking care to stretch a little farther each time develops flexibility. At night to relax, *static-passive stretching* can be employed. Try holding in a stretched position for at least 30 seconds. This will make the muscles grow longer and relax the PPS. Ensure that the muscles are moved around after the static stretch or one will lose speed of movement.

Manners, deportment, and decorum will "make or break" a PPS quicker than anything else. Proper dining etiquette and the ability to understand such aspects of corporate protocol as the conduct of meetings are the everyday issues that Personal Protection Specialists are confronted with. In many cases, persons with a criminal justice background have great difficulty adjusting to upper class society. Some who previously had to adjust to lower class society must now switch gears and join the upper crust of society. This "double whammy" is quite stressful. Anyone wishing to become involved in executive protection must become adept at manners and dress. A trip to the library or world wide web for some information on this might be the most important career investment an aspiring PPS can make.

PROTECTING THE PRINCIPAL

The operational aspects of guarding executives, celebrities, political leaders—or witnesses—encompass a wide range of tasks and duties. Personal protection is a specialty that requires immense dedication. Here are a few things to bear in mind when acting as security escort.

1. Never leave the protectee unguarded.
2. Always be alert and ready to respond to emergencies.
3. Position yourself between the protectee and possible threats.
4. Enter rooms first to make sure they are safe. Completely scan the room. Consider closing the blinds to avoid being visible from outside adversaries.
5. When trouble starts, move the protectee to safety immediately. He or she is your first and only responsibility.
6. Carry items, such as briefcases, in the nongun or non-weapon hand.
7. Always watch the hands of potential assailants.
8. Review the itinerary and prepare for the day's activities well beforehand. Know it! At the same time be able to make necessary changes and adjustments.
9. Become acquainted with a wide range of sports and hobbies that the protectee may engage in so that you may accompany him/her.
10. Conceal your position as a Personal Protection Specialist from everyone except those who need to know. Blend in and be part of the principal's team, not an unwanted appendage! *Bear in mind that one of the biggest threats to executives and celebrities is embarrassment.*

HOSTAGE SITUATIONS

The taking of hostages has become a serious problem. The criticality of these incidents, (a life or lives are threatened) coupled with the myriad of emotional, legal, and public relations problems that accompany them, make hostage incidents a concern for all security practitioners. In short, the *direct* and *indirect costs* of these incidents make them a serious problem! Security personnel must be prepared to

deal with these situations; they are simply too dangerous not to worry about.

While there are many types of hostage takers and an infinite variety of hostage situations present, there are some basic steps that can be taken. One does not need to be a qualified hostage negotiator to utilize a few basic "first aid" techniques in the event of an incident.

1. **Isolate the area of the incident (crisis point).** Keep the perpetrators contained and don't allow anyone except negotiators or tactical personnel near the area.
2. **Obtain as much information as possible.** Use a pre-designed threat form when receiving a hostage/extortion call. Question available witnesses. Find out as much as possible about the hostages, hostage takers, and the immediate physical environment. This includes their prior life history, medical condition, and emotional condition. Building layout with access/egress points, structural strength, and utilities must be collected also. *Intelligence data is crucial to the successful handling of a hostage incident. Security forces play a key role here in having this information available to hostage negotiators and special response teams!*
3. **Notify the central alarm station or dispatcher of the incident and keep the information flowing.**
4. **Maintain perimeters, supply information, keep a low uniformed officer profile and await further instruction.**

Don't try to make a play or be a hero, simply *contain the problem* and *report* any and all relevant information. Isolation of the problem and information regarding it are the key concerns of protection officers at a hostage situation.

HOSTAGE THREAT RECEIPT

According to the U.S. Nuclear Regulatory Commission (NUREG 0219 Task 57), the following procedures should be followed whenever a hostage threat call is received:

1. Stay calm.
2. Attempt to verify that the caller actually has a hostage by asking for information about the hostage and asking to speak to the hostage.
3. Record precise details of the call.
4. Notify the central alarm station or the security shift supervisor.

Obviously there should be a Hostage Threat contingency plan that is operational and updated periodically. A Hostage Threat Report form should be readily available to security officers and telephone operators.

IF TAKEN HOSTAGE ...

If a security officer is taken hostage *or* is in close proximity to the hostage taker, there are several key points to bear in mind.

1. **Do not do anything to excite or aggravate the hostage taker**. Accept your fate, speak little and lower your voice. Speak a little slower (*"slower and lower"*). Assume a passive/*supportive* body posture. Display palms, keeping hands at your sides or folded in your lap. Shoulders should be rolled slightly forward and your head a bit forward and down. This must be comfortable and natural; it needs only be a very slight change in posture to be effective.

2. **Identify yourself by your first name and use the hostage-taker's first name**. This will aid in having him or her view you as a *person* rather than an *object* with which to bargain.

3. **Don't speak unless spoken to and weigh your words carefully**. As with any emotionally charged individual, avoid the words **"you," "should,"** and **"why."** These are too direct/pointed and tend to place the person's reasoning process on trial.

4. **Be patient, remain calm, and try to rest**. Conserve your energy! This helps to prevent becoming stressed out, preserves your ability to think objectively, and prepares you for what will probably be a long ordeal.

5. **Analyze the hostage taker(s) as much as possible.** Try to see things through his eyes. **Empathic listening** is key.

6. **Analyze the physical environment as much as possible.** Look for cover, escape routes, means of communications, and obvious hazards.

MANAGING THE HOSTAGE INCIDENT

Management of a hostage situation—or other crisis event—consists of several key elements. These are **control, coordination, communication,** and **information.** By employing each of these concepts, the incident can be successfully negotiated without anyone getting hurt.

1. **Control access to the area.** Set up an **inner perimeter** around the crisis point where only negotiation and tactical personnel are authorized to go. An outside perimeter excludes members of the public and any other unauthorized personnel. Within the outside perimeter is the command post. All communications and agency liaison emanate from the command post. Media personnel should be restricted to a secured location within the outer perimeter that is not too close to the command post. The media's needs should be facilitated as much as possible in terms of access to power supplies, office/work rooms, and telephones. Their comfort and work needs should be met as much as possible by a public information officer. They need to do their job, yet they cannot be allowed to roam around unescorted.

2. **Coordination is also handled through the command post.** Persons who have a "need to know" information should be supplied with that information; actions of the negotiator(s) are not to be divulged to tactical personnel.

3. **Communication is centered in the command post.** Communications with the hostage taker should be set up immediately, preferably by telephone. The communications monitoring capabilities of the hostage-taker and the media must be carefully assessed and restricted.

4. **Information is the key to successful resolution be it through negotiation or assault**. Everything possible concerning the psychological, physical, and background characteristics of all those involved in the incident should be collected at the command post. Details regarding the physical layout of the crisis point, such as the location of utility lines, room layout, and building structure, should be obtained.

NEGOTIATION

While hostage negotiation is a complex professional skill demanding education in psychology and years of interviewing experience capped off by specialized training, it is important for security personnel to understand something about it. Security personnel must be able to render "first aid." They must be able to provide immediate, necessary actions to reduce the level of violence. Hostage negotiators may not be immediately available.

Hostage takers may initiate the negotiation process with someone close at hand and simply not want to talk with negotiators when they arrive. These are the basic concepts of negotiations.

1. Stall for time as much as possible. Say that you have to check with your boss.
2. Don't give the hostage taker something without getting something in return.
3. Make the hostage taker think. Wear him out mentally by forcing him to constantly decide things. *Slow it down.*
4. Never give hostage takers weapons or intoxicants.
5. Don't make promises or threats that you cannot keep.

FOR THE FUTURE

Counterterrorism and VIP protection will continue to evolve with the threats that confront protection officers. In order to meet the challenges of the future—*and be a part of that future*—there must a greater emphasis on the following:

1. The study of various types of threat groups and individuals by individual protection officers. There must also be research on this published in the professional literature. It cannot be the exclusive domain of political science or the general news media. Security magazines and journals must feature recent, relevant articles on threat groups and individuals.
2. The development of theoretical and practical aspects of conducting searches so that training programs can produce graduates who are truly proficient and professional at the searching function. **This must be studied!**

3. An emphasis on manners and deportment by protection officers so that they can join the management team and have a voice in the organization.
4. More academic programs in Security & Loss Control at colleges and universities so that both theory and technology can be studied. This will also aid in making Security a more visible career option to students who are the future of the industry. Currently the Foundation website at IFPO.ORG has links to college programs. ASIS International's website also has an extensive list of colleges offering Security courses (ASISONLINE.ORG).
5. Embracing of the principles of Risk Management by protection officers. This assists in more creative solutions to threat problems. It also helps to marry Security to Insurance and accepted business practices. Simply requesting more resources and inconveniencing people to harden a target is not the way to "win friends and influence people!"
6. Elevation and professionalization of the protection officer. Government agencies must see the role that they play in counterterrorism. So must the general public and the legislators who mandate training and licensing. In particular, the role of the protection officer in collecting intelligence and assisting in emergency response must be appreciated. "The biggest issue in public safety is private security."

REFERENCES

Abanes, Richard. (1996). *American Militias: Rebellion, Racism & Religion*, Intervarsity Press, Downers Grove, Illinois.
Anti-Defamation League. (1996). *The Web of Hate: Extremists Exploit the Internet*. ADL, USA.
Bolz, F., Dudonis, K. & Schultz, D. (2002). *The Counterterrorism Handbook: Tactics, Procedures, and Techniques*. CRC Press. Boca Raton, FL.
Braunig, Martha. (1992). *The Executive Protection Bible*. Executive Security International, Inc. Basalt, CO.
Kobetz, Richard W. (1991). *Providing Executive Protection*. Executive Protection Institute. Berryville, VA.
Kobetz, Richard W. (1994). *Providing Executive Protection Volume II*. Executive Protection Institute. Berryville, VA.
Pierce, William L. (1980). *The Turner Diaries*. New York, NY, Barricade Books.
Strentz, Thomas. (1990). "Radical Right vs. Radical Left: Terrorist Theory and Threat." THE POLICE CHIEF, August 1990.
U.S. Department of Justice (1993). *Terrorism in the United States: 1982–1992*. Federal Bureau of Investigation, Washington, D.C.
United States Nuclear Regulatory Commission. (1978). *Nuclear Security Personnel for Power Plants: Content and Review Procedures for a Security Training and Qualification Program.*. U.S. Nuclear Regulatory Commission, Washington, D.C.

RESOURCES

ASIS International has an Information Resource Center at their Web sit,e which is available to members. There are also a variety of books and videos in the ASIS bookstore. ASIS also hosts seminars relating to Terrorism and has a Council on Global Terrorism. Visit ASISONLINE.ORG.
AST Corporation (ASTCORP.COM) has numerous CD Rom and online programs within the HITS Program on Executive Protection and Homeland Security. IFPO members receive discounts on AST Corporation programs.
BSR (Bill Scott Racing School) (304/725-9281) provides training in Evasive Driving and Executive Security Training.
CRC Press **(CRCPRESS.COM) offers a variety of books such as *The Counterterrorism Handbook* by Bolz, Dudonis, and Schulz.**
Butterworth-Heinemann, an imprint of Elsevier Science, is a leading publisher of security books. There are a wide variety of titles relating to terrorism and related topics. Please visit http://stbooks.elsevier.com/security or call (800) 545-2522, 200 Wheeler Road, 6th Floor, Burlington, MA 01803.
Executive Protection Institute (540/955-1128) offers numerous programs relating to Executive Protection, Corporate Aircraft Security, etc. They also publish *Providing Executive Protection* and *Providing Executive Protection Volume Ii* . In addition, the Institute administers Nine Lives Associates, a professional organization of Personal Protection Specialists.
Executive Security International (800/874-0888 or 303/927-3383) provides training courses in Executive Protection and Counterintelligence. They also offer an outstanding book, *The Executive Protection Bible*, and distance education courses.
The **International Foundation for Protection Officers** (IFPO.ORG) maintains an Article Archives on the Web site, which contains articles on detection equipment, terrorism, and related topics.
PAASIS.ORG is the website for the Central Pennsylvania Chapter of ASIS International. The site contains numerous articles on terrorism and WMD response.
The **Professional Security Training Network (PSTN)** offers a monthly subscription service, various series on and single video tapes. The Network has many programs on Bomb Search, Vehicle Search, and Executive Protection. Visit PSTN.COM. Note that IFPO members receive substantial discounts on PSTN programs.
Scotti School of Defensive Driving (888/644-8722 or SECURITYDRIVER.COM) offers courses in Evasive Driving and other aspects of Executive Protection.

SECURITY QUIZ
Counter Terrorism / VIP Protection

1. Personal Protection Specialists should attempt to _____ in with the principal's entourage.
2. Personal Protection Specialists should, in effect, be " _____ consultants."
3. A principal is about to enter a room. List three things that should be done by the PPS.
   A _____
   B _____
   C
4. When in the presence of a hostage-taker or other violence-prone individual, _____ your voice to calm the person.
5. There has been a hostage taking in a building on your employer's property. List five items of information that should be given to police hostage response teams.
   A _____
   B _____
   C _____
   D _____
   E _____
6. List five of the principles of searching.
   A _____
   B _____
   C _____
   D _____
   E _____
7. When assuming a supportive body posture, the _____ should be slightly down and forward, the _____ rolled slightly forward, and the hands should be _____ in the lap or kept at the sides so that the _____ can be seen.
8. Counterterrorist security personnel should read and become intimately familiar with detection _____ manuals.
9. When speaking with a hostage taker, robber, or other emotionally charged individual, the protection officer should try and avoid using the words _____, _____ and _____.
10. List ten considerations to be addressed when employing detection equipment.
    A _____
    B _____
    C _____
    D _____
    E _____
    F _____
    G _____
    H _____
    I _____
    J _____

WEAPONS OF MASS DESTRUCTION: THE NBC THREATS

By Michael Stroberger, CPO, CLSO, CSS, CPOI, CLSD, CPP

Within the realm of possible incidents, the possibility of a Weapon of Mass Destruction (WMD) being used is, by far, the most devastating. These weapons are designed not only to impact a wide area, numerous persons, and often, extensive amounts of property; they are also usually intended to strike terror in the hearts and minds of those who survive them or even simply hear of their use.

Title 10, U.S. Code, Section 1403 defines WMD as "weapons or devices intended, or having the capability, to cause death or serious injury to a significant number of people through the release, dissemination, or impact of toxic poisonous chemicals or their precursors; a disease organism; or radiation or radioactivity."

These weapons are the potential tools of terrorists, criminals, and even the mentally disturbed. As the name suggests, these are capable of truly enormous amounts of damage; to the point that it often seems well out of proportion with the size of the device which causes it. Make no mistake, the proper WMD designed, manufactured, and delivered in accordance with the optimal use of that type of device or substance is capable of catastrophic amounts of damage and loss of life.

It is also important to note that some conventional devices, inclusive of improvised applications, can have the effects of a WMD. To the general public, a commercial airliner was thought to have, at most, the potential to end the lives of its occupants and perhaps some unfortunate souls on the ground if it were to be forced to crash. On September 11, 2001, this false sense of security was stripped away when airliners became the weapon of choice for a small group intent on causing massive damage and loss of life. As we all know by now, the secondary intent, the instilling of fear, was immediately fulfilled.

Within the realm of WMDs, there are three primary categories, commonly referred to as "NBC" types, that are considered the most likely threat types.

Nuclear
Biological
Chemical

Each one carries certain limitations based on the needed materials, methods of construction or development, and the vector of delivery. Each one, when properly executed, has the ability to produce results that are devastating.

NUCLEAR THREATS

Despite the images that immediately come to mind, the threats that fall within this category do not necessarily include the use of advanced delivery systems, such as missiles and aircraft. Due to advances in technology, the amount of space required to transport the materials, and initiate detonation, have been so dramatically reduced that it is possible to be contained within a man-portable bag or case. In addition to this, there is the threat of devices which do not utilize fissionable materials in the process of detonation, but which have radiological material packed in and around it to expose those in the area to radiation. These are commonly referred to as "dirty bombs." At the extreme end of this line of thought, a device planted within a reactor sufficient to destroy the containment structures would also fall within this category.

In all cases, the primary consideration one must make is the exposure to radiation, both during and after detonation. Those caught in the actual blast would find the effects mirror to those of devices, which are purely of a nonradioactive composition. The obvious difference being that actual nuclear devices produce blast effects on a monumental scale.

Regardless of the preblast phases, the primary threat in an on-going sense is the residual radiological effects.

One final possible scenario might involve simply placing highly radioactive materials where it is unshielded and can expose persons in the area. This type of threat may not be immediately obvious, as it would have no blast effects associated with it.

BIOLOGICAL THREATS

This category includes all pathogens or toxins that could be used to cause sickness or death. Pathogens are viruses, bacteria, and similar living organisms, and toxins are defined as the substances that are produced by certain living organisms. Specific examples of pathogens would include Anthrax, Plague, and Ebola. Toxins would include ricin and botulinium toxin. Biological threats, in the case of pathogens, present a very serious issue as they can easily spread over vast areas as a result of persons coming in contact with those already infected, and the possibility that recognizable symptoms may take days to appear. The initial exposure may be initiated through placement of a relatively small container, while the peak effects could include a vast area and an enormous number of people as a result of being transmitted from person to person.

CHEMICAL THREATS

Chemical threats could include a range of substances which have been created or fabricated by man. Some of the better known examples may be Sarin, VX, and Tabun. Going into the historical military uses, in some cases not very far back, examples of the use of mustard gas and hydrogen cyanide can easily be found. Chemical weapons can be further broken down by the nature of their effects. These subcategories would include nerve agents, blood agents, blister agents, choking agents, and incapacitating agents. As a general definition, these threats create the intended effects through a physiological reaction within the victim's body. Each substance is also described in terms of its persistence, meaning how long it will pose a threat, based on the effects of residue and length of effectiveness in the immediate area. Substances considered persistent would pose a continuing threat if one should come into contact with the droplets or possibly residue. Non-persistent substances are typically only a hazard when there is the potential for inhalation.

Unlike biological agents, chemical threats must originate from relatively large containers if they are to have impact over a vast area. Contamination of a room or relatively small area of a structure may involve containers as small as would fit in a backpack or bag, but contamination of venues, such as a stadium, would involve immense amounts of the same substance.

DEVICE DETECTION AND INCIDENT PREVENTION

As previously stated, these types of threats can come from relatively small packages. In their attack on the subway system, Aum Shinrikyo utilized Sarin. According to one witness, they observed a person put a bag or backpack on the floor and then drive the point of an umbrella into it. The result was a rupture of the pressurized canister that was inside of the bag and dispersion began immediately.

Given the wide range of possible containers and delivery types, it is not realistically possible to truly prevent such incidents. Through prudent and efficient security measures, it is possible to minimize this possibility, though. A well-executed program of bag and package inspections, obvious security program awareness, and participation and professional security staff all contribute to the creation of an environment where the proper placement of such a device is perceived to be more difficult. This is the basis of the defensive concept utilized in sporting arenas, large public functions, and other mass gatherings. Given a reasonable

chance of detection, persons looking to place such devices may be prompted to find a less secure target.

The actual detection of a specific device is somewhat difficult. In general, containers which appear to be out of the usual should be closely examined. This is the basic theme of mail inspections. When searching incoming mail, those performing the search typically look for some key indicators that a package may be a threat. Some classic indicators may be the following:

- Excessive postage, given the weight of the package
- Lack of a return address, or return address clearly differing from the area of origin, per the postmark
- Addressing to a person by title rather than name ("Mr. General Manager")
- Excessive tape or wrapping material
- Unbalanced and heavy contents
- Stains on the packing material

In each case, the presence of one or more of these indicators would suggest that the package might be suspect. Based on the nature of the business, person, or location, it might be prudent to isolate the package and contact the proper authorities. For biological and chemical threats, placing such a package into a large storage box (plastic, with a reasonably airtight lid), provides a much higher degree of safety prior to the arrival of the authorities. In case the device contains any form of explosive, it is also recommended that this storage box be away from high volumes of human traffic, or any other areas of concern. Once any such object is contained, all persons that came into contact with it, or into contact with anything in the immediate area, must thoroughly wash their hands. Application of self-drying disinfectant gels may also be prudent after the hands have been washed.

With the exception of some chemical agents, there is often no distinct indicator of the presence of these threats apart from the observed effects. In most cases, there is no telltale odor, colored cloud, or similar indicators.

IMMEDIATE RESPONSE

Obviously, the immediate response to any case must be obtaining outside support from law enforcement and EMS, and then assisting in identifying the actual nature of the threat by relaying all observations and initial findings. In the case of a nuclear blast, this will be very obvious. In exposures to chemical agents, it may be difficult. In biological exposures, due to the time delay in the onset of symptoms and other challenges, it may be impossible without medical examination and testing. It is essential that law enforcement be contacted, as they will have access to the proper reporting lines of communication for all other responsible agencies.

The following are some possible indicators of chemical exposure:

- Increased salivation
- Decreased visual clarity
- Headache
- Fatigue
- Slurred speech
- Nausea

Biological agents may present any of a number of indicators. Based upon the specific nature of the threat, it can appear as any number of illnesses. In general, this type of threat should be considered when large numbers of cases involving similar symptoms are reported within a short period of time and have a common location. It is important to note that the common location may have been within the recent past, possibly as much as a few days.

Those persons exposed to radiological effects may show a wide range of symptoms, depending on the level of radiation to which they were exposed and the period of time in which the exposure occurs.

One set of indicators that may be present in any of these types of incidents are the environmental impact on the area surrounding the point of origin. In most cases, the immediate area will be found to be devoid of animal life, with potential impact even on the plants. In cases of radiological involvement, you may find fragments of the device or other materials that radiate an inordinate amount of heat, even well after the actual blast. Unfortunately, those present in any area where this can be observed are most likely contaminated, unless properly utilizing protective clothing and equipment.

TREATMENT AND LONG-TERM RESPONSE

In looking at the primary responses and the treatment, it is essential that the health and safety of the responders be of the utmost concern. Proper precautionary equipment should be utilized if available, and all persons should be decontaminated as thoroughly as possible after contact with the area in question or any victims. Always seek to identify the area of effect, and approach all such areas from an uphill/upwind position to avoid any wind-borne particles or the possibility of runoff from liquid spills or fire control efforts from contaminating your person.

In all cases, contaminated clothing should be removed. Flushing the victims with water alone may remove a large amount of biological and chemical agents that have remained on the skin. The removal of residual agents can be improved through the use of hot soapy water, as this will aid in breaking down some compounds. In chemical and biological exposure cases, the addition of a bleach and water solution will greatly increase the effects of this decontamination. In all cases, the removal of surface contaminants is to be viewed as an attempt to prevent a continued exposure. These efforts obviously will not reduce the impact of any substances that have already entered the victim's body.

Depending on the exact nature of a chemical or biological incident, there may be certain medical responses which will mitigate the effects of the substance involved. In radiological incidents, it is commonly suggested that doses of potassium iodide be taken to prevent or reduce the effects of any airborne or food borne radioactive iodine, which would harm the thyroid glands of the victim. Dosages are based on age/weight of the victim. The FDA publishes these guidelines.

In all contamination cases, the area must remain secured until such time as the threat has been removed. In many cases, this will be an extended period of time. From the moment that a law enforcement, fire, government agency, or military person is on scene, they are in charge. It will be their decision as to when the scene is released back to the owner and under what conditions this will occur. All requests must be made through the proper channels until that time.

Weapons of mass destruction pose a potential threat on a monumental per-incident scale. WMDs could be viewed as a strong tool in attempting to strike fear into the population of a country, as well as in seeking mass media coverage for a cause.

WMDs may be broken down into various threat categories, but an underlying theme is carried throughout: these are devices that are designed to produce massive numbers of casualties and/or property damage. In many cases, the actual size of the devices may not appear to be threatening, although the effects are not directly related to comparative size due to technological advances.

The unfortunate truth is that there is little within the private sector that can be done to specifically address these threats beyond an adherence to sound physical security concepts and incident prevention strategies.

The first step in the immediate response must be to seek outside assistance. No nongovernmental entity will have the equipment to properly handle a large-scale incident of this nature. Contact the local EMS, and ensure that they are aware of your suspicions.

In the treatment of those exposed, decontamination must occur, as well as required medical attention. The removal of a continued exposure threat is essential if the victim is to be given a better chance of recovery.

All contaminated areas are under the command and control of the senior responding agency until such time as it is formally released back to the owner. In some cases, this may not be possible for an extended period of time.

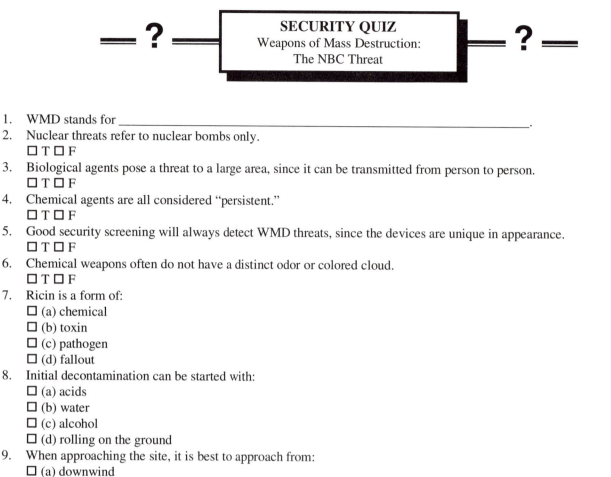

SECURITY QUIZ
Weapons of Mass Destruction:
The NBC Threat

1. WMD stands for _____.
2. Nuclear threats refer to nuclear bombs only.
    ☐ T ☐ F
3. Biological agents pose a threat to a large area, since it can be transmitted from person to person.
    ☐ T ☐ F
4. Chemical agents are all considered "persistent."
    ☐ T ☐ F
5. Good security screening will always detect WMD threats, since the devices are unique in appearance.
    ☐ T ☐ F
6. Chemical weapons often do not have a distinct odor or colored cloud.
    ☐ T ☐ F
7. Ricin is a form of:
    ☐ (a) chemical
    ☐ (b) toxin
    ☐ (c) pathogen
    ☐ (d) fallout
8. Initial decontamination can be started with:
    ☐ (a) acids
    ☐ (b) water
    ☐ (c) alcohol
    ☐ (d) rolling on the ground
9. When approaching the site, it is best to approach from:
    ☐ (a) downwind
    ☐ (b) the east
    ☐ (c) upwind
    ☐ (d) the south
10. What type of threat can result in the production of material that radiates heat for an extended period of time? (Nuclear or Radiological) _____

Unit 9

Crime Scene Procedures
Foundations for Surveillance
Interviewing Techniques
Investigations: Concepts and Practices for Security Professionals

CRIME SCENE PROCEDURES

By Martin A. Fawcett, CPO

At some point in time during your career as a protection officer you will likely discover a crime scene. Your actions or inactions at this critical time will determine to some degree the outcome of any ensuing investigation into the crime.

In order to properly preserve and protect a crime scene, it is important that the protection officer understand what a criminal crime scene is and what is it that is expected in terms of officer roles and duties.

DETERMINING THE CRIME SCENE

Many crimes do not have a crime scene in the sense that there is a physical location that the protection officer can see and protect. This would include crimes such as fraud or embezzlement where there is seldom any physical evidence left other than a document or various kinds of records.

On the other hand, some crime scenes can cover very large areas. On first examination, the boundaries of a crime scene may not be easily determined. It is important not to establish the limits of a crime scene until after an initial investigation. A premature definition of the crime scene may cause loss or destruction of evidence outside the established area defined as the crime scene.

DETERMINING BOUNDARIES

Once the boundaries of the crime scene have been established, close off the area to all persons who are not required for investigation purposes. This includes fellow officers, occupants, employees, and the public. The limits established should exceed beyond what is believed to be the actual crime scene. It is better to contain too much of an area than late to discover you did not include enough, causing a possible loss of valuable evidence. The area can always be reduced, but it is difficult to expand.

Always remember that in order to commit a crime, the culprit(s) must pass from one point to another. This can be further broken down into three areas: point of entry, location of crime, and point of exit.

By following a logical sequence in the reconstruction process, it is possible to determine in most instances all three areas, thereby deciding the probable limits of the crime scene. At this point, backup, support officers or investigators (police/security) are required.

Once a crime scene is established, how can we best affect protection of the scene and at the same time preserve any evidence that may be found at the protected area (crime

scene)? It can be accomplished by the observance of the following three rules:

1. Protect
2. Preserve
3. Make notes

PROTECT THE SCENE

As the officer is usually the first person on the scene of a crime, or the first person to be called, it is imperative that he/she arrives as quickly as possible to the location of the scene. When there is a time lapse between being notified of the crime and arrival of the officer, it should be stressed to the caller not to do anything until the officer arrives. Once the officer arrives, the first priority is to prevent unauthorized access to the crime scene area.

This means that all personnel, bystanders, and anyone else who happen to be in the area or stop to look, be prevented from entering the crime scene area. All unauthorized personnel must be told to leave the area and remain outside the area until told to return by security/police.

The reason for this is that people are creatures of curiosity and will often look and touch articles that appeal to them, thereby inadvertently destroying evidence.

If the location is a large one, then it is imperative that the officer summon enough assistance to ensure that unauthorized persons are kept out of the area. A word of caution: In your efforts to remove and keep out unauthorized persons, do not forget that they may have witnessed part or all of the crime and be waiting for someone to ask them for their story.

Many witnesses will silently stand around and then be sent on their way without the officer ever taking the time to question them about the crime. Remember, be polite when asking them to move away, and also ask if they know anything about the crime.

PRESERVE THE CRIME

After unauthorized personnel have been questioned or removed, the next important step is to preserve the scene exactly as it was when first discovered. Nothing must be moved, removed, or altered in any way; and no evidence, real or suspect, may be added to the scene. This merely confuses the scene for the qualified experts who must reconstruct the crime from the evidence.

Complete crime scene protection will enhance the protection officer image and greatly improve crime solution potential

The best way to preserve a scene is to remember: **Keep your hands to yourself.** This means that you do not touch anything. Should you have to touch, move, or remove anything from the crime scene for safety reasons, such as an article on fire that has to be extinguished, it is essential to remember exactly what you did, heard, or viewed respecting possible evidence. If anything was moved or altered in any way, an explanation must be provided.

If contamination has occurred in any way, it may lead investigators and technicians to false conclusions or blind leads which can prevent the successful solution of a crime.

In order to preserve a crime scene, it becomes necessary to understand what might be considered "evidence."

MAKING NOTES

In the initial stages of protecting a crime scene, there is normally a certain amount of confusion. It is important that the officer realize that time is vital and that many details he/she has seen will quickly be forgotten unless committed to a notebook. The moment the officer arrives, he/she should commit important information to the notebook format. The date and time of arrival, the date and time of the occurrence, who was present upon arrival and what happened. Also who initiated the call in the first instance, and all other pertinent information (see chapter on notebooks/reports) pertaining to the crime scene. In some instances, a small sketch in the notebook showing the scene as it was found can be of great value for future reference.

Ensure that the notes you make are accurate and complete. They may prove to be invaluable as the investigation progresses.

RECONSTRUCT THE CRIME SCENE

As soon as is possible after arriving at a crime scene, the protection officer should attempt to reconstruct, in his mind, the crime scene to be protected. Reconstruction may lead to further evidence that was not readily apparent upon arrival or after an initial search of the area.

PUBLIC RELATIONS

It is important during the crime scene investigation to not overlook the victim. During the rush of activity that follows the discovery of a crime scene, the victim is often pushed from the scene and left unattended. He/she may resent the fact that this is occurring and could become hostile.

It is important that the protection officer explain to the best of his ability just what is happening and the reasons for actions taken. This keeps the victim informed which could enhance communications and aid in the ensuing investigation. It will also show that the protection officer knows his/her job and cares about the people he/she is responsible to protect. This step takes very little time and greatly improves public relations and the protection officer's image.

PHYSICAL EVIDENCE

At a crime scene you can expect to discover any number of different forms of physical evidence. Physical evidence simply stated is anything that the culprit(s) could be connected to or associated with. The importance of physical evidence is that it can be used to link an accused person to the scene of a crime. These are some of the more common forms of physical evidence that could be encountered.

1. Fingerprints
2. Palmprints
3. Tool impressions
4. Footwear impressions
5. Tire impressions
6. Torn metal
7. Headlight glass
8. Torn paper
9. Penny match cases
10. Hair and fibers
11. Blood
12. Bullets and casings
13. Paint chips
14. Cut wires
15. Dirt and soil
16. Anything that appears out of place

The preceding list is by no means complete. Physical evidence can be visible or invisible. Some forms of evidence require complex scientific procedures to collect and identify. As a protection officer required to attend a crime scene, it is important to realize that physical evidence is usually present.

It is therefore imperative that you follow the guideline set forth by your supervisors, and **protect, preserve,** and **make notes.**

EVIDENCE COLLECTING

Evidence left at the scene of a crime should be left for the trained investigator or identification technician. These professionals understand the scientific procedures for the collecting and identification of physical evidence. These experts are responsible for gathering evidence. Again, "hands off" approach.

Another factor to consider when dealing with physical evidence is that the purpose of collecting it is to link the culprit to the scene and eventually enter the evidence as an exhibit(s) in court, with a view to gaining a conviction.

In order to enter physical evidence in court, a number of procedures are required or the evidence gathered will be ruled inadmissible. In order to reduce this threat, it is best to let the professional gather and identify the evidence because they are more familiar with all the rules of the court relating to the admissibility of physical evidence.

Should the occasion arise that it is impractical to await the arrival of the police or a senior member of the security force is not available, then the protection officer will have to take the initiative and gather the evidence that is found at the scene. If this becomes necessary, then there are a number of points to be remembered.

1. Assign **one** officer to collect **all** evidence.
2. Record all information in detail in notebook.

3. The "exhibit" officer must maintain possession of all exhibits.
4. For each exhibit, record the following:
   a) Time
   b) Date
   c) Location
   d) Officer 's initials
5. In a notebook, record the following:
   a) Time
   b) Date
   c) Location
   d) Who seized exhibit
   e) Description of exhibit
   f) Disposition of exhibit

The admissibility of any physical evidence in court will depend in part upon the manner in which it was collected and the safeguards followed to ensure its integrity. The protection officer must be able to demonstrate to the courts that:

1. The evidence introduced can be positively identified from other items of a similar description.
2. The evidence has not been altered in any way.
3. That "continuity of possession" (or "evidential chain of custody") has been maintained.

"Continuity of possession" simply means that there is an unbroken chain of possession from the first instance to presentation in court. Anyone coming into physical contact with any form of evidence joins the chain and will be required to testify in court as to his/her handling and disposition of the exhibit.

As you can well imagine, it is not only more expedient, but much safer to limit the number of persons involved with each exhibit. If for any reason, the chain cannot be proven, then the evidence may not be accepted by the courts, and if accepted, its value in the proceedings is greatly reduced.

CONCLUSION

When a crime scene is discovered, it is essential that the protection officer seek backup or support personnel. The person(s) responsible for the commission of the crime may well be on or near the scene. Criminals are dangerous. Your job is to protect innocent people and yourself. Capturing suspects is a job for the police. Your job is to report and observe. Protect life and prevent loss or damage to evidence. Your report will reflect your crime scene actions. Do first things first; that means prevention, not crime detection, and apprehension.

SECURITY QUIZ
Crime Scene Procedures

1. Sometime during your career as a protection officer, you will be called upon to investigate a crime scene and your _____ or _____ will have a great bearing on the outcome of any ensuing investigation. (Fill in the blanks.)
2. A premature definition of a crime scene may cause evidence that is later discovered outside the crime scene boundaries to be _____ or _____. (Fill in the blanks.)
3. The competent protection officer will always make sure that his notes are _____ and _____. (Fill in the blanks.)
4. The importance of _____ is that it may be used to link an accused person to the scene of the crime. (Fill in the blank.)
5. Elements to be considered when determining the boundaries of a crime scene are:
   ☐ (a) point of entry
   ☐ (b) location
   ☐ (c) point of exit
   ☐ (d) All the above
   ☐ (e) None of the above
6. The protection officer's prime responsibility with regards to crime scenes can best be described as:
   ☐ (a) protect, preserve, arrest
   ☐ (b) investigate crimes
   ☐ (c) seize evidence
   ☐ (d) All of the above
   ☐ (e) None of the above

7. Once the protection officer arrives on the scene, his first priority is:
    □ (a) to get the names of all those present
    □ (b) to lock all the doors and wait for the police
    □ (c) to preserve evidence found at the scene
    □ (d) to call for assistance
    □ (e) None of the above
8. Many crime scenes do not have a physical location on a site or facility.
    □ T □ F
9. The boundaries of a crime scene will be immediately evident once the protection officer arrives on the scene.
    □ T □ F
10. It is necessary to establish the boundaries of a crime scene before an investigation can begin.
    □ T □ F

FOUNDATIONS FOR SURVEILLANCE

By Michael Stroberger, CPO, CSS, CPOI, CLSD, CPP

In most popular media, the concept of surveillance is either portrayed as a man in a wrinkled, coffee-stained suit or an extremely large, sophisticated and complex electronic array, which requires three or more people to monitor. In reality, the typical surveillance operation falls between these.

The basic goal of surveillance is the obtaining of information, which might not be immediately available, without a concerted effort and a focused attention. In most cases, it is the watchful, knowledgeable, and sometimes lucky selection of points of focus that yield the best results. In other cases, it is the act of watching that produces results, as will be discussed later.

Of utmost importance in all surveillance operations is a proper understanding of privacy and the limits to which one can surveil another without violating legal restrictions, company policy, or common sense.

GENERAL TYPES

Surveillance operations can be broken down into a matrix of sorts with the headers being *covert* and *overt* on one side, and *personal* and *electronic* on the cross-referenced edge. As such, it is only appropriate that the bulk of this discussion be framed within the four possible combinations of these types.

- Covert operations are those done in secret without the knowledge of those being observed. Blending with the surroundings is critical to the success of these operations.
- Overt operations are out in the open, and can usually be easily identified as what they are.
- Personal operations are those carried out in person by individuals or teams of operatives. Although the initial set-up of such an operation may not be overly expensive, the continued use of manpower quickly increases the amount of required funding and quickly outweighs the cost of electronic alternatives.
- Electronic operations can range from CCTV systems to transmission interception and receipt of other electronic information. Usually, the operators are well out of sight, even if the equipment is clearly visible.

COVERT PERSONAL SURVEILLANCE

The act of watching another from a location of concealment, or in a manner in which this act is not obviously being carried out. This is the main focus of the services of some investigators in dealing with cases such as marital strife, insurance fraud, and even in law enforcement investigations. In referencing the fact that this is personal rather than electronic, it should be noted simply that some electronics are usually involved, but this is often limited to a camera, a voice recorder for the retention of comments on the observations, and similar low-end electronics. The primary advantage of this method is that it provides for the human decision making option as the situation evolves. By being on the scene, the operative(s) can determine how to refocus the operation to obtain better results. The major drawback is that this is extremely manpower intensive. In order to not attract too much attention, it is best to randomly exchange operatives so that the same person is not in the area for an extended period of time drawing potential interest though being conspicuous. When performing vehicle surveillance, this is even more of an issue, as specific vehicles can be easily recognized if they are continuously passing into and out of view.

These operations can yield interesting results stemming from the fact that, when properly executed, those observed are not aware that others are paying attention to them.

OVERT PERSONAL SURVEILLANCE

This type of operation ranges widely in its application. Most people in the field of protection engage in this type of operation on a regular basis without realizing that it falls within this type of category. This is the execution of visible and open inspection, such as when on patrol. The act of gathering information is shared in importance with the deterrent value of such an operation. The person executing these duties may be looking for specific types of incidents or situations. Through their presence, and the fact that they are paying attention to their surroundings and the persons in those surroundings, this may cause those in the area to reconsider intentions of violating company policy or legal restrictions.

The performance of this type of operation is most likely to alter the behaviors and responses of persons in the observed environment due to the fact that there is clearly a person paying attention to those present.

COVERT ELECTRONIC SURVEILLANCE

The use of hidden cameras, voice and electronic recording equipment, and similar devices falls within this category. It is within this type of operation that the surveillance agent must pay the closest attention to privacy issues, as the unwelcome observation of persons, under certain circumstances, may violate the state or federal restrictions on such actions. Care must be taken and counsel sought when designing such operations, so that the violation of such restrictions does not occur.

Some equipment options might include: pinhole cameras; cameras concealed in sprinkler heads, clocks, books and other non-descript items; scanners, tuned to permissible frequencies; and even long-range audio amplifiers as permitted. The equipment selection, given the right budget, can look very much like the property of a movie spy. The actual selection is often limited only by the budget of the operation.

Much like personal covert operations, this method often yields very interesting results. Those being watched are not, if properly executed, aware of the fact that they are being observed. As a result of this, they will act in a manner that is completely natural to them in the given environment.

OVERT ELECTRONIC SURVEILLANCE

The classic examples would be the pan/tilt/zoom camera domes found in most department stores. These do provide a significant amount of information to a trained operator, but also a very visible deterrent to certain types of crime. Often, if the recordings of such a system are replayed, persons can be seen behaving in one manner, then looking up to find that a camera is in the area and immediately altering the previous behavior to bring it more in line with the expectations of that environment. It is not that the devices themselves have any potential to bring harm to the individual. It is the concept that, absent of a clear view of the operator of the system, there is no way to know if the camera watching that specific area is being paid attention to at the given moment. It is the fear of possibly being observed that provides the deterrent factor in this case. It is because of this that CCTV systems, in such setting as industrial locations and employee-only areas of other types of businesses, should be placed in such a manner as to make it plainly obvious that CCTV is in use, but without providing a view of the monitors themselves. Those in the area should know that observation occurs, but not be able to determine which area at any given time is being observed.

EQUIPMENT REQUIREMENTS

As previously stated, the equipment may range widely. In the case of personal surveillance, either covert or overt, it may be as simple as binoculars, a camera, a mini-recorder, and a note pad. The initial outlay might be as low as a few hundred dollars, and the equipment retained over a period of many operations. In electronic operations, the initial outlay may be thousands, or tens or hundreds of thousands, of dollars. This is based upon the scope and sophistication of the intended operation. As an example, moderate grade pan/tilt/zoom camera operations require not only the camera dome itself, but also a Control Unit, video cabling, power sources and cable, and a method of recording the input. A single P/T/Z camera, in a stand-alone system,

could be thousands of dollars and would still have to be manned at least occasionally.

The equipment must be appropriate to the nature and scope of the operation if it is to be of optimal effectiveness. Experience and common sense will dictate the exact requirements.

Regardless of the nature and method of the operation, the underlying goal of obtaining information must also be addressed in the equipment. If this information is to be used in a truly effective manner, it must be recorded in some way. Certainly in cases of criminal and civil actions, the best possible method of recording the information should be sought. To appear in court without physical evidence, which could be inspected and reviewed, would be of almost no use at all. In many cases, simple still photographs can make a significant impact. If videotape can be made through camcorders or more complex systems, this often makes cases, such as insurance fraud.

PRIVACY ISSUES

Although the pursuit of justice and the protection of personal or company property are highly important, it is also critical that the laws protecting privacy be honored and protected. As such, it is essential that the basic concepts be understood in addition to the researching of laws, which would have bearing on the specific operation to be undertaken. Do not ever assume that the privacy laws of one area apply wholly to another area.

As an example, in some states, the recording of a telephone conversation may not be done without the prior knowledge and consent of both parties on that call. In other states, only one person must be aware of the fact that a recording is being made. In some cases, the employer may listen in to employee telephone conversations, resulting from legal permissions, specific content in the employee hiring agreement or employee handbook, or through the fact that the telephones are owned by the employer, and provided only for the execution of work-related duties. Without a clear understanding of the laws and restrictions that apply to the location in which you intend to perform a surveillance operation, it could be very easy to violate those laws.

Although there are many "rules of thumb" on this issue, the fact is that local laws vary so widely that there is no single clear message that can be sent, other than to research those that apply to your target area.

RECORDING AND RETENTION

As identified in the equipment topic, it is best to make some durable record of the surveillance operation's results. In some cases, this can prove a suspicion; in others, it could be used to defend the execution of practices of those involved in the operation. The materials produced by such activities should be retained for a period of time that is appropriate for the material and actions identified through that investigation, or for the locally defined period of time that those involved might be allowed to enter into a civil action, whichever is the longer period of time. In short, be prepared to prove your case for however long it might be an issue, and be prepared to defend your operation against civil accusations. In some cases, there are companies that have a policy that directs all closed case materials to be destroyed after a certain period of time. In some cases, this is a two-year retention policy. Research these directives before executing them. In some states, those involved are permitted as long as four years to file civil suits. It would be in the best interest of those involved that they have supporting evidence should this occur within the allowed period of time. Again, research the laws and restrictions that apply to not only your location, but also the specific location where the operation takes place.

Save everything if possible. Especially in retaining video and imagery evidence, as you never know what might be seen in the secondary areas of the image. Some cases have begun and been proven based on the background scene in video recordings. Even when the primary action, the focus of the video, did not prove to be a violation as previously thought. Pay attention to your background, and review all materials with this in mind. If storage space becomes an issue, it might be that noncritical materials have to be discarded. Review these materials prior to removal to ensure that there is nothing of value in them.

= ? — SECURITY QUIZ
Foundations for Surveillance — ? =

1. Covert operations is intended not to be known or recognized.
   □ T □ F
2. Personal operations are the least expensive in the long run.
   □ T □ F
3. Equipment requirements vary depending on the location, nature, and goal of the operation.
   □ T □ F
4. A proper understanding of privacy issues is only important if the case goes to court.
   □ T □ F
5. Electronic surveillance could include:
   □ (a) CCTV
   □ (b) interception of radio transmissions
   □ (c) interception of other electronic information
   □ (d) All of the above
6. Considerations for the retention of records could include:
   □ (a) company policy
   □ (b) statutes of limitation
   □ (c) storage space
   □ (d) All of the above
7. Overt personal surveillance:
   □ (a) relies on being properly concealed
   □ (b) could deter some incidents
   □ (c) Both of the above
   □ (d) Neither A nor B
8. A simple camera surveillance system will often include:
   □ (a) a camera
   □ (b) a recorder
   □ (c) a cable and connections
   □ (d) All of the above
9. A uniformed officer is an example of a _____ _____ operation.
10. The recording of a video signal from a camera located behind the air vent of an elevator is an example of a _____ _____ operation.

INTERVIEWING TECHNIQUES

By R. Lorne Brennan, CPO

Much of a protection officer's time is spent giving directions, answering questions, and dealing with the various enquiries related to the facility where he/she is working.

In the course of their duties, the protection officer is also required to investigate numerous complaints and offenses involving any number of people. The protection officer must assemble information gathered from these various sources, obtain the facts necessary to conduct the investigation, and, ultimately, to submit a complete report giving an accurate account of actions taken.

In order to fulfill this role, it is necessary for the protection officer to have a basic understanding of proper interviewing techniques. It is imperative that the protection officer control the conversation and keep control until the termination of the interview. Without control, time will be lost, facts may become distorted or forgotten, and the protection officer may lose the psychological advantage of being "in charge" of the interview.

The content of this section can be used in part for interviewing witnesses to an offense, crime victims, suspects, and potential employees. This is an overview of basic techniques that can be applied to most situations encountered by the protection officer. First, let's take a look at some of the areas that will be covered.

Conducting the Interview

1. Getting acquainted
2. Developing rapport
3. Motivating the subject
4. Keep the subject talking
5. Listen to what's said

Obstacles to Conversation

1. Avoid specific questions
2. Avoid yes/no questions
3. Do not use leading questions
4. Avoid rapid-fire questions

Encouraging Conversation

1. Open-ended questions
2. Use of the long pause
3. Nondirective approach

Ending the Interview

1. Winding down

Preliminaries: It is important for the protection officer to go into an interview with a game plan in mind and with all the facts that are available to him readily at hand. The success or failure of an interview is dependent on many factors, some beyond the control of the officer. The more factors that can be controlled by the officer, the greater the chances are for a successful interview.

Your first approach to the subject is very important. Many people will be emotionally upset, angry, hostile, physically injured, and so on. It will be necessary in some instances to tend to the subject's needs first before attempting to conduct a meaningful interview. Try to calm the subject, make him/her more comfortable, and enlist their active cooperation. Do not be rushed into an interview by the subject. Take your time, and obtain all the facts and as much background information as possible before taking any action.

At times, this approach will upset the subject, who feels that you should be taking swift action on his behalf; however, it is important to remember that you are in charge and you are responsible for actions that you take.

Make sure you have **all** information before committing yourself to a course of action. If at all possible, the location of the interview should be one that is chosen by the officer and should be as free of distractions as possible.

CONDUCTING THE INTERVIEW

Getting acquainted: The greeting should be cordial and sincere. Identify yourself, and if not uniformed, produce your identification. Your initial approach can be formal or informal, depending on the circumstances.

Attempt to set the subject at ease by entering into a general conversation with him/her before getting to the matter at hand. People like to talk about themselves and their interest; and this is a useful tool in obtaining information regarding your subject and locating a common ground for communication with the subject. At this stage, allow the subject to become accustomed to your presence and to the surroundings by setting the pace.

Developing rapport: Your immediate objective is to establish a common ground on which you can communicate with the subject. By following the preliminaries, you should have a good idea of what the subject's educational background is and at what level it is best to talk with him or her. If you are dealing with a laborer, you are not going to speak down to him by using terminology and words that he is not accustomed to.

By the same token, you would not speak to an executive as you would the laborer. Find your common ground and speak to the subject at his level. By finding areas of common interest, such as sports or hobbies, you can establish a rapport with the subject which will lead to easier communications.

In developing a rapport with another person, you must be able to put aside your personal feelings, respect the subject as a person, and show your understanding of the subject and the circumstances that have brought you together. If you are unable to establish a rapport with the subject, an unbridgeable gap will be created that will make further communication difficult, if not impossible.

Motivating the subject: Most people you will be interviewing will be in a strange and stressed situation which makes them uncomfortable. It will be necessary for you to remove any fears they may have. Many people are afraid of "authority" as presented by the uniform, appearing as a witness, incriminating themselves or others, or may simply be unsure of what they are to do.

If you have developed a rapport with the subject, it is a simple matter to convince the subject of the need to tell the truth and enlist their active cooperation.

Keep the subject talking: Once rapport has been established and the subject is motivated, turn the conversation towards the topic you wish to discuss. Allow the subject to give a complete account of their involvement without interruptions, but be alert for inconsistencies or omissions.

At times, you may have to interrupt to guide the subject back in the direction you wish the conversation to go. You must control the conversation to the extent that the subject keeps talking until you have all the information you require.

Listen to what is said and how it is said: The officer must not only induce the subject to freely relate information he may possess, but be must also evaluate the persons and the conversation. In many instances, it is not what the subject says that is important, but the manner in which he says it or what he does not say.

The officer must be constantly alert for signals from the subject that indicate he/she is telling the truth, lying, or merely withholding information. A wealth of information is available to the officer who wishes to advance his interviewing abilities by learning how to interpret body language.

OBSTACLES TO CONVERSATION

In most instances the content of an incident will be covered in more than one conversation. The subject will be asked to repeat his story again in order to properly fill in gaps and correct statements. It is important that one officer not interrupt the subject during the initial stages and that the subject be allowed to recount his version in full.

After the initial story has been told, the officer may then ask the subject to repeat the story, this time taking notes and stopping the subject from time-to-time in order to get the "full" story "straight." It is important to note that most people will never include all the details in the first attempt as they usually blurt out the information in rapid fire succession. After the initial telling, they will relax a bit and become more specific and provide greater detail.

Avoid specific questions: By asking specific questions, the officer diverts and limits the interview rather than letting the subject give a narrative of the whole, or part of the story. Direct questions may also lead the subject into a false line of thinking as to what you consider to be important areas of the story and as a result, the subject may omit some details in an effort to supply the information that he/she "thinks" the officer considers important.

Direct questions do have a place in an interview, but they should not be asked until the subject has given a complete narration. Direct questions can then be used to clear up various areas within the narrative. If the subject hits a block and stops talking, then a direct question can be used to lead him back into the conversation.

Avoid yes/no questions: In order for the officer to obtain full and detailed facts, the subject must respond with an explanation detailing the events. If a question is asked that only requires a yes or no answer, the information that may have been gained will be lost.

By avoiding yes or no questions, you also eliminate problems with the subject not understanding your question, agreeing or disagreeing based solely on what they perceive the 0fficer wants to hear, or what the subject wants to tell the officer..

Do not use leading questions: Leading questions have the same effect as yes/no questions. They may cause the subject to give false or misleading information to the officer. This may be done either mistakenly or on purpose.

Avoid rapid-fire questions: These may seem appropriate to the inexperienced investigator; however, they only lead to confusion, emotional tenseness, and resistance to the rapport that may have been developed. It also stops the cooperative witness from completing his statement, thereby possibly losing information.

ENCOURAGING CONVERSATION

Open-ended questions: By asking a series of questions in the early stages of an interview, you may be conditioning the subject to believe that if you want to know any information, you will be asked, no information is expected.

On the other hand, asking relatively few questions leading into a conversation will give the subject the feeling that everything he tells has significance. Any questioning of the subject's narrative is withheld until he has finished his story.

Typical of open-ended questions are general queries such as "Tell me what you saw"; "Can you tell me more about that?"; "What happened next?" These types of questions do not permit yes or no answers and allow for no misunderstanding of what the officer wants. The subject is forced to give a narrative in order to answer the question.

The use of the long pause: Sometimes during an interview, the subject will stop talking and a silence will descend on the room. To the inexperienced officer, this can be unnerving and cause the officer to lose control of the interview and start talking. Pauses in conversation are normal and are never as long in duration as they seem to be.

The subject is as ill at ease as you are during these silences, and the experienced officer will use these to advantage. Be patient and wait—many times the subject will resume talking and will frequently volunteer additional information just to break the silence.

Nondirective approach: The nondirective approach is a technique that turns the subject's statements into questions calling for more information. In using this method, simply repeat the subject's last phrase, but with a rising inflection on the last word so that it becomes a question.

During such an interview, control your emotions. Do not register surprise or anxiety, but merely restate the subject's statement. The effect of this technique is that further information is drawn out without giving direction or restricting the thinking as in direct questioning.

ENDING THE INTERVIEW

No interview should be abruptly terminated with a curt dismissal of "Thank you" or "OK," and so forth. When it is apparent that the interview is ending, close the conversation in a courteous and friendly manner. You may wish to summarize what has been said and ask the subject if there is anything else he/she wishes to add.

Let the subject know that you appreciate what he/she has done and that he/she has performed a valuable service. Thank the subject for their time and assistance. Treating the subject with concern and good manners will help in assuring that, should you or another officer need to speak with the subject in the future, the subject will be more cooperative and ready to assist instead of resist.

Recognition to Sgt. Steve Cloonan, Michigan State Police (Ret.) for assistance in development of this chapter.

SECURITY QUIZ
Interviewing Techniques

1. It is important for the protection officer to establish common _____ during an interview. (Fill in the blank.)
2. It is important for the protection officer to go into an interview with a game _____ in mind. (Fill in the blank.)
3. Leading questions have the same effect as _____ and _____ questions. (Fill in the blanks.)
4. By asking specific questions, the protection officer may divert or _____ the interview, rather than letting the subject give a narrative of the whole story. (Fill in the blank.)
5. Direct questions do not have a place in an interview.
    ☐ T ☐ F
6. Leading questions have the same effect as direct questions.
    ☐ T ☐ F
7. Any questioning of a subject's narrative need not wait until he has finished his story.
    ☐ T ☐ F
8. While conducting an interview, the witness stops talking. You should:
    ☐ (a) start talking yourself
    ☐ (b) tell the subject to start talking
    ☐ (c) be patient and wait
    ☐ (d) None of the above
9. During an interview using the nondirect approach, you should:
    ☐ (a) control your emotions
    ☐ (b) not register surprise
    ☐ (c) restate the subject's statement
    ☐ (d) All the above
10. Yes and no questions should be avoided because:
    ☐ (a) the subject may agree with you
    ☐ (b) the subject may not understand your question
    ☐ (c) the subject may disagree with you
    ☐ (d) All the above

INVESTIGATION: CONCEPTS AND PRACTICES FOR SECURITY PROFESSIONALS

By Christopher A. Hertig, CPP, CPOI

Investigation comes from the Latin word *investigere,* which means to track or trace (Bennett & Hess, 2001, p. 3). Investigation can take many forms—from the simple asking of a few questions and noting it in a report to the full-scale forensic examination. An unfortunate reality is that many people greatly underestimate the importance of investigation within the security field. Few texts on criminal investigation even mention private investigation or security investigation. Save for the obligatory treatment of Pinkerton, the texts are mute on the topic.

There seems to be a feeling that investigation is a highly specialized process that is performed only by police or supervisors. The popular image of private detectives who wear trench coats with their collars turned up and have cigarettes dangling from their lips has been created by the entertainment media. And it is reinforced by that same media. The public has been inundated over the years by movies and television. Perhaps it is rooted – at least in part – by a condescending attitude towards security officers. Security officers are, after all, "the Forgotten Soldiers of the Invisible Empire."

Whatever the cause(s); there needs to be a readjustment of attitudes by the public, managers, academics who write texts, and officers themselves. With the threat of terrorism and the proliferation of organized criminal groups, security personnel must become involved in the investigative process. And they need to be recognized for their contributions.

The fact of the matter is that investigation is performed each and every day by entry level protection officers as well as specialized investigators. The work of these persons rarely makes it onto the evening news. But it aids the asset protection process in innumerable ways. The contemporary protection officer acts as a management representative, A legal consultant, an enforcement agent, and an intelligence agent.

The roles of intelligence agent and legal consultant are perhaps most closely related to investigative activity. In the former role, the protection officer reports the presence of actual and *potential* loss-causing situations to management. In the legal consultant role, the officer must be conversant with the legal ramifications involved in searching persons, vehicles, and so on. They must appreciate the privacy considerations related to surveillance. They must understand the laws of evidence when conducting an investigation which may result in disciplinary or criminal action.

Investigation—from the simple to the complex—is "part and parcel" of what protection officers do. It is essential to acquiring information that may be useful in taking legal actions after a loss. It is also critical toward obtaining intelligence on organized criminal activity so that preventive actions can be taken.

Perhaps a start toward a better understanding is to see the scope of investigative activity that is performed by various entities.

INVESTIGATION TYPE	INVESTIGATING ENTITY
Criminal—felonies, misdemeanors, summary offenses, or ordinance violations	Police officers, protection officers, corporate investigators, state or federal agents, private investigative firms
Accident—work stoppage mishaps involved in production; slips and falls, vehicle accidents	Police officers, security officers, private investigators, insurance investigators, regulatory agency investigators (OSHA)
Personnel—violations of employer policy; may or may not be a crime or tort (civil offense)	Supervisory or managerial personnel, private investigators (undercover), corporate investigators, protection officers
Background—prior employment checks, criminal or credit checks done for hiring or promotion to sensitive positions or for bonding	Private investigative firms, human resources departments, corporate investigators, federal or state agency investigators

Investigations are performed by police, government agencies at the federal (FBI), state (attorney general's office), or local levels (municipal police). They are also performed by corporate staff—either investigators or supervisors—as well as private investigative firms. Most investigative activity is conducted "in-house" on a proprietary basis by and for the investigator's employer. Some are contracted out to private investigative agencies that are licensed to perform investigative services to another for a fee.

Private investigators can be useful if the client entity (corporation or government agency) does not have the expertise or manpower resources to conduct the inquiry. Some cases of complex financial inquiries or computer crime require the hiring of specialists. Undercover investigation is almost always outsourced. Insurance companies may use private investigators to conduct surveillance in areas where travel by a proprietary investigator would be impractical. Surveillance also requires some equipment; specialists in this field have the expensive equipment necessary for conducting difficult inquiries. Background screening firms are often used as they rely on local personnel to conduct records searches at courthouses. While some data can be obtained via computer, there is a real need for an old-fashioned hand search of records in many cases.

Private investigators must generally be licensed. They and their employees must meet regulatory standards often set by state agencies, which also regulate security officers. There may be restrictions on offering investigative or security services on a contractual basis without a license to do so. There may also be a requirement to work for only a single licensed firm at a time, or to carry an identification card, pay an annual registration fee, recertify by taking training periodically, and so on. The Fair Credit Reporting Act in the United States also places extensive requirements on third parties who conduct background investigations. It is important that persons working with investigative firms as employees or clients fully understand the legal requirements of such arrangements! In North America, the International Association of Security and Investigative Regulators lists state and provincial regulations on their Web site at **iasir.org.**

Investigation is an integral aspect of a protection officer's job functions.

Investigation and asset protection go hand-in-hand.

Uniformed protection officers on patrol or plainclothes loss prevention agents must be intimately familiar with their patrol environments. They must be able to discern when something isn't right. In many cases, unusual or unexplained situations indicate criminal activity. The investigating officer on patrol must be able to first recognize things that aren't quite right. This could be a vehicle parked in an unusual place, persons taking photographs, unusual trash disposal procedures, graffiti, hand gestures, clothing or "colors" worn around the area, persons conversing with others in an unusual way, etc. The list goes on and on. Each indicator could mean a variety of different things; terrorists or criminals conducting surveillance on a target, theft of materials, gang activity, or drug dealing.

One lesson of investigation is that major cases are solved via minor incidents. Murderers get caught parking illegally or shoplifting. While detectives and other investigative specialists may piece incidents together, it is the patrol officer who takes note of something and acts upon it that supplies the key information. Small observations often yield big results:

"Minor Is Major"

Along a similar vein, a review of accidents, terrorist attacks, or acts of workplace violence all have indicators that they are about to take place. After the unfortunate event has happened, it is often noted what all the cues, signs, or indicators were that should have been seen earlier. Perhaps better playing of the intelligence agent role is one means of taking corrective action before tragedy strikes.

In order to fulfill the intelligence agent role effectively, protection personnel must also be able to report what they observe in an articulate manner. They must "get it right" on paper. And they should always reinforce the written report with a verbal report to the appropriate personnel.

Investigation has nothing to do with attractive members of the opposite sex, great clothes, gunfights, or flashy cars. It is not glamorous. It is tedious and exacting. It has to do with *fact-finding* and *research*. **Investigation is simply an objective process used to discover facts about a situation, person, or behavior.** Once those facts are discovered, they are recorded in an appropriate manner. Investigation has a great deal to do with research; those who like to do Web or library research may acclimate themselves to investigative activity better than those who disdain research. Investigation requires precision and attention to detail. It culminates in writing reports about the known facts. These reports are the product of the investigation.

Investigation is important because without facts, management cannot make the correct decisions. As the security officer is an adjunct member of the management team, it is his/her duty to provide management with information. He/she reports this information after conducting some type of investigative activity (searching for something, questioning people, observing something, etc.).

INVESTIGATIVE LOGIC

Investigation is a logical, systematic process. Investigators use two types of logic: *inductive reasoning* and *deductive reasoning*. With inductive reasoning, a hypothesis is constructed about what has occurred. Facts are then gathered that either support it or reject it. There may be only a few "pieces of the puzzle" available so that the investigator must try and logically search for other "pieces." The investigator must look at what is most likely to have occurred so that investigative efforts are not wasted. Note that investigation often seeks to *narrow the focus of the inquiry*: instead of pursuing a vast array of possibilities, the investigator seeks to reduce them logically to a more manageable number. Inductive reasoning may aid in doing this. Inductive reasoning is also more likely to be used in intelligence analysis. When assessing intelligence information, it may be necessary to construct a theory about what may occur. A prediction of some sort must be made.

In deductive reasoning facts are collected. Next, a theory about what occurred is formulated. The "pieces of the puzzle" are obtained and put into place. The fictionalized Sherlock Holmes and the real-life Allan Pinkerton used deduction. Investigation of crimes, accidents, or work rule violations may be better served using deductive reasoning.

Each form of reasoning has its place. An investigative inquiry may begin with inductive reasoning and then become deductive. Investigators must always make sure that they are logical and objective. Investigators must never let their prejudices or preconceived notions interfere with their work. If exculpatory evidence—evidence which tends to disprove that the suspect committed the offense—is discovered, it cannot be ignored!

HISTORY

History teaches some important lessons regarding investigation, including the following:

1. **Writing and investigation go hand in hand.** Henry and John Fielding, Allan Pinkerton, and J. Edgar Hoover of the Federal Bureau of Investigation all published books. Henry Fielding wrote the famous novel *Tom Jones.* Henry and John Fielding also published the *Covent Garden Journa,l* which described wanted persons. Based on the ideas of Patrick Colquhoun, the *Covent Garden Journal* was similar to many Loss Prevention Department newsletters, *America's Most Wanted* television show, the "Crimestoppers" items placed in newspapers, and the FBI's tip line on the Internet. Pinkerton wrote about his detectives and in retirement wrote dime novels (these were popular forms of entertainment, comparable to contemporary videos or DVDs). Pinkerton is credited with starting the terms *sleuth* and *private eye,* which were popularized through his true life accounts of detective work as well as the fictionalized dime novels that he wrote.

2. **Advertising and media relations are essential for continued investigative success.** This seems to be true for public entities as well as private investigative firms that depend on direct customers for fees. The Fieldings published *The Covent Garden Journal.* Howard Vincent, an attorney who was placed in charge of Scotland Yard in 1878, had detectives who befriended the famous novelist Charles Dickens. Dickens wrote about detectives in his novels. Pinkerton used posters to advertise. These posters featured a large eye and the saying "We Never Sleep." John Edgar Hoover who ran the FBI from 1924 until 1972 had a weekly radio show and hired a publicist. It would appear that what the Fieldings started in terms of marketing/public relations were taken to new levels by Allan Pinkerton and J. Edgar Hoover.

3. **Reward systems tend to breed corruption.** Jonathan Wild, for whom the saying "It takes a thief to catch a thief" originated, worked under the Parliamentary Reward System. This system paid government rewards to those who captured felons. Wild also received a percentage of the value of stolen property returned to clients. He used the Parliamentary Reward System to great effect. He would have an associate steal the property, collect the fee from the client for its return, and perhaps turn in the associate and get the Parliamentary Reward. In America, private detectives used criminal informants extensively and collected rewards. They were the predecessors of municipal police detectives, who also collected rewards. Allan Pinkerton forbade his agents from obtaining rewards, even though in the mid to latter 19th century, municipal police detectives in the United States commonly did so. Present-day civil demand in retailing can be thought of as a type of reward system. A civil demand letter is sent to apprehended shoplifters requiring them to pay a fee under fear of civil suit. This may create ethics issues: is the Loss Prevention Department in existence to prevent loss or gain profit from the fees collected from shoplifters?

4. **Ethics is crucial to success.** Individuals and organizations that don't have good ethics may profit initially, but in the long run they fail. The same is true of investigators and investigative organizations. Jonathan Wild was hanged. Allan Pinkerton's firm became the largest investigative and security firm in the world. And it is still around after 150 years.

5. **New markets and new investigative services must be explored.** Whether the customer is internal as with a proprietary security department or external as with a private investigative agency; it is essential to envision the needs of end users. Currently background investigations are being used by more and more organizations. Certainly computer and internet crime are growing concerns; some firms are moving into that market. The key question is

"What investigative services could our organization offer that it currently does not?"

PRELIMINARY INVESTIGATIONS

This is the most important aspect of the investigative process. It is also the investigative stage that security personnel (or uniformed police officers) generally get involved with. The preliminary investigation is the initial fact-finding component of the investigative process. It is performed when the crime or incident is first discovered and is crucial to the success of the follow-up investigative effort. Preliminary investigation consists of several key steps.

1. **Attending to injured persons.** This must be the first priority!
2. **Detaining those who have committed the crime.**
3. **Finding and questioning witnesses.** A neighborhood canvass of the area to seek out witnesses should be performed as soon as possible.

4. **Preserving the crime/incident scene for evidentiary purposes.** *Protect, preserve, make notes!* Control access to the scene, take photographs, and note observations.

5. **Forwarding information about the incident to the dispatcher, central alarm station (CAS), or the shift supervisor.**

6. **Completing a preliminary report so that the follow-up investigators have** *adequate information* **with which to proceed.**

FOLLOW-UP INVESTIGATION

This step in the process begins where the preliminary investigation ends. It is a process of examining the information provided by the preliminary report and proceeding to uncover additional data until the case is solved - a complete understanding of the event is attained.

Obviously, the success of the follow-up investigation is heavily dependent upon the preliminary investigative effort. Without adequate records, evidence or witnesses, little or nothing can be determined, even if the follow-up investigator is extraordinarily proficient.

Follow-up investigations may be completed by the officer who performed the preliminary investigation, but in most cases they are handled by investigative specialists, police detectives, or supervisory personnel. For this reason, close liaison must exist between those conducting the preliminary investigation and these with follow-up investigative duties.

INTELLIGENCE

Intelligence is information, data, facts regarding current, past, or future events or associations. Intelligence collection can be thought of as a part of the follow-up phase of investigation. However, in many cases, intelligence is collected as an ongoing process, not after a specific event. One reason for collecting intelligence is to be proactive; to be able to see problems developing rather than investigating them after they have occurred. Protection officers play several key roles. One of them is the "intelligence agent" role. In order to perform this role effectively, officers must do the following:

1. Be observant.
2. Know what to observe.
3. Report the information in an effective manner.

Being observant is self-explanatory. Alert, attentive patrol officers will gather information. Inattentive ones will not.

Knowing what to observe comes from being properly trained and socialized by management. It also includes ongoing professional development such as knowing the signs and colors of local gangs, the types of drugs that are being distributed, and the indications that extremist groups who may resort to acts of terror are in the area (handbills, graffiti, and the observation of extremists congregating together). Educational sessions sponsored by local police are a good way of keeping up to date on these topics. So too is reading professional literature.

Proper reporting is essential. Good writing skills are part of this. Proper management of the information within an intelligence system is another key component.

A structured, highly developed intelligence process consists of the following steps:

1. **A need to collect the information is identified.** No information should ever be collected until a demonstrated need for it exists. There must be a clear connection between collecting the information and the protection of assets. There must also be a management decision to begin the collection; there must be a policy regarding it. In very simple terms, management will instruct protection officers on what type of information they are to collect as part of the "intelligence agent" role that they play.

2. **The actual collection process.** This is where the observations of protection officers and investigators comes in. It is also where data searches are performed and information from other agencies is obtained. In order to be effective, the collection process cannot be impeded by having protection officers involved in too many tasks so that they don't take the time to notice things or the care to report them. Officers must also receive positive feedback from managers regarding their observations. An additional concern here is the liaison that is conducted with other organizations. It must be positive and productive.

3. **The information is evaluated and collated or organized.** The information is evaluated to determine if it is worthwhile and correct. It must be timely. It should be verified. It is filed in an organized manner and collated so that it can be compared with other information. The establishment of files for cross referencing is important. Without this step, information is not referenced with other bits of data and "the pieces of the puzzle" don't get matched together. The use of computerized data systems such as the PPM2000 report writing software aids this effort.

4. **The information is analyzed and interpreted.** The meaning of the information is determined. After collation of the data, a professional intelligence officer will make a hypothesis on what the data means.

5. **The information is disseminated.** The information is given to authorized users within the organization or to external agencies. This must be done in accordance with policy and based on a "need-to-know."

6. **The information is reevaluated.** Intelligence and the process used to collect and analyze it are reviewed. This is the "feedback loop" of the intelligence cycle. This enables the process to be improved upon.

Robert Metscher's chapter on investigations in *Security Supervision: Theory and Practice of Asset Protection* (Elsevier Science) provides useful information on establishing intelligence files.

LIAISON

In many—if not most—cases, investigative efforts are undertaken in cooperation with other organizations. A simple example is counterfeiting. The problem is discovered by a teller or cashier who notices a suspect bill. The teller or cashier contacts a manager and/or the security department. Next, the local police and United States Secret Service are brought in. Each plays a role; counterfeit currency is not simply the domain of the U.S. Secret Service. Another example would be an accident in a parking lot. Security and maintenance would be involved. If there are injuries, local emergency medical services and police are called. In the wake of the accident, there may be an investigation by an insurance company. Many investigations involve more than one organization.

In order to be effective; liaison with other organizations must be developed *and* maintained. During the development phase of liaison, it is important to note the following:

1. Understand the role and purpose of each organization. This begins with the employing organization! Protection officers or investigators who do not know their employers mission statements or philosophies are in trouble to begin with! Once this is done, the external organization is studied. Their mission statements, goals, and philosophies note that with a contractual relationship—security service firms working for a client entity—he entire scenario becomes more complex. Employer, client firm, *and* external agency must all be studied.

2. Examine the capabilities of each organization. With the flow of funding, these are in a constant state of flux. Determine what specific services each is capable of offering to the other. Surveillance equipment, surveillance locations, vehicles, software, and so on.

3. Meet with and get to know the key persons in other organizations. For a protection officer, this may be the local police officers and their sergeant. For an investigator, it may be his or her counterparts with different organizations. For a manager, it would be the agency heads. The major point is to develop a comfort level for working with the people from different organizations.

4. Consider meetings or joint training exercises, or hosting seminars that various organizations can attend. In many cases, corporations have conference rooms and other resources that can be used by external entities. Informal "talking shop" is fostered at these fact-to-face get-togethers. Informal intelligence exchange occurs.

Once a liaison is developed, it must be maintained. The need for a positive working relationship with an outside agency cannot be overstated. Such a relationship requires continuous care to maintain.

1. Be respectful. Ask how you can help. Oftentimes protection officers can perform simple tasks for outside investigators such as holding the end of a tape measure at an accident scene.

2. Get to know people individually. Introducing oneself with local police and other investigators is a start toward building a trusting relationship.

3. Know the law! One way of doing this is to ask police and government investigators questions. An investigator who works a specific area of investigation (identity theft, auto theft, check fraud, etc.) usually knows the legal aspects of the offense.

4. Know policy! Complying with employer policy is necessary. Appreciating another organization's rules and values is also important.

5. Protect incident scenes effectively. Providing another agency with a safe, secure, sterile scene from which to carry on their inquiry is critical.

6. Be proficient at preliminary investigation. If calling on local police detectives to initiate a follow-up investigation; providing them with a quality, *professional*, starting point is a necessity.

7. Be proficient at case presentation and testifying effectively. Being able to present a case effectively is important as it is the culmination of an investigation. Deficiencies at this juncture can sour relations between cooperating agencies.

8. Keep the other agency informed. Keep them "in the loop."

9. Provide external agencies with resources as appropriate. Accommodate their needs for working space, phone lines, etc. A police department doing an interview or interrogation may need to use a conference room. They may also need to review surveillance tapes from CCTVs. There are also equipment needs that can be met such as loaning vehicles, surveillance equipment, and so on to police agencies.

10. Joint training sessions or seminars are an excellent way of both growing professionally and developing closer working relationships with other investigators.

11. Consider joining law enforcement or investigative organizations. Having membership in a professional or social organization that local police also belong to may be an effective way of forming a bond with them.

NOTES AND REPORTS

Notes are the *foundation* of a report. It is sometimes said that testifying—the *last* step in the investigative process —*begins* with note taking. Without adequate notes on the crucial details, there can be no effective report, follow-up investigation, or testimony. Reports are what make or break investigators. They are the summation of the investigator's or protection officer's work. The saying **"You are what you write."** is very true. Here are some key points on note-taking and report writing.

- Think of notes as aids in remembering key details. Don't think of them as another chore to do.
- Headings should be placed at the beginning of notes so that the notes are organized. The type of incident, date, time, and place can be recorded first at the top of

the notes. This keeps the notes organized. This same principle applies to notes taken during classes!

- Start each set of notes on a new page. Also make sure to skip a few lines after each entry so that additional information can be added. This also applies to notes taken in classes!
- Always have a notebook available; even if tape recorders or computerized systems are being used; old-fashioned paper and pencil are needed as backup and supporting note-taking aids.
- Periodically check notes. Summarize what is written to witnesses giving statements so that you are sure to get the information correctly recorded. This should always be done at the conclusion of an interview; it can also be done at various junctures throughout the interview process.
- Use abbreviations judiciously. If they are commonly known abbreviations, use them. Make certain that the abbreviation used is correct and that anyone reading the notes would understand it. **"If there is any doubt, spell it out."**
- Use rough sketches in notes to pictorially represent incident scenes. Simple, hand drawn figures can aid in making the notes useful later on.
- **Treat notes as the part of the official record that they are.** Start each set of notes on a new page. Number each page. Write in ink and cross out and initial each correction that must be made. The best evidence rule requires that the original, best and highest quality of proof must be used in legal proceedings. For this reason, original notes should be maintained.

AUDITING

Auditing is something in which loss control personnel should be involved. An audit is simply a check (or investigation) as to whether or not operations are proceeding as expected. There are operations audits which determine if procedures are being followed as well as financial audits to see if there are any fiscal irregularities. Audits can take many forms, depending upon the organization's present need.

- Security officers audit locks and alarms to maintain the integrity of the physical security system. They may also do audits of the fire protection system or of safety procedures on a weekly/monthly/quarterly basis.
- Security supervisors audit reports, procedures, personnel performance, and training/certification records of protection officers to ensure that things are being done the way they are supposed to be.
- Both contract and proprietary security managers audit policies, procedures, and training records to see that services are being properly given to client firms.
- Increasingly, we will see managers and supervisors auditing for compliance with standard setting organizations, such as government agencies and insurance carriers. Also, professional organizations, such as the Joint Commission on the Accreditation of Healthcare Organizations, International Association of Campus Law Enforcement Administrators and others will establish sets of standards. As the security industry professionalizes, such developments are inevitable.
- Accountants and/or fraud examiners perform financial audits of records such as payroll, accounts receivable, purchasing, or petty cash.
- Forensic accountants may review individual points of sale in retail facilities, parking garages, restaurants, or bars.

Audits enable the auditor to spot irregularities. This can mean a lack of commitment to proper work procedures caused by inadequate training, poor supervision, or demoralized jobholders. It may mean that the level of service being given by the organization is not up to standard and changes are necessary! It can also signal attempts at thefts, completed thefts, or simply the presence of the opportunity to commit thefts. Audits are often the starting point of an investigation; the basic leads being uncovered during routine audits. In other cases, they are part of the follow-up investigation. In these instances, the investigator needs to either expand or narrow the focus of the inquiry. Conducting an audit can help to make this determination. Additionally, they can be part of a corrective approach taken to remedy any problems that have been uncovered.

When conducting an audit, there are several important points to remember.

1. Compare what is being audited (job behavior, procedures, or conditions, etc.) with clearly defined, measurable standards. These can be written instructions, procedures, post orders, and so on. The analysis of the job behavior (e.g., not signing in visitors), procedure (price checks on merchandise) or condition, (e.g., faulty alarms) must be *objective*. It cannot simply be the auditor's professional opinion.
2. Communicate the purpose of audits to all employees. Obtain the positive cooperation of those who have input into the audit process.
3. Conduct audits in a fair and uniform manner with a set standard that relates to everyone and is used to evaluate everyone.
4. Utilize a variety of techniques. Each technique gives the investigator a specific type of information. Each provides the auditor with a particular perspective. Use a combination of techniques to see the whole picture.
5. Document the results of audits. Professional reports are essential.
6. Evaluate and review audits with relevant personnel. An exit briefing is one means of doing this. In an exit briefing, the auditor briefly discusses his or her findings with management prior to the submission of a complete report. This gives management rapid feedback upon which to make necessary modifications.

7. Follow the chain of command, be tactful, and make sure the information gets to the right people, and only those people.

As with any type of investigation, there are a variety of approaches to auditing. Each approach has its strengths and weaknesses; each has its time and place. Some that may be of use include:

1. Document review by either systematic (every document in a set) or random selection (a sample of documents in a set).
2. Deliberate error technique where an error is deliberately made to see if it is detected. An example would be a mispriced item at a point of sale (POS) terminal.
3. Drills are good ways to evaluate the performance of both systems and personnel. These must be done safely and in such a manner that they are not overly disruptive! In most cases, drills can be "compartmentalized" so that someone only needs to describe (orally or in writing) the procedures to be followed. Another method is to have the scenario limited to a single department or unit. Full-scale scenarios are often not feasible—even though exercises involving the entire protection operation and outside agencies is the best "final examination" possible for a security system.
4. Observation of job behavior or systems is a simple technique which can still provide useful information. This can be with the unaided eye or by reviewing videotape (openly taken) of someone performing job tasks.
5. Interviewing personnel is a method which may be used to investigate practices. In addition to one-on-one interviews, survey forms can be used.
6. A conference held with supervisors is a technique often used by managers to investigate workplace, problems, practices, and procedures. This can be scheduled with regular supervisor meetings or as a separate meeting prior to an external audit by a government agency or accrediting body.

INTERVIEWS

The conducting of interviews is something that security officers do all the time. In many cases, these interviews are conducted informally. Whether formal or informal, *an interview is a conversation with the objective of obtaining information.* Loss control practitioners who are adept at their jobs can collect information from every conversation. Here are some basic rules of interviewing.

1. Be pleasant, friendly, and helpful to the interviewee. They are taking their time out to help you!
2. Thank people for their help and always end an interview on a positive note. Providing them with a business card to contact you with if they can think of anything else is a positive way to continue the relationship.
3. Ask open-ended questions that require an explanation rather than a simple yes or no answer. "Can you tell me

what you saw?" or "Could you describe that?" are examples of open-ended questions.
4. Use silence ("the long pause") after the person has answered a question. Most people will feel obligated to continue the conversation and add more detail.
5. Interview in private—to the greatest extent practical; a quiet, relaxed, private setting will yield more information. The interviewee must feel comfortable. They cannot be distracted by noise or activity.
6. Be approachable and friendly. Pleasant people are easy to talk to; astute protection professionals are approachable and can gain the trust of people. Put the person at ease with a smile, joke, or off-the-subject questions (sports, family, current events). Also make the person comfortable; offer them a seat and sit next to them (picture the seating arrangements that TV talk show host use). This helps to establish rapport.
7. Take notes in a manner that records the key data but does not impede the interview by making the interviewee uncomfortable. Oftentimes, note taking should take place after the incident has been related by the witness. Going over the information again and taking notes on it often does not upset the interviewee's comfort level.
8. Summarizing and then taking notes may help. The interviewee may add information that was previously overlooked. It is also a good way to make sure that all the information is correct. It is in effect, an audit of the interview.

INTERROGATION

Interrogations are different from interviews in that an interrogation is an interview which focuses upon a person as a suspect. It is conducted after a substantial amount of information from other sources indicates guilt of an individual. Interrogations are conversations with the purpose of acquiring information, but with the obtaining of admissions or guilt or a full confession from the subject as the final objective. They are *focused interviews.* They should not be conducted by inexperienced and untrained individuals! Investigative specialists should be performing them. Unfortunately, there are instances where a protection officer without extensive information may come upon someone committing a crime or policy violation. In these cases a brief focused interview is appropriate.

These are some interrogation techniques.

1. **Be nonaccusatory.** Do not blame or accuse the subject. If the facts are wrong and they are not guilty, there is an obvious problem. Additionally, setting up a hostile relationship does no good. The investigator must "sell" the subject on telling the truth.
2. **Discuss the seriousness of the incident with the person being interrogated.** This is helpful in those cases where the individual falsely believes that they can act with impunity, that it is "no big deal."

3. **Request that the subject tell the story several tines.** Inconsistencies can be better noted in this way.

4. **Appeal to the emotions of the subject.** Let him/her know that everybody makes mistakes. Allow the subject to *rationalize* what they have done. Allow them to *minimize* the harm that has occurred. Allow them to *project* blame onto someone or something else.

5. **Point out inconsistencies in the story to the subject.** This is better done later in the interview. Anything done to make the interviewee defensive should be used as a last resort.

6. **Confront the subject with part of the evidence.** Be careful!

There are various legal restrictions active during interrogation. Basically, these standards do not allow any use of force, threats, or intimidation. The **Miranda** decision required all law enforcement personnel in the United States to advise suspects of their rights before asking them any questions which focus upon them as the suspect and which are asked in a "custodial" setting. Failure to follow these procedures will result in all evidence obtained via the illegal questioning being excluded from criminal proceedings (the Exclusionary Rule).

While in most states, private security personnel are not bound to the Miranda decision, a few courts have placed this obligation upon them. All U.S. courts place Miranda standards on private individuals who are acting at the direction, request of, or in close cooperation with public law enforcement personnel. Obviously Miranda relates if the security officer has any type of police powers. Such officers are in fact, agents of the government.

Another standard that the United States Supreme Court imposed upon employers is the **Weingarten Rule**. Under Weingarten, any time that an interview is held with an employee that could *reasonably be expected* to result in disciplinary action, the employee is entitled to representation by a union steward or another individual. This rule is limited to those employees who are represented by a collective bargaining unit. Failure to comply will result in an unfair labor practice charge being filed through the National Labor Relations Board. Discipline imposed as a result of the illegal interview may be set aside in an arbitration hearing. Employees that have been terminated may be reinstated and given back pay for the time that they were off.

While unlike Miranda in that management is not obligated to advise the employee of this right; once the employee asks for a representative (union steward or coworker), the interview must cease until the representative arrives—provided the representative is reasonably available. Employees cannot ask for a rep on vacation simply to avoid being interviewed. In these cases, the interview may proceed without the representative present. Alternatively, the interview may cease. Employees can be told that management will take action with the facts that they have. As a general rule, it is best not to force an interview with anyone!

MIRANDA	WEINGARTEN
Police interrogation of suspects in a custodial setting.	Employer questioning of employees concerning violations of employer rules.
Warnings are required before questioning.	Warning is not required—the employee must make the request for the representative.
An attorney is the representative of the accused.	A union steward or interested coworker is the representative; not an attorney.
The Exclusionary Rule prohibits statements made in violation of the law from being used in a criminal proceeding.	An unfair labor practice charge may be filed; this may result in the setting aside of discipline.

There are legal obligations to caution persons being interrogated. There are also other considerations to be addressed within the legal arena. As a general rule, the following procedures can save security practitioners a considerable amount of trouble in court:

1. **Review the case thoroughly before starting the interrogation.** The more that is known about the incident or scheme, the better. This is where good preliminary investigation comes into play.

2. **Interrogate in private, but remove all possible suggestions of duress, such as weapons, locked doors, and intimidating individuals from the environment.**

3. **Avoid making threats or promises.**

4. **Never physically touch a subject!**

5. **If the subject is of the opposite sex, do not question alone.** Have a member of the same sex present.

6. **Advise the suspect of his/her rights, if there is any chance of an obligation to do so.**

7. **Have the suspect sign each page of the statement and initial all corrections.** (There should be some corrections so that the integrity of the document can be clearly demonstrated in court).

8. **Have someone witness the statement.**

9. **Use the statement as supporting evidence; not the entire case!** Corroborate the statement with other evidence. Back it up as much as possible.

10. **Make sure the statement is in the subject's own words; that it is dated and signed.**

INFORMANTS

Informants are a key tool in many types of investigation. Often informants provide basic leads that alert loss control personnel to the presence of a problem. They are of particular importance when investigating the activities of a social network such as substance abuse, sabotage, gambling, and internal theft investigations. There are several kinds of informants operating under different types of motivation.

1. A desire to assist the investigator, either through public spiritedness or a feeling of indebtedness to the investigator.
2. A need to "play cop" and act like the police.
3. Revenge against a criminal competitor such as a rival drug dealer.
4. Manipulation of the investigator. This is common with criminal informants; they are called "cons" for a reason!
5. Financial gain such as the collecting of rewards from the investigator.
6. The investigator "having them over a barrel" and the informant wants leniency from charges.

Investigators using informants should try and understand the informant's motivation. They should investigate their background and fully comprehend any and all relationships that they have had with the subjects. One can never be too careful with informants. These are some tips for dealing with informants.

1. **Treat all informants with dignity and respect.** While most informants are good people, the occasional criminal informant will also be used for leads/information. Avoid using demeaning terms to describe informants; they perform a valuable service! Also, the use of such terms is hardly professional.
2. **Keep informants "at arm's length."** Avoid close personal involvement with them. Many informants are master manipulators who attempt to obtain confidential information from the investigator.
3. **Closely evaluate the value of the information that has been given by them.** Be vigilant against attempts to mislead the investigator or exaggerate the importance of the information they have provided.
4. **Attempt to verify through independent sources the accuracy of the information.** Don't rely solely on the information that an informant provides to build a case for prosecution! Corroborate with other evidence.
5. **Keep a "tight rein" on the informant; don't let them represent themselves as members of the security or police organization.** Don't allow them to do anything that is unauthorized or illegal. Some informants perceive that they have some sort of license to commit crimes!
6. **Take care of the legitimate needs of the informant.** Assist them when possible in finding work, transportation, child care, and so forth.

7. **"Telephone tipsters" should be kept on the line as long as possible!** They should be *interviewed.* They should NOT be given any confidential information. They should be thanked and asked to call back in the future if they have any additional information.

UNDERCOVER INVESTIGATIONS

Occasionally there arises the need for an undercover investigator. Generally there is no need for them except when other techniques (surveillance, informants, etc.) have failed to yield information or when the special perspective available to an undercover operative is needed.

Undercover investigation is a very expensive and risky method to use! There are numerous problems that can occur during an undercover investigation. For this reason, it should not be used unless it is absolutely necessary. **It should only be performed by competent professionals who specialize in this type of work.** The proper training, education, and experience are necessary to prepare the agent for the role they will be playing. The proper supervision and control over the agent is essential to ensure that the overall operation is effective. Controls need to be in place to reduce the risk of danger and legal problems from arising.

In order to use undercover investigation to the greatest advantage, the following considerations must be weighed:

1. **The objectives of the investigation must be clearly defined.** Management must know exactly what information is required and for what purpose the investigative effort will be initiated.
2. **The entire situation must be carefully weighed from all perspectives (legal, labor relations, economic, operational).** UC investigations can easily cause more serious problems than they rectify!
3. **Strict confidentiality on a "need to know" basis must be maintained.** Many operations are compromised due to the persons being investigated finding out about it.
4. **The proper agent must be selected.** They must have the necessary job skills to fit in with the work environment. They must be sociable and dedicated enough to see things through when difficult decisions (turning in friends, accompanying suspects during illegal activities, staying on the job when illegal activities are not occurring) must be made. Simply "looking the part" is not enough.
5. **Liaison with law enforcement agencies for the purpose of gathering information or prosecuting suspects must be done.** This can compromise the agent. It can also create numerous other problems if not done properly. Always assess the goals and objectives of the organization a liaison is being affected with so that conflicts are kept to a minimum.
6. **Corroborate the agent's testimony with other evidence.** Agents may not be credible with arbitrators, judges, or juries!

SHOPPING SERVICES

Shopping services are a type of "short-term undercover" inquiry where the investigator poses as a shopper. They are designed to achieve the following purposes:

1. **Uncover criminal or unauthorized activity.** Sometimes called "honesty shopping"; this may involve making purchases and observing what the cashier/waitress/bartender does with the money. Attempts to under-ring a point-of-sale terminal, pocket money, etc., are noted. Other investigations may audit how items are priced, how return merchandise is handled, or items without price tags are processed.
2. **Assess customer service and employee efficiency.** This involves "shopping" a location and seeing how attentive the sales personnel are to customers.

Shopping can be done by specialized investigative firms or in some cases on a proprietary basis. In the latter instance, a manager from another store may be used. This provides an expert view on how things are supposed to be done.

SURVEILLANCE

Surveillance is an essential investigative activity to loss control practitioners. It can be stationary ("plant" or "stake-out"), mobile, or contact (electronic tracking devices or invisible dyes). There are various objectives that surveillance can accomplish.

1. Identify suspects in a crime.
2. Record the movements and associations of suspects.
3. Identify patterns of criminal or unauthorized activity.
4. Collect information for prosecution.
5. Locate and apprehend suspects.
6. Prevent crimes from being committed. This can be done via overt or covert surveillance.

Once objectives have been identified, the planning process can begin. The entire planning process consists of the following steps:

1. **Establish the objective of the surveillance.** Write a clear, concise sentence as to why the investigator is doing the surveillance. What is the purpose behind the investigation?
2. **Reconnoiter the area that the surveillance will be conducted in.** Examine it for avenues of entry and exit as well as vantage points from which to observe. There should be several of these!
3. **Collect as much information as possible on the background(s) of subject(s).** The more known about the person being observed; the better. Having a firm idea of the person's appearance is essential to ensuring that the right person is being surveilled. Knowing the person's habits or potential for danger is also critical.
4. **Calculate the manning requirements.** A minimum of two (2) people will be needed if the surveillance lasts for any appreciable period of time or if there is danger present.
5. **Establish communication.** Cell phones, radios, and phone booths as a backup method can all be used. Security and continuity of communication is essential!
6. **Calculate equipment needs.** Equipment may consist of binoculars, videotape units, log or report forms, possibly weapons, and disguises such as hats, coats, and glasses.

If surveillance operations are planned properly, the chances for success are much higher. As the costs of initiating surveillance activities are high, it certainly behooves the loss control investigator to carefully scrutinize all aspects of the operation before precious time and money are wasted. Special attention must be devoted to communications and the response to incidents. Investigators must decide what may occur and how they will react to it. When this is considered, manning and equipment needs can be addressed in a logical manner.

Recording of activity observed during a surveillance must be done with care. The following is a sample outline for a surveillance log:

Location/objective (an introductory paragraph should be written):
Date:
Time (all activity occurring at a specific point in time is detailed):
Attachments (photographs, sketches, etc.):
Summary (brief concluding comments on observations):

BEHAVIOR CONDITION ANALYSIS

Another tool that investigators can use is behavior analysis. Whenever there is a crime or accident, the behavior of the perpetrator and/or victim can be examined and analyzed. The behavior can be divided into three segments.

1. **The behavior that occurred before the incident.** This can provide valuable insight into the criminal method of operation *and* can also be used for analyzing vulnerability. A better understanding of what took place can be developed and future prevention efforts can be more effectively developed. Examples of this might be the approach/entry used by a robber at the target. What protection was given to the target? Who would know what the target was? Who would be attracted to that type of target ("score")? What kind of insurance coverage was held by the victim? When applied to crimes or accidents, contributing factors to the event can be identified. What was the physical, mental, and emotional condition of the victim? What was the lighting and noise level in the environment? Would anyone gain by making a false report? What was the victim doing at the crime/accident scene?
2. **The actual incident itself.** What actually took place during the robbery? What did the robber say and do? What happened during the accident? What did the burglar do when inside the premises (the burglar's "prowl")?

3. **The behavior immediately after the incident should be identified and examined.** How did the robber make his escape? Where did the burglar exit from? How was the accident handled? What did the victim or perpetrator say? Who reported it? To whom was it reported? When was it reported?

Once all the behaviors in an incident are identified, it becomes much easier to analyze and understand the incident. Developing a list of questions for each phase of the event also helps to unfold lines of inquiry and perform a more complete investigation. While this technique is commonly used to investigate robbery, burglary, and homicide, there is no reason to limit its application to these types of cases. Embezzlement, passing bad checks, credit card fraud, accidents, bombings, fires, and chemical spills can all be dissected in this manner. Behavioral analysis aids in understanding the human factors in a loss event.

TESTIFYING IN LEGAL AND QUASI-LEGAL PROCEEDINGS

Once a case has been investigated, it may become necessary to present it in a court, disciplinary hearing, or labor arbitration. Officers are also called upon to give depositions in civil suits. **In many cases, the officer will testify in several different legal arenas; one never knows precisely where an incident will be decided!** Each of these proceedings has a different format and takes place in a different environment, but all require the providing of factual information in a professional manner. Each of these proceedings places the officer on the opposing side of the defendant, plaintiff, and so on. It is usually "your word against his." It is a "credibility battle." **During these proceedings, the successful investigator does everything possible to win the "battle of credibility."**

Here are some things to bear in mind when testifying in court.

1. **Always be positive.** Project a positive, affirmative image. Sell yourself to the judge, magistrate, jury, and so on.

2. **Be neat, clean, and conservatively dressed, as if you were going on a job interview.** Project a businesslike, professional image. Avoid dressing or talking like a cop or a soldier.

3. **Sit and stand erect with shoulders squared.** Face and look at the jury and judge. Be serious! You are accountable for what you say.

4. **Project your voice to the jury or judge.** Maintain eye contact with them. Address them when you're talking to them. Project your voice to the person farthest from you. This will ensure that you are heard by everyone who needs to hear you.

5. **Answer "yes" or "no" to questions posed by counsel or the judge.** Don't clarify or elaborate on you're answers unless it is necessary to do so. If you must clarify a point, choose your words carefully and know what you're going to say before you open your mouth. Consider before the proceeding what questions may be asked!

6. **Have the case prepared before trial.** Any reports or evidence presented must be carefully prepared. Consult counsel about the case beforehand to ensure that preparation is adequate. Go over the case, review evidence, and plan a strategy with the guidance of counsel. Review your notes before the proceeding starts.

7. **Any notes or reports taken to the stand may be examined by the opposing attorney.** Be critical of and careful with notes for this reason. Don't simply read from notes; consult them only if necessary. Don't take something that could cause embarrassment and a loss of credibility. Be critical of notes and reports!

8. **Avoid any show of sarcasm, conceit, or disgust with the defendant.** Be objective and unemotional. Don't be afraid to say something positive about the defendant.

9. **Never try to argue with the judge or attorney.** Be polite and professional, addressing them appropriately as "Sir," "Ma'am," or "Your Honor." Find out how to properly address them beforehand.

10. **If unsure as to what occurred, say so.** Don't be afraid to admit you don't know something or aren't sure. If you are sure, state so in a positive, affirmative manner. Try to avoid saying "I think" or any other expression which displays uncertainty.

11. **If you don't understand a question, ask that it be repeated or say that you simply don't understand it.**

12. **Don't be afraid to admit that you're wrong and be honest in all matters.**

13. **Critique your performance so that future testimony can be improved upon.** Experience is a good "teacher" for giving testimony. Look at every occasion as a learning experience. Don't be afraid to watch others testify or to ask for critiques from others on your testimony.

MANAGING INVESTIGATIONS

Just as investigation is an integral part of management, so too is management an essential element within the investigative process. If the investigative effort is not carefully controlled, man-hours will be wasted, confidentiality may be compromised, and objectives will not be met.

To begin with, the individual investigator must have personal management skills. He or she must set objectives, make daily priorities, and manage time effectively. Proper filing and administration of records is important. Critically evaluating one's work is crucial.

In an organizational sense, investigations must be managed by a series of procedures and controls. These are some of the techniques that should be considered when supervising an investigation.

1. Selecting and assigning investigators properly. Only the most qualified and efficient personnel should be entrusted with investigative duties. Individual cases should be assigned in accordance with the individual expertise of the investigator.
2. Investigators must be properly trained in the basics of investigation (interviewing, report writing, surveillance, interrogations, etc.) before assuming investigative responsibilities. They must also be trained in specialized areas (narcotics, fraud, espionage, undercover, etc.) should they be assigned these investigative duties. Training needs must be analyzed carefully. Periodic upgrading must be done in regards to legal and technological development.
3. All investigations should have clearly defined objectives. These objectives should be observable and measurable. The effectiveness of the investigative effort can be gauged by assessing whether or not the objective was met, how quickly it was met, and what the total cost in man-hours expended and other expenses were.
4. Case work sheets should be designed to meet the needs of individual organizations. These forms list dates, investigator's names, case numbers, persons contacted, time invested, expenses, and results of contacts. Their efficient design and utilization is a must for the investigative effort to be properly administered in a cost-effective manner.
5. Forms for efficiently reviewing reports can also be used to great effect. These forms enable supervisors to objectively audit reports submitted by security officers or investigators. Their use helps to streamline the investigative process while at the same time ensuring that errors are caught early enough to prevent disaster.
6. Coordination of the investigation with persons who have a "need to know" is important. Law enforcement agencies and victims should be kept informed of the progress of the investigation for several reasons, such as maintaining supportive relationships and receiving additional information. Special concern must be given to the victim who needs moral support and a clear explanation of judicial procedure if they are to feel comfortable with seeing through the prosecution process.

Investigations can be supervised and evaluated through a number of techniques. As with auditing, no single technique is adequate to provide a complete assessment. Using several methods in concert with each other provides the best results.

1. Statistical analysis of numbers of apprehensions, conviction rates, recovery amounts, and numbers of complaints against the investigator can also be used as an indicator of job performance.
2. On-the-job visits can always be used as a technique. Good supervisors are "coaches" to their subordinates. As an assessment method, it is limited in effectiveness and lacks objectivity; it *must* be used in conjunction with other evaluative methods.
3. Review of investigative reports. This gives the supervisor a "quick feel" for how the investigator is performing.

CONCLUSION

Investigation and asset protection are interrelated functions. Neither can exist in any real sense without the other. The contemporary protection officer serves as an intelligence agent for management. As such, he or she is tasked with collecting and reporting all manner of information on potential loss causing conditions. Information relating to crimes, accidents, and unethical/unprofessional practices has traditionally been collected by protection officers. Contemporary concerns with terrorism mandate that intelligence relating to potential terrorist activities be collected. Future officers will probably perform more auditing functions designed to catch errors and minimize waste.

In most cases, protection officers are involved in performing preliminary investigations. As the preliminary investigation is the most important phase of the investigative process, it is essential that it be conducted in a professional manner. This ensures that both security management and public police agencies can uncover facts necessary for the completion of their respective missions.

With increasing privatization, it is likely that a greater proportion of investigative tasks will be performed by private investigative agencies and proprietary security departments. Driving forces for privatization are decreased budgets for public agencies and the need for specialized expertise. Public police agencies will probably contract out for various types of investigative services in the future more than at present. Investigative functions not currently envisioned will be carried out by both proprietary and contract security organizations.

Proficiency and future growth and development in Investigation depend on a mastery of the basic skills. Protective service professionals must master interviews (*every conversation is an interview*), note taking (edit and review notes at various stages of the investigation), and report writing (*"you are what you write"*). Efforts must also extend to testifying in legal and quasi-legal proceedings. Effective oral communication skills are a necessity if cases are to be presented effectively. They are also integral to the development of a professional image and more productive relations with management, police, clients, and the public at large.

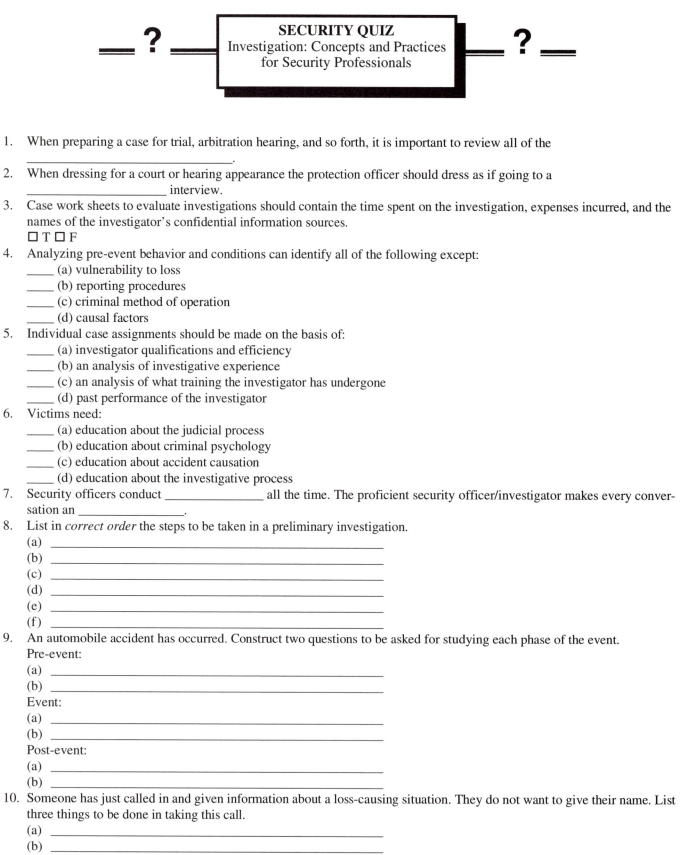

SECURITY QUIZ
Investigation: Concepts and Practices
for Security Professionals

1. When preparing a case for trial, arbitration hearing, and so forth, it is important to review all of the
    _____.

2. When dressing for a court or hearing appearance the protection officer should dress as if going to a
    _____ interview.

3. Case work sheets to evaluate investigations should contain the time spent on the investigation, expenses incurred, and the names of the investigator's confidential information sources.
    ☐ T ☐ F

4. Analyzing pre-event behavior and conditions can identify all of the following except:
    _____ (a) vulnerability to loss
    _____ (b) reporting procedures
    _____ (c) criminal method of operation
    _____ (d) causal factors

5. Individual case assignments should be made on the basis of:
    _____ (a) investigator qualifications and efficiency
    _____ (b) an analysis of investigative experience
    _____ (c) an analysis of what training the investigator has undergone
    _____ (d) past performance of the investigator

6. Victims need:
    _____ (a) education about the judicial process
    _____ (b) education about criminal psychology
    _____ (c) education about accident causation
    _____ (d) education about the investigative process

7. Security officers conduct _____ all the time. The proficient security officer/investigator makes every conversation an _____.

8. List in *correct order* the steps to be taken in a preliminary investigation.
    (a) _____
    (b) _____
    (c) _____
    (d) _____
    (e) _____
    (f) _____

9. An automobile accident has occurred. Construct two questions to be asked for studying each phase of the event.
    Pre-event:
    (a) _____
    (b) _____
    Event:
    (a) _____
    (b) _____
    Post-event:
    (a) _____
    (b) _____

10. Someone has just called in and given information about a loss-causing situation. They do not want to give their name. List three things to be done in taking this call.
    (a) _____
    (b) _____
    (c) _____

REFERENCES

Bennett, W. & Hess, K. (2001). *Criminal Investigation*. Belmont, CA; Wadsworth.

Fiems, R. & Hertig, C. (2001). *Protection Officer Guidebook*. Naples, FL; International Foundation for Protection Officers.

Horan, D. (1999). *TheRetailer's Guide to Loss Prevention and Security*. Boca Raton, FL; CRC Press.

Kuykendall, J. (1986). "The Municipal Police Detective: An Historical Analysis." CRIMINOLOGY. Vol. 24., No. 1.

Metscher, R. (1999). "Investigations" in Davies, S. & Minion, R. *Security Supervision: Theory and Practice of Asset Protection*. Woburn, MA; Butterworth-Heinemann.

Nemeth, C. (2000). *Private Security and the Investigative Process*. Woburn, MA; Butterworth-Heinemann.

Purpura, P. (2002). *Security and Loss Prevention: An Introduction*. Woburn, MA; Elsevier Science.

Swanson, C., Chamelin, N. & Territo, L. (2003). *Criminal Investigation*. New York, NY; McGraw-Hill Higher Education.

Veney, L. (2002). "Security Focus: Better Relations/Liaison with Police" Security Works, Professional Security Training Network (August).

RESOURCES

ASIS International (703/522-5800 or www.asisonline.org) has a Standing Committee on Investigations. ASIS also has an extensive library of books and videos for members to borrow (Information Resource Center)or purchase (ASIS Bookstore). There is also a professional certification program for investigators who have case management experience.

Association of Certified Fraud Examiners (800/245-3321 or www.cfenet.com) The Association sponsors the Certified Fraud Examiner (CFE) designation as well as producing a number of computer-based home study programs. There are also local chapter meetings and seminars in various locations.

AST Corporation (astcorp.com) provides an array of CD-ROM and online programs for investigative and security personnel. Persons who complete these programs may receive certificates from the International Foundation for Protection Officers.

Butterworth-Heinemann, an imprint of Elsevier Science, offers numerous investigative texts such as: *Legal Guidelines for Covert Surveillance in the Private Sector, Corporate Crime Investigation, The Art of Investigative Interviewing, The Process of Investigation,* and many others. Visit http://stbooks.elsevier.com/security, or call (800) 545-2522.

CRC Press Inc. (800/272-7737 or crcpress.com) offers several investigative texts. *The Retailer's Guide to Loss Prevention and Security* by Donald Horan is an outstanding book with chapters on investigation, audits, and employee dishonesty.

The International Foundation for Protection Officers (877/247-5984 or ifpo.org) publishes *Careers in Security and Investigation,* as well as, *The Private Investigator's Professional Desk Reference.* The Foundation sponsors both the **Certified Protection Officer (CPO)** and **Certified Security Supervisor (CSS)** designations and has membership opportunities available to protection officers and investigators.

LPJOBS.COM features jobs, educational programs, and articles in the magazine *Loss Prevention* dealing with retail loss prevention.

The National Association of Investigative Specialists offers books and membership to private investigators. Visit pi-mall.com/nais/home.html or call 512/832-0355.

The Professional Security Training Network (pstn.com or 866/727-7975) has a variety of video programs dealing with investigation, interviewing, and testifying.

John E. Reid and Associates specializes in interrogation and the detection of deception. Reid offers videos and training courses on interrogation. See reid.com or call 800/255-5747.

Security Supervision: Theory and Practice of Asset Protection has chapters on Investigation, Report Writing, and Testifying. The Investigation chapter details how investigations can be managed and provides useful information on intelligence. The book is the text for the IFPO Security Supervisor Program and is available from Elsevier (elsevier.com).

Wicklander and Zulewski (w-z.com) offer a variety of investigative services. They specialize in interrogation training.

Unit 10

Legal Aspects of Security
Protection Officer Law (U.S.)
Protection Officer Law (Canadian)

LEGAL ASPECTS OF SECURITY

By David L. Ray, LL.B.

INTRODUCTION

The purpose of this section of the manual is to introduce the student of security to the law. The law is a complex and constantly changing field and the security professional cannot be expected to have more than a fundamental understanding of the basics. It is important, however, to understand the rights and duties which are exercised in the everyday security roles.

This chapter will look at what the laws are, the sources of our laws, and the differences between some of the more important parts of the legal framework. It will look at some of the powers of the security officer including arrest and search, and it will also look at some of the duties that come with those powers.

OBJECTIVE

The objective of this section is to help you to understand the authority that is provided to you with your duties. The security officers who understand the nature and extent of personal authority do the best possible job for their employer without unnecessary exposure to liability.

Court actions for false arrest and illegal search can be costly in terms of legal fees and damages if the case is lost. It is the duty of every security officer to minimize the risk of exposure to those actions by acting within the law.

WHAT IS THE LAW?

There have been many attempts to define what the law is, but there has never been a universally accepted definition. The word *law* is used to describe a wide variety of things, from individual statutes (e.g., immigration law) to a whole system of justice (e.g., the law of England). It is also used to describe things outside the justice system (e.g., the law of gravity).

For our purposes, here we will describe laws as follows.

Laws are rules governing society.

Laws are everyday guidelines established by us, by our forefathers, and by the governments elected to rule us. Laws govern all of our everyday behavior—from the way we do business to the way we spend our leisure time. The purpose of our legal system is to do the following.

1. Set down our obligations to each other.
2. Set penalties for breaching those obligations.
3. Establish procedures to enforce those obligations.

THE SOURCE OF OUR LAWS

We tend to think of laws as being words written in books and passed by a government authority, but actually that is only one source of our laws. There are actually three.

1. The Common Law
2. Case law
3. Statutes

1. The Common Law

Before the introduction of a justice system in England, people went to the feudal lord to resolve disputes. The lord was expected to be consistent in his decisions from one trial to the next and he would rely on local custom. It was therefore believed that laws were **common** throughout the land, even though they were not written down. In fact, this was far from true and many disputes were settled by combat or by ordeal so that the lord would not be required to make a decision.

Even after the establishment of the royal courts, throughout England the judges met at the Inns of Court to discuss their decisions and ensure some degree of consistency in the whole jurisdiction. The common law eventually found its way to North America and even today plays a strong role in our judicial system.

The common law still provides authority which is not set down in statute, it provides defenses at criminal trials and it provides interpretation for statutes. The common law is still changing to adapt to changes within our society.

2. Case Law

Discussions by judges at the Inns of Courts in London during feudal times were the first example of the attempt to ensure that they follow each other's decisions. Once cases were reported in books, it became much easier to refer to those decisions and follow universal principles. This "case law" is also referred to as "precedent" or "the doctrine of stare decises." The principle of case law is fairly simply stated.

A court must stand by previous decisions.

In application, however, the doctrine becomes extremely complex. The weight that will be given to any previous decision will depend on a number of factors.

- Whether the court was the same legal jurisdiction
- The level of the court where the decision was made
- The similarity of the facts

3. Statutes

Statutes are the law in black and white. In feudal times, statutes would have been of little use because the common man could not read or write. As education became more commonplace, the government authorities began to pass statutes which would guide everyday life.

Statutes may be passed by any one of several levels of government from municipal right up to federal. Like the common law, statutes are constantly being amended, new statutes are passed and old ones are repealed. Our society is constantly changing and so it is necessary that statutes change to meet new requirements. They are created to fill a need in our society. Sometimes the need is economic (for example, an amendment to income tax laws, to "plug a loophole") and sometimes the need arises as a result of changes in society (for example, new computer crime legislation).

4. Conclusion

The security officer exercising the authority to arrest someone will not have to understand whether that authority comes from statutes or common law, or whether case law will uphold the matter in court. It must simply be understood that authority comes from one of several sources.

TYPES OF LAW—CRIMINAL AND CIVIL

The security officer should also understand the fundamental difference between criminal and civil law.

1. Criminal Law

Many criminal laws may appear to be set up to protect people. For example, it is an offense to assault someone. But, the criminal law is set up to protect the state, not the individual. A crime is an act against society and it is the state which will take action to obtain punishment (although in some cases, there are provisions for private prosecutions).

In general, the prosecutor will act on behalf of the state, not on behalf of the victim. Any fine that the accused pays will go to the state, not to the victim, and he may be sentenced to serve a sentence in a government institution.

2. Civil Law

The purpose of civil law is to protect private rights and not public rights. It is the individual who has been wronged, who must undertake the civil action. The prosecutor will not make that decision for him. He must pay for his own lawyer and hire an investigator if one is required. Any amount of money that the court orders the defendant to pay will go to the victim and not to the state, as in the case of a fine.

Often a particular action will be both civil and criminal. If a security officer were assaulted, the police may be called in to investigate a criminal assault and the person responsible may be charged with that criminal offense.

At the same time, however, the security officer may decide to sue civilly for damages for the assault and battery. Both cases may proceed at the same time, although through a different court system. The person responsible may be sentenced to jail in the criminal court and ordered to pay the officer damages in the civil court.

There are several major areas of the civil law. These are some of them.

Area	Example
Contracts	The law covering binding agreements between two or more parties. For example, a contract to provide security services for a building.
Warranties	A special type of promise or statement. For example, a guarantee that a fire extinguisher is effective on a certain type of fire.
Agency	A very important concept in the security industry. A question of whether one person is acting on behalf of another. For example — a security officer uses excessive force in subduing a suspected shoplifter. If the security officer is liable, is the store also liable because the officer was the store's agent?
Torts	Torts may be intentional civil wrong (e.g., assault, battery, wrongful imprisonment, libel or slander), or it may be negligence (e.g., the failure to provide the proper level of security in a dark employee parking lot).

Civil liability has caused increasing concern to the entire business community over the past decade. Damages in court actions in the United States and Canada have skyrocketed and insurance premiums for some types of liability insurance have become prohibitive.

Executives have found it necessary to take measures to defend against these crippling costs by increased security measures and by stringent screening, training, and security procedures. The security officer has a strong role to play in protecting business against civil liabilities.

ARREST

It is seldom necessary for the security officer to undertake an arrest, but the occasion does arise from time to time and the officer must be aware of what an arrest is and the power of arrest.

What Is an Arrest?

In order for an arrest to take place, it is not necessary that the person be handcuffed, tied up, or locked in a room. An arrest can take place with a simple assertion of the security officer's authority.

A court may find that an arrest has taken place if the officer says, "Sit there until the police arrive." It is important that the security officer understands this concept because if the arrest is found to be outside his authority, he or his employer may be found liable even though no force was used to affect the arrest, and even though the person willingly complied.

The Powers of Arrest

The powers of arrest are very complex and unfortunately vary from one jurisdiction to the next. The security officer would be well advised to become familiar with the local powers of arrest and ensure a good understanding of them. There are two methods by which a person may be legally arrested.

1. With a warrant
2. Without a warrant

Warrants are issued to the police and are executed by them in the course of their duties. Both the police and private individuals have the power to arrest without a warrant under certain circumstances. The police have wide latitude for arrest without a warrant, but the security officer can arrest only under specific circumstances and for certain types of offenses.

The authority to arrest will depend upon the following:

1. Whether or not the security officer found the person committing the offense
2. The seriousness of the offense

SEARCH

The security officer stops an employee driving out of the plant gate. He asks to look into the employee's lunch bucket which is sitting on the front seat. Does he have authority?

Often it is a condition of employment that employees will submit to a search upon leaving company property. In those circumstances and where the employee voluntarily complies, the security officer has authority.

Searches may be conducted with consent of the party being searched. But where the employee refuses to allow the security officer to look into the lunch bucket (he is withdrawing his consent), then the officer must not force the issue.

He does have a couple of alternatives, however.

1. Where he has reasonable grounds to believe that the employee is in possession of stolen property (not just a mere suspicion), he can call the police and turn the matter over to them.
2. He can report the matter internally and the employee can be disciplined for refusing to submit to the search.
3. Or he can do both of the above.

A NOTE ON FORCE

The amount of force that a security officer may use will always depend upon the circumstances of the case. The general guideline that is used is—only as much force as is necessary. Several other considerations must be applied to this principle.

1. The force itself must be necessary. The fact that a person is legally arrested does not give the arresting officer authority to mistreat him.

2. The force must suit the circumstances. A security officer does not have authority to shoot a suspect fleeing from a shoplifting.
3. As a general guideline where force is necessary, it should be a restraining type of force—not an attempt to incapacitate the person (unless it is a life-threatening situation).

EVIDENCE

Evidence is the proof that is required to establish the guilt or innocence of the accused. Evidence may be one of the following.

1. Real—a physical object, a gun, a piece of stolen property
2. Documentary—a contract, a bad check.
3. Testimony—the oral statement of a witness while under oath

Evidence must meet certain requirements in order to be admissible in court. For example, a security officer seizes a stolen calculator from an accused, but fails to secure the evidence before it is turned over to the police.

Several months later, the officer is called to testify in court. He is presented with the calculator and is asked if it was the same one that was taken from the accused. He is forced to admit that he cannot be certain. The judge refuses to admit the evidence and the accused goes free.

Any one of the three forms of evidence indicated above may be direct or circumstantial.

Direct evidence   Evidence that proves the facts in issue directly.

Circumstantial   Evidence that proves the facts in issue indirectly

A smoking gun does not prove that the person holding it pulled the trigger, but the inference may be drawn and it is therefore circumstantial evidence that is admissible in court.

It is a common misconception that a person cannot be convicted on circumstantial evidence. If the evidence is admissible and the case is strong enough, then it does not matter whether it is circumstantial or direct.

CONFESSIONS

Confessions are a special exception to the rule of hearsay (that one person may not repeat the words of another in court). Confessions are admissible as evidence in court only if they are first proven to be voluntary.

There can be no threats, intimidation, or promises to the accused which may induce him to make the statement. The police are required to advise the accused of the following:

1. His right not to make a statement
2. That the statement will be used against him
3. That he has the right to counsel

There is no similar duty on the private individual, however, and so the security officer need only ensure that the statement was willingly given.

The security officer may receive a confession from an accused in the course of an investigation of an incident. A confession need not be a lengthy statement in writing—it may be a simple oral statement like "I shouldn't have taken it." The officer should ensure that any statements by the accused are noted so that there will be no confusion later in court as to exactly what was said.

If the officer has occasion to interview a suspect, the following steps will help to ensure the admissibility of a confession:

1. Don't make any threats or promises.
2. Ask questions that are direct and pointed. If questions are ambiguous, the suspect will later be able to claim that he did not understand.
3. Give the accused time to explain.

THE BURDEN OF PROOF

The burden is always on the prosecutor in common law jurisdictions to prove that the accused is guilty "beyond a reasonable doubt." The onus is not on the accused to show that he is innocent. This has been referred to as the "golden thread" that runs through our judicial system. Because of this rule, the security officer must take steps to protect the admissibility of any evidence that is collected.

1. Any real or documentary evidence must be protected from the time that it is obtained. If possible, an identifying mark (for example, initials and the date) should be put on it so that the officer can later identify it in court. (Evidential "chain of custody.")
2. Extensive notes should be taken during the inquiry or immediately after—while it is still fresh in your mind. The judge will place a great deal more weight on testi-

mony where your memory can be refreshed from notes. The time that passes from the event to the trial can be several months or even years. The importance of notes cannot be overemphasized.

3. Make sure that your reports are accurate and detailed. The report itself may be entered into evidence and you may be required to explain discrepancies. Make sure that any statements you take from witnesses are also accurate and detailed.
4. Make sure that you are well prepared for the trial. Answer questions as clearly and directly as possible and don't be afraid to admit that you do not know the answer to a question.

CONCLUSION

The information in this chapter will help the security officer to understand basic legal concepts which can be used in the day-to-day execution of security duties. It touches on the following:

- The source of our laws: statutes, the common law and case law;
- The difference between civil law and criminal law;
- Powers of arrest and search and the use of force; and
- Evidence, confessions, and the burden of proof at criminal trials.

The security officer who understands these basic concepts will be better equipped to ensure that powers and duties provided by law are properly used and are not abused. It will also assist the officer to avoid situations which will expose the employer and the owner of property to liability.

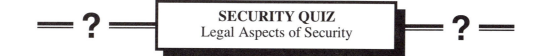

SECURITY QUIZ
Legal Aspects of Security

1. A person is arrested only when there is an assertion of _____. (Fill in the blank.)
2. A security officer may search an employee where it is a condition of _____. (Fill in the blank.)
3. A store can be liable for the actions of its security officer if it can be proven that the officer was their _____. (Fill in the blank.)
4. A person can be convicted on _____ evidence alone. (Fill in the blank.)
5. If a law is not written down and passed by government, we are not affected by it.
   ☐ T ☐ F
6. The purpose of our legal system is to:
   ☐ (a) set down our obligations to each other
   ☐ (b) set penalties for breaching those obligations
   ☐ (c) establish procedures to enforce those obligations
   ☐ (d) All of the above
7. The common law is not used in North America today.
   ☐ T ☐ F

8. You cannot sue someone and press criminal charges. It is double jeopardy.
    ☐ T ☐ F
9. At criminal trials, the prosecutor must prove the accused guilty:
    ☐ (a) on a balance of probabilities
    ☐ (b) beyond a reasonable doubt
    ☐ (c) by a preponderance of evidence
    ☐ (d) without a shadow of doubt
10. The police will investigate:
    ☐ (a) civil matters
    ☐ (b) criminal matters
    ☐ (c) whatever they are paid to investigate
    ☐ (d) All of the above

PROTECTION OFFICER LAW (U.S.)

LEGAL ASPECTS

The previous section covers important legal matters that are generic to all Protection Officers. Federal, State, and Provincial laws all have significant impact on the application of criminal law in the Security profession. For this reason it was felt prudent to prepare two additional chapters that deal exclusively with American and Canadian Law, which of course is all based upon British Common Law.

The Unit X examination process of the Certified Protection Officer (CPO) program is based entirely on the previous chapter (Legal Aspects of Security), which is necessary knowledge for all Protection Officers. We strongly suggest, however, that each candidate study the two additional chapters; Protection Officer and the Law (American), Protection Officer and the Law (Canadian). At the conclusion of each of these two chapters, CPO candidates will find five true/false and five multiple choice questions. While these questions do not comprise part of the CPO examination process, the reader should be able to answer each question correctly.

This unit includes a number of legal terms. CPO candidates should know the meanings of these terms and how they relate to the role of the Protection Officer.

By Jeff B. Wilt, CPP, CPO

INTRODUCTION

The protection officer is in a unique, albeit unenviable, position. The responsibilities and job duties of the protection officer require him or her to perform law enforcement type functions. In many cases, the required uniform of the protection officer closely resembles that of law enforcement officers. If authorized to carry handcuffs, a baton and/or a sidearm, the law enforcement image projected by the protection officer is greatly increased.

The inherent hazard presented by this law enforcement image lies in the possibility that the protection officer may begin to think of him or herself as an accredited law enforcement officer and acts or reacts accordingly. By acting as a law enforcement officer, the protection officer can expose him or herself and the employer or client to both criminal and civil liability.

Personal knowledge of the state statutes and local ordinances concerning the legal authority of protection officers can minimize this liability exposure.

The purpose of this chapter is to provide the protection officer a brief and generic summary of his or her legal authority.

LEGAL AUTHORITY OF THE PROTECTION OFFICER

In most states, the protection officer has no more legal authority than any other private citizen. There are two exceptions to this general rule.

1. Accredited law enforcement officers working off-duty (i.e., moonlighting) as protection officers retain their police authority. However, they are also still subject to the legal restraints placed on their authority by the U.S. Constitution, state statutes, and local ordinances.

2. A few states require that protection officers be "commissioned" or accredited as peace officers by the state. Protection officers in these states are granted full or limited police authority and are also subject to the same legal restrictions placed on this authority by the U.S. Constitution, state statutes, and local ordinances.

The vast majority of protection officers obtain their authority from their employer or client. In these cases, the employer or client has designated the protection officer as their legal agent responsible for the security of the employer's or client's property, resources, and assets. This agent designation is conveyed either through an employment agreement (proprietary security) or a service contract (contract security service).

In either case, the extent of the protection officer's authority and the methods by which he or she may exercise this authority should be documented as policy directives, standard operating procedures, and/or post instructions.

If instructions are issued verbally, the protection officer would be wise to document them in his or her notebook. Include the date and time of issue, and by whom the instructions were issued.

The bottom line regarding the general legal authority of a protection officer is; the protection officer has no more authority than a private citizen. As a result, many of the Constitutional and statutory restrictions that apply to law enforcement officers do not affect the protection officer.

To determine exactly what legal authority you do possess, and what legal restrictions apply to your position, protection officers should refer to the state statutes and local ordinances of their employment location.

SEARCH AND SEIZURE

A law enforcement officer with reasonable cause may stop an individual and require him or her to produce identification or submit to a search without the need of a search warrant.

Without a search warrant, law enforcement officers may make a reasonable search of persons, vehicles, and/or property incidental to an arrest.

With a valid search warrant, law enforcement officers may make a more thorough search of vehicles and property as specified by the warrant.

Generally, protection officers do not enjoy this legal authority. Before taking any action that could be considered a search of persons or property, the protection officer must first obtain the consent of the individual(s) involved. Consent can be obtained by several methods, including the following:

1. Required by the employer or client—proprietary or contracted employees may be required by their employment agreement, union contract, or service contract to submit to a reasonable search of their property by the protection officer.
2. Public notice—signs posted conspicuously at public entrances notifying nonemployees that any packages, containers, and similar objects are subject to search upon entering and leaving the premises.
3. Tacit approval or submission—the subject does not verbally object to the search and his or her behavior would lead a reasonable person to believe that they have consented to the search.

However, the subject can withdraw their consent at any time. Employees may prefer to face personnel actions by management rather than submit to a search or allow a search to continue. Nonemployees can withdraw their consent with relative impunity from punishment by the employer or client providing they were originally authorized to be on the property.

In both cases, the protection officer should not press the issue by demanding to conduct or continue the search unless the officer has reasonable cause to detain the subject. The protection officer must consider the possibility that consent was denied or withdrawn because the individual feels embarrassed rather than is guilty of a crime. No matter how professionally a search is done, it is a very personal and sometimes offensive action.

The protection officer must consider other alternatives when consent is denied or withdrawn. Among them are: simply letting the subject go on his or her way and reporting the details of the situation to management or detaining the individual, if sufficient reasonable cause exists, until local law enforcement officers arrive. Upon their arrival, let the police officer(s) conduct the search and accurately

document it. Be sure to include the officer's name and ID number.

During the course of a consent search, the protection officer has the right to seize items found such as the following:

- Property of the employer or client that the officer is required to protect and for which the subject has no obvious permission to possess
- Evidence of the commission of a crime (i.e., company property, burglar tools, controlled substances, etc.)
- Weapons that could be used to injure the officer, an innocent third party, or the subject
- Items that could help the subject escape detention

If no consent exists, the protection officer has no right to conduct a search. Any items found as the result of an illegal search cannot be seized nor entered as evidence in judicial proceedings.

However, any of the previously listed items that are IN PLAIN VIEW may be seized because the seizure is not the result of a search.

All authorized searches and seizures must strictly comply with established procedures developed by the employer or client. Additionally, protection officers should be familiar with state statutes and local ordinances concerning search and seizure by private persons. This will minimize the possibility of criminal or civil actions against the officer and the employer or client.

Familiarity with the local laws will also help assure that the employer's or client's policies and procedures concerning search and seizure are in compliance with the statutes and/or ordinances.

Remember, searches are very personal and can cause great embarrassment even if the subject has committed no crime. Searches should be conducted discretely to minimize public embarrassment for the subject and adverse public/employee reaction to the officer conducting the search.

TRESPASS

Both the common law (i.e., socially accepted practices over a period of time) and statutory law (i.e., written law) recognize the property owner's right to control access to, use of, activity on, and protection of their property. As mentioned in Section I, the employer or client designates the protection officer as their agent to protect their property and enforce their guidelines concerning it.

Many protection officers are responsible for property to which the public has access for business or recreation. As a result, it may seem difficult to determine when a trespass occurs.

Generally, one or more of the following must be present for a trespass to occur:

- The subject does not own or have other legal rights to the property involved.
- The subject must know this.

- The subject does not have permission of the property owner or agent (i.e., the protection officer) to enter upon or remain on the property.
- The property is posted in accordance with local ordinances with signs prohibiting trespass or fences and/or other barriers are present that would cause a reasonable person to believe they are not to enter the property.
- The property owner or agent has lawfully requested the subject to leave the property.
- The subject enters the property and/or refuses to leave after seeing posted notices and/or physical barriers, or receiving a lawful request to leave.

Again, the protection officer should be familiar with state statutes and local ordinances concerning trespass to assure that he or she is acting within the law when dealing with a possible trespass. Generally, the protection officer will not have to arrest a trespasser unless the subject is suspected of or known to have committed other crimes on the property.

In most cases, the subject will leave when advised they are trespassing. In others, the subject may not leave unless the protection officer tells them the local police will be requested to arrest the individual for trespass.

However, if the protection officer must make an arrest, he or she must know state statutes and local ordinances concerning arrests by private persons.

ARREST

Before discussing the aspects of arrest, let's first look over three definitions of crimes.

1. **Felony.** Generally, a crime for which the penalty includes a fine, imprisonment in a Federal or state prison for more than one year, or death.
2. **Misdemeanor.** Generally, a crime for which the penalty includes a fine or imprisonment in a county (parish) or local jail for one year or less.
3. **Breach of the Peace.** Generally, a misdemeanor involving conduct that is disruptive to a segment of the public (i.e., fighting, causing a disturbance, etc.).

Elements of an Arrest

1. **Intent.** The person making the arrest must have the intent to deprive the person being arrested of freedom of movement. This does not necessarily mean physical force like using handcuffs. It simply means the subject may not move about of his or her own free will.
2. **Communication.** The person making the arrest must communicate their intent to the person to be arrested. Additionally, the reason for the arrest must be communicated. This communication must be very clear so the subject does not misunderstand.
3. **Physical action.** In some cases, the protection officer may have to clarify the verbal communication of his or her intent to arrest by a physical action. This action can be as simple as pointing at the subject or touching the subject's shoulder or arm.

There is an inherent hazard in some contacts a protection officer makes on a daily basis. An officer may be involved in a potential arrest situation but has determined an arrest is not necessary. The officer's words, tone of voice, physical actions, or a combination of the foregoing may cause the subject to believe he or she has been arrested. For this reason, care must be exercised to ensure that the subject understands the verbal or non-verbal communication of the officer.

Despite the fact that the officer did not have the intent to arrest, the subject could believe an arrest was made. This could result in a criminal or civil action against the officer and his or her employer or client for false arrest.

It is the ultimate responsibility of the protection officer to clearly communicate his or her intent through verbal and physical communication.

We now have the definitions of certain crimes and the requirements for an arrest. Next, we'll see when and under what circumstances the protection office may make an arrest. In most states, all of the following must be present before a private person (i.e., protection officer) can make an arrest.

- A felony or misdemeanor amounting to a breach of peace must actually have been committed.
- Felony—The person intending to make the arrest must know the felony has been committed. This does not mean the felony had to occur in the protection officer's presence but the officer must have more than "reasonable belief" that the felony occurred. The protection officer requires reasonable belief the person to be arrested actually committed the felony.
- Misdemeanor, breach of the peace—The person intending to make the arrest must have witnessed the misdemeanor.
- Additionally, the protection officer must know that the person to be arrested actually committed the misdemeanor.
- The person making the arrest must release the subject to the custody of an officer of the court (i.e., police officer, constable, justice of the peace, etc.) as soon as practical.

To minimize the possibility of criminal or civil actions for false arrest, the protection officer should refer to the state statutes and local ordinances concerning arrest by a private person and give some conscious thought to both words and actions when involved in a potential arrest situation.

USE OF FORCE

The most common cause of criminal and civil actions against protection officers and their employers or clients is the officer's use of both physical and/or deadly physical force. Even when force is justified, the officer can expect to be the subject of both internal and police investigations.

Therefore, it is the ultimate responsibility of the protection officer to consider all other alternatives available before resorting to force. The officer must also consider his or her own moral convictions concerning the use of force.

The bottom line is the protection officer must know *when* force may be used and *how much* force may be used.

When to Use Force

Force should be used only as a last resort after the officer has exhausted all of his or her other options. Depending on the circumstances, the officer may not have had a chance to try other alternatives. Force should be used *only* to protect the officer, an innocent third party, or the subject from serious injury or imminent death.

How Much Force?

The protection officer should use only that amount of force necessary to overcome physical resistance to the performance of his or her lawful duties or to prevent serious injury or imminent death to the officer, a third party, or the subject. Once the resistance has been overcome or the threat neutralized, the officer may have an opportunity to try other available alternatives.

As with the preceding sections, it is to the benefit of the protection officer and his or her employer or client, to know the state statutes and local ordinances concerning the legal use of force.

STATEMENTS

Interviewing witnesses and suspects requires techniques that not everyone can master to the same degree. (Generally, the protection officer will interview witnesses, victims, and/or suspects during a preliminary investigation.) More thorough interviews may be done later by investigators or law enforcement personnel during the follow-up investigation.

A bad interview during the preliminary investigation can cause information obtained during later interviews to be unusable. The protection officer should know what he or she legally can and cannot do during interviews.

Remember, even though the protection officer as a private citizen is not required to "Mirandize" (i.e., give the Miranda Warning) suspects, any statements given by the suspect, victim, or witnesses must be voluntary.

The fact that the protection officer has been delegated

authority by the employer or client may be sufficient coercion to cause an employee to make an involuntary statement out of fear of losing his or her job or other punishment if they don't cooperate. The protection officer must be aware of this possibility.

The officer should make note of any statements made by the suspect prior to the formal interview. If possible, the protection officer should have the person being interviewed sign a declaration to the effect that all statements made are voluntary and not the result of threats or promises.

A second officer should be present to verify that the statements documented are both accurate and voluntary.

If the protection officer uses any kind of coercion or promises of rewards, the statements obtained will be declared inadmissible in court. Additionally, statements gained by such actions may affect the admissibility of information obtained later by investigators and/or law enforcement personnel.

Should the subject refuse to speak to the protection officer or wishes to end a voluntary interview, the officer should note this fact and not press the issue. If the officer insists on continuing the interview process, any statements the subject makes could be considered involuntary and inadmissible in court.

CONCLUSION

You have probably noticed at this point that the catchphrase of this chapter has been, "Know the state statutes and local ordinances of your location of employment." As boring and tedious as it may seem, it's been repeated for a very good reason.

The legal authority of law enforcement officers is well defined and subject to specific Constitutional restrictions. Conversely, the legal authority of the protection officer (i.e., private citizen) is not so well defined and varies from state to state and city to city. Additionally, the protection officer is not subject to all the Constitutional restrictions that apply to police powers.

However, just like the enforcement officer, the protection officer can be subject to criminal and/or civil action for violation or abuse of his or her legal authority. These actions can also affect the officer's employer or client.

FOR FURTHER INFORMATION

Butterworth–Heinemann, an imprint of Elsevier Science, offers an array of security texts including *Protective Security Law* by Inbau, Aspen and Spiotto and *Prosecuting the Shoplifter: A Loss Prevention Strategy* by James Cleary, Jr. Visit http://stbooks.elsevier.com/security **or call (800) 545-2522, 200 Wheeler Road, 6th Floor, Burlington, MA 01803.**

Gould Publications (199 State Street, Binghamton, NY 13901 (607) 724-3000) specializes in legal texts. Gould has a full line of state criminal codes, complete with annual updates.

Spain & Spain Inc. (4426 Mulberry Ct., Suite J, Pittsburgh, PA 15227 (412) 884-8185) provide seminars on "Civil Law for the Security Manager" as well as other topics. Spain & Spain also publish *The Spain Report,* a security law training newsletter.

The following websites have text and instructional programs dealing with legal topics: gouldlaw.com; hits.astcorp.com; looseleafelaw.com; PSTN.com.

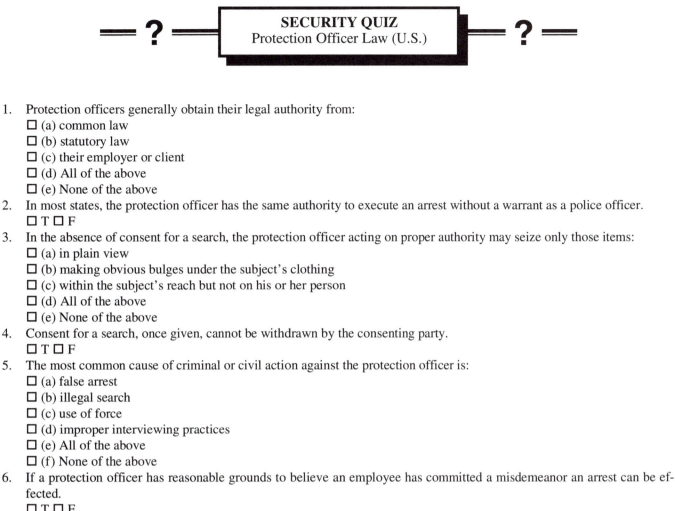

1. Protection officers generally obtain their legal authority from:
   ☐ (a) common law
   ☐ (b) statutory law
   ☐ (c) their employer or client
   ☐ (d) All of the above
   ☐ (e) None of the above

2. In most states, the protection officer has the same authority to execute an arrest without a warrant as a police officer.
   ☐ T ☐ F

3. In the absence of consent for a search, the protection officer acting on proper authority may seize only those items:
   ☐ (a) in plain view
   ☐ (b) making obvious bulges under the subject's clothing
   ☐ (c) within the subject's reach but not on his or her person
   ☐ (d) All of the above
   ☐ (e) None of the above

4. Consent for a search, once given, cannot be withdrawn by the consenting party.
   ☐ T ☐ F

5. The most common cause of criminal or civil action against the protection officer is:
   ☐ (a) false arrest
   ☐ (b) illegal search
   ☐ (c) use of force
   ☐ (d) improper interviewing practices
   ☐ (e) All of the above
   ☐ (f) None of the above

6. If a protection officer has reasonable grounds to believe an employee has committed a misdemeanor an arrest can be effected.
   ☐ T ☐ F

7. The elements required for an arrest are (check one item only):
   ☐ (a) reasonable cause, communication and action
   ☐ (b) intent, communication and action
   ☐ (c) intent, reasonable cause and action
   ☐ (d) All of the above
   ☐ (e) None of the above

8. Statements made to the protection officer must be voluntary.
   ☐ T ☐ F

9. The protection officer should know state statutes and local ordinances concerning the legal authority of a private citizen to (check one item):
   ☐ (a) make more arrests
   ☐ (b) impress the employer or client
   ☐ (c) minimize the possibility of criminal/civil actions
   ☐ (d) All of the above
   ☐ (e) None of the above

10. A protection officer could jeopardize the follow-up investigation by forcing a suspect to give an involuntary statement.
    ☐ T ☐ F

PROTECTION OFFICER LAW (CANADIAN)

By David L. Ray

Protection officers are given broader responsibility within the Canadian legal system because of their duties to protect life and property. The protection officer is often involved in activities that are inherently dangerous, either because they involve the enforcement of the law on property that they have been assigned to protect or because they are required to implement life safety procedures, such as dealing with bomb threats, fire, or evacuation. The public, employees, and occupants of the buildings and property being protected will look upon the protection officer as a symbol of authority that is there to protect them. Trespassers and criminals will view the protection officer as someone who is there to intervene if they do something wrong. The protective duties may require the officer to make decisions that could raise questions of liability against the officer, the property owner, or the employer. In conducting enforcement duties, the protection officer may be required to arrest, detain, use force, seize property, and testify in court where charges are laid. For all of these reasons, it is important that the protective officer understand the duties and responsibilities that are assigned under the Canadian legal system and the potential liabilities which could arise.

The purpose of this chapter is to provide information on the legal rights and duties afforded to the protection officer and some tools to ensure that those issues of responsibility and potential liability can be met.

LIABILITY AND NEGLIGENCE

Negligence may result in liability in the performance of security duties as a result of several different elements in the Canadian legal system. Negligence is a cause of action at common law so someone who suffers damages as a result of the negligence of another may sue to recover their loss. That negligence may be as a result of a failure to provide an appropriate level of security, a failure to have contingency or evacuation plans in place, or a failure to warn someone who is at risk as a result of a security exposure. Negligence can also be established through statutes such as occupiers' liability or occupational health and safety legislation. Those statutes require that the occupier of premises provide a safe work environment for not only employees, but also visitors to the property and sometimes even to trespassers. It is security's duty to provide the property owner with advice on risks that may exist on the property and to recommend appropriate methods of handling those risks. It is also security's duty to ensure that emergency procedures are properly followed and that training takes place to ensure

that those procedures work and that everyone is familiar with them.

AUTHORITY

The authority of the protection officer comes from the agency relationship with the property owner, occupier, or employer that they are assigned to protect. Those authorities may be addressed in the contracts issued or by internal policies set up by the customer or employer. Most of the provinces, with the exception of Prince Edward Island, have legislation that regulates the contract security industry. The provincial legislation will stipulate a number of requirements including provisions, such as licensing, age, and uniform, and where a protection officer is under contract, he/she must comply with that legislation. There may also be a number of written procedures, manuals, or post orders that provide instructions on the completion of duties whether the protection officer is contracted or in-house. These written instructions also give the officer authority as directed by the property owner or employer.

THE CHARTER OF RIGHTS AND FREEDOMS

The Charter of Rights and Freedoms (The Constitution Act) was passed in Canada in 1982 to protect the fundamental rights of Canadians. Many of those rights were already protected at common law but the Charter entrenched those rights in a statute. For example, there was a requirement on the police that they caution someone before taking a confession if they wished to see the confession entered as evidence. That requirement was under the common Judges' Rules but it is now entrenched in the Charter. The Charter may have an effect on the protection officer in terms of dealing with the rights of citizens against unreasonable search and seizure, arrest and detention, the right to be informed of the reason for an arrest, and to instruct counsel. Those issues will be addressed below. Where a person's Charter rights are breached through an inappropriate arrest or seizure of evidence, the only outcome may be that the subsequent prosecution may fail in court.

YOUNG OFFENDERS

The Young Offenders Act provides for the special treatment of the accused that is under 18. It provides for a requirement to notify a parent or guardian on the arrest of a young person. The protection officer will generally be able to rely on the police to meet the notification requirements, but there is also a requirement that the identity of the young offender remain private and, therefore, any reports of the protection officer will have to be properly secured.

TYPES OF A CRIMINAL OFFENSES

In order to understand your powers of arrest, it is important that you understand the different types of criminal offenses in our legal system. Criminal offenses may be summary conviction, indictable, or dual procedure. Summary conviction offenses are the less serious offenses in the Criminal Code or other punitive statutes. They include offenses such as disturbing the peace or offenses under the highway traffic or liquor control legislation. Indictable offenses are the more serious offenses, usually in the Criminal Code, and they include infractions such as breaking and entering or theft and fraud where the loss is over $5000. With dual procedure offenses, it is up to the prosecutor to decide whether to proceed by way of indictment or summary conviction. Dual procedure offenses include infractions such as theft or fraud where the value is under $5,000, mischief (damage or interference with property), or unauthorized use of a computer. For the purposes of understanding powers of arrest, the protection officer has the right to assume that any dual procedure offense is an indictable offense. Unfortunately, the only way to find out whether an offense is summary conviction or indictable is to refer to the Criminal Code.

ARREST

Generally, a protection officer will not have to arrest in the course of security duties or an investigation. There may, however, be occasions where an arrest may be necessary to identify a culprit, to recover stolen property or other evidence, or where someone is drunk or violent, to protect them and others. Under the Criminal Code, an arrest may be with or without a warrant but only the police have authority to execute an arrest warrant.

When does the intervention by a protective officer with a culprit become an arrest? Unfortunately, the law is not completely clear. Mr. Justice Roger Salhany stated the following:

> Mere words, however, do no constitute an arrest. There must be some actual restraint of the person of the arrestee or he must submit in a situation where the officer has the power of control. So to merely say to the accused that he is under arrest is not enough unless he submits and the officer is in a position to effect a seizure if desired.[1]

This question will become important if a person is charged with resisting arrest, if someone sues for false arrest, or if the protection officer is accused of assault in conjunction with an arrest. There have been cases where the accused has been acquitted on charges of assaulting a protection officer because they were found not guilty of the theft for which they were arrested.

The courts have also held that there does not necessarily have to be a laying of hands on the individual and an arrest may be complete by a "restraint by an assertion of authority" or words used to show a sense of compulsion. The courts will also look at whether the person submitted to the authority of the protection officer in deciding whether an arrest took place.

What about the right to search someone incidental to an arrest? The common law provides that the police have the right to search someone when they are being arrested and that right probably extends to someone other than a peace officer. Certainly if the accused has weapons or evidence in plain view on his person, the protection officer should take steps to secure the items, but, in most cases, the person should be watched until the police arrive so that they can conduct the search. In some cases searches by security personnel have been held to breach the accused's charter rights and property seized was not allowed into evidence at trial.[2]

THE CHARTER OF RIGHTS EFFECT ON ARREST

The Charter provides for the protection of the citizen on being arrested and three of those rights are important for the protection officer to understand.

1. The right to be informed of the reason for the arrest
2. The right to retain and instruct counsel without delay
3. The right to be informed of the right to counsel

Mr. Justice Beckett in *R. v. J.A.* stated the following:[3]

> I conclude the law to be that any arrest by a private person, which includes a security officer, would trigger the application of the Charter whereas if an accused is merely detained, in a situation that does not amount to an arrest, then the Charter does not apply.

A protection officer who effects an arrest has four duties.

1. **Call the police**—Section 494(3) of the Criminal Code states:

> Anyone other than a peace officer who arrests a person without a warrant shall forthwith deliver the person to a peace officer.

> This simply means that the protection officer must call the police and wait for them to arrive to take the prisoner into their custody.

2. **Notify the prisoner of the reason for the arrest**— This notification is required by the Charter but it is not necessary that technical language be used or that the section of the Criminal Code be quoted. It is sufficient to use words such as "You are under arrest for breaking into this building."

3. **Advise the prisoner of the right to counsel**—Following is a sample of a Charter caution used by the police.

---

1. Salhany, Canadian Criminal Procedure, fifth edition, page 39

2. R. v. Lerke (1986) 24 C.C.C. (3d) 129 (Alta. C.A.) was a case where bouncers at a bar arrested an underage patrol, searched his pockets, and found marijuana. The subsequent drug charge was dismissed because the search was found to offend the Charter.

3. [1992] O.J. No. 182 (O.U.F.C.)

I am arresting you for

_____.

You have the right to retain and instruct counsel without delay. This means that before we proceed with our investigation you may call any lawyer you wish or get free advice from duty counsel immediately. If you want to call duty counsel, we will provide you with a telephone and telephone numbers. If you wish to contact any other lawyer, a telephone and telephone book will be provided. If you are charged with an offense, you may also apply to Legal Aid for assistance.

Do you understand?

Do you want to call duty counsel or any other lawyer?

The prisoner must be given the opportunity to carry on a private conversation with the lawyer, subject to the officer being able to maintain proper custody.

4. **Protect the prisoner until the police arrive**—Once you have arrested someone, he/she is your responsibility and you must protect him/her and protect others from him/her.

POWERS OF ARREST OF A PROTECTION OFFICER

There are three powers of arrest provided to the protection officer in the Criminal Code. The first is the citizen's power of arrest in section 494(1). That section provides that anyone may arrest without warrant.

(a) A person whom he finds committing an indictable offense.[4]

(b) A person who, on reasonable and probable grounds, he believes:

(i) Has committed a criminal offense.

(ii) Is escaping from and freshly pursued by persons who have lawful authority to arrest that person.

In order for the protection officer to execute a valid arrest, the perpetrator must be "found committing" in relation to the offense and it must be an indictable (more serious) or dual procedure offense. The second part of the section allows a citizen to assist the police when they are in "fresh pursuit" of a suspect.

Section 494(2) provides for the second power of arrest.

(2) Anyone who is:

(a) The owner or a person in lawful possession of property.

(b) A person authorized by the owner or a by a person in lawful possession of property may arrest without warrant a person whom he finds committing a criminal offense on or in relation to that property.

This section gives a much broader power of arrest because it applies to all criminal offenses, both summary conviction and indictable. Note, however, that it still requires that the person arresting finds the perpetrator committing the offense. This section applies to the owner of the property, others in lawful possession, or a person authorized by the owner or person in lawful possession (e.g. a protection officer hired or contracted to look after the property). The section allows the protection officer to exercise powers of arrest for an offense committed on the property either against the property or someone on it, but also an offense committed off of the property but directed at it (e.g., a rock thrown through the window).

The third power of arrest in the criminal code is arrest for breach of the peace under section 30. It provides that anyone who witnesses a breach of the peace may detain someone who commits the offense or is about to join in the offense for the purposes of turning the prisoner over to the police. This section provides power to the protection officer where someone may be drunk, fighting, or molesting others on the property being protected.

THE USE OF FORCE

One of the more difficult questions is "How much force may I use in effecting an arrest?" Section 30, referred to above, uses the words "if he uses no more force than is necessary to prevent the continuance or renewal of the breach of the peace or than is reasonably proportioned to the danger to be apprehended from the continuance or renewal of the breach of the peace." This "reasonableness" test is the one that the courts will use in deciding whether a person arresting went beyond what was necessary to effect the arrest. The protective officer should use a restraining type of force. Once an offensive type of force or an attempt to incapacitate is used, there may be a question of liability for civil damages or a criminal offense of assault. Force should only be used to protect you or an innocent third party. In deciding how much force to use, the protection officer effecting the arrest must also consider the nature and seriousness of the offense.

Section 25 of the Criminal Code allows a person enforcing the law to use "as much force as is necessary" as long as they are acting on reasonable grounds. The section also states, however, that you are not protected if you use force intended to cause death or grievous bodily harm unless it is necessary for the preservation of you or someone that you protect from death or grievous bodily harm. Section 26 makes us criminally responsible for any excessive force used.

CONFESSIONS

Usually the police will be involved in interviewing an accused to receive a confession, but there may be occasions where a statement made to a protection officer will amount to a confession and may later be used as evidence in court. A confession is simply a written or oral statement made by an accused against interest. Even a denial by the accused

---

[4]. Remember that a dual procedure offense is assumed to be indictable until the prosecutor elects how to proceed.

may amount to a confession if the prosecutor is able to prove that the accused lied in making the denial (e.g., an attempt to set up an alibi). The protection officer should keep detailed notes of anything that an accused says because it may later contradict a statement made to the police. For example, an accused may tell you that he wasn't in the area when the offense was committed and he may later tell the police that he was in the area but he didn't do it. The two statements constitute a lie and may be admissible in court as proof of guilt.

In order for a confession to be admissible in court, it must be proven that it was made voluntarily. The courts will undertake an examination before a confession is admitted to ensure that there were no threats or promises to the accused that may have elicited the confession. A threat does not necessarily have to be a threat of violence. A threat to terminate someone's employment if they don't tell you what happened may be enough to question whether the accused confessed because he really did it or whether he confessed because he wanted to keep his job. Similarly, a simple promise that "Things will go better for you if you tell us what happened" may be sufficient to question the reliability of a confession.

A protection officer may be considered "a person in authority" by the courts and the result may be that a confession will not be accepted if the accused was not cautioned before giving the statement. One form of standard caution used by the police is as follows.

You may be charged with _____.
Do you wish to say anything? You are not obliged to say anything unless you wish to do so, but whatever you say may be given in evidence.

Where an accused is providing a statement to a protection officer, the following principles should be observed:

1. The suspect must be offered a chance to contact counsel and should be given the opportunity to carry on a private conversation with counsel.
2. The object of the interview is to learn the truth, not to induce a pattern of deceit or obtain answers that the questioner wants to hear.
3. There should be no actual or implied threats or promises.
4. The accused should be given the opportunity to give a full explanation.
5. The accused should be questioned in a language and phraseology that they understand—"legalese" or technical terms not known to the accused should be avoided.
6. The interviewer should not ask ambiguous questions.
7. The interviewer should not be aggressive or abusive to the person being interviewed.

SEARCH AND SEIZURE

What are the rights of the protection officer to conduct searches and seize property at the work site? Many employers have policies that establish procedures for searches of vehicles, lockers, or personal effects in order to deter theft or misuse of company property or the possession of illicit drugs or alcohol on site. When these policies are challenged by labor unions or the courts, the company must establish that the search was reasonable and that there is some evidence to believe an employment offense has taken place and that the search will result in discovery of evidence of the offense. The company must also be in a position to show that the policy is applied consistently within the work force and that it does not target specific individuals or groups. Courts and arbitrators will try to strike a balance between the rights of the employer and the right of privacy of the employee, and they will look at whether the company considered all other reasonable investigative means before embarking on search procedures. This is especially true in cases where searches are conducted on employees or their personal effects, as the company will be required to show that they established procedures to protect the privacy of its employees.

Many companies also have policies requiring people to submit their vehicles to search on leaving the property. These are usually in conjunction with a notice at the gate indicating that the vehicle will be subject to search. Even though an employee or visitor may imply that they will allow their vehicle to be searched by entering the property, they have the right to change their mind while on the property and may refuse to comply with the search when leaving. The protection officer should not force the issue and should simply report the matter. Management then has the opportunity to treat it as a disciplinary infraction if it is an employee or has the right to refuse further entry if it is a contractor or visitor.

TRESPASS

The owner or occupier of property has a right to place control and restrictions on its use. There are a number of methods for dealing with the trespass to company property. Where it is someone who deliberately impedes lawful access to property (e.g., a protest group), the police may charge the offenders with mischief under the Criminal Code. The company may also undertake a civil action against the person or group that has impeded their use of the property. Sections 38 and 41 of the Criminal Code give the right to a property owner or designate to prevent a trespasser from taking possession of personal, or real property, and to use no more force than is necessary to prevent them from entering onto or removing them from real property. There is also a Criminal Code offense for trespassing at night (section 177) but this must be done in relation to a dwelling house and the section was established mainly to deal with "peeping toms."

The provinces all have trespass legislation that provides for the method of giving notice restricting access to the property, placement of signs, fines, and, in some cases, powers of arrest. The protection officer should become familiar with the legislation for their jurisdiction.

CONCLUSION

With the increased legal rights and powers of the protection officer comes increased responsibility. It is important to understand those rights and the liabilities that may go with them so that the protection officer can act within the law and ensure that there is no undue liability imposed on their clients or employers.

FOR FURTHER INFORMATION

The Professional Security Training Network (PSTN) has a video series on Canadian Law for Security Officers. Visit www.pstn.com.

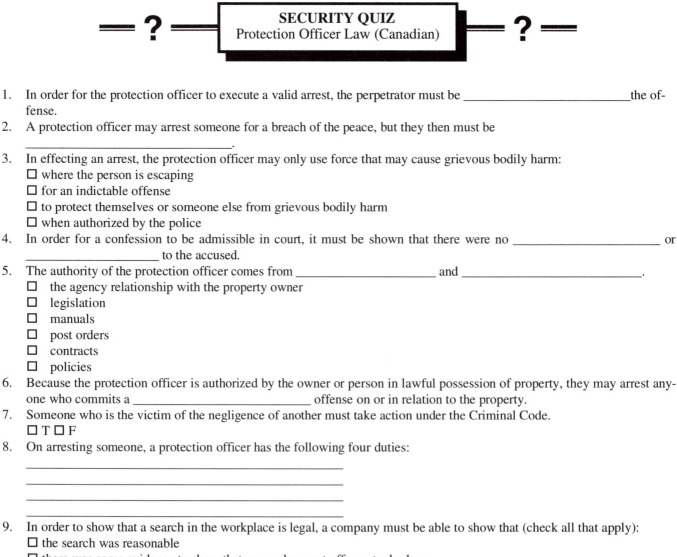

SECURITY QUIZ
Protection Officer Law (Canadian)

1. In order for the protection officer to execute a valid arrest, the perpetrator must be _____ the offense.
2. A protection officer may arrest someone for a breach of the peace, but they then must be
   _____ .
3. In effecting an arrest, the protection officer may only use force that may cause grievous bodily harm:
   ☐ where the person is escaping
   ☐ for an indictable offense
   ☐ to protect themselves or someone else from grievous bodily harm
   ☐ when authorized by the police
4. In order for a confession to be admissible in court, it must be shown that there were no _____ or
   _____ to the accused.
5. The authority of the protection officer comes from _____ and _____ .
   ☐ the agency relationship with the property owner
   ☐ legislation
   ☐ manuals
   ☐ post orders
   ☐ contracts
   ☐ policies
6. Because the protection officer is authorized by the owner or person in lawful possession of property, they may arrest anyone who commits a _____ offense on or in relation to the property.
7. Someone who is the victim of the negligence of another must take action under the Criminal Code.
   ☐ T ☐ F
8. On arresting someone, a protection officer has the following four duties:
   _____
   _____
   _____
   _____
9. In order to show that a search in the workplace is legal, a company must be able to show that (check all that apply):
   ☐ the search was reasonable
   ☐ there was some evidence to show that an employment offense took place
   ☐ there was some indication that there may be evidence in the place being searched
   ☐ that the search was being conducted to prove an indictable offense
   ☐ that any search policy is consistently applied
   ☐ that the right of privacy of the employee was considered
   ☐ that the company used all other reasonable means to investigate the offense
10. Occupiers' liability and occupational health and safety statutes may require that we provide safe work environments to trespassers:
   ☐ T ☐ F

Unit 11

Use of Force
Defensive Tactics and Officer Safety
Apprehension and Detention Procedures

USE OF FORCE

By Charles T. Thibodeau, M.Ed., CPP, CSS
Christopher A. Hertig, CPP, CPO

USE OF FORCE

The legally and socially acceptable use of force by private protection officers is a key issue in our contemporary—and future—society. As security personnel, we enforce rules, and ensure compliance with them. We are the "preservers of the corporate culture"; management's representative, charged with keeping an orderly, safe, and productive environment, in accordance with the organizational philosophy of our employer. We are the ambassadors of the organization, and serve a substantial public relations role. We enforce rules. We extend ourselves to help others, and assist in making the organization run more smoothly. We must be the "iron first in the velvet glove."

Obviously, the use of force is something that is unpalatable; yet at times very necessary. We need to decrease the frequency and degree of force used as much as possible, without creating a personal safety hazard. Generally speaking, the more proficient and professional we are, the less that force is needed.

If we find ourselves resorting more and more to the use of force, it is indicative of a systemic failure. Either we are not following instructions, we are a little shortsighted in our planning, or we have failed to be alert enough to observe imminent danger. When this happens in private security settings, the potential exists for extensive damage, injury to people, and loss of expensive assets. The potential also exists for increased legal liability and expensive court litigation. Simply put:

> "If you have to force it, you're doing something wrong." *H. H. Thibodeau*

Private security, at least ideally, implies a stable, relatively predictable environment, in which an individual, group, or community may pursue its ends without disruption or harm, and without fear of disturbance or injury. This definition necessarily includes personnel safety, fire safety, and emergency medical response, as well as safe and secure streets, homes, commercial businesses, parking areas, and work sites.

To accomplish our society's need to maintain order, we have formed governments based on laws, which express the desires of its citizens. In addition, we rely on physical security, which consists of those countermeasures required to promote a state of well being, to protect life and property, and to avoid or minimize the risks of natural or man-made disasters and crimes. Unfortunately, from time to time, things go wrong, systems break down, and we have no alternative. We have tried verbal persuasion. We have set limits. We have used loud, repeated, verbal commands. We have no time or place to retreat. We can only accomplish the necessary by using force.

The information in this unit of study will deal with this important aspect of the security officer's responsibilities. It is presented as a general educational guideline; specific procedures must be developed and adopted by the officer's employer. It is a starting point. **Each officer is strongly recommended to obtain additional education and training in this important area of a security officer's professional development.**

USE OF FORCE IN GENERAL

A definition that attempts to describe the reasonable use of force as "an amount of force equal to or just slightly greater than the force used by the aggressor" is sometimes misleading. Use of force is much better defined with respect to the concepts of **belief, reasonableness,** and **necessity.** For instance, you may choose to use pepper spray to disarm a person with a knife. In that case you actually use less force than the aggressor. At the same time, the choice of a less than lethal defensive weapon supports the assertion that the officer's use of force was reasonable.

Use of force is any tactic used to control, disarm, capture, restrain, or otherwise physically manage an aggressive or uncooperative subject. Force is predicated on the security officer's reasonable belief that the choice of weapons and the amount of force used were necessary, reasonable, and the only alternative.

Each use of force must accomplish a legitimate and lawful purpose. At the same time, each use of force must appear, to a prudent and reasonable person under identical circumstances, to be reasonable and necessary. Reduced to its lowest common denominator in a court of law; the appropriateness of each use of force will be measured by an "objective reasonableness and necessity standard" versus whether the use of force was a "deliberate and wanton infliction of pain."

In use of force litigation, the following motives will most likely not help to acquit the security officer: fear, retaliation, punishment, accident, or loss of control. If the officer claims that the subject was inadvertently injured while in custody, that admission may be viewed in court as an indication of negligence. All force used by private security must be based on the officer's **BELIEF** that the use of force was the **REASONABLE** and **NECESSARY** solution, and that the execution of force was **CALCULATED, MEASURED, AND DELIBERATE!** Failure at any one of these tests and you could be in jail, while the bad guy is out walking around free.

The reasonableness of any force used by a security officer is largely dependent upon the circumstances of the incident. Where the subject presents no threat to the officer, no use of force is permitted. For example, where an arrested person does not resist arrest, any use of force is excessive. Several cases have similarly held that the use of force during interrogation of a suspect is not justified in the absence of evidence that the suspect attacked the officer. Note: interrogation (or focused interviewing) should never involve the touching of a person.

JUSTIFYING THE USE OF FORCE

Your primary defense in a charge of excessive use of force will have to do with the question of assault. That is, did the suspect give the officer cause to use force due to the subject's assault of the officer? It is therefore helpful for you to know that the claim of assault consists of four parts: ability, imminent jeopardy, intent, and preclusion. These are the questions that will be asked after the officer's use of force.

1. Did the aggressor have the **ability** to harm you?
2. Were you in **imminent jeopardy** of being harmed?
3. Did the aggressor exhibit **intent** to harm you?
4. Were you **precluded** from escape or other defensive/control actions, so that your only way out was to use force?

If the officer cannot answer all of these questions in the affirmative, that officer may have serious trouble justifying his or her use of force.

There are four primary justifications for using force. These justifications consist of the officer's reasonable belief:

1. That harm would come to the officer or to someone else if force was not used.
2. That the actions taken were necessary.
3. That the actions taken were reasonable.
4. That the actions taken conformed to employer policy and training.

It is always better, of course, if force was used under the definition of an assault described above. Using force to defend property may be legally permissible, but it is generally frowned upon by the courts. Courts prefer that property owners utilize legal options, such as civil recovery to gain back property. When using force to protect property it is wise to remember this.

Property can be replaced; people can't.

If a security officer is arrested or sued for use of force there are several additional factors which will have an impact on the outcome of that litigation. Courts will consider the following issues:

1. Did the officer act under a reasonable belief?
2. Did the officer have a duty to retreat?
3. Did the officer give the aggressor a request or command to desist?
4. Did the officer follow department policy and procedure?
5. Did the officer follow department training?
6. Did the force used produce the desired results?
7. Did the officer place any third party in jeopardy?
8. Will the truth be relevant?
9. Will the witnesses tell the truth?
10. What or who will the jury believe?
11. What or who will the judge believe?
12. What or who will the public believe?

FORCE ALTERNATIVES DEFINED

Alternatives to the use of force amount to any method or tactic which can be used to de-escalate incidents, without the use of defensive weapons, gratuitous threats, or aggressive action. This definition necessarily connotes the use of verbal deescalation, removing persons from the "conflict zone," negotiating conflict resolution, maintaining a non-combative atmosphere, and calling in public law enforcement. These are some of the many alternatives that should be attempted before using force.

1. Take your time—slow down the action. Haste gets people hurt! "Haste makes casualties."
2. Awareness— recognize potential threats. Be alert.
3. Evaluate—get all the facts and pieces of evidence that are available. Understand the problem before acting to solve it.
4. Don't respond in anger! Take a step back. Take a few deep breaths. Take your time.
5. Be an actor—preclude the problem from escalating and erupting—not a reactor.
6. Maintain a safe distance.
7. Smile. Be as pleasant as appropriate under the circumstances.
8. Be polite—show respect to everyone, including the aggressor.
9. Really care about people! If you do, it is projected in your demeanor.
10. Apply active listening techniques to show interest in what another is saying.
11. Call for backup before acting, including the police when necessary.
12. Recruit assistance from persons nearby if necessary.
13. Ask perpetrator's friends and relatives to speak to the perpetrator.
14. Be slow to speak, slow to anger, fast to listen.
15. If all else fails, expect to get hit.
16. Expect any hit to hurt, brush it off. *It is not the end of the world.*
17. Engage in tactical retreat when things get hot; back off and get behind cover.
18. Use loud assertive commands: "STOP!" and "NO!" "Hit him with your voice."
19. Use repeated commands: "DROP THE KNIFE!" "DROP IT." "DROP IT!" "DROP IT!" "DO IT NOW!" "NOW," "NOW!"

20. Continue verbal deescalation. Be patient for as long as it takes.

EXCESSIVE FORCE LIABILITY

An examination of use of force cases, which resulted in injury and/or liability, shows that these cases commonly involve the following:

- Use (or threat) of any force where subject offers no resistance.
- Negligent use of normally nonlethal force, resulting in death or serious injury.
- Excessive force as an overreaction to subject's resistance to officer commands (continued past point of no resistance).
- Intentional infliction of pain (excessive force), as summary punishment.
- Use of deadly force in situations where it is not permitted.
- Failure to provide medical treatment for injuries from officer's use of force.
- An officer deliberately strikes or inflicts pain upon a subject after the subject is placed in restraints—using force to punish.
- An officer entices or provokes a subject in reacting aggressively, so as to create cause for using force. Poor interpersonal skills create crises!
- Death of a subject under the officer's control due to positional asphyxia. Proper restraint techniques, which do not impede breathing, are critical!
- Officer mistakenly reacts to a subject with a severe medical problem, such as confusing diabetic shock with alcoholism. First-aid training and constant monitoring of the subject are necessary for his/her safety and welfare.
- Officer is injured by taking a bad position, such as standing directly in front of the subject, too close to the subject, or not using cover.
- Officer is injured by having the wrong attitude. Carelessness, overconfidence, demeaning tone of voice, cockiness, and so on all cause problems with others.
- Officer is injured by relaxing too soon. "It's not over till it's over."
- Officer is injured by failing to search suspect—always do a visual search at a minimum!
- Officer injured by failure to watch suspect hands—see the palms!

DUTIES THAT ACCOMPANY USE OF FORCE

Private security officers must exhibit restraint and self-control within permissible limits at all times. Public and private protection officers are responsible for responding to the medical needs of subjects against whom force was used. Supervisors and line officers have a duty to intervene when another officer is using excessive force against a subject.

A FORMULA FOR SELF-CONTROL

Use of force is all about control. Sometimes pro-active preventive security plans break down, and force is required to maintain control. The question is: "Who is the person we most earnestly want to control?" Is it the drunk, the jealous spouse, the angry employee? No, it is OURSELF! In order to maintain control of others, we first must find a way to control ourselves when under great pressure. Remembering this formula might help keep everything in perspective, when faced with high-stress, potentially aggressive situations. Carefully examine the following equations:

$$CONTROL = I/E$$
$$I/E + P = E/I$$
$$E/I + T = I/E$$
$$I/E = CONTROL$$

This formula means that control is equal to "I" (intellect) over "E" (emotions). Thus, we are in control when our intellect rules our emotions. When we introduce "P" (problem) to the equation, it may have the effect of turning the equation upside down. Thus, $I/E + P = E/I$. Emotions then are in control of our Intellect! When we are running on raw emotions, we can get hurt, or we can lose control and hurt someone else. We can use more force than is necessary. We can use excessive force.

However, if you add "T" (training) to the equation, then the tendency is to reverse the negative effects of "P." You then have: $E/I + T = I/E$. Finally, $I/E = Control$.

What all of this means is, that by developing a trained response to perceived use of force situations, your emotions can be held in check, and with the intellect in charge, you can more effectively maintain control. That is why verbal deescalation, if practiced regularly, is an excellent weapon to use in aggressive situations. It can eliminate the use of force in the vast majority of situations. It can also help the officer to get along better with those in the work environment. Resolving conflict amiably is the essence of a protection officer's job. Those who are good at it have long and rewarding careers. Those who do not, get into all sorts of trouble.

Conflict resolution is the cornerstone of officer survival.

RESPONSE TO AGGRESSIVE BEHAVIOR

Dr. Kevin Parsons developed "The Confrontation Continuum" over a decade ago. The "Continuum" serves as a guideline for police officers when specific force applications are appropriate. Since then other entities such as PPCT Management Systems, REB Training International, and Larry Smith Enterprises have developed similar police-types of models. The following outline is not necessarily the model that the private security officer would want to follow, as the officer is generally not armed with a baton or firearm. Also, individual situations can modify the steps used in the application of force. The confrontational continuum outlined below can best be thought of as a general guide. In the final analysis, security officers must always follow the use of force policy established by their employers!

CONFRONTATION CONTINUUM

Step 1. Officer presence is the first step in the continuum. The mere presence of an officer establishes some degree of psychological control. Nonverbal communication can also be employed to control a subject.

Step 2. Initial communications can be thought of as the second step in the use of force. The use of questioning of a subject, as the initial communication, will give the officer an edge. By asking questions, the officer is increasing his/her psychological control over the situation. Persuasion and limit-setting can be part of this step.

Step 3. Commands are the next step. "Heavy control talk" used to direct the subject, such as "Stop," "Back," "Drop it," "Do it now," etc., provides a psychological control factor. Note that there should be short, simple, emphatically verbalized, commands given to a subject who is physically resisting or aggressive. Doing so ensures that the use of force follows a logical, justifiable, continuum. It also dramatically increases the effectiveness of any physical force exerted. Additionally, witnesses to the event will hear the command, and will be better able to place the use of force in its proper perspective.

Step 4. Soft empty hand control, such as grasping the subject's elbow and wrist, and leading them away (escort hold) may be required to remove the subject from the conflict zone and out of the public eye. **WARNING:** At this point you must expect to get hit and expect it to hurt. You should not allow yourself to be surprised by a "sucker punch." Whenever you touch an aggressive person, expect an immediate response; an escalation of aggression. You could get stabbed, hit with an object, or shot. You would do best to evaluate the situation carefully before you try to intervene at this stage in the continuum.

Step 5. At this point, if you are not working out regularly and practicing defensive tactics religiously, do not attempt to participate on this level of aggression response. You will not be qualified to respond to required increased levels of aggression. Call for public assistance, and use verbal deescalation until the police arrive.

Step 6. In extreme cases you will be forced to use a chemical incapacitation device, normally oleoresin capsicum aerosols (pepper spray), on the subject to protect yourself or others, or to obtain compliance with handcuffing or come-along. This chemical incapacitation device is considered a less than lethal defensive weapon. Be very careful of weapon retention and spray-back. Try to avoid bringing a weapon to the confrontation that can be used against you. If you take yourself out of the equation by becoming incapacitated by your own spray, you will be of no use to anyone. Remember, it is required that you administer first-aid to the subject immediately after you have restrained the subject, if you have used this spray.

Step 7. The next level of confrontation escalation is the hard, empty-hand control such as joint manipulation and decentralization. **WARNING:** Don't attempt this unless you have had documented, professional training. If you have no specialized training, do not attempt to participate in increased aggression escalation. Get lots of help, continue verbal deescalation, and overwhelm the subject until the police arrive.

Step 8. The next level of escalation is the empty hand impact. Deliver stunning techniques to motor points and other soft tissue targets. **WARNING:** Don't attempt this unless you are properly trained and proficient. If you have no specialized training, do not attempt to participate in increased aggression escalation. Get lots of help, keep up the verbal deescalation, and overwhelm the subject until the police arrive.

Step 9. The next level of escalation is the use of aerosol chemical agents, such as CS and CN gas. These can, if improperly used, cause serious injury. Be careful of weapon retention, spray-back, and the spraying of by-standers inadvertently. Also, remember it is required that you administer first-aid to the subject immediately after you have restrained the subject whenever chemical spray was used.

Step 10. The next level of escalation is the use of intermediate weapons such as batons and other impact weapons, stun guns, and tasers. **WARNING:** Don't attempt this unless you are trained and experienced in the use of batons and other impact weapons. If you have no specialized training, do not attempt to participate in this level of aggression escalation. Get lots of help, and overwhelm the subject until the police arrive.

Step 11. The next level of escalation is the use of lateral vascular neck restraint, which compresses the carotid arteries in the neck, causing the subject to pass out. Improper use of this hold could cause death. Also included would be impact weapon strikes to joints, which can cause serious bodily injury—and can be considered deadly force. **WARNING:** Don't even think about this unless you have received specialized training, and there is absolutely no alternative! In addition, don't attempt this level of escalation unless you are trained and experienced in the use of batons and other impact weapons. Also, certain techniques and unusual weapons may be perceived as being brutal by the public. Using them may constitute some inherent liability risk, even if they were used properly.

Step 12. The next level of escalation is the use of deadly force such as firearms, impact weapon strikes to the head or neck, or empty hand blows to the head, neck, throat, and so forth.. There is only one acceptable reason for use of deadly force, and that is the protection of human life. Use of deadly force to protect property will open you up to serious civil law suits and possible criminal prosecution. **WARNING:** Don't attempt this unless you are trained and experienced in the use of deadly force. Remember that after deadly force is used you have a duty to give first-aid until emergency medical assistance arrives. If you kill someone in the line of duty, even though you were 100 percent right, expect to be sued. You could even be arrested and go to jail. Expect to go to trial for a civil and criminal proceeding.

ESCALATION/DEESCALATION CONTINUUM

To better understand the application of the confrontation continuum, the following escalation/deescalation continuums have been prepared. If you are a police officer or a member of a highly trained private security contingent, you will be trained to participate in an escalation/deescalation procedure that will look something like the following:

1. Officer arrives on the scene, observes the situation, and engages the aggressor immediately. Officer gives verbal commands.
2. Aggressor escalates aggression; officer escalates force. Officer combines verbal commands with escalation of force.
3. Aggressor deescalates aggression; officer deescalates force and evaluates the situation. Officer combines verbal commands with deescalation of force.
4. Officer escalates choice of defensive weapons in response to the aggressor's choice of offensive weapons. If aggressor has a club the officer might choose a firearm.
5. This escalation and deescalation back and forth will continue until the aggressor succumbs to the force of the officer.
6. The officer must win every round of aggression. If striking the aggressor is required, the officer will use the element of surprise and strike decisively.
7. The officer will administer first aid immediately after the subject has been subdued.
8. The subject will also be debriefed. This means that they should be talked to so that their ego is restored. This can include an interview with the subject for use in assisting him/her, as well as for documentation of the event. Note that the subject may admit to being wrong or may apologize. This should be accepted and noted! A brief statement as to why the subject was restrained and what the violation entailed may be made. This could include the words such as "I had to handcuff you because you were assaulting me," or "I had to search you for your safety and mine." Debriefing is used to set the subject at ease, prevent future problems, and obtain information for the report.
9. The officer will thoroughly document the entire event. Statements made during debriefing that are admissions or apologies should be recorded. Steps to be taken by the subject during the next crisis situation should also be included. In many cases, a "contract" can be written where the subject agrees not to repeat this behavior in the future. This should be noted in the final report.

If you are a member of the average security contingent, with no training in self defense or the use of weapon, you would want to follow an escalation/deescalation procedure that looks more like this.

1. Officer arrives on the scene, observes the situation, and radios for help. Officer chooses a safe distance and location before commencing verbal deescalation. The communication procedure will commence as soon as the officer has reported the incident, and taken a safe cover.
2. The officer identifies escape routes, items to use to block aggression if needed, weapons of opportunity that could be used in an emergency, and evaluate each person in the immediate vicinity of the aggressor.
3. Aggressor escalates aggression, officer backs off, takes cover, keeping a safe distance. Officer combines verbal deescalation techniques with his move to safety.
4. Aggressor deescalates his aggression, officer continues verbal deescalation techniques. Officer opens up a dialogue and keeps it going.
5. Officer avoids personal confrontation at all costs except in deadly force situations. If the officer is in the grasp of the aggressor, the officer uses force to break away, give or get space, put something between the officer and the aggressor, and then continues the dialogue at a safer distance.
6. The officer must ensure that the aggressor is not forcing him into a state of preclusion, where maximum force will be necessary to escape. At the same time, the officer must ensure that the aggressor has a back door or escape route, and is not being backed into a corner. If the aggressor escapes from the area, the security officer will secure the area and the individuals in that area.
7. The officer must win every round of aggression. If striking the aggressor is required, the officer will use the element of surprise and strike decisively. The only purpose of the escalation of aggression is to break a hold, which the aggressor has put on, and which creates the risk of injury. The officer must break the hold and get to safety. There should be no attempt to force this aggressor into submission, as a trained, armed protection officer would be expected to do.
8. If a physical confrontation occurs, the officer calls for medical assistance and renders first-aid until the medics arrive.
9. Obviously, communication skills are of paramount importance! **This is the essence of defensive tactics; officers dealing with violent, aggressive persons should become devoted students of interpersonal communication.** In this way, the use of force must be precluded by verbalizing and retreating, where possible.

OFFICER SAFETY ISSUES

There are four individuals or groups who the security officer is concerned with protecting. They are: the security officer himself of herself, the apparent victim, the general public, and the perpetrator. It is important to understand that the order of importance is that the officer comes first on the list. Officer safety is primary, because if the officer is taken out, there may be no hope for the victim or anyone else. However, the officer may be his or her own worst enemy in times of stress, especially if the "body and mind" turns in on itself. That happens when the "tachy-psyche" effect takes over.

As pointed out above, self-control is the most important factor when engaging in the use of force. It is not unusual, when faced with an aggressor, for the officer to become extremely nervous, tense, and shaky. These signs indicate that the officer is afraid of confrontation. Left unabated, this shaking and fear may escalate into something called the "tachy-psyche" effect. That is when you can really get hurt. "Tachy" means rapid or accelerated. "Psyche" means the mind, functioning as the center of thought, feeling, and behavior, and consciously or unconsciously adjusting and relating the body to its social and physical environment. Some identifying characteristics of this phenomenon are the following:

- Rapid heart beat
- Rapid mental processing
- Sweating
- Dilated pupils
- Tunnel vision occurs
- Auditory occlusion blocks out sound
- Numbness and heaviness felt in extremities
- Loss of dexterity in fingers, arms, legs
- Shortening of breath
- Everything goes in slow motion
- Loss of bodily functions—stop breathing, bladder release, pass out or paralysis

If this happens to the officer, as the officer approaches an aggressive person, there is no telling what might result. Either the officer will be rendered defenseless, or the officer may respond with excessive force. If you feel this happening, take a tactical retreat until you can regain your composure. Only deep relaxation can counter this condition and alleviate the symptoms. Unfortunately, in most critical incident situations, there isn't enough time to retreat. The only prevention of this condition is training. An officer who is trained to handle critical incident situations, including handling aggressive persons, is not as prone to experience these symptoms.

OPTIMAL DISTANCE

It is possible that while approaching an aggressive subject, you can inadvertently set off an act of aggression, simply by getting too close to the aggressor. That is, if you enter the aggressor's private space, you can make the aggressor so uncomfortable that the aggressor will strike out in anger.

Optimal distance is a term that defines that area which extends out in all directions from an individual, within which the person feels safe and secure. Invasion of this space will result in a reflex reaction. This space is also known as a person's "comfort zone." Unwelcome invasion of a person's optimal distance could result in escalation of conflict, even if you don't touch the individual. It is important that security officers respect this optimal distance. Our job is to be part of the solution, not part of the problem.

One reason, other than for officer safety, that we recommend communication at 10 feet or more from the subject, is so that you will not inadvertently encroach on the subject's personal space, and set off an aggressive reaction. While this is a great distance, violent persons often have an extended personal zone. They need lots of space!

As for additional safety, the officer must be aware of the different distances that the officer must honor to keep safe, called the "reactionary gap." This gap is the distance between the subject and the officer, within which, if the subject decides to punch, stab, or hit the officer, the officer may, or may not, be able to defend against the attack. The officer should be aware that a reactionary gap of 8 to 10 feet away from the subject will provide a reaction time for the officer to defend against the punch. However, the reactionary gap for using a firearm in defense against the knife is approximately 25 feet.

The reactionary gap to defend against the gun, works in just the opposite way. In fact, the closer to the gun the better to allow disarming techniques, if you are trained in those techniques. Other than in a disarming attempt, reactionary gaps are fairly irrelevant when it comes to guns. Taking shelter and running might work, depending on a number of variables. Let the circumstances be your guide.

Whatever you do, don't rush in and attempt to touch the aggressive subject. If you wish to escort the subject, approach from the side or rear. Even then, unless the aggressor is handcuffed, try to control the subject without bodily contact. Verbal commands and gestures should be employed.

DEFANGING THE SNAKE

"Defanging the snake" is a term that is used to mean the elimination of the means of aggression from an aggressive person. It could include the removal of weapons, or the rendering of arms and or legs useless, either by pain, paralysis, breakage, or use of restrains. The fangs of the snake are where the poison that can hurt us is located. In our case, the knife blade, the bullet, the club, and the fists, are the "fangs" that can cause us harm, and possibly permanent injury or death.

Another way to defang the snake is to eliminate the fuel of the aggression. Separating warring parties, or removing the combatants from the conflict zone, could have the same effect as pouring water on a fire. Take away the fuel and the fire goes out. Thus, in many cases, if you remove the more aggressive of the two combatants, you can achieve the same effect as taking the weapon away from the aggressor. *A word of caution here, though:* You should only do this with backup present. Always keep in mind officer safety.

ELEMENTS OF AGGRESSION

An aggressive situation is usually more complex than a simple case of one person being upset with another. There are usually highly charged emotions driving the aggression. The trick is to attend to the business of assisting, without getting dragged into one side or the other of the controversy. It is important to recognize that aggression has two parts, the fuel of aggression and the means of aggression. The fuel of aggression consists basically of the emotional side of the confrontation, and may include any number of the following:

- Perceptions/attitudes
- Belief systems
- Rebellion
- Mental/medical conditions
- Chemical abuse problems
- Revenge, jealousy, passion
- Feelings of inadequacy

The means of aggression consists basically of the weapons of the confrontation, and may include any number of the following:

- Hands, feet, elbows and head
- Nonlethal weapons (chemical sprays)
- Lethal weapons (knife, gun)
- Vehicles
- Weapons of opportunity (things lying around)

DEALING WITH AGGRESSION

The most dangerous situation you may ever face is a violence-prone situation. Violence-prone situations can easily lead to injury to yourself, or to others. In addition, a lawsuit could result. What can you do in violence-prone situations to reduce the risk of using excessive force? The following are a few ideas on safely managing violence-prone encounters:

1. **Recognize your own emotions.** In itself, this causes the professional to calm down. In most people, violence is reached in stages—from anxiety, to defensive behavior, to physically acting out violent behavior. Cooling off the escalating violence-prone situation is best done by remaining calm and professional.
2. **Remember that when a person is in a rage, options cannot be seen.** As people grow angrier, they fail to realize that they have several options. They usually see their options of FLEEING or FIGHTING. Other options, such as discussing the problem and seeking a solution, may not be considered. Rage takes over cognition. The formula for rage is clearly C = E/I.
3. **Avoid humiliating subjects.** Some officers will create problems when speaking to a subject in a sensitive situation. When this happens, the subject will shut down communication, a condition that could become explosive. The best policy is to play it low key. Protect your space, and be ready to execute self-defense plans at the first indication of aggression. Remember that EVERYBODY—even the serene, little old lady—is potentially violent under the proper circumstances.

Slowing down the action, respecting the subject's personal space, and using emphatic listening skills help to deescalate.

4. **If the encounter becomes tough, get or give space.** As the aggression level escalates, the best relaxant is space. CLEAR THE CONFLICT ZONE! If two people are exchanging heated words, both should take a walk—in opposite directions. Immediate separation of antagonists can prevent a confrontation. At the same time they both should be "out of sight" and "out of sound" of each other. Get them turned around and as far away from each other as is practical. If possible, use walls to separate the subjects.
5. **Proactive prevention works better than reaction.** Officers must be receptive to warning signs of violence, rather than be reactionary. Understand that people who are antagonized by others may go from calmness to rage in seconds.
6. **Sharpen your observation skills.** Observing alcohol use and levels of intoxication can be obvious warning sings, as can playful pushing and shoving, and loud in-your-face type of communication. Boyfriend/girlfriend jealousy situations and domestic problems can also become volatile.

Some provocateurs will try to provoke a hostile, angry response from you. This is often done with a reference to your ethnic or racial background, or a derogatory statement about your mother. You must recognize that the name caller is trying to cause you to lose control, permitting escalation of violence

When you lose your temper, someone else has control over you.

Remember the formula for control: C = I/E. Remember, WHOEVER LOSES CONTROL—LOSES! Therefore it is in your best interest to identify indicators of aggression, which we call "red flags" of aggression.

Weapons of opportunity
Disguised weapons
Weapons in plain sight
All edged weapons
Perpetrator's hands
Relatives, friends, others in close proximity
Subject's red face
Subject's direct prolonged eye contact
Subject's quick and deep breathing
Subject's head and shoulders back
Subject's standing as tall as possible
Subject's hands pumping
Subject's finger pointing
Subject's moving in and out of your personal space
Subject's belligerence, yelling, cursing
Subject's pounding fist on walls and tables
Subject's verbal threats

VERBAL DEESCALATION

Verbal deescalation is just about anything you can say that fits the situation you find at the incident scene. The successful deescalation will be more a product of your attitude and level of professionalism, than of the actions you take.

At some point you may be surprised by the aggressor, or overwhelmed by more than one aggressor, and you will find yourself in a fight/flee/flow situation. That is, if you can't fight and you can't flee, then *flow*! By "flow" we mean verbal deescalation. You will have to talk your way out of the predicament. There cannot be a prepared list of canned verbal communication that will fit every situation. You will be more successful drawing on your own words, customized for the particular circumstances. The key to a successful verbal deescalation is in your level of professionalism with regards to caring, empathy, command of the language, personal sincerity, and candor.

WARNING: When practicing verbal deescalation, don't let down your guard. Keep in mind officer safety.

APPLYING VERBAL DEESCALATION TO AGGRESSIVE SITUATIONS

If you are called to a routine confrontation, where the participants appear to be reasonable and the likelihood of injury to yourself or to others is low, then you may wish to follow some of the following deescalation suggestions:

- Respect subject's dignity.
- Do not shout commands.
- Be careful not to become part of the problem.
- Assume officer safety distance (10 to 15 feet).
- Provide a pleasant greeting such as "How can I help you?"
- Assume a noncombative attitude.
- Use non-threatening questions. Avoid "Why?" questions.
- Slow everything down, take your time. "Calmness is contagious."
- Keep hands and chest high and ready to react.
- Attempt to move subject away from conflict zone.
- Listen intently to subject's words.
- Project empathy with subject's cause.
- Observe subject's hands and body language.
- Conduct a visual frisk, check for observable weapons.
- Look for weapons of opportunity.
- Listen to peripheral persons. They can be witnesses, "cheerleaders," or assailants.
- Keep talking and negotiating a solution.
- Practice officer safety at all times.
- Make the decision to arrest or release.

Procedures for dealing with a violence prone individual differ somewhat from dealing with the average aggressive situation. If the likelihood of injury is certain or extremely high, then you may wish to follow some of these suggestions:

- Subject's dignity is not the main priority. "Defanging the snake" is the priority!
- You will still want to respect the subject's dignity.
- Respect officer safety distance.
- Assume a self-defense attitude.
- Use loud, clear, directive commands for officer safety.
- Keep hands on your choice of weapons, or have weapons drawn.
- Call for backup before entering the conflict.
- Give subject directives to reach a solution.
- Keep talking and negotiating a solution.
- Listen intently to subject's words.
- Project empathy with subject's cause.
- Observe his hands and body language.
- When backup arrives conduct a search for weapons.
- Cuff and search for officer safety.
- Continue dialogue with subject.
- Listen to witnesses; take names, addresses, and phone numbers.
- Take notes of what witnesses have said. Use quotes from the witnesses.
- Make the decision to detain, arrest, or release.
- Use deadly force only when a life is threatened or serious bodily injury is imminent.

LETHAL AND LESS-THAN-LETHAL WEAPONS MANAGEMENT

The employment of weapons is often grasped at by protection officers in the wake of a frightening experience. Fear is usually the primary motivator for protection officers asking management if they can be armed. Unfortunately, weapons do not solve the threat problem all by themselves. They are tools that are necessary in certain circumstances. They require increased responsibility and skill to be employed in an acceptable manner. Handcuffing a resistant subject is difficult, and must be done tactfully. Spraying an assailant does not negate the threat; it merely helps to control the person. The officer must still step out of the way of the aggressor and take appropriate follow-up measures. The same is true with impact weapons, and even firearms. Protective body movement out of the danger zone, employment of the weapon, and proper follow-up, must be done for any weapon.

Weapons are only useful when in the hand of someone proficient at using them, in a situation where they are the appropriate tools to use.

Weapons offer added protection—if properly selected and employed—but they also increase the professional obligations of the protection officer dramatically. Their use involves substantial judgment and skill on the part of the officer. Such judgment and skill only comes after extensive instruction and practice in interpersonal communication, deescalation, interviewing, unarmed defensive tactics, legal considerations, etc. These are some of the proficiency areas that must be mastered, prior to the effective use of weapons. The following saying helps to put this into perspective.

You can't use a weapon if you can't use your hands. You can't use your hands if you can't use your voice. And you can't use your voice if you can't use your brain.

Whatever weapons are being employed, be they handcuffs, pepper spray, firearms, or impact weapons, the following guidelines will help to maintain that they are handled in a safe, appropriate manner:

1. Weapons should only be handled by persons who have been trained in how to use them. Training must be refreshed periodically. It must also be thoroughly documented.
2. Weapons should remain holstered or locked up unless they are to be employed in an actual confrontation, cleaned, or used during formal, supervised training. There must be no showing of weapons to curious persons, and absolutely no playing with weapons.
3. All weapons should be thoroughly checked by the officer carrying them prior to starting on duty.
4. The supervisor should check weapons on a regular basis.
5. A maintenance system should be in place for all weapons to include routine maintenance, as per the manufacturer's instructions, as well as work by armorers or manufacturers when needed.
6. Weapons should be supplied by the employer. The employer must exercise and retain control over the weapon.
7. Weapons, ammunition, holsters, and so on should not be modified except by a manufacturer's representative or qualified armorer.
8. All laws, property owners' wishes, and insurance carrier regulations on the carrying and use of weapons must be respected.

Unfortunately, weapons are occasionally "sold" by someone to management without management really assessing them fully. Seemingly impressive demonstration of a weapon's capability, put on by an expert who stages the demonstration, is not the reason to select a weapon for a protective force! Neither is the following of a fad, or the securing of a "bargain!"

Weapons selection is a serious decision, which must be made only after extensive research. On the other extreme, vacillating on a weapons decision—and not arming security officers when this is needed—raises unacceptable levels of risk to protection forces, and to those they are employed to protect. The following is a list of considerations which managers should review when selecting a weapons/weapons system:

1. For what specific need was the weapon selected?
2. How is the weapon most likely to be used (tactical research)?

3. What was the selection process used for adopting the weapon?
   a) Why was the specific weapon chosen over other weapons?
   b) Who made the decision?
   c) What was the decision making process?
      • Independent research studies?
      • Medical research?
      • Comparative bids?
4. What type of initial training is required?
5. Who can provide this training?
6. What type of refresher training is given?
7. Who can provide this training?
8. Can instructor qualifications be clearly demonstrated to the satisfaction of a court?
9. Is training adequately documented?
10. Is a continuous tactical review of the weapon's use in place, which shows how it is actually being used?
11. What training have supervisors had in the use of the weapons?
    a) Initial training?
    b) Periodic training?
    c) Training or education above and beyond what line officers receive?
12. Are reasonable and enforceable policies governing the use of the weapons in effect?
13. Are weapons carried by, or accessible to, officers who are off-duty?
14. Is weapon retention addressed?
15. What is the skill level required for the use of the weapon?
16. Does the weapon fit in with other weapons used by the organization or other agencies that the organization may interact with during an emergency?

REPORT WRITING IN USE OF FORCE CASES

What is involved in writing the report of an incident, where a use of force was necessary and reasonable? It should be enough to just sit down and write, in chronological order, the truthful facts of the case. Unfortunately, in our litigious society, where cash-hungry lawyers and an aggressive media lie in waiting for the next abuse of force case, the officer cannot be carefree. The report must be written, taking into consideration the technical requirements of criminal and civil liability, in both state and federal court.

Know your audience! You must assume that the paper you are about to write will be in the hands of an opposing attorney, and you will be in front of a judge in the near future. If the use of force required a firearm pain compliance, a chemical or electronic incapacitation device, baton, kicks, or other physical confrontation, your report must be thorough, concise, and accurate. In addition to all of this, the report must be absolutely true, as you witnessed the truth.

While writing the report, the officer must cover the following:

I. NECESSITY (What the Perpetrator Did)
   A. Self-Defense
   B. Defense of Others
   C. To Prevent Escape
II. REASONABLENESS (What You Did)
   A. Department Policy
   B. Department Training
   C. Supervisor's Instructions
   D. Conscious, Deliberate, Controlled, and Intentional Use of Force
   E. Caused By Aggressiveness of the Perpetrator
   F. Medical Follow-up (First Aid)
III. THE REPORT MUST BE BALANCED AND COORDINATED
   A. The Report Follows a Chronology
   B. The Report Has No Contradictions
   C. Times Stated Match Other Reports and Records
   D. Facts Stated Match Other Reports and Records

Any one of the above components that are lacking in the report will provide an opportunity for the plaintiff's attorney, or the prosecutor, to attack the integrity of the report, and ultimately your testimony could fall apart. You may have performed perfectly, followed all the rules, provided a truthful report, and still lose the case over the fact that you failed to write a proper report.

In reviewing the report, play "devil's advocate" with yourself. Try to anticipate what the lawyers or media might try to make out of what you are about to write. Review your organization's policy before writing it. Leave no gaps in the report to be filled in later. Don't assume anything. Never leave out a fact because you thought everyone would understand the fact without having to write it down. What you may think is common sense may be distorted by the plaintiff's lawyer or prosecutor to appear to the jury or judge as a cover up or a deception.

Keep in mind that the main thrust of the defense lawyer, or the plaintiff's lawyer, is to present their client as the victim in the case, not the perpetrator. They will work hard to accuse you of being the perpetrator and using the "but for" test, they will say, "but for the illegal or negligent acts or omissions of the officer, this poor client would not have sustained the injuries that he did." Be sure that nothing in your report supports the assertion that your acts were illegal or negligent.

Your report should pass the "reasonable person" test. That is, either the jury or the judge should be able to use your report to get into the scene sufficiently to be able to form a mental picture of what actually took place. From that picture, he or she should be able to determine what he or she would have done under exactly the same circumstances. If the report follows the above guidelines, it should lead that person to the logical conclusion that the officer acted in a reasonable and necessary fashion.

CONCLUSION

Ultimately, use of force comes down to something to be avoided. Just review all that has been presented here. There are so many traps and pitfalls in this area of a security officer's duties. Careful consideration must be taken before the officer knows about use of force and proper procedure. The better equipped officer will be able to participate successfully, win every round of aggression and escape personal injury and law suits. Personal training is the key to successful aggression deescalation. The general education provided in this chapter is offered to start the officer's professional development. Every person who puts on the uniform of a security officer should become an earnest student of the legal and tactical aspects of the **Use of Force.**

REFERENCES

Fisher, Robert J. and Green. Gion. *Introduction to Security,* Fifth Edition, Stoneham, MA, Butterworth-Heinemann, 1922, p. 3.

The American Heritage Dictionary, Second Edition.

Ouellette, Roland. *Management of Aggressive Behavior*, Powers Lake, WI, Performance Dimensions Publishing, 1993, p. 8.

RESOURCES

American Society of Law Enforcement Trainers (302/645-4080 or 302/645-4084 fax) sponsors seminars, an annual conference, and publishes *The Law Enforcement Trainer*. Visit www.aslet.org.

Butterworth–Heinemann, an imprint of Elsevier Science, is the largest publisher of Security texts. *Use of Force By Private Security Personnel* and *Private Security Law: Case Studies* are some of the titles available. Visit http://stbooks.elsevier.com/security or call (800) 545-2522, 200 Wheeler Road, 6th Floor, Burlington, MA 01803.

Calibre Press (800/323-0037) is the premier officer survival organization. They provide seminars, books, and videos covering a vast array of officer survival topics.

Crisis Prevention Institute (800/558-8976 or 414/783-5906 fax) is a leader in violence management. CPI provides certification in Nonviolent Crisis Intervention. They have an extensive collection of video-based instructional programs such as "Breaking Up Fights," "The Art of Setting Limits," "Documentation: Your Best Defense," etc.

Professional Training Resources (800/998-9400) is the leading supplier of Security books and videos. Hundreds of titles are available from various publishers on topics ranging from Self-Defense to Civil Liability.

REB Training International (603/446-9393 or 603/446-9394 fax) is a leader in Oleoresin Capsicum Aerosol Training ("pepper spray"). REB also has various training programs for security officers, such as PR-24, and the Management of Aggressive Behavior (MOAB).

SECURITY QUIZ
Use of Force

1. Reports written after use of force must have no _____.
2. Use of force can be defined according to the concepts of _____, reasonableness, and _____.
3. Did the aggressor have the _____ to harm you?
4. Pepper spray is lower on the Use of Force Continuum than mace or tear gas.
    ☐ T ☐ F
5. Security officers may have a legal obligation to use of force under certain state statutes.
    ☐ T ☐ F
6. "Conflict _____ is the cornerstone of officer survival."
7. List five things the officer who is authorized to carry a weapon must bear in mind.
    (a)_____
    (b)_____
    (c)_____
    (d)_____
    (e)_____
8. Handcuffing a resistant subject is easy.
    ☐ T ☐ F
9. The _____ gap is the distance between the subject and the officer within which the officer may not be able to defend him or herself if the subject decides to attack.
10. Persons engaged in fighting should be made to sit facing each other in the same room.
    ☐ T ☐ F

DEFENSIVE TACTICS AND OFFICER SAFETY

By Michael Stroberger, CPO, CSS, CPOI, CLSD, CPP

One of the basic intentions behind protective operations is the prevention of harm to people. The methods of achieving this, with regard to the clients, employees, visitors, and even unwelcome persons are usually fairly well defined. We observe, report and, in certain environments and situations, lend support. One thing that should be paramount in every officer's mind on a continuous basis is that they are responsible for protecting themselves as well.

To do this, each officer must understand that they are in the best position to provide for their own safety. They must be aware of some of the basic concepts involved in conflict and must be prepared to operate within that environment if the situation calls for this. While it is impossible to train for every given possibility, we can look at some more common factors, and how to manage them.

BASIC GOAL

The basic primary goal of every person is to prevent himself or herself from being injured. Secondary to that would be the protection of others, then the protection of property or other items deemed to be of value.

In most cases, the avoidance of direct conflict is the ideal tactic! Officers are often told to "observe and report," yet rush into conflict despite this. The execution of our duties can be achieved, in most cases, without being directly in harms way. Observing an intruder, the typical response of maintaining observation, while calling the incident in to dispatch or local law enforcement would be ideal, and would provide the relative safety of distance from the subject. Trying to apprehend them would be directly entering into a hazardous environment.

PREVENTION OF COMBAT

In the execution of a patrol, an officer encounters many areas where potential aggressors might be. This is a part of our jobs, and part of the reason that protective officers are employed. One of the most critical aspects of defensive tactics is the avoidance on unnecessary conflicts. When performing protective duties, one should do the following:

1. Use caution at all times. Do not rush into areas which provide concealment for potential aggressors, or which contain what might be the goal of an intrusion or attack.
2. Call for support when suspicious of a person or area.
3. Use lighting to your advantage. When patrolling an area at night, walk behind any ground-mounted lights, so that they illuminate your area of observation without highlighting your presence.
4. Use all of your senses. Often, the sense of smell or hearing will give away a potential threat, long before it is seen.

Of course, the underlying theme is that potential threats should be watched for and responded to accordingly. Do not rush into potential conflicts, as this does not allow time for consideration of additional threats, or a full understanding of the incident itself.

WHAT IS COMBAT?

Combat is the interaction between two or more persons with the intent to cause harm, for any reason, or to control or eliminate them. This is a simple and direct definition. With this in mind, entering into apprehensions, breaking up a fight, or even physically removing a person from an area in which they do not belong, are all forms of combat. It is also true that combat can escalate in intensity, very rapidly. It is because of this that caution must always be a consideration when dealing with others.

The basic mechanics of combat dictate that it is a struggle to impose your own control over another, or others, through manipulation of timing, space, and damage.

Control of timing means that you can achieve a goal faster than those opposing you. As there are many methods of achieving most goals, the quicker one, without giving up effectiveness, usually achieves that success. A person throwing a wide, sweeping punch is less likely to succeed, than the opponent that executes a quick linear technique, by virtue simply of the fact that the fist has less distance to travel.

Control over space is related to being in the most advantageous position at a given time. This provides the ability to execute techniques with speed, and to be more selective in your choice of a course of action. A person standing to the side of his/her opponent has not only options of where to strike, if this is appropriate, but also an improved chance of disengaging if they so choose. The person with an opponent at his/her side, has only half of their body immediately available to deal with them, and can only accelerate in an attempt to achieve separation, in directions that are completely within the field of view of that opponent.

Control of damage is related to choice of techniques and the probable injures that result. This is strongly linked with the legal aspects of justified use of force, as well as the mechanics of how it factors into the overall concept of combat.

Having described the three basic factors, it should also be obvious that each one strongly influences the other two. As examples, a person with good speed and mobility can more easily move into advantageous positions. A person in the proper position will find a strike to disable or slow an opponent and is more easily executed. A person whose attacker is slowed by an injury will have an increased speed advantage, when altering positioning or technique selection. Each is linked to the others, as well as being an independent factor.

KNOW YOUR LIMITATIONS

A thorough understanding of what you can do, and what you are permitted to do, is absolutely essential. Without this, any combat situation can result in extreme physical injury, followed by emotionally painful litigation.

Become familiar with your own physical conditioning. Most people do not know how quickly they tire when faced with a prolonged combat encounter. Certainly a fight which ends up on the ground in a grappling situation is extremely tiring. Regular cardiovascular conditioning, within a physician-approved program, will not only benefit your ability to endure such stresses, but will give you a better understanding of what you are physically capable of sustaining.

On the legal side, prepare your mind. Study your local laws, and determine what is permitted in your area, with regard to responses to aggression, observed crimes, and similar situations. You must act within these guidelines to reduce the likelihood of litigation. If a person is injured as a result of your actions, or in an incident in which you participated, chances are you will be facing litigation. If you have acted within the guidelines of that jurisdiction, this will be easier to defend against. A good rule of thumb is to never exceed the level of force directed against you. In many cases, a lesser level of force, applied with more thought and preparation, will effectively defend against an aggressor. Find out your limits and prepare accordingly.

STROBERGER'S RULES OF SEVEN

One set of general rules, identified over time and found to hold true in almost all situations, can be summed up as follows:

1. Most exchanges of gunfire occur within 7 feet to 7 yards.
2. As much as 14 percent of people do not react strongly to certain chemical sprays. Do not assume that any weapon or defensive tool will always be effective!
3. An aggressor can cover 21 feet at a full run before most people can draw and accurately fire their weapon. Maintain at least this distance from subjects that are dangerous, potentially armed, or highly excited.

As you can see, these basic rules of caution also reference the fact that timing, space and damage must be controlled to achieve success.

USE OF FORCE

Critical to the understanding of how one responds to a threat, is the concept of a relative level of force. In the following model, the various types of responses are ranked, based upon the relative level of force which they represent.

When following this progressive chart, one should note that the responses appearing at the top of the chart are generally perceived to be less forceful than those that appear near the bottom of the chart. With this in mind, it is essential that any response to a situation fall as close to the top of this chart as possible, while still allowing those responding to protect themselves or others from great bodily harm. In most cases, beginning your response at the top of this progressive flow, then moving toward more forceful responses if the current level of force is not sufficient, will show that the responder did not intend to cause great harm in defending themselves, but tried less forceful options initially. Often, it is this attempt to do less harm initially, which convinces courts that an officer responded with only due care and required force to an existing threat. It is the officers that immediately jump to the bottom of the chart, when responding to a threat, which more often find themselves on the loosing end of a civil suit or facing criminal charges.

In the following chart, you will note that the situation and perceived level of force are indicated in the following manners:

Control of Cooperative Persons—These are people who simply do not carry out a lawful order but are not threatening or resistive in their actions. They require some convincing to do as they are ordered.

Control of Passive-Resistive Persons—People who refuse a lawful order and attempt to pull away from being led in the right direction. These persons do not attempt to harm or manipulate the officer but continue to refuse to cooperate.

Control of Active-Resistive Persons—This would be a situation in which the subject is not only refusing a lawful order but intentionally pushing the officer away, trying to manipulate the officers hands or arms, in such a manner as to make Low Force options ineffective. These persons may make occasional aggressive movements or lash out in a disorganized and relatively ineffective manner.

Control of Active-Aggressive Persons—These subjects are believed, through their verbally or physically expressed intentions, to intend to inflict harm upon those attempting to impose a lawful order upon them or to others that might be within their ability to immediately harm.

Control of Active-Combative Persons—These subjects are believed, through their verbally or physically expressed intentions, to intend to inflict great harm, including attempting to kill, to those attempting to impose a lawful order upon them or to others that might be within their ability to immediately harm.

THE USE OF FORCE CONTINUUM

Situation	Perceived Level of Force	Officer Response or Actions
Control of Cooperative Persons	No Force	Verbal Persuasion
Control of Cooperative Persons	No Force	Body Language and Positioning
Control of Cooperative Persons	Low Force	Physical Contact Controls
Control of Passive-Resistive Persons	Low Force	Joint Control Techniques
Control of Passive-Resistive Persons	Low Force	Pressure Point and Pain Controls
Control of Passive-Resistive Persons	Medium Force	Chemical Controls
Control of Active-Resistive Persons	Medium Force	Weapon Assisted Controls
Control of Active-Resistive Persons	Medium Force	Weapon Assisted Pressure Point and Pain Controls
Control of Active-Aggressive Persons	High Force	Striking Techniques
Control of Active-Aggressive Persons	High Force	Weapon Striking Techniques
Control of Active Combative-Persons	Deadly Force	Striking Techniques to Critical Targets
Control of Active Combative-Persons	Deadly Force	Firearms

The perceived level of force would be an indication of how the average reasonable person, upon witnessing the techniques performed, might assess the aggressiveness of the officer's response. In general, it is better to respond with as low a level of force as possible, while still acting to preserve the health and safety of all persons involved.

The specific responses can be explained as follows:

Verbal Persuasion —Describing the lawful order to the subject without placing the officer's body in their intended line of movement, or in any manner intimidating or directing them through physical motion or presence. In most cases, this is the first moment of contact with a subject. **Often, if handled properly, the level of force does not need to progress beyond this point!**

Body Language and Positioning—The placing of an officer in a doorway, which the subject is attempting to enter. Position an outstretched hand, palm forward, to indicate that entry would be resisted if attempted. There is absolutely no physical contact at this level of response!

Physical Contact Controls—By making contact with the body of the subject, the officer is now utilizing perceived force. This level of contact would include actions as simple as a hand on the arm to guide the subject to the proper exit door. Any contact made with the subject will fall into this level of force, or a higher level of force.

Joint Control Techniques—These are techniques that rely on manipulation of limbs to entice the subject to move in a desired direction, cease or initiate a desired action, or comply with the wishes of the person executing the technique. An example would be grasping the arm at the wrist and elbow, then turning the arm in such a manner that the subject is inclined to walk forward, to relieve stress upon the elbow joint.

Pressure Point/Pain Controls—Applying pressure to key parts of the body with the intent of causing pain. These are usually nerve bundles or muscle and connective tissue locations, which cause an inordinate amount of pain, if manipulated properly. In contrast to the previous level, where joints are manipulated to produce the expectation of pain, if the desired order is not complied with in this phase, the actual sensation of pain is the motivator.

Chemical Controls—The use of such tools as OC sprays, commonly referred to as "pepper spray," to cause great deals of pain, and limitations to vision and ability to resist in a coordinated manner are the limit of what most observers would call "low force" responses. In fact, some observers might rank this response higher in the use of force continuum when noting the extreme level of pain that the subject suffers. In most cases, these tools do not result in permanent harm, although any officer utilizing them should have some form of decontaminating wash or spray available, in case the subject does have an unusual reaction to the chemicals utilized.

Weapon Assisted Controls—The use of an expandable baton, night stick, and even a radio to physically manipulate the subject falls into this level of force or a higher level. Through the introduction of the use of a weapon or tool, the officer has increased the overall level of force of the situation. This phase would include not only directing a person with the use of a tool or weapon, but also the use of these to increase the effectiveness of joint manipulation techniques as well.

Weapon Assisted Pressure Point and Pain Controls— Utilizing a weapon to increase the level of pain that a subject experiences as a result of applying it to critical points, such as nerve bundles. In many cases, observers could perceive this type of response to be excessive, unless the subject has clearly made a reasonable attempt to cause physical harm.

Striking Techniques—The use of techniques, without the assistance of any weapon or tool, to strike the subject in areas of the body that are not critical in nature. It is essential that this limitation on the target areas be well understood. A strike to the head or neck will usually be considered "deadly force," and would be a higher level of force.

Weapon Striking Techniques—The use of weapon or tool assisted striking techniques to strike the subject in areas of the body which are not critical in nature. As with the "Striking Techniques" phase, targeting areas which could have life-threatening effects will be considered a higher level of force. As these types of techniques tend to develop more impact energy, the areas considered critical are generally accepted to include the torso of the body as well. For example, a strike to the lower areas of the ribcage with an expandable baton is likely to cause fragmentation of the floating ribs, and punctures of the internal organs, as those fragments travel inward. Weapons striking techniques, in the phase, are generally to the long bones of the limbs in an attempt to limit the subject's ability to inflict injury upon others.

Striking Techniques to Critical Targets—The intentional targeting of critical areas of the subject's body in response to a reasonable perception that they intend to inflict great bodily harm or death upon the officer or others. These techniques should only be employed when no other, lesser force options exist.

Firearms—The use of firearms, in any form, is a final phase of the continuum. In the eyes of most courts, firearms are designed and used simply to kill the intended target. They should only be deployed in response to situations where the subject is believed to intend to kill or cause great bodily harm to others, has the ability to do this, and is in a position to do so immanently. This is the "last chance" response.

In all interactions with subjects, it must be the officer's goal to utilize the least amount of force possible while continuing to protect the lives and safety of themselves and others. When an officer finds themselves engaged at a level of force greater than the "no force" levels, options to reduce the level of force, deescalation of the conflict, should be sought. Officers facing a potentially dangerous subject should consider disengaging from the conflict as an alternative to escalating the level of response, if doing so does not increase the danger to others in the area.

As a general rule, the subject will not typically attempt to deescalate the level of force. It is up to the responding officer to try to reduce the level of threat reasonably.

TRAINING FOR SUCCESS

When designing a training program, the most critical factors should be realism and repetition. Without these, you will either be working toward a goal, which will prove ineffective, or you will be unable to execute the techniques due to lack of effective experience. Both factors should be present to be an effective program.

Design the training around the types of threats that you perceive to be likely within the environment in which you will be present. It does no good to practice handgun skills if your client will not let you carry such a weapon. Likewise, if you are designing a program for a location that will be staffed with armed officers, has a history of exchanges with firearms, and rarely involves physical contact with subjects, your training program should be divided in those proportions between armed and unarmed response techniques.

It is essential that this training be conducted with a strong sense of reality. Train in the actual environment when possible and under less than ideal conditions. Does it make sense to train in loose clothing on a floor with good traction when you wear a bulky uniform and patrol an area that frequently ices over? The program must reference the environment if it is to be effective within that environment.

When dealing with physical techniques, the ideal training will provide sufficient repetition that the specific techniques will be a reflexive response. Without this, the moment of decision that is interjected will reduce your control over the combat timing. To develop this level of response, it unfortunately requires extensive periods of repetition. As many as 7,000 repetitions may be required before the technique begins to be reflexively performed. It is essential also that these repetitions be technically sound. It is highly counterproductive to do your first thousand repetitions with incorrect technique. Vast amounts of time and energy will be wasted in this effort and the retraining required to retune the beginnings of the reflexive response. Once a specific level of skill is achieved, regular review and practice will be required to retain that skill over time.

On the mental side, the training must instill an understanding of the flow and dynamics of combat. The more realistic the training, the better the trainee will be able to handle the actual situations if they occur. This is why it is essential that some time be spent in training to confront multiple opponents. This type of encounter is often reported and can prove to be far more dangerous than a single aggressor. Effective training in this type of environment will allow one to understand how to use movement and speed to shift position effectively. Despite the presence of multiple aggressors, a combatant with a superior understanding of movement and a good use of the environment can find ways of interacting with only one person at a time.

MARTIAL ARTS AS DEFENSIVE TACTICS TRAINING

Although there are many good things to be gained by proper instruction in the martial arts; the selection of one and the proper instructor to be effective for this purpose is very difficult. Many schools focus too tightly on the sport or competition aspects of the martial arts, and the limitations that those bring with them. In competitions, there are usually targets, which are considered off limits and often restrictions on the level of force, which may be applied to an opponent. Within these environments, those fit well with the stated goals. In a conflict with an aggressor that is intent on ending your life and clearly has the ability to do so, there may not be any option other than one of these "off limits" target areas.

You will do, under stress, what you have trained to do with repetition. This means that, if you have trained under a set of restrictions which does not allow strikes to certain body areas, these possibilities probably will not occur to you, even when faced with a deadly threat. Even if they do, you probably will not know the most effective methods of utilizing them.

The selection of a martial art, if this route is chosen, must be very careful. Care should be taken to ensure that the basic philosophy of the style and the instructor are in line with the guidelines under which you will be operating, and that the training is as realistic as is safely possible. Again, train in your work environment and under normal conditions if possible. Be wary of instructors that insist that a single style will solve all combat situations. As an example, Jiu-jitsu is an extremely popular fighting system with some highly effective techniques. Unfortunately, most schools emphasize bringing your opponent to the ground where you can gain a tactical advantage by utilizing a superior understanding of leverage to gain body positioning. What if you are facing two or more opponents? If you go to the ground with one, the other(s) may gain a dramatic tactical advantage over you.

WEAPONS IN DEFENSIVE TACTICS

The possession and use of a weapon is typically controlled by the employer, client, and local law. In many cases, the possession of a weapon is prohibited, in others, required. In any case, a thorough understanding of the policies and laws that apply to your specific situation is critical.

Obtain and review all legal and company or client imposed regulations, prior to carrying any form of weapon. The expectations of all involved parties must be clearly understood, if one is to follow them. Once this is achieved, they must be followed at all times. These are typically designed to protect the weapon carrier from increased liability related to improper usage. If you have any questions related to those regulations, it is essential that you seek proper explanation and clarification.

Once the regulations under which this will be carried and used are understood, the training factor must be considered. As with training for unarmed techniques, the level of realism must be high and the repetitions numerous. Continuing training, to retain an achieved level of skill, is also critical. Having been an expert at one time does not guarantee that the skill will remain at a high level over time. Constant review and practice is required if one is to retain an achieved level of proficiency.

It is also absolutely essential that you know and understand the specific function and ability of any weapon, which will be carried. As an example, officers issued a firearm should be aware of not only their own level of accuracy at various ranges, but also the penetration characteristics of the ammunition, which they will carry. In this case, when deciding to either shoot or not shoot, the informed officer will be aware of potential penetration risks in the areas behind the target or even over-penetration of the target itself.

When dealing with firearms, learn what in your environment is cover, and what is simply concealment. Objects that provide cover are those that will block or significantly reduce the level of threat from an attack. Such things as brick and cement walls make great cover. Concealment simply reduces one's ability to be seen. Shrubs are one example of concealment. It is difficult to see a person through a shrub, but a firearm will still be a significant threat to them if fired through the shrub. Some things might seem to be cover when dealing with a certain level of force and become less effective when facing a different level of force. A car door, for example, might provide reasonable cover against an assailant with a .22, but might barely slow a shot from an assault rifle. A familiarity with your environment is essential when identifying these areas. When working in your area, constantly look around you, identify where you could go for cover, and what would only provide concealment.

The carrying of a weapon is a great responsibility. The proper and effective use of that weapon is an even greater one. Ensure that all restrictions are known and followed, that all properties of the weapon and its use are understood, and that sufficient training is obtained and maintained.

When dealing with an opponent that is armed, there is one critical concept to remember:

ASSUME THAT YOU WILL BE INJURED!

This does not mean give up or wait for it to happen. This means, if the aggressor has a knife, do not be surprised when you get cut. Failing to mentally prepare for an injury results in increased mental and emotional reaction to that injury. This, in turn, means that you give your opponent the benefit of extra time as you mentally regroup. This pause, usually referred to as a stunning effect, often results in additional injuries as it gives the aggressor a window of opportunity. In effect, allowing this to throw you off can give the aggressor complete command of the control of the timing aspect of combat. This can be very difficult to overcome.

When facing a weapon, the nature of that weapon must always be taken into consideration. As an example, when an aggressor has a blade weapon, it is best to avoid blocking techniques, which utilize the inside of the hands or wrists. Should these parts of the arm be used, it exposes the more accessible blood vessels and tendons to potential damage.

DEFENSIVE TACTIC TIPS

The following are some basic tips to improve the officer's understanding of the basic concepts of defending themselves. While no tactic is guaranteed to work in every situation, these can be generally applied to most situations.

1. Understand speed limitations. Become used to how quickly you can cover a given distance, execute a given technique, or retrieve and utilize a given tool or weapon.
2. Be aware of your surroundings. Use objects around you to aid in your control of movement and space.
3. When faced with a weapon, and no options of escape, gain control of the weapon as quickly and safely as possible.
4. Never assume that defensive equipment will always work! Ballistic clothing is a great tool, but should not be relied upon to guarantee your safety.
5. Use your energy efficiently. You should know how long you could operate under stress and strain. Use this effectively and with caution. Try to always keep some of your stamina in reserve.
6. When faced with potential hazards, get support. If possible, never face conflict alone.
7. Utilize your knowledge of cover and concealment to properly protect yourself.
8. If one technique does not work, keep going! Do not dwell on that failure and give your opponent time to counter you.
9. Never assume that the aggressor you see is the only one present. Always maintain awareness of your surroundings. Train for multiple aggressors to get a feel for the changes in the flow of action that it requires.

Through proper training, awareness, and an understanding of personal limitations, each officer will be better prepared to handle defensive situations. Conflict situations are around us every day. It is how we deal with them that determines our levels of exposure to the threat.

═ ?═ ┤ SECURITY QUIZ ├ ═? ═
Defensive Tactics and Officer Safety

1. Caution should be used at all times.
   ☐ T ☐ F
2. Additional support will never be required if you are cautious.
   ☐ T ☐ F
3. Most exchanges of gunfire occur beyond 7 yards range.
   ☐ T ☐ F
4. Firearms are the final phase (highest level) of the range of responses.
   ☐ T ☐ F
5. The critical factors when designing a training program are:
   ☐ (a) realism
   ☐ (b) repetition
   ☐ (c) Neither A nor B
   ☐ (d) Both A and B
6. The possession and use of weapons may be controlled by:
   ☐ (a) the employer
   ☐ (b) the client
   ☐ (c) applicable law
   ☐ (d) All of the above
7. The three basic factors of combat include:
   ☐ (a) weapon selection
   ☐ (b) control over space
   ☐ (c) body armor
   ☐ (d) None of the above
8. Points of consideration when entering into a physical confrontation include:
   ☐ (a) your limits of physical ability
   ☐ (b) the number of potential opponents you face
   ☐ (c) your legal restrictions
   ☐ (d) All of the above
9. An object that obstructs your opponent's ability to see you but does not to cause you harm is an example of
   _____.
10. An object that prevents or greatly reduces the ability of another to cause you harm is an example of
    _____.

APPREHENSION AND DETENTION PROCEDURES

By Richard P. Fiems, MA, CPO, CSS, CPOI

There is probably no topic in the security profession that generates as much discussion, and misunderstanding as apprehension and detention. It is not only the source of many complaints by the clients we serve, it can also be the beginning of a very lengthy and costly legal action. For these two reasons alone, it is worth a long look by people in the business. But that is not where it ends. We also have to look at the possibility of injury, and even death, that could result in a misunderstanding of just how much authority a security officer really has to control the movements of another person. For that reason we have to start from the beginning. We need to look at a few basic definitions.

Black's Law Dictionary defines an arrest like this: "To deprive a person of his liberty by legal authority." Note the use of the word "authority." That implies that the person making the arrest has the legal ability to do what they are attempting to do. *Black's* goes on to define an arrest by saying, "Taking, under real or assumed authority, custody of another for the purpose of holding or detaining him to answer to a criminal charge or civil demand."

The second portion of that definition has two big components. First, assuming the authority to do something does not necessarily mean that the authority really exists. The person could be basing the assumption on bad information or they could be just mistaken about the amount of authority that they really have. Either way, the end result could be problems for the officer. Second, all arrests have to be made with the intention of bringing the arrested person before a judge of some type. An arrest of any kind is never made to inconvenience someone, or delay their departure, or as a way to get even for some perceived wrong. If there was no intent to take them before a judge, the arrest is unlawful. *Black's* goes on to further define an arrest by saying, "Arrest involves the authority to arrest, the assertion of that authority with the intent to effect an arrest, and the restraint of the person to be arrested."

What that means is this. In order for an arrest to be legal and binding, the person making the arrest and the person being arrested both must know the following:

1. The authority to arrest is real.
2. That authority is being intentionally used.
3. The person being arrested must be restrained in some way.

So what does it mean to be restrained? *Black's* definition of an arrest goes on to say: "All that is required for an 'arrest' is some act by an officer indicating his intention to detain or take a person into custody and thereby subject that person to the actual control and will of the officer; no formal declaration of arrest is required." In other words, if someone who assumes the authority to make an arrest indicates by words or by actions that they are taking another person into custody, and that other person believes that they are being taken into custody, an arrest has happened.

This is why police officers are told to make their intention to take someone into custody as clear as possible to the person being arrested. They are trained to tell the person that they are under arrest and then give them clear orders and commands about what they want them to do in order to submit to the custody.

Since citizens are legally required to submit to an arrest by a police officer, this places the citizen in the position of facing charges for resisting if they don't comply. But security officers are not police officers. Security officers have the same authority to make an arrest as a citizen, unless some special circumstances exist.

A "citizen's arrest" is defined by *Black's Law Dictionary* as follows: "A private person as contrasted with a police officer may, under certain circumstances, make an arrest, generally for a felony or a misdemeanor amounting to a breach of the peace."

Security officers generally fall into the category of a private citizen. There may be certain instances, such as a local ordinance, that grants certain police and/or arrest authority to a security officer. Your obligation as a professional is to find out what laws and ordinances apply in the place where you are working.

DEVELOPING A WORKING MODEL

The law in most jurisdictions allows for a security officer to detain people when such a detention is for a reason that falls within the security officer's authorized duties. Authorization can come from one or more of three basic places.

1. The law can outline the statutory authority of a security officer within the arena that they are working. That can be a federal, state, or local law. Look for phrases in the law like "special officer," "auxiliary officer," "special police," or "special deputy." Be sure to be very clear of the definition as stated in the law. They can be very specific.

2. The security company that the officer works for can have a contractual agreement with the client for the officers to exercise a certain level or degree of authority on their property. The source of this authority then is

the contract that exists between the client and the security company.

3. Authority can also come from a job description for security personnel in a proprietary department. The contract of a particular company or the handbook from a human resources department might contain language that establishes the authority of the officer, too.

The bottom line is simple. It is, and always will be, the responsibility of the individual security officer to get totally familiar with the basis for the authority that they carry with them onto the job. Ask questions, check around and, by all means, get the verification in writing. This is one area of the job where it will pay huge dividends to do your homework.

WHAT CONSTITUTES AN ARREST?

Being arrested is one of those situations where the perceptions of the arrested person are what really matter. In short, an arrest does not really happen unless the person being arrested submits to the authority of the person making the arrest. A few examples might help at this point.

Let's assume for the sake of explanation that you are working as a security officer in an area that gives you limited authority to detain trespassers. While you are on walking patrol you meet an elderly lady who has gotten separated from a group that was taking an escorted tour of the facility. You question her about how she came to end up in a restricted area and she is cooperative, but very nervous. While you are trying to sort out the problem so you can locate the rest of the group, you get an emergency call to respond to an accident where someone had been injured. You take off running to the accident after telling the woman to "Wait here!" Forty-five minutes later you are just finishing up the accident call and you remember the elderly lady. You go back to the restricted area and find her still standing there. She stayed there because she thought she had been arrested. Her background and experiences in life have taught her to respect authority figures and do what they told her to do. The determining factor here is that she REASONABLY BELIEVED that she was NOT FREE TO LEAVE. She submitted to your authority. You may not have intended to give the impression that she couldn't leave, but it was reasonable under the circumstances for her to feel the way she did.

Contrast that with a small change in location and subjects. You are on motor patrol in the same facility and you happen across three young boys who are riding skateboards in a clearly posted restricted parking lot. You are on the opposite side of a chain link fence. You stop the boys and tell them to stay where they are. You then drive down the road and through the gate to get into the lot and by the time you get there the three boys are long gone. They took off as soon as you drove away from them to get to the gate. If you did happen to locate them later, you would have a very difficult time getting them charged with trespassing or resisting your authority in any way. They took off like jack-rabbits because they did not believe for one second that they were under arrest. There was not arrest because there was no submission to authority.

THE IMPORTANCE OF REASONABLENESS

As with most things legal we find the word REASONABLE popping up in any discussion about apprehension and detention. It is the common sense standard that you are going to be held to in almost everything that you do as an officer. It has particular application here because we are talking about taking an action that essentially deprives another person of their liberty, even if only for a short time. That has never been something that has been taken lightly in a free society. While it may be true that the security profession does not have the same restrictions placed on it as our counterparts on the police department, the standards are still the same.

When we take an action that limits the freedom of another person, we have to make sure that we are acting in a manner that would seem logical and obvious to a reasonable and cautious person.

WHAT GETS SECURITY OFFICERS IN TROUBLE?

When a security officer is placed in the position of having to take control of another person, a world of opportunity for trouble begins to open up. It has to be stressed that the security officer who acts in a reckless or indefensible way will be in for a rough ride. This fact stresses the importance of documentation. Whenever a physical contact is made with a citizen, for any reason, the security officer should sit down as soon as possible after the event and write a detailed report about what happened and why they felt that they had to do what they did. Basically the laws that can cause the problems come from two directions: criminal and civil.

CRIMINAL LAWS THAT CAN GET A SECURITY OFFICER IN TROUBLE LOOK LIKE THIS

Assault

Contrary to popular belief, at least in most jurisdictions, you do not have to touch someone to be looking at a criminal assault charge. You only have to place another person in a reasonable fear of being battered. Attempting to lay hands on someone and failing to do so can still be classified as an assault. In many cases, all you have to do is have the means at your disposal to commit a battery and communicate to the other person that you intend to do just that. For example, if you yell across a football field that you are going to put someone on the ground and handcuff them, the court would probably not consider that an assault. You were too far away to actually take control of the person and it would not be reasonable for them to think that you could reach all the way across the field and grab them. However, if you were standing right in front of the person, with the handcuffs in your hand, and you made the same statement, it would be reasonable for them to think that you were going to do what you said. You have the means and the proximity. If you do not have cause to take them into custody, you could be looking at an assault charge.

Battery

Battery is the actual physical touching of a person that is either hurtful or insulting in nature. A reasonable person wold think that being taken into custody, which involves being stopped, searched, secured in some way, and not permitted to leave, would be a hurtful or insulting set of circumstances. Once again, this stresses the importance of being right in your assessment of the situation and reasonable in taking the actions that you take.

False Arrest

This involves taking someone into custody without the legal authority to detain. Most jurisdictions, and it is your responsibility to find out the law in the one where you work, will allow for a citizen to take another citizen into custody for an offense, other than a misdemeanor or an ordinance violation, that is committed in the arresting person's presence. In other words, the violation must be a serious one and the person who makes the arrest must have direct knowledge of the commission of the violations. You cannot rely on hearsay or rumors. You can only act on firsthand knowledge.

Civil law violations that can get a security officer in trouble look like this. (*Note:* A civil violation, also known as a tort, does not carry with it the same burden or amount of proof necessary to establish responsibility in court. In criminal court, the State must prove its case "beyond a reasonable doubt." In civil court, the plaintiff must prove their case by a "preponderance of the evidence." Stated another way, guilt in criminal court requires 99 percent proof. Guilt in civil court requires 50.1 percent proof. Torts are somewhat easier to prove than crimes.)

1. **Assault.** Once again, the act of placing someone in reasonable fear of being battered. The belief of the victim must be reasonable.
2. **Battery.** Intentionally touching someone in a nonconsensual, no-privileged manner. Consensual touching means that you have the other person's permission. Privileged touching would be the act of giving someone first aid if they were unconscious.
3. **False imprisonment.** This is the unlawful detention of someone else for no reason, within fixed boundaries.
4. **Malicious prosecution.** This happens when a security officer detains someone with no intention of bringing criminal charges against them, or filing criminal charges without probable cause.
5. **Invasion of privacy.** This is an unjustified intrusion into the privacy or personal business of another person.

What are the keys to avoiding criminal and civil liability? Good human relation and communication skills are a crucial part of the process. But, basically, you can go a long way toward avoiding problems by following these simple guidelines:

1. Do your job in a reasonable manner. Know your responsibilities and know your limitations. Get familiar with the laws and regulations in your area and stick to the rules.
2. Conduct yourself in a reasonable manner. You are doing a job in an arena full of spectators. It is your responsibility to behave as if someone is watching every move that you make. If the time ever comes that you do have to take control of a person, it would be a great benefit to have the witness testify that you did what you had to do in a tactful and professional manner.
3. Keep detailed notes and records about what happened. It is no secret that memories fade over time. Complaints are seldom filed about an officer's actions right after the incident occurs. It is not unusual for a period of several months to lapse between an incident and a complaint. There is no such thing as too much information in a report describing an apprehension or detention. Be specific and be thorough.
4. Keep your supervisor informed. Any contact between you and a citizen or employee that could be looked upon as confrontational or potentially explosive needs to be reported to the people in your up line. The sooner the better. Supervisors are not particularly fond of surprises in the first place and late information about what a security officer did or said in a confrontation with someone else will not help your cause at all.

DETENTION AND APPREHENSION METHODOLOGY

What follows is a discussion that centers around tactics. As you know, there is no way that a trainer or teacher can outline a set of tactics that will work in every situation that you are going to be working with as a security officer. So, these are going to be presented to you as tactical guidelines and are intended to get you to think about the situation before things get to the point of having to take physical control of another person. A good team never goes to the competition without a game plan. A good security officer never goes to a situation without a tactical response in hand.

Lets assume that the situation that you are dealing with has developed, or degenerated, to the point that you have made the determination, based on the totality of the circumstances, that you have to take physical control of another person. As with most things on the job, the first rule of security work comes into play: Go home healthy at the end of your shift!

1. Get some backup headed your way. The Latin term "non solis" (never alone) should be the first thing that comes to your mind. Often the presence of another security officer will deter someone from resisting or causing further problems. Some departments like to use what is called a 'swarming technique' that involves getting as many officers there as they can to aid in the situation. At the very least you should be communicating with your department and should also contact the

local police as soon as possible. Remember, NON SOLIS.

2. Maintain a safe distance and good positioning. You should know what your reactionary gap is. That is the minimum amount of distance that you need to respond to a threatening move made by someone else. Blade your body so that you are balanced and ready and hold your hands up in front of you with your palms facing the person you are dealing with, about shoulder high. This will allow you to protect yourself and deflect an object or a blow if you need to. Leave yourself a way out of the area if you can and try to avoid cornering the other person. You could be injured if they feel that the only way out is through you.

3. Communicate your intentions. Tell the person that they are under arrest or apprehension, whichever is appropriate for your jurisdiction. In many States the intention to arrest or detain someone must be communicated clearly to the person being detained. It is also possible that they could be held responsible for resisting the arrest if it is made clear to them exactly what the situation is. If the person demands to know why you are detaining them, tell them in as few words as possible. It is not generally necessary for you to be able to quote the law they have violated to them chapter and verse. Just be clear about what you saw them do and your intention to hold them there until the arrival of the police or a supervisor.

4. Give the person simple, direct commands. Do not yell or threaten. Use a calm and clear tone of voice and tell the person what you expect them to do. If you want them in a chair, ask them to "Sit down, please." If you want them to move to another spot in the room, point to the location and simply say, "Over here, please." If they start to shout or become loud say, "Lower your voice, please." You have to maintain a cool and professional demeanor throughout the entire process. The people who are watching, even if there are none, should be able to testify that you were not the problem, the other person was. In the interest of your safety, you should not hesitate to say, "Keep your hands where I can see them, please." if they start to reach inside a coat or a pocket. There is not a requirement that I have ever seen that stipulates or even encourages you to do anything that would compromise your safety. So don't.

5. Move in with extreme caution. If you make the determination that the person needs to be placed in handcuffs, you must proceed with a great deal of caution. The closer you get to them, the more vulnerable you are. Handcuffs should only be used when you are convinced that not using them poses a greater threat to your safety or someone else's than letting them stand there until the police arrive. In any event, you must remember that handcuffs are TEMPORARY RESTRAINING DEVICES. They in no way guarantee

your safety once they are put on another person. Caution is still the rule. Have the person turn around and face away from you. Tell them to place their hands behind their back with the backs of their hands touching. Grasp their right hand with your right hand and place the handcuff on their right wrist with your left hand. Then grasp the loose cuff in your right hand and grab their left hand with your left hand. Using your right hand, place the remaining cuff on their left wrist. DO NOT strike their wrist with the handcuff. It looks cool in the movies but it really seldom works without causing harm to the subject you are cuffing. Tighten the cuffs until they are snug, but not so tight as to reduce the person's circulation. ALWAYS lock the cuffs in place! Always!

Handcuffing techniques should be practiced under the watchful eye of a trained instructor. Your goal is to restrain the person as quickly as possible. This is one of those situations where you will most definitely play the way you practice.

THE USE OF FORCE

The most critical time of your professional life will come when you or someone you are protecting is in imminent danger from the actions of another and you have to use force of some kind to protect yourself or them. It is never an easy situation to be in or an easy decision to make. Common sense tells you that the only time you can use force against another person is when there is absolutely no other choice. Security professionals are trained to use the escalating scale starting with voice commands and moving upwards in the scale to physical force if nothing else will work, or clearly would not have worked under the circumstances. Remember, too, that security officers are not authorized to use overpowering force like police officers are. We can use the same kind of force that a citizen can, neutralizing force, and nothing more. When the person we are dealing with stops using force, we have to stop too. Neutralize, don't overpower.

Prior to the development of that kind of a circumstance, you need to be comfortable with the decision making process that you have used. In other words, you have to ask yourself some questions.

1. Was I in imminent (that means immediate) jeopardy? This has to be clearly established by the circumstances known to you at that point in time.

2. Was someone whom I have a duty to protect in imminent physical jeopardy? What, exactly, is your duty under your orders and rules and regulations?

3. Was my mission as a security officer in imminent jeopardy? Was the action taken to protect property in proportion to the value or criticality of the property itself? In other words, did you behave in a reasonable way given what you were protecting?

4. Did I have any alternatives to using the force that I did? Force can only be used if there is no other way to respond and solving the problem is something that must be done immediately.

5. Is the harm I am trying to prevent greater than the harm I might cause? Property is replaceable, people are not. Deadly force is NEVER permitted to protect property.

6. How will the actions that I took be viewed by others? Was I reasonable? Did I do what needed to be done and nothing more?

These are hard questions. That is why they need to be thought about and mulled over before you find yourself in a situation where force may be required. Your head will need to be clear if the situations call for you to go tactical.

DEALING WITH THE AFTERMATH

If you are careful and reasonable in your apprehension and detention procedures, you are going to be able to justify what you do. But, if a complaint is made or a lawsuit is filed, you need to know that you are not going to go into litigation defenseless. The law does provide some rationale for you in building your case. They are called affirmative defenses.

1. **Self-defense.** There is no requirement under law that you have to allow yourself to be attacked. Under law everyone has the right to defend themselves. Just be sure that when you defend yourself, you don't go too far and become the aggressor.

2. **Necessity.** If you shove someone out of the path of a speeding car you have committed a battery. You had to in order to protect them from great harm or death. No court in the world would hear a charge against you for that.

3. **Mistake of fact.** If you are acting in good faith and believe that you are doing something legal and above board, and it turns out that you were misinformed, you have made a mistake of fact. Ignorance of the law has never been an excuse for violating the law, but a good faith mistake defense can still protect you if the circumstances are believable.

The defenses listed above have the effect of taking "INTENT" out of the equation. If you did not do something in a criminal state of mind you can defend yourself from a claim that you violated a law or committed a tort. The concept of reasonableness still applies.

CONCLUSION

No one really likes the thought of having to take someone else into custody. Hopefully, we can be proactive enough in the way that we do our jobs and we will avoid having to deal with this kind of situation. However, it is your job to be prepared. Keep up with the changes in the law and be very conversant in the rules, regulations, guidelines, and policies of your department when it comes to this subject. You cannot go into one of these situations half prepared and expect that everything is going to be all right. Murphy's Law has been around since before laws were written. Be ready.

SECURITY QUIZ
Apprehension and
Detention Procedures

1. *Black's Law Dictionary* defines an arrest like this: "To deprive a person of his liberty by legal authority."
   ☐ T ☐ F

2. In order for an arrest to be legal and binding, the person making the arrest and the person being arrested have to know:
   ☐ (a) the authority to arrest is real
   ☐ (b) that authority is being intentionally used
   ☐ (c) the person being arrested must be restrained in some way
   ☐ (d) All of the above

3. Security officers do not have the same authority to make an arrest as a citizen unless some special circumstances exist.
   ☐ T ☐ F

4. A "citizen's arrest" is defined by Black's Law Dictionary as follows: "A private person as contrasted with a police officer may, under certain circumstances, make an arrest, generally for a _____ or a _____ amounting to a breach of the peace."

5. It is, and always will be, the responsibility of the individual _____ to get totally familiar with the basis for the authority that they carry with them onto the job.

6. Contrary to popular belief, at least in most jurisdictions, you do not have to touch someone to be looking at a criminal assault charge. You only have to place another person in a reasonable fear of being battered.
    ☐ T ☐ F

7. _____is the actual physical touching of a person that is either hurtful or insulting in nature.

8. Guilt in civil court requires what percentage of proof?
    ☐ (a) 99 percent
    ☐ (b) 50.1 percent
    ☐ (c) 75 percent
    ☐ (d) 100 percent

9. Malicious prosecution happens when a security officer detains someone with the full intention of bringing criminal charges against them, or filing criminal charges without probable cause.
    ☐ T ☐ F

10. Under law everyone has the right to defend themselves.
    ☐ T ☐ F

Unit 12

Public Relations
Police and Security Liaison
Ethics and Professionalism

PUBLIC RELATIONS

By Charles T. Thibodeau, M.Ed., CPP, CSS
Christopher A. Hertig, CPP, CPO
George A. Barnett, CPO

Public relations consists of a mutual understanding between an organization and its constituent publics.[1] The term "*publics*" is defined as the general community, the people as a whole, or a group of people sharing a common interest.[2] With respect to Private Security, we would define the term "public" as primarily a group of people sharing a common interest relative to our work environment, plus the general public. The actual people we come in contact with changes from work-site to work-site with the exception of that one constant - the general public.[3]

If we are working in entertainment security, where crowd management is the main responsibility, we have a very broad and diverse constituency. If we are working in executive protection, we deal with a much more restricted group of people. However, no matter what the primary responsibility is, and no matter what our primary constituency is, the general public has an interest in how we perform our duties.

For the sake of example, assume we are security at a factory. Our primary constituency would be the employees who work for the company, and any number of vendors, repair persons, and other visitors. However, we cannot forget the general public. The factory is located in a community, and is an integral part of that community. The community has a number of interests including health interests, financial interests, image interests, and so on.

Health interests can be in the form of working conditions within the factory that may make employees from the community sick or injured. There may be toxic smoke belching from the factory, reducing air quality in the community. Either of these conditions would be of great concern to those affected by the factory, and would result in very poor public relations.

The financial interest might be in form of a paycheck for employees who live in the community, resale of the products made in the factory to members of the community, or sales of raw materials to the factory by other businesses in the community. This would be a positive impact on the community and therefore would result in very good public relations.

As for image, if a factory is making bombs for the military, it projects a different image in a community than a factory that is making baby formula or toys for children. The community may become quite disturbed having a bomb factory in their back yard, and they may revolt. Thus, the venture of the business will have either a positive or negative image in the community that reflects directly on public relations.

No matter what the business is involved in, the security officer is many times the "out front" person for that company, is frequently the first contact that anyone will have with the company, and therefore must pay particular attention to the topic of public relations. Based on the wide variety of responses the general public may have to your company, that first contact could be anything from very friendly to very unfriendly. Therefore, a sincere "How can I help you?" must be permanently at the ready when making that first contact. Being a helper, being a pleaser, and being a "can-do" problem solver, are the traits of a successful public relations minded security professional.

PUBLIC RELATIONS PLANNING

In maintaining a good public image, the security officer must not only look good, and perform in a reasonable and necessary manner, but the officer must appear truly concerned, speak with a pleasant and polite voice inflection, and show respect. The officer must make the person being served feel like his or her needs are very important, and that they are about to receive superior service. Most importantly, the officer must come to the job equipped with the skills of being capable of delivering what is promised. These things are all part of a well planned public relations program.

To carry out a successful public relations program, the security department cannot do it alone. The entire parent or client organization must be involved. However, the security contingent has no control over the entire company and is not responsible for what the other departments in the company do. Security can only be responsible for their own conduct. In the area of public relations, the security contingent must conduct themselves in a planned and organized fashion, sometimes with blinders on. It would be most unfortunate if the security contingent followed bad examples set by those in other departments.

To accomplish the goal of projecting a positive image, the security contingent must first have a quality program in place. Image is meaningless if it is a false veneer. Once this is done the Ten Rules of Public Relations in Private Security can be applied.

The customer is not always right or wrong. Public relations has little to do with judging others. The key words in public relations are "mutual need satisfaction."

While you may disagree with this from a security perspective, the most important thing to remember is to never tell the person with whom you are dealing that they are wrong. It is to the benefit of all concerned that the security officer works toward a position of mutual cooperation and prevent all situations from escalating into a win lose proposition. The person you are dealing with must be skillfully redirected into appropriate behavior, not bullied. This person must, as often as possible, leave a situation feeling that they were well served by the advice and assistance they received from the attending officer. This is not to say that issues of self-defense and defense of others will never be the case for the officer. We mean to say here that you will probably go in the "direction your nose is pointed," so keep things upbeat and positive. The officer must be a part of the solution, not a part of the problem!

Know your department's capabilities, as well as other department capabilities.

Successful salespeople always know their product inside and out. They are then in the position to continuously fit the product and service to the needs of the purchaser. A good security officer should be able to do the same. However, it is not good enough for the security officer to just know his or her products and services; the truly successful protection officer will know every other department's products and services as well. This will be a valuable asset in situations where a referral is required to another department. Thus, the successful public relations minded security officer will spend many hours studying the inner workings of the organization he or she is assigned to protect.

Always accentuate the positive.

People don't want to hear negative things; in many cases the negative is obvious and needs no introduction. Emphasize the positive aspects of your service or the situation and you will seldom go wrong. Emphasize the negative and you'll be treated accordingly.

Image is a valuable asset.

Organizations spend considerable amounts of time and money developing and maintaining a certain image. Single negative events can destroy that image. Chronic unprofessional job behaviors can erode it. The image you project as a representative of the company you work for can, and will, help to mold the company's image. Included in the image building perspective of a security officer are the following ten qualities:[4]

1. Be dependable.
2. Be courteous.
3. Show interest and concern.
4. Use tact.
5. Be discreet.
6. Respect confidences.
7. Be impartial.
8. Be calm.
9. Be patient.
10. Be helpful.

Remember that the most powerful advertising is negative customer service.

People who are dissatisfied with an organization's service tell their friends and associates—lots of them! This interpersonal message sending is very powerful. You can achieve ten great tasks of service in a day, but one cross word, one failure to satisfy someone, will be the service task remembered far into the future. You cannot afford to fail in the arena of public relations. You may not be successful in every attempt to help, but the person you were trying to serve must be convinced that you did everything possible. If you can achieve this level of success, you have not failed that person.

Be attentive to the other person's needs.

Each person has his own individual needs. Find out what they are and do what you can to address them. You may feel that this is a bit like soliciting work and you have enough to do already without asking people to give you more. However, with a little gentle coaxing you can get a reluctant person to express what it is they are really after. Serving those needs will be very well received and a great boost to the public relations record of the department.

Never "cut someone off cold."

When someone asks for assistance or information and you aren't able to help that person immediately, ask the person to let you get back to him or her after you have researched the problem. Then do so. Ask others for assistance, do the research and solve the problem. Help that person. Remove the following phrases from your vocabulary:

- "No, we do not do that."
- "No, we cannot help you with that."
- "It is not security's job."

When you can help someone, do so.

Whenever possible, help others. If necessary, volunteer to help them. This can make a lasting impression. It can also be a deterrent to crime as it puts would-be criminals on notice that someone is aware of their presence and behavior. Be friendly; don't be afraid to speak with those who seem to be in need. If helping someone won't create other problems, then there is no acceptable reason for not doing so.

Have something tangible to give the person.

People like to receive things. Even if the tangible item is of little consequence, people seem to be pleased whenever you put something in their hands. Just as the salesman is able to respond to requests for literature on the product he is selling, so must the security officer have brochures, maps, phone books, or even your handwritten instructions. No good salesman would do any less, and neither should you.

Have a "can-do" attitude.

The U.S. Navy SEEBEES have a motto: "Can-do." They say they can do anything given enough time, and the impossible just takes a little longer. What a great motto for your department to follow. Eliminate the words "can't do" as pointed out above, and replace them with the words "can do." Whenever a person comes to you with a request just say Yes! Then figure out how you will serve that person's needs. Pride yourself in being able to do the impossible when it comes to serving others. This does not eliminate the need for referral of some requests to other departments. However, always try to check back to see if the person received adequate service from your referral.

PROMOTING EFFECTIVE CUSTOMER RELATIONS WITHIN THE SECURITY FORCE

There are a number of steps that security supervisors can take affect the customer relations capabilities of their subordinates.

1. To start with, the supervisor's basic personnel management skills should be effective enough to minimize the "malcontent syndrome." Security officers should not be forced to work long hours without relief, get "shafted" out of vacations and days off, or be constantly given less than desirable assignments.

2. Security supervisors should conduct an inspection and briefing of each shift prior to that shift going on duty, and "on stage." Security supervisors should take this opportunity whether it is done formally in groups, or informally with individual officers. This inspection should include a physical inspection of equipment, officer appearance, and officer demeanor. It should also encompass an evaluation that each officer knows what has happened on previous shifts and what is going on that day in the work site.

3. Brief each department member on current events within the work site as well as current problems and changes in procedures. This helps to make the protection force members function as ambassadors for the organization. In addition to this daily refresher training, supervisors should make certain that the following work behaviors are adopted by all security force members during periodic staff meetings or other methods of professional development:

    *   Have necessary references at the ready. These include staff directories, maps, telephone books, procedures, and anything else that the person you serve is likely to inquire about.

    *   Be ready and capable of responding to security problems such as fires, bomb threats, disorderly persons, and other critical incidents in a prompt and professional manner. **Developing proficiency in dealing with people in crisis is a good investment for anyone in security.**

    *   Present a professional appearance at all times. Neatness and precision should be obvious attributes of all security officers; easily seen by even the most casual observer. Alertness, openness, and concern must be radiated by posture and behavior.

*   Be prepared to do the job by having the necessary tools for the job. Always have a pen or better yet, two pens—and a small note pad to write down important notes or to give someone directions on. Never come to work without a watch, a small pocket knife, and pocket flashlight. If your job calls for other hardware such as keys, handcuffs, mace, or defensive weapons, be sure they are all in place on the utility belt, and in top operating condition.

*   Two additional pieces of equipment that project the image of security are the officer's ID card and the two-way radio. The ID card should be worn in an obvious location on the front of the uniform. Avoid using a strap around the neck to hold the card for this would place the officer in jeopardy during physical confrontations. Likewise, the two-way radio should be worn in a holster or fastened to the belt by a belt clip. This leaves the officer's hands free.

*   The officers should be instructed to make personal introductions properly. A smile, a look in the eye, and firm handshake are all important aspects of human relations that security personnel must master. **Security personnel must be salespeople.** As representatives of management, they must sell themselves, the department, and the work site, to everyone who enters the work site.

*   Be especially attentive to the security officer's breath. They should be instructed to never ingest alcohol, garlic, tobacco, onions, or other items which might leave an offensive odor when speaking to someone. Breath mints are a necessary tool for the public relations minded security officer. Making it a rule that no one on the security team be allowed to drink alcoholic beverages 8 hours prior to a shift, and no smoking or tobacco chewing be allowed during the hours of work, will go a far way in ensuring that the officer's breath will be pleasant to be around.

*   Encourage the officers to be "professionally connected." This means that officers should complete certification programs that clearly demonstrate to other members of the parent organization, and customers alike, the officer's professional achievement. Seniority alone is not the answer to this. Neither is employment in a "previous life."

*   Aside from certification programs, the officers should belong to professional organizations for *security* and *safety* professionals. There should be professional literature available for officers to read; something which generally comes automatically with membership in professional organizations.

*   In addition to the above suggestions, the officers must be introspective regarding their own world views, their beliefs, fears, suspicions, biases,

prejudices, and insecurities in dealing with certain categories of individuals.[5]

- The International Chiefs of Police Training Key 94 contains suggestions for improving the one-on-one communications, which would be greatly helpful during attempts to serve the needs of others. The following recommendations are adaptations taken from those suggestions:[6]

  - Officers should always remain polite, respectful, and sensitive to the needs of the person being served. Use empathy, not sympathy, in dealing with people. Remember that you have no more power than that of any other citizen, you are not a police officer (even sworn officers must realize that *power struggles* are unproductive). Remain detached and ignore personal insults. You are only enforcing your employer's policies and procedures; they are not your policies and procedures. The insults are actually directed at your employer, not at you.

  - Be businesslike at all times. Treat the person you are interacting with the way you would want to be treated under similar circumstances. Anger, impatience, contempt, dislike, sarcasm, and similar attitudes, have no place in public relations.

  - Treat each contact as a *process*, consisting of several phases, instead of a happening. Slow everything down, and take time to evaluate the environment you are about to enter. Size things up as accurately as possible before making the contact.

  - Remember that although you intend to deliver customer satisfaction with each contact, be it conflict resolution, or simple assistance, it must be resolved within the guidelines of the civil law, criminal law, administrative law, policy, procedure, and ethics. Be sure not to stray outside these parameters.

  - Avoid arguing at all times. Never back the person you are dealing with into a corner. If the situation becomes heated, give or get space, and continue to use verbal de-escalation to defuse the situation.

  - Avoid giving the impression that your presence should be interpreted as a threat. Your demeanor should project your concern and care for the needs of the person you are interacting with. A great opening statement is **"How can I help you?"**

  - Even if the person you come in contact with is being aggressive, avoid physical contact if at all possible. Use verbal de-escalation whenever possible. If physical contact is necessary, be sure that your physical response is in self-defense, reasonable, and necessary. Most of all, remember that your physical response may be witnessed by the general public and therefore it must look *professional*. It must appear that you are in *control*.

  - You are under no obligation to disarm an assailant with a knife or a gun, or to chase down an assailant. Officer safety comes first. Instead of disarming the bad guy, or capturing the bad guy, evacuate the area, create a safety zone and keep your distance until assistance can arrive. This will look a lot more professional to the media, and will keep everyone safe.

HANDLING CUSTOMER COMPLAINTS

While constant practice of the principles of customer relations will preclude most complaints from occurring, there are still times when security officers must play the role of ambassador or diplomat. In some cases they must even act as "referees." A few points to remember about handling complaints are:

1. **Treat all complainers with respect.**

   Every complaint or objection should be handled with respect for the complainant, no matter how absurd it is. Always treat the person with dignity. Never argue. There are no winners in an argument.

2. **Allow the complainant an opportunity to save face.**

   Don't embarrass a person who has been abusive or mistaken. Say, "I can understand why you misunderstood. This policy is very confusing!" This rule is integral to conflict resolution, as well as situations where actual physical restraint may be necessary.

3. **Build the ego of the complainant.**

   Give them credit for their contribution. "You have a good point there. Not many people would have thought of that," is a technique that can be applied.

4. **Show genuine courtesy and respect to the complaining party.**

   Be respectful and considerate to the complainant. Interview the person and allow for venting of frustrations. Use active listening techniques to demonstrate your concern about the person's irritation and the problem.

SERVICE THAT CAN MAKE THE DIFFERENCE

Protective service departments must be just that: service departments. Persons who wish to survive in contemporary security/safety environments must be willing and able to take on new responsibilities. In essence:

Security Only Exists for the Services It Can Provide

Some service options that may be feasible within a security/safety department include those listed here.

Communication

- Administration of a central operator/voice-mail system
- Whole facility intercom communication systems

- Two way intercom access controls at each perimeter door
- Use of tape dialers with sensitive equipment to enunciate system failures
- Utilization of computerized remote dial up networking for critical system diagnosis
- Emergency call stations in remote parts of the facility tied to the CCTV system
- Two-way intercoms installed near all overhead CCTV cameras

Transportation

- Employee transport within the work site complex
- Visitor transport within the work site complex
- Administering the parking garage

Risk Analysis

A risk analysis is a detailed evaluation of identified threats, probability and criticality hypothesis, vulnerability studies, and security surveys of facilities and systems (manmade and natural crisis, critical incident response, sensitive information losses, and so on.). By performing a risk analysis, the Security department is placing itself in a consulting relationship with the parent organization. Risk analyses also help in the *loss control* effort, and pay for themselves many times over. A risk analysis can be performed for the following situations:

- Executive/employees homes
- Work site offices
- Satellite facilities
- New construction/renovation
- Proposed property acquisitions

Training

Training and educational services help to integrate the Security department within the organization and make it more visible. Here are some options for providing training services.

- New employee orientation
- Periodic safety/security training
- Nonviolent crisis intervention
- Employee college tuition reimbursement programs for security officers.
- Security officer cost reimbursement programs for attainment of certifications
- Employee tuition reimbursement for security officer CEU attainment

THE MEDIA: GOOD DREAM/BAD DREAM

With respect to the media, it can be the thing you have been dreaming of, to promote the good work the security department is doing, or to send the message that your security department is not soft on crime, or to help at budget time to make your department look good, or any number of helpful messages. **In today's society, no organization can survive without positive media relations.**

If you save someone's life, intervene in an assault and arrest the bad guy, or drag someone from a burning vehicle at a crash scene just moments before the vehicle blows up, the media wants to know. They will break their necks to get to the scene and start looking for heroes to interview. They will usually arrive with the first responders because they are out there listening to the emergency scanner frequencies.

On the other side of the ledger, if you mess up, the media can be your worst nightmare. That negative story will hit the media with bigger headlines, more repeat stories and sidebars, than anything positive you can do. The negative story will seem to last forever. From that day on, your security department will be known by that negative story line. Because bad news sells better than good news, the media's motto is that if you can't say something bad, don't say anything at all!

Regardless of the story the media finds when they arrive at the scene, if it is too bland, unexciting or lacks titillation, the media will fill the gap. They are more than willing to create filler-parts to make their stories more appealing to the general public. If you have ever been quoted by the media, you probably found that the words you said during the interview, and the words which were attributed to what you said, don't match exactly. Something has been deleted. Something has been added, and sometimes the entire quote is a fabrication. You then wonder how that can be since you spoke into a tape recorder during the interview!

Now imagine that you have an incident at your place of employment. The media shows up and the first place they stop is at the first person they see. Who would that be on most occasions? You! The security officer. You have a choice. Give them an interview or direct them to the public information officer for your company. You have no other choices! Here are some ideas of what to do.

- Use your very best pubic relations skills as pointed out previously.
- Be polite and give the media the number to reach the public information officer (PIO).
- If they press you for a statement, be polite, and continue to refer them to the PIO.
- If the PIO is on site, direct them or take them to the PIO.
- If they press you further call in your supervisor who will repeat the above.
- NEVER, NEVER, NEVER give an interview!
- NEVER say, "No comment!"
- NEVER be discourteous.

Other problems with the media that are of a security nature can be anticipated at the scene of a critical incident. These include:[7]

a) Access control
b) Disruption of business operations

ACCESS CONTROL AT THE SCENE OF A CRITICAL INCIDENT

Access control is an absolute priority at the scene of a critical incident. However, access control can set up a power struggle between security and the media. Under most circumstances and for any number of reasons, mainly safety and legal reasons, security must deny access to anyone who is not a public assistance professional; police, medical, or fire professionals. That includes the media.

The media will sometimes utilize devious means to attain a story. They may try to sneak in a back door, or simply walk in when you are not looking. They may even be involved with diverting your attention to allow a reporter to scoot in the front door. They may overwhelm you with numerous reporters attempting access at the same time on the theory that some will get through the lines. Fortunately, in most cases, after meeting a modicum of resistance, the media will back off and revert to other ways of getting the story. Once they have made contact with the PIO, the pressure is usually off the security department.

The "feeding frenzy" of reporters at the critical incident scene relates back to what we pointed out in the beginning of this unit. We told you that the public has a "right-to-know" because they have an interest in what businesses are doing in their community. The media are the keepers of that public right-to-know, and they go after the facts like salmon swimming up stream during spawning season. The key for security is to know where to draw the line on the media. However, you cannot reduce perimeter access control to appease the media. That is why it is so important that the pubic relations department of your company appoints a public information officer to take the pressure off security during critical incidents.

DISRUPTION OF BUSINESS

Disruption of business operations is another area of concern for security. If the critical incident is of such a nature, like a murder or rape or other crime, the place of business is intact and continues to operate. The valuable security processes must remain intact. Patrols must be maintained, property must be protected, alarms must be responded to, restricted traffic control within the business must be maintained, and so on. This is true even if the business is shut down due to a fire, explosion, or accident. That means that there must be a contingency plan to meet the needs of all types of incidence. For that purpose the company has two alternatives:

- Create a Plant Emergency Organization (PEO)
- Call in a contract security contingent

PLANT EMERGENCY ORGANIZATION CONTROL

The Plant Emergency Organization (PEO) is a group of people who work in other departments who are trained to respond to emergencies. Usually a group of a dozen to two dozen individuals, scattered over all shifts, will make up the PEO. During critical incidents, this group stops what they are doing and they report immediately to a predetermined assignment or location. This immediately expands the private security capabilities so that both the critical incident and the critical security procedure continue to be serviced at the same time.

These trained PEO people regardless of who they work for, are under the direction of the security director. The best candidates for this detail usually are the maintenance workers and facilities workers. However, anyone can be used in the PEO, and they sometimes take volunteers from all departments.

CONTRACT SECURITY CONTINGENT ACCESS CONTROL

Your security department will want to identify a local contract security company to be called in during certain emergency situations. The contract security company will commit to a certain number of emergency staff, each hour, until the required number of personnel can be assembled. Special pricing will be established to ensure immediate response. For instance, during the first hour of the emergency, the contract security company will ensure that at last six security officers will respond. Another six officers will arrive within the next two hours, and the remainder of individuals required will arrive within the next three hours. At that point, three shift contingents will be set up until the emergency is over. Flexibility will be built into the plan, so that the security director can control the number of individuals sent by the contract security company.

With these PEO and/or contract security people available, they can block all the perimeter doors and set up emergency access control to help control the media. In addition, the security department will have special color coded large tags for everyone to wear during the emergency. If the employees are sent home, everyone who enters the building will have to enter through one door, and receive their special tag at that door. These tags will signify times of access and levels of access and whether or not escort is required. Large brightly colored tags with the word "MEDIA" printed on them are reserved for use by the media, and these tags should always require escort.

Anyone found without a tag, except public service personnel, should be required to report to the main door and log in or leave the property. If the employees are not sent home, then they should be required to show a badge for access, and should be asked to remain in the building and avoid talking with the media. All employees who are also witnesses to the events surrounding the incident should be asked to go to a debriefing room set up by security, and they should be asked to give statements of what they have witnessed. Public law enforcement may want to be in that room under certain circumstances. These witnesses should be given special instructions to keep out of the public eye until the issues are resolved. Public disclosure of information vital to the prosecution may destroy the prosecutor's case.

The preceding security measures are not exclusively set up to control the media. Relatives of injured parties, children, and other innocent parties may be placing themselves in danger by gaining access to an emergency scene under certain circumstances. Your job is to prevent that from happening. However, your primary responsibility is to do your job while maintaining good public relations, and that means maintaining good relations with the media. The media must be accommodated — they need to do their job. They also must be managed so that they don't jeopardize that asset which is valuable to every organization's image.

1. *Encyclopedia Americana*, 1995 Edition, Vol. 22, P. 760.
2. *American Heritage Dictionary of the English Language,* 1973 Edition, p. 1057.
3. See Media section, this unit, below.
4. PSTN (Professional Security Television Network) "Basic Security Officer Training Series, Field Notes."
5. Hess, Karen M. and Wrobleski, Henry M. *Introduction to Private Security,* Fourth Edition, St. Paul, MN., West Publishing Co., 1996, p. 328.
6. Fay, John J. *Encyclopedia of Security Management*, Techniques & Technology, Stoneham, MA., Butterworth-Heinemann. 1993, p. 592.

FOR MORE INFORMATION

International Association of Health Care Security and Safety has various publications and training/certification programs. The safety certification process is an ideal method of enhancing both image and providing additional services to the parent organization. IAHSS can be contacted at P.O. Box 637, Lombard, IL 60148 (630) 953-0990.

International Foundation for Protection Officers is a nonprofit educational organization that sponsors the Certified Protection Officer (CPO), and Certified Security Supervisor (CSS) programs. The foundation also publishes a newsletter and several short books on various topics. Associate and corporate membership opportunities also exist. IFPO's address is P. O. Box 771329, Naples, FL 34107 (239) 430-0534 or http://www.ifpo.org.

Powerphone, Inc. is a leading company in telephone answering and dispatching. They offer seminars and manuals. Their address is P.O. Box 1911, Madison, CT 06443-0900 (800)53-Power, chris@powerphone.com or visit http://www. powerphone.com.

Professional Security Television Network (PSTN) produces a wide variety of videos dealing with public relations and related issues. Their address is, 1303 Marsh Lane, Carrolton, TX. 75006 (800) 942-7786 or (214) 417-4302.

"Public Relations" is a course that is offered on campus, and at client locations, by the Special Programs Office York College of PA, Country Club Road, York, PA 17405-7199 (717) 846-7788, fax (717) 849-1607; bpavlick@ycp.edu or visit http://www.ycp.edu/.

SECURITY QUIZ
Public Relations

1. Public relations consists of _____ understanding between an organization and its constituent publics.
2. The key words in public relations are: "_____ need _____."
3. All of the following should be carried by protection officers except:
   ☐ (a) a small pocket knife
   ☐ (b) duct tape
   ☐ (c) two pens
   ☐ (d) a watch
4. "Never _____ someone off _____."
5. Volunteering to help someone is good PR and can be an effective _____ to crime.
6. The "out front" person for the organization is usually the:
   ☐ (a) public information officer
   ☐ (b) protection officer
   ☐ (c) maintenance worker
   ☐ (d) human resource manager
7. If protection officers are pressed for a statement by a media representative, they can respond "off the record."
   ☐T ☐ F
8. Each contact with another person should be thought of as a _____ consisting of phases rather than a happening.
9. A risk analysis is an informal appraisal of physical security measures.
   ☐T ☐ F
10. The security department must first have a _____ program in place before a public relations effort can be launched.

POLICE AND SECURITY LIAISON

By Johnny May, CPP, CPO
Chris C. Lipnickey, CPO

For years the security industry has been negatively stereotyped. A 1971 study, conducted by the Rand Corporation, described the typical private security guard as an aging white male who was poorly educated and poorly paid. The average age was between 40 and 55, with little education beyond the ninth grade. The Rand researchers further reported, "The fact is, the average security guard in this country is underscreened, unrestrained, undersupervised, and underpaid."

This negative stereotype has followed us into the 21st century. Let's take a look at some recent incidents that have made the media.

- At the Republican National Convention in San Diego, a security guard stole 16 TVs from NBC. The officer, who pleaded guilty, was wanted in another burglary before he was hired.
- Three security guards were arrested at Simon Fraser University in Vancouver, Canada, for selling some computers and athletic clothing.
- The Whitney Museum of Art in New York was involved in a lawsuit because the security guard wrote "I love you, Tushee" and "love buns" on a borrowed painting worth more than $1.5 million.
- A female executive of Saks Fifth Avenue is suing the company for $50 million. She was raped in 1994 by a store guard. A preemployment background check on the guard failed to turn up his 1989 conviction for the sexual assault of an 11-year-old girl in Kentucky. The guard is serving 1½ to 4 years in prison.

The sad reality is that yes, these types of incidents sometime occur in our industry, but why don't heroic deeds by security professionals get the media's attention? Chris Hertig refers to private security as "The Invisible Empire" of the criminal justice system, and the security officers are referred to as the "Forgotten Soldiers" of this invisible empire.

In a recent *USA Today* article ("On Guard: Bad Guys Behind the Badge of Honor: All companies are looking for is a warm body in a uniform," September 12, 1996), Robert McCrie, editor of *Security Letter*, said, "Heroic deeds by security officers don't get media play. There are scores, thousands of noble, self-sacrificing security officers, including some who have rescued people from flaming buildings before the fire department arrived."

One example is Brandon Ford of First Security Services, who received the prestigious Brownyard Award in Atlanta, GA, for going above and beyond the call of duty. Ford tackled a man who was shooting a male nurse outside of a hospital in New Haven, CT. Ford, who was on duty, likely saved the nurse's life. "I was just doing my job," Ford said. The perception that security officers are merely rent-a-cops with very little education and training has greatly hampered the relationship between law enforcement and private security personnel. In 1976, the Private Security Advisory council, through the U.S. Department of Justice, identified two main factors that contributed to poor relationships between law enforcement and private security: (1) their inability to clarify role definitions and (2) they often practiced stereotyping. The Council cited various areas of conflict and ranked them in order of importance.

1. Lack of mutual respect
2. Lack of communication
3. Lack of cooperation
4. Lack of law enforcement's knowledge of private security
5. Perceived competition
6. Lack of standards
7. Perceived corruption

In the early 1980s, relationships between law enforcement and private security were rated fair to good, at best, by law enforcement executives. Research has confirmed that longstanding obstacles to interaction and cooperation between law enforcement and private security continue to exist.

One step for change is to have both law enforcement and private security personnel understand the differences between the two professions.

Law enforcement	*Private security*
Apprehension/ enforcement	*Loss prevention/asset protection*
Prosecution	*General services*
Reactive	*Proactive*
Protect a society	*Protect an organization*

Another way to bridge this gap is to find common ground between the two professions. That common ground for interaction between law enforcement and private security is crime. The following are several functions that both professions perform:

- Personal safety—The private sector has a responsibility to ensure the safety of its employees, clients, and anyone else with whom it comes in contact. Local law enforcement is responsible for the safety of the general public.
- Crime prevention—Both professions have obligation to develop crime prevention programs. Most police departments have acknowledged that it is better to prevent criminal behavior than to combat it after the fact. A large number of metropolitan police departments now maintain a crime prevention unit within the department.
- Order maintenance—The police are responsible for

maintaining public order. In areas maintained by private industry, the job of order maintenance is the responsibility of private security.

Liaison plays an important role in our day-to-day functions as security professionals. In fact, the (CPP) Certified Protection Professional examination, which is administered by the American Society for Industrial Security, dedicates 5 percent of the examination to liaison.

According to the *Hallcrest Report II, Private Security Trends* (1970–2000), private security is America's primary protective resource in terms of spending and employment (see Figure 12-1).

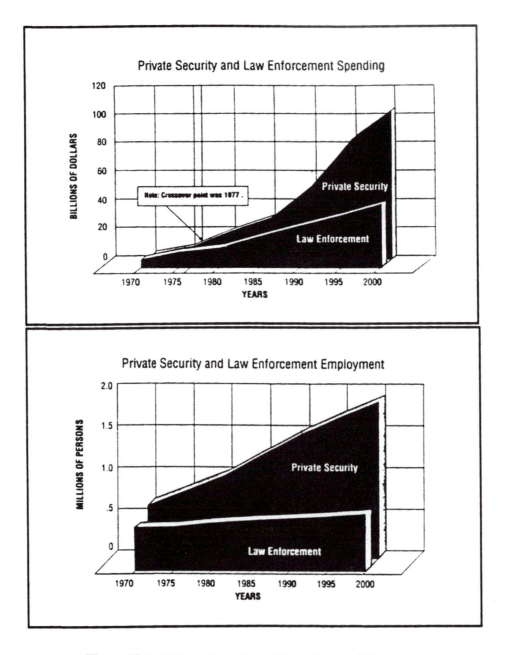

Figure 12-1   Private Security and Spending and Employment

By the year 2000, security officers will outnumber law enforcement officers 3 to 1. Private security currently employs almost 1.5 million people, with annual expenditures of $52 billion. By comparison, roughly 600,000 people work in federal, state, and local public law enforcement, and expenditures for those services are roughly $30 billion. These are some of the major findings of the report.

- The increasing growth of private security and the limited growth of public law enforcement is due to 4 main factors.
  a) Increasing workplace crime
  b) Increasing fear of crime
  c) A decreasing rate of spending for public protection
  d) Increasing awareness and use of private security effective protective measures
- The cost of economic crime in 1990 was estimated at $114 billion. At 2 percent or more of the gross national product, economic crime is out of control and on the rise.
- Private security personnel are younger and better educated than they used to be. The number of academic security programs has grown significantly, from only 33 certificate and degree programs in the mid 1970s, to 164 such programs in operation currently. Furthermore, employment in private security is projected to grow at 2.3 percent annually to the year 2000. The U.S. Department of Labor predicts that the national workforce will grow by a little more than half of that projected figure.

Privatization is the trend for the 1990s! For some time, there has been a shift in service industries toward assuming duties once left to government. In 1990, the Mercer Group, an Atlanta, Georgia based research firm that tracks prioritization of services, conducted a survey which revealed that roughly 33 percent of respondents, composed of local and municipal governments, special districts, and homeowner associations, contract security services to augment law enforcement.

According to James Mercer, President of the Mercer Group, "the basic reason is that the government can't afford to have a sworn officer with all the fringe benefits that come with that appointment—not when they can hire a security officer for a lot less money."

Private Security and Police in America: The Hallcrest Report, published in 1985 by the National Institute of Justice, Washington, DC, found that law enforcement officials, proprietary security managers, and contract security managers, agreed on the transfer of certain police related activities to private security. Those activities were burglar alarm responses, preliminary investigations, incident reports when victims decline prosecution, certain misdemeanor incident reports, and transporting people taken in citizen's arrest. A number of these activities are already being handled by private security in many areas of the United States.

There appears to be a growing potential for contracting private security to perform the following activities:

- Courtroom security
- Executive protection
- Parking lot security
- Parking enforcement
- Traffic control
- Housing project patrol
- Special event security
- Public building security

In Michigan, a large number of shopping malls and hospitals have opted to employ their own security police under what is known as Public Act 330 (see appendix #2). Public Act 330 is regulated by the Michigan State Police, and gives the security officers arrest powers while on duty at their establishment.

Listed here are some general recommendations for improving the working relationship between police and security personnel.

- *Establish credibility with local law enforcement.* Only contact the police (1) When you have information to exchange; (2) to have someone arrested; or (3) when there is an immediate danger or need for additional manpower. Knowledge of local codes assists in the arrest process, and helps the security officer testify more effectively in court.
- *Establish and/or follow a code of ethics.* Security personnel should realize that those individuals who are unethical do not have rewarding careers. They are snubbed by colleagues and superiors, passed over for promotions, and terminated from employment in the more serious cases. The most extreme cases result in revocation of licenses the officer may possess, and/or civil/criminal liability. The International Foundation for Protection Officers Code of Ethics is as follows:

  (a) Respond to employer's professional needs.
  (b) Exhibit exemplary conduct.
  (c) Protect confidential information.
  (d) Maintain a safe and secure workplace.
  (e) Dress to create professionalism.
  (f) Enforce all rules and regulations.
  (g) Encourage liaison with police officers.
  (h) Develop good rapport within the profession.
  (i) Strive to attain professional competence.
  (j) Encourage high standards of officer ethics.

- *Always maintain the highest level of professionalism.* In our society we are judged by how we look, what we say, and the manner in which we perform our job (e.g., uniforms should be clean, pressed, and properly worn. Written reports should be neat and detailed, use of proper English is recommended, and always be courteous.).
- *Increase police knowledge of private security.* This can be accomplished through shared training pro-

grams or seminars which explain the role of private security to law enforcement personnel. A one hour lecture, at the local police academy by security professionals is one example. In Michigan, the Detroit Police Department's Crime Prevention Section, and the Detroit Chapter of ASIS cosponsor an annual professional development seminar, entitled "Update," which focuses on current trends and topics, which are of interest to both sectors. One of the primary aspects of the seminar is the cooperation displayed between the two sectors in the development, planning, and coordination of the seminar. The law enforcement and security attendees network among themselves to form new relationships, and to share common problems and work out mutual approaches and solutions.

- Support licensing and regulation of security officers as a mechanism to upgrade private security.
- Law enforcement agencies should appoint private security liaison officers within the department for problem resolution and information exchange with private security personnel.
- Establish mutual assistance agreements between security and law enforcement personnel.
- *Develop and/or attend cooperative programs.* Beginning in the mid-1980s, cooperative programs between the private and public sectors have emerged at a faster pace than ever before. This creates the opportunity for valuable information exchange, and builds long lasting working relationships. One of the earliest cooperative programs, PRIDE (Pooling Resources in Defense of our Environment), was established in Southfield, Michigan (1981), by the Southfield Police Department, to regularly exchange crime-related information, to integrate protective services wherever possible, and to form a better working relationship between the police and private security. Another model cooperative program is the Area Police Private Security Liaison. APPL was established in Manhattan, New York (1986), to chance public/private cooperation in protecting people and property, to exchange information, and to help eliminate the "credibility gap" between police and private security.
- *Nurture professional growth and development.* Get all the education, certifications and specialized training that you can. One can never learn or know too much. Life is a learning process. Stay abreast of current trends and technologies (see Appendixes 1 and 3).

The key to maintaining a good working relationship with law enforcement personnel is to maintain a good public perception. Public perception plays a very important part in our day to day operations as security professionals. We must constantly work to improve our image. We must act as professionals if we ever expect to be accepted as such.

APPENDIX 1
Academic Programs (colleges which offer degree/courses in security)

York College of Pennsylvania
Country Club Road
York, PA 17405-7199
(717) 846-7788

Southern Illinois University
Woody Hall
Carbondale, IL 62901
(618) 453-5701

Northeastern University
360 Huntington Avenue
Boston, MA 02115
(617) 437-2200

University of Detroit-Mercy
4001 W. McNichols
Detroit, MI 48219
(313) 993-1245

John Jay College of Criminal Justice
899-10th Avenue
New York, NY 10019
(212) 237-8638

Wartburg College
222 Ninth Street, NW
Waverly, IA 50677
(319) 352-8200

Henry Ford Community College
5101 Evergreen
Dearborn, MI 48128-1495
(313) 845-9856

Indiana State University
Holmstead Hall, Room 208
Terre Haunte, IN 47809
(812) 237-2192

Michigan State University
560 Baker Hall
East Lansing, MI 48824-1118
(517) 355-2192

Missouri Southern State College
3950 Newman Road
Joplin, MO 64801-1595
(417) 625-9651

Southern Vermont College
Monument Avenue
Bennington, VA 05201
(802) 442-5427

*Webster University
470 E. Lockwood Avenue
St. Louis, MO 63119-3194
(314) 968-7000

University of New Haven
300 Orange Avenue
West Haven, CT 06516
(203) 932-7369

Eastern Kentucky University
253 Stratton
Richmond, KY 40475
(606) 622-1976

Central Missouri State University
305 Humphrey
Warrensburg, MO 64093
(816) 543-4616

St. John's University
Grand Central & Utopia Pkwys
Jamaica, NY 11439
(718) 990-6161

Pennsylvania State University
Fayette Campus, P.O. Box 519
Uniontown, PA 15401
(412) 430-4232

*City University
919 W. Grady Way
Renton, WA 98055
(800) 422-4898

*Correspondence Degrees

For a complete listing of college programs, visit
asisonline.org.

APPENDIX 2
MINIMUM TRAINING CURRICULUM FOR PRIVATE SECURITY POLICE

The curriculum herein described is minimum basic training required for private security guards to which Act 330, PA 1968, as amended, the Private Security Guard Act, is applicable.

SUBJECT	HOURS	EXAMINATION
Regular Training Requirements		
Exemptions from Regular Requirements		
INITIAL ORIENTATION	2	Required
Initial Orientation	1	Required
Professional Responsibility	1	Required
Human Relations and Police Liaison		
LEGAL SECTION OBJECTIVES	38	
Constitutional Law	1	Required
Roots of American Jurisprudence	1	Required
Courts	1	Required
Arrest Procedures	4	Required
Criminal Procedures	9	Required
Admissions and Confessions		
Search and Seizure		
Evidence	2	Required
Criminal Law	10	Required
Juvenile Law	4	Required
Civil Liability	4	Required
Cultural Diversity	4	Optional
SPECIAL CURRICULUM	53	
Firearms Proficiency	24	Required

Pressure Point Control/Defensive Tactics	24	Required
Bloodborne Pathogens/Hepatitis B	1	Required
Risk Management	2	Required
Narcotics and Dangerous Drugs	2	Optional
CRITICAL INCIDENT CURRICULUM	13	
CPR	8	Required
Fire Extinguisher Use	1	Required
Non-Violent Crisis Intervention	2	Required
Emergency Preparedness	2	Required
PATROL OPERATIONS CURRICULUM	14	
Report Writing	8	Required
Crime Scene Investigation and Witness Interview	2	Required
Radio Communication and Civil Disorder	1	Required
Access Control Systems	2	Required
Crime Prevention	1	Required
MAINTENANCE CURRICULUM SECTION	20 (16)	Required

REFERENCES

Cunningham, Strauch and Van Meter, *Private Security Trends: 1970–2000. The Hallcrest Report II*, Butterworth-Heinemann 1990.

Cunningham, William and Taylor, Todd, *The Hallcrest Report: Private Security and Police in America*, McLean, VA: Chancellor Press, 1985.

Fay, John J. *Encyclopedia of Security Management.* Stoneham, MA: Butterworth-Heinemann, 1993.

Hertig, Christopher "Liaison with Law Enforcement: Security Officers Should Only Call When," *Protection Officer*, July-September 1988.

Hertig, Christopher "Who Are the Forgotten Soldiers?" *Security Management*, February 1993.

Nemeth, Charles P. *Private Security and the Law*. Cincinnati, OH: Anderson Publishing, 1989.

Newborn, Ellen and Jones, Del. "On Guard: Bad Guys behind Badge of Honor: All Companies Are Looking For Is a Warm Body in a Uniform," *USA Today*, September 12, 1996.

Ortmeier P.J. "Adding Class to Security," *Security Management*, July 1996.

APPENDIX 3
Professional Certification Programs

(CPO) Certified Protection Officer
(CSS) Certified Security Supervisor
International Foundation for Protection Officers
P. O. Box 771329
Naples, FL 34107
(239) 430-0534

(CPP) Certified Protection Professional
American Society for Industrial Security
1655 North Fort Meyer Drive, Suite 1200
Arlington, VA 22209-3198
(703) 522-5800

(CST) Certified Security Trainer
ASET Secretariat
Route 2, Box 3644
Berryville, VA 22611
(703) 955-1129

(PPS) Personal Protection Specialist
Executive Protection Institute
Arcadia Manor, Route 2, Box 3645
Berryville, VA 22611
(540) 955-1129

(CSP) Certified Safety Professional
Board of Certified Safety Professionals
208 Burwash Avenue
Savoy, IL 61874-9571
(217) 359-9263

(CFE) Certified Fraud Examiner
Association of Certified Fraud Examiners
716 West Avenue
Austin, TX 78701
(800) 245-3321

(CHPA) Certified Healthcare Protection Administrator
International Association for Healthcare Security and Safety
P.O. Box 637
Lombard, IL 60148
(708) 953-0990

(CFSP) Certified Fire Protection Specialist
EMACS
P.O. Box 198
Ashland, MA 01721
(508) 881-6044

(CDRP) Certified Disaster Recovery Professional
Disaster Recovery Institute
1818 Craig Road, Suite 125
St. Louis, MO 63146
(314) 434-2272

The IAHS also offers certification programs for security officers. They offer a 40-hour basic security officer certification, a 20-hour supervisory certification, and a 20-hour safety certification. All 3 programs can be utilized in a self-directed (home study) program.

APPENDIX 4

The following is a good model to follow while working to establish a good professional relationship:

COOPERATE

- ➢ **C**ommunication
- ➢ **O**rganization
- ➢ **O**pen Mind
- ➢ **P**rofessionalism
- ➢ **E**mployee/Employer
- ➢ **R**espect
- ➢ **A**ttitude
- ➢ **T**raining
- ➢ **E**ducation

COOPERATE gives an outline for numerous issues that have been plaguing successful working relationships between police and security agencies and other business factions that security may work with. Some of the main points that are included in COOPERATE are listed below along with some other ideas.

COMMUNICATION

Keeping an open line is vital to a strong relationship; liaisons should keep in touch with other departments by professional means. This should include, but is not limited to, the following:

- ➢ Company letterhead
- ➢ Telephone contact
- ➢ Conference calls
- ➢ E-mail
- ➢ Meetings
- ➢ Presentations
- ➢ Boards/ Committees

ORGANIZATION

Keeping track of one's own company is critical to the way security liaisons operate. An individual acting to establish liaisons must be able to keep dates and times open. This allows them to work effectively with outside individuals in similar positions in other departments. Liaisons should master the following to help aid them with organization:

- ➢ Personnel rosters
- ➢ Timetables
- ➢ Logistical information
- ➢ Networks

OPEN MIND

Security professionals working as a liaison must keep an open mind. Tunnel vision is dangerous and can destroy any strong relationship. This can lead to unproductive behavior and hinder productivity in organizations. Security liaisons should be able to see past the differences in departments and perceive situations from others' viewpoint.

Avoid:

- ➢ Turf protection
- ➢ Stereotyping
- ➢ Prejudicial analysis

Do:

- ➢ Determine what the agency does.
- ➢ Why they do it.
- ➢ What type of education they have.

"Thinking outside the box"—such as going beyond security thoughts.

PROFESSIONALISM

Perhaps the most important part of a liaison is to act professional. Law enforcement has always seen itself as the "high man on the totem pole." Thus the only way to counter an ego such as that is to act professional. Steps to professionalism may include the following:

➢ Certifications
➢ Business appearance
➢ Knowledge of topics and laws
➢ Knowledge of related disciplines
➢ Credible sources of knowledge

EMPLOYEE/ EMPLOYER

Not to be overlooked by a security liaison are the relationships that are built with their employer and employees who are in the working environment. Liaisons should not overlook the following:

➢ Unions
➢ Management
➢ Customer relations
➢ Local community
➢ Media
➢ Ergonomics

RESPECT

Protection officers and police officers have always had conflict between them, mainly because they do not keep and open mind. To aim for respect, do the following:

➢ Keep an open mind.
➢ Avoid distrust.
➢ Act professional.
➢ Communicate.

ATTITUDE

Individuals who are chosen to be a representative and communicate with other companies must have a good work ethic. The way in which a liaison comes to work every day will affect the relationships he or she builds. A positive attitude can be built upon such ideas as these:

➢ Being optimistic
➢ Leaving personal problems at home
➢ Exercising good ethics
➢ Being a good listener
➢ Not being egocentric
➢ Wanting to learn more
➢ Having a positive image

TRAINING

It is also the job of the liaison position not only to develop a professional working relationship, but to also develop a training relationship as well. In the past, training was not consistent, and different departments had contrasting standard operation procedures. Liaisons should work in training to develop some of the following:

➢ Mutual training programs
➢ Drills
➢ Open houses
➢ Similar SOPs
➢ Similar training interest
➢ Seeking positive results
➢ Continuous training

EDUCATION

Security professionals appointed to be liaisons working in the discipline should have essential education needed to work in diverse, challenging, and changing fields. High professional standards of education should include the following:

➢ College degrees
➢ Certifications
➢ Elective courses
➢ Field studies
➢ Passion for knowledge

SECURITY QUIZ
Police and Security Liaison

1. A 1971 study conducted by the Rand Corporation described the typical private security personnel as _____, _____ and _____. (Fill in the blanks.)
2. The common ground for interaction between law enforcement and private security resources is:
    ☐ (a) education
    ☐ (b) patriotism
    ☐ (c) career development
    ☐ (d) crime

3. In the early 1980s, relationships between law enforcement and private security were rated _____ by law enforcement executives.
   □ (a) Fair to good
   □ (b) Excellent
   □ (c) Extremely bad
   □ (d) Very good
4. *Hallcrest Report II* found that private security personnel are younger and better educated now than they used to be.
   □T □ F
5. Cooperative programs between the private and public sector are on the decline.
   □T □ F
6. Law enforcement expenditures far exceed those of private security.
   □T □ F
7. Private security and law enforcement both perform the following functions:_____, _____, and _____.
8. The key to maintaining a good working relationship with law enforcement personnel is to _____.
9. By the year 2000, private security personnel are expected to outnumber law enforcement personnel by a ration of:
   □ (a) 2 to 1
   □ (b) 3 to 1
   □ (c) 4 to 1
   □ (d) 5 to 1
10. According to *Hallcrest II,* American Business losses were estimated at:
   □ (a) $114 billion
   □ (b) $53 billion
   □ (c) $241 billion
   □ (d) $16 billion

ETHICS AND PROFESSIONALISM

By Christopher A. Hertig, CPP, CPO

The business realities of contemporary management require that security (asset protection) efforts provide protection for **ALL** of an organization's assets, including people, property, information, and image. Asset protection should incorporate Bottom and Kostanoski's WAECUP Model in order to address these concerns. This model asserts that losses stem from waste, accident, error, crime, and unethical/unprofessional practices. under unethical/unprofessional practice are dissemination of confidential information, lying to clients, discrimination, profanity in public, poor relations with law enforcement and other security organizations, and slovenly dress. Most of this loss relates to negative public/client image. Additionally, within organizations that are stricken by a serious scandal, there are legal costs, increased personnel turnover, and lowered efficiency by a demoralized workforce.

An additional concern regarding ethics and professionalism is the role that protection officers play for the public at large. As protection officers increase in number and take on an increasing array of functions which place them in contact with the public; it becomes readily apparent that there is an acute need for higher standards of professionalism. Consider the following trends:

- A steady increase in the number of security personnel, particularly in the contract service sector.
- More contact with the public-contemporary protection officers is more commonly found in shopping centers, office buildings, and parks, than in the warehouses and industrial facilities guarded by their predecessors.
- Gradual—yet often unrecognized—assumption of duties formerly performed by public entities, such as maintaining order at special events, transporting prisoners, and responding to alarms (privatization).

Obviously, the role played by security officers is changing! When one looks at future trends (see PRIVATE SECURITY TRENDS: 1970–2000 by Cunningham, Strauchs and Van Meter, Butterworth-Heinemann) it becomes apparent that:

The greatest issue in public safety is private security.

From a personal perspective, officers should realize that those individuals who are unethical and unprofessional do not have rewarding careers. They are snubbed by colleagues and superiors, passed over for promotion, and terminated from employment in the more serious cases. The most extreme cases result in revocation of licenses that the officer may possess, and civil and criminal liability.

Those who make the wrong choices do not last.

Protection officers must be equipped with the decision-making skills and professional knowledge to make the right choices. For too long words like "professional" have been used indiscriminately without a complete examination of their meaning. Understanding what the terms represent is a necessary step towards adopting and implementing professional behavior!

KEY TERMS AND CONCEPTS

Ethics: the study of good and bad conduct within a profession. Ethics deals with the examination of moral philosophy combined with the duties and obligations within a certain profession. Ethical behavior results when the correct ethical decisions have been made and carried out. The International Foundation for Protection Officers Code of Ethics is:

I.	Respond to employer's professional needs.
II.	Exhibit exemplary conduct.
III.	Protect confidential information.
IV.	Maintain a safe and secure workplace.
V.	Dress to create professionalism.
VI.	Enforce all lawful rules and regulations.
VII.	Encourage liaison with public officers.
VIII.	Develop good rapport within the profession.
IX.	Strive to attain professional competence.
X.	Encourage high standards of officer ethics.

Duty: a professional obligation to do a certain thing. Protection officers have a duty to protect the lives and property of employees, conduct professional investigations, maintain order and assist visitors/employees/customers. Duties may be established by statute, custom, or contract.

Professionals think in terms of their duties and obligations, not their authority!

Professional: One who practices a profession. One who has special knowledge and skill which results from advanced training and education. Often an apprenticeship is required, such as the experience qualifications necessary for professional certification (Certified Protection Officer, Certified Security Supervisor, Certified Protection Professional, and so on). Professions have professional codes of ethics and professional organizations which members belong to. A professional is loyal to his or her chosen profession. A true professional has the following:

1. Education relating to the profession.

2. Training for the tasks and duties that must be performed.
3. Experience within the profession.
4. A *commitment* to the profession marked by continuously striving for excellence.

The acronym **"PROFESSIONAL"** outlines the attributes of a professional:

P - precise, exact, detailed
R - responsive to clients and the public
O - Objective in thought; free of prejudice and preconceived notions
F - factual in all reporting processes; honest
E - ethical
S - sincere about doing the best job possible
S - striving for perfection by trying to constantly improve one's job performance
I - informed about events and trends within one's profession
O - observant of people and the work environment
N - neat and orderly in dress and work
A - accommodating and helpful to others
L - loyal to one's employer, clients and profession

Deportment: How one carries oneself, bearing, outward manifestation of attitude and image. A few things to bear in mind about deportment are:

- Dress should be neat, precise, and conservative.
- Shoes should match belt.
- No purses for women.
- Socks should always match the pants and cover the calf.
- Conservative ties, properly tied; silk is a good choice of material.
- Jewelry worn judiciously!
- "Less is more" with makeup and cologne.
- Uniforms should be worn uniformly. All officers should have the same placement of insignia and equipment.

The acronym **"DEPORTMENT"** provides additional insight into the meaning—and practical application—of the term.

D - dress as a representative of your employer and/or client.
E - efficient in performing both routine and emergency job duties.
P - precision. Ironed shirts, neatly combed hair, all buttons, zippers, and pins properly secured.
O - organized on the job.
R - responsive to customers, clients, visitors, and community members; approachable.
T - talk as a professional does, using proper English.
M - manners - respect for others - exhibited at all times.
E - edit and review interviews and notes before concluding these segments of an investigation.
N - nurture professional growth and development at all times, Strive to learn!

T - timely, Being on time is essential. "Fashionably late" is out of style in professional settings.

Manners: Manners are simply accepted means of conducting oneself in public. Politeness. They consist of *consideration* and *respect* for others. They are *social graces*. A few basic tenets of proper manners are:

- Allow people to talk and express their views; DO NOT INTERRUPT—not only is this good manners, it is effective interviewing—and the truly professional protection officer makes every conversation an interview.
- Be respectful of people's input. *Compliment rather than criticize.*
- Praise others when appropriate. **Be genuine in doing this.**
- Stand up to greet people entering the room, especially a woman, client, or VIP. This is a show of respect and consideration. It is an opportunity to create a personal bond that no true professional can afford to pass up.

ETHICAL DECISION MAKING

Protection officers must be equipped with the ability to make *professional judgments*. They need to be proficient at decision making as it applies to ethics. Basic **decision making** consists of **problem solving.** Problem solving consists of the following steps:

1. Problem identification. There should be a descriptive definition of the problem. Inadequate problem definition often results in poor decisions being made.
2. Determination if a decision needs to be made immediately or if it can wait.
3. Research among the various options that are available - *many poor decisions stem from a failure to fully explore all of the options.* Professional knowledge of law, technology and organizational structure/chain of command is important in understanding all of the options.
4. Choosing an option. Pick that one which seems best.
5. Implementing the decision. Put it into effect.
6. Evaluating the decision and following it up. This means seeing how it works and reporting/documenting it. Keeping superiors informed is always important! Soliciting feedback from them is essential.

A practical, "real world" method of dealing with ethical dilemmas can made use of simple, easy to remember acronyms. Once the problem has been identified, the ethical dilemma can be managed by use of the **PORT** acronym:

P - problem—define and describe it. If possible write a sentence or two describing it.
O - options—what are they? Be sure to list all of them.
R - responsibilities to employers, family, the public, the profession, and so on.
T - time; the test of—"How will I feel about my decision in 20 years?"

Ethical decision-making must be real. It must exist in everyday work situations. Using the PORT acronym can help to maintain ethical conduct by protection professionals.

WHY UNETHICAL BEHAVIOR OCCURS

It is important to understand why unethical and unprofessional behavior occurs so that it can be prevented. Some of the more common causes of ethical lapses are:

- Protection officers—or any other person in a position of trust—must possess good character. As past behavior is the most reliable indicator of future behavior, it is necessary to do a check of prior employment. There can be no substitute for screening!

- Taking the "path of least resistance." This is human nature. Unfortunately, doing what is easy does not always solve the problem. Taking a "short cut" usually means *problem avoidance* where the person confronting the dilemma just hopes the problem will either go away or solve itself. It won't! Avoiding the problem almost always causes the problem to become larger and more damaging over time.

- Conflict with full-time and part-time employment. The practice of "moonlighting," with its inherent division of loyalties between the full and part-time employers, can create a breeding ground for unethical conduct.

- Fatigue. People often make the wrong choices simply because they are tired. Fatigue and stress impede good decision making. This can set up a vicious cycle where poor decisions are made and more stress is the result!

- "Traditionalism" and a resistance to change. Just because protection officers haven't been trained in first-aid and CPR doesn't mean that the practice should continue! Just because protection officers have not had a full and complete orientation to the organization they are protecting, does not mean that this should remain as standard practice. A pertinent example of "Traditionalism" is the practice of handcuffing. Handcuffs are rarely double-locked. Not doing so can cause the cuffs to cinch tightly on the subject's wrist which may result in permanent nerve damage. Another example is traffic control. Many organizations do not train their officers to direct and control traffic, in spite of the fact that this is a key safety issue, not to mention a crucial juncture in public relations!

REFERENCES

Black H.C. (1990). *Black's Law Dictionary*. St. Paul, MN.

Fulton, R. (1993). "How to Stay on the Team" in Nowicki, E. (Ed.) *Total Survival.*, Power Lake, WI Performance Dimensions Publishing.

Hertig, C.A. (1993). *Protection Officer Guidebook*. Bellingham, WA; International Foundation for Protection Officers.

Hoffman, T.W. (1996). *Duties And Responsibilities For New York State Security Officers*. Flushing, NY: Looseleaf Law Publications.

Merriam, G. & C. Co. (1972). *Webster's Seventh New Collegiate Dictionary*. Springfield, MA: G & C Merriam.

Minion, P.R. (1992). *Protection Officer Training Manual*. Stoneham, MA: Butterworth-Heinemann.

Pollock, J.M. (1994). *Ethics In Crime And Justice: Dilemmas And Decisions*. Belmont, CA: Wadsworth.

Tasks Force on Private Security (1976). *Report Of The Task Force On Private Security*, Washington, DC: Law Enforcement Assistance Administration.

Trautman, N.E. (1993). "Dealing with Attitude Anger, Lust and Greed" in Nowicki, E. (Ed.) *Total Survival*. Power Lake, WI: Performance Dimensions.

Walters, R.W. (1984). *Executive Guide To Behavioral Sciences Terminology*, Mahwah. NJ: Roy J. Walters and Associates.

```
=  ? =  ┌──────────────────────────┐  = ? =
          │      SECURITY QUIZ       │
          │  Ethics and Professionalism │
          └──────────────────────────┘
```

1. List three reasons why ethics and professionalism are important to the employer, public, and individual officer.
   (a) _____
   (b) _____
   (c) _____

2. Complete the acronym "PROFESSIONAL."
   P _____
   R _____
   O _____
   F _____
   E _____
   S _____
   S _____
   I _____
   O _____
   N _____
   A _____
   L _____

3. List five steps that can be taken to enhance one's professional development.
   (a) _____
   (b) _____
   (c) _____
   (d) _____
   (e) _____

4. List three methods by which the protection officer can dress to create professionalism.
   (a) _____
   (b) _____
   (c) _____

5. When looking at the increasing role of private security personnel in contemporary society, it becomes apparent that the biggest issue in _____ safety is _____ security.

6. List three reasons for unethical conduct.
   (a) _____
   (b) _____
   (c) _____

7. List three common errors in decision-making.
   (a) _____
   (b) _____
   (c) _____

8. Professionals think in terms of their _____ and obligations rather than their authority.

9. A true professional has the following:
   (a) _____ relating to the profession.
   (b) _____ for the tasks and duties that must be performed.
   (c) _____ within the profession.
   (d) A _____ to the _____ and continuous striving for excellence.

10. Fill in the blanks of the PORT Model of ethical decision-making. List a question that needs to be addressed in each of the letters of the acronym.
    P _____
    O _____
    R _____
    T _____

APPENDIX
BASIC KEY CONTROL FOR
ALL LEVELS OF SECURITY

By Cecelia Sharp

Prior to setting up a Masterkey system, do the following:

1. Consult all levels of management and the different operations within the organization.
2. Review the blueprints (if applicable) or draft plants of the area or buildings.
3. Determine future requirements or operations expansion.
4. Define the level of protection or security required. (See Figure A-1.)

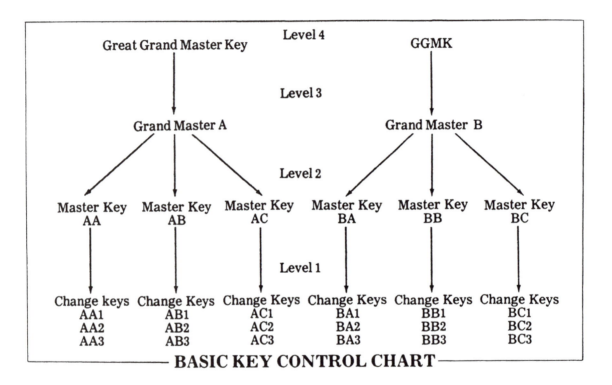

Figure A-1   Basic Key Control Chart

PATROL PREPARATION

Equipment (Foot Patrols)
- Flashlight
- Handheld radio
- Pen and notebook
- Whistle (if required)
- S.O. ID
- Keys
- Access cards, combinations

Equipment (Mobile Patrols)
- All previous (foot patrol)
- First aid kit
- Fire extinguishers
- Auxiliary lights—flares
- Radio communications
- Flashers—Spotlights
- Camera

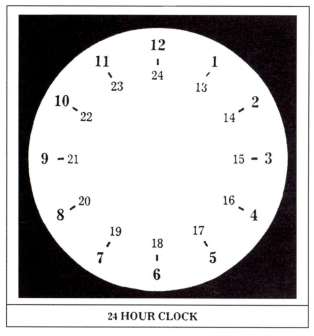

Figure A-2   24-Hour Clock

RADIO TEN CODES

The use of handheld, portable radios, radio telephones, and other forms of mobile communications are often an integral part of the protection officer's role. While codes and related messages may vary, the following is a generally acceptable guide for security personnel. The purpose of coded radio messages is to enhance and improve confidentiality.

10-3	Repeat		10-11	Returning to office
10-4	O.K.—Will comply		10-12	Will telephone
10-5	Stand by		10-20	Your location, please
10-6	Busy—Will call		10-30	Ready for assignment
10-7	Out of service (location - time)		10-70	Message for all cars
10-8	In service		Mayday	Emergency
10-10	Continuing patrol			

PHONETIC ALPHABET

As in the case of radio codes, the phonetic alphabet is not always identical in all security organizations. It is essential that all members of a particular department are conversant with the letters and accompanying words that are utilized. The following list is a generally used and accepted method of attaining greater clarity in transmitting messages by radio or telephone:

A	Alfa		N	November
B	Bravo		O	Oscar
C	Charlie		P	Papa
D	Delta		Q	Quebec
E	Echo		R	Romeo
F	Foxtrot		S	Sierra
G	Golf		T	Tango
H	Hotel		U	Uniform
I	India		V	Victor
J	Juliet		W	Whiskey
K	Kilo		X	X-ray
L	Lima		Y	Yankee
M	Mike		Z	Zulu

Index

Page numbers followed by "f" denote figures; those followed by "t" denote tables